Bilingual First Language Acquisition

PEFC/16-33-111
CATG-PEFC-052
www.pefc.org

MM Textbooks bring the subjects covered in our successful range of academic monographs to a student audience. The books in this series explore education and all aspects of language learning and use, as well as other topics of interest to students of these subjects. Written by experts in the field, the books are supervised by a team of world-leading scholars and evaluated by instructors before publication. Each text is student-focused, with suggestions for further reading and study questions leading to a deeper understanding of the subject.

MM Textbooks

Advisory Board:

Professor Colin Baker, *University of Wales, Bangor, UK*

Professor Viv Edwards, *University of Reading, Reading, UK*

Professor Ofelia García, *Columbia University, New York, USA*

Dr Aneta Pavlenko, *Temple University, Philadelphia, USA*

Professor David Singleton, *Trinity College, Dublin, Ireland*

Professor Terrence G. Wiley, *Arizona State University, Tempe, USA*

Full details of all the books in this series and of all our other publications can be found on http://www.multilingual-matters.com, or by writing to Multilingual Matters, St Nicholas House, 31-34 High Street, Bristol BS1 2AW, UK.

MM Textbooks
Consultant Editor: Professor Colin Baker

Bilingual First Language Acquisition

Annick De Houwer

MULTILINGUAL MATTERS
Bristol • Buffalo • Toronto

Library of Congress Cataloging in Publication Data
A catalog record for this book is available from the Library of Congress.

De Houwer, Annick
Bilingual First Language Acquisition / Annick De Houwer.
MM Textbooks: 2
Includes bibliographical references and index.
1. Language acquisition. 2. Bilingualism. I. Title.
P118.D373 2009
401'.93--dc22 2008053069

British Library Cataloguing in Publication Data
A catalogue entry for this book is available from the British Library.

ISBN-13: 978-1-84769-149-1 (hbk)
ISBN-13: 978-1-84769-148-4 (pbk)

Multilingual Matters
UK: St Nicholas House, 31-34 High Street, Bristol BS1 2AW, UK.
USA: UTP, 2250 Military Road, Tonawanda, NY 14150, USA.
Canada: UTP, 5201 Dufferin Street, North York, Ontario M3H 5T8, Canada.

Copyright © 2009 Annick De Houwer.

All rights reserved. No part of this work may be reproduced in any form or by any means without permission in writing from the publisher.

The policy of Multilingual Matters/Channel View Publications is to use papers that are natural, renewable and recyclable products, made from wood grown in sustainable forests. In the manufacturing process of our books, and to further support our policy, preference is given to printers that have FSC and PEFC Chain of Custody certification. The FSC and/or PEFC logos will appear on those books where full certification has been granted to the printer concerned.

Typeset by Saxon Graphics Ltd, Derby
Printed and bound in Great Britain by MPG Books Ltd

Dedication

This book is dedicated to Professors Hugo Baetens Beardsmore and Eve Clark.

Hugo Baetens Beardsmore's undergraduate 'Sociolinguistics of English' class showed me how interesting linguistics could be. Through his classes, I found out that bilingualism was a scholarly topic. Professor Baetens Beardsmore later became my PhD advisor at the Free University of Brussels. He was also Multilingual Matters' first book author (*Bilingualism: Basic Principles*, 1982).

Eve Clark was my main teacher during my graduate Fulbright year at Stanford University. Through her many inspiring classes I gained a firm foundation in developmental psycholinguistics. Especially the seminar in research methods that I was lucky enough to be able to follow (it was only offered every other year) taught me many important things that later helped me in the work for my doctoral dissertation and far beyond.

I owe both these teachers a lot. Thank you.

Contents

Acknowledgements	xi
Preface	xiii

1: Introducing Bilingual First Language Acquisition — 1

What is Bilingual First Language Acquisition (BFLA)?	2
The family as the primary socialization unit for BFLA	7
Is BFLA a common phenomenon?	9
A brief history of the study of BFLA	10
Summary box	14
Suggestions for study activities	15
Recommended reading	15

2: Bilingual children's language development: an overview — 17

Early interaction, socialization and the child's own developmental path	19
Language learning in the first year at the intersection of interaction, socialization and maturation	20
An outline of bilingual development in the first five years of life	29
Normal variation in BFLA and MFLA	40
Bilingual children's language repertoires	41
Language choice	46
The relation between BFLA children's two developing languages	47
Summary box	50
Suggestions for study activities	50
Recommended reading	51

3: Research methods in BFLA — 53

Why this chapter is important even if you are not embarking on a study of BFLA	54
Need for bilingual researchers	56
Subject selection: making sure you are dealing with BFLA	57
Deciding on how many subjects you should study	57
When and where to collect data: need for sociolinguistic authenticity	59
Data handling: transcription and coding	60
CHILDES as an important tool in BFLA for corpus-based work	66
Bilingual corpora available through CHILDES	69
The CDI as an important tool for lexical research in BFLA	71
Other recommendations specific to BFLA	76
Need to clearly describe the BFLA learning context	77
Summary box	79

	Suggestions for study activities	79
	Recommended reading	80
4:	**Socializing environments and BLFA**	**83**
	Preliminaries	**86**
	It all starts with love... and positive attitudes	86
	Attitudes and beliefs	90
	Bilingual children's language learning environments	96
	What BFLA children hear	**98**
	Young BFLA children's linguistic soundscapes	98
	Language models	104
	The role of language presentation	107
	Language orientation	116
	Input frequency in BFLA	119
	What BFLA children say	**127**
	Changes in BFLA children's linguistic soundscapes and their effects	127
	Speaking the 'right' language and what it depends on	132
	Explaining the composition of young BFLA children's linguistic repertoires	145
	Summary box	148
	Suggestions for study activities	148
	Recommended reading	149
5:	**Sounds in BFLA**	**151**
	Breaking the code	153
	The sounding world of BFLA children	156
	Early bilingual speech perception	160
	Speech perception and word learning	164
	Making the melody of speech	166
	Bilingual babbling	167
	More on melody	171
	Syllable structure and stress as used by BFLA children	172
	Bilingual speech segments	175
	Phonological processes	180
	Perfecting their skills	183
	In conclusion	185
	Summary box	187
	Suggestions for study activities	188
	Recommended reading	190
6:	**Words in BFLA**	**191**
	The words that BFLA children hear	193
	Early bilingual word comprehension	198
	Translation equivalents in comprehension	202
	The Mutual Exclusivity Bias in BFLA	205
	Early comprehension vocabularies: BFLA and MFLA compared	206

	Comprehension and production: two sides of the same coin?	209
	Words and meanings in early production	212
	Early bilingual word production	217
	The rate of lexical development in bilingual production	223
	How many words do BFLA children produce?	226
	The size of BFLA early production vocabularies compared to MFLA	228
	Translation equivalents in production	230
	What drives the production of TEs, or what hinders it?	236
	Translation equivalents and language choice	238
	In conclusion	241
	Summary box	246
	Suggestions for study activities	247
	Recommended reading	248
7:	**Sentences in BFLA**	**251**
	The need for more meanings	253
	The grammatical status of early word combinations	254
	Different paths in learning to combine words	255
	When do BFLA children first start to combine words from scratch?	256
	Lexical development and the transition into sentences	259
	Beyond early word combinations: sentences	263
	Sentences and BFLA children's language repertoires and language choice	267
	Unequal skill in Language A and Language Alpha	272
	The Separate Development Hypothesis: BFLA children's sentences develop separately in each language	277
	The Separate Development Hypothesis: methodological issues	280
	What makes separate development possible?	284
	Crosslinguistic influence in unilingual utterances	287
	BFLA compared to MFLA	288
	BFLA compared to ESLA	290
	The structural features of mixed utterances	291
	The development of narrative	293
	In conclusion	295
	Summary box	298
	Suggestions for study activities	299
	Recommended reading	301
8:	**Harmonious bilingual development**	**303**
	The whole child	305
	BFLA: good or bad?	307
	Comparisons with monolinguals	308
	Harmonious bilingual development or the lack of it	310
	And what happens when BFLA children get older?	324
	Needed: an alternative research paradigm	326
	In conclusion	327

Summary box		330
Suggestions for study activities		330
Recommended reading		331
Resources for parents and educators		331

Appendices

Appendix A	Subject selection: making sure you are dealing with BFLA	333
Appendix B	Behavioral studies of early speech perception in BFLA infants	337
Appendix C	Behavioral studies of early phonetic word learning in BFLA infants	341
Appendix D	Studies of the use of speech rhythm in young BFLA children	343
Appendix E	Studies of the use of speech segments in young BFLA children	346
Appendix F	Studies comparing lexical development in MFLA and BFLA/ESLA	348
Appendix G	Studies of BFLA supporting the Separate Development Hypothesis	350
Appendix H	Main morphosyntactic topics investigated in empirical studies of BFLA supporting the SDH	354
Appendix I	*Not* using particular kinds of grammatical elements and what this might mean in terms of crosslinguistic influence	356

Glossary	359
Bibiliography	371
Child index	405
Language index	407
Subject index	409

Acknowledgements

When Multilingual Matters first approached me with the question whether I would write a textbook on Bilingual First Language Acquisition, I didn't hesitate a moment. I am very happy to have been given the opportunity to draw together what I have learned about the topic since I first started to work on it, and I thank Multilingual Matters for the fact that they initiated this book, and that they put their trust in me to take it to where it is now.

Working on this book hasn't just involved writing down what I already knew. In fact, it has been a wonderful learning experience. In drawing together research findings that had not so far been related to each other, I discovered many new things. You will find them throughout the book.

One of the other great pleasures in writing this book has been that I had a good excuse to get in touch with many colleagues throughout the world. I would like to thank the following scholars who provided feedback and/or helped me obtain literature and citation information: Jessica Barlow, Ruth Berman, Agnes Bolonyai, Matthias Bonnesen, Marc Bornstein, Ferenc Bunta, Tracey Burns, Krista Byers-Heinlein, Katja Cantone, Philip Carr, Barbara Conboy, Annette de Groot, Margaret Deuchar, Christopher Fennell, Steven Gillis, Harriet Jisa, Ghada Khatab, Astrid Klammler, Agnes Kovacs, Madelaine Krehm, Judith Kroll, Imre Kuchenbrandt, Pat Kuhl, Brian MacWhinney, Virginia Marchman, Karen Mattock, Jürgen Meisel, Elena Nicoladis, Kim Oller, Gabriele Pallotti, Maren Pannemann, Janet Patterson, Barbara Pearson, Diane Poulin-Dubois, Suzanne Quay, Marta Ramon-Casas, Stefan Schneider, Ludovica Serratrice, Carmen Silva-Corvalán, Guillaume Thierry, Yamamoto Masayo and Quin Yow.

I am grateful to Ellen Van Bael for helping me out with some Japanese examples.

Part of this book was prepared while I was a Visiting Scholar at the University of Virginia[1]. Special thanks to John Bonvillian and Filip Loncke at UVA for being such gracious hosts. Filip also helped me obtain some articles I needed. Thank you.

Special thanks also to my collaborator at NIH, Diane Putnick, for her invaluable help in getting me many articles that were not easily available in Belgium, and to Wolf Wölck and Antje Wilton for helping me structure the book.

Marc Bornstein, Madalena Cruz-Ferreira, Ghada Khattab, Elizabeth Lanza, Natasha Ringblom, Megha Sundara, Antje Wilton and Wolf Wölck took the time to read portions of the manuscript and give me valuable comments. At 20 years of age, and without any prior knowledge of bilingualism research or linguistics, my daughter Susan Clynes was also a very helpful reader of portions of the manuscript. She gave some useful tips about how to make the text more appealing to a generation of students who are perhaps more visually oriented than past generations.

I am grateful for the time and feedback that all my readers gave to this project. Because of their help, the book is now better than it would have been.

One very special reader, though, was my editor at Multilingual Matters, Colin Baker. Throughout the writing process, his feedback and support were invaluable. What surprised me most though, and what was quite helpful indeed, was the sheer speed with which Colin's comments would land in my mailbox. The turnaround was very fast indeed. This in itself was encouraging, and made it possible to incorporate more general comments regarding style and structure from the beginning of the next chapter I happened to be working on. Thank you, Colin, for your help.

Colin Baker's enthusiastic support of my work-in-progress was a great encouragement and means a lot to me. I also want to thank the many colleagues and friends – too many to name – who encouraged me throughout the writing process. Special thanks, though, to Aliyah Morgenstern, Anat Ninio and Gabrielle Varro for their great enthusiasm and support. Writing a book is by necessity a fairly lonely affair and when you then get warm email messages of support that really helps. *En Susan, dank voor je blije steun en je vertrouwen in mijn kunnen!*

Anna Roderick of Multilingual Matters has been a wonderful partner in this enterprise. Whenever I had a question or idea, she was open to making it happen. Thank you, Anna, for this 'can-do' attitude, and the trust you put in me.

But above all, I want to thank all the bilingual children and their families who allowed me to learn so much from them throughout the years. I hope this book can at least be a down payment on my debt.

Lasne, August 7, 2008

Note

1   Partial funding was provided by a BOF-NOI-grant from the University of Antwerp. This support is gratefully acknowledged.

Preface

Bilingual First Language Acquisition (BFLA), or the development of two languages from birth in young children, has become a prominent topic in the last decade. More and more students are interested in the topic, either just in order to learn more about it, or to start their own investigations. Advanced students interested in Bilingual First Language Acquisition in different departments and programs have different overall specializations. The main ones are Psychology, Linguistics and Education. In addition, there are also students in Speech Therapy, Communication Disorders, and Health and Social Work with an interest in the topic.

At the same time that students' interest in the topic has increased, BFLA has often become a topic in many different kinds of courses. BFLA may be a topic in a sociolinguistically oriented course on Bilingualism. Or it may be taught as part of a psycholinguistically oriented course on Child Language Acquisition. In Education programs, BFLA may be discussed in the framework of a course on Second Language Acquisition. In Speech and Hearing programs, bilingual acquisition is often discussed in a course on Communication Disorders. There are now also courses on bilingual language development that have BFLA as their main or only topic.

The readings for courses that have BFLA on their subject list often include a selection of key primary publications, as well as overview chapters published in handbooks. For instructors wishing to give their students a more in-depth and teaching oriented coverage of BFLA, however, there are no texts available. This textbook aims to fill that gap.

The book's intended audience consists of students who have at least two years of college education behind them. At the same time, it is also aimed at graduate students. The study questions or suggestions for projects at the end of each chapter that carry the indication 'advanced' are meant particularly for them. Also, more in-depth coverage is included in some explanations and illustrations ('Boxes') that are meant primarily for advanced students in linguistics or psychology.

This book starts from the assumption that knowledge about bilingual children's language development is grounded in adequate empirical research methods. The aim is to educate readers from many different backgrounds both about bilingual acquisition and about some of the methodological approaches that have been and can be used to gain insight into its development.

Central to the book is the notion that how children in a bilingual setting learn to speak is variable and will very much depend on the specific environments they find themselves in. These environments will, among others, influence whether they speak two languages or only one. Because of their fundamental importance I will pay much attention to the possible environments for the acquisition of two languages from birth.

After the general introduction in Chapter 1 in which I set the stage for the rest of the book, I give an overview of bilingual children's language development in Chapter 2. This overview chapter starts with a discussion of how early language development takes place at the intersection of interaction, socialization and maturation. Chapter 2 also introduces some basic linguistic concepts that are necessary for a good understanding of the rest of the book for those students who have little background in linguistics. It also gives a very summary overview of the main developmental course taken by children who hear two languages from birth. Before I embark on a more detailed discussion of bilingual development and its context, I discuss some important methodological issues specific to studying BFLA in Chapter 3. I also explain some of the methods that have been used to investigate bilingual acquisition. Although some of Chapter 3 is directed at students wishing to pursue their own research projects on BFLA, the methodological issues I cover are important as background for the rest of the book. In Chapter 4 I explore the BFLA learning context, bilingual socialization practices and the role of the speech heard by children. Chapter 4 is divided into two main parts: one that focuses on children's bilingual environments and another that focuses on how these environments affect development.

After the first half of the book, I describe BFLA children's bilingual acquisition in detail. I take the developmentally determined route of starting with the earliest signs of developing linguistic knowledge, namely, how very young bilingually raised infants perceive the sounds in their linguistic environment and how they tackle the task of producing sounds themselves. This is discussed in Chapter 5. After this, I look at the words that bilingual children understand and use in Chapter 6. These words are soon combined into sentences, and this brings me to Chapter 7 on the structure and ordering of words as they are used in utterances produced by bilingual children. Sentences make up a conversation or a narrative, and aspects of the use of these larger linguistic structures by bilingual children are also discussed in Chapter 7.

Chapter 8, the final chapter, talks about what I call 'harmonious bilingual development', how it can be fostered, and offers a general conclusion to the book. It also outlines some directions for research that I see as important.

My overall focus in this book is on children under the age of six. The most obvious reason for this is that most BFLA research concerns children under this age as well. The underlying cause of this restriction is that as in monolingual child language acquisition research, the emphasis in bilingual acquisition studies is on the young child's acquisition of language in an informal setting, without formal language instruction at school. Since many children start school and concomitant formal language instruction around the age of six, it becomes more difficult after that age to study language development as it evolves in an uninstructed setting.

Throughout the book I pay attention to the specifically 'bilingual' aspects of early bilingual development such as the relationship between bilingual children's two languages and the use of two languages in one word, sentence or conversation. I also compare aspects of BFLA with monolingual acquisition and, to a lesser extent, with the acquisition of a second language in early childhood. The reader will hopefully forgive me that when I discuss findings from monolingual acquisition I often draw on data from the acquisition of Dutch, my first language, besides, of course, English, the most substantially investigated language-in-acquisition in the world.

On the whole, I will focus more on the empirical research findings about bilingual acquisition than on theoretical issues, although of course my basic stance with regard to the importance of children's learning environments represents a theoretical position in itself. For advanced students, I include references to sources that address current theoretical debates in the Recommended reading sections found at the end of most chapters.

The multidisciplinary interest in BFLA reflects the fact that BFLA should be studied from a variety of perspectives. Regardless of one's particular perspective or research question, however, a real understanding of BFLA requires at least some background in two distinct areas of specialization: the field of child language development and the field of bilingualism. This textbook combines insights from both the fields of bilingualism and child language development and thereby hopes to offer a richer perspective than either of these fields can by themselves. These fields, which are interdisciplinary, are rarely offered as courses of study within the same program. Also, there are few senior faculty members who are specialists in both. I have been fortunate enough to have been able to incorporate both fields in my own training: the sociolinguistics of bilingualism mainly under the guidance of Professor Hugo Baetens Beardsmore at the Free University of Brussels, and child language acquisition under the guidance of Professor Eve Clark at Stanford University, who also taught me about the importance of research methods. I dedicate this book to both of them.

I bring to this textbook my now 30-year-long experience as a bilingualism scholar. That experience has included reading widely in the bilingualism and child language literature and carrying out my own empirical research on early bilingual development up until today. In my capacity as a bilingual children's specialist, I have had occasion to meet and talk to many people in bilingual families all over the world. I have learned a lot from them, and from the many educators, speech therapists and social workers involved with bilingual children that I have met throughout the years. I also bring to this book my nearly 50-year-long experience as a bilingual (and later, multilingual) person, and my background as the mother of a bilingual child. I have very much enjoyed bringing all this experience together in this book and hope that you, the reader, can benefit from it.

Some technical notes about this book

1. Although many of the examples throughout this textbook are anonymous, they are always based on actual people's behavior.

2. Twenty years ago, the field of BFLA was quite small. It has fortunately grown considerably, and it is no longer possible to give comprehensive overviews. This book is no exception. It is necessarily selective. This does not imply that what is not mentioned is not worthwhile.

3. Most of the references are limited to readily available published material. Unpublished doctoral dissertations and master's theses are not generally referenced. Neither are internal research reports or unpublished conference presentations, except where they

represent new work in areas that previously had not been studied. Some key references are identified at the end of most chapters in a short Recommended reading section. All citations are referenced in the Bibliography at the end of the book, but readers may refer to the book's website for separate bibliographies for each chapter at http://www.mmtextbooks.com/bfla/.

4. Because bilingualism is by definition not limited to a single language, I have tried to reference publications in many different languages. For the examples, I have also tried to span a variety of languages. I apologize to authors of texts in languages that I do not read but whose work is pertinent to BFLA.

5. In view of the broad intended audience I have chosen to define rather more than fewer terms. Terms are either defined in the text, in separate 'boxes' and/or in the Glossary at the end of the book. Terms that appear in the Glossary are highlighted in the text at their first appearance. I strongly recommend that readers look up these terms when they first meet up with them. Sometimes, I have explained terms only in the Glossary, and not in the text, because explaining them in the text would be too disruptive for the flow of the 'story'.

    Readers with training in linguistics may find some of the definitions and explanations of linguistic terminology rather too general and theoretically ambiguous. I hope they will bear with me and see those definitions and explanations for what they are: aids to help readers without linguistic training understand the facts of bilingual acquisition.

6. Children's ages are usually indicated as year;month. For instance; 1;6 means one year and six months. For younger children, indications in months (e.g. 4.5 months) may be used as well. For easy reference, I have added a key that 'translates' between months and years in Box 2.8 in Chapter 2.

7. Especially for Chapters 5, 6 and 7 this textbook has not been able to do full justice to the many complexities of the methods, empirical evidence and theoretical issues involved in the study of BFLA children's phonological, lexical and morphosyntactic development. These chapters are brief summaries of the major issues and findings so far. They should be seen as starting points for a deeper understanding.

8. Throughout the book I have differentiated between text, illustrative boxes and study activities for less and more advanced students. Paragraphs that are particularly geared towards more advanced students with a background in linguistics or psychology are shaded in gray. Other students may skip these portions and will still learn about the main issues and findings. Some boxes are also meant more for advanced students. This is indicated by the abbreviation 'adv.' after reference is made to a particular box number. Endnotes are not crucial for understanding the main chapters, but offer additional and/or nuancing information for more advanced readers. The Appendices are meant for advanced students as well.

10. Study activities that involve students 'going out into the field' and doing their own small projects are labelled *Project*. Study activities that specifically feature an internet resource are marked *WEB*.

11. When I refer to children as 'English–Spanish' or as 'monolingual French', for instance, I am referring to the languages they are learning, not their citizenship or nationality.

Disclaimer

This book sometimes refers to specific languages to exemplify situations relevant to Bilingual First Language Acquisition. Sometimes these situations are not altogether positive. These references to specific languages are by no means intended to express any disrespect for those languages or their speakers. In most cases, another language could have been chosen to exemplify a particular situation (with then, again, possible negative connotations for that language...).

1

Introducing Bilingual First Language Acquisition

What is Bilingual First Language Acquisition (BFLA)?	2
The term	2
The process	2
BFLA, MFLA and ESLA	4
The family as the primary socialization unit for BFLA	7
Is BFLA a common phenomenon?	9
A brief history of the study of BFLA	10
More than 50 years ago	10
Renewed interest after a fairly quiet time	11
Interest from the public at large	12
The foundations laid in the 1980s	12
An explosion of research interest	13
BFLA research today	13
Summary box	14
Suggestions for study activities	15
Recommended reading	15

What is Bilingual First Language Acquisition (BFLA)?

The term

Bilingual First Language Acquisition (BFLA) is the development of language in young children who hear two languages spoken to them from birth. BFLA children are learning two first languages. There is no chronological difference between the two languages in terms of when the children started to hear them. This is why in referring to these languages it is best to use a notation that does not imply a notion of 'first' and 'second'. Following Wölck (1987/88) I will refer to BFLA children's two languages as Language A and Language Alpha.

Although many processes of the acquisition of *three* languages from birth may be very similar to what happens when a child is learning just two, empirical research on trilingual acquisition is just starting to receive serious research consideration. It is too early to make any generalizations based on the few existing studies so far. This book, then, will use the term 'bilingual' to refer just to the use of two languages, rather than to also more than two.

It appears that Merrill Swain was the first to introduce the term Bilingual First Language Acquisition. Swain used this term in a brief summary of her dissertation work (Swain, 1976). As far as I have been able to determine, however, the term did not appear in print again until Jürgen Meisel briefly used it in his much cited chapter published in 1989. I took up his lead and proposed a definition for this 'new' term in my case study of a Dutch–English bilingual child (De Houwer, 1990). Prior to this, various terms were used to cover the concept of BFLA, but many of these also referred to more than just BFLA. It was often impossible to really know what scholars meant when they wrote of 'incipient bilingualism', 'childhood bilingualism' or 'simultaneous bilingualism'. The term BFLA is now widely accepted and has the advantage of having a clear definition.

The process

The fact that BFLA children hear Language A and Language Alpha from birth does not necessarily mean that they will actually learn to speak these two languages. It is not uncommon for BFLA children to speak just one of the languages they have been addressed in since birth. When BFLA children understand two languages but speak only one, they may be called 'passive' bilinguals, although there is nothing passive about understanding two languages and speaking one. If BFLA children do not learn to understand and/or speak either of the languages spoken to them, this is a cause for concern: maybe they have a hearing problem, or maybe there are neurological problems. Just as in children raised with just one language who do not understand much language and/or do not speak, the lack of comprehension and/or speech in any language in BFLA children is a severe problem and needs to be discussed with a speech and language pathologist. In Box 1.1 I outline four main patterns of language use in BFLA children and briefly evaluate them.

| Box 1.1 | Four patterns of language use in BFLA children over the age of 1;6 [a] |

	Child understands Language A	Child speaks Language A	Child understands Language Alpha	Child speaks Language Alpha
Pattern 1	yes	yes	yes	yes
Pattern 2	yes	yes	yes	no
Pattern 3	yes	no	yes	no
Pattern 4	no	no	no	no

Pattern 1 is the normal, most frequent case. Pattern 2 is another normal, but less frequent case. Pattern 3 is a worrisome infrequent case. Pattern 4 is a very worrisome infrequent case.

[a] Before the age of one and a half, it is quite normal for children not to speak at all, and the absence of speech in any language is normally developmentally determined; however, children should be able to understand words around the first birthday (see Chapter 6).

The expectation for normally developing BFLA children, then, is that they will learn to understand two languages from early on and speak both languages, or just one of them (Patterns 1 and 2 in Box 1.1). In Box 1.2 I give an example for Pattern 1 and Pattern 2. Chapter 2 gives a more in-depth overview of bilingual children's linguistic skills.

| Box 1.2 | Two examples of normally developing BFLA children |

An example of the more frequent case (Pattern 1 in Box 1.1)

Carlo is the son of an American father and an Italian mother. His family resides in Scotland. For the first five months of his life, Carlo's father addressed him in English and his mother spoke Italian to him, as did his older brother, who is five years his senior. When Carlo was five months old he started to attend a half-day English-speaking day care center on weekdays and his father started to address him in Italian rather than English. He continued to hear Italian from his mother and brother, and also had Italian-speaking care providers on weekdays when he was not in the English-speaking day-care center. His parents spoke to each other in English, as they did to an older stepbrother living in the same household. Carlo understood and spoke both English and Italian (Serratrice, 2001, 2002).

An example of the less frequent case (Pattern 2 in Box 1.1)

'Il ragazzo' (the boy) is the son of linguist Walburga von Raffler-Engel. He grew up in Florence, Italy, and his mother always addressed him in Italian while his American father always spoke English to him. Among each other, the parents spoke English. The child's broader environment was almost exclusively Italian-speaking. Von Raffler-Engel (1965) reports that her son understood both English and Italian, but that he would speak Italian only. She writes: 'Il suo desiderio di perfezionarsi nell'inglese è quasi nullo' (p. 176: 'his desire to speak English is just about zero' – my translation). Von Raffler-Engel is not very surprised about this, since in her circle of acquaintances with lots of other Italian–American bilingual families it is very common for the children to speak just Italian, and no English, in spite of one of their parents addressing them in English.

People often assume that BFLA children know each of their languages equally well. This is not always the case, though. When we look at children's skills in a language we need to distinguish between **comprehension** and **production**.

For language comprehension, there could be large differences between a child's two languages in how well they are understood. However, because of the small number of studies on comprehension in BFLA children we don't really know just how large these differences can be and whether it is possible that a child understands very little of one language but a whole lot of another, even though he or she has heard both of them frequently from birth. What little **empirical research** is available, however, suggests that there is a lot of variation between children in how many **words** they understand in each of their languages. This research is reviewed in Chapter 6 on the **lexicon**, which summarizes the research on the kinds and numbers of words that bilingual children know.

For language production or speaking, there is ample evidence for large, and quite normal, differences between BFLA children's two languages: there are children who do not speak Language A at all but who are fluent in Language Alpha. At the other end of the continuum there are children who are more or less equally fluent in Language A and Language Alpha, and then there are all the variations between these two extremes, with children speaking one language better than the other to various degrees.[1]

It is not easy, however, to measure differences in how well children speak a particular language (I discuss this in more detail in Chapter 3). But there is a consensus in the field that BFLA children who actively speak two languages do not necessarily speak them equally well. A possible reason for this may be that children do not hear each of their languages to the same extent. I will return to this issue of variable knowledge throughout the book.

BFLA, MFLA and ESLA

Note that BFLA is defined in terms of a particular learning context. Certainly, it is a different context from **Monolingual First Language Acquisition (MFLA)**, in which children hear just one language from birth (their **Language 1**), and **Early Second Language Acquisition (ESLA)**, where monolingual children's language environments change in such a way that they start to hear a second language **(Language 2)** with some regularity over and above their Language 1. Often this happens through day care or preschool.

The language learning contexts MFLA, BFLA and ESLA have in common that they are contexts in which very young children acquire language without formal instruction. I outline these three main different learning contexts for children under age six in Box 1.3.

In Box 1.3 you will see the word **input**. I will be using this term a lot throughout this book, and will use it to refer to the speech that children hear, whether it is addressed to them or not (see Chapter 4 for further explanation). Note that in Box 1.3 reference is made not just to 'input' but to 'regular input'. Regular input here refers to daily or almost daily contact with a language through interpersonal interaction or overhearing a language (see further, Chapter 4).

Box 1.3	Three main learning contexts for the acquisition of language before age six
Monolingual First Language Acquisition (MFLA)	
Language 1: regular input from birth	
age 0 ———————————————————————— age 6 and up	
Bilingual First Language Acquisition (BFLA)	
Language A: regular input from birth	
age 0 ———————————————————————— age 6 and up	
Language Alpha: regular input from birth	
age 0 ———————————————————————— age 6 and up	
Early Second Language Acquisition (ESLA)	
Language 1: regular input from birth	
age 0 ———————————————————————— age 6 and up	
Language 2: regular input in the preschool years	
ages ca. 1;6 to 4 ———————————————————————— age 6 and up	

Box 1.3 indicates the age range of 1;6–4 years of age as the typical time of first regular exposure to a second language in ESLA. This age range indication is not meant to be exclusive: ESLA contexts might well exist before age one and a half, or after age four. The younger cut-off age of one and a half is meant to reflect the fact that in toddlerhood many hitherto monolingually raised children gain access to various group settings outside the home, such as playschools and nurseries, through which they are introduced to a second language. The older cut-off point was chosen because in many societies children start to learn to read at preschool at age five, including children for whom the school language is a second language. If children's introduction to a second language coincides with literacy programs, even if children are only five years old, we can speak of formal second language acquisition rather than ESLA.

Each of the three main language learning contexts (MFLA, BFLA and ESLA) has quite distinct effects on early language development. MFLA children learn to understand and speak only one language. BFLA children learn to understand two languages concurrently, and when they start to speak, they usually say words and sentences in each of their two languages. ESLA children learn first to understand one language and start speaking in one language only, their Language 1 (in fact, then, ESLA children start off as monolingual children). Subsequently, they learn to understand a second language, their Language 2, which they may also start to speak at some point.

Box 1.4 summarizes the main developmental trajectories for the three major language learning contexts that young children may find themselves in. In Box 1.4, language comprehension is assumed to start at age one, but children may start to understand language prior to that. It is usually not until around the age of one, however, that we can start to reliably measure <u>lexical comprehension</u> using commonly available methods such as <u>parental rating instruments</u> (I discuss these at length in Chapters 3 and 6).

> **Box 1.4** Language learning contexts and typical developmental trajectories for the acquisition of language comprehension and production before age six

Comprehension

MFLA
By age 1: Language 1, and increasing knowledge of Language 1 until age 6 and up

BFLA
By age 1: Language A, and increasing knowledge of Language A until age 6 and up
By age 1: Language Alpha, and increasing knowledge of Language Alpha until age 6 and up

ESLA
By age 1: Language 1, and increasing knowledge of Language 1 until age 6 and up
Much later: Language 2, and increasing knowledge of Language 2 until age 6 and up

Production

MFLA
By age 2: Language 1, and increasing knowledge of Language 1 until age 6 and up

BFLA: most children
By age 2: Language A, and increasing knowledge of Language A until age 6 and up
By age 2: Language Alpha, and increasing knowledge of Language Alpha until age 6 and up
BFLA: some children
By age 2: Language A, and increasing knowledge of Language A until age 6 and up

ESLA
By age 2: Language 1, and increasing knowledge of Language 1 until age 6 and up
Much later: Language 2, and increasing knowledge of Language 2 until age 6 and up

Box 1.4 gives the age of two as a starting age for language production. This again is a fairly conservative indication. There are many children who start to speak well before the age of two. However, the second birthday usually coincides with children's production of short sentences, and certainly, if children are not speaking at all by the age of two, this is cause for concern.

So far, there is no terminology to refer to early language learning contexts in which children start out hearing just one language but very soon, in the first year of life, are confronted with a second language. Is this context more like a BFLA context, or more like an ESLA context? And, more importantly, does these children's language development look more like that of BFLA children with input in two languages from birth, or does it look more like the development of children who started hearing a second language at age one and a half? The answers to these questions are not clear and studies have yet to systematically investigate this issue. Since there are major differences between 'clearly' MFLA, BFLA and ESLA children in the early language skills they develop and in the timing of their overall linguistic development, it is to be expected that children with initial monolingual input but very early input in a second language will, in fact, exhibit some important differences in their initial acquisition stages compared to the language development of BFLA children and to that of ESLA children.

Even though there are quite major differences between MFLA, BFLA and ESLA children in the number of languages they know and in the timing of their initial knowledge of these languages, there are also many similarities between these three types of early language development. The emphasis in this book is not on comparing these three types. However, where relevant and appropriate I will note similarities and differences in so far as they are known.

The family as the primary socialization unit for BFLA

If children hear two languages spoken to them from birth, they will most likely hear them within the (extended) family. As such, the family is the primary socializing agent for the development of BFLA. There are, of course, many different kinds of families, and children grow up in many different kinds of family settings (see the end of this section and also Chapter 4).

The typical BFLA situation is one where a child's parents are speakers of different languages and speak those languages when addressing the baby. The chances are that during pregnancy the unborn infant was hearing two languages, both as spoken by the mother and as spoken by people in close proximity to the mother (see Chapter 5). But it is equally possible that up until the child's birth only one language was used, and that the birth of the child brought with it a change in the patterns of language choice (see further Chapter 4).

Childless monolingual couples often become instant bilingual families upon the birth of their first child. This is most often the case when children are born to couples where the spouses have different language backgrounds but speak only one language between them. After the birth of the baby one of the spouses then starts speaking another language to the infant, and continues using the other language in addressing the other parent. Such changes in home language use patterns can have profound effects on the couple's relationship (for a book that addresses such issues for bilingual couples in the French–German-speaking town of Freiburg/Fribourg in Switzerland see Brohy, 1992).

Alternatively, parents-to-be may both be bilingual and speak two languages at home. When the baby arrives, this pattern is just continued. There are also situations where bilingual couples decide to address their infant in just one language, thereby effectively blocking the possibility of BFLA (see Chapter 4). At the other end of the spectrum, monolingual parents may hire a nanny or 'au pair' out of the desire to raise their child with two languages from the very beginning. Box 1.5 shows two 'real-life' examples of couples-turned-parents and their language choices.

> **Box 1.5** Becoming a bilingual family: two examples
>
> *From bilingual couple to bilingual family*
>
> Monique and Laurent have been married for two years. They were both raised in Dutch and French, and use Dutch and French between each other. Their relatives speak Dutch and French every day as well. When their twin boys are born, Monique and Laurent continue to speak Dutch and French at home between each other and to their newborn babies. This feels the most natural and normal to them.
>
> *From monolingual couple to bilingual family*
>
> Hiroko and Marc speak English together. Marc understands some Japanese, but does not speak it. His family speaks only English. Hiroko's family only speaks Japanese. Hiroko herself is fluent in English. When Marc and Hiroko's baby girl Toshie is born, Japanese enters their home when Hiroko finds she does not feel comfortable addressing her in English. After a long conversation, Hiroko and Marc decide that Marc will speak to Toshie in English and Hiroko will talk to her in Japanese. Marc will try to learn more Japanese so that he will understand what's going on, and Marc and Hiroko decide that if Marc feels left out once Toshie is a bit older, Hiroko could still use English when Marc is around and switch back to Japanese when he's not.

It depends very much, then, on whether parents start speaking two languages to their baby whether a child will be raised in a BFLA setting or not. For some parents, it is a conscious decision to raise their child with two languages. For many, however, speaking two languages at home is just a matter of course and not a matter of choice, very much the way that it is not a real 'choice' for completely monolingual parents to address their newborn child just in the one language they happen to know.

Not all children are born into a family that has at its core a parent pair. Their mother may be single and raise the new child on her own. Children may be given up for adoption and be institutionalized immediately after birth. BFLA is also possible in these exceptional circumstances. However, the bilingual acquisition literature almost exclusively looks at children who are born to a set of biological parents and who live with their families. Thus, this scenario will also be the focus in this book.

Parents may transfer part of the care for their young children to other people such as grandparents or nannies. Nevertheless, parents remain a central part of children's lives, whether directly or indirectly. In most societies, parents decide about their children's residence and education, even if such decisions are implicit, for instance, when parents do not change their residence once a child is born. Of course, children usually meet up with other individuals besides their parents, and are influenced by these people as well. In Chapter 4 I discuss in more detail the various bilingual first language acquisition learning contexts and the role that families play in the creation and perpetuation of bilingual development.

Is BFLA a common phenomenon?

We do not know much at all about the history of BFLA in centuries past, nor about how widespread the phenomenon was or is. Census and survey data can only indirectly reveal anything about children's linguistic environments. There are most likely large differences between societies in the proportion of BFLA children, depending on how common bi- and multilingualism is in the society as a whole.

However, a survey on 'hidden' bilingualism that I conducted in Flanders, Belgium in the 1990s shows that in around 8% of the over 18,000 families with school-aged children sampled, the parents speak two languages at home (De Houwer, 2003). This means that when mothers' and fathers' home language use is combined, two languages are spoken by the parent pair. Given that the sample did not include families with children at international schools or at schools with a large proportion of immigrant children, the actual figure for parental home bilingual language use in Flanders is probably well above 10%.

Because of a lack of information generally on the languages that young children hear at home, it is impossible to provide reliable estimates for other areas or countries. However, if you consider that Belgium has seen a lot of immigration since the 1960s and is demographically similar to many Western and Northern European countries, the situation in such other countries in Europe is probably quite similar. Studies in France and the Netherlands that have looked at home language use by children and teens confirm this general idea (Deprez, 1995; Extra *et al.*, 2002).

Results from the Flanders survey study also show that, in spite of hearing two languages at home, many children do not, in fact, actively speak these two languages (De Houwer, 2007). All children speak the majority language (in this case, Dutch) but only in 71% of the 1356 two-parent families do the children also speak the minority language (any one among the 73 languages found in the study).

This average of 71% masks the fact that the children's use of the minority language depends on how home language use is divided among the parents. When both parents speak the minority language at home and one parent in addition also speaks the majority language, children also usually speak the minority language (this was the case for over 93% of the relevant families). It is a different story for families in which both parents speak the majority language at home and just one parent also speaks the minority language. In this case, only a little over a third of the families (a low 36%) have children who speak the minority language. Parents who both speak both languages at home have a 79% chance of raising children who speak two languages. The figure for the single-parent families in the study where the single parent speaks both Dutch and a minority language at home is the same. In these 75 single-parent families, 50 (or around 80%) had children who spoke both languages (these results are based on additional analyses of data presented in De Houwer, 2007). I summarize these findings in Box 1.6.

> **Box 1.6** Parental home language input patterns and child bilingual use: data from the Flanders survey

	In how many families do the children speak both the majority and a minority language?
Two-parent families	
(1) Both parents speak just a minority language or at most one parent also speaks the majority language	in **96%** of the 665 families
(2) Parents both speak both languages or one parent speaks a minority language	in **79%** of the 562 families
(3) Parents both speak the majority language and one parent also speaks a minority language	in **36%** of the 353 families
Families headed by a single parent	
(4) The single parent speaks just a minority language	in 42 of the 46 families
(5) The single parent speaks both a minority language and the majority language	in 50 of the 75 families

All children speak the majority language. The differences between 100% and the figures above reflect the families where the children only speak the majority language.
Adapted from De Houwer, 2007

My conservative estimate for countries in Western and Northern Europe is that every tenth family uses two languages at home and thus would appear to constitute a typical BFLA learning context. However, child active language use in these BFLA families is bilingual only in about 70% of the cases. We do not know what the situation is in other regions of the world.

A brief history of the study of BFLA

More than 50 years ago

The first extensive, book-long study of a child growing up with two languages from birth was published almost 100 years ago. It is the classic case study that the French linguist Ronjat (1913) made of his son Louis, who heard German and French at home from birth. Ronjat gives many important insights into bilingual development but is mainly known for advocating his linguist friend Grammont's 'one person, one language' rule, stating that the best way for children to become bilingual is for each person who talks to them to use just one language.

Ronjat is unfortunately not much cited these days. His book has as its great merit, though, that it provides a good global description of a particular child's bilingual development. Given today's increasing emphasis on minute detailed descriptions of very specific aspects of language functioning only, it is easy to forget the larger picture. Yet, BFLA research should aim to understand bilingual children's language development in its entirety. This is impossible, of course, for any one researcher or group of researchers, but studies like Ronjat's help to provide a much needed larger perspective.

Ronjat's study is also significant in that he followed the lead of the founders of modern child development, the German psychologists Wilhelm and Clara Stern, in describing language development against the backdrop of children's overall development, but for a bilingual child instead of the monolingual children that the Sterns had a few years earlier reported on (that was in 1907; this work has been republished as Stern and Stern, 1965). I will refer to Ronjat's work quite frequently in this book, especially in Chapters 5 and 6.

It took almost three decades before the next large study of BFLA appeared. This is the four-volume study (in English) by the German–American phonetician and linguist Werner Leopold, published between 1939 and 1949 and reprinted in 1970. These volumes form the currently most precise and comprehensive longitudinal description and analysis of a single child's language development. They are a prime example of the benefit of having a parent-phonetician with a well-trained ear act as child language observer. Leopold's work inspired many scholars in the 1970s working on the then fairly new field of child language research, even though most of these researchers studied monolingual acquisition rather than BFLA. As Hatch (1978: 24) noted in her introduction to an article by Leopold, each of his four volumes 'has served as a resource for some of the finest work in first language acquisition'.

Leopold studied the acquisition of his German–English learning daughter Hildegard. He describes her language development in great detail (he also adds some comments about his second daughter Karla's language development). For anyone wishing to do any 'serious' empirical work on BFLA, Leopold's book is an important resource. Of course, you will not find any reference to current theories about bilingualism, child language acquisition or early bilingual acquisition. However, reading Leopold's work will impart a wealth of information about a bilingual child's development in a relatively short time, and often you will feel you are right there, in the Leopold household, and getting to know Hildegard and her family. I refer to Leopold's work quite often, especially in Chapters 5 and 6. One drawback of his work, however, is that Leopold could only describe Hildegard's signs of language comprehension and her language use when he was present. I return to this issue in Chapter 3.

Renewed interest after a fairly quiet time

The 1970s saw a spate of articles and books on young bilingual children's language development, but their quality was variable, and it was not always clear whether children were growing up in a BFLA environment or not. Although Leopold's work has been influential in studies of child language development in general, it was not until the end of the 1970s that another study on BFLA took up the more specifically bilingual points made by Leopold. In their influential but also lately much criticized article on two German–Italian learning children, Virginia Volterra and Traute Taeschner concur with Leopold in positing a developmental period in which young bilingual children speak a mixed sort of language rather than each language as a separate set (Volterra & Taeschner, 1978), a position which is no longer upheld (see Chapter 7).

Interest from the public at large

In the early 1980s came the publication (by Multilingual Matters) of George Saunders' (1982a) popular first book on his bilingual family, and the same decade saw many other books which were primarily meant to satisfy parents' growing interest in bilingual development. This includes the thoughtful book by Bernd Kielhöfer and Sylvie Jonekeit (1983) that uses examples from Ms Jonekeit's German–French-speaking sons to illustrate issues relating to raising bilingual children.

While the focus in Saunders' and most other books directed at a wide audience was mostly on the earlier stages of bilingual development, Saunders' second book (1988) on his bilingual family spans a much wider age range and includes information on, among others, the development of literacy in two languages.

George Saunders and his wife Wendy raised their three children in German and English in Australia. Thus, just as was the case for Leopold's family, the father spoke German to the children and the mother English in an English-speaking environment. Although Saunders' books are very different from Leopold's in, for instance, their level of detail, they give readers a good idea about how two languages can work in a bilingual family, how different children even in the same family can and do develop differently (at least as far as the details are concerned), and how a bilingual family is not an island but part of a larger community, even if it is a monolingual one.

More recently, Stephen Caldas (2006) has written a fascinating book spanning 19 years in the life of his English–French-speaking family. Like Saunders, he describes his three children's bilingual language and literacy development in a monolingual setting, but now the setting is that of Louisiana in the United States.

The interest in early bilingual development from parents and educators continues unabatedly, and the quarterly *Bilingual Family Newsletter* launched by Multilingual Matters in 1984 can still count on many subscribers. More and more, however, parents, educators and scholars alike are turning to the World Wide Web for information on bilingual acquisition. The quality of the many available websites is, again, variable. In Chapter 8 I return briefly to a discussion of information sources that parents and educators can use.

The foundations laid in the 1980s

Yet another case of German–English BFLA (after those of Leopold's and Saunders' children), now with an English-speaking father and a German-speaking mother living in Germany, was the subject of Donald Porsché's (1983) book, which focused mostly on his oldest son's early lexical development. While Porsché's book contains a lot of useful information that I will come back to, especially in Chapter 6, it has had surprisingly little impact on the field.

In contrast, the 1980s saw five sites in five countries starting to carry out research on BFLA that turned out to have a continuing impact on the field of BFLA research. These are the projects initiated and directed by Jürgen Meisel in Germany (German–French), Fred Genesee in Canada (French–English), Elizabeth Lanza in Norway (Norwegian–English), Margaret Deuchar in Britain (Spanish–English) and myself in Belgium (Dutch–English). These projects were focused primarily on **language choice** and **morphosyntactic development**, and on the relationship between the young bilingual child's two languages, an issue that will come up again and again in the remainder of this book, but especially in Chapter 7.

An explosion of research interest

I critically reviewed most publicly available publications on early bilingual development published prior to 1988 in my 1990 monograph (De Houwer, 1990). As I hinted at in the Preface, it is quite impossible now to comprehensively review most publicly available research on early bilingual acquisition. There is simply too much of it!

The 1990s saw an explosion of published work on BFLA, and it continues to grow at a high rate. The main novelty in the field of BFLA of the 1990s lay in the expansion of the topics addressed. In particular, the work on bilingual lexical development by Barbara Pearson, Kim Oller and colleagues, and by Suzanne Quay opened up a whole new area.

In **morphosyntax**, the 1990s saw a great expansion as regards the particular pairs of languages investigated in order to explore the relationship between a child's two languages. More and more attention was given to the contextualized nature of child bilingual use, and a few notable studies ventured into the difficult realm of early bilingual **phonological development**. With the publication of exciting new research on early speech perception in bilingual infants the field of BFLA gained even more momentum (Bosch & Sebastián-Gallés, 1997), and more recently this momentum has increased with the initiation of studies investigating bilingual infants' neurological response to speech and language stimuli (e.g. Vihman *et al.*, 2006).

BFLA research today

The number of scholars studying BFLA has greatly increased over the last 20 years, and the field has really 'come into its own'. Not only has the number but also the geographic diversity of the researchers studying BFLA grown dramatically. Previously, BFLA scholars were mainly of Western European descent; nowadays, BFLA research is carried out by scholars of different ethnic backgrounds in many countries across the globe, spanning from Australia over China to Russia, Norway, Portugal and the Americas. This geographic diversity of researchers brings with it a much needed diversity in the languages that are being studied. It also holds the promise that soon we will be able to start teasing apart those aspects of BFLA that are specific to particular cultural contexts and those that are of a more universal nature.

After all, as Dan Slobin and many other prominent child language researchers have stated repeatedly, it is only by studying language acquisition in crosslinguistic contexts that we will be able to gain full insight into the features of acquisition that are universal and those that are specific (see, e.g. Bowerman, 1985; Slobin, 1985).

BFLA children offer a unique opportunity for investigating this important issue, since they are a 'natural linguistic laboratory' in the sense that they are always at the same level of socio-psychological development. Any differences between their skills in either language must then be related to linguistic factors, rather than to differences in socio-psychological development. Such differences could be the reason for different acquisitional paths between monolingual children learning different languages.

Studying BFLA children, then, can contribute significantly to the study of issues in child language research. In fact, some of the most influential work on child language acquisition was inspired by the observation of young bilingual children (Leopold, 1970; Slobin, 1973). Studying BFLA children can also contribute to our knowledge of bilingualism in general. If you know how something came about this tells you a lot about what that something is. It is no wonder, then, that BFLA has become a topic for handbooks on child language as well as on bilingualism (see, for instance, Hoff & Shatz, 2007; Kroll & de Groot, 2005).

Of course, in order to get to know how learning two languages from birth works, nothing can compare to real-life contact with bilingual children and their families. Important books like the ones mentioned above that open the door to how other families and children have experienced a BFLA setting, however, are a good basis for putting your own ideas and observations into perspective.

Notes

1. The notion of 'fluency' is very much linked to age, at least in young children. Children cannot be called 'fluent' speakers until they start to regularly and unhesitatingly say sentences that have three or more words in them.

Summary box

- If children regularly hear two languages spoken to them from birth they are growing up in a Bilingual First Language Acquisition (BFLA) situation.
- BFLA children typically hear their two languages spoken in the home.
- BFLA children learn to understand two first languages concurrently.
- In a quarter of the cases BFLA children will also speak two languages from early on.
- Quite a few BFLA children speak just one language.

Suggestions for study activities

1. *Project:* Ask around in your circle of friends and family about whether they know anyone who was raised with two languages from birth. Try to get in touch with them and have a conversation with them about their early bilingual experience. What languages were involved? Did they learn to understand them? Did they learn to speak them? How do they feel about their early bilingualism?
2. *Project:* Ask around in your circle of friends and family about whether they know anyone who is raising a child with two languages from birth. Try to get in touch with them and have a conversation with them about their child's overall linguistic development. What languages are involved? Does their child *understand* them both? Does their child *speak* them both?
3. Locate either of Saunders' two books (1982a, 1988), skim through it and choose a chapter to read in depth. Write a short summary of that chapter.
4. Do activity 3 in a group and divide the chapters among the group members. After writing chapter summaries, present each chapter to the other group members and discuss the entire book.
5. Find five recent articles in the *International Journal of Bilingualism* whose titles suggest they deal with bilingual children. Determine whether or not they deal with BFLA.
6. *WEB:* Read an early review of Leopold's four volumes by Otto Springer in *The German Quarterly* in 1955 via the following link: http://www.jstor.org/view/00168831/ap020114/02a00200/0?frame=no frame&userID=8fa9c13f@ua.ac.be/01c0a8487300504b048&dpi=3&config=jstor
Which points did you find most interesting?
7. Find out where you can get easy access to Leopold's four volumes and spend a few hours reading in them so you get an idea of the book (advanced).
8. If you read French, try to locate a copy of Ronjat's book and dip into it for a few hours (advanced).

Recommended reading

Leopold (1978) summarizes some of his monumental work in article format. Meisel's (1989) chapter pulls together a lot of theoretical and methodological issues that are still important today (only recommended for readers with some background in linguistics). Equally important has been Lanza's emphasis on input and interaction in BFLA (Lanza, 1988, 1992).

2
Bilingual children's language development: an overview

Early interaction, socialization and the child's own developmental path	19
Language learning in the first year at the intersection of interaction, socialization and maturation	20
Maturation, imitation, turn taking	20
Joint attention	21
Early sounds	22
Infant-directed speech (IDS)	23
Phonemes	24
Learning to tune in to phonemes	26
The role of experience	27
The early developmental processes relevant for language are highly similar for children everywhere	28
Learning about language starts very early	29
An outline of bilingual development in the first five years of life	29
Before take-off	29
Sounds and words	30
Holophrases	31
Putting words together	32

Making sentences	*32*
Utterance length	*37*
Bilingual milestones	*38*
Normal variation in BFLA and MFLA	**40**
Bilingual children's language repertoires	**41**
Different kinds of utterances in production	*41*
Using mixed utterances	*43*
Variation between BFLA children in the kinds of utterances they produce	*44*
Language choice	**46**
The relation between BFLA children's two developing languages	**47**
Summary box	**50**
Suggestions for study activities	**50**
Recommended reading	**51**

Early interaction, socialization and the child's own developmental path

Young children are at first not really able to communicate much. When they are born they are 'speechless', they are 'infants'.[1] Gradually, babies learn to communicate with people they know. It is through these early **interactions** that babies become able to understand their world and the people in it. Early interactions with familiar people are the contexts in which babies develop **intersubjective learning**, that is, they learn through and in communication with others.

This early intersubjective learning through interaction is the cornerstone of children's overall development and communicative functioning (e.g. Papoušek, 2007). Because of its crucial importance to children in any kind of linguistic setting, including a bilingual one, this section and the next focus on the time frame in which this basic intersubjective learning takes place, i.e. in the first year of life.

The people that young children interact with on a daily basis typically are those who take care of them, educate them and thus 'socialize' them. Typically, these people are the baby's parents, grandparents or other adults that take their place. In some cultures, older siblings play an important role in the care of young children (cf. Kulick, 1992; Zukow-Goldring, 2002). Thus, infants and toddlers tend to interact mostly with individuals who are several years older. Simply because of the difference in life experience, most of the people that young children interact with will have more skills and competence than they do, and will act as a guide and a model for them (Vygotsky, 1975).

Young children come to rely upon these important people in their lives, trust them and know them. Affective bonding with these people is very important, and children are eager to receive emotionally positive feedback from them. Thus, young children are not simply 'passive consumers' of the attention they receive, they bring their own developing minds and personalities to their interactions with the people familiar to them.

With the passage of time, interactions between young children and familiar individuals become more and more the dynamic result of a shared history. As children become older, they will develop their own interactional styles and preferences within each of the relationships in which they are engaged. Nevertheless, it is ultimately the caretaking or older partner in the relationship who will be able to set the limits for what is acceptable and appropriate. Some children may love to talk at dinner, but if their parents forbid them to speak at the dinner table and show anger if they do not obey, then even the most talkative child will 'shut up'. Yet often it is enough to model a particular behavior so that children follow the lead: in cultures where dinner-table talk is just 'not done' and everyone eats in silence, children will generally also be silent and will not need to be told. Thus, two important parts of **socialization** are **modeling**, that is, showing by example, and explicit teaching or telling.

Children grow and change all the time. This process is called **maturation**. How much of the socialization around them that children are able to interpret and act upon themselves very much depends on their level of maturation. There is a particular timetable or developmental path that all normally developing babies follow. As many young parents know all too well, it makes no sense to try and tell a three-month-old baby to stop crying. Very young babies are simply unable to understand what you say to them, and their crying appears to be something they cannot really control anyhow. And it makes no sense to teach nine-month-old babies to jump – at that age most cannot even walk.

Most parents know instinctively what their children will be able to do and 'take in' as they closely monitor their children's development and respond to the continuous changes in their children's abilities. There is also evidence that children's cognitive development at least partially depends on their socializing environments (e.g. Bornstein, 2002; Bornstein *et al.*, 1996, 1998; Hart & Risley, 1995). Thus, children's development is the result of a complex interplay between their own developing neurological and physical abilities (their maturation) and the way their caretakers interact with them. Children's language learning is an integral part of their overall development and takes place at the intersection of interaction, socialization and maturation.

Language learning in the first year at the intersection of interaction, socialization and maturation

Maturation, imitation, turn taking

Children do not learn language in a vacuum. For instance, they are able to learn language because they can perceive sounds,[2] can see,[3] have an increasing cognitive ability to make sense of what they hear and see, have an increasing ability in motor skills that allows them to control the movements of the articulatory organs needed for speech (mostly the oral cavity, tongue and lips), and have an increased cognitive ability to interpret and respond to other people's actions and speech. These aspects of maturation are not enough, however. Without people to interact with them and actually talk to them children will not learn to speak.

Parents don't really talk a lot to babies just after they are born. But they do interact with them through smiling, cuddling, tickling, rocking, singing, nursing and so forth. These interactions serve many different functions. One very important function is that in these early interactions, babies learn to pay attention to other people. That makes it possible for them to try to mimic or imitate some of the things these other people are doing or saying (for an example, see Box 2.1).

Box 2.1 Newborns are able to mimic facial gestures

Adapted from Figure 1 in Meltzoff & Moore, 1977

Babies don't (and can't!) imitate just anything, though. In fact, adults interacting with babies are very sensitive to the sorts of things that babies of different ages might be able to imitate. Adults select some action they find worth imitating (such as waving bye bye) and then encourage infants to pay attention to that action, which they then model (show) for the baby. Imitating, then, is not something that babies 'just do' at random. Rather, imitation is embedded in social interaction (Zukow-Goldring & Arbib, 2007). For language, the early imitation of vocal sounds is also firmly grounded in reciprocal interaction with a supportive adult (Papoušek & Papoušek, 1989).

In order for babies to be able to imitate or otherwise act or 'say' something themselves, though, they have to learn to wait until their **interlocutor** has said or done something first (Masataka, 2003: 44–63; Snow, 1977). This is called turn taking.

These two basic things, being able to imitate and being able to take turns, are crucial foundations for language learning. These skills develop as children's cognitive abilities mature. In using language, however, it is also important that you can actually talk about something. You must have something to say that others will attend to.

Joint attention

In the first few months of life, interactions between caregivers and babies mainly just involve caregivers and babies. It is the interaction itself and the participants in the interaction that are the focus of attention. As babies get a bit older, though, caretakers do their best to try and establish what is called **joint attention**. They try to get babies to attend to a third element in the interaction: an action, an object, an animal or another person (see Box 2.2).

Only when both partners in an interaction are focused on the same entity can they start to talk about it and refer to it by means of words. Of course, at first it is only the older participant in the interaction who can actually talk. But babies can show through their non-verbal behavior, such as gaze (what they are looking at) and pointing, that they are focused on what their interlocutor is talking about. Through repeated hearing of words in specific settings they can very gradually come to understand what their interlocutor is saying.

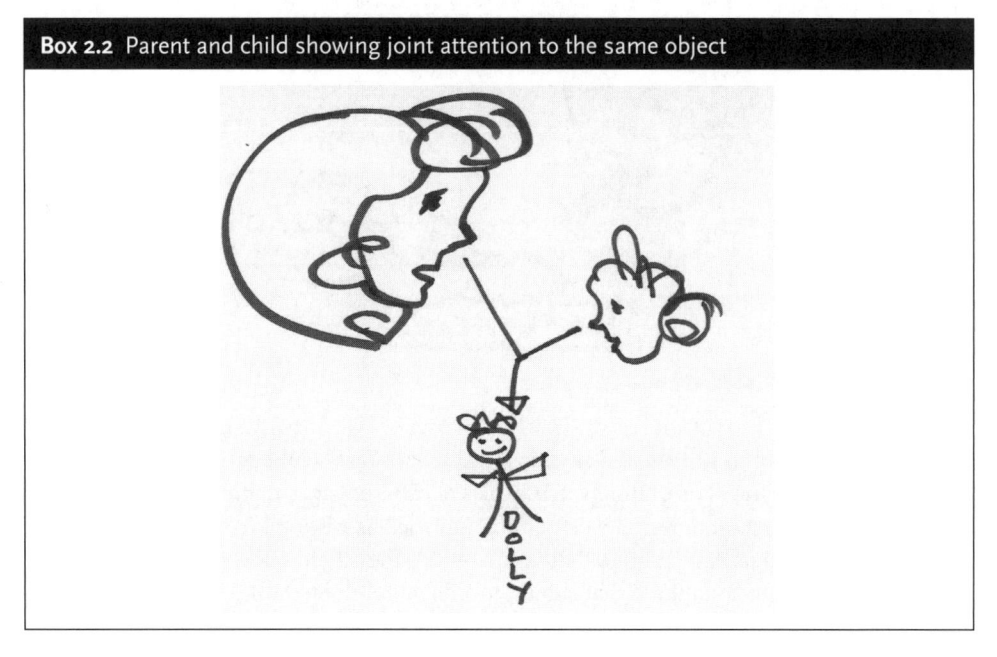

> **Box 2.2** Parent and child showing joint attention to the same object

It is not only the older participant who takes the lead in interactions, however. Babies can take the initiative, too, in focusing another person's attention either on themselves, on their wishes or on objects, animals and people in their immediate environment. Indeed, in the first year of life, the meanings that are involved in interactions between an infant and an older interlocutor tend to be limited to the here and now.

Early sounds

When babies take the initiative in an interaction, they often do this using a vocalization, a sound. When caregivers then respond with speech, this makes it easier for babies to respond in turn with speech-like sounds (Masataka, 2003: 67, 121–123; van der Stelt, 1993). Babies are thus supported and encouraged in their efforts.

At first, infants' repertoire of possible sounds is quite limited. Crying is a universally known vocalization that young babies use a lot. They can also make cooing sounds. Adults usually like these much better! Gradually, the crying becomes less and less frequent and older babies learn to use their lips, tongue, oral cavity and vocal cords to produce all kinds of sounds. Before they are three months of age it is difficult for them to do so because their tongue just about fills their mouths.

Putting **articulators** such as the lips, tongue and oral cavity into different positions has an effect on how sounds will be produced and perceived. The vocal cords are responsible for the **pitch** of sounds. The lungs play an important role in their volume. By using the vocal cords and having the mouth open a bit babies can in a fairly controlled manner produce 'melodies', or **pitch contours**, well before they are able to control their oral articulators.

Babies will often try out all sorts of sounds when they are alone in their cribs. Aside from just enjoying themselves, however, babies are thus actively practicing. Not all their speech sounds, then, are meant to communicate with others, and these practicing sessions are sure signs of maturation taking place in the absence of immediate interactive stimulation. Also, they show that babies are actively involved in their own learning.

Around the beginning of the second half of the first year of life, babies may already start to sound more and more language-like. They may have started to babble, which means that they produce sounds that make you think of **syllables**. Syllables are the basic units around which babies' speech production evolves (Oller, 2000), although of course **prosody** is important as well (Masataka, 2003).

Towards the end of the first year, babies often say what their parents think are real words. People who do not know a particular baby, though, will not be so sure. The way that these first words are articulated can be very different from day to day. Babies need to get their articulators around the sounds that are needed in the language or languages they are learning, and it takes quite some time to do this well. Depending on the particular language they are learning, two year olds in fact still have a few years to go before their **consonants**, **vowels** and **diphthongs** (if their language has these) sound fully **adult-like**.

I discuss children's early sound production in more depth in Chapter 5.

Infant-directed speech (IDS)

In order for children to be able to learn to say the sounds of their language, however, they first have to hear them. This means they first need to be able to pay attention to speech sounds and to **intonation**. This is again where interaction is important. When people talk to babies, they will tend to use a very specific, exaggerated way of speaking. Babies love this typical kind of **infant-directed speech (IDS)**.

In fact, infants are very interested in people talking to them from the very beginning. Cruz-Ferreira (2006: 99) reports that her three children, who heard Portuguese and Swedish from birth, all turned their heads in the direction of human voices when they were one week old. By the time they were one month old, they showed a great interest in facial expressions and in speech addressed to them. They soon learned that sounds they made themselves gained an immediate reaction from their parents. As Cruz-Ferreira (2006: 99) writes: 'vocal sound acquired meaning then, not as a spontaneous effect of bodily discomfort, but as a cause of something pleasurable, namely company and attention'.

Infant-directed speech contains much larger differences between high and low pitched sounds than speech addressed to adults. Also, IDS contains a high proportion of high pitched sounds. These attract infants' attention to speech sounds (Masataka, 2003:

129–138).[4] As babies grow older and appear to understand more, parents will use less and less of the typical characteristics of IDS (Kitamura & Burnham, 2003). We see here a wonderful example of the interplay between infants' own maturing perceptual and cognitive systems and socialization patterns.

Phonemes

A crucial element of early language learning is that infants have to learn which speech sounds are important in their language, that is, which sounds carry communicative meanings and which do not. This is what I call 'tuning in' to important speech sounds.

Before I can say more about this process of 'tuning in' I need to explain what makes certain speech sounds important. At the single speech sound level, the important speech sounds are called **phonemes**. Simply put, these are speech sounds that carry different meanings in a language. I explain this at length in Box 2.3.

Box 2.3 Phones and phonemes

A multitude of different speech sounds
There are many different sounds that humans can produce with their tongues, lips, mouths and vocal cords. If you measure the sound waves produced by these sounds they are all different, however subtly so. One reason is that people's slightly different anatomies produce different resonances.

Phones
The world's languages depend on sounds for meaningful communication. Languages have developed a very efficient system for using different types of sounds as building blocks for speech. The many languages in the world have divided up the staggering multitude of acoustically different human speech sounds to a total of just a few hundred types of important sounds that include consonants, vowels, clicks, tones and word stress. These speech sounds are 'phones' and are represented using a specially designed phonetic alphabet; the consonants and vowels in this alphabet are written between square brackets, as, for instance, [b] and [i]. You can see an inventory with audio examples on the following website sponsored by the International Phonetics Association: http://web.uvic.ca/ling/resources/ipa/charts/IPAlab/IPAlab.htm

Phonemes: meaningful clusters of (allo)phones
Not all languages of the world use all the sounds in the phonetic inventory. The 'click' sounds used in the South African language Xhosa, for instance, do not function as a speech sound in many other languages (but people who do not speak Xhosa sometimes 'fool around' with these click sounds just for fun).

Some languages use only a few of the sounds in the world inventory, others quite a lot more. Also, languages cluster sounds in different meaningful categories. The types of sounds that each language treats as sounding the same are called phonemes (written with slashes around them, as in /p/ and /i/).

A phoneme is a kind of abstract sound, a category, which groups together different individual articulations of sounds that speakers of a particular language will treat as basically sounding similar. These are called 'allophones'. For instance, the Dutch phoneme /b/ may be pronounced like a

> **Box 2.3** Phones and phonemes continued

voiced [b], but sometimes it will be pronounced more like a voiceless [p] (for instance, in the middle of a word due to influence from a neighboring sound). This won't bother speakers of Dutch in their understanding: both the voiced [b] and, in some cases at least, the voiceless [p], are thus allophones of the Dutch phoneme /b/.

Native contrasts: phonemes differ according to language
Languages have different ideas about what sounds similar and what does not. English, for instance, treats [r] and [l] as two very different sounds: these are two separate phonemes. It means something else to say 'read' or 'lead': these two words differ in meaning because they start with what are different phonemes, at least, in English. When this is the case, we can speak of **native contrasts**: these are a pair of sounds that differ from each other in one particular language because they can be used contrastively, that is, using each of them in a word leads to a difference in meaning.

In fact, though, the actual sounds that English speakers hear as /l/ and /r/ are not all that different from each other in their articulation. They are both 'liquids', that is, they are pronounced without a total closure of the mouth, and the air in the mouth just swirls around the tongue. The difference between the sounds [r] and [l] mainly depends on the position of the tongue.

In Japanese, the sounds [r] and [l] do not constitute different phonemes, but there is just a single phoneme /r/ that could be pronounced like English /l/ or /r/. It doesn't make any difference! So if you pronounce the Japanese word 'arigato' ('thank you') as 'aligato' you would be perfectly understood in Japan. In Japanese, then, [r] and [l] do *not* form a pair of native contrasts.

Japanese speakers, however, have trouble distinguishing what to them is the non-native contrast between English /l/ and /r/ (Miyawaki, Strange, Verbrugge, Liberman, Jenkins & Fujimura 1975). They often cannot hear the difference between them, and that makes it very difficult for them when they want to speak English to use /r/ where needed (you might have heard jokes that play on this).

English speakers, however, do not always fare better. For instance, they have great difficulty hearing the difference between French 'rue' ('street') and 'roue' ('wheel'). That is because they are not used to there being an important difference between [y] (the vowel sound in French 'rue') and [u] (the vowel sound in French 'roue').

> **Box 2.3** Phones and phonemes continued
>
> Similarly, speakers of Spanish generally hear no difference between English 'feel' and 'fill'. That is because in Spanish there is just a single phoneme /i/ that can be pronounced either very briefly and with a just slightly open mouth, or with more length and with the lips spread vertically - it does not matter in Spanish. In English, these two different pronunciations make a big difference!
>
> *See Clark and Yallop (1995) for a comprehensive introduction to phonetics and phonology (the field in linguistics which study speech sounds).*

Learning to tune in to phonemes

Just imagine that you are in a rain forest and you've never been in one before – you will be hearing all sorts of new and different sounds. At the beginning, you won't know what they mean, and each sound you hear may startle you and you may not know how to interpret it. But as you spend more time in the rain forest, you will soon start to recognize that some sounds are quite similar, and you will have figured out they come from a spot of rain dropping on leaves, for instance, and are nothing to worry about. But once you have heard a very strong whooshing sound several times and have found yourself in a massive downpour each time you will have learned the difference between these two different kinds of rain sounds. You have learned to put individual instances of different sounds into two major categories: the raindrop sound, which is harmless and the downpour sound, which tells you to find shelter.

Babies have to go through a similar process. They have to learn how the speech sounds they hear pattern into phonemes.

When they are born, babies can distinguish between all sorts of acoustically different sounds. They can hear the difference between [r] and [l] and [b] and [p] and [i] and [y] and [u] and so forth – in fact, they probably hear each sound as being very different from the next. You'll understand that's not very efficient and in fact can be quite chaotic, just like your first days in the rain forest. It pays to try and make sense of the myriad different (speech) sounds that babies are hearing, and in fact, babies do manage to do this.

By the end of the first year of life babies are able to distinguish pretty well between the sounds that are meaningful in the language they are learning. As I explained in Box 2.3, these are called 'native contrasts'. An example for English is the distinction between the /s/ of 'silly' and the /f/ of 'filly'.

However, unlike before, one-year-olds may now have trouble hearing differences between non-native contrasts, which, as I explained in Box 2.3, are sounds that are acoustically different but where this acoustic difference does not really matter in the particular language they are learning. An example for Russian-learning babies is that they would no longer be able to hear the difference between the vowel sound in 'leave' and 'live'. Like Spanish, Russian doesn't use a long (also called 'tense') ee-sound ([i:]) as in English but just has one phoneme /i/ that can be pronounced somewhere in-between the long vowel sound of English 'leave' and the short vowel sound of English 'live'. Because of that, Russian adults may also have trouble hearing the difference between English 'leave' and 'live'.

Just as you learned to distinguish raindrops from a downpour in the rain forest, the way one-year-old infants perceive speech sounds is guided by categories of sounds that they have constructed in their minds based on previous linguistic experience (Sebastián-Gallès, 2006; I develop this point further in Box 2.4). This most probably makes it easier for babies to focus on the particular language they are learning. They no longer have to figure out for each separate sound they hear whether it is an important one and thus they can move on to focusing on bigger things: words and sentences.

> **Box 2.4 Learning to listen for phonemes in infancy**
>
> Box 2.3 contrasted the use of English [l] and [r] with their use in Japanese. The sounds [l] and [r] represent different phonemes in English (viz., /l/ and /r/), but not in Japanese.
>
> It is not surprising that American–English-learning infants can distinguish between [l] and [r] around six and a half months of age (and perhaps earlier). They do far less well than American-English speaking adults, however, so there is room for improvement. And indeed, by the time they are about one year old, American–English-learning infants are doing much better at distinguishing between [l] and [r] than earlier (Kuhl *et al.*, 2006).
>
> In the course of the second half of the first year of life, then, infants become better at distinguishing among sounds that are used to carry different meanings in the language they are learning. This is crucial in helping them understand these different meanings. The experience that infants have with language input in natural settings alters their perception (Kuhl, 2007).
>
> Now consider infants learning Japanese. When they are about six and a half months, they are as good as American–English-learning infants in distinguishing between [l] and [r] (Kuhl *et al.*, 2006), even though this contrast is not relevant to Japanese.
>
> Although they can still distinguish between them occasionally, just four months later Japanese-learning infants are much worse at distinguishing [l] and [r]. Also, they are significantly worse than slightly older American–English-learning infants in distinguishing them (Kuhl *et al.*, 2006).
>
> Japanese-learning infants hear sounds like [l] and [r] in their environment (Kuhl, 2007), but these sounds are not used in a meaningfully contrastive way in Japanese and thus infants do not need to distinguish between them in order to understand Japanese. If they did, and tried to look for different meanings of Japanese words depending on whether they were pronounced with l- or r-like sounds, they would be on the wrong track. It would not aid them in understanding their world.

Babies also need to learn that specific intonation patterns in their input language carry specific meanings. For instance, they need to be able to distinguish between an angry tone of voice and a soothing, sing-song kind of voice. Or, for instance, they need to distinguish between question intonation and intonation patterns that signal a command. However, little research has been carried out in this area. It is not clear just when and how babies learn these meanings (in Chapter 5 I talk more about intonation and its importance).

The role of experience

Babies need to hear a lot of the sounds of their language to be able to learn which sounds in that language are used as building blocks for words and sentences. Generally, they need about a year's experience with people talking to them on a daily basis before they are really 'tuned in' to the language they are learning. Some of that 'tuning in' has already happened by the time infants are six months old, however.

Infants learning different languages that differ with regard to the frequencies of use of particular sounds in the input show different patterns of speech perception that reflect these input differences (Kuhl, 2007; Kuhl et al., 1992). There is also evidence that variations in infant-directed speech in a particular language have an effect on variations between infants in how well they are able to perceive native contrasts (Liu et al., 2003).

Thus, various properties of the naturally occurring input that infants hear affects how they perceive their input and, hence, how they can respond to it.[5] Again, it is social interaction that impacts on early language development (Gallaway & Richards, 1994; Kuhl, 2007; Snow & Ferguson, 1977).

The early developmental processes relevant for language are highly similar for children everywhere

My brief overview above of some of the earliest stages in language development makes it clear that regardless of which language babies are hearing, a lot of specific linguistic developments take place well before children are able to speak.

Later language development builds on the speech perception abilities that infants have developed when they are only six to seven months old (Conboy et al., 2005; Newman et al., 2006; Tsao et al., 2004). Early speech perception abilities, in turn, very much depend on the way people interact and talk to infants.

In fact, infants in the first year of life need human interaction in order to start learning a particular language. Nine-month-old English-learning babies learned to distinguish a Chinese Mandarin **phonological contrast** that does not exist in English. They learned this after exposure to the contrast through interactions with a human who used IDS. However, when the infants heard the contrast through just audio or video recordings they did not learn it, even though the recordings were done using intonation patterns and stylistic features of IDS (Kuhl et al., 2003).[6]

The complex interplay between children's own maturation, interaction and socialization is basic to children's development regardless of which language they are learning – at least, for the languages and monolingually raised children studied so far.

This interplay is most likely also basic to children growing up with two languages from birth, although the evidence for this claim consists of just a single study to date. In a study I co-directed in Belgium, we compared a group of 30 infants learning just Dutch and 31 BFLA infants learning both Dutch and French. The children were growing up in similar demographic and sociocultural backgrounds (Bornstein et al., in preparation). We observed the infants as they interacted with their mothers in the home at the age of five months. We coded and analysed a large number of different aspects of mothers' and their infants' behaviors, both vocal/verbal and non-verbal. We found no differences between the monolingual and bilingual groups other than that some mothers in the bilingual group spoke French whereas all the monolingual mothers spoke Dutch. It doesn't seem to matter for the way mothers and children interact, then, whether children are part of a monolingual or a bilingual family.

Learning about language starts very early

As I mentioned earlier, babies are already learning about the specific language they are hearing in the first six months of life. What they are learning about a specific language in that very early period of life helps to shape their later development of that same language.

Learning about a specific language starts even before children have seen their mothers! We know this thanks to studies of newborn babies. Newborn babies already have some skills that are language related. For instance, they can already pick out the rhythm of their mother's language from other rhythms (Nazzi *et al.*, 1998). The only logical explanation for this feat is that babies have already started to learn about language before they are born. In fact, there is growing evidence from research with unborn babies that they can already respond to selected aspects of their mother's language prior to birth (Krueger *et al.*, 2004). It will be interesting to find out what the response to language is by unborn infants whose mothers regularly spoke two languages during pregnancy. Do these unborn children already respond differently to either language? Right now, we can only guess, but exciting recent work on newborn infants whose mothers regularly spoke two languages during pregnancy also suggests that these children are learning about language before they are born (Byers-Heinlein *et al.*, 2008; see also Chapter 5).

Bilingual First Language Acquisition and Monolingual First Language Acquisition both involve the learning of language from birth or even before. The importance of this early learning of the foundations for language suggests that BFLA will be closer to MFLA than to Early Second Language Acquisition (ESLA). As we shall see, generally speaking this does, indeed, appear to be the case. Before we can start to compare BFLA to other acquisition settings, however, we need to take a closer look at BFLA itself.

An outline of bilingual development in the first five years of life

Before take-off

Children who hear two languages from birth do not say much in the first year of life. Through interactions with people who talk to them regularly they do learn to understand words and phrases in two languages by the end of the first year. In the second half of the first year of life, bilingual infants start to babble. This babbling lays the foundation for speech (see Chapter 5).

Then, in the second year of life, bilingual infants start to say things that sound like words. At first, children produce mainly single words. Some BFLA children may try to say longer things, but although the melodies of these longer **utterances** might sound like **sentences** it is impossible to make much sense of them. As bilingual children start to say more and more 'real' words, their babbling all but disappears.

Towards the end of the second year, bilingual toddlers speak in longer utterances comprising two or three words. In the third year, language production really takes off, with children producing multi-word utterances. From then on, the sky is the limit, and it is often difficult to keep bilingual children quiet!

You cannot say words without being able to say their sounds, and you cannot say sentences without knowing how you should put the words together (and, of course, you have to have something meaningful to say). In learning to speak two languages, then, learning about sounds, words and sentences are all part of one complex whole. Yet at the same time, each of these different learning tasks also has its own special features. In the following subsections I focus on those features in a little more detail. Chapters 5, 6 and 7 are the places where you will find more in-depth discussions.

Sounds and words

Bilingual children acquire the phonological patterns of their two input languages slowly. They start out using **substitution** and **deletion** patterns as well as **adult-like** sounds, that is, phonemes that sound the way that adults would say them (apart from the general difference in the pitch range of the voice between children and adults).

Substitutions involve the use of a related phoneme instead of the adult phoneme, that is, the one you would expect to hear from an adult. For instance, instead of the /k/ phoneme in Dutch 'kapot' (broken) which is pronounced in the back of the mouth like English /k/, young children often say [t], which is pronounced much more forward in the mouth, but apart from that is really the same (the air flow from the lungs is completely blocked at one point in the mouth and the vocal cords are not vibrating – the sound is **voiceless**). In deletion, children omit a phoneme where there should have been one. For instance, they might pronounce the first two sounds of the French word for cars, 'voiture', as [w] rather than /vw/.

Gradually, adult-like phonemes prevail, and BFLA children become much easier to understand, to unfamiliar people as well. Around the age of three and a half much of what bilingual children say is quite understandable to people who meet them for the first time.

Children must not only learn to say words properly, they must also learn where the word boundaries are and what the words mean. How are they to know that when you point to the cat and say in French 'Regarde, le chat!' (look, there's the cat) you are referring to that animal and that only the word 'chat' (cat) in fact refers to it and not 'regarde' (look), or indeed, the whole utterance.

It is amazing how children do learn to understand many words from very early on. It is difficult to test just what they think the meanings of these words are, but when they themselves speak we realize that their developing meanings are not necessarily ours. A child might say 'chat' but point to a dog! Perhaps this child has interpreted 'chat' as referring to furry pets. This is an example of what is called **overextension**: the adult meaning is made 'bigger'. Or another child might say 'chat' only to refer to one particular cat. This is called **underextension**: the adult meaning is made 'smaller'. Phenomena such as over- and underextension are called **semantic** processes. What little information there is on these processes in young bilingual children shows that they use them in addition to apparently adult-like use (e.g. Leopold, 1970).

Holophrases

When BFLA children first start to say things that adults interpret as words, they appear to use these words with very 'big' meanings. When a bilingual English–Dutch-speaking child says 'apple', for instance, depending on the circumstances adults might interpret this as having a meaning like 'that's an apple and I would like you to confirm that' or like 'I want to eat an apple'. Similarly, the child's Dutch 'uit!' (out) might be interpreted as 'I want to get out of my high chair'.

These 'big' single words have often been called **holophrases**. They are not sentences but parents often seem to interpret them as such: BFLA children seem to express just what is to them the most important word of a sentence and parents try to figure out the 'story' around this word. Parents and children's caregivers will attribute these holophrases with a larger meaning than single words usually have in adult speech.

Typically, BFLA children *want* something when they talk. For instance, they want to draw someone's attention to something, or they want to get something to eat or drink or play with. They use holophrases for this purpose.

From early on, in fact, BFLA children learn to use language to reach particular communicative goals such as getting someone's attention, getting some object they want, persuading someone, asking for information, stating their beliefs and so forth. These meaningful actions effectuated by means of language are called speech acts. Using speech acts is part of what is called **pragmatics**.

Bilingual children's early words, then, are not necessarily **referential**, but often have a **pragmatic meaning**: they are used for communicative effect. An example is the Dutch 'uit!' above, or Portuguese–English Sofie's 'aqui? aqui? aqui?' (here? here? here?) said while she was quickly leafing through a magazine in search of a favorite picture. Her utterance had the effect that her mother started to help her find the picture (Cruz-Ferreira, 2006: 107). Bilingual children make use of holophrases in the second year of life (Leopold, 1970; Porché, 1983; Ronjat, 1913; see Chapter 6).

The meanings of BFLA children's early words are linked to the here-and-now. Children will tell you what food they want, or they'll comment that an ambulance is coming by, but don't expect them to discuss the caloric value of food or how ambulance services are organized until some years later.

I discuss BFLA children's early words further in Chapter 6.

Putting words together

In order to sound a bit more like adults and in order to increase their communicative power, young BFLA children do not stick with holophrases but eventually start to combine words with each other. This is an important milestone in bilingual children's language development.

At first, bilingual children occasionally start to say two words in a single breath, with or without a short pause between them. Once bilingual children start to do this they often have a **production vocabulary** of about 50 words or so (Patterson, 1998). I give an example of a BFLA child's earliest words and word combinations in Box 2.5.

> **Box 2.5** Early words and early word combinations: examples from a German-English speaking boy
>
> The boy Nicolai heard German and English from birth and grew up in Germany. When he was 21 months old, Nicolai first started to occasionally say two words in one breath. At that time, he had been heard to say at least 66 different words. These 66 words constituted his total repertoire. This repertoire contained:
>
> 1 German words like 'Ei' (egg) and 'ja' (yes);
> 2 English words like 'nice' and 'pee-ta' (peacock);
> 3 Words that could belong to either German or English like 'Teddy' and 'house/Haus', and
> 4 A separate category of words that mostly consisted of onomatopoeic words or 'babytalk' items such as 'dada' for 'bye bye' and 'au/ow' for 'cat', modelled after 'miaow'.
>
> Nicolai's first word combinations were 'die da' (two German words meaning this-there) and 'tickticktick uhuh' (two words that could be either German or English).
>
> Nicolai said 'tickticktick uhuh' with amazement when he discovered that an alarm clock was not in its usual place – he was basically saying that the alarm clock wasn't there; 'uhuh' probably sounded like [∂h∂]. The utterance 'die da' was one that he had heard his mother and other German speakers say, but 'tickticktick uhuh' was his own creation.
>
> *Adapted from Porsché, 1983: 90, 100*

Most bilingual children start using two word combinations between the ages of 18 and 23 months (Patterson, 1998). At the same time, the number of words that they know in each language increases quite dramatically also. This increase in the number of words goes together with an increase of words that are needed to make sentences, such as verbs. It is perhaps not surprising, then, that with increased vocabulary knowledge in each language bilingual toddlers' grammatical knowledge increases as well (Conboy & Thal, 2006). I start discussing this issue more in Chapter 6 and take it up again in more depth in Chapter 7.

Making sentences

You and I don't usually speak in utterances of just two words. Also for BFLA children it's not enough to just put one word after another one. In order to express more meanings, they need to combine more words! That's what speakers of different languages all over the world do when they make sentences.

Indeed, people combine words into sentences to express all sorts of quite complicated ideas. In Box 2.6 I give a brief summary of what sentences consist of and of some of the devices that languages use to construct sentences. Readers with a background in linguistics may wish to skip this box.

Box 2.6 Morphosyntax: Some basic sentence elements

It is impossible to capture the variability in the languages of the world in a brief description. This box is meant simply as a basis from which to better understand some of the discussions and descriptions later in this book and is by necessity highly selective. The selection is based on the languages that will be referred to most often in the remainder of the book.

Words, free morphemes, word roots
Languages construct sentences out of words. What we call 'words', however, can differ quite a lot between languages. Some languages don't really have words like English does. They use word roots to construct sentences (an example is Inuktitut, a language spoken by the Inuit).[a] It is more accurate, in fact, to say that most languages construct sentences on the basis of **free morphemes** or **word roots**. Free morphemes or word roots each have some sort of dictionary meaning.

In principle, free morphemes are words with referential meaning that can be used on their own. Often, however, they need other elements attached to or combined with them to be properly used. Word roots cannot be used by themselves but always need other elements to be attached to them.

An example of a free morpheme that can be used by itself is Spanish 'llave' (key). An example of a word root is Italian 'parl-' (talk, speak). In Italian, you need to add some element to this root to make any sense. For instance, you could add 'o' to make 'parlo', which means 'I speak'. Some languages have very few free morphemes while others have very few word roots.

Combining free morphemes and/or word roots into sentences
Free morphemes and/or word roots are used to build up a bigger sentence meaning. This is done through a combination of basic mechanisms.

(1) *Word order* (the term 'word' is shorthand here for both free morphemes and word roots) Speakers of all languages have in common that they cannot say two different words at once. Therefore, words are said one after the other.

Just putting one word after another in some random order is not good enough. We need to put words into a particular order. Languages differ in the typical word orders that they use for the basic building blocks of sentences (**subjects**, **verbs** and **objects**; see below). If I were to say: 'the in look drawer' people might figure out that I mean to express that they should look in a particular drawer, but if they are English speakers they will understand me much better if I say: 'look in the drawer!', with the words in an order that makes sense in English.

(2) **Morphology**.[b]
Most languages make use of at least a few **bound morphemes** to help construct sentence meaning (some languages have a lot of these). Bound morphemes are elements that can be very short (a single phoneme) or longer (several syllables) and that are closely attached to free morphemes or word roots.

> **Box 2.6** Morphosyntax: Some basic sentence elements continued
>
> Every language has a set number of bound morphemes. They form what is called a 'closed class'. This means that it is very rare that new bound morphemes appear. This is in contrast to many kinds of free morphemes and word roots.
>
> There are several kinds of bound morphemes. I list the three main ones:
>
> (2.1) Prefixes: these come before the free morpheme or root. An example from Swahili is the **noun** prefix 'wa-', which indicates a plural on word roots referring to animate beings. For instance, if you add the prefix 'wa-' to the word root '-tu' you get 'watu', which means 'persons, people' in Swahili
>
> (2.2) Infixes: these are inserted somewhere inside the free morpheme or root (usually the latter). Infixes are common in the original languages of Australia and in Semitic languages such as Arabic and Hebrew. Languages originally spoken in Western Europe have traces of infixes. For instance, the German verb stem 'lass' (let) changes to 'ließ' (let) to form the past tense. There is a change inside the word from 'a' [a] to 'ie' [i].
>
> (2.3) Suffixes: these are attached at the end of the word or root, as in the Spanish '¿Hablas ingles?' (do you speak English?), where the '-as' at the end of the root 'habl-' is a suffix that refers to the second person singular present tense.
>
> A single bound morpheme can also consist of a combination of prefixes, infixes and suffixes. An example is the Dutch bound morpheme used to make past participles of verb stems. The regular past participle consists of a combination of the prefix 'ge-' and the suffix -[t]. Thus, the past participle form of the verb stem 'maak' (make) is 'ge-maak-t'. German uses a similar process.
>
> (3) *Grammatical words*
> There may be separate word-like elements that do not attach themselves to particular words as do bound morphemes but that serve a similar function. Like bound morphemes, these also form a 'closed class', but they are free morphemes. These closed class **grammatical words** include categories we know from English, French and German such as **pronouns** and **determiners** but also **particles** as used in Japanese. Languages rarely introduce new words in these categories.
>
> An example of a grammatical word is the Dutch second person singular pronoun 'je' that means 'you', as in the Dutch 'Spreek je Duits?' (do you speak German?).
>
> *Verbs, subjects and objects*
> In sentences, **verbs** are usually the central element (one per sentence). In fact, you can have sentences that contain just a single verb, as in the command 'Go!'. Verbs can consist of just one word or more.
>
> If you want to add more meanings, you can add more specific information around the verb. For instance, you could express who or what was doing the action that is expressed in the verb (as in 'She has gone'). The sentence element that expresses this agent is called the **subject**. Note, though, that subjects aren't limited to expressing actions expressed in verbs, and that verbs aren't limited to expressing actions: for instance, 'seems' in 'That seems OK' doesn't exactly express an action. Also, some languages do not always express the agent of an action through the subject.

> **Box 2.6** Morphosyntax: Some basic sentence elements continued
>
> The sentence elements expressing something that is affected by whatever the verb refers to are called **objects**. Verbs, subjects and objects are the most important elements in a sentence.

^a Often the term 'stem' is used for word roots that consist of verbs.
^b I here only discuss inflectional morphology, that is, word formation devices that are grammatical in nature and express things like gender, tense, person, direction, definiteness, passive, number, case and much else besides (an example from English, a language poor in inflectional morphology, is the plural '-s' in 'verbs'). Inflectional morphology differs from derivational morphology, which tends to be used to make new words and change their grammatical class (e.g. '-ize' in English turns adjectives into verbs, as in 'modernize', which is based on the adjective 'modern').

Young bilingual children try to make themselves understood as well as possible from early on. This implies that they will try to build little sentences that make sense in the languages they are learning. Although young bilingual children are trying to build sentences for the very first time in their lives, they can pretty much already do this according to the patterns that exist in their two input languages. They usually don't just put words together in a random order, as in 'the in look drawer'. Nor do they say things like 'put want go look', where you find four different **lexical verbs** put together in one utterance.

Instead, bilingual children mostly use language-appropriate word orders from early on. Examples are Italian 'vuoi il cioccolato?' (do you want the chocolate?) and English 'dat a dog' as said by English–Italian Carlo at age 2;2 (Serratrice, 2002). In 'dat a dog' there is something missing (the copula 'is') but the order of the words is right.

Many languages in the world use bound morphemes (I explain what these are in Box 2.6). Bilingual children who are learning a language with a lot of bound morphemes will start to use some of these from early on. However, the total number of bound morphemes they use at a particular age is still relatively small in comparison with adult usage. Also, BFLA children will at first use their limited repertoires of bound morphemes in fairly limited ways. Gradually, bilingual children use more and more different bound morphemes, and use them in more diverse ways.

Languages that do not use a lot of bound morphemes typically rely more on special kinds of words to help construct meanings such as pronouns and determiners (see Box 2.6). From now on, I will refer to these as grammatical words (see also Box 2.6). Again, bilingual children who are learning a language that uses more grammatical words than bound morphemes will from early on start to use at least some of these important building blocks. As they grow older, the diversity of these closed class items will expand.

Starting at around age two and a half, then, BFLA children will start to construct real sentences that consist of three or four words. They will usually put these words into the right order for the language they happen to be speaking, and they will use bound morphemes and grammatical words from the right language. Moreover, studies of bilingual children's morphosyntactic development have provided ample evidence for the **Separate Development Hypothesis (SDH)**, which states that children regularly exposed to two separate languages from birth develop two distinct morphosyntactic systems, in that 'the morphosyntactic development of the one language does not have any fundamental effect on the morphosyntactic development of the other' (De Houwer, 1990: 66; 2005). I discuss the SDH in more detail in Chapter 7.

In Box 2.7 I give some examples of sentences that bilingual children say from an early age and of the sentence elements they use to construct those sentences.

> **Box 2.7** Basic sentence elements: some examples from bilingual children
>
> *All word orders in these examples are* **target-like***; I use the* **CHAT transcription** *conventions from* **CHILDES** *for representing utterances (for explanations of CHILDES and CHAT, see Chapter 3).*
>
> *CHI: yes, what happened (English)
> yes   = sentence particle
> what   = closed class grammatical word (interrogative subject pronoun, inanimate)
> happened = verb consisting of the free morpheme 'happen' and a past tense bound morpheme -ed (suffix)
>
> *By Timmy, who heard Cantonese and English from birth; age: ca. 2;10; source: CHILDES archive, Yip and Matthews corpus*
>
> *CHI: é aí meu carro (Brazilian Portuguese)
> gloss: is-there-my-car
> é   = free morpheme, copular verb
> aí   = closed class grammatical word (adverb)
> meu   = closed class grammatical word (possessive pronoun, first person, singular)
> carro = free morpheme, noun
>
> Note: the word order here is a bit unusual, but still target-like
>
> *By Daniel, who heard German and Brazilian Portuguese from birth; age: ca. 3;01; source: Hinzelin, 2003*
>
> *CHI: ora devo fare una casa bella (Italian)
> gloss: now-I have to-make-a-house-beautiful
> ora   = closed class grammatical word (adverb)
> devo = verb consisting of the word root 'dev-' and the first person singular present tense bound morpheme -o (suffix)
> fare = verb consisting of the word root 'fa-' and the infinitive bound morpheme -re (suffix)
> una   = closed class grammatical word (indefinite pronoun, feminine, singular)
> casa = free morpheme, feminine singular noun
> bella = adjective consisting of the free morpheme root 'bell-' and the singular feminine bound morpheme -a (suffix)
>
> *By Lina, who heard Swedish and Italian from birth; age: ca. 2;11; source: Bernardini, 2003*

In their fourth year of life, BFLA children will start to be able to say **complex sentences**. These combine simple sentences with each other. Together with their increased knowledge of how to connect sentences with each other, being able to produce complex sentences allows bilingual children to carry on better conversations and to tell stories. For a more detailed discussion of bilingual children's morphosyntactic development see Chapter 7.

Utterance length

Regardless of the specific language they are learning, the average length of young children's utterances is indicative of their overall level of language development. In general, the longer an utterance is, the more complex it is. This is why often the **mean length of utterance** is used as an indication of young children's language development.

Mean length of utterance or MLU is the average length of the utterances that a person says during a particular time frame. For instance, if a child's MLU is 2.5 at age three, this means that on average, that child's utterances are 2.5 words long. What this will actually mean is that there will be some utterances consisting of just a single word, quite a few consisting of two words and many consisting of three words. A child speaking the same language who at age three has an MLU of 3.0 will be saying longer utterances and this will usually mean that those utterances are on the whole more complex in terms of their grammatical structure. BFLA children's MLU in each language goes up as they get older.

Typically, MLU is computed on the basis of at least 100 consecutive utterances (this follows the guidelines of Roger Brown, who introduced the MLU measure – see Brown, 1973). Length can be measured in morphemes or words. Because the notion 'word' is more difficult to properly define, it is customary in child language research to count the number of morphemes that occur in an utterance. In Chapter 3 you will find a more in-depth discussion of the use of the MLU measure in studies of bilingual acquisition.

Box 2.8 Milestones in BFLA children's early language development

When? (roughly)	What?
6 to 12 months	babbling in syllables
By 12 months	comprehension of many words and phrases in each of two languages
Soon after 12 months	production of what sounds like single words in one or two languages
18 to 24 months	noticeable increase in the number of different words produced
Around 24 months	production of combinations of two words in one breath
30 to 36 months	production of short sentences with at least some bound morphemes and/or closed class grammatical words
Around 42 months	child is mostly understandable to unfamiliar adults who speak the same language(s)
Around 48 months	production of complex sentences
54 to 60 months	ability to tell a short story that hangs together

For easy reference, here is a key to some age indications:

12 months = first birthday, age 1, start of the second year of life
24 months = second birthday, age 2, start of the third year of life
36 months = third birthday, age 3, start of the fourth year of life
48 months = fourth birthday, age 4, start of the fifth year of life
60 months = fifth birthday, age 5, start of the sixth year of life

Bilingual milestones

Box 2.8 summarizes some of the points discussed in this section in the form of an overview of the ages at which you can expect certain linguistic behaviors from BFLA children (see the next section on 'Normal variation', though). I call these 'milestones' because they are important stages in bilingual development.

The last age indication in my overview of milestones in young BFLA children's language development coincides with children's fifth birthday. This does not imply, however, that language development is complete by that age. There is still a lot to learn after the age of five (see, e.g. Berman, 2004). The very fact that no adult wants to sound like a five-year-old in any language is clear evidence of that. Not only do BFLA children learn a lot more words, idioms and phrases after age five, they also learn to construct more and more complex monologues and become better conversationalists. They may also learn to read and write. I discuss a few studies that have looked at later developments in BFLA children at the end of Chapter 7.

In this overview I have focused on BFLA children's overall language development, regardless of which languages they are learning and without referring much to the specifics of the bilingual setting. After all, this course of language development is of fundamental importance in a BFLA child's life.

If you are familiar with patterns of MFLA you will have noticed that the general patterns of bilingual development for children regularly addressed in two languages from birth are identical to those for monolingual children (see also De Houwer, 2002a, 2005).

Box 2.9 What the belief that bilingual children develop more slowly can lead to

This pediatrician thinks that bilingual input leads to language delay. Therefore, she is not surprised

> **Box 2.9** What the belief that bilingual children develop more slowly can lead to *continued*
>
> to see a bilingually reared two-year-old who does not speak at all yet. She sees no need for a detailed examination and sends the father away with the advice to drop the minority language. She tells the father that all will soon be fine.
>
> But after a year the child is back, and still does not speak. Upon examination (finally!), the child is found to be profoundly deaf. Most likely, the child's hearing was not good at age two, either. In this case, the doctor's prejudice has sadly resulted in lack of proper care for this young child.

There is a particular order in overall language development that all young children follow. Babbling occurs prior to saying sentences, for instance, and comprehension precedes production.

However, people often worry that bilingual children are hampered in their language development because they have to deal with two languages. Many people believe that bilingual children will develop language slower than monolingual children. If pediatricians or other 'authorities' believe this, it can have disastrous effects for children and their families (see Box 2.9). In the next section I put this belief into perspective and show that there is no evidence for the claim that as a group, children with bilingual input from birth develop language more slowly than children with input in just a single language.

Normal variation in BFLA and MFLA

The time frame in which the major developments in language take place is similar across MFLA and BFLA children: it takes about five years to develop enough language skill to tell a good story. However, there is a wide variation regarding the ages at which children reach important linguistic milestones. This variation exists in both monolingual and bilingual children. There are also large differences between children – regardless of whether they are learning one or two languages – in how many words they know, how talkative they are, how easily they speak how well they speak or how clearly they speak.

Let us take a closer look at the timing of important milestones. It might not seem much of a difference from the perspective of an adult life, but a difference of six months in the life of a two-year-old is quite a large difference: six months in the life of a two-year-old means a quarter of their lifetime. But the six months between 18 and 24 months of age are the normal age range in which children may have reached the word combination milestone. Some children will be saying two-word combinations when they are one and a half, while others will be ready only at the time of their second birthday. Both possibilities represent the 'normal' variation, that is, the variation that occurs between children that you don't have to worry about. This normal variation is the same for MFLA and BFLA children (Patterson, 1998).

At the younger end of the normal variation in language development we are dealing with precocious children. More worrisome is the older end. When children are not saying word combinations soon after their second birthday, parents should consult a speech-language pathologist to see what might be the reason for this delay in language development. This goes for children reared monolingually as well as children reared bilingually.

Within the normal variation pattern, however, MFLA and BFLA children who are developing faster definitely have an advantage over the slower developers. This is particularly the case for word learning. There can be huge (and normal) differences between bilingual toddlers in the number of words they say (Marchman et al., 2004). As Hart and Risley (1995) have shown for monolingual children, early differences in the numbers of different words that children produce when they are three years old become even greater as children grow older: Children who knew far fewer words than same-age peers simply cannot catch up with them. And since word knowledge is so important for academic achievement, the better word learners will have an advantage over the less good word learners (Marchman & Fernald, 2008).

It is indeed important, then, to find out about the possible reasons for the differences between children within the normal range of variation. It would be nice to know whether some of that variation can be linked to factors that you can manipulate; if so, you could increase the chances that a particular child develops faster. Hart and Risley (1995) have explained differences in word learning in the monolingual group of children they studied in terms of the cumulative effect of the number of words per minute that children hear around them. In Chapter 4 I discuss input frequency effects in bilingual learning.

In conclusion, whether you grow up with one or two languages, as long as you have no major problem such as hearing loss, neurological disorders or lack of human interaction you will learn to speak pretty well by the time you are five. Yet you may speak much worse or much better than another child your age. Why this should be the case isn't quite clear, but it does not depend on the number of languages you are learning.

Bilingual children's language repertoires

As I have indicated above, BFLA children's overall course of language development is like that of monolingual children. This shows the robust nature of the early language acquisition process: its general course is fairly universal and not influenced by whether children are learning one or two languages. However, there is a large and obvious difference between MFLA and BFLA children in that the former are learning to understand and speak one language, whereas the latter are learning two.

But what does it mean to be learning two languages? This section reviews to what extent BFLA children show any evidence of learning two languages rather than just one.

Different kinds of utterances in production

Most BFLA children mentioned in the literature actually speak two different languages. This means that they are able to produce utterances with words and structures from one language exclusively, and that they do this for two different languages. Utterances with words from one language only are **unilingual utterances**.

Bilingual children may also use words or morphemes from both their languages in one utterance. These are called **mixed utterances**. Typically, mixed utterances by young bilingual children consist of borrowings of one free morpheme (usually a noun) from Language A into an utterance in Language Alpha (e.g. Cantone, 2007: 173; Quay, 2008).

BFLA children hardly ever insert just a bound morpheme from Language A into an utterance that is otherwise entirely in Language Alpha. Genesee (2005) reports that in a corpus of 10,000 utterances by several young French–English-speaking children only six such instances were found, as in 'Bross-ing dents' ('brushing teeth', said by the child Gen at age 2;7), where the English '-ing' bound morpheme is inserted into an otherwise entirely French utterance (for more on the structure of mixed utterances, see Chapter 7).

Depending on the actual languages that they are learning, BFLA children also produce utterances that could belong to either of their languages. Following a suggestion by Wolf Wölck, I will call these **indeterminate utterances**. Typically, languages that are historically closely related also have some overlap in their lexicons. When children then say a word that sounds and means the same in both languages you cannot really decide which language they are speaking.

The possibility for the use of indeterminate utterances depends very much on which two languages a child is learning. The more closely related the two languages are, the more chance there is that they will be part of a BFLA child's repertoire. The longer an utterance is, however, the less chance there is that it will be indeterminate, simply because there is not all that much overlap even between closely related languages.

Indeterminate utterances can be heard at any age (including in the speech of bilingual adults). Since it is mostly young children who tend to produce relatively more short utterances, the proportion of indeterminate utterances will usually decrease with age.

Finally, for very young bilingual children you can sometimes not find any clear connection between what they are saying and either of the languages they are learning. Also for very young monolingual children the link between what they say and the words from the language they are learning is sometimes impossible to find. These utterances I will call **'floating' utterances** since their origin is unknown to adults, but must be 'floating around' in the child's mind somewhere.[7]

Floating utterances are typical of very young children (up until around the age of two) and will only occasionally occur later on. They are children's own language-like creations and are usually not taken very seriously by the people around them. Ultimately, these floating utterances disappear or become the stuff sound-games and poetry are made of.

In Box 2.10 I list the five categories of utterances that bilingual children might use, with examples for each.

Box 2.10   Five categories for BFLA child utterances

1. Unilingual utterances in Language A: the entire utterance (short or long) is in Language A only
Example 1(a)   **itata?** '(did it) hurt?' (the adult form would be: itakata)
          ita(i) = have hurt; (ka)ta = simple past morpheme
Japanese; by English–Japanese-speaking Ken at 2;3 (Mishina-Mori, 2005: 304)

Example 1(b)   **kore watashi no?** '(is) this mine?'
          kore = this; watashi = I; no = particle indicating possession
Japanese; by English–Japanese-speaking Rie at 3;3 (Mishina-Mori, 2005: 305)

2. Unilingual utterances in Language Alpha: the entire utterance (short or long) is in Language Alpha only
Example 2(a)   **you get, I eat**
English; by English–Cantonese-speaking Timmy at 2;02 (Yip & Matthews, 2005: 2428)
Example 2(b)   **me want to eat**
English; by English–Cantonese-speaking Sophie at 3;00 (Yip & Matthews, 2005: 2429)

3. Mixed utterances that combine elements of Language A and Language Alpha
Example 3(a)   **[kak]** ('cake')
Blend of English /keik/ and Norwegian /ka:ke/ by English–Norwegian-speaking Siri at 1;11 (Lanza, 1997: 164)
Example 3(b)   **og jeg er boy** ('and I am (a) boy')
          og = and; jeg = I; er = am
Utterance with three Norwegian words (og, jeg, er) and one English word (boy) by English–Norwegian-speaking Tomas at 2;3 (Lanza, 1997: 348)

> **Box 2.10** Five categories for BFLA child utterances continued
>
> 4. *Indeterminate utterances that could either be entirely in Language A, or entirely in Language Alpha (these sorts of utterances are typically short)*
> Example 4(a)   **[ba]** 'ball'
> Attempt at Dutch 'bal' [bal] or French 'balle' [bal], which both mean 'ball'; by a French–Dutch-speaking boy aged 20 months (from my unpublished data collected in cooperation with Marc Bornstein)
> Example 4(b)   **papa**
> This word could be either Dutch or French (and other languages besides!); by a French–Dutch-speaking girl aged 20 months (from my unpublished data collected in cooperation with Marc Bornstein)
>
> 5. *Floating utterances: apparently meaningful utterances whose language provenance cannot be determined*
> Example 5   **[pi:pi:]**
> Onomatopoeic word used by a German–Italian-speaking child at age 22 months to refer to a car or the sound of a horn (Klammler, 2006: 45)

You will have noticed that some of the unilingual utterances in Box 2.10 are not really adult-like. 'You get, me eat' and 'me want to eat' are not 'proper' English. But they do consist of only English words. That makes them unilingual rather than mixed. Also, it is clear that the words are English and not Cantonese or another language. This means they are not in the category 'indeterminate' or 'floating'. To what extent these unilingual utterances may show influence from Cantonese grammatical structure, however, remains to be seen.

The fact that the categorization of utterances here is lexically based means that comparisons with utterances from monolingual children are possible. Monolingual children's unilingual utterances also have words from one language, but are not necessarily adult-like (in fact, they often are not).

Using mixed utterances

Even when children are not yet speaking in short sentences, they may produce mixed utterances. These are not very easy to identify, however. After all, when children are in the one-word stage, their sound production is still very much in flux. This makes it often difficult to identify to which language a child's vocalization belongs.

The difficulty of identifying the language provenance of early utterances means that mixed utterances at the one-word stage have only rarely been reported. Porsché (1983: 103) mentions that he heard his English–German son Nicolai produce such mixed utterances only once or twice. He is sure of the following example, where Nicolai said 'tsow' (rhyming with 'foe'). One of Nicolai's toes was hurting and his word 'tsow' was apparently a mix of German 'Zeh' (toe), where the first sound is pronounced as 'ts' and English 'toe'. These kinds of mixes at the word level, called '**blends**', have also been reported for monolingual children, where they combine elements from two free morphemes in a novel creation (see also Chapter 6).

There certainly is no evidence for the often-heard claim that all BFLA children go through a period in which they use almost exclusively mixed utterances. In fact, in a recent detailed longitudinal study of the mixed utterances used by five young German–Italian-speaking children, none of the children used more mixed than unilingual utterances. Up until the time when the children were producing mainly two-word utterances, their use of mixed utterances was no greater than 10%, and not all children reached the level of 10%. At later stages, each child's proportion of use of mixed utterances remained fairly constant (Cantone, 2007). Serratrice (2005) reports that her Italian–English-speaking subject Carlo produced only two mixed utterances in a corpus of 457 early multi-word utterances. There is, however, a great deal of variation between BFLA children in the extent to which they use mixed utterances.

Mixed utterances are not a sign of confusion. Rather, since many of the mixed utterances that young children produce are not used by the people around them, mixed utterances are highly creative features of speech (Vihman, 1999). Mixed utterances can be enhancements to communication. They are exclusively available to bilinguals.

Variation between BFLA children in the kinds of utterances they produce

As I already indicated in Chapter 1, not all BFLA children actually speak two languages. They may speak only one (cf. also Schlyter, 1994).

BFLA children's repertoires, then, may vary quite a lot from child to child. Somewhat older bilingual children's repertoires, say, from age two and a half onwards, typically consist of unilingual utterances in at least one language. Many BFLA children also produce mixed utterances. And then there are many BFLA children who regularly produce unilingual utterances in Language Alpha and unilingual utterances in Language A. Many of these bilingual children who produce unilingual utterances in two languages may also occasionally or more frequently produce mixed utterances (I leave aside indeterminate and floating utterances here).

BFLA children, then, have different language use repertoires. In Box 2.11 I give examples of the possible variation between BFLA children. This variation is a very normal thing for bilingual children, but it is very different from monolingual children, who have only two options: speak their one language all the time or not speak at all. The latter, **mutism**, is however not within the range of the expected normal variation.

The six children in Box 2.11 represent the range of the normal variation between BFLA children. Note that all children produce unilingual utterances in at least one of their input languages. Not all of them produce unilingual utterances in their other input language and not all of them produce mixed utterances. Also, there is not a single child who only produces mixed utterances. In fact, the proportion of use of mixed utterances in BFLA children differs from child to child, but is usually no higher than 35%. That means that young BFLA children minimally produce about twice as many unilingual as mixed utterances.

> **Box 2.11** Differences in BFLA children's language repertoires: an example from four-year-olds
>
> The six four-year-olds whose language repertoires are shown below have all been addressed in Dutch and French from birth onwards. The information in the table gives a general impression of the proportion of use of three kinds of utterances in recordings lasting about three hours that gave the children the opportunity to speak both their input languages. These proportions of use are consistent with the children's mothers' assessments of their language use in the month prior to the recordings. The shaded cells highlight the fact that a particular category of utterances was absent from the children's repertoires.
>
> | BFLA child produces... | Unilingual utterances in Language A (= Dutch) | Unilingual utterances in Language Alpha (= French) | Mmixed utterances combining A and Alpha |
> | --- | --- | --- | --- |
> | Arthur | about half the time | about half the time | none |
> | Ben | about half the time | none | about half the time |
> | Cecilia | most of the time | some of the time | some of the time |
> | Daniella | most of the time | none | some of the time |
> | Eric | most of the time | some of the time | none |
> | Francis | all the time | none | none |
>
> These data come from the same group of Dutch–French BFLA children who were reported on in De Houwer *et al.* (2006a) when they were 13 months old; so far, we have not published on the four-year-old cohort, but see Neiss *et al.*, 2008; the names used in this Box are pseudonyms.

BFLA children such as Francis in Box 2.11 who produce unilingual utterances in one language only and who produce no mixed utterances are like MFLA children and like some ESLA children who have just started to hear a second language. The other five possibilities for BFLA children (represented by Arthur, Ben, Cecilia, Daniella and Eric in Box 2.11) are all possible for ESLA children as well.

Not only is there variation between different BFLA children in their language repertoires, there can also be quite a lot of variation within the same BFLA child across time. BFLA children may start out speaking just one language but after some time they may speak two. It can also go the other way: they may start out speaking two languages and may speak these fluently after a while, but lose one along the way. Early fluency and ease in two languages, then, is no guarantee for continued fluency and use. I describe an example of this in Box 2.12. Finally, some BFLA children replace one language fully by another one.

In Chapter 4 I discuss some possible reasons for some of the very different language repertoires that BFLA children have and for changes in these repertoires across time.

> **Box 2.12** Changes in young BFLA children's language repertoires: an early example
>
> Perhaps the earliest documented example of drastic changes in young bilingual children's language repertoires is the case of Adelheid, one of Wilhelm von Humboldt's daughters (Wilhelm von Humboldt is acknowledged as the eminent founder of comparative and typological linguistics, and was active in the late 18th and early 19th centuries). Adelheid lived in Italy with her parents, who both spoke German to her but who were also fluent in Italian. Childminders spoke Italian to her from when she was born. She spoke German and Italian fluently at the age of 3;9. Her mother then left on a long trip and stayed away for 11 months (fairly common in those days for upper middle-class families). The only person speaking to Adelheid in German after that was her father, who presumably didn't spend that much time with her. At first, Adelheid continued to speak German to him. She spoke Italian when she was playing by herself and to her little sister Gabriele, who spoke no German. But soon, six months after her mother had left, Adelheid no longer spoke German to her father, but just Italian. She also started to make derogatory comments about German. And when her mother returned when Adelheid was 4;8, Adelheid could not speak to her in German. Only very slowly did Adelheid start to speak German again, after her mother made a lot of effort to get her to change.
>
> *We see here, then, that early fluency in two languages is by no means a guarantee for continued fluency and use.*
>
> We know about all this from von Humboldt's letters to his wife during her trip; Porsché (1983) gives excerpts from these on pages 68–72, and Ronjat (1913: 110) refers to them as well.

Language choice

The fact that many BFLA children are able to produce different kinds of utterances means that they have a choice as to when to produce a particular kind of utterance, but also that they must choose. It is impossible to produce a mixed utterance and unilingual utterances in two different languages at once.

'Choosing' a particular kind of utterance is not necessarily a conscious process. But it does seem to follow particular regularities. Children's **language choice**, so their use of one particular kind of utterance rather than another, is not random. From a very early age, most young bilingual children are able to use the language that is expected of them in a particular situation. Some studies have found that children can do this as early as the second year of life (e.g. Sinka & Schelletter, 1998).

From the onset of speech, young bilingual children seem to switch easily between unilingual utterances in Language A, unilingual utterances in Language Alpha and mixed utterances. Their switching is determined by sociolinguistic factors such as their interlocutor's language choice, their interlocutor's expectations, the place of interaction and the topic (see, e.g. De Houwer, 1990; Deuchar & Quay, 2000; Genesee *et al.*, 1996; Lanza, 1997). Both in the fact that they easily switch, and that they usually switch for clear sociolinguistic reasons, bilingual children resemble bilingual adults right from the start.

Once children acquiring a second language are able to produce mixed utterances and utterances in their L2, their language choice resembles that of BFLA children.

I discuss BFLA children's language choice in more detail in the section 'Speaking the "right" language and what it depends on' in Chapter 4.

The relation between BFLA children's two developing languages

The levels of knowledge and skill that BFLA children have in one of their languages can differ quite dramatically from the levels of knowledge and skill in the other. They may speak one language fluently and the other one not at all. If they do speak two languages, one language may appear to be far better developed than the other.

Thus, young bilingual children do not necessarily develop each of their languages at the same pace. They may have a stronger and a weaker language, which means that one language is much better developed than the other. Box 2.13 shows an example of this.

Box 2.13 Uneven development of a BFLA child's two languages: one stronger, the other weaker

Céline grew up in Hamburg, Germany. She heard German and French at home from birth. Céline spoke much more German than French. Also, her German was much better than her French: the overall length of her French utterances was steadily much shorter than that of her German utterances. In addition, the variety of verbs that she used was far greater in German than in French. German was clearly her stronger language and French her weaker.

The table below shows some data from recordings with Céline made by two different researchers on the same day. One spoke German with her while the other was doing the taping. Then they switched, and the one who had been taping before now spoke French with Céline, while the other one did the taping (the order could be different, too). The length of the French and German sessions was the same.

Céline's age (approximately)	Language	Number of utterances	Number of verb types[a]	Mean Length of Utterance[b]
2;0	German	nearly 200	nearly 30	2.0
	French	just 1 or 2	1	n.a.
2;7	German	about 125	about 45	about 3.8
	French	50	about 9	just under 2
3;1	German	250	60	nearly 4.0
	French	about 120	10	about 1.4

[a] This refers to the number of different verbs used.
[b] Not clear whether this was computed on the basis of words or morphemes.
Adapted from Kupisch, 2003; numbers extrapolated on the basis of graphics used in her Figures 4, 5 and 6

At the same time, there are BFLA children who speak two languages at similar levels of complexity. Also, as I show in Chapter 4, within one child Language Alpha may be stronger at one point but might become the weaker one later on (see also Box 2.12 earlier). Again, then, there is a lot of variation between BFLA children in how well they speak each of their languages at a given age.

There may also be differences between the two languages in how well a particular child understands each of them. Not much is known about this, however. I discuss the few studies that have looked at comprehension in BFLA children in Chapter 6.

There can be quite an **uneven development** between a BFLA child's two languages, then. Although sufficient empirical information about this is lacking, I suspect that uneven development of two languages in a BFLA child is the rule rather than the exception.

Theoretically, the existence of different levels of proficiency in two languages at any one time does not preclude influence from one language on another. Once different levels of proficiency in BFLA children are apparent, however (generally, starting from age two onwards at the very earliest), young bilingual children can speak each of their languages without noticeable systematic influence from the other. There may be some influence from one language on the other, but generally speaking, children over age two develop their two languages independently from each other. This has been shown in the area of morphosyntactic development especially.

Whether separate development also occurs prior to age two, and in the realm of phonology, is difficult to say for several reasons, one being the overall immaturity of infants' and toddlers' language skills. However, the relation between a BFLA child's two developing languages continues to be a research focus in many studies of BFLA. I will come back to the issue of the relation between a BFLA child's two developing languages throughout the remainder of this book, but especially in Chapters 5, 6 and 7.

Although BFLA children might have different levels of skill in each of their languages, they usually speak one of their languages well and at an age-appropriate level. An age-appropriate level is the general level of language functioning that people would expect of a child at a given age. This is different in different societies, but for most Western-European languages this would mean that one-year-olds are not expected to talk beyond maybe a word or two, two-year-olds are expected to know quite a few words and start to put them together, and so forth (the 'milestones' I referred to earlier).

Here we see a similarity between BFLA and MFLA children: under normal conditions, they both produce utterances in one language that are of an age-appropriate level.

In terms of not being able to produce long utterances with ease, some BFLA children may resemble ESLA children who are just starting to make their own utterances in their new language. But on the whole, BFLA children resemble MFLA children more than ESLA children in the kinds of things they say.

However, for one of their languages, BFLA children may lag behind in comparison to MFLA children acquiring that same language. They may also develop some elements of that language faster than MFLA children (see, e.g. Kupisch, 2006). One problem with detailed comparisons between MFLA and BFLA children for the course of development of a particular language is that there are very few data available for comparison. Because of the wide variation between children acquiring a particular language it is possible that these comparisons happen to compare children at extremes of this variation. Much more research is needed to obtain an accurate idea of the range of similarities and differences between the acquisition of a particular language by bilingual children on the one hand, and monolingual children on the other.

More fundamental, however, is the purpose of comparisons between BFLA and MFLA children. Often it seems as though BFLA is only 'acceptable' if it resembles MFLA, except that BFLA children are learning two languages. Bilinguals, though, including bilingual children, are not some strange kind of monolingual who happens to know another language as well (see also Grosjean, 2008). Bilingual acquisition is a phenomenon that is worth studying on its own. And given the many bilingual children in the world we owe it to them to understand how they are developing language. Such understanding may form the basis for practical advice to parents, educators and speech clinicians involved with bilingual children and thus eventually help them in their development.

Notes

1. This word is derived from the Latin 'infantes', literally, 'not able to speak'.
2. Sadly, not all children have good hearing. The present book does not focus on bilingually reared children who have hearing problems, but bilingualism certainly is possible in children who cannot hear well. For instance, they may learn to sign in one of the many sign languages such as American Sign Language, British Sign Language or Sign Language of the Netherlands (e.g. Morgan & Woll, 2002) and also understand lip reading as well as a gestural system, and they may learn to express themselves using at least one of these (see, e.g. Baker & van den Bogaerde, 2008; van den Bogaerde & Baker 2002). When they are older, they may also learn to read and write in one or more languages.
3. There are unfortunately many children who are born with or develop vision problems. These children can certainly learn to talk but some of them may show a different language acquisition profile than sighted children (see, e.g. Baker, 2006).
4. The reasons for why this is the case are not quite clear.
5. There have been surprisingly few detailed studies, however, of the actual language input to infants in their first year of life.
6. You should not conclude from this that children cannot learn language from television. It all depends on children's ages and on quite specific circumstances. For instance, many 12-year-old Dutch monolingual children in Flanders know quite a bit of English based on many years of viewing English television programs with English subtitles (Kuppens & De Houwer, 2006).
7. In my earlier book on BFLA (De Houwer, 1990) I called these 'floating' utterances 'non-language specific'.

Summary box

- Early language development does not take place in a vacuum. Instead, children learn language through a combination of interaction, socialization and maturation.
- Learning the sounds of a language starts prior to birth. This learning about sounds is fundamental to learning a particular language.
- Bilingual language development is a gradual process that works on different levels of functioning at once. It takes at least five years for BFLA children to be able to tell a good story.
- There is a lot of variation between children in when they are able to say certain kinds of things. This variation exists regardless of whether one or two languages are being acquired.
- On average, BFLA and MFLA children reach similar milestones in their early language development around the same ages.
- Unlike MFLA children, BFLA children can understand and use two languages, can switch between them and can produce utterances that combine elements from two languages.
- BFLA children differ in their language repertoires but normal bilingual development implies that children speak at least one language at an age appropriate level

Suggestions for study activities

1. *Project:* Find a friend or relative who has a baby anywhere between eight and twelve months of age. Ask if you can observe the baby for about ten minutes when she or he is wide awake and being fed (other than getting a bottle). Observing here means sitting quietly with pen and paper – not with a video recorder. Jot down anything you find interesting about what the baby is doing or saying and what the person feeding her or him is doing or saying. On the same day of your observation session, re-read the first two sections of this chapter and see whether what you observed fits (most likely you did not observe everything that was discussed; also, you will have observed different things depending on the baby's age).
2. Take the language you know best. Then try to think of strange pronunciations you have heard other people say who do not know that language well. Explain to a classmate who does not know your best language why these pronunciations sounded so strange.
3. Find a classmate who knows the same other language than English that you know. Translate the sentence 'I am reading this book on how children learn two languages' into that language. Each of you should then divide up the new sentence into morphemes. Discuss with each other your solution and try to find a compromise if you don't agree.
4. *Project:* Visit a local childcare center and ask for a short interview with one of the caregivers there. Have a conversation with them about the language use of the children in their care. Do they understand the children? Do the children understand them? Can they remember any strange or funny words that they heard children use? Do they feel that they can communicate well enough with the children to get them to do what they want? Do the children talk to each other? Write up a brief report of your interview and compare notes with classmates who have done the same.
5. Obtain a copy of the chapter by Kupisch (2003) and plot out the levels of French language use by the monolingual child Grégoire and the bilingual children Alexander and Céline as done in Box 2.13. Look at five similar age points two months apart (e.g. age 2;0, age 2;2, age 2;4 and so forth). Describe what you found to your classmates: compare the children to each other and see whether they showed any development (advanced).
6. *Project:* If you did not do study activity 2 in Chapter 1, do it now!

Suggestions for study activities continued

7. *WEB:* Watch http://www.youtube.com/watch?v=-iBtLiVWk7Y&NR=1 for an example of a child who cannot yet speak. There are features in the child's vocalizations, however, which are language-like. What are they? Is this child able to communicate something? If so, what?

8. Download a few files from the bilingual corpora in CHILDES (see Box 3.5 in Chapter 3 for an overview) where the child in question speaks at least one language that you know. Look at the files and make a listing of at least 20 unilingual utterances in the language you know and five mixed utterances. (advanced)

9. Do the same as in point 8 but instead of limiting yourself to 20 unilingual utterances find 50 of them. Divide these 50 utterances into morphemes. Count the number of morphemes and calculate the mean length of utterance. Try to decide whether this child has reached any significant milestone as presented in Box 2.8 for the language you are looking at. (advanced)

10. *WEB:* Choose a friend from your class to do this activity with. Watch http://www.youtube.com/watch?v=g8rOy33sUok, which is an interview with developmental psychologist Dr Stephen Reznick (now at the University of North Carolina in the United States, and one of the collaborators on the CDI – see Chapter 3). Listen carefully to what Dr Reznick has to say, especially about the importance of early language comprehension and consider what this might mean for bilingual children. Discuss your thoughts with your friend. (advanced)

Recommended reading

Bornstein and Lamb (2008) offer an excellent introduction to developments in infancy. A clear, recent and fairly brief overview of the research on early parent–child interaction and the development of intersubjectivity can be found in Papoušek (2007). An article that goes beyond the earliest stages of development but also focuses on the importance of social aspects of early language learning is Tomasello (1992). Lois Bloom's (1993) book explains how children come to understand the world through language. Sebastián-Gallès (2006) offers a clear and succinct overview of how infants become more and more attuned to the particular sounds of their input language in the first year of life. And for the more advanced student, Werker and Yeung (2005) give a summary of how infant speech perception relates to early word learning.

3 Research methods in BFLA

Why this chapter is important even if you are not embarking on a study of BFLA	55
Need for bilingual researchers	56
Subject selection: making sure you are dealing with BFLA	57
Deciding on how many subjects you should study	57
When and where to collect data: need for sociolinguistic authenticity	59
Data handling: transcription and coding	60
Transcription	61
Categorizing utterances	61
Language choice codes	63
Utterance length count and MLU	64
CHILDES as an important tool in BFLA for corpus-based work	66
CHAT	67
CLAN	68
Comparisons with other corpora	68
Bilingual corpora available through CHILDES	69
The CDI as an important tool for lexical research in BFLA	71
What is the CDI?	72
The CDI as a screening tool	73
Using different raters in CDI studies of BFLA	74

Other recommendations specific to BFLA   **76**

The importance of being familiar with the language models that BFLA children hear   *76*

Terminological issues   *76*

Experimental studies   *77*

Need to clearly describe the BFLA learning context   **77**

Need to be clear about the age at which children first started to regularly hear each of their two languages   *77*

Other things that are important to mention   *78*

Summary box   **79**

Suggestions for study activities   **79**

Recommended reading   **80**

Why this chapter is important even if you are not embarking on a study of BFLA

This chapter focuses on some important **methodological issues** that researchers studying BFLA should take into account. You might think that you can skip this chapter because you are not thinking of starting on a study of BFLA any time soon. However, it will be helpful to read this chapter now, because it will help you to understand better the remainder of the book. For instance, in later chapters I will refer to methodological tools that are explained in this chapter such as the **CDI**. Also this chapter will help you to evaluate critically and assess the merits (or drawbacks) of published studies that you might want to read as a follow-up to the book.

More so than in other chapters, though, I have shaded portions of the text in grey for more advanced students in linguistics or psychology. Other students can skip these portions and will still learn about the most important issues.

The chapter is organized around the chronological steps you need to undertake for an empirical study of language use. You need to determine whether you as a researcher are the right person to carry out a particular study; then you have to recruit subjects and decide on how many you are going to study and in what kind of research design; then after you've collected the data you will need to process them in some way so that you can start to analyze them; and after you have finished analyzing you will need to report them.

I cannot cover all the kinds of studies that exist or that you might want to embark on yourself at some point. My main focus in this chapter is on **observational studies** of what is often called 'naturally occurring interaction'. These are so-called **naturalistic studies** that make audio- and/or video-recordings of children interacting with people in ways that are not determined by a pre-set 'protocol' or set of instructions.[1] The latter usually happens in **experimental settings**, in which researchers try to get children to respond to specific verbal stimuli that are highly controlled.

Experimental studies of BFLA children's language use are quite rare so far.[2] With increased knowledge of specific aspects of BFLA children's language use, experimental methods could teach us even more.

Aside from focusing on observational studies I will also pay a lot of attention to studies relying on the CDI. As I explain in detail below, the CDI is a tool that collects data (information about that which you want to study) indirectly, that is, researchers in fact are asking other people (e.g. children's parents) to tell them about children's language development. The data collected by the CDI, then, are reported data, not observational data. Survey or census data are another type of reported data. I will not discuss these here (for more information on research methods used in bilingual settings, see Li & Moyer, 2008).

Need for bilingual researchers

Researchers who want to study BFLA should have a good knowledge of the two specific languages involved. This may seem obvious, but there have been quite a few studies of BFLA where the investigator was familiar with only one of the languages, and therefore could only report on that single language.

There is in principle nothing against studying only one of the languages that a bilingual child is learning (but see below for an important exception). There always has to be some sort of selection, since it is impossible to study all aspects of a particular child's language development.[3]

However, if the selection of one particular language is made on the basis of the researcher's lack of knowledge of the other language rather than on the basis of theoretical issues, there is a problem. In BFLA one basic issue is to what extent children's language development in one language is influenced by the other language. Researchers who share only one language with the BFLA children studied can only investigate those language forms that appear to be entirely in that language. This might work to some extent, if indeed, such forms appear (which they may not! – see the end of Chapter 2).

However, researchers who share only one language with the BFLA children studied will always be limited in trying to attempt to explain any developments found. There would always be the possibility that whatever they thought they found would be due to the child's knowledge of the other language – and they would not be able to check on that. For instance, an English-speakng researcher studying Spanish–English BFLA children may be lucky enough to find that these children say a large number of English utterances. However, if some of these English utterances have strange word orders, the researcher would not be able to check on whether these might be influnced by Spanish.

This basic issue, then, of the relation between the languages that bilingual children are acquiring is the main reason why researchers studying BFLA must have a good knowledge of the two languages their subjects are in the process of learning.

This knowledge of the two languages should primarily consist of a high degree of familiarity with the specific **oral varieties** that the children are learning. Knowledge of just a formal and written variety of a language is not good enough since there are too many differences between oral language use and written styles.

Above I noted that there is one exception in which you *must* take into account both of a BFLA child's languages, and that is when you are wanting to compare the number of words that BFLA children know with the number of words that MFLA children know (Patterson, 2004 *et al.*, 1993). Since for MFLA children you are trying to get an idea of their total lexical knowledge, it is only fair and appropriate that you do likewise for BFLA children, and this means you will have to investigate their lexical knowledge in both their languages, the sum of which gives you their total lexical knowledge (see Chapter 6 for a more in depth discussion).

Subject selection: making sure you are dealing with BFLA

When you want to start on an empirical study of BFLA, you can study children, their families, or both. In either case, you should recruit subjects who have clearly had experience with two languages from birth or who as a family have offered input in two languages from the moment a child was born.

It is not always easy to ascertain that indeed there was bilingual input from birth, especially if you meet up with the possible subject for your study in the preschool years. Parents might have forgotten exactly how they spoke to their infant. Or they may not be very much aware of their own language use. Or they may be convinced that they started speaking two languages to their child from the time he was born, but in fact if you ask grandma about it she denies it.

Before you recruit a family or child for a study on BFLA, you should take some time trying to find out as well and as much as you can about the target children's language background. As I show in Chapter 4, BFLA children's language backgrounds are important to help explain and interpret fundamental aspects of their linguistic development.

For the interested reader I have written an overview of what it is important to know about at the subject selection stage in case you want to study BFLA. You can find this overview in Appendix A at the end of the book.

Deciding on how many subjects you should study

At the start of the previous section I wrote that a BFLA study could have as research participants a family, a particular child in that family, or both. Of course, you could decide to study many bilingual families or many bilingual children, or many of both. In any event, you will need to have the sort of background information listed in Appendix A for all the families and/or children you end up recruiting.

This brings me to a discussion of the number of subjects to be recruited for a BFLA study. For instance, you could study just a single child. Typically, such so-called case studies are longitudinal, so they follow a particular child for a long time (normally at least half a year; often, much longer). Case studies have been used a lot in BFLA research and are very important to find out about the course of development for a particular pair of languages (I list some recent examples in the 'Recommended reading' section).

Case studies used to be quite common in MFLA research as well, but they seem to be used much less nowadays. It is really the field of BFLA research that has in the last 15 years or so been contributing relatively more case studies. Especially for language pairs that have not been studied it is important to design a case study (see some references in the 'Recommended reading' section to publications that discuss the advantages – and disadvantages – of the single case study in BFLA research).

Typically, a case study is manageable if a sole researcher has the opportunity to collect data for about a year, and has the time to work on the material for a few years. This is usually possible in the framework of a doctoral dissertation. If more resources are available, a good alternative to an intensive longitudinal case study of one family and child is the use of multiple longitudinal case studies within the same project in which the input languages are the same and the input situation similar (for some examples, see the 'Recommended reading' section). Such a study will, in principle, be able to furnish data that are more generalizable than is the case for a single case study. Care should be taken, however, not to collapse the data across children.

Each child's course of development is unique. It will show similarities with other children's development, but there will be differences as well. Because of these differences, different bilingual children's data should not be collapsed in an attempt to reflect the course of 'all' bilingual children's language development. Hence, using a **cross-sectional design** in which data taken from different children at various ages are assumed to reflect any single child's development is not quite appropriate for BFLA research (it is no longer that popular in MFLA research either; researchers are more and more aware of the individual differences between also monolingual children in their language development – see, e.g. Bates *et al.*, 1995).

It depends very much on what you want to study, though, on whether you will want to opt for a longitudinal design using the single or multiple case study approach or not. If you are interested in tracing the course of development for particular phenomena, you will need to use a longitudinal design.

Typically, a longitudinal design involves the frequent collection of data, for instance, data are collected at least once or twice a month. This high frequency of data collection is one reason why it is often not feasible to study more than one or a couple of children, the work involved would just be too much for a single researcher. Given sufficient resources, of course, a greater number of children and families could be followed using frequent data collection points.

The more children we have information on, the more we will be able to find out about the general course of development in BFLA. In principle, then, we need to know about as many children as possible. Findings about just one child are not necessarily generalizable to other children, although findings from one child can falsify general theoretical positions. For instance, Volterra and Taeschner (1978) claimed that young bilingual children do not start to speak two separate languages, but one sort of 'muddled' language in which the syntactic rules of both languages are mixed. Findings from just a single case study have shown that this general claim cannot be upheld: Deuchar and Quay (2000) describe how Manuela, a child who regularly heard Spanish and English from birth, used two separate syntactic rule systems as soon as language-specific morphology appeared.

The fact remains, though, that the more children are studied, the more generalizable the findings become. If you have enough time and resources, you can start on a longitudinal group study, but there will always be limitations on how often you can collect data and on how many participants you can include. Also, it can be very difficult to find enough subjects who meet the requirements for your study. For a longitudinal group study of BFLA children that I have been directing in Belgium in cooperation with Dr Marc Bornstein, NICHD, United States of America, it took nearly two years to find the group we needed: 30 first-born infants under the age of five months who had regularly heard Dutch and French in the home from birth and whose families were prepared to cooperate for at least 15 months.[4]

It may be easier to find a group of age-matched BFLA children if there is no longitudinal design. Families may be more willing (and able) to cooperate for a 'once-off' data collection effort. Even so, recruitment problems may explain why recent group studies on young bilingual children, such as the ones by Frank and Poulin-Dubois (2002) and Conboy and Thal (2006) do not limit their subject pool to just BFLA children, but include children with early input to a second language as well.

When and where to collect data: need for sociolinguistic authenticity

In the section on subject selection I stressed the importance of detailed background information in order to decide whether to include a particular family and child in a study of BFLA or not. Such background information is not only important for recruitment purposes, but also for deciding on what would be sociolinguistically appropriate methods for data collection.

Even if you are going to use only parent reports such as the CDI (see below for an explanation of what that is), you need to know who are the main speakers of each language to help you decide who you should ask to fill out the CDI forms. I discuss this issue more in the section where I explain the CDI.

If you are going to carry out an observational study of bilingual children, whether it is in a naturalistic or an experimental setting, you will need to know what the bilingual children's normal language environment looks like. And you will need to make data collection decisions that approach this normal environment as much as possible.

If you collect observational data from bilingual children (or their families) you will need to take into account the kinds of sociolinguistic settings that the children are used to and will find authentic, that is, real. Also, you will need to make sure you set up observations in all the major sociolinguistic contexts that your subjects are used to. If you do not, you may miss some crucial information (see Box 3.1).

> Because of the need to take into account the sociolinguistic contexts of language use in BFLA, and because of the need to collect data in each of the major sociolinguistic settings

a child or family find themselves in, it is often necessary to have at least two data collectors, one for each language. In some studies, parents are used to help collect data. There is in principle nothing against this. Working with two research assistants is perhaps more of a guarantee that recordings will be made according to schedule. A combination of both is probably the best.

> **Box 3.1** Leopold's mistake
>
> Werner Leopold made an exemplary diary study of his daughter Hildegard (Leopold, 1970). However, he made one fundamental mistake: he only had observations of his daughter Hildegard when he was present (see also Myers-Scotton, 2006: 330).
>
> Leopold spoke German to Hildegard and his wife mostly English (she did speak some German and understood it, though). Often, his wife was also present when he was taking notes. No data were collected when Leopold was not there (Leopold's wife did take some occasional notes in his absence but Leopold was doubtful of their quality).
>
> On the whole, then, Hildegard's data were collected in a bilingual environment and not in a monolingual English-speaking setting, although much of Hildegard's early life was spent in the latter. Thus, there is no information on what Hildegard said when she was just with English-speaking monolinguals. Leopold on occasion makes wide-ranging claims about Hildegard not speaking either English or German – he claims she often spoke a 'mixed' language. The problem is that he could not know what she spoke when he was not there, and whether in conversations with just English monolinguals Hildegard spoke 'proper' English instead of a 'hybrid system', as Leopold calls it.

For more experimental studies sociolinguistic contexts are of prime importance as well. In early perception studies, for instance, it may matter where the study takes place and who greeted the child and accompanying adult at the entrance of the laboratory. Using a particular language just prior to the experiment may orient (or cue) the child to just that language and may impact on the research results. Hence, also in more experimental studies **language orientation** (Chapter 4) has to be taken into account.

Finally, you should realize that no data collection method is perfect. Any type of data collection is necessarily selective. Even with very 'dense' corpora such as have been recently collected by Elena Lieven and colleagues in MFLA (see, e.g. Lieven *et al.*, 2003), selectivity is unavoidable. Still, thinking carefully about how best to proceed and being aware of the merits and drawbacks of specific approaches are crucial and will make it possible to collect data that can really tell us something more about how children go about learning two languages from an early age.

Data handling: transcription and coding

Once you have collected your data you will need to process them in some way or other. Of course, different types of data will have to be processed differently. I focus here on what is still the most commonly used type of data today, namely audio and/or video-recordings of interactions or child speech, whether in a more structured, even experimental setting, or in a more naturalistic one.

Transcription

Typically, you will need to make a written record, called a **transcript**, of the recordings you made. The totality of the transcripts you make constitutes your **corpus** (plural: corpora). Without a transcript, your data will be unmanageable. Your aim in making this transcript should be to stay as close as possible to the original recording, and not to interpret too much into it. In the section below where I discuss **CHILDES** I will give examples of portions of transcripts. In this section I want to discuss some aspects of transcription that are important specifically for BFLA research.

In MFLA research, you can assume that children are attempting to speak the one language they are hearing. In BFLA research, you cannot be sure which language children are aiming at, or indeed, whether they are aiming at just a single language or some amalgamation of two. In BFLA research, one basic methodological issue is to try to identify the language that young BFLA children are aiming at (see also Navarro et al., 1998).

If you have recordings of very young children (infants or toddlers) you will ideally have video recordings as a basis. The advantage of having a video record is that you have some idea of the context in which the recordings took place. Typically, very young children's language use is highly context dependent, and in order to have some idea of what is going on you will need to be able to take the context into account. But before you can start and try to interpret what a bilingually raised toddler is trying to say you will need to write down the sounds that the child is saying using **phonetic transcriptions** (for specific tips, see Cruz-Ferreira, 2006: 55–59). You cannot assume that you can just write down what the child says in ordinary, orthographic spelling. Very young children typically pronounce words very differently from adults, and they are often very difficult to understand (I explain this further in Chapter 5).

> It is best if a team of two bilingual people carries out the phonetic transcriptions: one person who knows Language A very well, and another one who knows Language Alpha very well. Sometimes each of these people will hear very different things (that happens in MFLA research as well) and then you just won't be able to decide. But often both will agree on what the child has said in terms of the sounds.

Categorizing utterances

During transcription the question is what language children's words belong to. In order to write down the word, you need to decide what language it is. This is, in fact, already a coding decision. You should ideally involve two people in this process. In order to make a decision, you will need to take both the verbal and non-verbal context into account (what could the child be trying to say?). It is an arduous task, but it is crucial that you do it carefully.

If you are lucky, the child you were recording speaks very clearly, has a well-developed sound system and is already a good talker. But if that is not the case it is often very difficult to decide what language the child's word or word-like form relates to. And, of course, for any later analyses you will ideally have to know which form relates to which language.

For any word or word-like form the choice is not just between Language A and Language Alpha. There are two additional language categories: a word or word-like form could be both

Language A and Language Alpha, such as the word 'coucou' (hello), which could be French or Dutch. A word could also be a mixture of two languages (a blend; see Chapter 2), for example, 'liket', as said by Dutch–English Kate, in which a Dutch third-person singular present tense suffix was added to an English verb (De Houwer, 1990: 10). And, of course, there is always the 'rest' category of forms that you are sure are meaningful to the child, but for which you cannot decide the adult target (and by implication, its language provenance).

If a child's utterance consists just of a single word or word-like form, as is common in children under age two, then whatever language that form was in will be the language of the utterance: unilingual in A or Alpha, indeterminate, mixed or floating (see Chapter 2 and especially Box 2.10).

When you are observing a somewhat older child (say, soon after the second birthday) the transcription hurdles become less difficult but you will still need to be very careful not to make hasty decisions about what word form in what language a child is saying. If you are not very sure at first what language a particular form is in, it is better to use phonetic transcriptions and try to determine the form's language provenance later.

When children are well into their third year, they start to speak more clearly and in longer utterances. Other than for MFLA research, you will always need to determine the language provenance of each of the transcribed child utterances: unilingual in A or Alpha, indeterminate, mixed or floating (see Chapter 2 and especially Box 2.10). Depending on your research goals you may need to categorize the adult utterances as well.

The older children are, the fewer utterances you will have that fall into the 'indeterminate' or 'floating' category. Mostly, you will be dealing with unilingual utterances on the one hand, which are either completely in Language A or completely in Language Alpha. Alternatively, you will have mixed utterances that clearly combine elements from both languages.

By elements from both languages I mean words or parts of words from both languages. A sentence with words from just Language A, but a word order that makes you think of Language Alpha is still a unilingual utterance. Perhaps it is showing the influence of the other language, but when you are categorizing utterances you will have to put it in the 'unilingual' category. Later, in the analysis stage, you can try to determine to what extent there is any influence from the other language. In Box 3.2 I give a few examples of unilingual and mixed utterances as produced by young BFLA children (these complement the ones in Box 2.10 in Chapter 2).

> Finally, a common coding problem for language pairs that are historically related is that many words are shared by these languages. For instance, what do you do with the word 'is' in the utterance 'That is a bad doggie' by a child who also hears Dutch? Is that an English unilingual utterance, or a mixed utterance, or is it indeterminate? After all, the word 'is' also exists in Dutch, and has exactly the same meaning (third person singular present tense form of the copula). Theoretically, you could argue that the source of this 'is' in this otherwise English utterance is actually the child's concurrent knowledge of Dutch. You might indeed be able to construct an argumentation for this, but only after you have analyzed a whole lot of utterances. You cannot make any real decision at the coding stage.

> **Box 3.2** Some unilingual and mixed utterances produced by BFLA children (in CHILDES format)
>
> *Unilingual utterances*
> *THO: hat dein hemd ein loch da drin?
> gloss: has your shirt got a hole in it?
> language: German
> age: 4;2
> Source: Saunders, 1988: 59 (reporting on Thomas)
>
> *LIS: cosa state facendo?
> gloss: what are you doing?
> language: Italian
> age: 3;4
> Source: Taeschner, 1983: 130 (reporting on Lisa)
>
> *Mixed utterances*
> *THO: I (a)m just schraubing this on
> gloss: I'm just screwing this on
> languages: English and German
> age: 4;0
> Source: Saunders, 1988: 182 (reporting on Thomas)
> Comment: 'schraubing' is a mix of the German verb root 'schraub' and the English bound morpheme '-ing'
>
> *LIS: jetzt faccio ein fisch
> gloss: now I'm doing a fish
> languages: German and Italian
> age: 2;10
> Source: Taeschner, 1983 (reporting on Lisa)
> Comment: the Italian verb form 'faccio' is inserted into an otherwise entirely German utterance

For coding, when in an otherwise clearly unilingual utterance you hear words that could belong to either language it is best to start from the question 'Could a person without knowledge of the other language have said this utterance?'. If the answer is clearly 'yes', then you give the utterance the status of 'unilingual'. Later you can examine whether there are grounds to change that decision or not.

Language choice codes

Coding for the language provenance of each utterance in a transcript can be done by adding a coding line after each utterance in a transcript, a language choice code. While you are doing this it may also be useful to code the language of the preceding utterance and the person who produced it (if the present utterance is a response to that utterance). If the utterance is an initiation, that is, not a direct response to a preceding utterance, you may add a code for the person or persons you think are being adressed. In Box 3.3(adv.) I explain this language choice code further.

> **Box 3.3(adv.)** Language choice codes in transcripts
>
> *Each utterance in a transcript that you are interested in analyzing later needs to get a language choice code. You can also add two more codes that may be useful for later analyses.*
>
> (1) The first term of the language choice code indicates the language provenance of the utterance you are coding. Choose one code among the following:
>
> A = unilingual in Language A (or: choose another letter such as S for Spanish)
> Alpha = unilingual in Language Alpha (or: choose another letter such as B for Basque)
> M = mixed utterance
> IND = indeterminate
> F = floating
>
> (if either of the two languages you are working with starts with M, I or F, you can of course use substitutes)
>
> (2) Before you can add the second term, you need to decide whether the utterance was a response to a preceding utterance or not. In the case it was a response, you code the language provenance of that preceding utterance (A, Alpha, M, I or F – see above). In the case it was not a response, you add the code 'INI', for 'initiation'.
>
> (3) The third term of your code expresses which person or persons are being addressed. You can again work with capital letters, but you can also use other abbreviations. Whatever system you use, make sure there is no overlap with the language provenance codes (so no 'M' for 'mother' or 'F' for 'father'). It isn't always clear who exactly was the addressee, though.
>
> *Three examples of a three-term language choice code are:*
> A INI gran   Language A as an initiation to grandma
> M Alpha sis   Mixed utterance in response to an utterance in Language Alpha said by the child's sister
> IND INI XX   an indeterminate utterance that is an initiation, but it is not clear to whom the utterance was addressed
>
> With this system, it will be quite easy later on to filter out the unilingual utterances in each language and the other types. It will also be fairly easy to analyze to what extent a particular language is used in response to another language, and whether there is any pattern in a speaker's language choice when addressing a particular interlocutor.
>
> The three-term language code is not a requirement in order to be able to use CLAN (see further in this chapter), but I recommend it in any case. It allows the quick counting of the number of utterances per language in each transcript, as well as the number of utterances in each language as addressed to a particular speaker, and so forth, even before you run CLAN on the transcripts.
>
> *Code structure adapted from Table 5.1 on p. 92 in De Houwer, 1990*

Utterance length count and MLU

Language choice codes are not needed in MFLA research. One sort of code that is very common in transcript work in MFLA, however, is a count of the length of a child's utterance, expressed in morphemes. If you add up the counts for each utterance and then divide that number by the number of utterances you get what is known as the MLU, the mean length of utterance.

As I already noted in Chapter 2, MLU is a relatively quick measure of child language development, although it is certainly not without its problems (Crystal, 1974). In principle, the idea is that the longer children's utterances become, the more skilled children most likely are in a particular language (see also Chapter 2). In other words, a measure of length is at the same time a measure of complexity – at least, this has been shown to be the case for English, the language for which the MLU measure was first developed (Brown, 1973).

The MLU measure was developed in response to the fact that children of a particular age differ a lot from each other in terms of how well they speak, and a combination of using the MLU and the count of the longest utterance in a transcript (the Upper Bound or UB; Brown, 1973) was proposed as a better basis on which to compare children to each other who are learning the same language.

As a measure of *comparing across languages*, however, MLU is highly problematic. That is because languages differ quite dramatically in their use of bound morphemes.

> Languages may either rely heavily on the use of bound morphology or much less so (Chapter 2). Even historically related languages may differ quite a bit in how many morphemes they need in order to express the same thing. In English you can say 'I won', which consists of just two morphemes. In German, this translates into 'Ich habe gewonnen', which consists of four morphemes (ich-habe-won, and the discontinuous past participle morpheme ge-/-en). A child learning English will need just two, but a child learning German will need four.

> Suppose that on average you find that a child has an MLU of 2 in English, and another child an MLU of 4 in German. Can you then conclude that the German-speaking child is more advanced linguistically than the English-speaking one? Certainly not! The difference between the MLUs is due to the difference between the structures of the two languages. Because of such differences between languages, the rules for calculating MLU as proposed by Brown (1973) for English cannot be applied to morphologically more complex languages (see also Fortescue, 1984).

A major implication of this is that MLU cannot be compared across different languages (for a discussion of this problem in BFLA, see Cruz-Ferreira, 2006: 145). For bilingual acquisition, researchers often want to know whether a BFLA child is more skilled in Language A than in Language Alpha. Simply comparing MLU counts based on morphemes will not say anything about a child's relative skill in each language. Yet, in BFLA, it is indeed important to try and compare children's levels of linguistic development in each language.

What can be done, then? Perhaps one could compare a BFLA child's MLU in each set of unilingual utterances to that of children acquiring those languages as their only language, and factor in age to see whether in each language a BFLA child is functioning at a level that is age appropriate in monolingual children. There are several problems with this approach.

> First, this approach presumes that bilingual children should function similarly to monolingual ones in each of their languages. In other words, bilingual acquisition is measured in function of monolingual acquisition. There is no reason for this. Why should the comparison not go the other way round? After all, bilingual acquisition is most likely as common as monolingual acquisition.

Second, this approach presumes that bilingual children's use of unilingual utterances is similar to that of monolingual children. While in all the cases investigated so far this does seem to be the case (see Chapter 7), too few languages-in-acquisition have been compared to date to be able to state with certainty that the acquisition of a particular language by a BFLA child runs exactly the same course as its acquisition by a monolingual child.

Third, there is the practical problem that for many of the languages studied in BFLA research there are insufficient data from monolingual acquisition available as comparison material.

Some studies that recognize the problem with counting morphemes in each language and then comparing the two with each other have proposed to use a length of utterance measure that counts words, not morphemes. Even just counting words, however, is not without its own problems.

Many people would say that the overall word structure of Spanish is quite similar to that of English (compared to, for instance, Inuktitut or Hungarian). Yet here there are important differences on the word level, with for instance English 'get up' consisting of two words but its Spanish equivalent 'levantarse' consising of only one, which means that you cannot be sure you are really comparing the same thing (Silva-Corvalán & Sánchez-Walker 2007: 11). In any case, Silva-Corvalán and Sánchez-Walker (2007) find word MLU comparisons more appropriate for Spanish and English than morpheme MLUs. The question of whether MLU comparisons (at the word level) are at all appropriate will very much depend on the actual pair of languages involved.

The fact remains that there are no easy ways of measuring overall skill in a language. This makes it very difficult to compare a BFLA child's skill in one language to the other. Quite obvious differences such as the use of very simple and short utterances in the one language but the frequent use of complex sentences in the other are easy to see. In other cases, only fine-grained analyses that take into account the specific nature of each language involved will be able to decide on a BFLA child's relative overall skill in each language at a particular age.

CHILDES as an important tool in BFLA for corpus-based work

CHILDES (Child Language Data Exchange System; MacWhinney, 2000; MacWhinney & Snow, 1985) is a large public archive available over the Internet that contains transcribed speech data from many different languages. Its main initiators (in the 1980s) were Brian MacWhinney and Catherine Snow, supported by a board of eminent child language scholars. Currently, CHILDES is being maintained and further developed under the direction of Brian MacWhinney at Carnegie Mellon University.

Although the main focus of CHILDES is on speech produced by children, it contains speech produced by adults addressing those children as well. All these transcripts were donated to CHILDES by researchers worldwide. Some transcripts in the system are accompanied by linked audio and/or video files of the original recordings the transcripts were based on. The CHILDES database is continuously expanding and researchers are invited to contribute their transcripts, preferably with the audio or video files that they are based on.

CHAT

The transcripts available through CHILDES follow the same transcription system, CHAT (Codes for the Human Analysis of Transcripts), which has been developed over the last 25 years or so in close collaboration among child language specialists worldwide. CHAT is now the international standard for transcribing human speech.

A basic form feature is that CHAT transcriptions are made in a line-by-line format, with one utterance per line (see Box 3.4 for examples). Each of these speaker lines can be followed by code lines that refer to the immediately preceding speaker line. There are a few basic rules for how utterances are to be transcribed. In addition, there are many additional features and levels of complexity. However, all these follow a standard format. This is necessary to allow for the later analysis of the transcript by the software package that is part of CHILDES, viz., CLAN (Computerized Language ANalysis).

Box 3.4 Two examples of transcripts in CHAT

- The lines preceded by an asterisk are speaker lines
- Other lines are code lines or comment/explanation lines

1. Excerpt of a transcript without coding lines: Hayashi corpus, Japanese–Danish (target child: Anders, referred to as CHI)

*CHI:	&ukunbah &uhuh
*MOT:	un
*CHI:	&ukungeya hvad er det
*MOT:	xxx
*MOT:	hvad er det?
*CHI:	hvad er det
*MOT:	hmhm
*CHI:	det
%act:	touching MOTs clothes
*CHI:	det
*MOT:	un seetaa
*MOT:	itte

2. Excerpt of a transcript with coding lines: Genesee corpus, French–English (target child: Olivier, referred to as CHI)

*CHI:	oh oh oh
%pho:	o o o
%cod:	$LAN:B $ADD:FAT

Bilingual First Language Acquisition

> **Box 3.4** Two examples of transcripts in CHAT continued
>
> | *CHI: | o |
> |---|---|
> | %act: | puts the microphone in his mouth, takes it out, puts it back in then screams |
> | *FAT: | Olivier, fais une belle chanson |
> | %cod: | $LAN:F $ADD:CHI |
> | %act: | CHI gives microphone to OBS |
> | *OBS: | <je vais> [?] chanter |
> | %cod: | $LAN:F $ADD:CHI |
>
> The line preceded by %pho here shows a phonetic transcription (in a standard CHAT format); the lines preceded by %cod include information about which language was used and who was being addressed (CHAT has alternatives for including this information, such as the %lan or %add coding lines; see also Section 12.1 'Code-Switching and Voice-Switching' in the CHAT coding manual, available online at http://childes.psy.cmu.edu/manuals/chat.pdf).

CLAN

The analysis programs in CLAN can do a number of things. For instance, they can make lists of all the different words that appear in a transcript and how many times they were used. They can also automatically select portions of your transcripts and put those in new files that you can then do further work on. They can count the frequency of occurrence of particular codes in the coding lines or words or word combinations in the speaker lines, and much more.

You can use the CLAN programs in CHILDES to analyse your own transcripts, as long as you have followed the CHAT transcription system. This is obviously a great advantage. For instance, you can use CLAN to help separate out the different languages so you end up with a partial corpus in Language A, one in Language Alpha and a set of mixed (or floating, or indeterminate) utterances. You can then easily analyze each of these sets separately. Of course, you can continue to run analyses on the entire corpus as well. There are many possibilities.

Comparisons with other corpora

A great advantage of CHILDES is that you can use the available corpora (both monolingual and bilingual) to compare your own data to. You can also run re-analyses of these data using CLAN. If you want to see whether the BFLA children you are studying are using Language Alpha in ways similar to monolingual children speaking just Language Alpha, you might be lucky enough to find a monolingual corpus in CHILDES that you can use as a basis for comparison.

You could, of course, also compare your own data to the bilingual corpora in CHILDES. An example of a study that compared new, original data to bilingual data available through CHILDES is the one by Berger-Morales and colleagues (2005). They compared new data that they had collected on a German–Italian bilingual child with data from Spanish–English-speaking Manuela. The Manuela data were originally collected and transcribed by Margaret

Deuchar and made available to CHILDES several years ago. In an earlier study, I had also relied on the Manuela data in a comparative study of BFLA children's mixed utterances (De Houwer, 1995b). The following section gives an overview of the bilingual child language corpora that are currently available through CHILDES.

Bilingual corpora available through CHILDES

Box 3.5 gives an overview of corpora available through CHILDES on children under the age of six who were raised with two languages from birth.

Box 3.5 Overview of BFLA corpora in CHILDES (up to date as of August 2008)

Corpus	Languages	Child(ren)	Age range	Location
De Houwer	Dutch–English	Kate	2;7–3;4	Belgium (Antwerp)
Deuchar	Spanish-English	Manuela	1;3–3;3	United Kingdom
Genesee	French–English	Leila	1;2–2;3	Canada (Montreal)
		Olivier	1;10–4;0	
		Jessica	1;11–2;0	
		Gene	1;11–3;7	
		Joelle	2;4–2;5	
Hayashi	Japanese–Danish	Anders	1;0–2;6	Denmark
Klammler	Italian–German	Manuel	1;9–2;1	Italy (Naples)
MCF (Cruz-Ferreira)	Portuguese–Swedish	Karin ♣	0;1–5;7	Sweden, Portugal or Austria
		Sofia ♣	0;1–3;9	
		Mikael ♣	0;1–1;6	Austria or Portugal
Pérez-Bazán	Spanish–English	Alberto	1;3–3;0	USA (Ann Arbor, MI)
		Antonio	2;11–3;1	
		Carla	2;0–3;3	
		John	2;0–3;3	
		Shelia	2;2–2;8	
		Tina	2;2–2;11	

Box 3.5 Overview of BFLA corpora in CHILDES (up to date as of August 2008)

Serra/Sole	Catalan–Spanish	Marti	0;10–4;0	Spain (Barcelona)
		Josep Andreu	0;10–4;0	
		Antoni	1;4–3;1	
		Caterina	1;1–4;4	
Vila	Catalan–Spanish	Maria del Mar	1;9–5;4	Spain (Barcelona)
Watkins	French–English	Pauline ♦	1;3–2;7	No information
		Stephanie ♦	1;6–5;2	
		Christophe ♦	1;11–7;2	
		Annick ♥	2;3–4;10	
		Olivier ♥	2;5–4;8	
		Jeremy	2;5–2;9	
		Timmy ♠	1;6–3;7	
Yip–Matthews	Cantonese–English	Sophie ♠	1;6–3;0	Hong Kong
		Alicia ♠	1;3–3;1	
		Kathryn	3;7–4;6	
		Llywelyn	2;0–3;4	
		Charlotte	1;9–3;0	
		Janet	2;9–3;11	

Ages have been rounded off to the nearest month
♣ These three children are siblings and many of the transcripts involve more than one child
♦ These three children are siblings and many of the transcripts involve more than one child
♥ These two children are siblings and some transcripts involve more than one child
♠ These three children are siblings
Source: http://childes.psy.cmu.edu/data, Bilingual Acquisition; information about each corpus can be found in the Bilingual Acquisition section of the CHILDES manual at http://childes.psy.cmu.edu/manuals/

The bilingual corpora can be accessed through the CHILDES website http://childes.psy.cmu.edu. If you follow the link to the Database Manuals you can download the file 'Bilingual Acquisition'. This file gives you detailed information on all the bilingual corpora in CHILDES (including those of second language learners). If you follow the Database link and click on Downloadable Transcripts you will see the link to 'Bilinguals' under 'Zipped Transcripts'. Clicking on that link gives you access to the list of bilingual corpora, which you can download to your computer. If you want to work with any of these corpora you should check what the conditions are. Usually, authors of corpora want you to cite a particular publication of theirs if you use their data.

You should be aware that the corpora in Box 3.5 differ greatly from one another in terms of their length and density. Also, some include various coding lines, whereas others do not. If you are thinking of using any of the corpora (including the monolingual ones), you should carefully read the documentation about them first.

For a quick summary of the bilingual corpora, see Box 3.6(adv.). The combination of the number of transcript files for each corpus and the information about the number of children and the age ranges does give some idea of the magnitude of each corpus. However, some transcript files may cover half an hour of interaction, whereas others may cover just a few minutes or less.

Box 3.6(adv.)   Summary of BFLA corpora in CHILDES (up to date as of August 2008)

Corpus	Number of children	Number of files	Age range
De Houwer	1	19	2;7–3;4
Deuchar	1	20	1;3–3;3
Genesee	5	35	1;2–4;0
Hayashi	1	17	1;0–2;6
Klammler	1	10	1;9–2;1
MCF	3	34	0;1–5;7
Pérez-Bazán	6	51	1;3–3;3
Serra/Sole	4	84	0;10–4;4
Vila	1	50	1;9–5;4
Watkins	6	73	1;3–7;2
Yip–Matthews	7	387	1;3–4;6

Ages have been rounded off to the nearest month
Source: http://childes.psy.cmu.edu/data, Bilingual Acquisition; information about each corpus can be found in the Bilingual Acquisition section of the CHILDES manual at http://childes.psy.cmu.edu/manuals/

The CDI as an important tool for lexical research in BFLA

Transcriptions of recorded interactions can yield a lot of useful information. In particular, they are necessary as a basis for investigating language choice, the use of particular speech acts and morphosyntax. Transcriptions are not very useful for investigating lexical knowledge. Certainly, you can get a list of the words used in a particular transcript, but this will tell you little about a child's production lexicon and nothing about the words that a child understands.

For a study of BFLA children's lexical knowledge, it is better to use other means of data collection. There are several tools that can be used to assess children's vocabulary knowledge, but here I will focus just on the one that I think is particularly useful for the study of BFLA, and that is the CDI.

What is the CDI?

The CDI is an abbreviation for the American English MacArthur–Bates Communicative Development Inventory (Fenson et al., 1993, 2006) or adaptations of it in other languages. It is a standardized set of lists that contains a number of items and open questions. Adults who know a child well (mostly parents) are asked to check off whether the child has any knowledge of a particular item and to answer the questions. As such, the CDI is a parent report instrument through which the researcher is asking a third person to assess particular features of a child's knowledge and behavior. Thus, the researcher need not have any direct contact with the child themselves.

The CDI consists of three main parts: (1) the CDI: Words and Gestures (Infant Form), designed for use with 8- to 16-month-old children; (2) the CDI: Words and Sentences (Toddler Form), designed for use with 16- to 30-month-old children; and (3) the CDI III, to be used for children between 30 and 37 months of age. The particular items and questions included in each part are developmentally determined and thus different, although there is some overlap between the different parts.

The CDI: Words and Gestures focuses mostly on the gestures that children use and on word comprehension and word production. The CDI: Words and Sentences no longer asks about gestures, but focuses on word production and on the child's use of morphosyntactic elements. Finally, the CDI-III is a short list which includes a fairly short vocabulary section and items and questions meant to assess grammatical complexity, semantics, pragmatics and comprehension.

In the following I focus only on those parts of the CDI that assess the lexicon.

For the vocabulary items on the Infant Form, parents are asked to check off whether a child just understood an item (comprehension) or both understood and said it (production). The Toddler Form only asks whether a child both understood and said an item.

The vocabulary items on the CDI forms are grouped into various categories such as 'Names for people', 'Things outside the house'. There are also more grammatical categories such as 'Action Words', but these also form part of the vocabulary items.

Box 3.7 shows examples from the American English Infant and Toddler Forms.

> **Box 3.7** Examples from the American English Infant and Toddler CDIs
>
> **CDI: Words and gestures**
>
> D. Vocabulary checklist
>
> 1. Sound effects and animal sounds
>
> | | understands | understands and says |
> |---|---|---|
> | baa baa | O | O |
> | choo choo | O | O |
> | cockadoodledoo | O | O |
> | grrr | O | O |
>
> Parents are asked to check just one O in each column, and not to check anything if their child does not know the item.
>
> **CDI: Words and sentences**
>
> D. Vocabulary checklist
>
> 16. Words about time
>
> | | |
> |---|---|
> | after | O |
> | before | O |
> | day | O |
> | later | O |
>
> Parents are asked to check an O if their child says the item in question, and not to check anything if their child does not say the item.
>
> *Adapted from Fenson et al., 1993*

The CDI can, of course, not yield information about all the possible words that a child knows, but reliability studies have shown that the greatest part of children's early vocabularies is well represented in the CDI word lists (Fenson *et al.*, 1994). In a bilingual setting, it has been shown that English and Spanish CDI word production results correlated significantly with observational data (Marchman & Martínez-Sussmann, 2002; Patterson, 2000).[5]

There are currently CDI lists available for a total of 48 languages or language varieties (but not necessarily for all three main parts of the CDI). These adaptations are culture-specific adaptations, and not simple translations. The adaptations of the CDI into other languages are carefully monitored by the CDI Advisory Board. On its website (http://www.sci.sdsu.edu/cdi) you can find more information about all the CDI versions, the structure of the CDI, publications that are based on the CDI and much more.

The CDI as a screening tool

The CDI can be used for research purposes but is also meant as a screening tool for language learning problems. This is why for many of the languages in which the CDI is available there are norming studies, which offer information about large numbers of children and which allow researchers to determine whether a particular child is doing well or less well compared to others at a given age.

This is done on the basis of so-called 'percentile scores', which take a child's raw number of words known at a particular age and compute how that raw score compares to the raw score of many other children at the same age. Speech therapists can then compare a child who was not part of the norming study to the percentile scores, and see whether a child's raw score falls into a lower, average or higher percentile. The lower the percentile that a child falls into, the less knowledge that child has compared to other children of the same age.

So far, the norming studies for the CDI have focused mainly on monolingual children. It is therefore not unproblematic to compare CDI data from bilingual children to the percentile scores obtained for a monolingual sample, whether for research or screening purposes (see also Thordardottir *et al.*, 2006). Whether it will ever be possible to construct valid norming data for BFLA children is a big question (see also Pearson, 1998), but in the mean time, I suggest that BFLA researchers using the CDI's work only with raw CDI scores.

Using different raters in CDI studies of BFLA

Usually, the CDI is filled out by just one person who knows a particular child very well. In a BFLA setting, that is of course not good enough. Asking just one person may give you information about just a single language. If you want to obtain data on BFLA children's two languages then you most likely will have to ask two people, one for each language.

Of course, some people in BFLA children's linguistic environment will address a child in two languages (Chapter 4). If so, they may have access to that child's knowledge of both languages. Also, even if a person addresses a BFLA child only in Language A, the child may respond in Language Alpha, or that person may overhear conversations between the child and other people in Language Alpha.

The point here is that the people who regularly interact with a BFLA child may know about the child's lexical knowledge in both languages, regardless of whether they themselves address the child in one or two languages.

In the group study of 31 Dutch–French BFLA children that I have been conducting with Dr Bornstein which focuses among other things on these children's early lexical knowledge as assessed by the CDI, considerations like the ones above led us to ask all the people familiar with a particular child to fill out CDI forms for the two languages involved. Using this method, we hoped to gain the most comprehensive information about the children's lexical knowledge in both languages (see also Marchman & Martínez-Sussmann, 2002). We also asked people to fill out the forms on their own, because we wanted to get as many different words as possible. If people were discussing with others whether or not the child knew a particular word they might start to doubt what they first had in mind.

In our study, there were often three people we could ask to fill out a CDI in each language: both the child's parents and the child's regular caretaker such as grandma or a nanny. Of course, if a person did not know the other language they could fill out the form for one language only (for a study in which we report on some results based on this method, see De Houwer *et al.*, 2006a).

In order to get one vocabulary score per language, the cumulative score, we had to bring together the information from all the people who had filled out a form for one particular language. In Box 3.8(adv.) I explain how this was done (reading this Box will be of interest in particular to students wishing to pursue their own CDI study or with a special interest in lexical development; others may skip it).

> **Box 3.8(adv.)** How to compute cumulative CDI scores if more than one rater filled out a CDI form
>
> In the longitudinal study of 31 Dutch–French BFLA children that I have been conducting with Marc Bornstein we asked up to three people to fill in a CDI form in each language when the children were 13 and 20 months old. This Box explains the scoring method used to obtain the number of words understood (comprehension), and the number of words both understood and produced (production) in each language.
>
> We usually obtained at least two filled out CDI forms per language at each age.
>
> For each child, at ages 13 and 20 months separately, we combined two or three completed CDI forms for Dutch, and determined the best rating given by any one rater for each vocabulary item on the form.
>
> At age 13 months (Infant form) a word was counted as understood if at least one of the raters, but not necessarily all, indicated that the child understood the item. A word was counted as produced if at least one of the raters indicated that the child had said it. If one rater indicated that the child had produced an item, and another rater had indicated only comprehension, the child was credited with the 'best' rating, i.e. the child was credited with production. The '13 months Dutch cumulative comprehension score' was the total of the number of words that at the age of 13 months a child understood according to at least one rater, based on the item-per-item comparison. The '13 months Dutch cumulative production score' was the total of the number of words that at the age of 13 months a child said according to at least one rater, based on the item-per-item comparison.
>
> For the Toddler form administered at age 20 months a child was credited with saying a word if at least one rater had checked it off as 'understood and said'. The '20 months Dutch cumulative production score' was the total of the number of words that at the age of 20 months a child said according to at least one rater, based on the item-per-item comparison.
>
> We followed the same procedure for the French CDI forms and thus computed a '13 months French cumulative comprehension score', a '13 months French cumulative production score' and a '20 months French cumulative production score'.
>
> If for either French or Dutch only a single form was completed for a particular child, the cumulative score was identical to the single rater's score.
>
> We used a similar method for CDI data for a matched group of 30 Dutch-speaking children.
>
> *Adapted from De Houwer et al., 2005, 2006a*

The CDI is a relatively quick and easy method for obtaining a lot of information about a lot of children. CDI measures for the same children can also be taken at several time points.

In BFLA research, if care is taken to collect enough forms for both languages, use of the CDI can greatly increase our knowledge of many aspects of the bilingual acquisition process, not just the lexicon. Certainly, in combination with other data collection methods the CDI is a powerful research tool.

Other recommendations specific to BFLA

The importance of being familiar with the language models that BFLA children hear

There will usually be at least one person in a BFLA child's linguistic environment who is bilingual. It is possible that this person's speech in either of the two languages shows influence from the other one. It is important that in a study of BFLA this possibility is taken into account. BFLA children, then, do not necessarily hear a 'purely' monolingual model in each language (see also Chapter 4).

Especially if a BFLA child's input in Language Alpha is provided by one person only, you will need to know more about how this person speaks Language Alpha and it may be wise to record that person's speech as addressed to the child in question.

If you are studying children in a more stable bilingual community, the chances are that each language shows some influence from the other one that you cannot necessarily find documentation for in textbooks. Textbooks on the sound structure of languages, for instance, tend to focus mainly on 'standard' varieties that may in fact differ quite a bit from the specific varieties that the BLA children you are studying are hearing. If you do not know what the specific features of BFLA children's language input are, you may come to the wrong conclusions about aspects of these children's linguistic development.

Terminological issues

So far, I have not used the term 'dominance' in this book. Many bilingualism scholars use the term, but often do not explain what they mean by it or how they have measured it. Even when scholars do explain what they mean by the term 'dominance' they fail to satisfactorily measure it (see also Myers-Scotton, 2006: 33; Romaine, 1995: 180).

Another term that is used a lot in the BFLA literature is the term 'language mixing'. Once again, this term is often used without a clear definition, and appears to be applied to phenomena that are quite different in nature (see also Myers-Scotton, 2006: 330).

It is important that any technical term that you use is well defined. If it is not possible to clearly define a term, it is better not to use it. In this book, the terms 'dominance' and 'language mixing' are not used because it is not clear what they mean or should mean. Furthermore, the term 'language mixing' has a negative connotation that I wish to avoid.

Experimental studies

In this chapter I have not paid much attention to experimental studies of BFLA. That is not because experiments are not useful, on the contrary. The main reason is that doing good experiments requires a lot of training that can only be gained from instructors and advisers who are experienced in carrying out experiments themselves (there are of course textbooks on how to carry out experiments that can help as well).

Another reason is that anything I could write here would have to be all too brief and not very useful. The general recommendations that I gave in the second to fifth sections in this chapter, however, apply to experiments as well. In particular, it is important to pay attention to setting up the right sociolinguistic contexts prior to the experiment proper so that the experimental results can be properly interpreted. Also, experiments will have to take fully into account the wide range of variation that can exist between bilingual children in how well they know a particular language, but also within one bilingual child when one language is compared to the other.

Need to clearly describe the BFLA learning context

It is one thing to carry out a study of BFLA. Quite another still is writing it up. It is very important to accurately describe the bilingual learning context for your study. This will make it possible for your readers to properly interpret your findings and will also make it possible to compare your findings to those of other studies.

Need to be clear about the age at which children first started to regularly hear each of their two languages

One common problem is that when researchers report on young bilingual children's language development they fail to be specific about the time at which children's first regular exposure to each of their languages started (see also Myers-Scotton, 2006: 330). Scholars sometimes just mention which language each parent spoke at home. Or they just say that two languages were learned simultaneously. Or they just say that the parents each spoke just one language to the child. Or they state that the children studied grew up in bilingual homes.

It is important, however, to specify explicitly whether there was bilingual input from birth. Parents could be speaking two languages at home at the time of recruitment, but did they do so since the child's birth? And, indeed, a child can be learning two languages simultaneously, but this is also the case for ESLA once a second language has been added to a first. If each parent spoke one language to a child, did each parent speak a different language to the child, and did they do so from birth? And if a home is bilingual, does this automatically mean that the children in it heard two languages from birth?

Even when scholars use the term BFLA, it is not always the case that they use it to refer to bilingual input from birth. They sometimes equate it with simultaneous bilingualism (e.g. Paradis, 2007), which often means that children had bilingual input before the age of three, but not necessarily from birth (age three was the cut-off point for simultaneous bilingualism in McLaughlin's widely cited book from 1984).

> When you describe the subject(s) for your study, then, it is imperative to state quite explicitly when input in both languages began, which, in your case, will be at birth. Only then will it be clear to readers what the input pattern was. But there is more.

Other things that are important to mention

Other aspects that are important to report in studies of BFLA are when each of the languages involved was spoken, what language(s) the parents spoke between each other, how parents, live-in relatives and caregivers addressed the child, and whether whatever pattern they used had remained the same up until the time of study. Another important issue is whether both parents understood both languages involved. Failure to mention these aspects makes it hard to determine exactly which type of learning context a child was raised in.

> As I will discuss in Chapter 4, learning contexts have a large effect on BFLA children's language use. In writing up any study of your own on BFLA, then, you would need to take this into account and give a description of your subject's or subjects' language background.

In Chapters 5 to 8 I will, as a rule, only review published work that clearly indicates that a child was raised with input in two languages from birth. This, after all, is the most basic issue.[6] When I do review a study that is not a case of BFLA, I mention this explicitly.

Notes

1. Studies may also rely on hand-written notes (see later on the diary method).
2. Experimental studies of how BFLA children perceive sounds, however, are more common (see Chapter 5).
3. It is only after you have established that a particular module of language development you are interested in in Language A is not influenced by Language Alpha that you can safely limit your analyses to Language A only. Many researchers working in the DUFDE-project in Hamburg, Germany have been taking this route; DUFDE stands for Deutsch und Französisch – Doppelter Erstspracherwerb (German and French – Double First Language Acquisition); for overviews, see Köppe (1994b) and Schlyter (1990a).
4. Once the number of subjects in a group is around 30, it becomes possible to carry out reliable statistics if you are going to compare individual children to each other. Reliability is quite reduced with, for instance, groups consisting of just 10 or even 20 children.

5. The children in the study by Marchman and Martínez-Sussmann (2002) included clearly ESLA children, as well as children who had heard two languages from before the age of three months. Most of the children in the Patterson (2000) study were BFLA, but some were ESLA (Janet Patterson, personal communication).
6. Unfortunately, few studies actually state that there was bilingual input from birth. In cases where I suspected that there was bilingual input from birth, but a study did not mention it, I tried to get confirmation directly from the authors.

> *Summary box*
>
> - For a study of BFLA you need to get to know your potential subjects' language backgrounds very well. That way you can design data collection methods that are appropriate for your subjects.
> - If you do an observational study, you will need to make written transcripts of the recordings. For these you can make use of the standardized transcription system that is part of the CHILDES archive. In CHILDES, you can also find transcriptions from scholars around the world as well as special software to help you process your material.
> - If you are more interested in studying lexical development, a good tool to use is the CDI. This involves asking parents to fill out checklists in both languages.
> - An important point when scholars write up their studies on BFLA is that they describe the language input setting very precisely so it is clear when each language was heard and in what circumstances.

> *Suggestions for study activities*
>
> 1. *WEB*: Download the transcripts from the CHILDES bilingual database (see Box 3.5) for a child who is acquiring at least one language that you are familiar with (including English). Look at the last transcript (so the oldest age for which there are data available). Print out the transcript and blacken any coding there may already be. Code each utterance in terms of whether it is unilingual or mixed (even if you do not know the other language, you will recognize the words from the language you do know). This study activity does not want to suggest, though, that it is OK for a researcher to know just one of the two languages involved (see the section 'Need for bilingual researchers').
> 2. *WEB*: Download the transcripts from the CHILDES bilingual database (see Box 3.5) for a child who is acquiring at least one language that you are familiar with (including English). Look at the last transcript (so the oldest age for which there are data available). Print out the transcript and blacken any coding there may already be. Identify all the unilingual utterances that are in the language you know. Count the number of words in each of these utterances and reflect on some of the problematic cases you might have encountered (so where you were not sure whether you were dealing with one or more words). Also count the number of morphemes and reflect on the difficulties of some of the decisions you had to make here. Compare your counts on an utterance-by-utterance basis. Which do you think is the best method: the word count, or the morpheme count? Or does it not matter much in this case? (advanced)
> 3. *WEB*: Check whether there are any CDI lists available in at least one language that you know other than English. Find out through http://www.sci.sdsu.edu/cdi/adaptations_ol.htm.
> 4. Select one journal article on an aspect of bilingual acquisition cited in each of the following four chapters that you have easy access to and check whether it clearly explains that there was bilingual input from birth. If not, was there any other indication that suggested that there might have been?

Suggestions for study activities continued

5. Select one journal article on an aspect of bilingual acquisition cited in each of the following four chapters that you have easy access to and check whether it clearly explains the subject's or subjects' language learning environment up until the time of study. Do you feel that you have a sufficiently good idea of the language learning environment of the child(ren) studied in the articles? Why (not)?

6. If you are in fact planning to carry out a study of BFLA yourself, draw up a five page rough outline of the steps you will be taking to carry out your study. Decide on the number of subjects you will need, what you want the main focus of your project to be and what type of data you are going to collect (observational, reported, experimental or a combination of these), and how you are going to collect those data. You could, of course, also do a CHILDES-based study, which would not necessarily involve collecting new data. Discuss your outline with two other students in your class and edit it before submitting it to your advisor or instructor. (advanced)

Recommended reading (advanced)

On the process of subject selection

In her 1997 book, Elizabeth Lanza gives a rare overview of the process she went through to find the participants for her study (see pp. 82–86).

Advantages and disadvantages of the use of the case study in BFLA research

Discussions of the merits and drawbacks of the use of the case study in BFLA research can be found in Deuchar and Quay (2000: 2–4) and Lanza (1997: 81–82).

Some recent examples of case studies in BFLA research

Almgren and Idiazabal (2001) report on a case study of Mikel, a Basque–Spanish bilingual boy. Serratrice (2001) presents a case study of an English–Italian boy, Carlo. Qi, di Biase and Campbell (2006) trace aspects of the language development of James, who is acquiring English and Mandarin.

The use of multiple case studies in the same project: Some recent examples

The project *Bilingualism in early childhood: Comparing Italian/German and French/German* collected data on five Italian–German bilingual children (see Cantone, 2007). The Hong Kong Bilingual Child Language Corpus contains longitudinal speech data of seven bilingual children exposed to Cantonese and English from birth (six of these are reported on in Yip and Matthews, 2007).

Data collection in BFLA

In Chapter 2 of my 1990 book, I give a methodological critique of many studies of bilingual children published prior to 1988. This includes a critique of Leopold's data collection method (see in particular De Houwer, 1990: 29, 37–39). In her 1997 book, Elizabeth Lanza gives a very useful summary of Leopold's Hildegard study. She ends the summary with some points of basic methodological concern (see pp 18–23).

In my introduction to a Special Issue on Bilingual Acquisition of the *International Journal of Bilingualism* I elaborate on the need to take into account the sociolinguistic contexts for data collection in BFLA (De Houwer, 1998). An in-depth discussion of the role of the context for data collection in the interpretation of language choice data can be found in Deuchar and Quay (2000: 102–103).

Fortunately, more and more attention is being paid to this need for sociolinguistic authenticity. A prime example is Lanza's (1997: 93–101) description of how she tried to make sure that her observations of her subjects Siri and Tomas were authentic. Lanza also evaluates her efforts to reach this goal. Poulin-Dubois and Goodz (2001) relied entirely on parental help for their study of babbling in bilingual infants, and they made quite sure that recordings were made in distinct, natural sociolinguistic contexts. For their quite different study of bilingual preschoolers' language choice (not all BFLA, though), Paradis and Nicoladis (2007) describe how they tried to make sure that the sociolinguistic make-up of their data collection settings was as natural as possible.

In her study of BFLA and Early Third Language Acquisition, Madalena Cruz-Ferreira includes a very nuanced discussion of the merits and drawbacks of various methods of data collection (Cruz-Ferreira, 2006: 40–50). Lanza's Appendix VI to her 1997 book gives some pointers on how to collect bilingual diary data based on the recommendations by Braunwald and Brislin (1979).

Transcribing bilingual data

Cruz-Ferreira (2006: 52–59) offers a very helpful discussion of how she transcribed her data. She followed the CHAT protocol from CHILDES and explains why she used an IPA-based phonetic transcription method.

Terminology in BFLA

In my introduction to the Special Issue of the *International Journal of Bilingualism* (see above), I also focus on issues of terminology (De Houwer, 1998).

4 Socializing environments and BLFA

Preliminaries	**86**
It all starts with love... and positive attitudes	**86**
Becoming a bilingual family	*86*
Bilingual/monolingual couples: learning Language Alpha	*88*
Bilingual/monolingual couples: switching between Language A and Language Alpha	*88*
Bilingual couples	*89*
Attitudes towards child bilingualism and the desire to speak your own language to your child	*89*
Attitudes and beliefs	**90**
The effect of attitudes from people outside the bilingual family	*90*
Rejecting the idea that input matters	*92*
'Children just pick up language "like that"!'	*93*
The importance of having an impact belief	*95*
The link between attitudes and parental beliefs about language learning	*96*
Bilingual children's language learning environments	**96**
What BFLA children hear	**98**
Young BFLA children's linguistic soundscapes	**98**
Age of first regular input in each language	*98*

The people BFLA children interact with	99
The role of overheard speech	101
Overhearing language and pronoun use	102
The dynamic nature of BFLA settings	104
In conclusion	104

Language models — 104

BFLA children growing up in bilingual communities	105
Input from second language learners	106
BFLA children's actual input	106

The role of language presentation — 107

One person, one language (1P/1L)	107
The 1P/1L setting and mixed utterances	109
How common is the 1P/1L setting?	110
Diversity and uniformity in language presentation	111
The three basic parental input patterns	111
Fathers and speech style	113
'Mother language'?	114

Language orientation — 116

Input frequency in BFLA — 119

Do monolingual children really hear more words than bilingual children?	119
Frequency of input in a Dutch-German bilingual family: a re-analysis of 'old' data	121
Does the variation in how much children hear actually matter?	123
What if children hear one language more than the other one?	124
Comprehension and production	126
What determines how much talk children hear?	126
Category frequency	127

What BFLA children say — 127

Changes in BFLA children's linguistic soundscapes and their effects — 127

Losing a language	128
How fast do children lose a language?	129

Gaining more skill in a language	*130*
Changes in language presentation	*131*
Going off to school	*132*
Speaking the 'right' language and what it depends on	**132**
The rules of language choice	*133*
Parental discourse strategies	*134*
Using monolingual or bilingual discourse strategies	*137*
The effect of bilingual discourse strategies on children	*138*
How monolingual discourse strategies can support bilingual development	*139*
A particularly important time: going off to school	*140*
BFLA children's language choice in interactions with familiar people	*141*
BFLA children's language choice in interactions with people they have not met before	*142*
Prerequisites for language choice	*144*
Factors influencing language choice	*145*
Explaining the composition of young BFLA children's linguistic repertoires	**145**
Summary box	**148**
Suggestions for study activities	**148**
Recommended reading	**149**

Preliminaries

This chapter is by far the longest chapter in the book. The reason is that it discusses what I see as the most complex and most fundamental issue in the study of BFLA, namely, why do some children born to linguistically diverse couples grow up speaking two languages fluently, while others do not?

I tried to see how I could perhaps divide the chapter into two, but since all the issues are related to each other this was impossible to do. Because of the length of the chapter, I have divided it into three main parts. The first part, *Preliminaries*, discusses some basic issues about what leads to BFLA input or what prevents it from getting started or being continued, and then outlines the main aspects of BFLA children's language learning environments. The second part, *What BFLA children hear*, focuses mostly on various aspects of that environment. The third part, *What BFLA children say*, relates various aspects of BFLA children's language use to their language learning environments. This division into three main parts hopefully makes the chapter easier to handle.

It all starts with love... and positive attitudes

Becoming a bilingual family

BFLA starts with the use of two languages in the family once a new baby is born. Children may be born to couples who already speak two languages between each other, or who start speaking two languages only when their first baby is born.

Of course, children may be born to single mothers, or, in the tragic case where mothers die in childbirth, single fathers. Also, a child's biological parents may not be the people who take the newborn baby into their home.[1] While fully recognizing the many different family environments that newborn children may find themselves in, I will continue to use the term 'couple' and 'parents' to refer to the people who bear the main responsibility for the newborn child and who will be deciding about childcare arrangements and most other aspects of a young child's life.[2]

I give an overview of some of the main language use patterns in linguistically diverse couples in Box 4.1.

Many bilingual couples or couples consisting of a monolingual and a bilingual parent start addressing their newborn baby in each of two languages as a matter of course. The implication is that they have a neutral or positive attitude to both languages involved, and to child bilingualism.

Box 4.1 Four main patterns of language use in linguistically diverse couples

In linguistically diverse couples, at least one of the partners is bound to be bilingual (otherwise it is hard to see how partners could communicate sufficiently with each other to have a satisfying relationship).

Pattern	Partner Q	Partner P	Language used between Q and P
1	only **LA**	**LA** and LAlpha	**LA**
2	**LA** and **LAlpha**	**LA** and **LAlpha**	**LA**
3	**LA** and **LAlpha**	**LA** and **LAlpha**	**LA** and **LAlpha**
4	**LA** and **LAlpha**	**LA** and LX	**LA**

LA, LAlpha and LX refer to different languages spoken by partners in linguistically diverse couples even though they may not speak these between each other. In each pattern, LA is the overlapping language. There may be a second overlapping language. Overlapping languages are marked in bold.

The language(s) that couples use between each other need not be a bilingual partner's first learned or preferred language; in fact, bilingual partners in a couple often use a language in which they may not be all that proficient (for examples, see, e.g. Yamamoto, 2005).

Box 4.2 No bilingual input in spite of a bilingual mother

Luke is an English-speaking Briton and married to Martina, whose first language is Italian. Luke does not understand Italian but Martina is fairly fluent in English so they speak English together. They love each other very much.

When Martina got pregnant she and Luke discussed the possibility of raising the child with Italian and English. Luke thought it must be very hard for a child to learn two languages. He had never been able to, so how could a young child do it? Martina agreed, and although she was sorry she would not be able to speak Italian with her children, she started to speak only English to the twins when they were born.

Many other linguistically diverse couples do not become bilingual families, however. In the section on 'The family as the primary socialization unit for BFLA' in Chapter 1 I mentioned that such couples may, in fact, decide against speaking two languages to their newborn child. There could be several reasons for this, but a major reason often is the lack of a **positive attitude** towards one of the languages involved or the lack of a positive attitude towards bilingualism in children. In either case, parents won't have the motivation to start raising a bilingual family. For an illustration of this, see Box 4.2.

Bilingual/monolingual couples: learning Language Alpha

You might say: Yes, but what about the couples in pattern 1 in Box 4.1 where one person speaks two languages, A and Alpha, but the other one simply doesn't understand Language Alpha and speaks only Language A? Surely, even positive attitudes towards Language Alpha won't solve the problem that one half of the couple wouldn't understand what is going on if the child were addressed in Language Alpha or were to start speaking Language Alpha!

My answer to your question would be that positive attitudes towards both languages in these **bilingual/monolingual** couples can go a long way: the monolingual partner could make an effort to learn Language Alpha at least to such an extent that (s)he could learn to understand simple conversations.

In fact, many previously monolingual parents in bilingual families are able to learn quite a bit of a second language through observing interactions in that language between their partner and their young child. Parents are often proud that they are thus able to learn along with their child, and are happy that this way they have become able to understand and often say at least some things in what is often their partner's preferred language. Often, this learning experience encourages them to learn the other language even better through formal classes (I mostly know about situations like this because I have met many parents in such situations; there is not much information about them in the literature, but see Evans, 1987).

Of course, life is often too fast and too complicated for young parents to be able to take the time to learn another language. And yes, it is not good for family harmony if members of the family cannot understand the interaction between other members of the family. Does this mean, then, that bilingual/monolingual couples cannot raise a bilingual family unless the monolingual partner learns Language Alpha? Fortunately, it does not. I say 'fortunately' because there are many bilingual/monolingual couples, and the bilingual partners in those couples should not be 'punished' for falling in love with a person who does not understand the language they themselves were raised in. I return to this issue in the subsection 'Attitudes towards child bilingualism and the desire to speak your own language to your child' later in this section.

Bilingual/monolingual couples: switching between Language A and Language Alpha

Another possibility for bilingual/monolingual couples to become a bilingual family is to take the decision that the bilingual partner in the couple will speak Language Alpha with the new baby when the monolingual partner is not present, and to switch to Language A when (s)he is. Such a strategy seems to work well for many bilingual families. However, also in this situation, both partners need to have a positive attitude towards both languages. If the monolingual partner is in fact not supportive of the language that (s)he does not understand, there will soon be disharmony, and it will be difficult to raise a bilingual child.

One should also realize that linguistic choices are not emotionally neutral (Pavlenko, 2004; Piller, 2002; Yamamoto, 2005). Monolingual parents may come to resent their bilingual partner speaking a language with the children that excludes them, even though they are not present. I return to possible problems such as these in the final chapter.

Bilingual couples

Bilingual couples who speak two languages to each other as in pattern 3 in Box 4.1 will not have the problem that one partner may be excluded from interactions in the family, and most likely they will have positive attitudes towards the two languages before they start with a family.

There are also bilingual couples where both partners are **proficient speakers** of the same two languages, but where they use mainly or exclusively one of these between them (see pattern 2 in Box 4.1). Again, here there will be no problems of lack of understanding.

Bilingual couples include couples where one partner is a proficient speaker of two languages and the other knows one language well but has only a beginner's knowledge of the other language. In these couples **verbal interaction** will usually be restricted to the one language (LA) that both partners speak well (for a study of couples of different language backgrounds, see e.g. Piller, 2002). Understanding Language Alpha may be a problem.

There are also more and more couples who between them know three languages but share only one of them (pattern 4 in Box 4.1). These couples have the possibility of raising children monolingually, bilingually or trilingually (for an example of the latter, see Montanari, 2005). Regardless of their language use patterns before they became parents, linguistically diverse couples with a newborn baby will soon have to adjust to a new dynamic in their relationship that relates to language (e.g. Varro, 1998).

Finally (not shown in Box 4.1), there are also couples where both partners have different first languages, where both have some knowledge of the other partner's language, but where both use a third language for speaking to each other. Barnes (2006: 91) reports on such a couple, where the man is a Basque first language speaker who gained proficiency in English and the woman (Barnes herself) has English as a first language and is an intermediate learner of Basque. Before they had children, the couple spoke Spanish to each other. When the first child was born, the decision was made to speak English together in the presence of the children. As Barnes reports, that change took a lot of effort.

Attitudes towards child bilingualism and the desire to speak your own language to your child

In spite of positive attitudes towards the two languages that a couple could be speaking to a new baby, they may decide against bilingual input because of negative attitudes towards child bilingualism. If you believe that child bilingualism leads to language delay or to learning disabilities, you would not want to raise your child bilingually. I can assure readers that hearing two languages does not, in fact, delay children's language development (see Chapter 2). Also, hearing and learning two languages do not lead to learning disabilities.

Parents who could start a bilingual family may also decide against raising their children with two languages because of feelings of insecurity about becoming a bilingual family. Such feelings of insecurity are understandable, especially in situations where parents have no experience with being part of a bilingual family.

Negative attitudes towards child bilingualism or feelings of insecurity will be difficult to reconcile with most parents' desire to raise their children in the language(s) they learned when they were a child. Most people find it self-evident that they will raise their children in the language they themselves were raised in. This self-evidence is called into question when people fall in love with someone who does not understand or speak that language and want to build a family with this person. People who themselves have been raised with two languages in childhood will, of course, be influenced by their own experiences, and this could go either way – for or against a bilingual upbringing for their own offspring. Again, their attitudes towards child bilingualism will play a role in their decision.

Many couples with different language backgrounds who are expecting a baby do not discuss what language or languages they will be speaking to the new baby. Any attitudes they have towards the languages involved and child bilingualism do not really surface until they start to talk to the baby or the baby starts to speak. Some of these families will have started with bilingual input, while others will not. Parents may both speak one language to their infant in the first year of life, but once their child starts to say a few words one of the parents may realize that they would, in fact, like the child to speak their native language as well, and may then switch to also addressing the child in that language.

More and more though, expectant couples with different language backgrounds look for sources about child bilingualism before the baby is born to help them make a decision about whether to become a bilingual family or not, and if so, how to go about it. The quality of these sources is variable, however (see King & Fogle, 2006b). Still, discussing the options beforehand is a good idea.

With positive attitudes towards the two languages involved and a favorable view of child bilingualism, many new parents from different linguistic backgrounds become part of a bilingual family once they start to speak two languages to their newborn child. As we will see in the next section, positive attitudes remain important as their child develops.

Attitudes and beliefs

The effect of attitudes from people outside the bilingual family

Attitudes towards the two languages involved and towards early bilingualism help determine whether potentially bilingual families actually start with bilingual input once a new baby is born. They also help determine whether bilingual input is kept up.

Positive attitudes that parents had before they started a bilingual family will most likely not change, but parents may be confronted with negative attitudes from people around them which eventually make them decide to stop talking one of the languages with their children. In the previous chapter I already referred to the pediatrician who advised monolingual input as a 'cure' for the fact that a bilingually raised child was not speaking at age two.

Negative attitudes can be less open and direct, and can come from people such as neighbors, relatives and even friends. Nannies, childcare workers, doctors and preschool teachers may also express negative attitudes.

These negative attitudes may surface only very subtly (e.g. by the question: 'Don't you think your child will be confused?') or more strongly (e.g. 'I read somewhere that bilingual children are way behind other children in school. Is that really what you want for your child?'). In the final chapter on harmonious development in BFLA I come back to this issue.

Young parents want the very best for their children, and questions and comments like the ones above can lead them to doubt their decision, wonder if they are good parents and, ultimately, give up the bilingual input. Box 4.3 describes the sad experiences of a young couple in that situation.

> **Box 4.3** Positive parental attitudes turned around in the face of negative attitudes from outside the bilingual family
>
> After his studies in agriculture, Danish-born Bent spent two years in Vietnam helping to set up a farm cooperative there. During his stay, he learned to understand some Vietnamese and even speak a little. He met the girl of his dreams, Phuong, and they were soon married.
>
> After his stint at the Vietnamese cooperative, Bent was offered a good job back in Denmark and the couple decided to move there. Phuong started to take Danish classes in Denmark and set up a small import business. After a few years Bent and Phuong decided it was time for a family, and soon their son Tuan was born.
>
> It was self-evident for Bent and Phuong that they would raise their son in Danish and Vietnamese. They both understood enough of the other one's first language to follow the kinds of conversations that adults have with small children, and they were both eager to learn more. And in due time they hoped to return to Vietnam. Until that time they visited Vietnam once a year, and Phuong's mother, who knew no Danish, came to visit twice a year.
>
> At first Tuan stayed at home and was mainly taken care of by his mother. His father took care of him one day a week. That way Phuong could still look after her business a bit. When Phuong's mother was there she could take more time for the business. However, when Tuan was two years old and had started to speak in Danish and Vietnamese, the couple decided it was time for him to go to a playgroup and spend time with other children.
>
> The playgroup teacher was a sweet lady and the atmosphere was warm and fun.
>
> After a few weeks, however, the playgroup teacher started to make strange comments about Tuan. She thought he was overly shy and said he didn't really talk enough. Bent and Phuong replied that surely he needed some time to adjust to the new setting.
>
> But the teacher didn't change her mind, and called them in for a meeting. She explained that it is not good for children to learn two languages from a young age and she strongly advised the parents to no longer speak Vietnamese to Tuan. In fact, she likened bilingual input to child endangerment.

Bilingual First Language Acquisition

> **Box 4.3** Positive parental attitudes turned around in the face of negative attitudes from outside the bilingual family continued
>
> Bent and Phuon were in shock. They didn't know what to do. But it became clear that if they wanted Tuan to stay on at the preschool, they would have to comply with the teacher's admonitions. They were also worried that the teacher might make trouble with child services. And their belief that child bilingualism was fine for young children was starting to crumble.
>
> As a result, Bent and Phuong no longer spoke Vietnamese at home. Tuan was bewildered to hear his mother address him in Danish and cried when she did. It was very difficult for Bent and Phuong. When Phuong's mother came to visit, Tuan could no longer speak to her in Vietnamese.
>
> The experience made Phuong want to go back to Vietnam. She could not bear not being allowed to speak her language to her child, and thus transmit its culture. Bent agreed that this was a terrible price to pay and so they are looking for ways to move to Vietnam.

When people express negative attitudes towards early child bilingualism, they almost invariably 'recommend' that the language that is not the majority language be given up. Often, it appears as if people's concerns about child bilingualism are a disguise for negative attitudes towards the minority language.

Whatever the underlying cause of society's expressed negative attitudes towards early bilingual development, in order to counter them parents need help from good sources to guide them in their bilingual family journey (Harrison *et al.*, 1981; King & Fogle, 2006a). This may help in fostering bilingual development. I return to this issue in Chapter 8.

Rejecting the idea that input matters

Support for the development of bilingualism from one's environment is crucial. Without it, it is very difficult to raise bilingual children. But even with such support and parents' own positive attitudes, a bilingual upbringing may be at risk if parents do not realize the very important role of the input that the young bilingual-child-to-be receives from them and the other people in their child's life.

There are parents who actively reject the idea that the input they offer their children has any effect on their children's language learning. A sad example of this is shown in Box 4.4.

Henry, the 'Western' father in Box 4.4 actively rejected the possible role of the input in children's language learning. Thus, he lacked any sort of belief that he could have an impact on his child's language learning: he lacked an '**impact belief**' (De Houwer, 1999). In addition, however, this father strongly believed in the determining role of his child's own will in language learning, even already at the age of three.

Such a strong belief in children's own will also finds illustration in Don Kulick's wonderful book about language and culture in the Papua New Guinean village of Gapun (Kulick, 1992). Gapun adults believe that children have their own 'big heads' and cannot be taught anything against their will. Gapun parents do not see themselves as active agents in their children's learning, including language learning. In the next section I will explain what this lack of impact belief means for the transmission of the local language, Taiap, to the next generation.

> **Box 4.4** Positive attitudes but rejecting the notion that input is important
>
> Henry, an American with an MA in French–English translation, worked in Brussels, Belgium, as a translator. He lived with his family in Bruges, a Dutch-speaking city in Flanders. Bruges is about an hour and a half by train from Brussels.
>
> Because of his work and the time it took to travel to and from the office, Henry barely spent any time with his two young children during the week. He didn't really 'catch up' on weekends, though, because he often went out with friends. All in all, he spent about three hours a week in the company of his daughters (a baby and a three-year-old, Lia).
>
> Henry spoke English and did not speak Dutch, although he did understand it a bit. He only spoke English to his children, and found it very important that they learn English. He had very positive attitudes towards English and also towards child bilingualism.
>
> Henry's wife, who was from Bruges, spoke Dutch to the children but English to her husband. The children, then, heard Dutch all the time except when their father was home (for, on average, three hours a week): then they would hear their parents converse in English, and they would also be addressed in English.
>
> At age three, Lia understood very little English and only said 'yes' and 'no'. This angered Henry. He saw Lia's lack of English skills as a rejection of him and would not accept my suggestion that her limited knowledge of English might be related to the infrequent input she received in it. In fact, he quoted the renowned linguist Noam Chomsky to me as proof that amount of input does not matter.[a] This is why he considered it unimportant for language learning that he spent time talking to his daughters.
>
> [a] In his writings, Chomsky has indeed minimalized the role of the input (see, e.g. Chomsky, 1980), but whether he would go as far as to claim that input does not matter at all is not certain.

'Children just pick up language "like that"!'

In other cases, parents may have positive but unrealistic ideas about the nature of language learning and may not pay any attention to the possible role of the input. They may have very positive attitudes towards all kinds of languages and find it very important that their children are raised bilingually, but they may believe that 'children pick up languages "like that"!' – meaning, without any effort, as if by magic.

Language learning, however, is hard work and requires a lot of time. After six years of input in a language, six-year-olds sound just like six-year-olds – no adult would like to sound that way in any language. Six-year-olds still have a long way to go in their language learning process in order to be able to negotiate at high levels, tell good jokes and thereby be the center of a party, hold an audience captive with a persuasive speech, or read and write (see also Chapter 2).

It is true that some children can pick up accents very quickly. During a ten-day vacation where they meet up with children speaking the same language but with another accent (say, Canadian–English and Scottish–English children), many school-age children can pick up the other accent and use it for fun. They can also rapidly pick up a few stock phrases in another language.

> **Box 4.5** Positive parental attitudes but no attention to BFLA children's learning opportunities
>
> Sven's parents are both Swedish diplomats. They get posted to exotic countries but cannot themselves decide on where they will be next. Sven's parents firmly believe in the benefits of bilingualism and multilingualism and have positive attitudes to all the languages in the world. They lead very busy lives and do not have much time to spend with Sven.
>
> When Sven was born, the family was posted to Cairo, Egypt. They hired an Arabic-speaking nanny from the very beginning. Sven heard Swedish from his parents, so he was raised with two languages from birth. At age two and a half, Sven spoke Arabic fluently. He spent very little time with his parents, though, and spoke no Swedish, although he did understand some. This did not worry the parents: they were very happy that he spoke Arabic.
>
> Soon after, the family was posted to Brussels, Belgium. The parents were delighted because this way Sven could easily become multilingual: there are many international schools in Brussels. The parents waited until September to move to Brussels, so that Sven could start school there straightaway. The Arabic-speaking nanny did not move to Brussels and once he was in Brussels nobody spoke Arabic to him.
>
> His parents had chosen an excellent English–French school for him. They themselves were very busy with the move and their new jobs, and did not see Sven much. Luckily, there was a good after-school program.
>
> At school, Sven did not speak. Before, however, he had been very talkative in Arabic. He did not speak Swedish to his parents, either. His parents thought he just needed some time to adjust and expected him to speak English and French fluently after a few months.
>
> This, however, did not happen. Instead, Sven changed from a cheerful and dynamic little boy into a depressed, unhappy child. This made his parents unhappy, of course, but they never considered that the language setting could have anything to do with it. They thought he missed his nanny. They therefore arranged for the Egyptian nanny to visit when Sven was four years old, but were very surprised that Sven did not understand her Arabic anymore and that he did not speak to her. The fact that Sven spoke no Swedish the parents interpreted as a sign of anger towards them for moving away from Egypt.
>
> When he was four and a half, Sven was still not speaking. After finally consulting an expert on bilingual children, the parents decided to move him to a Swedish–French school so he would at least learn some Swedish. Now, after a year or so, Sven is speaking Swedish, but he is not a happy child and his Swedish sounds very foreign to native speakers. He understands the French that is used in the classroom but he does not speak it.
>
> *The parents in this example never considered that in order for children to learn a language there needs to be a lot of input. They thought that Sven would just 'pick up' any language he encountered, and when he did not, they explained it through other factors. These other factors might indeed have played a role, but at the time of the move to Brussels the parents would have done well to hire a Swedish-speaking nanny who could at least have given him the opportunity to build on the little Swedish he knew from before. This might have avoided a lot of his unhappiness. Also, a Swedish-French school from the start (there are no Swedish monolingual schools in Brussels) would have been a better idea than a school with two new languages.*

But this is very different from learning a whole new language from scratch. Yes, you will say, but children can in fact learn a new language very fast! Indeed, some children are capable of carrying on a simple conversation after only six months' experience in a new language environment. And the stock phrases that children may pick up in a new language at first can be enough to get them what they want for a few months.

However, such stock phrases and highly simple conversations are just a beginning, and second language learning children who are at this stage of development are far from being proficient speakers of the second language with a large, age-appropriate vocabulary in their new language. That is because even for these initially fast learners (who typically are over age four of five) language learning is a long drawn-out process. As Suzanne Schlyter reported (Schlyter & Granfeldt, 2008), it often took more than a year's input in a French-speaking school before Swedish-speaking preschoolers spoke enough French so that Schlyter and her colleagues could go and record the children's French. Likewise, there were only ten out of 25 L1 German preschoolers with daily input at a French-speaking school for three months to just over a year who said more than single sentences (Meisel, 2008).

Learning to understand a language requires that you have had opportunities to hear it. Learning to speak a language implies that you have had opportunities to speak it. These opportunities are vital. Unfortunately, some parents in bilingual settings do not realize this. A particularly sad example of this is shown in Box 4.5 (you may not believe this example. As with any example in this book, however, it is taken from real life and is, unfortunately, quite real).

The importance of having an impact belief

The Swedish parents in Box 4.5 did not see much of a role for themselves in their son's language learning. They expected him to learn to speak Swedish fluently without considering that it was up to them to offer sufficient learning opportunities. As such, they lacked an impact belief about child language development. Like the English-speaking father and the Gapun parents I discussed earlier who did not see themselves as playing much of a role in their children's language development, Sven's parents lacked any belief that how and how frequently they themselves communicated with their child had any effect on their child's language development.

Many parents, in fact, whether in monolingual or bilingual families, are not aware of the importance of their role as providers of language input to their children. In a monolingual setting, if the parents do not speak much to the child there will most likely be other sources of input to the child that can help the child in learning language. In a bilingual setting the input in one of the languages may be limited to just one parent and thus be much more fragile than a monolingual one, especially if that one parent does not speak much with the child (as in Box 4.4). In the next few sections I will explain more about just how important the actual input is for children growing up with two languages from birth.

Parents who have no impact belief about child language development will have very low chances of raising children who will actually speak two languages. Only parents with such an impact belief stand a good chance of having children who speak two languages. That is because parents with an impact belief will undertake specific steps to foster their children's language development. Even though their decisions here may not be very conscious, they may seek out opportunities for their children to hear more of a particular language. Or they may talk to their children in ways that encourage children to speak both of their input languages. Again, I will come back to this issue in later sections.

The link between attitudes and parental beliefs about language learning

Attitudes and parental beliefs about the role of the language environment in young children's language learning, then, are crucial for the creation and maintenance of a bilingual input situation. They can be so because they are the basis for parents' own linguistic behavior towards their children and for parents' management of their children's linguistic environments. Later sections in this chapter will return to this issue.

If parental and/or environmental attitudes towards the two languages involved and child bilingualism are negative, there will be little support for child bilingual development. With positive attitudes, parental beliefs about the role of the language environment in young children's language learning become important. A belief that the language environment matters and can be manipulated (an impact belief) supports children's speaking of two languages. Lack of such an impact belief does not support speaking two languages but may still lead to the understanding of two languages. Attitudes and parental beliefs thus are fundamental in determining whether young children will actively speak two languages or not. I summarize the importance of attitudes and parental beliefs for bilingual development in Box 4.6.

Box 4.6 Attitudes and parental beliefs: supportive of child bilingual development or not?		
Parental beliefs	*Attitudes towards the two languages and child bilingualism*	
	Positive	*Negative*
Impact belief	**yes**	no
No impact belief	no[a]	no

[a] In this case, however, children may have sufficient input to learn to *understand* two languages.
Adapted from Figure 3 in De Houwer, 1999: 88

Now it is time to turn to the nature of young BFLA children's language environments.

Bilingual children's language learning environments

Bilingual children's language learning environments can be described according to different aspects and from different perspectives.

You can look at the people who provide the input in the two languages. What are their roles in children's lives? Do they speak one or two languages? Do they differ a lot from each other in their language use patterns? You also have to ask yourself what input actually means. Does it include only speech directly addressed to children? Or does it also include overheard speech?

You can also study the way the languages are presented to children by means of media such as radio and television. The totality of the spoken language use that children encounter constitutes their personal '<u>linguistic soundscape</u>', so to speak. The concept as I use it here includes children's social networks such as, for instance, described in Li Wei's insightful book on language choice in Chinese–British families (Li, 1994). In addition, the concept of linguistic soundscape includes audio-media of all kinds and speech overheard from people who are not part of children's social networks.

> The term 'linguistic soundscape' is inspired both by the terms 'soundscape' and 'linguistic landscape'. 'Soundscape' as used by Finnegan (2005) refers to all the sounds that a particular person can hear at a particular time; 'linguistic landscape' has been used to refer to the written language that people meet up with on signs in public spaces (e.g. Gorter, 2006). For children who cannot yet read this written language is not yet relevant: they are limited to what they can hear. And since this book is about language, the soundscape of interest is that which has to do with language. Hence: linguistic soundscape.

Another major part of bilingual children's language learning environments is the way people verbally interact with children. These verbal interactions socialize children into particular language use patterns.

You can also look at bilingual children's language learning environments from another perspective. Rather than start out from the people that children interact with, you can start out from each of the languages that children hear, regardless of whom they hear talking. This way, you can focus on the frequency with which children hear each of their languages. That will involve looking both at absolute frequency, where you count the number of utterances or conversations (or another unit of analysis) in each language, and at relative frequency, where you express those absolute frequencies as a proportion of the total amount of input that children hear.

The combined effect of (1) BFLA children's linguistic soundscapes, (2) patterns of verbal interaction and (3) the input frequency with which they hear each language most likely are the foundations that can explain why some BFLA children become fluent speakers of two languages and others speak only one, and the whole range of possibilities between these extremes. The sections 'Young BFLA children's linguistic soundscapes', 'Language models', 'The role of language presentation' and 'Changes in BFLA children's linguistic soundscapes and their effects' focus on the people in BFLA children's lives and their language choices. The sections 'Language orientation' and 'Speaking the "right" language and what it depends on' mainly deal with socialization patterns and their effects. The section 'Input frequency in BFLA' focuses on this important missing link.

Of course, all the different aspects of bilingual children's language learning environments are connected with each other. Therefore some of the things I discuss in the separate sections might also have been mentioned in another section. The connection between all aspects of bilingual children's language learning environments is also exemplified by the fact that the order of the sections does not follow a neat division between the three major perspectives outlined above.

At the end of this chapter it should be clear that bilingual children's language learning environments matter a lot, and cannot be disregarded in any explanation of the bilingual acquisition process.

What BFLA children hear
Young BFLA children's linguistic soundscapes

Age of first regular input in each language

In Chapter 1 I defined BFLA as the situation in which children hear two languages from birth. In reality, few people will actually speak to a newborn baby. It takes a few days or even a few weeks for this to happen. People will initially focus more on non-verbal communication with newborn babies (see also Chapter 2), and if they 'speak' to them it will often be 'nonsense' (van der Stelt, 1993: 62). Babies will normally overhear 'real' language before they are directly addressed in it, however.

In order to qualify as BFLA, it does not matter whether at first babies were overhearing two languages or whether they were directly addressed in them. It is possible that they first heard the one language by overhearing only and the other one in speech addressed to them. What is important to qualify as BFLA is (1) that there was no long time lag between the baby's first hearing of Language A as compared to Language Alpha and (2) that after this first contact with both languages, Language A and Language Alpha were heard regularly.

The question is: what is a long time lag and what does the word 'regularly' mean? There are no empirically based answers to these questions. It is not known whether different definitions of 'long' and 'regularly' matter here. Also, I know of no reports in the bilingual acquisition literature with precise accounts of newborn babies' linguistic experiences.

In my 1990 book, in which I first formally defined the term BFLA, I allowed for a time lag of up to a week between first exposure to each language and I defined 'regularly' as being addressed in both languages almost every day. Regular input to two languages thus defined may be more of an ideal than a reality, though.

The people BFLA children interact with

For children to be in a BFLA setting, at least one person must speak another language than other people do.[3] It is not a definitional requirement for this person to speak *only* that other language (see the section 'The role of language presentation' for a discussion of the language–person link). Depending on the specific family and culture they are born into, babies will have many people to interact with or very few.

At first, infants and toddlers tend to interact mostly with adults, or in any case, with individuals who are several years older. In some cultures, older siblings play an important role in the care of young babies. Other people taking care of young children may include grandparents, aunts, nannies or professional childcare workers.

Contacts with peers, so with other babies and very young children, are usually much less frequent. What is more, on the whole, sustained peer interaction starts to be possible only when children are well into their third year (Holmberg, 1980). For later-born children, their older siblings are often their first peer group and thus they can learn specific peer-to-peer interaction through them (see the section on 'Input frequency in BFLA' for a discussion of the role of siblings in BFLA). First or only children have a different experience. They must make their own way in the world of child peers.

The quality of peer interaction is very important for social acceptance and social status. Already at age three, children judge peers on the basis of their verbal skills (Rice, 1993). Preschoolers who are liked best by their peers are children who are good communicators. Preschoolers dislike other preschoolers who are not able to respond appropriately to others (Hazen & Black, 1989). Thus, children in preschool or school will find it very important to do well in the school language. This may be part of the reason why in a bilingual setting the home language that is not used at school is usually at a disadvantage. In the later section on 'Changes in BFLA children's linguistic soundscapes and their effects' I further discuss what the effects can be of BFLA children's entry into preschool or school.

On the whole, children will interact or spend time with people they are familiar with, or become familiar with (see the section 'Early interaction, socialization and the child's own developmental path' in Chapter 2). As such, it will not matter much to very young children what the main language is of the society that their family lives in. What matters to young children under the age of three are the individuals they know on a personal level.

The societal language can have an effect, however, through media exposure. Early television and radio exposure can bring the societal language (and perhaps also others) into the home. Songs, books being read aloud, puppet theatre shows and the like are all part of developing young children's linguistic soundscapes.

Television doesn't have much of an effect on very young bilingual children's language development, though.[4] Rather, two-year-old bilingual children's word learning is much helped when parents read books to them (Patterson, 2002).[5]

Young children may be looked after mostly in their own homes, or they may be cared for elsewhere, at a day care center or in someone else's home. As children get older many will start to spend time away from home – at playgroup, preschool or school. Again, once children enter preschool or school this will often bring with it a major change in their linguistic soundscapes. At this point, the societal language (if it is the same as the school language) will gain in importance.

> **Box 4.7** Different linguistic soundscapes for BFLA children with small and large social networks
>
> *BFLA children at age two with small social networks*
> - Dana lives with her two parents and is taken care of by her mother. Her father works full-time and is not often home. Occasionally, the family visits the father's parents (the mother's parents are deceased). Dana spends most of her time with just her mother. They don't go out much.
>
>   Dana's mother mostly speaks to her in Irish, although she occasionally speaks English to her as well. Her father and his relatives speak to her in English. Dana hears much more Irish than English. Irish is strongly linked with just one person. She hears English from more than one person. In her linguistic soundscape, one language is limited to just one person, whereas the other one is not.
>
> - Diego lives with his two parents. They work at home and both take care of him. His father speaks Spanish to him and his mother French. The family rarely goes out for social occasions but when they do, they visit the mother's French-speaking relatives who also know Spanish and like to practice their Spanish with Diego. Diego hears his parents speak both French and Spanish together. He hears a lot of French and Spanish every day. In his linguistic soundscape, both languages are linked with more than one person.
>
> *BFLA children at age two with large social networks*
> - Stefania lives with her single mother. Her mother is a full-time nurse and works shifts. Stefania's mother speaks Greek to her. When Stefania's mother has to work, Stefania goes to her paternal grandmother's home. Her grandmother speaks Greek and Italian to Stefania.
>
>   There are always lots of people at grandma's home. These include friends of grandma's, about five other children that she also takes care of and a few cousins. Typically, when Stefania is at her grandmother's home, there will be four people present. Most of them speak only Italian, and some speak a bit of Greek as well, which they like to practice with Stefania.
>
>   Twice a month Stefania spends a weekend with her father, who speaks Greek and Italian to her. He remarried and his wife speaks Italian. Stefania hears Italian from many people, and Greek from at least three. In her linguistic soundscape, both languages are linked with more than one person.
>
> - Nikki lives with his two parents. His mother speaks Korean to him, but only when they are alone together. His father is monolingual in Japanese. Nikki's parents speak Japanese between each other. Nikki's mother takes care of him most of the time, but she takes him out a lot on weekdays. Nikki and his mother are part of a playgroup where the only language spoken is Japanese. While at the playgroup, Nikki's mother speaks Japanese to him. Nikki's mother has a few Japanese-speaking friends who come to visit regularly. They bring their own Japanese-speaking children along who are a bit older than Nikki and during the visit these children do their best to play with him.
>
>   On weekends the family usually visits the father's family. There, everybody speaks just Japanese. In Nikki's linguistic soundscape, Japanese is spoken by many people and Korean by just one.

The variety of people that young children will be in touch with is variable from child to child. Some children know many people and thus have large social networks, while others know very few. Children's social networks vary in function of their ages. All this means that children's linguistic soundscapes will also vary tremendously. Children with small social networks will tend to spend a lot of time with the same few people. This gives these few individuals a greater opportunity to have an effect on children's language development. Children with large social networks may tend to spend less time with individual people but will be exposed to more different ways of speaking. This may have its own particular effect on children's language development. In Box 4.7 I give examples of different linguistic soundscapes for BFLA children with small and large social networks.

The examples in Box 4.7 show how different children's experiences with both their languages can be. Regardless of whether children have small or large networks, however, one particular language can be associated with just one person, or with more than one person. To what extent such differences matter for BFLA children's language development has so far not been studied (but see the next section for a discussion of this point with reference to parental language use).

The role of overheard speech

In many societies adult caregivers talk to young infants. There are societies, however, in which this is not the case. One such society is that of the Gapun in Papua New Guinea (see also the section on 'Attitudes and beliefs' earlier). Until infants are about eight months of age and can no longer be easily quieted by the breast or an object to divert their attention, Gapun mothers do not speak to their infants (Kulick, 1992: 191). Babies will at first only overhear language not addressed to them.

In other cultures such as those of the Chilcotin in British Columbia, the local language is not for speaking to children (Pye, 1992). Children, in turn, should be seen but not heard. Such was also the case in many upper-class families in Europe until not long ago. However, in these families nannies and teachers were hired to educate children.

Young children growing up in socializing environments where adults do not usually speak to them directly do learn to speak, but it is not clear to what extent their linguistic development differs from children who are talked to from a much earlier age. As I discussed in Chapter 2, children who are talked to from the first month of life onwards have already learned a great deal about language by the time they are six months old. Do children need input addressed to them in order to be able to learn from it? Can children learn from language not strictly addressed to them? After all, children in all cultures hear language that is not directly addressed to them.

In a bilingual setting, there is some evidence that children can learn to understand a language through overhearing it. Again we turn to the Papua New Guinean village of Gapun, where adults speak both the local language, Taiap, and the more widely used language Tok Pisin (Kulick, 1992). Adults want their children to speak both too, but they do not really speak to very young children (see above). They leave this job to older siblings. When adults do start speaking to young children they speak mostly Tok Pisin. Among each other, but in the hearing range of young children, adults speak mostly Taiap. Children invariably show an understanding of Taiap, but much to the chagrin of their parents they do not speak it. This example suggests that in spite of little or no direct input in a language, children can learn enough of a language through overhearing in order to understand it.

The example from Gapun also shows that Gapun adults do not offer much of a supportive language learning environment for Taiap. As I explained in the previous section, the Gapun lack an impact belief about child language development. In spite of their fervent wish that their children learn to speak Taiap as well as Tok Pisin, no children in the village under age ten speak Taiap. This local language will, therefore, soon disappear. Gapun adults realize this too and are very sad about it, but they do not know how to stem the tide.

Overhearing language and pronoun use

Recent research for monolingual children suggests that direct input is not an absolute requirement for learning about specific elements of language. Children can learn words from overhearing them, so from conversations with third parties (Akhtar, 2005; Floor & Akhtar, 2006). However, the research on monolingual children is restricted to children who were actually talked to from when they were very young.

Box 4.8 Personal pronouns heard directly or overheard

Research on monolingual children has also shown that they can learn about the pragmatic functions of particular speech acts as they observe them from interactions between people that do not directly involve them (Lieven, 1994). In particular, the overhearing of pronoun use in some languages may help children to learn to use those pronouns themselves.

In many Western-European languages, first person singular pronouns (e.g. English 'I', French 'je', German 'ich', Dutch 'ik') refer to the speaker, and second person singular pronouns refer to the addressee (e.g. English 'you', French 'tu', German 'Du', Dutch 'jij'). Young children in these languages are addressed as 'you' (using a second person pronoun), but they have to learn that when they want to express something about themselves they need to use a different one, namely a first person pronoun. They also need to learn to address others with a second person pronoun, rather than the first person pronoun these people use to refer to themselves. All this is not easy to learn if children only hear speech addressed to themselves (see Box 4.8). How are they to know that, in fact, you have to say the *opposite* of what the other person is saying?

Indeed, many children learning English make persistent pronoun reversal errors until quite late in their development. That means that they address others with 'I' and talk about themselves as 'you'. It is only from observing conversations among third parties that children can find out exactly how the pronouns should be used (Oshima-Takane *et al.*, 1999; see Box 4.8). In such conversations, there are shifting references that show children how the pronouns depend on the interlocutors' speech roles. They cannot observe these shifts when they themselves are involved in a conversation. Here again, then, we have an example of the importance of overheard speech. In Box 4.9 I give an example of the role of overhearing conversations in a bilingual child's pronoun usage.

> **Box 4.9** Learning to use personal pronouns by overhearing them: an example of a BFLA child
>
> Susan was two and a half years old and lived with her parents in the United States. She heard English from everyone except her mother, who addressed her in Dutch (but others in English). Susan spoke well for her age, and this in both languages.
>
> In English, Susan was using the first and second person singular personal pronouns 'I' and 'you' correctly, without reversals. In Dutch, however, she did not use those pronouns, although they are part of Dutch in very much the same way as they are in English. Instead, she referred to herself as 'Susan' and to her mother as 'mama'.
>
> This difference between the two languages disappeared completely and immediately, however, on the day after a dinner at home to which two Dutch-speaking people had been invited. Susan had been present for part of the dinner and had overheard the adults speak in Dutch. This was the first time in six months that she had heard people other than her mother speak Dutch or that she had heard other people speak Dutch to her mother.
>
> The next morning, Susan addressed her mother with 'jij' (you in Dutch) and referred to herself as 'ik' (I). Her observation of the use of these pronouns at the dinner table had shown her how they should be used. She no longer needed the proper names 'Susan' or 'mama' as substitutes.

The dynamic nature of BFLA settings

One striking characteristic of BFLA settings is that they are quite dynamic. Typically, the parents in bilingual families have different nationalities, and in order to keep in touch with friends and family there is a lot of travel. Mother may take off with the children to spend a month at the grandparents in distant Russia, or daddy may take the children on a hiking trip with his best friend from the 'old' country. Of course, MFLA children also go on trips. But for them that usually does not imply the cessation of input in their language. For BFLA children, trips often do mean that one of their languages is no longer spoken to them (but at the same time that contact with their other language intensifies). I discuss the possible effects of such changes in the later section on 'Changes in BFLA children's linguistic soundscapes and their effects'.

In conclusion

BFLA children may hear their two languages from just a single person or from many different people. Not only do their linguistic soundscapes consist of the languages that people speak in talk directly addressed to them. These also include overheard speech and speech as heard on the radio or through other mass media. Thus, BFLA children's linguistic soundscapes are usually not limited to only their parents' talk.

Yet, parents play a crucial role in shaping BFLA children's linguistic soundscapes and offering them the opportunity for diverse linguistic encounters. As such, parents can and do influence their children's bilingual development quite a bit over and beyond the fact that they speak two languages to them.

There is a lot of variation in BFLA children's linguistic soundscapes. Variation is also present in the exact ways in which people speak around children, i.e. in the language models that BFLA children hear. These are discussed in the next section.

Language models

As Fred Genesee has pointed out in his seminal article from 1989, researchers should study the actual **language models** that bilingual children are exposed to, that is, the actual form of the languages they hear. It is crucial to know these models in order to help explain particular features of children's language production, such as the use of elements of two languages in one sentence or stretch of conversation. If you don't know whether children regularly hear such combinations of two languages in their linguistic environments there is no way of determining whether in using these themselves children are just doing what people in their environment are doing, or something novel.

I would like to add that it is particularly important to know to what extent the language models that BFLA children hear are relatable to just two separate languages or not. What I mean is that it is important to know whether children hear a particular language model in Language A that might be somewhat influenced by Language Alpha.

BFLA children growing up in bilingual communities

Some BFLA children grow up in communities where most of the people they interact with speak the same two languages and where the community has been bilingual for many years. The varieties of language that BFLA children hear in such bilingual communities may be varieties that are influenced by long contact with the other language (or other languages - see Box 4.10 for an example).

> **Box 4.10** Singapore Colloquial English: a variety of English influenced by long contact with other languages
>
> Singapore Colloquial English (SCE) is a type of English that developed mostly in the twentieth century as a result of the influence from different languages spoken in multilingual Singapore such as Hokkien, Cantonese and maybe also Malay.
>
> SCE is decidely English, but it has features that are not part of standard English as commonly taught all over the world through textbooks published by large publishing companies and as used in this textbook as well.
>
> For instance, in SCE it is not compulsory to express a subject if it is clear from the context. In standard English this happens very occasionally too (as in: 'Got what?' as a clarification request after someone said 'I got the tickets for the concert'), but in SCE it is common practice (as in 'make so much noise' – with 'they' not expressed). SCE will also often delete the auxiliary 'be', as in 'Today I going swimming'. These non-standard features can be seen as influences from the Chinese languages spoken in Singapore.
>
> *Source: Gupta, 1994: 10–11, 47*

In order to understand and to be able to explain certain features of bilingual children's speech, it is important to know what the models are that they hear. For instance, in the case of BFLA children hearing Singapore Colloquial English (as in Box 4.10) and Cantonese, it would be wrong to expect them to produce subjects in English, since they are hardly hearing such subjects in the particular variety of English that is spoken to them. It would be even more of a mistake to attribute the lack of subjects in these children's speech to influence from Cantonese, and to ignore the fact that there is little or no support for subject usage in any of the languages the children are hearing.

> When children grow up in bilingual communities where the varieties of the two languages they hear are influenced by the other language it may sometimes be difficult to say where one language stops and another begins. Also, in bilingual communities people tend to use a lot of mixed utterances (for a particularly insightful description of a bilingual community, see Zentella, 1997).
>
> As a result, sometimes the question can arise whether children in bilingual communities are, in fact, hearing two separate languages.[6] If children *only* hear utterances that linguists would describe as combining words from two languages, they are not in fact receiving bilingual input. They are not hearing two different ways of speaking that they need to differentiate between in order to learn to speak themselves. Rather, they are hearing one particular contact variety which happens to include elements that are relatable to two separate languages (see, e.g. Romaine, 1995: 120 ff.).

> Bilingual input is only present if children regularly hear unilingual utterances in Language A and unilingual utterances in Language Alpha (see also De Houwer, 2006). In addition, they may regularly hear mixed utterances that combine words from Language A and Language Alpha. Although it is impossible to say exactly what the proportion should be of each type of utterance in order to count as a bilingual input setting, and although it is not feasible to actually count the number of utterances that children in a potentially bilingual setting hear over a number of years, I would suggest that a BFLA input setting needs to consist of numerically more unilingual utterances in each language separately than mixed utterances.
>
> If children hear unilingual utterances in only one language and in addition mixed utterances that combine words from that language and another one it would depend on the nature and frequency of these mixed utterances whether they could be seen as an entirely different variety, and whether the input setting could be characterized as bilingual.

Input from second language learners

Many children growing up bilingually hear at least one of their languages spoken by people who learned this language later in life. This will often mean that some forms that BFLA children are hearing are not the kinds of forms that a monolingual person would use. Because of this, many people think it is best to speak only your 'first' or 'native' language with children. This is seen as a guarantee against children hearing less-than-good language models.

There are of course a large variety of second language learners. Some are good at learning and using second languages, others are not. Some may show influence from their first language only in their accent, some may show influence on many levels of language functioning (see also Chapter 5). The fact that good second language learners can provide appropriate models for children is amply evidenced by Saunders (1988), who spoke German, his L2, to his three children in Australia. Everyone else spoke English. The children learned to speak 'good' German (as commented on by teachers in Hamburg, Germany, who did not know that the children were bilingual) as well as English.

It remains to be seen to what extent hearing a language as spoken by second language speakers has an effect on BFLA children's language learning. The possible effect of hearing a Language A as spoken by second language speakers will depend not only on the level of proficiency that these speakers have, but also on whether in addition to these second language speakers BFLA children's linguistic soundscapes include individuals who speak Language A as their only language.

BFLA children's actual input

All too often, the bilingual acquisition literature appears to work on the assumption that children hear only standard, monolingual forms. In fact, they often do not. In explanations of particular forms that BFLA children are producing it is important to take into account the actual models for these forms that children hear. I discuss the few studies that have investigated aspects of the input in BFLA where relevant in Chapters 5, 6 and 7.

None of those studies have examined input to BFLA infants, though. An exception is van de Weijer's (1997) study, which looked at various pitch measurements of the speech directed at an infant growing up bilingually with Dutch and German. Van de Weijer did not examine specifically bilingual aspects of the input in a BFLA setting. Nor did he look at the way each input language approached monolingual norms. He did find, though, that as for speech addressed to monolingually reared children, adults in a BFLA setting speak slower to an infant in the first year of life than to other adults, use shorter utterances to the infant than to other adults, and use higher pitch when addressing the infant than when addressing other adults.[7] Infant-directed speech (IDS) to a BFLA child in the first year of life, then, offers the kind of simplified and supporting environment that has been suggested is necessary for children to learn to speak in the second year of life (see Chapter 2).

Another environment that has been claimed to be particularly supportive in a bilingual setting is the one where each person in a child's linguistic soundscape addresses the child using only one language. I look at the role of this and other kinds of language presentation in the next section.

The role of language presentation

Language presentation refers to who speaks which language(s) to a child and how many: one or two. I first look at the issue of how many languages the important people in a child's life speak to them.

One person, one language (1P/1L)

Many parents in bilingual families receive the advice to each address their children in one language only. In other words, they should follow a 'one person, one language' principle (1P/1L). Many parents take this advice and often see themselves as adhering to it in a very strict fashion. However, actual transcripts of parent–child conversations may show that parents who claim to stick to one language only, do not do so all the time (Goodz, 1989).[8] The 1P/1L strategy, then, is often more of an ideal than a fact. Nevertheless, in talking to their children many parents will stick to one language most of the time and some even *all* the time.

Following the 1P/1L principle is supposed to result in bilingual children who actually speak two languages and who do not, in a lay person's terms, 'confuse' them. This supposed result, however, is not supported by the available research.

First, following the 1P/1L strategy does not necessarily have the outcome of active bilingual use by children. As all too many parents in bilingual settings have experienced, their children speak only one language in spite of parents using the 1P/1L approach. In the large survey I conducted in Flanders, only 74% of the 198 families in the sample who used the 1P/1L approach had children who spoke two languages. Families where both parents spoke both languages (a 1P/2L setting) had a slightly better chance (nearly four in five) of having children who spoke two languages (De Houwer, 2007; I described the survey earlier in Chapter 1; see in particular Box 1.5).

Yamamoto (2001) found similar results. She looked at the language use by Japanese–English-speaking dual-parent families residing in Japan and their children. Of the 46 children who were addressed exclusively in Japanese by one parent and exclusively in English by the other, eight did not in fact speak English. On the other hand, only four of the 54 children whose two parents addressed them in two languages did not speak English. Thus, children's chances for speaking two languages were greater in a 1P/2L than in a 1P/1L setting.

The findings from Yamamoto's survey and my own do not directly say anything about why the 1P/1L language presentation is less successful than the 1P/2L setting. There could be many underlying reasons. Invariably, in a 'failed' 1P/1L situation, it is the non-societal language that loses out. This suggests that there may be an important effect of the frequency of input. This is discussed later in the chapter.

Second, let us take a look at the issue of 'confusing' the languages. This appears to refer to the use of mixed utterances. Whether the use of mixed utterances should, in fact, be seen as a sign of 'confusion' or not being able to keep languages apart is debatable (I come back to the issue of mixed utterances later in this chapter). Still, mixed utterances are often seen as something that should be avoided (see Box 4.11). The 1P/1L setting is often seen as a kind of 'vaccination' against children's use of mixed utterances that is more effective than other language presentation settings. Regardless of how one wishes to interpret mixed utterances, let us examine their use in BFLA and the link with the 1P/1L setting.

Box 4.11   Unwarranted bad press for mixed utterances

The 1P/1L setting and mixed utterances

Most of the case studies on BFLA involve children who were raised in a 1P/1L setting. Most of the reports on these children mention their use of at least some mixed utterances (see also Chapter 2). This already shows that using the 1P/1L approach is not a fail-safe method for avoiding children's use of mixed utterances.

But do mixed utterances actually need to be avoided? Perhaps it could be seen as a real problem if children were to produce only or mainly mixed utterances in spite of hearing mainly unilingual utterances in each of two languages, as, for instance, in a 1P/1L setting.

However, I know of no BFLA child who produces only or mainly mixed utterances in spite of hearing mainly unilingual utterances in each of two languages. Instead, all BFLA children that I know or that have been reported on in the literature produce unilingual utterances in at least one language (see also Chapters 2, 6 and 7). They may in addition produce mixed utterances but these are normally used with a much lower frequency than unilingual ones.

Bilingual children's use of mixed utterances, then, does not mean that they do not use any unilingual utterances. And their use apparently cannot be avoided, even in a 1P/1L setting. But perhaps there is less 'risk' of them in a 1P/1L setting than in other language presentation settings? The available evidence suggests otherwise.

Patterson (1999) looked at the relation between the use of mixed utterances by a group of 102 Spanish–English bilingual toddlers and the way the languages were presented to the children. She found no difference between the use of mixed utterances by children from homes where parents used the 1P/1L approach and by children from homes where both parents adressed children in both languages (1P/2L). Also, there were quite a few children from homes where both parents addressed them in both languages but who did not use any mixed utterances.

Patterson also examined the role of language presentation in function of children's attainment of that important milestone, namely the use of word combinations (see Chapter 2). Again, she found no differences between children from homes where both parents addressed them in both languages and children from 1P/1L homes in whether children had reached this important milestone or not.

It would appear, then, that the 1P/1L setting is not a 'fail-safe' approach for raising children who actually speak two languages and for avoiding their use of mixed utterances. Also, it is not superior to a 1P/2L setting for child language outcomes.

Parents who generally adhere to the 1P/1L principle will occasionally switch languages or will occasionally use mixed utterances. Such switches may have specific pragmatic functions: they may be used to attract a child's attention, to stress particular meanings or to discipline children (Goodz, 1989). Similarly, children's mixed utterances or use of the 'wrong' language may also function as attention-grabbers or for emphasis (Goodz, 1989). Parents may also use mixed utterances or language switches to make sure their children understand or to repeat what their child said. As Goodz (1989: 41) notes, adults seem to have an irresistible urge to repeat very young children's utterances. Such repetitions often act as a confirmation that the child's intended meaning was understood. As children grow older, such confirmations will occur less frequently.

The situation may be very different in families where the adults speak two languages and commonly switch between them, both within and across utterances. A rare study of such a family that had a BFLA child suggests that the child's early language repertoire reflected the type of language use and mixed utterances that he heard at home (Huerta-Macías, 1981). Similarly, Quay (2008) reports that the kinds of mixed utterances that a Mandarin Chinese–English BFLA child with input in a third language (Japanese) starting at age five months heard from her parents at home were very similar to the kinds of mixed utterances she produced between the ages of 1;10 and 2;4. Both the parents' and the child's mixed utterances usually consisted of insertions of nouns from one language into the other.

How common is the 1P/1L setting?

The majority of in-depth studies of BFLA children's language development concern children who heard each of their languages spoken by mostly one person or parent. A well-known exception is the Spanish–English girl Manuela whose language development is described by, among others, Deuchar and Quay (2000). Manuela was reared in a 1P/2L setting, in which both her parents addressed her in two languages and chose each language depending on the circumstances. To what extent does the literature reflect actual practices? Is Manuela's case indeed an exception, as the literature would suggest?

Information from two survey studies of parental language choice suggests that, in fact, the 1P/1L approach is the exception rather than the rule (De Houwer, 2007; Yamamoto, 2001). There are three main patterns of language presentation based on the number of languages that parents use in speaking to BFLA children: (1) 1P/1L, with each parent mainly using a single language that is different from the other parent's; (2) 1P/2L, with both parents addressing children in the same two languages, and (3) 1P/1L & 1P/2L, where one parent addresses children using only one language, while the other parent uses that same language plus another one.

Box 4.12 The three main patterns of parental language presentation in BFLA

1P/1L	1P/2L	1P/1L & 1P/2L	Totals	Source
16.75%	42.35%	40.91%	1457 [a]	De Houwer, 2007
23.00%	27.00%	44.00%	188 [b]	Yamamoto, 2001

[a] This is the total number of families in Flanders in which a particular pattern was used (regardless of the number of children in each family); the figures for 1P/1L and 1P/2L include single and dual-parent families; the figures represent new calculations based on the data in De Houwer 2007.
[b] This is the total number of input patterns addressed to 188 children in dual-parent families in Japan; the figures represent new calculations based on the data in Table 5.4 in Yamamoto 2001: 101.

As I show in Box 4.12, the 1P/1L setting is the least common. This suggests that the many published case studies on BFLA that concern children growing up in a 1P/1L setting are not representative of the full range of variation in BFLA. The 'exceptional' case of Deuchar and Quay's (2000) Manuela turns out not to be exceptional at all.

Diversity and uniformity in language presentation

As we have seen before, young children's linguistic soundscapes may include many more people besides the parents. The parents may use a 1P/1L approach and all other people may address children using two languages, or the other way round. Children may experience different person–language links, that is, they meet up with diverse patterns of language use across individuals: some people will be bilingual, others monolingual. Alternatively, they may meet up with people who all speak just a single language to them or who all speak two languages. This represents a uniformity in language presentation across individuals.

Many variations are possible. I show a few of these in Box 4.13. As I have suggested elsewhere (De Houwer, 2006), it is my suspicion that the pattern (D4) in Box 4.13 is the most common outside of stable bilingual communities. An example of pattern (D3) is the case of Joanna, who was addressed in German by her father, in English by her mother, in German and English by her paternal grandmother and only in English by most others (Clyne, 1987: 89).

Box 4.13 Diversity and uniformity in language presentation to BFLA children

Diversity
(D1) A BFLA child's parents use the 1P/1L approach and most other people speak two languages.
(D2) A BFLA child's parents speak two languages and most other people speak just one language (A or Alpha).
(D3) A BFLA child's parents use the 1P/1L approach, some other people speak just one language (A or Alpha), yet others speak two.
(D4) One parent speaks just one language (A or Alpha), the other parent speaks two languages, some other people speak just one language (A or Alpha), yet others speak two.

Uniformity
(U1) 1P/1L
All people in a BFLA child's linguistic soundscape speak just one language (A or Alpha).
(U2) 1P/2L
All people in a BFLA child's linguistic soundscape speak two languages.

It is possible that it makes a difference in the language development process whether children are used to uniformity or diversity in language presentation. It may also matter which specific pattern within each that they experience. So far, however, studies have yet to examine the precise role of language presentation beyond the family, either by itself or in combination with language presentation within the family.

The three basic parental input patterns

Given that, so far, only the parents' role in language presentation has been studied I return to a discussion of parental input patterns. If we compare the three main patterns of parental language presentation in terms of the main language outcome for children (i.e. whether children actually speak two languages or not), it would appear that the 1P/2L pattern is the most successful one (see Box 4.14).

Box 4.14 Three basic parental input patterns and their success

	1P/1L	1P/2L	1P/1L & 1P/2L
Children speak two languages	74.24%	79.18%	59.23%
Children speak only one language	25.76%	20.82%	40.77%
Totals	198	562	596

Adapted from Table 7 in De Houwer, 2007; the most successful case has been shaded

	1P/1L	1P/2L	1P/1L & 1P/2L
Children speak two languages	38 (82.6%)	50 (92.6%)	77 (87.5%)
Children speak only one language	8 (17.4%)	4 (7.4%)	11 (12.5%)
Totals	46	54	88

Adapted from Table 5.4 in Yamamoto, 2001: 101; the most successful case has been shaded

However, the figures in Box 4.14 mask the fact that within the 1P/1L & 1P/2L pattern there are two basically distinct situations: one, where the language that both parents speak is the societal language, and the other, where both parents share the non-societal language. When we distinguish between these we get quite distinct results, as shown in Box 4.15.

When we take into account which language is the shared language between parents in a 1P/1L & 1P/2L setting we see that this pattern emerges as the most successful one of all if parents share the non-societal language (compare Boxes 4.14 and 4.15). However, if parents share the societal language at home in a 1P/1L & 1P/2L setting, the chances of their children speaking two languages drop dramatically.

These findings suggest that language presentation in terms of whether a parent addresses a child in one or two languages is not the most decisive factor in whether children will grow up actually speaking two languages. Additional evidence is the small degree of difference of success between the 1P/1L and 1P/2L situations (see my survey data in Box 4.14).

Rather, it most likely matters whether parents offer differing levels of support for either language. In the 1P/1L and 1P/2L situations, both languages have similar levels of parental support: either they are both spoken by just one parent or they are both spoken by both parents. In the 1P/1L & 1P/2L setting, however, one language gets support from both parents and the other one only from one. In this more uneven situation, the societal language wins out if that is the language that both parents share.

> **Box 4.15** The 1P/1L & 1P/2L parental input pattern and its success, depending on whether both parents speak the societal language at home or not

Flanders	Children speak two languages	Children speak only one language	Totals
All	59.23%	40.77%	596
A. the parents' shared language is the societal language	35.70%	64.30%	353
B. the parents' shared language is **not** the societal language	93.42%	6.58%	243

Adapted from Table 7 in De Houwer, 2007; the most successful case has been shaded; the difference between A and B is significant at the 0.01 level; $\chi^2 = 196.191$

Japan	Children speak two languages	Children speak only one language	Totals
All	77	11	88
A. the parents' shared language is the societal language	16	11	27
B. the parents' shared language is **not** the societal language	61	–	61

Adapted from Table 5.4 in Yamamoto 2001: 101; the most successful case has been shaded; the difference between A and B is significant at the 0.01 level; $\chi^2 = 24.799$

The possible reasons for the advantage for the societal language are manifold. I already mentioned the importance of peer pressure at school (see the section on 'Young BFLA children's linguistic soundscapes' earlier). However, another factor that could be of great importance is the frequency with which each language is heard. This could also be an important factor that determines whether in a 1P/1L or 1P/2L setting children speak two languages or not. The role of input frequency is discussed later in this chapter.

The categorization of parental language presentation I used above (1P/1L, 1P/2L and 1P/1L & 1P/2L) only refers to one or two languages. As I indicated earlier, however, parental input to children does not only consist of utterances in each of two languages, but may also consist of mixed utterances. Also, a 1P/1L setting may be an ideal rather than 100% reality (see above). Thus, the three-way categorization of parental language presentation is an idealization of what is often a much more complex reality.

Fathers and speech style

As Pancsofar and Vernon-Feagans (2006) have shown for young monolingual children, fathers can contribute a great deal to their children's language development. As possibly the sole providers of input in a bilingual setting, the role of fathers there is even more crucial (for an example, see Juan-Garau & Pérez-Vidal, 2001; this example is discussed in detail in the section on 'Speaking the "right" language and what it depends on').

Even if fathers are not the sole providers of input in a language they may have a particularly important role to play in their children's language development. This is because they may contribute a unique style of interaction that will challenge and thus foster children's language development (e.g. Barton & Tomasello, 1994).

Everyone who talks to children does so in a particular style. This style may be very different from person to person. Also, particular kinds of speakers may have a consistently different style compared to others. For monolingual acquisition, both similarities and differences have been observed between mothers and fathers in how they talk to young children (Rowe et al., 2004). This has been found for BFLA as well. Lanza (1997) has shown how in one BFLA family the mother and father developed distinct interactional styles with regard to language choice (see the section 'Speaking the "right" language and what it depends on'), whereas in another BFLA family both parents had developed very similar interactional styles as concerns language choice.

Speech styles may not only differ according to who is talking but also according to who is being addressed. For instance, mothers have been found to speak differently to girls than to boys (e.g. Kitamura & Burnham, 2003). I know of no studies that have focused on gender differences in BFLA but there may indeed be differences in bilingual families as well depending on whether parents talk to daughters or sons.

'Mother language'?

A final point regarding language presentation is the question whether its matters what kind of person is the 'carrier', so to speak, of a particular language. Often people assume that bilingual children will develop faster in the language that their mother speaks to them. So far, however, no research findings have been able to confirm this (see also Goodz, 1994). Also, the survey of bilingual families that I undertook in Flanders showed no influence from the mother versus the father that could help explain why in some families children spoke a minority language or not (see Box 4.16).

Box 4.16 The role of mothers vs. fathers in supporting active bilingual use by BFLA children

	Mothers offer input in the non-societal language	Fathers offer input in the non-societal language
Children speak two languages	81.79%	80.30%
Children speak only one language	18.21%	19.70%
Totals	1477	1528

Adapted from Table 5 in De Houwer, 2007; the difference between mothers and fathers is non-significant; $\chi^2 = 0.9849$

Sometimes, it is also suggested that the mother's language will be BFLA children's stronger language. However, this assumption also appears not to be true. The mother's language is not necessarily a bilingual child's stronger language (for an example, see Box 4.17).

> **Box 4.17** The language that mothers speak to their bilingual children is not necessarily the one that children speak best
>
> Lina and Lukas are two children who have heard Swedish and Italian from birth. Lina's mother speaks Swedish to her, while Lukas's mother addresses him in Italian. Lina is growing up in Italy, and Lukas in Sweden. Lina speaks much better Italian than Swedish, however, and Lukas speaks much better Swedish than Italian.
>
> | BFLA child | Mother speaks to child: | Country | Child's better language |
> |---|---|---|---|
> | Lina | Swedish | Italy | Italian |
> | Lukas | Italian | Sweden | Swedish |
>
> How do we know that Lukas speaks Swedish better than Italian? The main evidence we find is the fact that at any given age, the longest utterances he says are always in Swedish, and there is usually a big difference between his longest utterance in Italian and his longest Swedish utterance.
>
> For Lina, we see a similar picture but she is saying longer utterances in Italian.
>
> *Source: Bernardini, 2003*

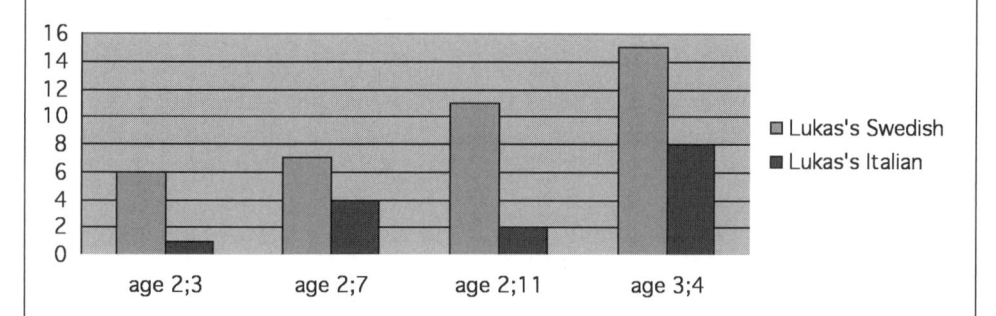

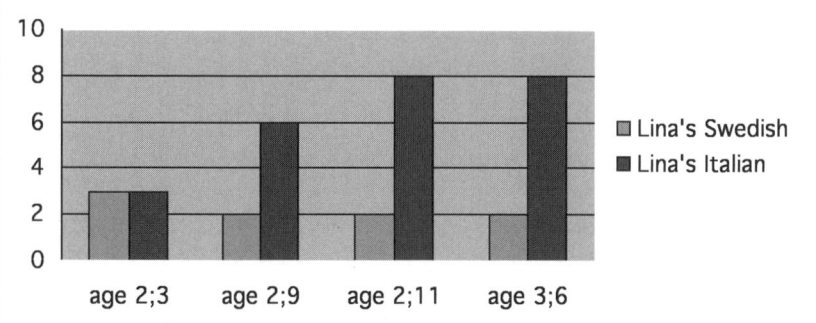

Parental gender, then, seems not to be an important factor for explaining bilingual children's language use. We have to look for other factors.

Usually, if bilingual children have a clearly stronger and weaker language, or, more dramatically, they speak one language but not the other, it is the environmental language, the language of the society in which they are growing up, that has the upper hand (e.g. De Houwer, 2007; Pearson, 2007; Yamamoto, 2001). This is most likely the result of the combined effect of peer pressure and the higher frequency of input of the societal language in both sheer amount of input as well as in the different contexts of use. In addition, the linguistic soundscape in terms of the number of different speakers is bound to be far more diverse for the societal language than for the non-societal language.

Language orientation

As Baetens Beardsmore noted several years ago (Baetens Beardsmore, 1982), in speaking to other bilinguals, bilinguals often feel free to use two languages. In conversations with monolinguals, however, they usually do not, and will try to stick to just one language.

In my first publication on Dutch–English three-year-old Kate (De Houwer, 1983), I noted a similar finding, namely that bilingual Kate apparently felt more free to use both Dutch and English with people she knew were fluent bilinguals (although they were speaking only Dutch to her), and tried to stick to just English with people who didn't speak any Dutch.

In my 1983 article, I explained this behavior in terms of a psycholinguistic construct that was quite in fashion at the time, viz., the monitor. In that particular study, the monitor was seen as a psychological processing mechanism that controlled language choice.

François Grosjean has suggested that it is particular neural activation processes that are involved in the ability to process languages in a bilingual individual. He has called these activation processes 'speech modes' (Grosjean, 1989) and later 'language modes' (e.g. Grosjean, 2001). As he wrote recently:

> at any given point in time and based on numerous psycho-social and linguistic factors, the bilingual has to decide, usually quite unconsciously, which language to use and how much of the other language is needed – from not at all to a lot [..]. If the other language is not needed, then it will not be called upon or, in neural modeling terms, activated [..]. The state of activation of the bilingual's languages and language processing mechanisms, at a given point in time, has been called the language mode.
> (Grosjean, 2008: 38)

The handbook edited by Kroll and de Groot (2005) contains many chapters which propose psycholinguistic theories as regards the activation of a bilingual's two languages.

Between the levels of observable behavior and processing in the brain I propose the concept of **language orientation**. Language orientation as understood here is a particular 'mind-set', a psychological orientation if you will, that has come about through bilingual speakers' experience with language and that helps them to function in a particular linguistic setting. It has a lot to do with attention, but also with expectations regarding language choice.

Monolingual and bilingual orientations are not usually a matter of 'all or nothing'. There can be degrees in each, with less monolingual orientations becoming more bilingual and the other way round.

If as a bilingual you are used to hearing only one language at the time from just about everybody you know, you will be used to a monolingual orientation for each language, and you'll expect people to just speak one language – either one of the two you know. Then if someone happens to use two languages in one sentence or conversation, you might at first not even understand – even if you know those two languages! You are simply not expecting anyone to actually use two languages in the same conversation. Some people might say that you are pretending not to understand (see, e.g. Métraux, 1965), but the lack of understanding can be quite genuine. Also, if you are used to having a monolingual orientation you will tend to stick to just one language with everybody.

If you have a more varied linguistic environment in which some people speak just one language with you and others regularly use two, you will probably have a more monolingual orientation with the former and a bilingual one with the latter (see Box 4.18). With the bilingual orientation, you will be expecting to hear two languages in the same conversation, and you will feel free to use two languages yourself. If you are used to everybody around you speaking two languages with you, you may also address them in two languages and you will generally operate in a bilingual orientation.

> **Box 4.18 One person, three language orientations**
>
> I am a fluent English–Dutch bilingual. Some of the people I usually speak English with understand and speak some Dutch, but most do not. Most of the people I usually speak Dutch with understand and speak English fairly well, but some do not.
>
> Depending on who I am talking to and depending on the circumstances, I am focused on just one language (monolingual orientation) or on either (bilingual orientation). I have been able to document the monolingual orientation examples below thanks to the existence of recordings I happened to have made of the relevant conversations. Without recordings, it may be hard to know that you have been operating in a monolingual orientation.
>
> *Monolingual orientation: Dutch*
>
> My daughter Susan was raised with English and Dutch from birth. I always spoke just Dutch with her, even when English speakers were present, and I expected her to speak Dutch to me, which she usually did from the very start.
>
> One day Susan and I were home alone in our house in Pennsylvania, USA. Susan was 19 months at the time and was at a stage where she was able to say three word sentences in either Dutch or English. I was busy cleaning up the kitchen and Susan was sitting at the kitchen table with her crayons. I sometimes made recordings of our times together. Also this time.
>
> I asked Susan in Dutch whether she wanted something to eat. She replied but I really didn't understand so I asked her again and then she said in Dutch: 'Rozijntjes!' (raisins).
>
> It was only later when I played back the recording that I heard Susan's first answer to my question: 'Raisins!', said loud and clear. I had not understood this simple English word, because I was not expecting to hear English. My mind was 'set' on Dutch and only Dutch.

> **Box 4.18 One person, three language orientations continued**
>
> *Monolingual orientation: English*
>
> In the early 1980s I was collecting data in English–Dutch bilingual families residing in Belgium. I went to their homes to play with their children and recorded these interactions. In these families the mothers were speakers of English with variable skills in Dutch. I spoke only English with the mothers.
>
> I have one recording where one of the mothers is explaining to me how her child is doing at preschool. In the middle of her explanation she says: 'on the *steenweg*' (the Dutch word *steenweg* refers to a particular kind of road), and I asked her a clarification question – I had not understood her, because I was simply not expecting her to use any Dutch (you might say that perhaps she didn't pronounce the word very well, but in fact she did, so a bad pronunciation was not the reason for my lack of understanding). My mind was 'set' on English and only English.
>
> *Bilingual orientation: Dutch and English*
>
> When I was his doctoral student, Professor Hugo Baetens Beardsmore usually spoke English with me, but he used some Dutch as well. He is fluent in English and Dutch (as well as other languages). During meetings in his office at the Dutch-speaking Free University of Brussels, I definitely had a bilingual orientation.
>
> I had no problem understanding Dr Baetens Beardsmore, even though he might be speaking English interlaced with Dutch asides. I was used to this pattern and was expecting the use of both languages in the same setting.
>
> *Names used with permission*

Your language orientation does not only depend on what you are used to from specific individuals, but is also connected with contexts of use (see Box 4.19).

> **Box 4.19 Two settings, two language orientations**
>
> The girl Kate who was the subject of my case study on early English–Dutch bilingual acquisition (De Houwer, 1990) was used to speaking Dutch with me. She also went to an English-speaking preschool, which was located in Antwerp, Belgium, where the main language is Dutch.
>
> In the year after I had finished recording her for my study, when Kate was four years old, I got a part-time job teaching music at her English preschool. Of course I had to speak English in the school, too. In this small international school, there was no room for Dutch. It was a little English-speaking island. All the children and staff were expected to speak English, regardless of their background. Kate happened to be in my class, so I spoke English to her there and she spoke English to me. We were both oriented just to English.
>
> The school was right around the corner from Kate's house and Kate's mother had asked me if I could take her home after school. I still remember vividly how I was escorting Kate from the classroom to the school's front door and how she was chattering away to me in English.
>
> Then I opened the door, we stepped down two steps onto the sidewalk, and she changed into Dutch! And I switched with her – I don't know how she would have reacted had I continued to speak English. But Kate obviously perceived the setting as very different, and switched back to what she had been used to with me from the time she was two years old: Dutch. And so we were both back in a monolingual Dutch orientation.

Language orientation, then, is strongly connected with language socialization and thus with sociolinguistic contexts. Even very young bilingual children may already have a more monolingual and/or a more bilingual language orientation. Although experimental evidence of this is lacking, young children's language choice indicates preferences for a monolingual or a bilingual orientation from early on. I discuss children's language choice in the section 'Speaking the "right" language and what it depends on'.

Input frequency in BFLA

Do monolingual children really hear more words than bilingual children?

In the literature on BFLA you often find the curious statement that bilingual children receive quantitatively less input in each of their languages than monolingual children do in their one language. This statement assumes that all monolingual children receive the same amount of input. That is most patently not the case.

There are huge differences in how much talk monolingual children hear. In one of the most impressive longitudinal group studies of monolingual children's language input to date, the average number of words per hour that young English-speaking American children heard from their parents differed vastly across families (Hart & Risley, 1995). On average, some children heard 2150 words per hour, others only 620 (Hart & Risley, 1995: 132). Parents' speaking rates, then, are quite variable. Box 4.20 shows how such variable **speaking rates** lead to huge differences between monolingual children in the number of words they will have heard from their parents by the time they are three years old.

Box 4.20 Differences in the cumulative number of words heard by three-year-old monolinguals based on their parents' different speaking rates			
Parents' average speaking rate	Low	Medium	High
	620 words/hour	1250 words/hour	2150 words/hour
Estimated number of words that three-year-olds have heard from their parents since birth [a]	10 million	20 million	30 million

[a] Estimates based on 14-hour waking days.
Source: Hart & Risley, 1995: 131–132

In addition to these variable speaking rates, there are large differences between children in how many hours they spend with other people. Just consider the fact that some children sleep a lot more than others. In the 1990s, I did a study of ten monolingual Dutch-speaking four-year-olds. I found that during the nights of the full school days in one month, some of the children were in bed for 164 hours, while others spent up to 200 hours in bed. That's a difference of 36 hours in just one month, or close to three waking days, that some children are not interacting with anyone but that others are (these are previously unpublished results of a study I described in De Houwer, 2000).

Regardless of their parents' speaking rates, the longer sleepers will have had less opportunity for interaction and hearing language than the shorter sleepers. Then, there is also the variation that exists between children in the amount of time they spend in a group situation or alone with a person who is talking to them. The amount of talk may be quite different in these two contexts.

Box 4.21 Input in two languages does not automatically imply less input in each of them compared to a monolingual setting

More input in Language A in a bilingual than in a monolingual setting (1)

	Bilingual input: 1P/2L	Monolingual input: 2P/1L
Input in Language A	1250 words/hr; 15 hrs/day = 18,750 words/day	700 words/hr; 13 hrs/day = 9100 words/day
Input in Language Alpha	1000 words/hr; 15 hrs/day	none

More input in Language A in a bilingual than in a monolingual setting (2)

	Bilingual input: 1P/1L	Monolingual input: 2P/1L
Input in Language A	2150 words/hr; 7 hrs/day = 15,050 words/day	900 words/hr; 14 hrs/day = 12,600 words/day
Input in Language Alpha	2150 words/hr; 7 hrs/day	none

The same amount of input in Language A in a bilingual as in a monolingual setting

	Bilingual input: 1P/1L	Monolingual input: 2P/1L
Input in Language A	2000 words/hr; 6 hrs/day = 12,000 words/day	1000 words/hr; 12 hrs/day = 12,000 words/day
Input in Language Alpha	1150 words/hr; 7 hrs/day	none

Less input in Language A in a bilingual than in a monolingual setting

	Bilingual input: 1P/2L	Monolingual input: 2P/1L
Input in Language A	1000 words/hr; 12 hrs/day = 12,000 words/day	1500 words/hr; 12 hrs/day = 18,000 words/day
Input in Language Alpha	1150 words/hr; 12 hrs/day	none

2P/1L refers to the fact that both parents speak one and the same language to the child.

The children in these imaginary examples are supposed to be three years old.

There are various other factors that can affect the amount of language that a child hears. These factors are, in principle, similar for bilingual and monolingual settings. I return to a discussion of factors affecting the amount of input later in this section, but for now I want to stress that the amount of input in a particular language does not depend on the number of languages that a child hears.

Box 4.21 shows how some three-year-old bilingual children may, in fact, hear more of a particular language than some monolingual children. It also gives an example of similar levels of language input and also of lower levels for bilinguals. It is important to remember that the total amount of input in a language depends primarily on the combination of the amount of time available for interaction and the overall speaking rates of the people interacting with the child, rather than on the number of languages a child hears.

The figures in Box 4.21 are entirely speculative, since we have no data on how many words people say to three-year-old bilinguals. The figures for monolingually reared children fall within the limits of Hart and Risley's (1995) study.

Frequency of input in a Dutch–German bilingual family: a re-analysis of 'old' data

For BFLA children we still lack the kind of study that Hart and Risley carried out. However, van de Weijer's (2000) study offers information on the overall frequency of actual language input to young BFLA children. Ironically, van de Weijer was not aiming to study BFLA. Rather, his purpose was to record all the language input to an infant between the ages of six and nine months and to study the nature of this infant-directed speech (see also earlier).

The infant studied happened to be growing up in a bilingual family and had a sister who was two years older. The children's mother often spoke German with them but used Dutch as well. All other people, including the children's father, spoke Dutch.

Because of his different research goals, van de Weijer (2000) did not focus his analysis on a comparison of the speech addressed to the infant versus the older girl, nor on the specifics of the bilingual situation. Because he did differentiate between the two languages, however, I have been able to analyze his data differently. I wanted to see what the distribution was of the languages addressed to each child (the infant and the toddler). I show the results of my analyses in Box 4.22 (adv.).

Box 4.22 (adv.)   A bilingual mother's input to her young children

The average number of utterances per day that a bilingual mother said to her young children and the average proportions with which she used German, Dutch and indeterminate utterances

Mother speaks...	To her infant	To her toddler
German	217 (42%)	596 (59%)
Dutch	46 (9%)	110 (11%)
Indeterminate	253 (49%)	310 (30%)
Average total number of utterances per day	516	1016

Data recalculated on the basis of Tables 1 and 2 in van de Weijer (2000)

> **Box 4.22 (adv.)**   A bilingual mother's input to her young children continued
>
> *The average proportion of utterances that a bilingual mother addressed to her infant vs. her toddler every day (per language category and in total)*
>
> | Mother speaks... | To her infant | To her toddler | Average daily number of child-directed utterances |
> |---|---|---|---|
> | German | 27% | 73% | 813 |
> | Dutch | 29% | 71% | 156 |
> | Indeterminate | 45% | 55% | 563 |
> | ALL | 34% | 66% | 1532 |
>
> Data recalculated on the basis of Tables 1 and 2 in van de Weijer (2000)
>
> The figures above are based on the mother's language input to her children on 18 days in the period when her youngest was between six and nine months old (the infant), and her oldest between 2;6 and 2;9 (the toddler).
>
> Source: van de Weijer, 2000

Van de Weijer used a three-way classification for each maternal utterance that was addressed to the children: Dutch, German or indeterminate. German and Dutch are closely related languages and so there are many utterances that could be classified as either Dutch or German (for instance, 'Ja!', which means 'yes' – it sounds exactly the same in German and Dutch and also means the same). Especially short utterances can sound exactly the same. Van de Weijer classified utterances with just the child's name as indeterminate.

As you can see from the tables in Box 4.22 (adv.), the mother here used not only unilingual utterances in Dutch and German, but also utterances that could be either Dutch or German. You can see that the proportion of these indeterminate utterances is quite a bit lower when this mother speaks to her toddler than to her infant (30% in the case of the toddler, 49% for the infant – a difference of nearly 20 points).

Since there is more chance for short utterances to be indeterminate, we can assume that the lower proportion of indeterminate utterances addressed to the older child indicates that the mother was speaking to her in longer utterances. This is indeed the case: as van de Weijer (2000: 159) explains, utterances directed to the infant were, on the whole, much shorter than those directed to the toddler. This finding reflects findings in monolingual settings that adults tend to address toddlers in longer utterances than they do infants. Van de Weijer's study is the first to have shown this for BFLA.

Another difference that is very clear from especially the second table in Box 4.22 (adv.) is that the mother spoke to her toddler nearly twice as often as to the infant. Of course, it wasn't only the mother who talked to the children. The children were also spoken to at their day care center and other people addressed the children at home.

On the whole, the toddler heard 2435 utterances per day addressed to her, and the infant 903, which is 2.7 times less (my recalculations of the data in van de Weijer's (2000) tables 1 and 2). The numbers for the toddler will in fact be even higher, though, since the recordings focused only on the 8.75 hours per day that the infant was awake. The toddler most likely was interacting with others for some of the time that the infant was asleep.

Also, when caregivers spent time with both the toddler and the infant they addressed just the toddler using on average 940 words per hour, while they addressed just the infant using only 300 words per hour (van de Weijer, 2002). The difference in language addressed to the toddler and the infant in this study would suggest that BFLA children get talked to more often as they get older. This mirrors findings for monolingual children (e.g. Hart & Risley, 1995).

The average number of utterances that the children in Box 4.22 (adv.) heard from just their mother is quite high. If you add the utterances that other adults speak to them you realize that children may hear quite a lot of speech in a day. Also, children hear speech addressed to them individually, speech addressed to them and others, and overheard speech. Both the infant and the toddler in the Dutch–German bilingual family studied by van de Weijer heard a combined total of 2990 words per hour (van de Weijer, 2002; this makes the estimates for bilingual settings in Box 4.21 earlier quite realistic).

Does the variation in how much children hear actually matter?

Children hear a lot of language, hour after hour, day after day, week after week, month after month, year after year. Thus, children have a lot of opportunity to learn.

The more opportunity they have to learn language, the more children will in fact learn. This has been shown quite convincingly by Hart and Risley (1995). At age three, the children in the 42 monolingual English-speaking families they studied varied widely from each other in the number of words they knew. Some children knew 1100 words, others just about half of that. Hart and Risley traced this variation to the language input the children received from their parents. They were able to show that the children who heard the most words per hour also had learned the most words. Because of the great importance of this finding, I summarize their results in Box 4.23. This box will remind you a lot of Box 4.20 earlier.

Box 4.23 Differences in the number of words known by three-year-old monolinguals in function of their parents' different speaking rates

Parents' average speaking rate	*Low*	*Medium*	*High*
	620 words/hr	1250 words/hr	2150 words/hr
Average number of words that their three-year-olds know	ca. 540	ca. 760	ca. 1100

Source: Hart & Risley, 1995

Up until Hart and Risley's monumental study, no clear link had been established between the frequency with which children heard words in the input and their level of lexical development.[9] The fact that the sheer magnitude of the number of words that children hear addressed to them has an effect on how many words children themselves will know by age three is very encouraging news.

So far, the direct effect of the **absolute frequency** of global language input on children's lexical development has only been specifically investigated for monolingual children.

However, there are published data on the total number of utterances used by caregivers and children in five English–Inuktitut families living in Inuit villages that offer some important insights for bilingual settings. The data are based on longitudinal recordings of natural conversations in the home for each child–caregiver pair and comprise an impressive total of 24,755 transcribed utterances (Allen et al., 2002; this study is summarized in Allen, 2007).

Allen et al. (2002) did not specifically focus on the overall amount of speech in the transcripts, but when I compared the rank orders found for the caregivers with those for the children, there was a clear relation between the two: the more the caregivers in each family talked, the more their children talked (see Box 4.24). There was just one exception, namely for the top two families, where the orders were reversed for the children. Still, these two families with the greatest amount of input had children who talked most, compared to the other three families. Thus, if caregivers are verbose they will have children who are too. This finding for bilingual children reflects the results demonstrated by Hart and Risley for monolingual families.

Box 4.24 The total number of utterances in caregiver speech and in BFLA children's language production

Family	Total number of utterances	
	Caregivers	Child
AW	4726 (1)	1771 (2)
AI	3990 (2)	2586 (1)
SA	3452 (3)	1572 (3)
SR	2363 (4)	1206 (4)
PN	2143 (5)	946 (5)

The numbers between brackets refer to the ranking per caregiver and child category.

Adapted from Tables 2 and 3 in Allen, 2007 (original data reported in Allen et al., 2002)

What if children hear one language more than the other one?

For monolingual settings, you can only look at the absolute frequency of utterances addressed to children. In bilingual settings, you can also look at **relative frequency**. Relative frequency concerns the proportion with which a particular phenomenon is present, in this case, the proportion with which a particular language is addressed to a child.

In an often-cited study, Pearson, Fernández, Lewedeg and Oller (1997) found that the more Spanish children heard in comparison to English, the more Spanish words they produced.

Proportions of English and Spanish in the input were based on parental estimates. However, there are no data on the total number of utterances that children heard on average, and it is not clear how mixed utterances are part of the equation, or on what basis parents decided that one language was spoken more often than the other one, especially since most people in the children's environments spoke both English and Spanish. Also, the balance between individual children's input in both languages changed quite a lot over time.

In spite of these issues, the fact remains that using an input measure of relative frequency that Pearson *et al.* themselves called 'crude' yields the finding of a link between relative input frequency in one language compared to another and bilingual children's lexical development: the more children heard Spanish rather than English, the more Spanish words they knew and the other way round.

Pearson *et al.*'s (1997) study relied on reported data only. A rare observational study that provides detailed information about the usage of unilingual and mixed utterances by both BFLA children and their caregivers is that by Allen *et al.* (2002) I referred to above. This study shows that the proportion of mixed utterances as used by five children and their bilingual Inuktitut–English-speaking caregivers is surprisingly similar within each child–caregiver pair. Yet, the five caregivers differed quite a bit in the degree of usage of mixed utterances (ranging from 2.1 to 8.0%), as did the children (ranging from 1.1 to 9.8%). On average, caregivers used mixed utterances 5.4% of the time and the children 5.3% of the time.

In addition, when we look at the rank orders among the five sets of caregivers for the proportion of unilingual utterances in Inuktitut and English we see that they are the same for the children being cared for by those same caregivers. I summarize the data in Box 4.25(adv.).

Box 4.25(adv.) Relative frequencies of mixed and unilingual utterances in caregiver speech and in BFLA children's language production

Family	Proportion of mixed utterances	
	Adults %	Child %
AI	8.0	9.8
PN	7.6	3.5
SA	6.7	4.1
SR	3.7	4.6
AW	2.1	1.1

Adapted from Tables 2 and 3 in Allen, 2007

Family	Unilingual utterances: Inuktitut		Unilingual utterances: English	
	Adults %	Child %	Adults %	Child %
AW	84.6	80.6	13.3	18.3
SA	72.4	50.9	20.9	45.0
AI	52.3	42.6	39.7	47.6
PN	41.5	20.3	50.9	76.2
SR	23.6	11.2	72.7	84.2

The columns headed by 'Adults %' refer to the proportion of utterances in each category as used by the children's caregivers in each family.

Adapted from Tables 2 and 3 in Allen, 2007 (original data reported in Allen et al., 2002)

Comprehension and production

We see, then, that there can be quite a close association between the relative frequencies of mixed utterances and unilingual utterances in Language A and Language Alpha in the input, and the relative frequencies with which young BFLA children use each of these. At the same time, as I have made abundantly clear before, many children do not actually speak two languages, in spite of regular input in those two languages. Clearly, here other factors besides input frequency are at work.

BFLA children with input in two languages who speak only one language do understand two languages (e.g. Jisa, 2000). Perhaps the relative frequency of input in each of their languages will have an effect on how much they comprehend and, also, on how well they speak the one language they do speak.

The fact that BFLA children may understand two languages but speak only one implies that the potential effect of input frequency (both absolute and relative) on children's language development in bilingual settings needs to be examined from two perspectives: that of comprehension and that of production. So far, however, there are no studies that have looked at the possible effect of bilingual input from these different perspectives. The few studies of input effects have focused only on production.

What determines how much talk children hear?

There are various factors that can affect the amount of language that a child hears. For instance, depressed mothers do not talk much and do not encourage their children to talk much. Children of depressed mothers soon learn to keep their interactions with their depressed mothers to a minimum, and as a result monolingual children who have depressed mothers may speak less than those who do not (Breznitz & Sherman, 1987).

Another factor relates to sibling status. Older siblings usually take up more 'language space' in the family. And mothers do talk and generally interact less with their second born children than with their firstborn children. A recent study of 54 mothers in interaction with their firstborn and second-born children showed that they were generally much less communicative with their second-born than with their firstborn children (Putnick et al., 2007).[10]

Thus, the difference we saw earlier in the bilingual input to the toddler and the infant in the German–Dutch-speaking family studied by van de Weijer most likely is not only age-related (people tend to talk more to children the older they are; see also Hart & Risley, 1995), but has to do with the toddler being the firstborn and the infant being the second born. Furthermore, Hart and Risley found that in monolingual families with newborn children the total amount of talk stayed more or less the same compared to before. Whatever level of verbosity there was before did not change. The same amount of talk was just divided differently.

Another factor that may influence the overall amount of speech to children is people's social class (Hoff, 2003). For instance, in Hart and Risley's (1995) study parents who were on welfare talked much less on average than parents who had a college degree and a high income from work. Different contexts for communication play a role as well (Hoff-Ginsberg,

1991). For instance, there may be less talk if parents are playing with their children in the park than when they are reading books to them.

There is no reason to assume that the major factors found to play a role in the amount of talk that parents address to MFLA children are any different for BFLA children. However, consistent differences between contexts for communication among BFLA children's two languages could play a decisive role in their development of each of these languages (see also Silva-Corvalán, 2003). Such consistent differences are more likely to occur if only one person or very few people speak one particular language to a BFLA child.

Finally, it should be realized that older siblings are also part of many BFLA children's linguistic environments. Evidence is emerging that sibling talk to younger BFLA children may influence proficiency in either language (Bridges, 2008).

Category frequency

Input frequency does not only concern the global amount of talk and within that the number and proportion of unilingual utterances in each language and mixed utterances. On a more local level, input frequency also refers to the frequency of particular words, structures and pragmatic functions in the speech addressed to children. Again, one can look at the absolute frequency which which a particular linguistic category occurs within a particular time frame, or one can look at the relative frequency of one category compared to another.

The effect of category frequency in the input for language development is an issue that has been of interest in studies of monolingual (e.g. Gathercole, 1986) and bilingual (e.g. Nicoladis *et al.*, 2007) acquisition alike. For bilingual acquisition, very few studies however have looked at the frequency of particular linguistic structures in the actual input that bilingual children are hearing. The few studies that have looked at specific input effects for specific linguistic developments will be discussed in the following chapters where relevant (e.g. De Houwer, 1997; Paradis & Navarro, 2003; Rieckborn, 2006).

Quite a few more studies on BFLA have shown how changes in children's linguistic soundscapes can affect children's overall bilingual development. I turn to this issue in the next section.

What BFLA children say

Changes in BFLA children's linguistic soundscapes and their effects

As I have suggested before, BFLA children's linguistic soundscapes can be very dynamic. That means that there can be major changes in these linguistic soundscapes.

For monolingual children trips do not involve the cessation of input in one language. For BFLA children, they might well do. Parental separation may also lead to quite drastic changes in BFLA children's linguistic soundscapes. The death or departure of a beloved nanny or grandmother may mean the end of input in a particular language, or a change from two or three people speaking that language to just one or two.

Losing a language

If there have been long periods of time that children were away from one of their languages, they will not have had regular and continuous input in their two languages. In such cases, children may experience some degree of language attrition or even loss, however transitional. Attrition is a severe restriction in linguistic skills; loss signifies that there are no more skills.[11]

We mainly know about individual language attrition and loss in BFLA children through anecdotes (for an exception, see the study by Berman, 1979 as described in Box 4.26). Métraux (1965), however, reports that eight mothers in a group of families who together had 47 BFLA children of varying ages (with some children belonging to the same family) said that their children had learned and forgotten at least one language before the age of six. This suggests that attrition and loss are fairly common in BFLA.

> **Box 4.26   Individual language loss in a BFLA child**
>
> *From birth up until 2;11: in Israel*
> Shelli was born in Israel. Her parents and her grandmother spoke English to her, but adult siblings, her babysitter, neighbors and relatives spoke exclusively Hebrew to her. Thus, Shelli was raised in a 1P/1L situation from birth. Shelli started attending an all-Hebrew nursery school at age two.
>
> In this age period, Shelli learned to understand two languages, but she spoke only one: Hebrew. In her third year, she spoke Hebrew at the level of monolingual Hebrew-speaking peers. But she understood English quite well, as evidenced, for instance, by translations into Hebrew of English utterances that she had heard.
>
> *The year between age 2;11 and 3;11: in the USA*
> Shelli moved to the USA with her parents, who continued to speak English to her there. Only occasionally were there any visits from Hebrew-speaking relatives (including Shelli's adult siblings) and friends. After a month in the USA, when Shelli was three years old, she started going to an all-English and all-day public nursery school.
>
> In the first month of her stay, Shelli continued to speak Hebrew to everyone, as she had done before (her parents, of course, understood Hebrew, but nobody else did). After another six weeks, however, Shelli no longer spoke any Hebrew but had switched over entirely to speaking English. She grew intolerant of anyone who occasionally spoke Hebrew to her, and by age 3;6, seven months after arriving in the USA, 'she seemed genuinely not to understand anything said to her in H(ebrew)' (Berman, 1979: 161).
>
> *For all intents and purposes, then, Shelli seemed to have forgotten her Hebrew entirely, although she had used it fluently at an age-appropriate level only about half a year before.*
>
> Source: Berman, 1979

BFLA children may realize, to some extent, that they are in the process of losing one of their languages. An example of this and strategies of how a BFLA child dealt with encroaching attrition is shown in Box 4.27.

> **Box 4.27** An interesting strategy in a case of language attrition
>
> Cruz-Ferreira (2006: 74) describes how the youngest of her three children, Mikael, reacted to the fact that his Swedish was rapidly losing ground when his father, his only Swedish interlocutor, was absent for a long time. Mikael had been raised with Portuguese and Swedish from birth. His mother and older sisters spoke Portuguese to him, and his father Swedish.
>
> Mikael spoke both Swedish and Portuguese by the time his father had to go and work abroad. Mikael was 1;9 at the time and the family lived in Portugal. Until he was 2;7, he saw his father only for two short days every month. In that time period, Mikael's ability to speak Swedish quickly deteriorated.
>
> But occasionally Mikael needed to use Swedish, for instance when he went along to pick up his sisters at the Swedish school they went to or when he met a Swedish person during shopping trips. On these occasions, Mikael started talking very quickly in the little Swedish he remembered. Mikael also did this when he talked on the phone to his father or Swedish relatives. The purpose of this, Cruz-Ferreira notes, 'appears to have been to show that he knew that the situation demanded Swedish, that he knew which language that was and, not least, that he was a sociable individual' (p. 75). Here follows a typical example.
>
> *Mikael (MIK) is two and a half years old here. All his utterances are in Swedish, and they are said in rapid succession to each other, with the gestures very quickly in between.*
>
> | *MIK: | hej! | ('hi!'; after this he stretches his two fingers to indicate his age) |
> | *MIK: | Micke så! | ('Mikael like this!'; after this he points at his shoes) |
> | *MIK: | skorna! | ('the shoes!'; after this he looks up and points at the sky) |
> | *MIK: | där plinnplan! | ('there aeroplane!'; the Swedish adult word is 'flygplan') |
> | *MIK: | så där, va? | ('so, right?') |
> | *MIK: | hejdå! | ('bye') |
>
> Adapted from Cruz-Ferreira, 2006: 74

The fact that changes in input patterns can have quite immediate and strong effects on bilingual children's language use is not limited to BFLA. Young ESLA children may show such effects as well. A Japanese girl, Atsuko, moved to the United States from Japan when she was five years old. After eight weeks of exposure to English, she was saying a large number of English utterances which were steadily increasing in length. After a few months, however, her input in English declined because school was closed for the summer vacation. This had an immediate effect on the length of her English utterances: they got much shorter. Once school started again she began saying longer utterances again (Rescorla & Okuda, 1987).[12]

How fast do children lose a language?

It is difficult to say anything with certainty about the minimum length of time without input in a particular language that will lead to language attrition or loss. Also, in order to assess attrition or loss we need a good description of the child's linguistic skills before the change in language environment.[13]

And then there is the question of how to precisely define language attrition or loss in young children, who are just on their way towards gaining linguistic skills and so have a very unstable and highly changeable proficiency profile to start with. Is language loss the inability to speak a language that children were somewhat able to speak before? Is it the inability to understand a language that they understood to some extent before? And for attrition, should we perhaps think in terms of 'difficulty'? And does this then mean that things were 'easy' before?

There are no easy answers to these questions at the moment. It does appear to be the case, though, that the younger children are, the faster they lose their ability in a language they haven't heard for some time. Evidence for this mainly comes from experience with internationally adopted children (Gindis, 1999; Nicoladis & Grabois, 2002).[14] That situation typically is one of 'successive monolingualism', however, where one language is fully replaced by another. As such, it is quite different from BFLA.

I know of one example of a BFLA child that suggests that the speed with which young children can lose ability in a language is remarkably fast. My daughter Susan was an outgoing and gregarious BFLA child who spoke fluent Dutch and English at the age of two and a half (she was using Dutch and English multiple clause utterances by then). She also understood both languages well enough to participate in conversations with strangers. Then she spent three weeks in an environment where nobody spoke English to her and she spoke no English either. When she happened to meet up with English speakers after just these three weeks, she did not understand them and certainly she did not speak to them. She seemed to have lost her English.

Gaining more skill in a language

In contrast to losing a language, children may also gain more skill in it as a positive result of changed linguistic soundscapes. Vacations or visits from relatives may bring a highly increased frequency of input in a language that previously had perhaps not been so frequently used (see also David & Li, 2008). The literature is full of examples of this.

Young Louis' use of German and French shifted in response to increased or decreased input frequency in either language (Ronjat, 1913: 7–10). The German–French BFLA girl Céline's skill in French suddenly increased during and after a long visit from her French-speaking grandmother (Kupisch, 2003: 17–18). Céline's French received another boost after a long holiday in France (you have already met Céline in Box 2.13 in Chapter 2). German–English Laura showed dramatic progress in her hitherto weaker language, English, after a holiday in the United Kingdom (Gut, 2000b: 216). Another example of increased skill after a trip is described in Box 4.28, which talks about German–English Hildegard.

Tiffany and Odessa experienced something very similar to Hildegard. They were raised with French and English from birth, but hardly spoke any English when they lived in France. Then their mother took them on a trip to the United States, and very soon the children's use of English increased dramatically. They also spoke it much better than before (Jisa, 2000). Likewise, English–Norwegian Thomas, who lived in Norway and hardly spoke any English at age 2;4 (see Lanza, 1997), increased his skill in English quite a bit after two trips to the United States (Lanza, 1998).

> **Box 4.28** Travel may bring increased skill in a language
>
> Hildegard was the daughter of linguist and phonetician Werner Leopold (who I introduced to you in Chapter 1).
>
> Hildegard spent most of her first five years in the United States. Everybody there spoke English to her except her father, who adressed her in German. He held a full-time job and hence could not spend all that much time with Hildegard.
>
> Leopold (1978: 30) reports that Hildegard spoke English fluently in her fifth year but that she spoke very little German, and if she did, it was mostly in the form of German nouns inserted into otherwise English utterances.
>
> Towards the end of Hildegard's fifth year the family went to Germany for six months. There, Hildegard was left in the care of German speakers for four weeks. That time was enough to 'give her complete fluency in German while English receded' (Leopold, 1978: 30).
>
> After her return to the United States, Hildegard experienced problems in speaking English, but after a few days she was speaking better again. After a few months she was speaking both German and English quite fluently and well, although German once again became her weaker language.
>
> Source: Leopold, 1978

A final example is that of the Florentine 'ragazzo' from Box 1.2 in Chapter 1 who didn't speak any English in spite of his father speaking it to him from birth. By the age of 3;3 the boy had only spoken Italian. When he then visited England with his parents he did speak some English there to monolingual English speakers (von Raffler-Engel, 1965).

In some of the cases where there is an increased input in one of the languages children's previously weaker language often just gets better and the previously stronger language does not appear to be affected. In other cases, the balance shifts and the previously stronger language becomes the weaker one (see the Hildegard example in Box 4.28). (For a discussion of 'weaker' and stronger' languages, see the section 'The relation between BFLA children's two developing languages' in Chapter 2).

Changes in language presentation

In addition to clear changes in BFLA children's soundscapes, there may be changes in language presentation. Parents living in a Language A environment who started using two languages with their children right after they were born might give up speaking Language Alpha in the course of time, thus effectively changing the bilingual environment to a monolingual one. The reasons for such changes are usually related both to attitudes and to how parents see their own role in their children's language learning (see the section 'Attitudes and beliefs' previously).

Many parents who have chosen to follow the 1P/1L principle (see the earlier section on language presentation) may start out using only one language when children are very young, but may use the other language more often as their children become older and more competent language users (Goodz, 1994). Also, the circumstances in which parents interact with their children change as children grow older, and these changed circumstances may bring with them some social pressures that make parents take a less strict stance with regard to the 1P/1L ideal. However, children themselves may not be ready for such a looser bond between a person and their language use and may object to it (see also the next section).

If children hear a lot of Language A in their larger language environment parents may decide to switch from using Language A to speaking Language Alpha in mid-course in order to maximize their child's exposure to Language Alpha (see, e.g. Caldas & Caron-Caldas, 2000 for the child John; Serratrice, 2005). Also, parents may change from a 1P/2L to a 1P/1L setting. The reason here may again be that parents feel their children need more input support in one of the languages.

In contrast to the effect of changes in the overall linguistic soundscape, little is known about the effect of changes in parental language presentation. Children may see the way that parents present themselves linguistically as an important aspect of their identity. Children may experience changes in parental linguistic identity that involve adding a language or dropping one as traumatic.

Thus, the dynamic that children bring to the language input situation and potential changes in it certainly plays a role. There are children who do not seem to care much in which language their parents address them. These children will most likely not protest if there is a change in language presentation. Then there are children who have made a strong person–language link. They are less likely to accept changes in those links.

Differences between children in how willing they are to accept changes in their parents' language presentation may, in part, depend on how they were socialized before with regard to language choice. I explain this more in the next section.

Going off to school

Finally, a major change in most young children's lives occurs when they start to go to school. For BFLA children this event often means a drastic change in their linguistic soundscapes, with an increased input in one of their languages and possibly an entirely different balance between their languages in terms of the number of people speaking each. The impact of school can be quite great. School is more than the temporary change in linguistic soundscapes represented by vacations and visits. It is a well-known phenomenon that once young BFLA children start to attend school in one of their languages, the school language (Language A) often 'takes over', as it were, and children may cease to speak Language Alpha or may cease to develop in Language Alpha. The extent to which this will happen may depend a lot on the discourse strategies that parents use. I now turn to a discussion of these.

Speaking the 'right' language and what it depends on

You cannot speak two languages at once. That means that if you know two spoken languages you must always choose between them.[15]

The rules of language choice

Bilinguals have the choice between unilingual utterances in Language A, unilingual utterances in Language Alpha and mixed utterances combining words from Language A and Language Alpha (see also the section 'Language choice' in Chapter 2). There are social rules that guide children's selection of each type of utterance.[16] These rules are usually not explicit, but still, they exist.[17] They can be different from family to family or even from person to person.

In some families the implicit rules are that when you talk about school you do it using Language A. When you talk about things around the house you use Language Alpha. In other families rules for language choice don't depend on the topic of conversation but may depend on where you are and/or on who you are with. Some people insist that children address them in just a single language, regardless of the topic. Others do not really care in which language children speak to them. In some families mixed utterances are frowned upon. In others, using mixed utterances is taken for granted. Or, in some families some people don't mind mixed utterances, whereas others find them unacceptable (e.g. Huerta-Macías, 1981).

Children have to learn these social rules for language choice. Thus, part of children's bilingual socialization involves getting them to speak the right language in the right circumstances. What is considered to be 'right', however, depends on adults' ideas about this. What may be right for the one parent is not necessarily right for another one. In Box 4.29 I show a few contrasting examples of this.

> **Box 4.29** Three fathers, three ideas about the 'right' language to use
>
> Manuel, Rubén and Julio are first-generation Mexican Americans who speak and understand Spanish and English. They each have a three-year-old girl that they address only in Spanish. Their wives are third-generation Mexican Americans who speak and understand Spanish and English and who address their daughters mostly in English, but sometimes also in Spanish. The families live in the same suburb of Los Angeles and have friends who speak both Spanish and English, or just Spanish, or just English.
>
> The families' daughters, Monika, Rosita and Julia, thus live in very similar linguistic soundscapes. Yet, they are growing up in different socializing environments as far as the expectations go for which language they should speak to their fathers.
>
> *Manuel*
> Manuel doesn't care really what language Monika speaks. He is just happy that she is able to communicate at all, in any language! Manuel does not care if that includes mixed utterances that combine words from Spanish and English. For Manuel, any language is 'right'.
>
> *Rubén*
> Rubén just expects Rosita to speak the same language as he does, Spanish. For Rubén, it is just a matter of course that Rosita speaks to him in Spanish. English would not necessarily be 'wrong', but just unexpected. Rubén hasn't really thought much about utterances with words from two languages. He hardly ever uses any and hasn't noticed that Rosita has.
>
> *Julio*
> Like Manuel, Julio doesn't really care which language Julia speaks, but he finds it unacceptable if she uses words from two languages in the same utterance. That he just does not find proper.

Parental discourse strategies

Parents' different ideas about which language they want their children to speak to them or about the use of mixed utterances are related to their attitudes regarding a particular language or the use of mixed utterances. These attitudes find expression in parents' explicit ideas about language choice. These attitudes also feed into the discourse strategies they use with their BFLA children (De Houwer, 1999). Such discourse strategies are also influenced by parents' impact beliefs.

Discourse strategies in BFLA are conversational patterns that express the speaker's wishes and expectations regarding language choice. Discourse strategies have the effect of encouraging or discouraging the use of a particular language. Elizabeth Lanza was the first scholar to draw explicit attention to these discourse strategies in BFLA and their potentially important role in child bilingual development (Lanza, 1992).

Some bilingual parents, like Manuel and Julio in Box 4.29, don't mind if their child speaks only one language at the beginning of speech. They are just happy that their infant can talk, and will respond to the child's utterances without focusing on the actual language the child used. They may answer a child's question in Italian with a response in German if that is the language they usually use with their infant. Regardless of whether they have an impact belief or not, these parents are using what Lanza (1997) has termed 'bilingual discourse strategies'. These allow the use of two languages within a conversation (see further below).

Other bilingual parents, like Rubén in Box 4.29, may just not expect the use of two languages within a conversation or may be much less tolerant of it. They may also see themselves as active agents in their children's language development. This impact belief and their attitudes will be at the basis of their use of 'monolingual discourse strategies' (Lanza, 1997). Through these, parents socialize their children into using mainly one language within a stretch of discourse.

Lanza has made a categorization of discourse strategies in a bilingual setting that shows different strategies on a continuum going from 'monolingual' to 'bilingual'. I explain her categorization in Box 4.30 and have added examples that might have been used by Manuel, Rubén or Julio, the protagonists of Box 4.29.

Box 4.30 Five parental discourse strategies in BFLA	
Note: everything in this Box that is not English is Spanish; the parents here usually address their children in Language A	
Monolingual discourse strategies	*These have the effect of keeping the conversation limited to one language only*
Minimal Grasp Strategy	In response to a child utterance in Language Alpha, the parent uses Language A to ask the child to clarify the Alpha utterance (the parent might, indeed, not have understood; see Box 4.18). This is a direct or indirect request for clarification (direct: e.g. 'Please say that again' or 'what did you say?'; indirect: e.g. 'I don't understand'). The expectation is that the child will respond to the request.
	e.g. when Rosita said 'I wanna go play', Rubén said: '¿Que?' (what?). Rosita then rephrased her wish in Spanish.

> **Box 4.30** Five parental discourse strategies in BFLA continued
>
> **Expressed Guess Strategy**   In response to a child utterance in Language Alpha, the parent uses a question in Language A to translate what they thought the child intended to say. This functions as a direct or indirect request for confirmation and takes the form of a yes-no question (direct: e.g. 'Did you mean to say book?'; indirect: e.g. 'A book?'). The expectation is that the child will respond to the request.
>
> *e.g. when Monika said 'I wanna drink', Manuel asked: '¿Quieres algo de beber?'
> (You want something to drink?). Monika replied with 'si!' (yes).*
>
> **Repetition**   In response to a child utterance in Language Alpha, the parent repeats the child utterance in Language A. There is no request for the child to respond, although some children may in turn repeat the parent's repetition in Language A.
>
> *e.g. when Julia said 'eso es un camel' (a mixed utterance meaning 'this is a camel'),
> Julio repeated the utterance completely in Spanish: 'eso es un camello'.
> Julia in turn then said: 'un camello'.*
>
> **Move On Strategy**   When the child produces a mixed utterance or an utterance in Language Alpha the parent does not use any of the three preceding strategies but just continues talking in Language A.
>
> *e.g. when Julia said 'I wanna go to the zoo!', Julio replied:
> 'si, Juliasita, mañana vamos al zoo!' (yes, Julia sweetie, tomorrow we'll go to the zoo').*
>
> **Language Switch**   When the child produces a mixed utterance or an utterance in Language Alpha the parent switches to Language Alpha or a mixed utterance and does not stick to Language A.
>
> *e.g. when Monika said 'I wanna go to the playground!',
> Manuel replied: 'OK I'll take you there now'.*
>
> *Bilingual discourse strategies*   *Their effect is that the conversation is carried on in two languages, or changes from one language to another*
>
> The five discourse strategies have been ordered from most monolingual to most bilingual
>
> Model adapted from Lanza (1997: 261–269); I rendered Lanza's term 'Code Switch' as 'Language Switch' because the term 'code switch' can have too many different meanings depending on particular theoretical perspectives.
>
> Monika, Manuel, Rosita, Rubén, Julia and Julio were introduced in Box 4.29.

Not all parental or adult responses to children's 'wrong' language choice can be fitted into the five-category model, but close (see also Cantone, 2007: 102–110). In fact, Cantone (2007: 104) suggests changing the name of the strategy 'Repetition' to 'Repeating and translating by guessing'. In her study of five German–Italian BFLA children in interaction with a German- or Italian-speaking researcher–interlocutor, Cantone found that the adults used such strategies quite regularly. An example is shown in Box 4.31.

> **Box 4.31 Repeating and translating by guessing**
>
> *At age 3;7, German–Italian Marta (MAR) is talking to an Italian-speaking investigator.*
>
> | | |
> |---|---|
> | *MAR: | cos – cos – aveva così un Kleid, lo sai (Italian, except for the German word 'Kleid') |
> | gloss: | like – like – she had a dress like that, you know |
> | *INV: | aveva? (Italian) |
> | gloss: | she did? |
> | *MAR: | così qualcosa (Italian) |
> | gloss: | something like that |
> | *INV: | che cos'è quello? (Italian translation) |
> | gloss: | what's that? |
> | *MAR: | un Kleid – Kleid – una gonna (Italian except for the German 'Kleid') |
> | gloss: | a dress – dress – a skirt |
> | *INV: | un **vestito?** un vestito (Italian) |
> | gloss: | a dress? dress |
> | *MAR: | così un vestito (Italian) |
> | gloss: | a dress like that |
>
> The adult here isn't quite sure what Marta means, and offers a translation of 'Kleid' with questioning intonation (see word in bold font). This is a translated repetition of the child's word that offers a suggestion as to what it is the child might mean. It is not a simple repetition in the other language, and takes place after it's already been made clear that the adult did not understand. More than with Lanza's 'Repetition' strategy there is here a negotiation going on about what something is called.
>
> *Adapted from Cantone, 2007: 104*

Another example of an utterance that does not really fit is listed in Box 4.32.

> **Box 4.32 Switching languages all round**
>
> Nicolas (age: 2;1.26) is a young Spanish–English bilingual who is talking to his Spanish-speaking grandmother who also understands English.
>
> | | |
> |---|---|
> | Nicolas: | That's mermaid? [pointing at pictures of women in a clothes catalogue] |
> | Grandmother: | Parecen, pero no son *mermaids*. |
> | | (seem to be – but – not – are – mermaids; |
> | | They look like it but they're not mermaids.) |
> | Nicolas: | Son niñas. Son mamis. |
> | | (are – girls. are – mommies; They're girls. They're mommies.) |
>
> *Source: Silva-Corvalán & Montanari, 2008*
>
> Nicolas asks his Spanish-speaking grandmother a question in English. She answers his question in Spanish but repeats an English word that he asked in his question. Although she replies using a mixed utterance, we can still categorize this utterance as an example of the rather more bilingual 'Move On' discourse strategy (see Box 4.30), where the adult just continues talking to the child in the language the adult usually speaks. This particular 'Move On' strategy here resulted in the child switching to the grandmother's language, and to a more monolingual conversation.

One particular strategy that can be subsumed under the Minimal Grasp Strategy in Lanza's five-category model (Box 4.30) is an explicit request for a translation (Lanza, personal communication, June 2008). Translation requests function as ways to keep a conversation in one language only. Therefore, they constitute a monolingual discourse strategy.

Requests for translations are fairly typical in early conversations with BFLA children, but perhaps not so common in conversations with children who have just started to speak in two-word utterances and who may not know that many words yet. As Lanvers (2001: 453) has noted, such requests for translation are quite challenging to young children. They only make sense if adults know that the child knows the **translation equivalent** (see Box 4.33). I discuss translation equivalents in more depth in Chapter 6.

Box 4.33   Request for translation

Anouk (age: 2;3,13) is a young French–Dutch-speaking bilingual who is talking to her French-speaking mother who also understands Dutch.

Mother:	ça c'est un fruit	(French for: that's a piece of fruit)
Anouk:	aabei	(Dutch for: strawberry)
Mother:	aabei, comment tu dis en français?	

Mother repeats child's Dutch word for 'strawberry' and then asks in French: how do you say that in French?

Anouk:	(child gives no answer)	
Mother:	non, comment tu dis en français aardbeien? comment je dis moi?	

In French: no, how do you say in French 'aardbeien' (= Dutch word for strawberries)? how do I say it?

Anouk:	faise	(French for: strawberry – without the 'r' after the f)
Mother:	fraise oui	(in French: strawberry, yes)

Source: van der Linden & Hulk, 1999: 45

Anouk's mother is teaching Anouk about the category 'fruit' (supposedly she is referring to a strawberry). Anouk does not quite accept the overarching term 'fruit' for what she knows to be a strawberry and 'corrects' her mother – but in the 'wrong' language. Anouk's mother asks Anouk for a translation into French. She repeats her request for a translation when Anouk doesn't answer. This may seem a bit demanding of a child who is not even two and a half years old, but Anouk does know the French word and finally provides it, and her mother acknowledges that she's got it right (about BFLA children's early translating abilities, see Chapter 6).

Using monolingual or bilingual discourse strategies

Discourse strategies as understood in this book can be used both by bilingual and by monolingual adults interacting with a child. However, monolinguals will only be able to use an explicit request for translation, as in Box 4.33, or a Minimal Grasp Strategy (the most 'monolingual' of strategies). Bilinguals who understand two languages but speak only one will be able to use an explicit request for translation and all the strategies in Lanza's five-category model (Box 4.30) except the most 'bilingual' one, viz., the Language Switch. Only bilinguals who are able to speak two languages will also be able to use the Language Switch in addition to the others.

Monolingual adults, then, can only use the more 'monolingual' strategies. Bilingual adults can use both the more 'monolingual' and the more 'bilingual' strategies. They have a choice. Through using mainly the more monolingual strategies, however, bilingual adults can present themselves to the child as more of a monolingual than a bilingual.

The strategies that bilingual adults use most likely have a profound effect on children's language choice.

The effect of bilingual discourse strategies on children

If parents do not insist that their children speak both languages they probably won't (see also, e.g. Bayley *et al.*, 1996). If parents use mainly the more bilingual discourse strategies ('Move On' and 'Language Switch') and thus allow children's use of 'the other' Language Alpha, children ultimately have no need for speaking Language A.

It is a broad observation that parents talk to their children in Language A but that children respond in Language Alpha. Following Saville-Troike (1987), I will call such conversations **dilingual conversations**. Typically, the children who participate in such dilingual conversations speak only the majority language. This has often been observed for Spanish and English in the United States (e.g. García & Carrasco, 1981; Schecter & Bayley, 1997).

The occurrence of just dilingual conversations is an extreme example of the use of bilingual discourse strategies by the interacting adult and may be the result of using more bilingual than monolingual discourse strategies when children were younger. BFLA children raised with bilingual discourse strategies, then, may soon become part of that large group of children raised bilingually who understand two languages but speak only one. Such children must have a bilingual language orientation (see the section 'Language orientation' earlier) when they interact with the bilingual parent.

An example of a BFLA child who speaks only the majority language is Alexei. He is growing up in an English-speaking environment but has always been addressed in Russian by his bilingual mother. His mother has never insisted on Alexei speaking Russian to her. She always uses the 'Move On' strategy. This most likely is the major reason why Alexei does not produce any Russian unilingual utterances. His repertoire consists only of unilingual utterances in English and mixed Russian–English utterances (O'Neill, 1998).

An example of a BFLA child who is probably on his way towards becoming a speaker of just one language is presented in Box 4.34.

Box 4.34 On his way towards speaking only one language?

Ken (age period: 1;11 to 2;2) is a young Japanese–English-speaking bilingual living in the United States. He receives Japanese input from his bilingual mother (and, for some time, from the researcher), and English from everyone else, including his father. His mother speaks only Japanese to him. Hence, Ken is growing up in a 1P/1L setting. His parents speak English to each other.

In his input setting, English is used more frequently than Japanese. Overheard speech is always in English except when the researcher visits the home.

Ken uses unilingual utterances in Japanese and English, as well as mixed utterances. He speaks mostly Japanese to his mother, and mostly English to his father. As such, he is adapting to each parent's input language. However, he speaks far less Japanese to his mother than English to his father.

> **Box 4.34** On his way towards speaking only one language? continued
>
> Ken's monolingual father mostly uses monolingual discourse strategies. Ken's bilingual mother, however, often uses bilingual discourse strategies. She mostly 'moves on' with Japanese when Ken addresses her in English.
>
> Source: Mishina, 1999
>
> | Average proportions... | To his mother | To his father |
> | --- | --- | --- |
> | ...of Japanese utterances | 66% | 6% |
> | ...of English utterances | 32% | 94% |
> | Totals | 490 | 402 |
>
> Adapted from tables 6 and 7 in Mishina, 1999 (I did not include mixed utterances)
>
> Why might Ken be on his way towards speaking only one language, English?
>
> In this setting, where Japanese is the less frequently used language, where it is not the school language, and the language used by just one or two people, Japanese is at a disadvantage. If this disadvantage is not countered by the creation of a communicative need to actually speak two languages through the use of strictly monolingual discourse strategies then English may soon be the only language that Ken speaks.

How monolingual discourse strategies can support bilingual development

If children are socialized by primarily monolingual discourse strategies (either by monolingual or bilingual adults), they will usually be compelled to use whatever language the interacting adult expects from them. In a study of four Japanese–English-speaking BFLA children, Kasuya (1998) demonstrated that monolingual strategies as used by the bilingual Japanese-speaking parents in these families usually had the desired effect of having the children switch from English to Japanese. Another example of the effect of using monolingual discourse strategies is offered in an exemplary study by Juan-Garau and Pérez-Vidal (2001). In this study, the authors show how a situation very much like the one described in Box 4.34, but now with English as the 'disadvantaged' language, is turned around.

This turn around is largely in response to a change in discourse strategies. Andreu's Catalan–English bilingual father always spoke English to his son, but until Andreu was three years of age his father did not insist on him speaking English in return and Andreu often spoke Catalan to his father (cf. the dilingual conversations mentioned above). When Andreu was three years old, his father decided to change his strategy and introduced two puppets from England, who could not understand Catalan, as aides in creating an English monolingual setting. The strategy worked and very soon it was just normal for Andreu to address his father in English and everyone else in Catalan.

These examples show that parents and children are not separate entities that each do what they like when they are talking together. Parents and children mutually influence each other. As noted in Chapter 2, the features of infant-directed speech change as children grow older. Similarly, the way parents negotiate a bilingual or a monolingual context with children may change in function of children's increased linguistic skills (Goodz, 1994). However, there is yet a lot to discover about how this happens in bilingual settings.

Children who have been used to monolingual discourse strategies from the beginning may have made such a strong link in their minds between a particular person and a particular language that they might respond quite negatively when that person uses another language.

A case in point is my daughter Susan who was raised with English and Dutch from birth. I always addressed her in Dutch and she spoke Dutch to me as well. As I explained in Box 4.18 earlier, I had a strictly monolingual language orientation when I was alone with Susan. The discourse strategy that I used in the example in Box 4.18 when I did not understand her was a monolingual one (without me being aware of it!). In response to this monolingual strategy, when she was 19 months old, Susan switched from English to Dutch. I cannot recall that she ever spoke English to me when she was a young child.

When she was three and a half, I had just finished a telephone conversation in English. Susan was in the room playing with her dolls. After the telephone conversation, I by accident asked her something in English and Susan started to cry and say in Dutch: 'Nee mama, nee! Niet Engels mama!' (no mommy, no! no English, mommy!). I quickly switched to Dutch but was taken aback by her strong reaction. I did not realize just how strong the link was that she had made between myself and the use of Dutch in addressing her.

The fact that a bilingual parent uses monolingual discourse strategies does not have to imply that that parent addresses their children in one language exclusively. Monolingual discourse strategies can be used in different languages in different circumstances. In conversations with the same parent, children can thus learn to use Language A at home, for instance, and Language Alpha outside the home.

A particularly important time: going off to school

Parental discourse strategies are just one of the many factors in BFLA children's socializing environments that can make a difference in how children develop bilingually (see also Kasuya, 1998). Juan-Garau and Pérez-Vidal (2001) stress that also in their study other factors besides discourse strategies played a role in Andreu's changed patterns of language choice. They mention a two-week stay in England as another contributing factor. However, the crucial role of discourse strategies cannot be denied. This role is particularly highlighted when BFLA children who speak two languages start going to school.

Bilingual parents have often complained to me that their children started to speak only one language once they had been at school for some time, even though children had been speaking two languages fluently before.

Going to school for the first time is a big event in children's lives. They are excited when they come back home from school and want to talk about what happened there. They are often still so full of their school experiences that they will tend to use the school language (Language A) even to people with whom they never spoke it.

Bilingual parents who never needed to use monolingual strategies before because their children always spoke the expected Language Alpha will perhaps not know what to do when children suddenly address them in Language A. Of course, it is important to let children tell their story and to be interested in what they have to say, regardless of the language spoken.

But if parents want to ensure that their children continue speaking two languages it is important to help children use Language Alpha from the first day that children come back home from school. This may involve asking children explicitly to repeat some of what they said in Language Alpha or to indicate to them that parents would like to hear about school in Language Alpha. Or it may involve giving children the words needed to talk in Language Alpha about things learned and experienced at school in Language A.

Especially the latter will be a concern for years to come. Whatever strategy is used, it is important to be sensitive to children's needs to talk about school, and children should feel supported in their efforts rather than 'punished' in any way for speaking the 'wrong' language.

BFLA children's language choice in interactions with familiar people

We do not know enough about the specific effect of discourse strategies on young BFLA children's language choice. We do know, however, about young BFLA children's language choice in and of itself.

Young children under the age of three tend to mostly interact with people they are quite familiar with. When they interact with these familiar adults, young bilingual children are able to show different language choice behaviors depending on whom they are talking to.

Even when they are not yet two years old, BFLA children can adjust their language choice to the parent they are talking to (Genesee *et al.*, 1995; Köppe, 1996; Nicoladis, 1998; Sinka & Schelletter, 1998; Wanner, 1996). Also a young trilingual child has been shown to adjust her language choice to her interlocutor before the age of two (Montanari, 2005). I discuss very young children's language choices in greater detail in Chapter 6.

In their third year of life, many bilingual children tend to use Language A more often than Language Alpha with the parent or person who mostly addresses them in Language A. At the same time, they will tend to mostly speak Language Alpha rather than Language A with the parent or person who usually addresses them in Language Alpha (e.g. Cantone, 2007; De Houwer, 1990; Genesee *et al.*, 1996; Mishina, 1999). As for instance Kwan-Terry (1992) has shown, the same children may show different behavior with people who usually address them in one language only (by sticking to one language with these people) and with people who are more flexible in their own language choice and address the child in two languages (by speaking two languages with these people as well).

Older BFLA children who speak two languages will normally also adjust their language choice to their interlocutor's expectations. Certainly, they will address monolinguals in the one language that these speak and understand.

BFLA children's language choice in interactions with people they have not met before

Children's language choices are most likely based on knowledge that they have of their parents and on habits and patterns of socialization, such as the discourse strategies discussed above to which they are accustomed.

What happens with people that children do not know?

Children are able to distinguish between familiar and unfamiliar adults from very early on and behave differently with both. They realize that people they meet for the first time are 'new'. Typically, toddlers in different cultures are quite inhibited when they meet up with unfamiliar adults (Rubin *et al.*, 2006). Therefore, on the whole, children under the age of three may be reluctant to talk to strangers. A certain inhibition that expresses itself in shyness and lack of speech is developmentally quite normal, and there is no reason to believe that BFLA children are generally less inhibited than monolingual toddlers.

Also for bilingual toddlers, then, one would expect different behavior with unfamiliar adults. It is all the more remarkable, then, that some young BFLA children who are not even two years old not only talk to unfamiliar adults but also adjust their language choice to the language spoken by these unfamiliar adults. Two studies have shown this to be the case.

The first of these was an experimental study that focused specifically on language adjustments to unfamiliar adults (Genesee *et al.*, 1996). Genesee *et al.* showed that BFLA children just over the age of two can adjust their language choice to the limited language abilities of unfamiliar adults if they are monolingual in one of the languages known to the children. Box 4.35 gives contrasting examples from two bilingual toddlers in this study who were both quite talkative with an unfamiliar monolingual stranger.

The second study did not focus on language choice with unfamilar adults but looked at the use of early mixed utterances by five German–Italian BFLA children (Cantone, 2007). At the first recording, the children were the following ages: 1;7,10, 1;8,14, 1;10,8, 1;10,23 and 2;1,3. These first recordings were made in two settings: first, with an unfamiliar stranger who spoke Italian while another unfamiliar German-speaking stranger handled the video-camera, and then with the same two adults, but now in reverse roles (Cantone, 2007: 93; it is also possible that the German-speaking adult was the first to interact with the child). Cantone's figures for language choice by each of these five children show how in the very first recording all children spoke mainly Italian to the Italian-speaking stranger and mainly German to the German-speaking stranger (Cantone, 2007: 117–122).[18]

Socializing environments and BFLA

> **Box 4.35** Two actively bilingual toddlers talking to an unfamiliar monolingual adult
>
> Jessica and Leila were both raised with English and French from birth in Montreal, Canada. When they were about 2;2, they were recorded in separate interactions with their mothers, fathers and an unfamiliar female adult ('the stranger'), each lasting 20 minutes.
>
> Jessica and Leila both speak English and French.
>
> Jessica's mother speaks mostly French to her, and her dad English. The unfamiliar adult talking to Jessica spoke only English. Leila's mother speaks mostly English to her, and her dad French. The unfamiliar adult talking to Leila spoke only French.
>
> Here is the breakdown of the number of unilingual utterances the girls addressed to each interlocutor during the three recording sessions:
>
> | | *To her mother* | *To her father* | *To the stranger* |
> | --- | --- | --- | --- |
> | Jessica: French | 68 | 25 | 13 |
> | Jessica: English | 56 | 101 | 100 |
> | Leila: French | 7 | 23 | 9 |
> | Leila: English | 109 | 55 | 68 |
>
> *Adapted from Genesee et al., 1996*
>
> In the table I have highlighted the unexpected language choices, so the choices you would not expect based on the language use of the addressee.
>
> Jessica's highlighted, unexpected choices are always less frequent than the non-highlighted, expected ones. And Jessica clearly accommodates to the stranger's lack of French by speaking much more English to her.
>
> Leila, on the other hand, only really follows her mother's language choice quite consistently. She does accommodate a little to her father, but does not seem to take much notice of the fact that the stranger speaks no English: she talks to her in English most of the time. Of course, we may assume that in each case the strangers also understood the other language – otherwise it is hard to see how any sort of interaction could have been sustained for as many as 68 utterances.
>
> *Source: Genesee et al., 1996*

What happens when children interact with familiar bilinguals (their parents) in the presence of an unfamiliar monolingual, even though this person is not taking part in the interaction? In talking to their children, bilingual adults will try to adjust their language choice to accommodate the monolingual. BFLA preschoolers, though, basically ignore the fact that the unfamiliar monolingual may not understand one of the languages they are speaking to their parents (Tare & Gelman, 2008). Whether such behavior is specifically bilingual or part of a more general developmentally determined characteristic of young children is not clear.

Prerequisites for language choice

Of course, in order for bilingual children to be able to adjust their language choice they must be able to express themselves in two languages (see also the section on translation equivalents in Chapter 6). Only then do they have the basis for adapting their language choice to a particular communicative setting in ways that are appropriate.

If bilingual children can express themselves only in one language and that language does not overlap with their unfamiliar interlocutor's language, they have the choice between speaking the 'wrong' language or not speaking at all. The youngest child in the Cantone (2007) study, Marta, was much more vocal with the Italian-speaking unfamiliar adult than with the German-speaking one (see p. 122). Marta did not, in fact, speak much at all to the German-speaking interlocutor at age 1;7,10. Significantly, however, Marta spoke no Italian to her either (except in one or two mixed utterances), although Marta could speak Italian fairly well. Rather than see silence as a sign of inhibition, then, you can also see it as a sign of sociolinguistic sensitivity. Some children prefer not to speak rather than to speak the 'wrong' language.

Silence may also be a sign of the general inhibition often shown in monolingual toddlers, and even actively bilingual children may be too shy to speak when they meet up with an unfamiliar adult. Speaking the 'wrong' language with a monolingual unfamiliar adult in toddlerhood is not all that unexpected, either. After all, toddlers are still very young and need to learn to communicate.

The fact that at least some bilingual toddlers can and do adjust their language choice to accommodate unfamiliar monolinguals, however, confirms that it is possible for very young children to develop a high sensitivity to their interlocutor's communicative needs.

These communicative needs can be signalled by the interlocutor's own language choice. In an experimental study, Comeau, Genesee and Lapaquette (2003) controlled the proportion of mixed utterances as used by research assistants in conversations with six English–French-speaking two-year-olds. Most of the children adjusted their proportion of mixed utterances to those of the assistants. The authors link this overall effect to the fact that more often than not, a mixed utterance by an assistant got a mixed utterance response from the child. This shows a very fine-grained tuning of children's own language choice to that of their interlocutor's.

Such fine tuning may crucially depend on children's linguistic skills. At age three, the child Joseph spoke Russian well, and English less so, but he always addressed his English-speaking monolingual mother in English and Russian speakers in Russian. After a drastic change in his language environment with a great increase in English input and a decrease in Russian input, Joseph started to lose his ability in Russian and increase his ability in English. He first started to speak English to monolingual Russian speakers, although he had never done so earlier. Later on, he no longer responded to Russian utterances (Turian & Altenberg, 1991). The use of English to Russian monolinguals was of course not very sensitive, whereas the use of silence was perhaps more so.

Factors influencing language choice

BFLA children who actually speak two languages may not only adjust their language choice to their interlocutor, but also to different circumstances. For instance, a Polish–Hebrew-speaking boy in Israel spoke Polish to his parents in the home but when he was walking towards nursery school with them would switch over to Hebrew, the language used at school (Herman, 1961).

More recently, Quay (1998) described how Spanish–English-speaking Manuela would speak Spanish with her mother at home and in the car, but would switch over to English once the car entered the gate in the fence surrounding Manuela's English-speaking crèche building. Deuchar and Quay (1999) show how the same child at the tender age of 19 months could already adjust her language choice according to the setting.

Earlier in Box 4.19 I described how Dutch–English-speaking Kate switched languages as she switched settings. Thus, bilingual children can and usually do adjust their language choice with bilingual interlocutors depending on what they perceive to be different settings for interaction.

However, there are many differences between BFLA children in the degree to which they speak the language that is expected from them. There have been many studies that have tried to determine causes for these differences between children and for within-child differences across time. Explanations have ranged from how language choice is being modeled to the child (do parents always use the 'right' language themselves?, see, e.g. Mishina, 1999), how parents respond when children use the 'wrong' language (discourse strategies; see, e.g. Lanza, 1992), whether children know the words in the expected language (e.g. Lanvers, 2001), whether children are proficient enough in both languages (e.g. Jisa, 2000) and whether children know that their interlocutor is proficient enough in both languages (e.g. De Houwer, 1990; Quay, 2008), to young children's developing self-awareness (e.g. Deuchar & Muntz, 2003). No study has come up with the final answer, and given the complexity of the matter, it is unlikely that any ever could.

Most likely a combination of factors determines whether BFLA children will speak the 'right' language – not in the least, their own motivation for doing so. It is clear, however, that knowing when to use what language is something that needs to be learned, and that can be learned very fast from very early on.

Explaining the composition of young BFLA children's linguistic repertoires

Language learning in monolingual children is commonly seen as the result of the interaction of many different factors, both child-internal and child-external (Chapman, 2000; Collins et al., 2000). No doubt it is also that way for BFLA. The BFLA setting, however, draws one's attention quite strongly to child-external factors, viz., the child's bilingual environment.

All the different aspects of the actual language input that children receive in a bilingual setting may converge to quite large differences between the two input languages. Differences may consistently be disadvantageous for one of the languages. Language Alpha may be overheard more often than Language A, it may be spoken less than Language A, it may be spoken by a depressed parent, and the people speaking Language Alpha may use bilingual discourse strategies much more often than the people speaking Language A. All these factors combined may result in Language Alpha offering less than optimal learning conditions and may explain why a particular BFLA child does not speak Language Alpha, or speaks it much less well than Language A.

The bilingual environment not only has an important influence on whether children will produce unilingual utterances in two languages. It most likely also affects the extent to which children use mixed utterances: children mainly use mixed utterances if they are speaking with other bilinguals who they know will understand them.

The effect of the input setting on BFLA children's repertoires is particularly noticeable when there is a major change in children's linguistic soundscapes. Often, children's linguistic repertoires will change quite soon after the change in the input setting. Changes in discourse strategies can also have quite an immediate effect. They may expand a child's linguistic repertoire from producing unilingual utterances in one language only to producing unilingual utterances in two languages, or indeed the other way round.

BFLA children's linguistic repertoires, then, depend to a large extent on their socializing environments. However, children also bring their own developing minds to the language learning experience. I turn to the outcomes of the interplay between those minds and children's socializing environments in the next three chapters, in which I look at BFLA children's learning of speech sounds, words and sentences.

Notes

1. Such is the case, for instance, for some homosexual couples or adoption parents.

2. The only study involving young bilingual children that I know of that pays attention to single-parent families is my own survey study as discussed in Chapter 1 (De Houwer, 2007).

3. The exception to this arises in the case of a single parent being the only person to interact with the child. For BFLA to apply, the single parent will have to address the child in unilingual utterances in each of two languages.

4. In an experimental study involving monolingual nine- to ten-month-olds who were frequently exposed to a foreign language through video and audio recordings, Kuhl *et al.* (2003) found absolutely no effect of foreign language learning while in contrast, other infants exposed to the same foreign language through human interaction were (see also

Chapter 2). This is in line with the findings from Patterson (2002) that television watching had no effect on language learning in two-year-old bilinguals.

5. Most of the children in this study were BFLA, but some were ESLA (Janet Patterson, personal communication).

6. In Zentella's (1997) study, however, there were two separate languages being used.

7. See Cruz-Ferreira (2006: 281–282) for some transcribed examples of exaggerated intonation contours that she used in addressing her elder daughter in a bilingual setting.

8. For a rare study that closely compares parental report of their language use with their child with observational data based on transcripts, see Quay (2008). Quay confirmed Goodz's (1989) finding of some discrepancies between parental report and actual practice.

9. In a study of 125 monolingual English-speaking children in Britain, however, Wells (1985) had earlier found various effects of the total amount of input on children's language development. However, since the Wells study was not really set up to study input the nature of that input could not be as meticulously described as in the Hart and Risley (1995) study.

10. Putnick et al. (2007) studied these 54 mothers in similar circumstances: the children were at the same ages when they were observed, so mothers took part in a longitudinal study; and mothers interacted with each child by themselves, without 'competition' from the other sibling.

11. Evidence is emerging, however, that adults who spoke a language fluently up until age seven had benefits when they re-learned that language in young adulthood (Au et al., 2008).

12. For a study documenting first language loss in somewhat older second language learning children, see Anderson (2001).

13. As exemplified in Berman's (1979) study and also in a study of attrition and eventual loss in an English–Russian BFLA boy (Turian & Altenberg, 1991).

14. It is very difficult to know what level of knowledge children had before they moved to the new country, however (Schaerlaekens et al., 1988).

15. Even in mixed utterances words or morphemes from two languages follow each other.

16. I use the term 'rule' here as overlapping a lot with the term 'norm', but I prefer to avoid the more group-oriented meaning of the word 'norm'; often, in BFLA families, only a few individuals are involved that have particular expectations regarding language use.

17. As Cantone (2007: 106) notes: 'Among bilinguals, there may be an implicit agreement of only using one of the two languages'.

18. Note that Cantone does not characterize these adults as 'strangers'.

Summary box

- Attitudes are very closely connected to ideas about parenting and the role that parents themselves can play in the bilingual acquisition process. In particular, an impact belief is important for the development of child bilingualism.
- The particular ways in which BFLA children come into contact with each of their languages may well have an effect on particular aspects of their language development. The linguistic soundscapes that BFLA children encounter can be quite diverse.
- The combined evidence suggests that the number of languages that each parent addresses children in does not really explain whether children will speak two languages or not. Rather, it is the particular parental input pattern that matters. Families where both parents speak a minority language to their children and one parent in addition speaks the majority language to them have the best chances of having children who speak two languages.
- There appears to be a central role for discourse strategies that create more of a monolingual or more of a bilingual context. Bilingual discourse strategies do not create a need for the child to actually speak the language that the interlocutor is using.
- Input frequency matters a lot as well. Children cannot learn a language without hearing that language a whole lot. In absolute terms, input frequency relates to how often each language is heard; in relative terms, it relates to which language is consistently heard more often. The amount of input in each of a BFLA child's two languages is quite variable, and thus also the proportions with which children hear each language. There will also be differences in the number and proportion of mixed utterances used.
- The role of input frequency is particularly noticeable when children experience large changes in their linguistic soundscapes. Changes in that BFLA environment can have dramatic results such as language loss, or a sudden increase in language skill.

Suggestions for study activities

1. *WEB*: Locate three websites in the language you know best (or, if you cannot find any, in another language you know) that discuss child bilingual development. Browse through those websites and rate them on three points: (1) whether or not they have a positive attitude towards child bilingualism; (2) whether they show an impact belief regarding things that parents can do to help their children become bilingual and (3) whether in general you find the information on the website accurate and realistic judging from your understanding of the first three chapters in this book. Explain why for each point.
2. *Project*: Ask around in your circle of friends and family about whether they know anyone who is raising a child with two languages from birth. Try to get in touch with them and have a conversation with them about what made them decide to raise their child with two languages. Or perhaps it was not a conscious decision? Do they feel good about their child learning two languages?
3. *Project*: Find people in your environment who because of their profession deal with young children (or, find people who are studying in preparation of such professions). Possibilities are: pediatric nurses, pediatricians, family health practicioners, preschool teachers, childcare workers, and the like. Have a conversation with two such individuals built around the following questions: would they advise people to raise their child with two languages? Why (not)?
4. *Project* Find people in your environment who because of their profession deal with young children (or: find people who are studying in preparation of such professions). Possibilities are: pediatric nurses, pediatricians, family health practitioners, preschool teachers, childcare workers and the

> **Suggestions for study activities continued**
>
> like. Have a conversation with two such individuals built around the following questions. What sorts of courses have they taken (if any) that have had as a topic bilingual child language development? How trained or educated do they feel they are to give advice on issues pertaining to bilingual development?
> 5. Read four recent issues of the *Bilingual Family Newsletter* or a similar magazine about bilingual or multilingual children and identify two main concerns that parents have about raising bilingual children.
> 6. *Project*: If anybody you interact with speaks another language than English, map out your own linguistic soundscape.
> 7. Select two transcripts from the Spanish–English Deuchar corpus in CHILDES (see Box 3.6 in Chapter 3 for information about where to find it) and analyze them in terms of the discourse strategies used. You can do this even if you only know English. (advanced)

Recommended reading

I describe the importance of the relation between attitudes, beliefs and linguistic practice in BFLA in De Houwer (1999). Heath's (1989) chapter offers a good overview with many concrete examples of studies showing the importance of culturally determined socialization patterns and expectations for children's language learning. Hart and Risley (2003) present a compelling summary of their pioneering work on the importance of how much parents talk to children and the damaging effects of insufficient input. A more encompassing recent overview of the role of the input in children's language development can be found in Gathercole and Hoff (2007). Lanza (2007) gives an excellent recent overview of socialization practices in bilingual families. Juan-Garau and Pérez-Vidal (2001) offer an in-depth example of the importance of parental discourse strategies in early bilingual development together with excellent discussions. In a novel but thought provoking approach towards explaining the use of mixed utterances and language choice, Serratrice (2005) tries to link the use of mixed utterances with children's overall learning strategies. Ervin-Tripp and Reyes (2005) offer an excellent discussion of the many factors underlying young and older children's language choice.

5
Sounds in BFLA

Breaking the code   **153**
    The importance of intonation   153
    Infant detectives   153
    Looking for cues   154
    Early speech perception   155

The sounding world of BFLA children   **156**
    Sound learning starts before babies are born   156
    Highly increased sound learning after birth   157
    Funny accents   158

Early bilingual speech perception   **160**
    Distinguishing between two input languages in BFLA   160
    Behavioral studies of early speech perception in BFLA   160
    Studying speech perception through brain response   162
    Back to behavioral studies   162
    Visual cues can help in learning to distinguish between two languages   163

Speech perception and word learning   **164**

Making the melody of speech   **166**

Bilingual babbling   **167**
    Early vocalizations   168
    Canonical babbling   168
    Is bilingual babbling language specific?   169
    Do babies continue to babble?   170

 In conclusion   171

More on melody   171

Syllable structure and stress as used by BFLA children   172

 Contradictory results   172

 Why are there contradictory results?   173

 BFLA children are not two MFLA children in one   174

 The importance of the language models that BFLA children hear   174

Bilingual speech segments   175

 Phones and phonemes   175

 Instability and variability in the production of early speech segments   176

 Do BFLA children's speech segments develop in language-specific ways from early on?   177

 What can we learn from studies of BFLA children's use of speech segments?   179

Phonological processes   180

 Are phonological processes language specific?   182

 Do children continue to use phonological processes?   182

Perfecting their skills   183

In conclusion   185

Summary box   187

Suggestions for study activities   188

Recommended reading   190

Breaking the code

In Chapter 2 I explained how different languages use different sets of partially overlapping sounds. Children must learn which sounds are used in the language or languages that they are learning.

Learning about sounds is not a task in and of itself. Learning how sounds are used to carry meaning is what it's really about.

The importance of intonation

At a general level, it is the 'melody' or global intonation contour of an utterance that can carry meaning. This includes both the pragmatic meaning and the more structural meaning. By pragmatic meaning I here refer to the functional meaning in terms of whether an utterance is a question, is a statement, expresses suprise and so forth: what does the utterance *do*? The pragmatic meaning also includes information about the speaker's emotional stance: for instance, a statement may be said in an angry tone or in an emotionally neutral tone. Try saying 'there's no more juice in the fridge' as just a simple statement or as an angry accusation and then just hum each of them, without the words, and you'll see what I mean. Languages differ in the link between intonations contours and the meanings they express. What sounds like an 'angry' tone in one language may just be a normal tone in another one.[1]

The intonation contour of an utterance also indicates where the utterance starts and stops, and what the important elements in it are. This is what I call the structural meaning of intonation contours. For instance, in American English, an utterance that is a statement (also called a declarative) will first have rising intonation at some point and then the pitch will go down. To see what I mean, try saying 'that was a really nice party last night', first with the words and then just by humming it. Speakers of American English know that the utterance is not finished as long as the pitch has not gone down. Also, a speaker of American English will give a different meaning to the utterance: 'did you see that?' depending on which of the words is stressed the most: 'did', 'you', 'see' or 'that' (try out the four possibilities).

Again, languages differ in how specific intonation patterns are linked to these more structural meanings.

Infant detectives

Babies know nothing about any of this when they are born, except that they can already perceive global differences between utterances in a language they heard before they were born, and other languages (see the next section). They must learn the particular sound-meaning correspondences that matter in their specific input language. Infants have to be like detectives, really, and must find out what speech sounds mean what.

BFLA infants have the added problem that they must detect and learn which set of sounds goes with one particular set of meanings, and which other set of sounds goes with another particular set of meanings.

It is quite a challenge, and a miracle, really, that both MFLA and BFLA babies do manage to make sense of the sounding world they find themselves in. Just imagine yourself in a foreign country where you do not know the language – and there is no one to translate for you and nobody speaks the languages you know. Yet you need to survive, get food, get shelter, stay in a safe place, be warm. As an adult, you already know about communication, and the power of smiles and looks and pointing. Newborn babies do not have that knowledge. Yet they need to make an entrance into their sounding world. They need to figure out what kinds of speech sounds carry important meanings.

How is it possible that infants can 'break the code'? Scientists have no conclusive answer to this complex issue as yet. The answers must lie in the dynamic relation between babies' own developing minds and bodies and the quality of their human environment (see Chapter 2). In addition, there is the specific nature of language, which is a system that is so well constructed that it can be learned. It contains cues that aid in learning.

Looking for cues

Each language or language variety has its own specific cues. But of course, like all good detectives, infants must be able to pick up on these cues.

You can only recognize something as a cue if you remember seeing something similar before. Things get even better when you can start to see patterns in what you see. Repetition is a key element here. And indeed, many of the important cues that infants need in order to break the code of their sounding world are repeated time and again.

For instance, caregivers will typically use a falling intonation and fairly low pitch to soothe infants who are upset or fussy. Such utterances are typically repeated several times within one 'soothing' episode (such repetition is typical of IDS – see Chapter 2). Infants need to be able to learn to discriminate such utterances from other types and to interpret their meanings.

Most likely, the frequency with which infants hear these patterns over and over again plays a crucial role in their ability to figure out how the multitude of sounds around them can be put into patterns that are meaningful, and so help them to understand what others are trying to say.[2] By the time they are six months old, infants are able to distinguish between different intonation contours in their input language.

Intonation contours and the meanings they are associated with are language specific. This means that they can signal a particular language. They are very important cues, and speech directed at infants takes this into account by exaggerating pitch variations. As I noted in Chapter 4, van de Weijer (1997) found such exaggerated pitch variations in the bilingual input to a Dutch–German BFLA child. Languages also differ in other sound cues, such as their phoneme inventories (see Chapter 2 for an explanation of what phonemes are), the intonation patterns associated with words (this is part of prosody) and the rules for combining phonemes (this is what is referred to as **phonotactics**).

Early speech perception

'Breaking the code' is part of what is called speech recognition, or early speech perception (you will also find the term 'processing'). The large differences between languages in the kinds of cues that are important for speech perception is one reason that the processes underlying speech recognition may vary from one language to another (Mehler *et al.*, 1996: 101). I give an example of this in Box 5.1.

> **Box 5.1** Why it is important that BFLA children learn to distinguish between the sounds of their two languages from early on
>
> Children have to develop strategies that help them to identify where a word begins and where it ends. It is the sounds of a language that can help children in that identification task. These sounds include the way words sound in a particular language.
>
> In some languages, one particular word can have different intonational patterns that each means something different. For instance, Thai has five lexical tones, meaning that the same word (e.g., 'mai') has meanings as different as those between 'wood' and 'not', depending on whether the word is said with a rising tone, a falling tone, in a steady high tone, in a steady mid tone or a steady low tone.
>
> English has no lexical tones, but different English words are marked by other cues such as stress patterns and the order in which phonemes can be put. Often, English stresses the first syllable of words that consist of more than one. You can see how this works if, for instance, you say the sentence 'did you put the vegetables in the fridge?'. You will notice that the final two syllables of 'vegetables' get very little stress indeed, and that 'in' gets more stress than these two syllables – stress helps in defining the boundaries of words.
>
> To see how the order of phonemes is important, take the word 'stick', for instance. 'Stick' is a fine word in English but 'tsick' is not - knowing that 'ts' cannot be at the beginning of a word in English helps you to know that 'gutsy' must be one word rather than two separate words 'gu' and 'tsy'. Word stress will also help you to figure this out.
>
> Infants learning Thai will have to pay attention to variations in pitch at the word level. That will help in learning Thai. But it won't help much if a BFLA child learning Thai and English tries to look for lexical tones in English. Whether 'cow' is said with a rising intonation, a falling intonation or a steady tone, it remains a cow.

> **Box 5.1** Why it is important that BFLA children learn to distinguish between the sounds of their two languages from early on continued
>
> Suppose that a Thai–English BFLA infant thinks that the word 'cow' if said with falling intonation means 'horse', and if said with steady intonation means 'cow'. And suppose that the infant is trying to find different meanings for all kinds of other English words pronounced with slightly different intonation patterns. This kind of strategy will get in the way of learning English. The cue that works for Thai doesn't work for English.
>
> On the other hand, a Thai–English BFLA child could, in theory, be approaching Thai on the basis of the sound rules for English words. The child could assume that the pitch and pitch variations for a word don't matter in Thai. A child with this assumption and learning strategy will not be able to understand many words in Thai, since word pitch contours are important in order to distinguish between various meanings.
>
> Clearly, BFLA Thai–English children need to discover the specific word-sounding cues for Thai and the ones for English, otherwise they won't to learn to identify Thai and English words, and to make sense of what people are saying.
>
> *(On how monolingual English- and French-speaking infants perceive Thai lexical tones, see Mattock et al., 2008a)*

In processing their language input, children are most likely guided by different characteristics of that input, depending on which language(s) they are hearing. In order to understand early speech perception in infants, then, researchers need to have a good knowledge of the specific sound-meaning patterns that are used in speech addressed to infants.

For BFLA children, it is important to specify the similarities and differences between the important sounds of the languages that are spoken to them. BFLA infants who hear two languages that are very different will need to develop different strategies for processing and perceiving them, while BFLA infants learning languages that are phonologically very similar may not need to (see also Bosch & Sebastián-Gallés, 1997: 36). This is all part of children's 'sounding worlds', the speech sounds that they hear.

The sounding world of BFLA children

Sound learning starts before babies are born

Children's opportunities for learning about language start a few months before they are born. Unborn children are capable of hearing sounds in the womb and of responding to them. In addition, unborn babies are already developing enough memory skills so they can learn from what they hear and retain it.

What is more, learning experiences in the womb can affect how newborn babies respond to the sound of talking voices. In particular, newborn infants in a monolingual setting prefer their mother's voice and language (for an overview, see Moon & Fifer, 2000). This means that babies can identify their mothers at birth, just on the basis of how they speak. You can imagine that this is important from an evolutionary point of view. This way, babies can orient to their mother when they hear her voice, and when they hear their mother's voice they can feel safe.

Unborn babies can learn about the melodic aspects of language, the intonation contours. Studies of monolingually raised children have shown that newborns are particularly responsive to the melodic or prosodic aspects of speech, namely variations in pitch, rhythm and stress. It is these aspects that children can best hear in the womb. The smaller building blocks of speech (phonemes), and especially consonants, are not very audible in the uterine environment (Gerhardt & Abrams, 2000; Moon & Fifer, 2000).

The evidence from unborn babies comes from monolingual settings. There is no reason, though, why bilingual environments should not have similar effects. Well before BFLA children are born, they may have heard two languages as spoken by their mothers. One pioneering study has compared newborn babies whose mothers spoke just one language during pregnancy (English) with a group of newborn babies whose mothers had spoken two languages during pregnancy (Tagalog and English). Infants were tested within the first five days after they were born. The results are very clear: newborn babies exposed to two languages prior to birth and newborn babies exposed to just one language prior to birth can both distinguish between English and Tagalog. However, whereas the newborn babies with monolingual exposure prefer just the language they heard prior to birth, the newborn babies with bilingual exposure showed no preference for either of their prenatal languages (Byers-Heinlein *et al.*, 2008).

This last piece of evidence shows that unborn children who regularly hear their mothers speak two languages can also hear these two languages, and that they can learn basic aspects of these languages.

BFLA children may hear two languages in the womb, or just one. So far, no studies have looked at whether there are any differences in how these two types of BFLA children later respond to sounds. In either case, BFLA children start to hear two different ways of speaking from birth at the latest.[3]

Highly increased sound learning after birth

Once children are born, they continue to hear the prosodic aspects of speech. But now, without their mother's body and bodily fluids enveloping them, they are in a different 'sounding world', one in which they will be able to hear much more than just the melody of speech. Both MFLA and BFLA children can now start to hear many more of the phonemes in the language(s) that they are exposed to. They also hear these phonemes combined in language-specific ways. BFLA children, thus, will hear two sets of speech sounds that differ in their use of prosodic aspects, phonemes and phonotactics.

But is it really true that BFLA children hear two totally separate sets of sounds? If you think about it for a moment you will realize that no, it is not true. Certainly, for one particular language, there is one particular complex combination of specific intonation contours, one particular phoneme inventory and the specific phonotactic rules that go with it. The overall constellation of all this will be unique to one particular language. In that sense, the last sentence of the previous paragraph is true, after all.

However, many of the specific sound features of a language will be shared with other languages. For instance, Language A and Language Alpha may both use rising intonation, word accents and the consonants /b/ and /t/. They may differ in a number of other ways. For instance, Language A may use a lot of falling intonation contours and Language Alpha much less so. Language A may use a consonant (e.g. /v/) that is lacking in Language Alpha. In any case, a child hearing any combination of Language A and Language Alpha will be hearing sounds that are similar in both and sounds that are unique to one of them.

Depending on the specific pair of languages that BFLA children are hearing, the extent of the differences between their two input languages in prosody, phoneme inventory and phonotactics is variable. Just exactly which of these cues BFLA children use to break the code, that is, to distinguish between their two languages, is still a mystery. Yet it is of crucial importance that BFLA children learn to make distinctions between the sounds of their two input languages. If they do not, they will have a hard time learning to understand words and sentences (see also Box 5.1 and Box 5.2 (adv.)).

Box 5.2(adv.) More on the importance in BFLA of distinguishing between two languages from early on

The point that BFLA children need to distinguish between their two languages from very early on was made quite forcefully by Jacques Mehler and colleagues (Mehler *et al.*, 1996). Mehler's laboratory has carried out some of the most influential research on the early capabilities of infants to perceive the sounds of their language. Mehler *et al.* (1996: 101) wrote:

'Because multilingual environments are the norm rather than the exception, infants must have the capacity very early in life to distinguish one language from another. Without such a capacity, infants might acquire linguistic systems that amalgamate properties of different languages. The ensuing confusion would be overpowering. Fortunately, this never arises, despite the intuitive fears of monolingual parents. Infants raised in multilingual societies do not become dysphasic. Nor do children who learn more than one language at once pay a high price in terms of time or effort. These informal observations constitute one of the central mysteries that psycholinguists are faced with.'

Mehler *et al.* published these considerations as a theoretical position, since in 1996 no publications had appeared on bilingual infants' early speech perception. In 1996, there was no empirical evidence that indeed BFLA infants can distinguish their two languages from very early on, nor for the claim that BFLA children in fact do *not* 'pay a high price in terms of time or effort' (see above). It was only in the following year (1997) that the first study on early bilingual speech perception was published. At the end of the section on early bilingual speech perception I discuss to what extent there is now empirical evidence for Mehler *et al.*'s a priori position.

Funny accents

You have to remember, though, that children do not hear 'languages', they hear people! And people don't always talk exactly the way that you would expect based on phonological descriptions for a particular language. This is particularly relevant for a bilingual setting.

Some of the sounds that BFLA children hear from people who are speaking Language A to them may show an influence from Language Alpha. As I explained in Chapter 4, many of the people that BFLA infants meet up with are bilingual. The language they are addressing to an infant may be a second or third language for them. It is well known that getting the accent right is something that many people have a lot of trouble with when they learn a second or third language after childhood. As a result, many people who are fluent in a second or third language speak it with a funny accent sometimes.

In Box 5.3 I give an example of what such 'funny' accents might mean for early speech perception in BFLA children.

> **Box 5.3** The nature of the input and its importance for early bilingual speech perception
>
> Even if they are very good speakers of their second or third language people may occasionally sound foreign in these second or third languages (and even in their first, but that's another story).
>
> A good friend of mine, Karl, is a very proficient speaker of English, and some people think he is of Scottish descent (he did spend some time in Scotland). Yet sometimes he betrays his real origin, German, because of the way he pronounces some of his 'l's in English. English uses a 'dark' /l/, and my friend usually does, too (this /l/ is pronounced with the tip of the tongue close to the upper teeth or the ridge just before the teeth). But often when he says an [l] it's not quite dark enough, and that's how he gives away the fact that English is not his first language.
>
> Karl is one of the people to talk a lot with Ronnie, who is learning English and French from birth. In French, 'l's are not dark. Ronnie mainly hears English from his father, a native of Scotland who only uses dark 'l's, and from Karl, who uses 'l's that are much less dark, and sometimes even clear (pronounced with the tongue touching the roof of the mouth).
>
> Based on this kind of input, Ronnie has no reason to make a distinction between dark 'l's for English and clear 'l's for French. If he were to take this strategy, he wouldn't know what to do with Karl's 'in-between' 'l's in English. If you tested Ronnie on this, he most likely would not be showing a clear distinction between dark and clear 'l's. A monolingual infant learning only Scottish English would most likely show such a distinction, that is, this monolingual infant would be able to distinguish between what she knows, dark 'l's, and what she does not know, clear 'l's.
>
> Would such a difference between a BFLA and a MFLA infant show that BFLA infants are slower in learning to perceive different kinds of 'l's? That is probably the wrong question: certainly, there is a difference, but it makes no sense to speak of any kind of 'delay'. The difference is a direct result of the differences in what the BFLA and the MFLA infants in this hypothetical but realistic example need to learn in order to make sense of their sounding worlds.
>
> Of course, a BFLA child who hears just 'native' Scottish English and 'native' French may distinguish between dark and clear 'l's just like MFLA infants learning each of these languages as their only language. This does not mean that this type of BFLA child is 'two monolinguals in one'. What this means is that like MFLA children, BFLA children learn to perceive what they need to perceive.

The example in Box 5.3 shows that it is important to take into account the actual models that individual BFLA children hear (see also Chapter 4). Specifically for early bilingual speech perception, Anne Fernald, who is an eminent specialist on infant speech perception, has emphasized this point in a commentary on studies of speech perception in BFLA (Fernald, 2006: 26). She has convincingly argued that these studies do not always sufficiently take into account the variability in the pronunciation of particular phonemes that individual BFLA children may be hearing.

The next section discusses these studies and what they can tell us about the ways in which BFLA children distinguish the sounds of their languages.

Early bilingual speech perception

Distinguishing between two input languages in BFLA

From early on, MFLA infants can distinguish between the language they have heard from birth and other languages. They show that they can distinguish these by responding in consistently different ways to recordings of sentences in a foreign language and in their own language (e.g. Mehler & Christophe, 1994).

A similar result for BFLA was found in the very first published study on speech perception in BFLA infants. In 1997, Laura Bosch and Núria Sebastián-Gallés from Barcelona, Spain, published a study that included data on 4.5-month-old BFLA infants who were acquiring two closely related languages, Spanish and Catalan. Their pioneering work showed that these BFLA infants responded differently to recordings of sentences in either of their own two languages than to recordings in languages that they had not heard before (English and Italian). This mirrors the findings for MFLA children, who likewise are able to distinguish between languages they have heard regularly since birth, and new languages.

For BFLA children, however, being able to distinguish between what they are used to (their two languages) and any other language is not nearly as important as being able to distinguish between the two languages they are hearing (see the previous section). As I noted earlier, newborn babies with bilingual prenatal experience in Tagalog and English can distinguish between their languages at birth (Byers-Heinlein et al., 2008), just as 'monolingual' newborns can distinguish between the one language familiar to them prior to birth, and another language. Bosch and Sebastián-Gallés (2001b) showed that BFLA infants acquiring Spanish and Catalan in Barcelona, which are very similar on the prosody level, can distinguish these two languages at the age of 4.5 months. This happens to be the same age that monolingual infants acquiring only one of these languages can distinguish them.

Behavioral studies of early speech perception in BFLA

Up until recently, the studies coming out of the Barcelona laboratory were the only ones examining how BFLA infants perceive speech. Just in the last few years, there has been quite an expansion in this area, and established researchers in the field of (monolingual) infant speech perception like Janet Werker in Vancouver, Canada, have turned their attention to the study of speech perception in BFLA infants.

One reason is that important theoretical issues in monolingual infant speech perception can be put to the test by using bilingual subjects. Explaining these theoretical issues is beyond the scope of this book, however. I refer interested students to the Recommended reading section below for more information. Another reason for the surge in interest in bilingual infants is that basic explanations of early speech perception should cover speech perception in all infants, not just monolingual ones.

Studies of infant speech perception are experimental studies. In Box 5.4(adv.) I explain some of the basic procedures that are involved in these studies. The studies I describe in Box 5.4(adv.) are also behavioral studies. In this case, that means that they observe infants' behavior in response to hearing certain sounds.

> **Box 5.4(adv.)** A note on typical procedures used in behavioral studies of infant speech perception
>
> Studies of infant speech perception are experimental studies. One type of study involves measuring infants' behavior in response to experimental stimuli. These are sound stimuli (e.g. recorded sentences or words) that the researchers have carefully constructed to investigate a particular point of interest.
>
> In the experiments, infants control how long they listen to specific sound stimuli by sucking, or looking at the screen. When they stop sucking, or looking, the sound stimulus stops playing. This is the essence of the testing procedures.
>
> Typically, babies visit a research laboratory with a caregiver. There, they are seated in a small room equipped with hidden loudspeakers and a video screen. Usually there is also a camera or other equipment that records the child's behavior.
>
> On the whole, the procedures used are variations on the following theme. Infants hear language samples when they look at an appealing image on the screen. The same sample is played over and over to familiarize them. Then a novel sample is played. If the infants can tell the difference between the familiarized and the novel stimuli, they look longer at the novel stimuli.
>
> There are many variations to the procedure described here. For instance, for newborns (and two-month-olds), studies often take infants' sucking rates as a behavioral sign of response. That is possible because infants tend to suck with a constant speed on a pacifier or bottle nipple. If they get excited by a particular sound stimulus, they start to suck faster and so their sucking rate increases. Once they are used to the stimulus that excited them they return to their own 'normal' sucking rate.
>
> Experimental settings like these investigate the degree to which infants respond to novel stimuli. These responses imply the detection of a difference between stimuli. In order to avoid undue influence from the accompanying adult on the infants' behavior, caregivers are usually given headphones and/or are masked.
>
> You can see that research with infants has its own very specific methods. Researchers need a lot of ingenuity to devise techniques that will be reliable and will work. For an illustration of some techniques, see some of the pictures on the trilingual website (Spanish, Catalan, English) of the Barcelona infant studies laboratory (e.g. http://www.ub.es/pbasic/sppb/ingl/estudi.htm). There is also a relevant picture in Figure 1(a) in Werker and Byers-Heinlein (2008).

Studying speech perception through brain response

There is another type of experimental study that can teach us about infants' speech perception. These are studies that investigate infants' brain activity in response to hearing certain sounds. In these studies, infants have a little cap on their heads that has electrodes attached to it (don't worry, this doesn't hurt). These electrodes pick up the electrical activity from the brain. That electrical activity depends on what the infants hear, and particular kinds of sounds in particular languages give off different patterns of electrical activity. By studying these patterns, scientists can find out more about early speech perception in infants.

The number of studies that use this neurological approach is growing steadily. The bulk of the studies concern MFLA infants (see Friederici & Thierry, 2008 for an overview). However, some laboratories have also turned their attention to the study of BFLA infants. It is too early to draw any general conclusions from these studies, but with the rapid advances in the methods used, increasingly easier access to the technical requirements and, most importantly, the increased interest from scholars in studying BFLA children, the future holds a lot of promise. I refer interested students to a few of the relevant published studies in the Recommended reading section.

Back to behavioral studies

> I now come back to behavioral studies on early speech perception in BFLA infants. Space does not permit a discussion of every study in detail. Rather, I give an overview of most of the relevant published studies so far in Appendix B, with some descriptive information on each study and an indication of its main findings. In reading this overview, students should keep in mind the discussion in Chapter 2 earlier, where I explained that monolingually raised infants are able to perceive all sorts of sounds at the segmental level, including sounds that do not have phoneme status or that are not relevant in their input language. This ability, however, all but disappears towards the end of the first year. By that time, infants are focused mainly on the sounds that are important in the particular language they are learning. Thus, perceptual speech learning undergoes a reorganization in the course of the second half of the first year.
>
> Below, I give a brief overall summary of what the observational studies in Appendix B, taken together, can tell us about bilingual infants' early abilities to perceive differences between their languages.

The scope of the published studies on early speech perception in BFLA today is quite limited in terms of the specific languages and language combinations that have been investigated. In addition, for each of these languages and language combinations, only a very small number of sound contrasts have been investigated. These are important points, since, as I have explained before, languages differ significantly in the extent to which they rely on particular phonological characteristics such as stress, phonemes and rhythm to express meanings (see, once more, Box 5.1 earlier for an illustration in BFLA). This means that results could be quite different depending on which languages and language combinations are studied.

Keeping these limitations in mind, we can nevertheless formulate some preliminary findings based on the combined results of the studies to date that have investigated behavioral aspects of bilingual infants' early speech perception.

BFLA infants learn to distinguish contrasts that are useful in each of their languages. Some studies find that bilingual infants learn to distinguish a particular type of sound from one of their languages at the same age as monolingual infants acquiring that language. Other studies find differences in the ages at which bilingual and monolingual infants learn to distinguish one particular type of sound. Certainly, before the middle of their second year, bilingual infants are able to distinguish sound contrasts that are relevant to the languages they are acquiring.

There is no evidence of a general 'slowdown' in the learning of sounds by bilingual infants in comparison to monolingual ones. At the same time, 'Infants raised with two (or more) languages should not necessarily be expected to resemble monolingual learners of each of their languages; they may develop perceptual, cognitive and linguistic systems that are unique responses to the conditions and demands of their bilingual input' (Kuhl *et al.*, 2008). Indeed, as I have stressed before, bilingual development is a phenomenon worthy of study on its own merits. There is no monolingual (or indeed, bilingual) standard.

All studies that have looked at the same sound contrasts for the same pair of languages over time find a reorganization in the perception of the same pair of contrasts by bilingual infants as they get older. This generally mirrors developments in monolingual infants.

> These overall findings are necessarily vague. The highly increased recent research interest in early bilingual speech perception hopefully is a sign of an upward trend that will yield many more studies involving different languages and language combinations. The available evidence at this point, however, does seem to suggest that bilingual infants 'place utterances from different languages in different files' (Mehler *et al.*, 1996: 111). And there is nothing in the evidence at this point that refutes Mehler *et al.*'s (1996) theoretical position that I mentioned in Box 5.2(adv.).

Visual cues can help in learning to distinguish between two languages

Breaking the code, that is, distinguishing between two languages in BFLA, may not only depend on sounding cues. Visual cues may play a role as well (Ronjat noted this already in 1913; see, e.g. p. 39). There is evidence from one BFLA infant study that children may be aided in learning to distinguish between their two languages on the basis of the different gestures that the people speaking different languages to them use (Test, 2001).

Also, there is evidence from 24 French–English BFLA six- and eight-month-old infants that they can distinguish between French and English on the basis of silent video clips of the same speaker saying sentences either in French or English (Weikum *et al.*, 2007). Matched eight-month-old infants learning just English were not able to distinguish between these silent video clips in French and English (although younger monolinguals were, at four and six months of age). In these silent video clips it was only the movement of the speaker's mouth that differed. These mouth movements, it appears, are very good visual cues that bilingual infants can rely on to help them discriminate between languages. A nice example of how speech perception and visual cues come together in BFLA is shown in Box 5.5.

> **Box 5.5** An example of early speech perception and visual cues coming together in BFLA
>
> Cruz-Ferreira (2006) writes about the language development of her three children, who heard Portuguese and Swedish from birth in a 1P/1L setting. Cruz-Ferreira addressed her children in Portuguese, and their father spoke Swedish to them.
>
> Cruz-Ferreira (2006: 62) notes:
>
> the mother was largely in constant contact with the infant children throughout the day, and there was, naturally, a lot of talking going on, involving the mother, to the child, or to and from siblings, all of it in Portuguese. One of the highlights of the children's day was their father's homecoming in the evening, which usually meant lengthy sessions of rough play and giggles. At age 0;4, the children started freezing in place, as it were, in the mother's arms, instead of reaching out to their father as usual. They would turn to stare intently at the mother's mouth as she used Swedish to address the father, frowning and firmly refusing to cuddle either parent until something else was made to catch their attention. For a few weeks, the children's disquiet at the mother's use of Swedish was clear.

Speech perception and word learning

Learning to distinguish between different sounds is crucial in being able to understand what people mean to say. A big part of that is learning to distinguish words and, eventually, to learn to comprehend them.

The link between early speech perception and the learning of words later in development seems obvious. But until the important study by Tsao, Liu and Kuhl (2004) this link had not been empirically investigated. In this study, Tsao *et al.* showed that individual differences in early speech discrimination when monolingual infants were six months old predicted later individual differences in various aspects of word knowledge in the same children at 13, 16 and 24 months of age. Children who had not been very good at discriminating sounds at six months were not doing so well (compared to the others) in later vocabulary knowledge. Other studies have since found similar results.

An important study on the link between early speech processing and later development has even found that the speed with which two-year-olds recognize spoken words, together with the size of their production vocabularies, predicts linguistic and cognitive skills at eight years of age in the same children (Marchman & Fernald, 2008).

In order to learn new words, infants must pay close attention to the phonetic detail of how people are talking to them (Swingley & Aslin, 2002). This is not a skill that infants are born with. They must learn how to do this, so they can start to isolate words from the speech streams they hear and thus have a chance of starting to figure out what these words mean.

Given that many infants already understand some words at the age of nine months and understand quite a lot more by their first birthday, infants have obviously already learned enough to isolate words from the speech stream and give them some meaning. Related to this, 11-month-old Welsh–English BFLA infants distinguished between words they were most likely familiar with, and unfamiliar, rare words. They did this in both their languages (Vihman et al., 2007). One-year-old infants still have a long way to go, though, in the level of phonetic detail that they are able to perceive and use in the learning of new words (see, e.g. Werker et al., 2002).

How good are bilingual infants at using small phonetic differences in order to learn new words? And how do BFLA infants compare to monolingually raised infants? Two pioneering experimental studies have examined this. I give more information about them in Appendix C.

> The first of these word learning studies looked at when BFLA children learning Canadian English and another language were able to learn new English nonsense words ('bih' and 'dih') that contrasted in their initial consonant (/b/ vs. /d/). In this study, Fennell et al. (2007) found that 17-month-old bilinguals did not learn these new words, but that 20-month-old bilinguals did. In an earlier study with the same set of stimuli of monolingual infants learning Canadian English, Werker et al. (2002) found that at the age of 17 months, infants were able to learn these new words, but not at age 14 months. The bilinguals, then, took longer to learn these particular English test stimuli than monolinguals.
>
> In the second of these studies, Mattock et al. (2008) found that by the time they are 17 months old, bilingual infants can learn new nonsense words ('bowse' and 'gowse') that contrasted in their initial consonant (/b/ vs. /g/). They took care to use stimuli that work well in both Canadian French and Canadian English, the BFLA children's input languages. They also presented these stimuli with French and English pronunciations. The experiments were repeated with monolingual infants learning French and English. These monolingual infants had trouble distinguishing the stimuli, though.
>
> A third study (not listed in Appendix C) found that a number of BFLA Spanish–Catalan children between the ages of 1;7 and 4;3 seemed quite tolerant of mispronunciations of words that involved substituting [ɛ] for [e] in cognate words (the contrast is phonemic in Catalan but not in Spanish). They thus resembled Spanish monolingual but not Catalan monolingual children. Importantly, relatively greater tolerance was found in those BFLA children who heard more Spanish than Catalan (Ramon-Casas et al., under review).

Research into the way that bilingual infants learn to use sounds for recognizing words has just started. It is too early to draw any general conclusions. We do not know whether the fact that BFLA infants have to learn sounds and words from two languages slows down their ability to recognize and learn words. Actually, the little evidence there is about the number of words that BFLA infants learn to understand by the age of 13 months in comparison to monolinguals suggests that there is no slowing down at all (see Chapter 6).

More research is needed about the very earliest stages of bilingual acquisition in order to address the important issue of how and when BFLA children distinguish between the sounds and words of their two input languages.

Making the melody of speech

Ronjat (1913: 11) begins his discussion of his bilingual son's production of sounds by saying that Louis sang the sound that the grandfather clock in his house made. This singing became the basis for Louis' later word for this clock (see Box 5.6). In her study of three BFLA children, Cruz-Ferreira (2006: 99) also notes the important link between music and language learning.

> **Box 5.6** An early bilingual example of the link between music and speech
>
> In his study of his German–French-hearing son, Louis, Jules Ronjat drew attention to the link between singing and talking. He writes that towards the end of Louis' first year, Louis says something like [i ɑ] when he is asked to say the word for pendulum clock. When the clock sounds, Louis turns to look at it and sings:
>
> (this is my rendition of Ronjat's drawing)
>
> Ronjat goes on to explain that at the age of 13 months this melody becomes a word [iɑ] that is pronounced without pause and without regular musical interval, and with two vowels with an approximately equal level of intensity.
>
> *Adapted from Ronjat, 1913: 11*

Previously I stressed the importance of intonation contours for early speech perception, but in production, the melody of speech is also of prime importance. As Cruz-Ferreira (2006: 96) writes, the prosody of speech is acquired first, before words (a review of relevant literature for monolingual infants also comes to this conclusion; see Snow & Balog, 2002).

There are, however, not many studies of prosodic development, neither in monolingual acquisition nor in bilingual acquisition.[4] An exception is the large body of research on young children's production of syllable structure and word stress (e.g. Ota, 2003). I discuss studies of bilingual acquisition that have looked at syllable structure and stress in the section below entitled 'More on melody: syllable structure and stress'.

Cruz-Ferreira (2006, chapters 5 and 6) focuses on the intonation contours that her three Portuguese–Swedish BFLA children used. As infants, all three children used two different kinds of speech melody patterns that reflected basic differences between their two languages in terms of the reliance on vowels, stress and intonational patterns (pp. 63–64). At a time when the children were not quite yet saying words, they were already using Portuguese-sounding utterances with Portuguese-speaking interlocutors, and reserved Swedish-sounding utterances for speakers of Swedish. The children's intonation patterns sounded like fluent Portuguese and Swedish, without the words.

A detailed auditory and acoustic longitudinal study of a number of prosodic aspects of the speech of three German–English BFLA children between the ages of two and five reveals that both languages show different developmental patterns (Gut, 2000a). This study also shows that the acquisition of sentence prosody is a long drawn-out process. The children that Gut studied had German as the clearly stronger language. They developed intonational patterns earlier in German than in English, and there was no evidence that patterns they had already acquired in German were transferred to English. For the child Laura, question intonation was examined and found to develop in a language-specific manner in each language (Gut, 2000a, chapter 9; see also Gut, 2000b).[5]

The importance of intonation patterns is shown throughout Cruz-Ferreira's (2006) study. For instance, when the infants were not sure of a word in a particular language, they would often replace it with a humming tone so that the overall intonation pattern of their utterance still sounded either Portuguese, or Swedish (p. 67). At a later age, the children produced many 'fillers'. These are syllables that appear in children's early sentences but that have no meaning from an adult point of view. As Cruz-Ferreira convincingly argues, fillers in fact 'represent child attempts at replicating the suprasegmental structure of the language in question' (p. 123); as such, fillers add prosodic fluency to utterances (p. 126).

Another example of the importance of prosody relates to babbling. The children's earliest vocalizations in effect constituted 'suprasegmental babbling' (p. 102), that is, the production of consonant and vowel-like sounds in sequences that differed in pitch, amplitude, tempo and length. As babbling became more and more word-like, with reduplicated syllables, the babbling sequences became more and more rhythmical and melodic wholes (p. 103).[6]

Cruz-Ferreira and Gut have shown how the full mastery of prosody takes several years of practice. This also goes for the learning of other aspects of phonetics and phonology. We start by taking a look at BFLA children's typical speech productions in the first year of life: babbling.

Bilingual babbling

Ronjat (1913) was the first to study what he calls 'Krähen' in a BFLA child, or what in English we would now call babbling. In Ronjat's time, scholars studying child language were just starting to discover more about the nature of infants' early vocalizations. As Ronjat notes, the distinction between babbling and the beginnings of what he calls 'l'imitation de langage des adultes' (the imitation of adult language; fn 1 on p. 38) hadn't always been noticed by students of child language at the time.[7]

This also means that Ronjat doesn't consider infants' early vocalizations and babbling to be specific to a particular language. While most scholars today would agree with that assessment for infants up until the age of around seven months, there is controversy about the extent to which the more word-like babbling of infants starting around that age is geared towards a particular language or not.

Early vocalizations

Before I discuss this word-like babbling let's go back a bit and look at infants' very early vocalizations (before the age of six months, say). These early vocalizations may globally sound like they come from all kinds of different languages, but they cannot easily be transcribed; that is because most of the time, they do not overlap with any adult phonetic units (Oller, 2000: 39, 49). For a good description of these early vocalizations, you need a different system entirely.

Researchers in the United States developed such a system in the 1970s. The system distinguishes between, for instance, squeals, coos and 'raspberries' (that's when pouted lips are made to vibrate; it's often considered a 'rude' sound! If you try it you'll see what I mean). The system also distinguishes 'marginal babbling', which is reserved for sounds that make you think of syllables but not quite (Oller, 2000: 50).

Children all over the world use these kinds of sounds, and so far, scholars have tended not to think of these early vocalizations as linked to any specific language. The three longitudinal case studies that report on BFLA children's early vocalizations in the first six months after birth (Cruz-Ferreira, 2006; Leopold, 1970; Ronjat, 1913) show that BFLA children produce very similar early vocalizations. These studies do not make any claim of language specificity either. Cruz-Ferreira (2006: 100–104) does emphasize, however, that early vocalizations by her three subjects relied heavily on intonation patterns that could already sound like Swedish or Portuguese (so they were language specific in a more global sense). It remains to be seen whether this finding can be generalized to other children.

Canonical babbling

Once infants start to produce a number of clear vowel–consonant combinations, they have reached the stage of **canonical babbling** (Oller, 1980). Canonical babbling consists of syllable sounds that could in principle be words (Oller, 1980: 180), such as [dæ] (noted by Leopold, 1970). Often, these syllables are part of a longer sequence of the same syllable, like [bɑbɑbɑbɑbɑ]. This type of canonical babbling is called **reduplicated babbling**.

Canonical babbling may start around the age of eight months. It does not replace the earlier types of vocalizations entirely, but as infants babble more, they use fewer of the earlier forms and, eventually, the earlier vocalizations all but disappear. There is a lot of variation between infants in how they babble (Oller, 1980).

The patterns described here occur in infants learning many different languages. They also occur in BFLA children, and there is no difference in the general timing with which they appear (Cruz-Ferreira, 2006 for three Swedish–Portuguese infants, Leopold, 1970 for German–English Hildegard, Oller *et al.*, 1997 for 20 Spanish–English infants and Ronjat, 1913 for German–French Louis). As a small point of interest, all three of the longitudinal studies here report the production of the very same syllable [bwa] at the age of eight months in Hildegard (Leopold), Louis (Ronjat) and Mikael (one of the three children studied by Cruz-Ferreira).

Is bilingual babbling language specific?

None of the above case studies on BFLA offer a language-oriented description of bilingual babbling.[8] This implies that they do not see the syllables made up of vowel- and consonant-like sounds produced in bilingual babbling as having any clear relation to either of the languages the children are hearing.

> In a study of the babbling of two English–Serbian twins, Zlatić *et al.* (1997) found some indication of an effect of the input languages. The twin siblings produced many more palatal glides than children growing up in monolingual English environments. The authors attribute this to the presence of a large number of palatal segments in the Serbian input that are absent in English.
>
> The Zlatić *et al.* study did not take into account the possible role of the sociolinguistic setting in bilingual babbling and the way that this setting might cue infants towards babbling differently.
>
> In contrast, two more studies that looked at the babbling of infants raised with English and French did take into account different sociolinguistic settings. The first of these examined to what extent 13 BFLA infants between the ages of 10 and 14 months in Montreal, Canada, showed a difference in their use of consonants depending on whether they were interacting with a French or an English-speaking parent (Poulin-Dubois & Goodz, 2001). More particularly, this study looked at the frequency and proportion with which the infants used consonantal sounds differing in place and manner of articulation. Poulin-Dubois and Goodz found no discernible differences in how infants babbled in the French vs. English interactional context. They did find, though, that 'most infants produced consonants more frequently found in the babbling of monolingual French-learning infants than in the babbling of monolingual English-learning infants' (pp. 104–105).
>
> However, the monolingual infants that Poulin-Dubois and Goodz used as comparisons (they relied on data published by de Boysson-Bardies and Vihman, 1991) did not hear Canadian French and English. Poulin-Dubois and Goodz recognize that differences between English as spoken in Montreal and the American English of the infants studied by de Boysson-Bardies and Vihman might explain why the bilingual infants differed quite a bit from the monolingual English infants.
>
> The second study that specifically looked at whether there was any difference between the babbling of a BFLA infant depending on the sociolinguistic setting is that by Maneva and Genesee (2002). This study followed a single English–French boy, Bryan, between the ages of 10 and 15 months. It looked in particular at a great number of characteristics of the syllable structure of babbling. The study concludes that Bryan showed some consistent differences depending on whom he was interacting with, but that other characteristics were the same in either the French or English setting.

Although it is recognized that babbling plays an important role in children's overall phonetic development, there is still a question to what extent canonical babbling is relatable to the specific input language that infants are hearing (e.g. see Grenon *et al.*, 2007).

A difficult problem for the analysis of babbling is that there is such a large variation between infants in how they babble. One reason is that different infants may differ in the kinds of sounds they prefer. Another reason is that infants differ greatly in their ability to control their articulatory organs. If you compare infants from different monolingual backgrounds it will be hard to keep these factors constant.

Studies of BFLA could perhaps keep these factors more constant. Presumably, individual children will prefer particular kinds of sounds. Certainly, one particular BFLA child will be at the same level of motor development. Carefully conducted studies with BFLA infants babbling when alone and when interacting with speakers of different languages could, in principle, offer the right kind of data to approach the issue of which aspects of babbling show language-specific influence and which do not.

However, the bilingual infant is not two monolinguals in one, and findings from BFLA would not necessarily be generalizable to monolingual acquisition.

At this point, it is too early to draw any conclusions about the exact nature of canonical babbling in BFLA children. Some of the findings in the few studies that have looked at bilingual babbling in more detail are intriguing, though. More research is needed to investigate to what extent prelexical BFLA infants already show some influence from their input languages in their babbling.

> A related issue is to what extent babbling relates to later phonetic development. I will not go into this issue except to point out that as infants gradually start to say word-like forms, their pre-existing babbling patterns may influence the sound-shape of these forms (Vihman et al., 1985), and if children still babble a lot concurrently with their first attempts at words, there may be quite a bit of mutual influence (Elbers & Josi, 1985). For BFLA, Leopold (1953: 5) reports that in the first stages of word-like productions, his English–German daughter used the low vowels that she had earlier used in her babbling, although one low vowel sound, [æ], was dropped.

Do babies continue to babble?

Babbling is generally not seen as communicative (Oller, 1980). The communicative nature of vocal sounds changes towards the end of the first year. That's when children start to say more word-like utterances, that is, single syllables or combinations of syllables that are recognized by parents as attempts to convey a particular meaning. This meaning could be more referential or more pragmatic, that is, children's word-like utterances could be naming something or just expressing a personal stance like interest or desire.[9]

Babbling may continue even once infants start to produce more communicative vocal sounds. Leopold (1953, 1970) noted this for German–English Hildegard as well. She used reduplicated babbling many months after she said her first 'real' word (pretty) at age ten months. In contrast, my diary notes for my Dutch–English daughter Susan, who did not use much reduplicated babbling at all, show that she stopped babbling altogether at the age of 9.5 months, when she said her first 'real' word, [noː] ('no'?), while shaking her head and refusing to eat. There is a lot of individual variation, then, in the extent to which babbling will continue to be used once children start to say word-like forms.

In conclusion

Close to Louis' first birthday, Ronjat (1913: 41) wrote that for his son: 'le bilinguisme ne semble avoir eu aucune influence particulière sur les modalités du Krähen ou sur la date des premières imitations'.[10] To what extent there are bilingual effects in babbling needs to be seen, but all the data to date show that the timing of babbling and its general characteristics are, indeed, not specifically bilingual but shared by monolingually and bilingually raised infants alike.

More on melody

As BFLA infants go into their second year, they continue learning to use the right 'melodies' for each of their languages. Languages differ in the rhythms they use. This gives rise to differences in the overall stress patterns. These global stress patterns influence a lot of other aspects in phonology, including how syllables are structured and what the typical stress patterns are at the word level (Fox, 2000).

All children, including those raised with two languages, need to learn the rhythmical properties of the particular language(s) that they are hearing. This is part and parcel of learning a language. Also, children need to learn to coordinate these prosodic properties with different types of sentence structures. This may take quite some time (Behrens & Gut, 2005; Gut, 2000a). Prosodical learning is also related to learning to use the proper duration of consonants and vowels. Especially consonant duration can take 10 years to acquire (Kent, 1976), and it is likely that learning most of the rhythmic patterns of a language can take that long as well (Whitworth, 2002).

As I wrote above, learning to use the right intonation contours takes a long time. At the same time, BFLA children can already use language-specific intonation contours from very early on (Cruz-Ferreira, 2006). In addition, BFLA children use language-specific word stress in many of their early words (Cruz-Ferreira, 2006: 64–66); for an example, see Box 5.7.

Box 5.7 An early bilingual example of different word stress for different languages

Karin heard Portuguese and Swedish from birth, and loves bananas.

The Swedish word for 'banana' has just two syllables, with the stress on the second syllable: 'banan'. In Portuguese, the word for 'banana' has three syllables, with the stress on the middle one, like in English: 'banana'.

At age 1;8, Karin was too young to pronounce the adult forms of Swedish banan and Portuguese banana. She used two forms to refer to 'banana'. They were: nana and nanu.

You won't be surprised to know that Karin said nana when she talked to her Portuguese mother and nanu when she talked to her Swedish father. Her 'Portuguese' nana deleted the first unstressed syllable of Portuguese 'banana' but kept the remaining stress pattern. English-learning children will also often say 'nana' when they mean 'banana'. Karin's 'Swedish' nanu mirrored the adult stress pattern in 'banan'.

Adapted from Cruz-Ferreira, 2006: 64

The example in Box 5.7 shows that young children's renditions of adult words may be very different from those adult words. Children will typically not produce many multisyllabic words, but will mostly produce words consisting of just one or two syllables, even if the corresponding adult word has more. This process is called **truncation**.

The intriguing part is that children do not 'truncate' at random. There are patterns in their truncations that can be related to the specific properties of their input language (Box 5.7). However, because of the fact that there can be such a large difference between adult and young children's versions of specific words, it is not always easy to discern correspondences between them. Furthermore, different theoretical viewpoints may yield different perspectives on the nature of these correspondences (for an overview of phonological theories relevant for acquisition, see Stoel-Gammon & Vogel Sosa, 2007).

Syllable structure and stress as used by BFLA children

Truncation, the deletion of syllables compared to adult target words, typically is seen in MFLA children between age one and two. Evidence from BFLA children shows that they also truncate in the second year of life (Cruz-Ferreira, 2006; Leopold, 1970; Ronjat, 1913).

The question arises whether BFLA children truncate according to the patterns of each of their input languages. More generally, since word truncation and word stress are very much linked up with syllable structure, the question is whether BFLA children show consistently different rhythms in their two languages, and if so, when. The answers here are not clear.

> I list most of the studies so far that have specifically investigated word stress, syllable structure and other aspects of speech rhythm in BFLA children in Appendix D.

Contradictory results

Studies of syllable structure and truncation in BFLA so far have shown some apparently contradictory results.

> Some studies find a clear difference between a BFLA child's use of syllable structure in different languages (e.g. Keshavarz & Ingram, 2002; Paradis, 1996). For the five children studied by Lleó *et al.*, (2003) the production of **codas** or syllable-final consonants in German was more advanced than their coda production in Spanish. This reflects the differences between the two input languages, where German uses many more codas than Spanish and where German codas are far more complex than Spanish codas (in German, codas may consist of more consonants than in Spanish, as in '**Strumpf**' (sock), which has three consonants in the coda, something that isn't possible in Spanish). It appears that the children are 'tuned in' to these differences between their input languages. Other

studies find little evidence of clear differences. Instead, they find evidence that the two languages interact, namely, that aspects of Language A influence Language Alpha (e.g. Lléo et al., 2007; Paradis 2001).

Three German–English BFLA children were found to develop specific word pitch and stress patterns in each of their two languages separately from the age of 2;1 onwards (Gut, 2000a: 166). Intonational patterns used in German were not transferred to English (or the other way round). However, French–English Tom first misused **iambic stress** in English words, as in [ba'bit] for 'rabbit', with the stress on the second syllable instead of the first one (which worked fine for his French words, as in 'can**ard**' (duck), with correct stress on the second syllable). Tom started to use the correct English **trochaic pattern** only at age 2;4, as in '**mon**ey', with correct stress on the first syllable. It appeared that Tom was first guided by French, which indeed has basic word stress on the final syllable. English word stress tends to be on the first syllable. Later on, Tom again misused iambic stress in new English words for a while (Brulard & Carr, 2003). Ronjat (1913: 14–15) notes that French–German Louis used correct French iambic word stress. Stress in German words was sometimes wrong (up until the age of 2;6), with stress on the second syllable instead of the first. Although Ronjat doesn't comment on this in terms of influence from French, the possibility exists that like Tom, Louis was influenced by his French to some extent.

Another bilingual boy, Arsham, who was also acquiring two languages with a similar difference to French and English, mostly used the right stress pattern in each of his languages: iambic for Farsi and trochaic for English (Keshavarz & Ingram, 2002). However, when he made mistakes, it was the iambic pattern from Farsi that was used in English words. The fact that Arsham usually used the correct stress pattern from the beginning in English is different from what Tom was doing. But the fact that Arsham's occasional errors showed an influence from the iambic stress pattern resembles the error pattern seen in Tom.

Studies of speech rhythm, that is, 'the alternation of timing and the perceived regularity of prominent units in speech' (Bunta & Ingram, 2007: 999), likewise, show both evidence of BFLA children using two different sets of rhythmic properties and interaction between them.

Why are there contradictory results?

The answer to the question whether BFLA children show consistently different speech rhythms in their two languages, then, is not clear. One reason is that, so far, there simply have not been enough studies. Also, the available studies have used divergent methods, which often makes it difficult to interpret the combined results.

Another issue is whether the question of separate rhythmical development can ever be answered in any general terms. Learning the speech rhythm of a language is a long drawn-out process that shows a lot of variability among children in the speed with which they acquire it.

There is also the more fundamental issue of whether all languages-in-acquisition stand an equal chance, so to speak, of showing language-specific effects as far as the pronunciation of words and syllables is concerned. There is evidence that some languages are 'harder' than others, that is, it takes more time for children to sound adult-like in one language than in another as far as the rhythm of speech is concerned (Grabe *et al.*, 1999; Vihman *et al.*, 2006).

BFLA children are not two MFLA children in one

Often the studies in Appendix D evaluate BFLA rhythmical patterns against patterns found for monolingual children. In many studies, this evaluation then is used as a basis for deciding whether BFLA children distinguish between their two languages or not. The assumption appears to be that evidence for different processes in the two languages depends on whether the same language-specific patterns can be observed in MFLA children.

By definition, a BFLA child is *not* two MFLA children in one, however. There is no a priori reason to assume that BFLA children should behave like two separate monolingual children.

Comparisons with monolinguals cannot serve as a basis for a within-bilingual comparison (see also Chapter 7). Furthermore, monolingual children learning the same language show quite a lot of interindividual variation. There will be even more variation among BFLA children acquiring the same set of languages. In such circumstances, it is difficult to see what is due to interindividual variation and what is due to influence from a particular language, or the fact that children are acquiring two languages rather than one.

There is also the problem that monolingual comparison data are often lacking (Gut, 2000a: 167).

The importance of the language models that BFLA children hear

Another important point, which I will repeat wherever relevant, has to do with the models that BFLA children hear. In second language learners, speech rhythm patterns are particularly vulnerable to 'infiltration' from a first language. Bilingual people speaking Language A may use some rhythmical patterns that a person who knows only Language A would never use. BFLA children cannot be expected to speak Language A in a 'monolingual' fashion if they hear it frequently spoken by such bilinguals.

One study of speech rhythm in BFLA has taken the potential role of the input into account. It specifically investigated parental speech patterns and compared these to the respective children's patterns.[11] This study concerns three German–English families with children between the ages of five and 13. The two siblings whose mother's speech patterns were different in German and English also acquired different patterns in German and English, whereas the other two pairs of siblings whose mothers did not use any different rhythms in their German and English did not either (Whitworth, 2002).

Another study that has compared characteristics of the input language with development in BFLA shows a close correspondence between the two. Keshavarz and Ingram (2002) found a high degree of similarity between the proportion of monosyllabic words in Farsi and English BFLA input to Arsham and Arsham's own use of these in Farsi and English, respectively.[12]

It is most likely these very local influences from the people who talk to children that can help explain some of the contradictory patterns that have been noted by scholars studying speech rhythm in BFLA. Especially if children's first word learning strategies are to try to match existing production patterns to input forms, as suggested by Vihman (2002), then the influence from both languages is very much guided by local influences, that is, by the precise ways in which specific people around the child produce particular words. Such local influences will most likely also have an effect on children's production of **speech segments**, to which I turn next.

Bilingual speech segments

Phones and phonemes

As Ronjat noted in 1913 (p. 12), children do not learn to say separate speech sounds. Rather, they acquire them indirectly as they attempt to say words. Obviously, the same goes for the learning of word stress and syllable structure as discussed previously. Children learn these things as they try to say words. A discussion of children's production of separate speech sounds, or rather, speech segments, then, is necessarily an abstraction. This should be kept in mind as I discuss bilingual children's use of segments.

When adults say words, they produce speech segments, which are called phones. The phones that adults use have phonemic status, that is, they relate to a particular phoneme (see Chapter 2). Phonemes are abstract ideas that people have of the meaningful single speech sounds in their language (remember from Chapter 2 how that abstract knowledge makes it difficult for adults to distinguish certain new phones in another language). The different phones that relate to one specific phoneme are called allophones. For instance, in English both an aspirated [pʰ] and [p] without aspiration refer to the same phoneme /p/. This means that in English [pʰ] and [p] are allophones, different renditions of /p/. Some phonemes have just one allophone, others several.

Phonemes and the allophones that can express them are language specific, as I explained in Chapter 2. Just to remind you, here is another example. In Spanish, for instance, the phoneme /b/ can be pronounced as [b] (which, phonetically, is a **stop consonant**, meaning that the airflow is stopped at some point in the mouth – in this case, by the lips). But when /b/ appears between two vowels, it is pronounced as [β]. This is a spirant or **fricative**, pronounced with a partial closure of the mouth. Spanish speakers understand the phones [β] and [b] as expressing the same underlying phoneme, /b/. To German speakers, in contrast, there is no 'spilling over' of stop consonants into fricatives. The phone [β] is not really part of the way German speakers pronounce any of their phonemes, but if they were to hear an L2 speaker of German use [β], they would think they are trying to say /v/, never /b/. Any notion of 'fricativeness' is foreign to the German phoneme /b/.

Young children have to learn that phones relate to underlying, abstract phoneme categories. They also have to learn which phones relate to what phonemes.

Towards the end of the first year, when infants are ready to start saying words, they will already have learned something about phoneme categories in perception (see earlier). Whether and how they use this knowledge in production, however, is not clear (Ingram, 1989).[13]

When children babble, they do not yet produce phonemes, that is, their speech sounds are not yet linked to a specific adult phoneme category. The segments or phones they produce are just phonetic elements that have no phonemic status as yet.

Infants' first apparently communicatively used utterances are produced without the frequent reduplication of babbling. They are proto-words, predecessors of 'real' words. Some scholars have also used the term 'phonetically consistent form' to refer to these rather more word-*like* than actual word forms (Dore *et al.*, 1976). In some children, it may take a long time before these proto-words develop into 'real' words with a fixed phonological shape and an adult-like meaning (e.g. see De Houwer & Gillis, 1985). In others, proto-words soon resemble 'real' words.

In any case, infants produce phones once they are in the single word stage. They gradually build up their ability to produce phones. The phonemic status of these phones is not clear, and much depends on scholars' theoretical position as regards phonology in general how they will interpret infants' and toddler's speech segments (Stoel-Gammon & Vogel Sosa, 2007).

Instability and variability in the production of early speech segments

At first, there is a great deal of instability in infants' articulatory abilities. One reason is that they have to try to control their lips and tongue and coordinate them both with how far their mouths are open.[14] That's quite difficult for young children in and of itself, especially since at the same time, their articulatory organs are growing (that includes their teeth).

Infants in the second year of life have variable articulatory control. Some are better articulators, others less so. This holds for MFLA and BFLA infants alike.

In addition to gaining articulatory control, children must match their developing articulatory capabilities to something they want to say.

There are children who appear to attempt to say long utterances that sound like real sentences in terms of the overall intonation contours. These don't work too well in communication, since such early long utterances without any discernible words don't mean much to children's interlocutors. Adults will often respond to such long utterances by saying 'oh, you don't say! do you now?' and smile (because they are delightedly surprised to hear entire adult-sounding intonation contours), or they will repeat the utterances in a questioning tone. But there will not be much more interaction, or any discussion of content, since these kinds of utterances are simply not understood. Infants will soon get the message and change tactics.

Changing tactics usually will mean that children try to focus on producing shorter utterances to get their meanings across: (proto-)words.[15] Most likely, infants have some holistic idea in mind of a particular word form, a 'template' (see, e.g. Vihman, 2002). It is to this template that they then try to match their own sound production. Thus, children indeed are most likely not aiming to say specific single sounds, just as Ronjat noted (see the beginning of the section).

Do BFLA children's speech segments develop in language-specific ways from early on?

As pointed out before, it is not clear to what extent and at what point in development the phones in children's early words can be called phonemes (e.g. see Vihman, 2002). This is an important point for BFLA, since it is mainly phonemes and their allophonic realizations that are language specific. Before BFLA children produce phones that are clearly relatable to phonemes, then, it is not possible to say much with regard to the language-specific nature of early bilingual phonetic–phonological development.

This implies that there really is no point in asking whether BFLA infants' earliest use of vowels and consonants reflects the use of a 'single' or a 'double' system (see also Deuchar & Quay, 2000 and Vihman, 2002). For there to be a 'system', there must be underlying rules, and there is no evidence that at this stage in development infants are relying on abstract rules that work with categories of sounds, i.e. phonemes.

For the most detailed study of early bilingual phonetic–phonological development to date, Leopold wrote: 'During the first two years of life [..] no clash of phonemes due to the presentation of two languages can be said to have occurred. [..] In examining the sound learning of my daughter during the first two years, I paid special attention to possible bilingual effects, and found very little' (Leopold, 1978: 25). It is hard to know what precisely Leopold meant by this (see also Leopold 1970: 183). Ronjat's (1913) claim that French–German Louis had two separate articulatory, phonetic and phonological systems in the second year of life is more straightforward. Given the theoretical issues involved, however, both Ronjat's and Leopold's positions are to be considered with great care.

Aside from the theoretical problems, there are also great methodological difficulties in investigating the extent to which young BFLA infants' production of speech sounds is language specific. It is very difficult in a monolingual setting to determine the phonemic status of early speech sounds. In a monolingual setting, however, one can work with a single set of phonemes that, presumably, infants are aiming at. In a bilingual setting, there are two sets of target phonemes involved, most likely with some degree of overlap between them.

If it is difficult in a monolingual setting to determine what phoneme an infant might be aiming at, just think how difficult that becomes in a bilingual setting. In Box 5.8(adv.) I explain in more detail what some of the methodological hurdles are. These methodological points are not limited to the study of phones, but also to the study of other aspects of phonological development (such as, e.g. syllable structure, discussed above), as well as lexical and morphosyntactic development in the second year of life.

Bilingual First Language Acquisition

> **Box 5.8(adv.)** Determining the target language of early words in BFLA
>
> Since young children do not speak in separate phones, but in words, scholars approach the study of early phones on the basis of words. They often then try to compare the child word with a presumed adult target word, and then go on to compare the form of both to each other, in order to determine to what extent the child's form approximates the adult word.
>
> In MFLA, determining the target language of monolingual infants' and toddlers' early words is not an issue.[a] It is a problem even in MFLA, however, to try and determine what specific word a child was aiming at. One reason is that early child meanings are very fluid (see Chapters 2 and 6). In addition, child forms may differ quite a bit from adult forms (see the next section on phonological processes).
>
> How can we as adults be sure what word a child was aiming at? For instance, in MFLA the form [dæ] as produced by a child acquiring English could be used while the child is pointing to a playpen filled with teddybears, to pictures in a book that show a girl that looks like his older sister Danielle, or it could be said when the child has completed a task such as building a tower. Thus, depending on the context, the adult target for [dæ] could be 'bear', 'Danielle' or 'there!', just to name a few possibilities.
>
> When he discusses his daughter Hildegard's use of words in the second year, Leopold (1970: 178) notes: 'The crude phonetic form of the child's words often precluded definite assignment to one language'. Ronjat (1913) doesn't voice such caveats, but it is clear that if it is difficult in a monolingual setting to know what word a child is aiming at, that is all the more difficult in a bilingual setting. My drawing on the right takes an example from Ronjat's son Louis, who said [pap] in reference to French 'patte' (animal's leg) and German 'Spatz' (literally, 'sparrow', but used as a term of endearment for Louis). It is possible that indeed 'patte' and 'Spatz' were the adult words that Louis was targeting, but often it will not be clear at all what words are being targeted.
>
> This makes it very difficult to study early phonological development in very young BFLA children. The question is until what age these difficulties exist. That will depend very much on individual children. Some speak quite clearly from the beginning, others not at all. But to give you an idea – in the study of 31 French–Dutch bilingual toddlers that I have been conducting with Dr Marc Bornstein we made phonetic transcriptions of video recordings of the children at age 20 months in interaction with their mothers. These transcripts were made by two to three bilingual transcribers who made the transcriptions separately and then discussed their transcripts with each other. Even with this labor-intensive procedure, 63% of the child utterances could not be assigned to a particular language (or to the category 'indeterminate' nor 'mixed').

Box 5.8(adv.)	Determining the target language of early words in BFLA continued

What Leopold wrote for Hildegard by age 21 months, namely 'The crude phonetic form of the child's words often precluded definite assignment to one language' (1970: 178), then, still holds true today.

[a] Although, perhaps, it ought to be, too; there is quite a lot of variation in how different adults speak, even in only one language (see also Khattab, 2002). Perhaps children are at first trying to talk like specific people in their environment, and try to adjust to individual differences between them? For a discussion of the importance of addressing variation in the input to both MFLA and BFLA children, see De Houwer, 2006.

What can we learn from studies of BFLA children's use of speech segments?

In Appendix E I list most of the studies that have looked at the production of speech segments in young BFLA children to date. Typically, the studies in Appendix E investigate phonetic inventories. Some of these studies talk about these sounds in terms of phones or phonetic shapes, others in terms of phonemes. Some studies discuss problems of interpretation, others do not. Some studies draw comparisons with monolingual children. Some of these find great resemblances for one particular language as produced by MFLA and BFLA children, others find differences.

The general picture of great variability and potentially great instability in the production of speech segments that is seen in MFLA is found in BFLA infants as well. In addition, as for MFLA children, BFLA's phonetic–phonological development is gradual, and by no means completed by age three or four.

At this point, it is not clear whether the specific early phonetic inventories that young BFLA children use are language specific for each language separately or not, and to what extent there might be an influence by one language on another. The theoretical and methodological hurdles are great and the number of studies addressing them small.[16]

I would like to add here that in all my reading of the literature on BFLA in areas other than specifically phonology, I have never encountered reports of BFLA children over the age of three sounding systematically 'funny' in terms of their sound productions. In a study that focused on an acoustic analysis of voice onset time (explained further below in the section 'Perfecting their skills'), Johnson and Wilson (2002: 284) report that their two English–Japanese subjects 'sounded to adults like native speakers of each of their two languages' (Johnson and Wilson are reporting on a girl aged 2;10 and her older sister aged 4;11).

Also in my own published and unpublished recordings of BFLA children over the age of three learning either English and Dutch or Dutch and French, I have never had the impression that children were systematically misusing speech segments from one language in the other, or were sounding very different in each language from Dutch and English monolingual children.[17] At the same time, the data set I have (which goes up to age five) does still show a general immaturity in comparison with adult speech. Of course, what I'm writing here is impressionistic and needs substantiation by systematic investigation.

However, there is research evidence that my impression here is most likely not all that far off the mark. In a series of auditory and acoustic studies of the same three English–Arabic-speaking children, including a five-year-old (and two older children), little evidence was found for interactions between the two languages. In addition, most of the aspects investigated in each language were also found in age-matched monolingual children in both languages. Yet some aspects of finer phonetic detail were not yet acquired by the age of ten (the findings are summarized in Khattab, 2006). The children studied by Khattab regularly started to participate in interactions with the L2, English, at age six months, even though they might have overheard English before.

According to the definition in this book, these English–Arabic-learning children were, strictly speaking, not acquiring two languages from birth. Yet the fact that even these very early ESLA children seemed to develop two separate segmental phonologies, at least by the age of five, suggests that BFLA children can do so as well.

A final but important point here is that few studies take into account the fact that some of children's main models in a particular language may be less typically 'monolingual' than others (see also Khattab, 2002, 2006). Since small children tend to spend a lot of time with the same few speakers, there is a large potential effect of the specific ways in which these speakers talk on children's attempts to say words. A recent study of how Spanish–Catalan children speak Catalan shows influence from the different kinds of Catalan they hear (Cortés et al., 2008). Especially if there is only one person who is the model for a particular language (as is common in BFLA – see Chapter 3), it is important to know just how that person speaks in order to find explanations for children's speech patterns.

A phenomenon that makes it particularly difficult to investigate infants' and toddlers' early words, including the sounds in these words, is their common use of **phonological processes**. In the next section, I explain what these are.

Phonological processes

Often the particular forms that infants use to express words are very far removed from the adult forms. Yet there are particular patterns that we as adults can see when we compare what children say with the adult words that they are attempting to say, such as 'bee' instead of 'Bambi' (where the first syllable is deleted), or 'appe' instead of 'apple' (where the last sound, /l/, is deleted).

In addition to deletion patterns, there may also be particular substitution patterns, such as 'stopping', which involves the saying of stop consonants (pronounced with a full closure of the mouth, as in [t] or [k]) instead of fricatives (pronounced with partial closure of the mouth, as in [f] or [z]).

Such deletion and substitution patterns are called phonological processes. BFLA children make use of these, as do monolingual children (see, e.g. De Houwer & Gillis, 1998: 10–22). I give a few examples from BFLA children in Box 5.9.

> **Box 5.9** Examples of phonological processes in BFLA children
>
> *Deletion patterns*
>
> - At age 10 months, Dutch–English Susan said Dutch [pʰu] for the word 'poes' (pussycat), so she deleted the final fricative.
> - At age 2 years, French–German Louis said French 'quai' (quay) and German 'Kuh' (cow) without the initial /k/.
> - At age 2;1, German–English Hannah said German 'pobieren' instead of 'probieren' (try), so she left out the 'r' after the 'p'. She said 'lease' instead of 'please' in English, so she left out the initial 'p'.
> - At age 2;5, German-English Laura said English 'tee' instead of 'tree', so she left out the 'r'. Children often simplify clusters this way. Clusters are groups of consonants or consist of a combination of a consonant (or consonants) and an approximant (that's a speech segment somewhere in between a vowel and a consonant).
>
> *Substitution patterns*
>
> - At age 12 months, Dutch–English Susan said [pʰuʃ] for the Dutch word 'poes' ('cat'), so she palatalized the final fricative.
> - At age 2;3, French–English Tom said French [mus] when he meant to say French 'mouche' (fly), so he replaced final /ʃ/ with [s].
> - At age 2;3, French–English Tom said something like 'pock' when he meant to say English 'cup', so he mixed up the two consonants, and substituted initial /p/ for /k/, and final /k/ for /p/.
> - At age 2;5, German–English Laura said German 'babut' instead of 'kaput', so she pronounced the velar /k/ much more in front of the mouth (by using the bilabial [b]), and at the same time she made two sounds voiced rather than voiceless ([b] instead of /p/, and in addition to the fronting of /k/, its voicing).
> - At age 3;6, German–English Adam said German 'kross' instead of 'gross' (big), so he pronounced the first, voiced sound of 'gross' as voiceless.
> - At age 3;6, German–English Adam said English 'heaby' instead of 'heavy', so he used a 'stopping' procedure, whereby he replaced a fricative with a stop consonant.
>
> *The examples for Susan are from my unpublished diary notes; the examples for Louis are from Ronjat, 1913; the examples for Tom are from Brulard & Carr, 2003; the examples for Hannah, Laura and Adam are from Gut, 2000a, Chapter 7*

The examples in Box 5.9 show that BFLA children use phonological processes in words from both their languages. Ronjat (1913: 18) notes that similar simplification processes are used in both the French and German words produced by his son Louis. Louis often left out the /r/ from adult clusters with a consonant such as /rp/ and /rm/ and said /j/ instead of /l/. He did this regardless of language.

The use of phonological processes is one explanation for why children may vary a lot in how they attempt to say a particular word from one time to the next (for Catalan examples of the resulting similar sounding words with different meanings – homonyms – in a Spanish–Catalan child, see Lléo, 1990).

The fact that children may say [p] instead of /t/, for instance, shows that their production of phones is not necessarily related to adult-like phonemes (in Dutch, for instance, the phoneme /t/ cannot be realized by [p]). Yet children's substitution patterns are not quite

> random. Children tend to replace particular kinds of sounds by specific other kinds of sounds. This shows that infants and toddlers are already making some kind of categorization in the sounds they produce.

Are phonological processes language specific?

Whether young BFLA children use phonological processes in language-specific ways is not certain. Gut (2000a: 88) reports **devoicing** of word-final consonants in English words in two and a half-year-old German–English Laura (she said 'lif' instead of 'live', for instance – so instead of saying a voiced consonant /v/, Laura said a voiceless, or devoiced, [f]). It isn't clear whether this happened under the influence of German, which normally devoices all final consonants.

Brulard and Carr (2003) present evidence that French–English Tom used a specific substitution pattern, **consonant harmony**, only for English words and not for French ones. For instance, he said 'pub' instead of 'tub'. Tom also used **reduplication** patterns only for French words but not for English ones. On the whole, Tom avoided saying fricatives in word-initial position and 't's at the ends of words. Tom was studied until the age of two and a half.

In his synthesis of Leopold's (1970) data on English–German Hildegard, Ingram (1989: 378) finds that the phonological processes used in Hildegard's English words were quite similar to those used by other American English-learning but monolingual children, except that Hildegard said [w] instead of word-initial /f/. This is a substitution pattern that has not been documented for other English-speaking toddlers, and this leads Ingram to suggest that maybe here we see an influence from the fact that Hildegard was also learning German.

At present, there have not been enough studies in BFLA focusing on phonological processes to know whether there is systematic influence from one language on the other. Again, the methodological hurdles here are quite formidable.

Do children continue to use phonological processes?

As they get a bit older, children continue to use phonological processes, but much less frequently than before (e.g. De Houwer & Gillis, 1998: 20–21 for MFLA). By age five or six, children may still use some of them, though (see Gut, 2000a, for examples for BFLA).

The use of phonological processes greatly impedes children's understandability. A rare experiment that tapped adult listeners' ability to understand recorded words said by Spanish and English monolingual and English–Spanish bilingual children between the ages of 24 and 28 months has shown that many of these words, which were played to the adults without any context, were very difficult, if not impossible to understand.[18] They simply lacked sufficient language-specific phonetic elements (Navarro *et al.*, 1998; see also Navarro *et al.*, 2005). Yet the children who supplied the words were thought of as developing well in their language(s) by the people who knew them.

As children use phonological processes less frequently, they start to sound more and more adult-like. Depending on which language is involved, children may have learned to correctly realize most of the phonemes in their input language(s) by the time they are four years of age. With the increased stability in the phonetic shapes of their words, it becomes increasingly possible to see systematicity in their use of speech sounds and to analyze them in terms of adult, language-specific categories.

A final point here is that the same BFLA children may show evidence of language-specific developments for one area of sound production, such as phonological processes controlling the production of segments, and of possible transfer in another area, such as word stress patterns, as found in French–English Tom (Brulard & Carr, 2003). This is possible because there is not necessarily a connection between the learning of stress patterns and segmental learning (Brulard & Carr, 2003; Gut, 2000a). Once again, though, detailed investigations of the input should be carried out to rule out the possibility that, in fact, children are showing rather direct effects of the perhaps less-than-normative input instead of creating transfer patterns that are not supported by their input models (see also Khattab, 2002, 2006).

Perfecting their skills

Once children are about four years old, they know how to say most of the phonemes in their language. However, some sounds are quite difficult to pronounce. A typical example is /r/. There are very many different ways in which 'r's are pronounced in different languages.[19] In Dutch, children often say [j] or [l] instead of /r/, because the rolled variety of /r/ pronounced with the tongue close to the teeth is articulatorily quite difficult. In Box 5.10, I discuss one BFLA child's learning of /r/.

Box 5.10 Learning to say the right /r/ in BFLA
Susan heard American English and Flemish Dutch from birth. The 'r's she heard in English and Dutch are very different: mostly, she heard the alveolar approximant in English, and an alveolar trill in Dutch.
Susan's English contained English 'r's from early on that sounded fairly adult-like. But in Dutch, Susan never pronounced any 'r's until the age of three. Until then, she replaced Dutch 'r's by [j], and talked about her favorite color, 'roos' (pink) as [jo:s].
When she was three years old, she met a Dutch-speaking girl who pronounced Dutch 'r's in a fashion that is also possible in Dutch (but that Susan had never heard before), namely as a voiced uvular fricative (sounds a bit like gurgling). The day after Susan met this girl, all her substitutions by [j] disappeared, and she now used the voiced uvular fricative herself (but only in Dutch, never in English). Apparently, this uvular sound was easy to say.
Given that Susan was now the only one in the family to use a uvular 'r', and that I didn't like her to use this uvular 'r' (a question of identity!), I took the opprtunity when I was in the United States with Susan at age five to try if I could get her to say the much harder alveolar trilled 'r'. Susan was happy to oblige, and after a half hour practice session in the car, she managed to say the trilled 'r' and has said it ever since.
In Susan's case, there was no influence whatsoever from one language on the other.
(Example based on my notes regarding my daughter Susan's language development.)

Similarly, Spanish 'r's are not easy, either. To sound really Spanish, you have to be able to say at least two kinds of /r/, a shorter one and one that's quite long in duration. They are both rolled and very different from English /r/. Using the Spanish version in English and the other way round gives rise to accented speech (Pearson & Navarro, 1996). In a rare study on a BFLA child's pronunciation of 'r's, González-Bueno (2005) describes how a four-year-old Spanish–English bilingual progressively pronounces Spanish 'r's in a more and more Spanish-like fashion (see also one of the study activities below).[20]

In contrast, for German and French, Ronjat (1913: 49) claims that his son Louis already pronounced 'r's correctly in all word positions at the age of 2;9.

Most of the studies of sound production in BFLA reviewed in this chapter have relied on transcriptions of speech. The studies by Gut (2000a, 2000b) and Cortés *et al.* (2008) also include acoustic measures of the speech signal as produced by bilingual children. One acoustic measure that has been of specific interest is that of **voice onset time**.

Voice onset time (VOT) refers to the time period between the release of air just after the production of a stop consonant (e.g. [b], [t] or [k]) and the moment that the vocal cords start to vibrate. It can also be the other way round: in languages like Spanish, the vocal cords start to vibrate *before* the air release that occurs in the production of a stop consonant. The vocal cords start to vibrate at different times for different sounds, and all this differs from language to language.

Differences in VOT will determine whether people hear a consonant as voiced or voiceless. It's important, then, to be able to control the VOT mechanism in order to sound right in a language. In Box 5.11(adv.) I list the small number of studies that have investigated the use of VOT in BFLA children's two languages.

Box 5.11(adv.) Acoustic studies of the use of VOT in BFLA children

Studies are ordered according to the ages of the children studied

Child	Age[a]	Languages[b]	Focus	Source
Manuela	1;7–2;3	English–Spanish	word-initial stops	Deuchar & Clark, 1996; Deuchar & Quay, 2000: 34–45
Robert	2;0–2;4	German–Spanish	word-initial stops	Kehoe *et al.*, 2004
Simon	2;0–2;6	German–Spanish	word-initial stops	Kehoe *et al.*, 2004
Nils	2;0–2;6	German–Spanish	word-initial stops	Kehoe *et al.*, 2004
Stefan	2;3–3;0	German–Spanish	word-initial stops	Kehoe *et al.*, 2004
Hinata	2;10–3;0	English–Japanese	stops	Johnson & Wilson, 2002
Nanami[c]	4;8–4;11	English–Japanese	stops	Johnson & Wilson, 2002

[a] Ages were rounded off to the nearest month.
[b] The language used in the greater community is listed first.
[c] Nanami is Hinata's older sister.

Again, these studies show a large degree of variability between the seven children studied so far. Some children show tendencies towards language-specific, adult VOT characteristics, while others do less so. It is too early for generalizations. An important consideration in the studies by Deuchar and Clark (1996) and Johnson and Wilson (2002) is that the adult parent models were analyzed as well (only for Spanish in the first, both for English and Japanese in the second), even though comparisons with their children's data are inconclusive. As Kehoe *et al.* (2004: 85) write, 'The voicing systems of young bilingual children are fragile and subject to change'. Khattab's (2006) study of the acquisition of VOT in three older very early ESLA children (see previously) shows that it may take quite a long time for children to fully control the VOT characteristics of their input languages.

In conclusion

This chapter has taken you around a great many intriguing aspects of the very earliest linguistic developments in young BFLA children. I have had to spend quite a lot of time explaining some of the complexities of the issues involved, only to then perhaps disappoint you by showing that methodologically, things are quite difficult, and there just have not been many studies that could really tell us much about the developing relationship between the sound patterns of BFLA infants' languages-in-acquisition.

However, the fact that there has been a lot of recent interest in studying early bilingual speech perception as well as production gives rise to the hope that more studies will be carried out in these exciting areas of research.

The very fact that there is so much variation between infants, with some apparently tracking each of their input languages quite closely, and others less so, is intriguing. Is this because the specific pair of languages being learned makes it somehow easier to do so? Is it because some speakers in children's environments speak more clearly than others? Clarity of maternal speech to young infants, after all, has been found to be quite important in explaining why some children perform better at a speech perception task than others (Liu *et al.*, 2003). There are many more possible reasons to consider.

It is important that the variation within BFLA children themselves is addressed. Yes, of course it is possible to compare children with monolinguals. But what does that really teach us about the bilingual acquisition process? In essence, not much. Bilingual infants are not the sum of two monolinguals in one. Monolingual acquisition is not the 'standard' for BFLA.

Rather, explanations for developmental patterns in BFLA should first and foremost take into account the very specific input setting of BFLA children. Furthermore, they should address the possibility that early developments could be related to quite local influences: the way mommy says a particular word, the way daddy always exaggerates the final stress on particular words.

In a bilingual setting, such local influences can be quite important, since often, only one or two speakers are the models for a particular language. This is quite different from most monolingual input settings. The chances are that if children hear only one person speak a language, they will model their own attempts at that language very closely on that person's speech patterns. If they hear a language spoken by three or more people, they will perhaps take different routes.

The development of phonology in young children is very much linked to the acquisition of word forms. Both are of major importance in ensuring that BFLA children become able to speak in sufficiently different ways so that they can successfully express meanings in two languages. This leads us into the next chapter on lexical development.

Notes

1. This can create a lot of problems in intercultural communication if second language learners stick to the intonation patterns of their first language.
2. I can here give only a highly simplified discussion. An excellent recent paper that discusses the complex link between intonation contours and their meanings in infant-directed speech, and how and when infants learn to discriminate between various types of intonation contours is that by Spence and Moore (2003).
3. That is, on top of the individually different ways in which people speak. A very important aspect of learning to distinguish between important sounds is making abstraction of the individual variation there is between speakers of the same language. BFLA children must in addition learn to do this for two different languages.
4. The fact that a recent overview of phonological development does not discuss the acquisition of different intonation patterns illustrates the point (Stoel-Gammon & Vogel Sosa, 2007).
5. The data for the other two children, Hannah and Adam, show that they use similar pitch contours in German and English (appropriate for each).
6. De Boysson-Bardies *et al.* (1984) have earlier suggested that adults are able to recognize babbling as being from a familiar or non-familiar language based on the intonation patterns present in longer babbling sequences.
7. More recent research has shown that infants can imitate adult vowels between the ages of two and four months (Kuhl & Meltzoff, 1996), but Ronjat was most likely referring to words and sentences in fluent speech.
8. Except, again, that Cruz-Ferreira points out the use of language-specific intonation contours in babbling, an issue that neither Ronjat nor Leopold talk about.
9. See Oller (2000: 194ff.) for a particularly insightful discussion of the problems that both parents and researchers meet up with when they try to interpret one-year-olds' apparent attempts at words.
10. Loosely translated as: 'bilingualism didn't seem to have any specific effect on the characteristics of babbling or on the appearance of the first imitations'.

11. Lléo *et al.* (2007) note that they analyzed the rhythmic properties of the input data of one of the mothers of their three bilingual subjects.

12. Comparisons of three Dutch-speaking mothers and their toddlers show that, on the whole, the proportions with which the toddlers use different word stress patterns correlates with the proportions used by their mothers. The mothers used different stress patterns in quite different proportions (De Houwer & Gillis, 1998: 76–77).

13. There is evidence that children's own early sound productions can, in turn, have an effect on their speech perception, which might aid children in their word learning (Vihman & Nakai, 2003).

14. They also have to learn to control their vocal cords so that they can produce voiced and voiceless consonants.

15. Another tactic could be silence. Some children don't want to make fools of themselves and prefer to wait a little longer until they think they can say something correctly (see also Schnitzer & Krasinski, 1996: 562). Note that many children do not try the 'long utterance' approach but go straight to attempting words.

16. There are rather more studies on phonological development in children who first started to hear one language, and after some time a second one. The recent volume edited by Hua and Dodd (2006) contains a number of these.

17. I cannot compare with French monolingual children, since I have so far too little experience with that population.

18. Most of the bilingual children here heard two languages from birth, though not all (it isn't clear how many did not).

19. That is, if they have an /r/ phoneme at all. Not all languages do.

20. A study of the pronunciation or 'r's in Welsh and English by bilingual children aged two and a half to five years of age shows just how difficult trilled 'r's are, also for this population (Ball *et al.*, 2001). Nothing is said about when the children in this study started hearing Welsh and English, though, so it is not sure that the study concerns BFLA.

Summary box

- Bilingual infants can discriminate various aspects of their two languages at an early age. Their early vocal development, including babbling, resembles that of children acquiring just a single language.
- Both MFLA and BFLA children's early sound production shows great interindividual variability.
- So far, it is not clear to what extent word stress patterns, patterns of syllable structure and the use of speech segments in young BFLA children reflect each of their input languages. Yet there are BFLA children who, in spite of sounding generally immature, do not sound 'foreign' in either of their languages. BFLA children use the same sorts of phonological simplification processes as children acquiring just one language.
- Learning to use the sounds of two languages takes a long time, as it does in monolingual children.
- In trying to explain BFLA children's phonological development it is important to take into account the way the people who talk to them actually speak.

Suggestions for study activities

1. *Project*: Find a television station in a language you do not know. Find a program on it that looks as though it is a soap, fictional series or movie. Listen to a few conversations. Close your eyes and listen again. Can you figure out whether people are having an argument? Or whether they are complaining? Or trying to convince someone of a point? Or seduce them? I predict that you will be able to interpret at least some of what is going on, even if you do not know the language in question. Do this study activity with a friend in your class and discuss each other's interpretations.
2. *WEB*: Explore the website of the Infant Learning Project under the direction of Dr Melanie Spence at The University of Texas at Dallas (United States) via http://bbs.utdallas.edu/ilp/. Although this laboratory does not currently study bilingual infants, a visit to this website will teach you more about early child development and how researchers go about studying it.
3. *WEB*: Visit the website of the Vancouver infant studies lab under the direction of Dr Janet Werker and, in particular, the part of it on visual language discrimination in infancy at http://www.psych.ubc.ca/~jwlabmgr/SiteNew/Pictures.html. Look at the various pictures and films. In particular, see the example of silent French and English stimuli. How are they different? And can you spot the difference?
4. *WEB*: This is an activity that links up to the previous one. Get a friend who knows English or French to watch the two stimuli videos (but don't tell them that they are in fact from different languages – so you'll have to adjust your screen). Ask them whether what they saw was the same or not. Talk about the issues and explain to your friend what these videos are about.
5. *Project*: This is again an activity that links up with the one about the Vancouver website visit (number 3). Find a friend who speaks a language Y other than French or English. Film your friend reciting a few sentences in language Y without moving their head and with a neutral expression. Play that recording to a friend of yours who doesn't know language Y. Ask them whether they think they know what language was being spoken. Talk about the issues and explain to your friend what this is all about.
6. Think about what the infants' behavior in Box 5.5 might mean for later language choice as discussed in Chapter 4.
7. *WEB*: For a unique example of early interaction between a father and a three-month-old BFLA child that has been transcribed in terms of intonation patterns, look at the file **mg10108.cha** in the MCF corpus on CHILDES (downloading this corpus is part of the study activity; for tips on how to access the bilingual data in CHILDES, see Chapter 3). I know that you will not understand what the codes are for the intonational patterns (although for a better understanding you could read the information about the MCF corpus in the Childes Database Manual), but this example will give you some idea of the length of the infant's vocalizations, even at this young age. It will also show you the typical way in which adults interact with children of this age. Finally, the example also shows the magnitude of the work involved in transcribing intonation patterns. (advanced)
8. *WEB*: Listen to especially the last bit of babbling on the example of precanonical speech at a website at Purdue University (United States) under the direction of Dr David Ertmer at http://news.uns.purdue.edu/audio/Precanonical.mp3 and focus on its melody. Play it a few times. Can you mimic what the baby is doing?
9. *WEB*: Go to the button 'Basic Canonical Syllables' at http://www.vocaldevelopment.com/ and listen to all the examples. Do these sounds sound like language to you? Why (not)? (This website was also developed by Dr Ertmer.)

Suggestions for study activities continued

10. Draw up the phoneme inventories for two languages that you are very familiar with. Determine which of the phonemes are overlapping or partially overlapping in how they are actually pronounced and which are not. Can you find potential problem spots for children acquiring these two languages from birth? Think of two sounds that are different phonemes in one language but that are 'covered' by just a single phoneme in the other, or look for cases where the phonetic realizations of certain phonemes are partly overlapping. And what about sounds that only exist in the one language and not in the other? (advanced)

11. *Project*: Find a child around the age of one and a half that parents will allow you to go and play with for an hour or so. It is important that the language that the child hears is one you know well. Bring a small set of age-appropriate, interesting toys and a simple book (with attractive pictures). Play with the child but try to elicit as much speech from them as you can. This may be a difficult task in itself. While you play with the child, record what is going on. (For the purpose of this activity, an audio record suffices.) On the same day, play the tape and try to identify which words the child was trying to say. How many of the words can you *not* identify?

12. *Project*: This is the same activity as in number 11, except now you should try to find a BFLA child who is acquiring two languages that you know well. Now you will need two recording sessions, though (a half hour for each). For data collection, involve a friend who knows one of the languages well for one of the sessions. Do the other session yourself.

13. *Project*: Find a child around the age of one and a half that parents will allow you to go and play with for an hour or so. It is important that the language that the child hears is one you know well. Bring a small set of age-appropriate, interesting toys and a simple book (with attractive pictures). Play with the child but try to elicit as much speech from them as you can. This may be a difficult task in itself. While you play with the child, record what is going on. (For the purpose of this activity, an audio record suffices.) On the same day, transcribe the child's utterances phonetically. For each word form or word-like form that you have been able to transcribe, make a comparison with the adult phonological form. Can you identify any phonological processes? Do you see any systematicity in them? (advanced)

14. *Project*: This is the same activity as in number 13, except now you should try to find a BFLA child who is acquiring two languages that you know well. Now you will need two recording sessions, though (a half hour for each). For data collection, involve a friend who knows one of the languages well for one of the sessions. Do the other session yourself. Once you have transcribed the child utterances, try to answer the questions in the previous activity. In addition, can you detect any clear differences or similarities between how the child is sounding in both sessions? (advanced)

15. *WEB*: Listen to Alicia, a four-year-old Spanish–English bilingual girl, trying to say 'r's in isolated words in Spanish: http://soe.ku.edu/faculty/gonzalez/ArticulatoryEvolution.php. Notice just how different these 'r's are from English. You can also hear Alicia speak spontaneously in Spanish via http://soe.ku.edu/faculty/gonzalez/Sounds/Sounds5/cuento2.wav (website under the direction of Dr Manuela González-Bueno at the University of Kansas, United States of America).

Recommended reading (advanced)

You will find an overview of bilingual infants' speech perception and comprehension in Werker and Byers-Heinlein (2008). Another excellent overview, which also discusses speech perception in older bilinguals, is Sebastián-Gallés and Bosch (2005). The interested student should also read Fernald's (2006) chapter, which draws together some important theoretical and methodological caveats.

Two book chapters that discuss bilingual (and monolingual) infants' neurological responses to sounds and other speech stimuli are Conboy *et al.* (2008) and Thierry and Vihman (2008). Other relevant studies are those by Conboy and Mills (2006) and Vihman *et al.* (2007). These studies, however, do not limit themselves to infants with regular input to two languages from birth. In order to understand the complex specialized techniques used, you would do well to first read an introductory text such as the one by Männel (2008).

Chapters 5 and 6 in Cruz-Ferreira (2006) offer highly engaging discussions of three Portuguese–Swedish BFLA children's early phonological (and lexical) development. Students interested in early speech production (whether in mono- or bilinguals) can gain a good introduction to some of the important issues by reading the informative online review that Cruz-Ferreira wrote of Oller's (2000) important book at http://linguistlist.org/issues/11/11-1317.html.

Ingram (1989: 189–219) discusses the issues involved in early speech production and proposes a method for characterizing early phonological development. Johnson and Lancaster (1998), Johnson and Wilson (2002) and Deuchar and Quay (2000: 25–29) discuss the methodological and analytical difficulties involved in interpreting BFLA children's early phonological development.

Khattab (either 2002 or 2006) offers very useful discussions about the need to pay close attention to input variation in studies of phonological development.

6
Words in BFLA

The words that BFLA children hear — 193
   Words in one language, words in two languages — 193
   The number of words that BFLA children hear — 195
   How adults use words in the input — 197
Early bilingual word comprehension — 198
   Learning to understand words — 198
   How many words do BFLA children understand? — 200
   Helping themselves learn to understand more words — 201
Translation equivalents in comprehension — 202
The Mutual Exclusivity Bias in BFLA — 205
Early comprehension vocabularies: BFLA and MFLA compared — 206
Comprehension and production: two sides of the same coin? — 209
   Comprehension precedes production — 210
   Number of words understood or produced — 210
   Understanding and producing translation equivalents — 211
Words and meanings in early production — 212
   Proto-words — 212
   The meanings of the earliest words — 214
   What about grammatical categories? — 215
   Semantic processes — 216
Early bilingual word production — 217
   First words — 217
   The make-up of BFLA children's lexical production repertoires — 219
   Lexical gaps and adding new words — 221

Creating new words 222
Changes in word production repertoires 222

The rate of lexical development in bilingual production 223
Overall rates of change 223
Do both languages develop at the same rate? 224
Stability in word production 225

How many words do BFLA children produce? 226
Large differences between children 226
Children who say more words in one language also say more words in the other 227
The number of words that children say in each language at a given time can be quite different 227

The size of BFLA early production vocabularies compared to MFLA 228

Translation equivalents in production 230
The status of translation equivalents in early BFLA production 230
First occurrence 231
How many TEs do young BFLA children produce and what is their rate of development? 233
The kinds of meanings expressed in TEs 234
Young translators? 234
A special status for TEs? 236

What drives the production of TEs, or what hinders it? 236
Similar sounding TEs 236
TEs that are quite distinct in form 237
Form similarity as a basis for TE learning? 237

Translation equivalents and language choice 238

In conclusion 241
BFLA input can speed up the rate of word learning 241
Two separate lexical 'systems'? 242
Bilingual lexical development beyond the toddler years 242
Fostering lexical development in two languages 243

Summary box 246
Suggestions for study activities 247
Recommended reading 248

'Words are indispensable. Without words, speakers are tongue-tied. Without them, they can't exemplify syntactic patterns, morphological structure, or even the sound patterns of their language. Words, in short, offer the primary linguistic means for conveying meaning.'

Clark, 1995: 393

The words that BFLA children hear

Words in one language, words in two languages

By definition, BFLA children hear words in two languages. They must learn to understand the words that people say to them, in whatever language they are. Otherwise, they will have trouble making sense of the world around them.

At the beginning, BFLA children's worlds are small. They typically live at home, and people talk to infants about food, drink, going to sleep, going for a walk, toys, the people in infants' environments, and not a whole lot more.

The chances are that if people talk about these fairly basic things to a child in two languages, some of the words will be translations of each other. Such words are commonly called 'translation equivalents'. Translation equivalents (or TEs) are cross-language synonyms. It is true, total synonyms do not really exist (Clark, 1993), but there are many words that in their normal, everyday meaning are quite acceptable translations of each other, such as French 'eau' and English 'water'. There may be French 'eaux' (waters) that simply have no equivalent in English, such as some well-known commercial brands, but if at home someone talks about 'eau' then this is really quite the same as talking about 'water'. I discuss the issue a bit further in Box 6.1.

In a normal bilingual household, then, you would expect children to hear words and phrases from both languages that refer to the same thing. When daddy says: 'Time to go to sleep!' and mommy says: 'Tijd om te gaan slapen!' (Dutch; time-to-to-go-sleep), you have phrases (and words) from two languages that mean the same thing. For the child, regardless of whether he hears 'Time to go to sleep!' or 'Tijd om te gaan slapen!', the effect will be the same: being scooped up and carried to bed. Or when mommy asks 'Noch ein Keks?' (German; another-a-cookie) and daddy comments 'encore un biscuit!' (French; another-a-cookie), again there are different words in each language that mean the same for the speakers in that particular context. Such words are called **translation equivalents** (see also Box 6.1).

Remember, though, that this is the adult view. To what extent children themselves know that 'sleep' and 'slapen' as in the example above are each other's translations is not clear.[1] Certainly, for their comprehension or production of 'sleep' and 'slapen' it is not necessary that they know that the one is a translation of the other (see also Leopold, 1970: 179). I focus in quite some detail on children's comprehension and production of translation equivalents throughout this chapter.

> **Box 6.1** Two words for the same thing in young BFLA children's worlds
>
> A Dutch–English BFLA child may hear the word 'fles' (bottle) in Dutch and the word 'bottle' in English. Both words will be used in speech adressed to the child (and overheard speech as well, maybe) to refer to a particular kind of bottle that children typically drink out of when they are little: a fairly short plastic drinking bottle with a nipple.
>
> Are 'fles' and 'bottle' really, truly completely equivalent across Dutch and English? Probably not. 'Bottle' can be a noun and a verb in English. The English verb 'bottle' means to put a liquid, like wine, in a bottle (Dutch uses the verb 'bottelen' for this). Dutch also has a verb that uses 'fles', but just the stem 'fles' as a verb is, I think, never used. Students sometimes say: 'Ik ben geflest' (I-am-bottled), so 'fles' is part of a past participle. That doesn't mean they were put in a bottle, though – it means they failed their exams.
>
> Let's take a look at the nouns 'fles' and 'bottle'. Pretty much the same sorts of containers for liquids can be called 'fles' and 'bottle' interchangeably in Dutch and English. When it comes to hot water bottles, though, Dutch no longer uses the term 'fles', but reverts to 'kruik', in this case, 'warmwaterkruik' (hot water bottle). And 'fles' in Dutch can also be used to refer to a particular way of making knots. I don't believe that 'bottle' has that use in English.
>
> The question is: how is all this of interest to a baby? If a baby only hears Dutch 'fles' and English 'bottle' in reference to that wonderful object with good tasting liquid in it, then for all intents and purposes 'fles' and 'bottle' are equivalent to that baby. In this particular context, 'fles' is an excellent translation for 'bottle', and the other way round: for an adult, they are what we call translation equivalents.

A special subgrouping of translation equivalents that children hear consists of a set of words that not only mean pretty much the same but that also sound pretty much the same. This set will be fairly large when children hear two languages that are very closely related on the lexical level, and much smaller for historically much less related languages such as Mandarin and English. Words that mean and sound pretty much the same across languages are commonly called **cognates**.

The similarity between cognates may be so great that you can't tell which language a particular word is – the word 'works' in both languages. Sometimes, the words sound almost identical, but not quite, like German 'Bett' and English 'bed' (example from Schelletter, 2002), or the first Italian, now international word 'pizza' – it can receive a slightly different pronunciation depending on which language a speaker is used to. Cognates are in fact neutral as to which language they are from – that is, compared to the other language a child is hearing (German 'Bett' stops being a cognate once you compare it to French 'lit' – then the two words are simply translation equivalents).

BFLA children will most likely hear many words from both their input languages that refer to the same thing. That's as if one and the same thing had two different labels. BFLA children will also hear labels for things in one language only.

There may be words that only mommy or only daddy says. Mommy may never play with the toy truck and so may not need to talk about it. And daddy may not be much involved with dressing the children and so doesn't talk about their clothes with them. In a bilingual setting, this may lead to a kind of language specialization for some topics.

You don't get this language specialization in a monolingual situation, even though different speakers may talk about different things. For instance, if it is daddy who usually takes the kids to the zoo without mommy there, daddy will be the one naming the animals. If mommy doesn't really discuss animals, she will not be teaching children the words for them. But MFLA children will still know the words in their one language, even though they heard them from only one person.

In contrast, if the one person who talks to them about animals speaks French and no one else talks to them about animals, children who hear French and German won't learn to understand or say any names for animals in German. Similarly, French–English Caroline only said English 'cookie' and not French 'biscuit', simply because she had never heard the word French word for 'cookie' (Celce-Murcia, 1978).

Influence of the input on the learning of translation equivalents is not limited to such local effects that refer to specific words. David and Li (2008) have shown that French–English BFLA children's own production of translation equivalents is correlated with changes in the proportion of exposure to each input language (see also Lanvers, 1999 for an English–German child and Mikes, 1990 for a trilingual child growing up with Hungarian, Serbocroatian and German). Increased exposure in one language relative to the other may give children more of a chance to get to know members of translation equivalents which until then were absent from the input.

In summary, the words that BFLA children hear are divided between two languages. Some of the words that young children hear in Language A will express things that they hear in Language Alpha as well. They may also hear some things discussed only in one language.

The number of words that BFLA children hear

Children experience vastly different 'wordscapes'. Some children hear a lot of words, others much fewer. A BFLA child might hear a lot of words in one language but far fewer in the other one. Alternatively, the input could be quite balanced in terms of the number of words that children hear in each language.

As I explained in Chapter 4, the number of words that children hear will have an effect on the number of words they learn to produce themselves; at least, this has been established for English (Hart & Risley, 1995).

For BFLA, we do not know as yet what the effect is of the number of words that children hear. We need group studies of BFLA children growing up in similar circumstances who heard different numbers of words in each of their languages to really address the important issue of the influence of the number of words that BFLA children hear on their own word production.

However, there is some evidence that input as a whole (so not measured in the number of words that BFLA children hear) can have an effect on word learning.

Ronjat (1913: 7) notes that in the second year of life, his son Louis produced many more words in German than in French. Ronjat attributes this to the fact that Louis heard German much more frequently than French. After his second birthday, Louis no longer displayed a big difference between his two languages as regards the number of words he said in each (Ronjat, 1913: 8). This followed a great increase in his French input, and continued large input in German.

Between the ages of 1;3 and 2, Leopold's (1970) Hildegard produced many more English than German words. This may be related to the fact that in the course of her second year, Hildegard heard much more English than German and interacted more frequently with English speakers than with her father, who at that time was her sole source of input in German. However, this had not been the case when Hildegard was younger, and as you can see from Box 6.2, this had quite an effect.

Box 6.2 Input and word knowledge: an early example

In the following table, I set out Leopold's Hildegard's input environment between birth and the age of one and a half years. In relation to that, I outline some basic aspects of Hildegard's early word comprehension and production (source: Leopold, 1970).

Age	Input environment	(Word) comprehension	Word production
Birth–0;11	USA: E from mother, servants and relatives; G from father [a]	• 0;6: understood her own name • 0;8: comprehension of several E words • after 0;8: comprehension of directions in both languages	• 0;8: first proto-word • 0;10: first 'real' word: E 'pretty' • a few more E words • a few G words
0;11–1;2	Germany: G only (including from mother)	• 1;1: understanding of a direction in G but not in E [b] • 1;2: no more understanding of E	• no more E words except for 'pretty' • several G words
1;2–1;6	USA: E from mother, servants and relatives; G from father and occasionally mother	• it took 13 days in the USA for her to start understanding some E again • G understanding still much superior • so much so that at 1;5, H did not understand long E explanations [c]	• 1;3: addition of a few new G and E words • 1;4: increased production of new E words

E = English; G = German

[a] in talking to each other, the parents each spoke their own language.

[b] 'At the end of 1;0 it was observed that, for the first time, a direction was understood and obeyed in German, but not in English. When she was asked, "Kannst du allein stehen?" she would delightedly demonstrate her new prowess of standing up without holding on. Her mother tried the same question in English, but the child did not react' (Leopold, 1970: 174) (the German question was: can you stand on your own?).

[c] 'Later in the month, she understood familiar commands in English and in German; but in many cases, especially for longer explanations, her mother, who does not speak German with ease, still felt impelled to resort to German' (Leopold, 1970: 175).

More recently, it was found that the proportion of the estimated time that children spend in the presence of speakers of both languages can, in many cases, explain why a particular child said more words in Language A than in Language Alpha (David & Li, 2008; Pearson *et al.*, 1997; see also Vila, 1984[2]). The most convincing evidence to date for the importance of input in early word learning comes from a study by Marchman *et al.* (2004: 217) that found a strong correlation between the relative amount of exposure to each language and a large group of English–Spanish BFLA children.[3]

Patterson (2002) found that the more children between 21 and 27 months old were read aloud to in Spanish, the more words they were able to say in Spanish. The same was true for English. These effects were significant even when children's overall degree of exposure to each language was controlled for.[4] Indeed, book reading can be of particular importance to BFLA children's word learning (see also Cruz-Ferreira, 2006: 182–184).

How adults use words in the input

Children hear words in the input just by virtue of the fact that adults talk to children by using words. In addition, however, adults will often explain what specific words mean, or they will contrast one particular word with another, by saying things like 'no, that's not a **red** ball, that's an **orange** one'. That way, adults can help children in their construction of a lexicon (Elbers & van Loon-Vervoorn, 1998). In a bilingual setting, adults will often tell children what the translation equivalent of a word in Language A is in Language Alpha. They may do this by saying the words from each language one after the other, as shown in Box 6.3 (as I discuss later, children may also ask for the words in the other language).

Box 6.3 Learning to produce translation equivalents from hearing them side-by-side

Jessie lives in Japan and heard Japanese and English from birth. We meet up with him at the age of 1;11, when he is talking to his English-speaking father, who is also fluent in Japanese.

Jessie says	Jessie's father says	Context
kagi kagi (twice 'key' in Japanese)		looking at a picture of a key
	that's a key yah, **kagi** key	
kagi		looking at the picture card with the key on it and holding it
	key	commenting on the card
key		looks at the picture of the key and holds it in front of him
kagi		puts the picture card in a box
	yah, key	Jessie gets up to get something else while his father comments
kagi key		Jessie picks up the card and looks at it again

Adapted from Wanner, 1999: 49

Another example of an adult teaching a child the name of a thing in the other language is shown in Box 6.4. Here, the adult just mentions one word in Language A that is a translation of a word the child had said in Language Alpha.

> **Box 6.4** Adult providing a translation equivalent
>
> German–Italian Jan is talking to a German–Italian bilingual investigator who speaks Italian with him. At age 3;8, Jan says a mixed utterance, with an article in Italian and a noun in German: 'un gespenster' (a ghost; but note that it should be 'Gespenst'). The investigator responds in Italian: 'un fantasma dici?' (a ghost you mean?). In this utterance, she told Jan the Italian word for 'ghost'. Jan confirms in Italian: 'sí un fantasma' (that's right, a ghost).
>
> Adapted from Cantone, 2007: 105

Adults will often ask children for the words for things, even though adults know the words very well themselves. Children are usually happy to respond to these test questions. Such test questions help children solidify their word knowledge. In a bilingual setting, parents will often ask children what a word in Language A is in Language Alpha. They do this by asking questions such as 'what does mommy say for....?'.

The emphasis on words here doesn't mean that adults speak to children in single words. Adults may indeed address children in single word utterances, but more often, adults speak to young children in short sentences that are made up of words. As Leopold (1970: 162) noted, children 'may understand the meaning of an utterance as a whole without being as yet able to analyze it in its component parts'.

The next section discusses what we know about where it all starts: early word comprehension.

Early bilingual word comprehension

Learning to understand words

Word comprehension may start very early. The timing of its apparent beginning, though, is quite variable from child to child. The ages at which four BFLA children first responded to their names were four months (Karin), five months (Sofia), six months (Hildegard), and seven months (Mikael) (Cruz-Ferreira, 2006: 146; Leopold, 1970). In MFLA, children also often first learn to respond to their names. I am here equating a particular response to a word with 'word comprehension', but to what extent the children really knew that their names referred to them is an open question.

It is in fact very difficult to say whether a young child understood a particular word or phrase, and how the child understood it (Tomasello & Mervis, 1994). Parents may say that a child understood a word if the child looked up in response to a word that was said to them, or if a child pointed to the appropriate entity in response to a 'where is X?' question. Whether such responses at first involve real word comprehension is debatable.

In this chapter, I will not try to define early word comprehension but will simply assume that if parents reported a child as understanding a particular word, they did, even though their level of comprehension was most likely not adult-like at all. Much of early word comprehension is very much bound to a specific context (as is early word production; see later). Children may give you their red ball at home if you ask them to give you the ball, but outside in the park, with another ball, they may not be able to oblige.

Thus, children may underextend in comprehension, i.e. they will understand a word with a smaller meaning than the adult one (see Chapter 2 earlier for an explanation of underextension). Children may also overextend in their early comprehension (Naigles & Gelman, 1995).

In BFLA, children have been reported to respond to simple commands starting at the age of seven months (Cruz-Ferreira, 2006: 146). Like MFLA children, they soon learn to respond appropriately to queries about where certain parts of their bodies are located (see Box 6.5 for an example). Such query–response patterns are part of frequent routines that parents and children engage in, often much to the delight of both parties.

> **Box 6.5** Responding to queries through actions
>
> - Portuguese–Swedish Karin is eight months old. Her mother asks her in Portuguese: 'onde é que está o pé?' (where is the foot?). In response, Karin grabs her own feet.
> - Portuguese–Swedish Mikael is eight months old. His mother asks him in Portuguese: 'onde é que está o relógio?' (where is the clock?). In response, Mikael points towards the clock on the wall.
>
> *Adapted from Cruz-Ferreira, 2006: 147*
>
> - English–German Hildegard is nine months old. When her mother asked her: 'where is the baby?' (referring to a picture of a child on the wall; Hildegard was sitting with her back to the picture), Hildegard would turn around in her high chair, look at the picture, and laugh with joy. The same effect was obtained with the German translated question 'wo ist das Baby?' (the word 'baby' is identical in both languages).
>
> *Adapted from Leopold, 1970*

Such routines gradually lose their stereotypical character, and children gradually become able to satisfy requests to get objects from another room (for BFLA, see Cruz-Ferreira, 2006: 147 and Leopold, 1970). They also become able to respond appropriately to queries about the identification of many more pictures and the location of many more objects (Cruz-Ferreira, 2006; Leopold, 1970). The children that Cruz-Ferreira studied recognized the names of colors by the time they were 17 or 19 months old (2006: 148). Color terms are quite difficult to learn to understand. You can see an example of this in Box 6.6.

From early on, then, BFLA children build up a comprehension vocabulary. So far, there have been no reports that in spite of continued and regular input in two languages, BFLA children understand only one language. The earlier example of Hildegard (see Box 6.2) does show that when input in a language is temporarily stopped, this can have quite an immediate effect on children's comprehension.

> **Box 6.6** Learning to understand color terms: an example from a BFLA child
>
> *María del Mar hears Spanish from her mother and Catalan from her father. She speaks both languages. A Catalan-speaking investigator is asking María del Mar (2;1) to identify which card out of a set of colored cards is which color.*
>
> | | |
> |---|---|
> | *INV: | ¿cuál es el vermell? |
> | gloss: | which one is the red one? |
> | *MAR: | este. (same word in Spanish and Catalan) |
> | gloss: | this one (while she incorrectly points at the green one) |
> | *INV: | ¡no! ¡este es el verd! es el verd. |
> | gloss: | no, that one is the green one. that's the green one. |
> | *INV: | ¿i el blau? |
> | gloss: | and the blue one? |
> | *MAR: | aqui. (same word in Spanish and Catalan) |
> | gloss: | here (while she correctly points at the blue one) |
> | *INV: | ¿i el verd? |
> | gloss: | and the green one? |
> | *MAR: | aqui. (same word in Spanish and Catalan) |
> | gloss: | here (while she correctly points at the green one) |
> | *INV: | ¿i el vermell? |
> | gloss: | and the red one? |
> | *MAR: | aqui. (same word in Spanish and Catalan) |
> | gloss: | here (while she incorrectly points at the blue one) |
> | *INV: | ¡no! (same word in Spanish and Catalan) |
> | gloss: | no! |
>
> Learning to understand color terms is not an easy task for children! (For an explanation, see Clark 2006.)
>
> *Adapted from Vila, 1984: 44*

How many words do BFLA children understand?

A very useful instrument for assessing children's lexical comprehension repertoires is the CDI (see Chapter 3). Just to refresh your memory: this instrument asks people who are familiar with a child to check off on a predetermined list which words a child understands. The CDI also asks about which words children understand as well as say. Scholars usually ignore the 'understand' portion of this and usually refer to the items checked as 'understands and says' as 'word production'. I discuss word production in later sections.

As I explained in Chapter 3, it is the Infant form of the CDI that asks about comprehension. The Infant form is meant for children between the ages of eight and 16 months. Data from monolingual infants acquiring different languages show that the size of children's comprehension lexicons can vary widely among children of the same age (Fenson et al., 1994, Zink & Lejaegere, 2002).

Box 6.7(adv.) shows that BFLA infants also vary widely in their word comprehension (De Houwer et al., 2007). Some 13-month-olds understand only 16 words in total, while others at the same age understand 564! That is quite a difference. Also within each language there is a wide variation between children in how many words they understand.

Box 6.7(adv.) Interindividual variation in BFLA children's comprehension vocabularies

The following results are based on analyses of CDI data for 31 children growing up with Dutch and French from birth. All children were 13 months of age.

13 months CDI	Mean	S.D.	Range
Comprehension Dutch	122.94	85.76	15–309
Comprehension French	109.68	75.99	1–304
Total comprehension	232.61	140.86	16–564

Adapted from De Houwer et al., 2007

For BFLA children you can compare their comprehension across languages. On the group level, De Houwer *et al.* (2007) found no statistically significant differences between the two languages. That means that in this particular group of infants, there was no 'advantage' for the one language compared to the other. Also, children who understood more in the one language also understood more in the other. Thus, BFLA children, like monolinguals, are just fast learners, or not so fast – and this doesn't depend on the specific languages they are acquiring.

The fact that BFLA children who understand more in Language A also understand more in Language Alpha does not imply that they understand the same number of words in each language. In fact, most of the infants studied by De Houwer *et al.* (2007) understood more words in one language than in the other. Only four of them understood equal numbers of words in each.

Helping themselves learn to understand more words

As children get older, they rapidly gain in word comprehension. They may experience a great sudden increase in the number of words they understand (Reznick & Goldfield, 1992).

They also start to be able to control their own learning in a sense. It's typical that children in the third year start asking about the names of things. They want to know what things are called. Sometimes that drives parents a little crazy, all these 'what's that?' questions. Young BFLA children also ask about the names of things. Leopold (1970) notes that this was driving English–German Hildegard's mother 'to exasperation' when Hildegard was two years old (Vol. IV, p. 15).

BFLA children will also ask what the names of things are in the other language (Leopold, 1970). A playful example of this can be found in Box 6.8.

Children may not just ask for the names of things verbally, but they may 'ask' by staring at the person they want to hear a word from, that is, from people who speak a particular language with them and not another (Cruz-Ferreira, 2006: 69). Such a strategy is perhaps unique to bilingual children.

> **Box 6.8** Asking the names of things in the other language
>
> *Mikael is one and a half years old. His mother, who speaks Portuguese to him, is helping him to put on his shoes. Just before that, Mikael asked her several questions about how his Swedish-speaking father says several words. It's a kind of game, and he loves it. Now he asks his mother how she says particular words.*
>
> | | |
> |---|---|
> | *MIK: | mamã sko? (mixed utterance; the first word is in Portuguese, and the second in Swedish) |
> | gloss: | mommy shoe? |
> | *MOT: | como é que a mamã diz sko?? (mixed utterance consisting of mostly Portuguese words, with the word 'sko' (shoe) in Swedish) |
> | gloss: | how does mommy say sko? |
> | *MOT: | então não sabe? (Portuguese) |
> | gloss: | don't you know? |
> | comment: | Mikael knows the Portuguese word for 'shoe' very well |
> | *MIK: | sapato!   (Portuguese) |
> | gloss: | shoe! |
>
> *Adapted from Cruz-Ferreira, 2006: 85; for another good example, see p. 79 in the same source*

Another aspect of comprehension that is unique to bilingual children is that they must learn to understand translation equivalents.

Translation equivalents in comprehension

Much of bilingual learning involves learning to understand two words from different languages for the same thing. Without such learning, it is hard to see how bilingual infants and toddlers could learn to make sense of their world.

BFLA children will need to sort out what each person is saying in whatever language comes their way. However, this process of trying to figure out what everything means need not involve any comparisons across languages. When mommy says 'schön!' (German; 'well done, nice') and daddy says 'muy bien!' (Spanish; 'well done, nice') when their daughter shows them a drawing, she may in each case understand that mommy and daddy liked it but she may not make the direct link between 'schön' and 'muy bien'. If children appear to understand words from each language that mean the same in adult day-to-day language use, we say they understand a pair of translation equivalents, or cross-language synonyms. This does not necessarily mean that children know that the one word is a synonym for the other.

Just as monolingual infants do not learn to understand all the words they hear at once, bilingual infants do not learn to understand all the translation equivalents in their input from the beginning. The process of learning to understand translation equivalents takes time. Yet, they can be learned from an early age. Porsché (1983: 87) mentions that his son, who heard German and English from birth, understood some cross-language synonyms 'sehr früh' (from very early on). Deuchar and Quay (2000: 55) also note that in the second year of life, English–Spanish Manuela could correctly point to specific parts of her body when she was asked to do so, and it didn't matter whether the request was made in English or Spanish.

The only quantitative data so far on the early comprehension of translation equivalents comes from the CDI study of the same 31 13-month-olds discussed in the previous section. De Houwer *et al.* (2006a) investigated the extent to which the Dutch and French words on the CDI understood by the 31 BFLA infants were translation equivalents. For an explanation of the procedure to follow that makes this possible, see Box 6.9(adv.).

Box 6.9(adv.)   Comparing different language versions of the CDI

(1) Get a version of the CDI for two different languages.
(2) Make a list of all the vocabulary items on each form. Make sure you indicate for each item what section it belongs to. (All lexical items on the CDI are organized into different sections; see Chapter 3.)
(3) Compare the two lists in terms of whether there are any identical items on them (i.e. cognates that are identical in sound and meaning). Make a separate list of these. The items on this list are the 'language neutral' words. Examples are French 'ouaf-ouaf' (Kern, 1999, for the European French CDI, henceforth F-CDI) and Dutch 'waf-waf' (Zink & Lejaegere, 2002, for the Dutch CDI, henceforth N-CDI) – both mean 'bow wow'. Children's knowledge or use of them says nothing about their knowledge of one specific language. Depending on the historical and linguistic connection between the two languages you are comparing, you will find more or fewer of these 'language neutral' items.
(4) Compare the remaining items. For each item, see whether you can find a translation equivalent in the other language. If you can think of any single context in which an item from the one language could be used just as well as a specific item from the list in the other language, you have found a 'doublet', thus a translation equivalent pair. List those doublets in a separate list.
(5) Be aware that when you find a doublet, you may find another one with one of the words that is already on your doublet list. For instance, the French word 'voiture' on the F-CDI can form two translation equivalents with items on the N-CDI: there is one doublet {voiture-auto} (car) and another one {voiture-kinderwagen} (child buggy).[a] Both {voiture-auto} and {voiture-kinderwagen} go on your doublet list.

[a] To make matters even more complicated, some Dutch speakers in Flanders also say 'voiture' for a child buggy, but this possibility is not listed on the N-CDI.

(6) The remaining items on both lists should be specific to each list. That is, they should not be translatable by any of the items on the other list. For instance, 'sieste' (nap) appears on the F-CDI, but there is no word on the N-CDI that comes close. Conversely, the word 'yoghurt' (yoghurt) only appears on the N-CDI, not on the F-CDI. Of course, children may hear the translation equivalents of these words, and may also know them, but it just so happens that they are not covered by the two CDI lists you are comparing, and so you cannot approach the issue of TE knowledge based on the language-specific items.

Make a third list of these language-specific items for both languages.
(examples here are from the Infant forms)

Procedure inspired by Pearson et al., 1993

> **Box 6.9(adv.)** Comparing different language versions of the CDI continued
>
> Here is what the results of the procedure above yielded for the F-CDI and N-CDI Infant forms:
>
> | N-CDI | Number of... | F-CDI |
> |---|---|---|
> | 434 | total of lexical items | 414 |
> | 89 (20.5%) | language-specific items | 47 (11.30%) |
> | 14 (3.20%) | language-neutral items | 14 (3.40%) |
> | 331 (76.30%) | items that have at least one TE on the list in the other language | 353 (85.30%) |
>
> *De Houwer et al., 2006a, Table 1*
>
> Items that have at least one TE on the list in the other language form a pair of translation equivalents that expresses one particular meaning. The total number of translation equivalent pairs or meanings formed by the 331 Dutch and 353 French items in the last row of the table is 361. *It is these pairs that are the basis on which to investigate children's knowledge of translation equivalents using the CDI.*

The first important finding of De Houwer *et al.*'s (2006a) study was that all infants understood both members of at least one translation equivalent pair. This De Houwer *et al.* (2006a) termed 'doublet knowledge', following Pearson *et al.* (1993) who introduced the term 'doublets' to refer to both members of a translation equivalent pair.

Second, there was a great amount of variability between the infants: some understood only very few translation equivalents, while others understood very many. Third, all children also understood words that were just one member of a translation equivalent pair (this De Houwer *et al.* (2006a) termed 'singlet knowledge'). This means that although they might have heard words from both languages for the same referent, infants understood the word from only one language. Of course, doublet knowledge is only possible if children have in fact heard both members of a TE pair. Unfortunately, so far there have been no systematic studies of the words that BFLA children hear.

> De Houwer *et al.* (2006a) also looked at whether the meanings represented by the 361 translation equivalents present across the Dutch and French CDI were more likely to be known as doublets or singlets. Infants who understood more TE meanings also understood more doublets. Although this study was not longitudinal, the finding of increased doublet knowledge as total TE meaning comprehension goes up suggests that, as BFLA children learn to understand more words, their increased understanding really means that they are learning more words for the same thing.
>
> De Houwer *et al.* (2006a) only examined the comprehension of the number of meanings expressed in the 361 TE pairs that happened to be found across the Dutch and French Infant CDI. Even this limited examination shows that BFLA 13-month-olds differ widely from each other in the number of meanings that they understand.

As I explained at the beginning of this section, the fact that very young children understand doublets does not necessarily mean that they make any kind of link between them. Also, children may attribute different meanings to the members of a translation equivalent pair.

For instance, they may think that Dutch 'fles' (bottle) means just the bottle they drink their milk out of, and when they hear English 'bottle' they may understand it to refer only to the kinds of bottles that contain their favorite juice. This could be a result of their Dutch-speaking mother usually fixing the milk bottle and their English-speaking daddy usually taking care of the juice.

We may never know whether very young BFLA children make a direct link between two translation equivalents in their comprehension of these words.

The Mutual Exclusivity Bias in BFLA

While learning to understand words is made possible in part by children's growing ability to use social and pragmatics cues in their language learning environment (e.g. Bloom, 1993), scholars have also shown that children are guided by specific word learning strategies in their attempts to understand (and produce) words (e.g. Clark, 1987; Markman & Wachtel, 1988; for a recent review of theories of early word learning, see Diesendruck, 2007).

One of those specific lexical strategies is the Mutual Exclusivity Bias, which leads children to assume that every class of objects can only have one name (e.g. Markman, 1989). This sort of assumption can help children to learn new words for things. After all, children are constantly exposed to objects which are new to them. At the same time, they are hearing new words all the time, words that they need to learn fast in order to make sense of what's going on. It helps if children have some strategies to help them in that task.

The Mutual Exclusivity Bias helps children to process new words in the presence of unfamiliar objects or in the presence of objects they do not yet know the name for. When children hear a word they don't know yet, they will assume that the new word refers to a new thing or to a thing they do not know the word for yet. If you think about it, this makes a lot of sense, and will usually work in order to make connections between a word form and an object.

The Mutual Exclusivity Bias has been shown to exist quite strongly for monolingual children (Markman & Wachtel, 1988; Markman, 1989). MFLA children may hear two different words for the same sorts of things (for instance, mommy calls a particular parakeet 'birdie' but daddy will call it 'the parakeet'), but this most likely does not happen frequently.

In contrast, BFLA children are used to hearing the same object referred to in two ways, namely by a word from one language and a word from the other. Given this quite different learning environment, the question then is to what extent BFLA children also rely on the Mutual Exclusivity Bias.

Anecdotal evidence suggests that BFLA children sometimes do not accept translation equivalents in conversations where adults discuss known objects with them (e.g. Vila,

1984: 41). But there are also plenty of examples where children actively seek out words for known objects from the other language for words they already know (see previously).

There have been several experimental studies of bilingual children's use of the Mutual Exclusivity Bias (e.g. Davidson *et al.*, 1997; Frank & Poulin-Dubois, 2002). However, it isn't clear to what extent most of the children studied had bilingual input from birth. Since the question is to what extent early and regular experience with hearing two words for the same thing makes any difference in children's use of the Mutual Exclusivity Bias, it is especially important to make a distinction between children who have had experience with two words for the same thing all their lives, and children who had much less experience with this phenomenon.

A recent study with mostly BFLA children shows that they rely much less on the Mutual Exclusivity Bias than a group of matched MFLA children (Yow & Markman, 2007). Instead, the bilingual children seemed to rely more on the experimenter's use of gestures to help them interpret unknown words. In a follow-up study, bilingual two-year-olds were able to use an experimenter's use of pointing to help them carry out the task much better than even four-year-old monolinguals (Yow & Markman, 2008). This leads Yow and Markman to suggest that the early experience of a bilingual environment may heighten children's sensitivity to what their interlocutors are attempting to convey non-verbally.

Early comprehension vocabularies: BFLA and MFLA compared

Many people want to know how bilingual children do in comparison to monolingual ones. There is especially a great interest in this question with regard to lexical development, also outside of the relatively small community of child language researchers. Parents and teachers may get worried when they think that a particular child knows few words or has trouble expressing herself through words (Patterson & Pearson, 2004).

Pearson *et al.* (1993) were the first to compare BFLA with MFLA early word comprehension. They used English and Spanish versions of the CDI. They compared 12 bilingual Spanish–English-learning and ten monolingual English-learning infants between the ages of eight and 16 months.[5]

For their comparisons, Pearson *et al.* (1993) developed an analytical procedure that has been very influential and offers a good basis for comparing BFLA and MFLA vocabulary sizes.[6] I outline this procedure in Box 6.10(adv.).

Pearson *et al.* (1993) used percentile scores as a basis for comparing the bilingual and monolingual children's early word comprehension. This means that they first compared the raw scores to norming scores obtained for monolingual children. Even using this perhaps less than adequate basis, Pearson *et al.* found a clear advantage for the bilingual children in comprehension.

Box 6.10(adv.) Comparing bilingual and monolingual children's vocabulary sizes using the CDI

(1) Language-specific vocabulary
- *Monolinguals*: Count the number of items known (understood or produced) on the single-language CDI. This is the only number one can obtain for the monolinguals (MonoVocA).[a]
- *Bilinguals*: Count the number of items known (understood or produced) on each single-language CDI. This will yield two numbers: vocabulary size in Language A (BilVocA), and vocabulary size in Language Alpha (BilVocAlpha).

A first comparison then involves comparing MonoVocA to BilVocA

[a] Ideally, one should have two groups of monolinguals: one for Language A and one for Language Alpha. In practice, studies usually include only one group.

(2) Total vocabulary
- *Monolinguals*: This is the same measure as above (MonoVocA), now called MonoVocTotal.
- *Bilinguals*: This is the sum of the measures BilVocA and BilVocAlpha (see above): BilVocTotal.

A second comparison then involves comparing MonoVocTotal to BilVocTotal

(3) Total meanings (also called total conceptual vocabulary [b])
This refers to the total number of 'concepts' or 'meanings' known. In monolinguals, the number of lexical items is assumed to coincide with the number of different meanings they know.
- *Monolinguals*: This is the same measure as above (MonoVocA), now called MonoMeanings.
- *Bilinguals*: This is the total of the word meanings they know across both languages: BilMeanings (see below for how to compute this).

A third comparison then involves comparing MonoMeanings to BilMeanings

[b] Term first introduced by Swain (1972) with reference to the fact that bilingual children's lexical knowledge in their two languages combined is not isomorphous with their knowledge of the concepts or meanings expressed in those words.

Computing BilMeanings

STEP 1: Compare the two different language forms as in Box 6.9(adv.). This yields four different sets of lexical items:
(1) N pairs of language-neutral items
(2) N pairs of translation equivalents
(3) N items specific to the CDI list in Language A
(4) N items specific to the CDI list in Language Alpha

STEP 2: Determine bilingual children's meaning knowledge (words understood or produced) for each of the four different sets as follows:
(1) and (2): Pairs of language-neutral items and translation equivalents: check for how many PAIRS the child shows knowledge of either one of the members of the pair, or both – that does not matter. Suppose a child understands both Spanish 'gato' and its English translation 'cat': the child gets credit for a single meaning. But also a child who just understands 'gato' gets credit for a single meaning, as does a child who just understands 'cat'.
(3) and (4): Each language-specific item known counts as one meaning known.

STEP 3: Sum up the results of step 2. That gives you BilMeanings.

Adapted from and inspired by Pearson et al., 1993

This trend in their results was confirmed by a study comparing the same 31 13-month-old Dutch–French BFLA infants I mentioned earlier with a matched group of 30 MFLA 13-month-old infants acquiring only Dutch.[7] Following the procedure outlined in Box 6.10(adv.), De Houwer *et al.* (2006b) found that 13-month-old BFLA infants understand 70% (!) more words than matched monolinguals. When we compared just the knowledge of Dutch, there was no difference between the two groups. Nor was there a difference between the number of meanings understood by the BFLA and MFLA group. It was only in the number of 'labels' that children understood that the bilinguals had a huge advantage.

Likewise, Pérez Pereira (2008) found no differences between bilingual Galician-learning children (their other language was Spanish, Portuguese or French) and monolingual Galician children in comprehension as measured by the Galician CDI (Pérez Pereira & García Soto, 2003).

> In order to know whether bilingual exposure somehow 'delays' or, indeed, accelerates the acquisition process in comparison to monolingual exposure we need to compare only BFLA children, not children with input in a second language some time after birth. That is because any fair comparison can only take place when the overall time for learning a language has been the same. Of course, individual BFLA children may have heard each of their languages with different frequencies, but this will be the same for individual MFLA children's only input language (see Chapter 4).
>
> An additional methodological requirement is that for the BFLA children, input in the language to be compared to monolingual children's should have been fairly regular up until the time of study (as the example from Leopold in Box 6.2 shows, drastic changes in the input can have quite a large effect on bilingual learning). The requirement for regular input in their single language is also important for MFLA (children with extended hospital stays or long periods of ear infections, can, up to a point, be likened to BFLA children with decreased input in one of their languages).
>
> A much cited study of 105 Spanish–English older (between the ages of 5;11 and 8;6) bilingual children's receptive vocabulary included about 40 BFLA children but for the rest consisted of ESLA children (Umbel *et al.*, 1992). It is striking that even in this mixed group of bilingual children Spanish receptive vocabulary fell within the norms developed for Spanish-speaking MFLA children.
>
> However, this was not the case for English. Umbel *et al.* rightly point out that in order to properly assess bilingual children both their languages should be taken into account. Umbel *et al.* also found that children who had input in two languages in the home (whether or not this was from birth onwards) knew more English than children with only Spanish input at home but who heard English outside the home. As a result, Umbel *et al.* propose that in order to assess bilingual children's knowledge their language input should be taken into account.
>
> As part of its careful methodology, a study of four-year-old BFLA and MFLA children that was not focused on comprehension but rather on speech perception checked on the children's language comprehension (Sundara *et al.*, 2006). As a measure of

comprehension Sundara *et al.* used a very commonly used testing instrument, viz. the French and English versions of the PPVT, the Peabody Picture Vocabulary Test (Dunn & Dunn, 1981; Dunn *et al.*, 1993).[8] No statistically significant differences were found between the bilingual and monolingual children's scores for English. In addition, there were no statistically significant differences between the bilingual and monolingual children's scores for French.

Likewise, another study of French–English BFLA children that was focused on another aspect of language (i.e. the use of repairs in conversation), also checked on children's language comprehension using French and English versions of the PPVT (Comeau & Genesee, 2001). In many of the 18 cases (there were 12 three-year-olds and six five-year-olds), the BFLA children's scores fell within the monolingual norms developed for each language.

Another study of English–French children (eight bilingual toddlers; they were not all BFLA, though; see Appendix F) found that their English scores were only a little below those for a group of ten somewhat older monolingual toddlers. The bilinguals' scores were still within the monolingual norm, though (Thordardottir *et al.*, 2006).

Word learning isn't only about comprehension, of course. Word learning is also about saying words yourselves. You might think that word comprehension paves the way for word production. The next section examines whether and to what extent this is true.

Comprehension and production: two sides of the same coin?

As for sounds, the knowledge of words involves a component where children are not actively speaking, comprehension, and one that does involve actively speaking, production.

Some aspects of word comprehension must be related to (word) perception, but as I indicated in Chapter 5, we know little about BFLA children's word perception. I have found no studies so far on the link between word perception and word comprehension. As I also explained in Chapter 5, early word production is closely linked with early sound production. The two cannot, in fact, be really separated (except in a book like this!). But what about the relation between word comprehension and word production?

You would think that once you understand a word, it's easy to say it. That may be the case for adults, but it isn't that way for young children. One problem is that they have yet to learn how to control their articulatory organs sufficiently in order to say a word they might have in mind (see Chapter 5). But that's most likely not the only explanation. It's more likely that word comprehension and word production are two fundamentally different processes (e.g. Bates, 1993). But of course, these need to be matched up at some point (e.g. Clark & Hecht, 1983). Just how this matching up works isn't clear, though.

Comprehension precedes production

You already know from Chapter 4 that two- and three-year-old children with input in two languages can carry on conversations with people who address them in another language (e.g. Jisa, 2000). Little Shelli (see Box 4.26 in Chapter 4) understood English and Hebrew but spoke mainly Hebrew at age 2;11, although she did produce some isolated English words and phrases (Berman, 1979).

Examples such as these show a very large difference between word comprehension and word production in bilingual preschoolers. Do younger BFLA children also show such a difference?

Monolingual children will show signs of understanding words several months before they attempt to say anything that adults interpret as being word-like (Stern & Stern, 1965). Their word comprehension, then, is well ahead of their word production.

There isn't much information for BFLA on these very early stages, but the little there is confirms that BFLA children follow the same route in development as MFLA children. Three Portuguese–Swedish infants started to be able to appropriately respond to simple commands at the age of seven months, and they started to increasingly show signs of understanding many more words just one month later (Cruz-Ferreira, 2006: 146–147). The children started to talk several months after that.

Leopold (1970: 163) also noted that English–German Hildegard started to say words much later than she first started to understand them. At the end of her first year, she thus understood many more words than she said. Curiously, Hildegard's first word, English 'pretty', persisted in her word production at a time when she no longer understood English at the end of a stay in Germany at age 1;2 (Leopold, 1970: 174). Deuchar and Quay (2000: 55) also note that in the course of the second year their BFLA subject Manuela understood much more than she produced.

Number of words understood or produced

The mismatch between early word comprehension and early word production is most noticeable when you look at the number of words that young children appear to understand and the number of words they say at one particular age. Data from yet again the 31 BFLA 13-month-olds mentioned previously show a large difference between the number of words children concurrently have in their comprehension and production repertoires (De Houwer et al., 2007). As shown in Box 6.11(adv.), these BFLA children understand many more words than they say. At the same time, there is a lot of variability between children in how many more words they understand than produce. De Houwer et al. (2006b) found similar results for a matched group of 30 monolingual Dutch-hearing infants at age 13 months.

We also found that at 13 months the size of BFLA children's early word comprehension repertoires did not relate to the size of their early word production repertoires (De Houwer et al., 2007). It seems that early word comprehension is one kind of thing and early word production quite another. Children can be good 'comprehenders' (a term introduced by Bates, 1993) or they can be good talkers. The two need not go together.

Box 6.11(adv.) Differences between early word comprehension and word production in BFLA

This table shows the size of differences between the number of words understood and produced by 31 13-month-old infants acquiring Dutch and French as measured by the CDI. For instance, a mean of 112.80 means that, on average, children understood 113 more Dutch words than they produced.

13 months CDI	Mean	S.D.	Range
Within Dutch	112.80	82.69	2–309
Within French	103.16	74.78	5–288
Within both	215.83	139.04	3–564

Adapted from De Houwer et al., 2007

You might wonder whether being able to understand a lot of words at an early age helps in saying a lot of words later. For young BFLA children, there seems to be no relation between the two: comprehension at age 13 months did not relate to later word production at 20 months in the same group of BFLA children (De Houwer et al., 2007). Dutch comprehension did not predict later Dutch (or French) production, French comprehension did not predict later French (or Dutch) production, and total comprehension did not predict later total production.

Understanding and producing translation equivalents

There can also be quite a mismatch between early word comprehension and early word production as far as translation equivalents are concerned. Children may understand doublets, that is, both members of a translation equivalent pair, but they may produce only one (see Box 6.12).

It isn't clear just how many doublets children understand but do not say. Porsché (1983: 88–89) mentions that his son Nicolai understood many more cross-language synonyms than he produced. Likewise, Quay (1995) reports that English–Spanish Manuela 'understood many more equivalent terms than she was able to produce' (p. 374). Studies have yet to quantitatively compare the number of doublets that BFLA children understand with their production of those doublets.

In the second year of life, then, word comprehension and word production appear to go pretty much their own separate ways in BFLA. The fact that they seem to represent different aspects of psycholinguistic functioning may partly explain why it is possible that somewhat older BFLA children can consistently speak Language A in response to utterances from Language Alpha.

Before I go on to discuss BFLA children's early word production, I briefly say a few things about why they use words in the first place: to express and communicate meanings.

> **Box 6.12** Translation equivalents and the mismatch between comprehension and early production
>
> *Hildegard*
>
> Hildegard said 'bye bye' in English starting at 15 months, and said it frequently afterwards (when she first started to understand it is not clear). She started to understand the German 'auf Wiedersehen' (bye bye) two months later, but it took her a full eight months to start saying 'auf Wiedersehen' herself.
>
> *Hildegard understood the words in both languages for the same thing, but showed a great discrepancy in the time between first comprehension and first production of one of the words.*
>
> *Adapted from Leopold, 1970: 181*
>
> *Louis*
>
> When he was just 14 months old, Louis' father had just given German–French-speaking Louis a piece of bread:
>
> father: 'dis merci' (French for 'say thank you')
> Louis: 'dan(k)e' (attempt at German 'danke', thank you)
>
> *Louis understood a word in Language A, but produced it in Language Alpha (in fact, around this age, Louis only said 'thank you' in German, never in French). Louis did understand 'Danke' in German, too.*
>
> *Adapted from Ronjat, 1913: 76*
>
> *Nicolai*
>
> When he first started to speak, German–English Nicolai understood German 'Wagen' and its English counterpart 'car'. Nicolai was very interested in cars. However, he never said 'Wagen' or 'car'. He did refer to cars using the German word 'Auto'.
>
> When his mother asked him: 'Gehen wir zum **Wagen**?' (German; shall we go to the car?) Nicolai would say: '**Auto**!' and run to the car. When his father asked him: 'Nico, can you say **car**?', Nicolai said: '**Auto**!'.
>
> *At age 19 months, Nicolai understood a specific pair of translation equivalents, did not say the words, but said a third word instead that was a synonym of a German word and a translation equivalent of an English one.*
>
> *Adapted from Porsché, 1983: 87–88*

Words and meanings in early production

Proto-words

The meanings of children's early words in production are quite elusive (for an overview, see Barrett, 1995). For adults, it is often very difficult to know what a child exactly meant by a particular word.[9]

This is especially the case for children's very earliest word-like forms. As I explained in Chapter 5, children may start out using 'phonetically consistent forms' or 'proto-words', which make adults think of words, but are still very far removed from adult targets or, indeed, the adult targets are not clear at all.

The word-like quality of these proto-words lies mostly in the fact that children use them with apparent communicative intent, in specific contexts or tied to specific events (De Houwer & Gillis, 1998: 54–59). Thus, they are not used at random. For an example, see Box 6.13.

Box 6.13   Examples of proto-words

A monolingual case
Maarten, a boy with monolingual Dutch input, regularly said a long 'sh' between the ages of 1;1 and 1;5. 'sh' is not a Dutch word (except to tell someone to be quiet, as in English).

Maarten first said 'sh' when someone lit up a cigarette and puffed out smoke (the data on Maarten were collected long before it was known that second-hand smoke can hurt you). A few weeks later, at age 1;2, Maarten said a long 'sh' when apparently he wanted someone to light a lighter. A month later, Maarten said a long 'sh' when a light was switched on. Nearly a month later, he said a long 'sh' when he saw steam coming out of a hot coffee cup.

There were several other different occasions when Maarten said a long 'sh'. For Maarten, 'sh' seemed to function like a word, in having a particular form that he used in specific circumstances and not in others (for instance, he didn't say 'sh' when he was playing with his cars – then he said another proto-word, 'brr').

Adapted from De Houwer & Gillis, 1998; data first documented in Gillis, 1984

A bilingual case
Mikael, who was learning Swedish and Portuguese from birth, said [kx:kx:] at age 1;4. This sound or 'word' doesn't mean anything in adult Swedish or Portuguese. However, it could have been modelled after the 'universal' word 'ski'. As Cruz-Ferreira (2006: 143) describes: 'Mikael said this word whenever skiing was discussed among the family in Portuguese or Swedish, or when looking at pictures or films of family skiing holidays or of ski resorts. He complemented his use of the word by adopting the forwards-tilting, knee-bent body posture of a skier, and jerking both arms rhythmically backwards with clenched fists, as if holding ski poles. If sitting on his high-chair, he would bounce his body and use the same arm movements.' Cruz-Ferreira goes on to say that it isn't clear whether [kx:kx:] referred to, for instance, ski equipment, the physical activity of skiing or the noise of skis scraping against snow.

Adapted from Cruz-Ferreira, 2006: 143

Few studies of BFLA have looked at these early proto-words. Wanner (1997), in a longitudinal study of the early word production by a Japanese–English BFLA child between the ages of 1 and 1;9, discusses a number of forms that most likely were proto-words rather than 'random vocalizations', as he interprets them.

Some children use proto-words for a long time, others go on very quickly towards attempting adult words. This doesn't necessarily mean that there will be any clear form-meaning correspondences. The forms may be unstable, as may be their uses.

The meanings of the earliest words

Early word use is very much bound to a specific context. Gradually, individual words become less and less linked to one specific context and start to be used more and more in adult ways. Infants' early words accompany their actions and express their desires, needs and feelings in general. Infants may also refer to classes of objects or use proper names to refer to specific individuals. They may also refer to various qualities and properties of actions and objects, such as German–English Hildegard's early use of 'pretty' (Leopold, 1970) and Dutch–English Susan's early use of 'more' as a way of asking her father to lift her up in the air again and again (my diary notes). Infants also use early words for purely pragmatic purposes, as in the ubiquitous 'no', said to refuse more food or drink.

Infants vary a lot from each other in the order with which they start to express particular kinds of meanings. Some children name objects in their environments from the very beginning, others first use a route of using solely 'pragmatic words' (sometimes also called 'social words') and words expressing how they feel before they are ready to start naming objects (for an overview of monolingual children's early use of words, see Barrett, 1995).

Social words, such as 'bye' or 'peek-a-boo' form a large part of most young MFLA children's vocabularies, though. Once they produce about 50 words they start to use far fewer of these in comparison to other kinds of words (Caselli *et al.*, 1999). That is, the proportion of social words is usually quite high in the period where children say up to 50 words. Afterwards, that proportion drops, because children learn to produce many more other kinds of words, such as names for objects, processes and characteristics of things and people.

Like MFLA children, a group of 13 English–French BFLA children used proportionally many social words in the first stages of word production. This pattern was the same for both languages. Once children started to say more than 50 different words in total, the proportion of social words decreased drastically (David & Li, 2005). Similar results were found for a CDI study of 64 English–Spanish bilingual children (Conboy & Thal, 2006).[10]

Holowka *et al.* (2002) classified the first total 50 words produced by three French–English BFLA children according to semantic category (for instance, animate objects, person-related non-objects). Their analysis looks at the global occurrence of these kinds of words and finds quite a few differences between the three children in the extent to which they use words in each semantic category.

Earlier, Leopold (1970) had classified Hildegard's words produced throughout her second year of life into semantic 'groups', as he calls them, such as 'food', 'persons', 'outdoor life and traffic'. It is interesting to see that these groups are quite similar to the groupings of words used in the CDI today. Leopold notes, though, that it is sometimes difficult to correctly classify a word. A cursory look at Leopold's classification shows that Hildegard produced words from both languages in most categories.

In contrast, Mandarin–English James showed quite different lexical acquisition patterns across his two languages (Qi *et al.*, 2006). James used lots of names for objects and people in Mandarin, which was not matched by his early English, where he mostly produced what Qi *et al.* (2006) call relational terms such as 'good' and 'no'.

As I explained in Chapter 2, children's early use of words is often called 'holophrastic', because infants often appear to use a single word with a very large meaning that is much bigger than the meaning of a single word, and not necessarily related to an adult meaning at all. Ronjat and Leopold had already noted their use in BFLA over 50 years ago. Box 6.14 shows an example from a more recent source.

> **Box 6.14** An example of a holophrase in BFLA
>
> For months in the second year of life (no further age indication), German–English Nicolai produced a single word: 'das' (could be the German version of 'that').
>
> Nicolai used 'das' with at least five different functions (and specific intonation patterns):
>
> (1) to ask a question (in this case, 'das' was pronounced first with falling intonation, and towards the end of the word the intonation rose);
>
> (2) to confirm the correctness of something or to express that he agrees with something (in this case, 'das' was pronounced in a very determined tone and with lightly falling intonation);
>
> (3) to express a desire (in this case, 'das' was pronounced with level intonation, and accompanied by a hand signal);
>
> (4) to repeat the expression of a desire (in this case, 'das' was pronounced with level intonation but much louder than in (3));
>
> (5) to express excitement or happiness (in this case, 'das' was first pronounced with a high, screechy voice, soon after which intonation fell sharply).
>
> *Adapted from Porsché, 1983: 85*
>
> *Note that the use of 'das' by Nicolai isn't entirely of his own creation. In German, adults also ask 'das?' with rising intonation (1), or in response to a question as to what they want, they might reply using 'das!', with final falling intonation (2). One can also imagine circumstances where they might pronounce 'das' in similar ways and with similar meanings as Nicolai in (3), (4) and (5).*

What about grammatical categories?

You will have noticed that I am describing children's very early words in terms of semantic domains rather than grammatical categories such as 'noun' and 'verb'. That is because children's very early word productions often defy description (see the next subsection).

At a very rough level, grammatical categories are related to specific kinds of meanings, although there is no precise one-to-one mapping. In English, for instance, actions are usually expressed by verbs, and nouns or pronouns are used to talk about objects.

Verbs, nouns and other parts of speech can also be defined more structurally in terms of where they should be placed in a sentence, what kinds of words can precede and follow them, and what kinds of bound morphemes can be used with them (see Chapter 2). It is not only the kinds of meanings expressed by verbs and nouns that differ, then, but also the ways in which they are used in a sentence. We can categorize words on the basis of their different uses in sentences and, in addition, on the basis of their contrasting global meanings.

Children who are just starting to learn individual words have no inkling of these grammatical categories, and it is quite debatable whether it makes any sense tocategorize their early word forms into adult grammatical categories. For instance, Dutch-speaking

> Maarten at the age of 1;10 often said the word 'zevalt' (De Houwer & Gillis, 1985). This word sounds like the Dutch past participle verb 'gevallen' (fallen), used with the wrong ending ('t' instead of 'en'). Maarten said 'zevalt' when something fell down, but he also seemed to mean 'ready', or even 'the tower has been built' – the opposite of falling down. Thus, he did seem to say 'zevalt' to refer to a process or the result of a process. This would seem to fit an interpretation of 'zevalt' as being a verb. However, maybe the occasional meaning we as researchers attributed to 'zevalt' of 'the tower has been built' actually referred to just the tower – thus the actual construction. This would imply more of a noun-like quality. The often quite fluid nature of the meanings that children seem to intend with their early words is an important obstacle in trying to decide what grammatical category their words fall into (see also Cruz-Ferreira, 2006: 149). The very fact that single word utterances do not allow an analysis based on structural elements is another impediment.

At a very basic level, categorizing children's earliest single words in terms of adult grammatical categories such as verb and noun may be quite pointless (Clark, 2003: 83). Eventually, though, children will have to learn to put words together in sentences that make sense in the language or languages they are learning. At that point, a description in terms of grammatical categories starts to make more sense as well (Clark, 1993).

I take up the issue of grammatical categories again in Chapter 7.

Semantic processes

Children's early meanings are quite fluid. It isn't always clear what exactly they are referring to, and often they refer to things in ways that are strange from an adult point of view (see the example from Maarten above). This is most obvious in their use of referential words, that is, words that are used to refer to an object, animate being, process, action or event.

As I explained in Chapter 2, children may use words in a much 'bigger' sense than adults do, that is, they 'overextend' the meaning of certain words. An example is saying 'ball' for everything that is round, including oranges and the moon. BFLA children also use this kind of semantic process (Cruz-Ferreira, 2006: 189–190; Leopold, 1970; Ronjat, 1913). Box 6.15 shows two examples.

Box 6.15 Examples of overextensions by young BFLA children

(1) At age 11 months, Portuguese–Swedish Mikael consistently said the same form of Portuguese 'água', which means 'water', to refer to any kind of drinkable substance (Cruz-Ferreira, 2006: 143).
(2) Before French–English Ed produced 50 words (no age indication), he often called a horse a cow.[a] Before French–English Jane produced 50 words (no age indication), she often said banana when she should have said apple or cucumber (Holowka et al., 2002: 233).

[a] *This is a mistake that two-year-old monolingual children make as well (Naigles & Gelman, 1995)*

Another type of semantic process is underextension. When children underextend the meanings of words they limit the scope of a word too much. For instance, they may say 'apple' only to refer to big green apples. They may simply not refer to red apples. This kind of error is much harder to detect.

Learning to match words to their adult meanings is no easy task, then. BFLA children must learn to match words from two languages to particular meanings. As we have already seen for comprehension, they appear not to be 'held back' by this apparently more difficult task, and in fact understand many more words than age-matched monolinguals. Let's see how BFLA children tackle the task of learning to produce words in two languages.

Early bilingual word production

First words

First word production usually occurs around children's first birthdays (Clark, 2003). A problem for specifying the youngest age for first word production, however, is that not all scholars use the same criteria for deciding on the word status of children's early word-like forms. Since nowadays so many scholars use parental reports such as the CDI and may also rely on parental diaries, however, it is increasingly 'folk' ideas about what constitutes a child's first word that determine what counts as the age of first word production. Since scholars have not been able to come up with better ideas, that's fine!

CDI norming data reveal that there are MFLA children who already produce words at the age of eight months (see Fenson et al., 1993 for English, Zink & Lejaegere, 2002 for Dutch and Kern, 2007 for French).[11] Although there are slight differences between the norming data for English, Dutch and French, children who have not produced their first word shortly after their first birthday are performing below average, and children who by age 15 months have not produced their first word are decidedly slow.

The normal period of time within which one would expect first word production, then, lies somewhere between eight and 13 months. This difference of five months in a young life of 13 months represents a long period of time and shows just how different young children's 'starting blocks' for communicative language use can be. Yet there are plenty of MFLA children who produce their first words between the ages of 13 and 15 months.

Hildegard produced her first word (a rendition of English 'pretty') at the age of ten months (Leopold, 1970). This is the same age that Dutch–English Susan produced her first word, a rendition of Dutch 'klok'. The English translation, clock, is very close in form to the Dutch word but since Susan had never heard the English version I interpreted it as Dutch; also, the quality of the vowel Susan used was very Dutch-like (my diary notes).

These two examples happen to note the same age of first word production in BFLA children, but there is in fact a lot of individual variation between BFLA children as regards the ages at which they produce their first words (see Box 6.16). The examples in Box 6.16 show a range of about six months in the appearance of BFLA children's first words. This reflects the range of differences between MFLA children in when they produce their first words.

BFLA children do not necessarily produce their first words in both languages on the same day. In some children, there is a very long time lag between their first production of a word in Language A and their first production of a word in Language Alpha. In others, there is a much shorter time lag, and in yet others, there is no lag at all. This is also shown in Box 6.16.

Box 6.16 First words in BFLA

Child	First word in Language A at age:	First word in Language Alpha at age:	Time lag	Source
Mikael	0;8 (P)	0;8 (Sw)	none	Cruz-Ferreira, 2006
Sophie	0;8 (P)	0;11 (Sw)	3 months	Cruz-Ferreira, 2006
Karin	0;9 (P)	0;9 (Sw)	none	Cruz-Ferreira, 2006
Roger	0;11,9 (S)	1;3,3 (C)	115 days	Vila, 1984
Jane	0;11,10 (E)	1;1,7 (F)	27 days	Holowka et al., 2002
Sue	1;1,15 (F)	1;2,11 (E)	26 days	Holowka et al., 2002
María del Mar	1;2,2 (C)	1;2,14 (S)	12 days	Vila, 1984
Ed	1;2,20 (E)	1,2,20 (F)	none	Holowka et al., 2002

C = Catalan; E = English; F = French; P = Portuguese; S = Spanish; Sw = Swedish

You might wonder what the reason could be for these differences between the age of first word production in Language A and Language Alpha. Perhaps it has something to do with the lexical relation between the specific languages that children are acquiring. Perhaps if languages have a lot of shared vocabulary it takes children longer to start using language-specific words. The little evidence there is suggests, though, that it doesn't matter whether languages are closely related on the lexical level or not.

In the same group of 31 Dutch–French BFLA infants mentioned earlier, three children did not yet say any words at the age of 13 months as measured by the CDI. The majority of the children did, however, and 26 of these 28 produced more than one word (De Houwer et al., 2007). On average, the children in this group produced a total of ten words (that's in both their languages combined). Four of the 28 children who were producing words only produced them in one language, and not yet in the other (De Houwer et al., 2007). French and Dutch are lexically quite different, one being a Romance language and the other a Germanic one.

Another group study of bilingual children, this time of 15 Spanish–Catalan BFLA infants, shows that all children produced words between the ages of 12 and 14 months (Águila et al., 2005, table 4). Seven of the children produced words in only one language, though. However, the parent report instrument that Águila et al. used contained only 148 items, so it is possible that children did produce words in the other language, but that these were just not 'caught' by the instrument used.[12] Spanish and Catalan are lexically very similar.

The combined evidence, then, shows that BFLA children produce their first words within the same age range as MFLA children. Bilingual children may first produce words in just one language, or in two languages from the very beginning.

The make-up of BFLA children's lexical production repertoires

Vila (1984) looked at the early word use of two Catalan–Spanish BFLA children, Roger and María del Mar. It took Roger close to four months to produce his first word in Catalan, although he was very young when he produced his first word, which was in Spanish. By the time Roger was 1;3, and first started to produce words in Catalan as well as Spanish, he did produce 21 words which could be either Catalan or Spanish. These two languages are very closely related and have a lot of overlapping vocabulary. Yet this didn't keep María del Mar, who was acquiring these same two languages, from constructing language-specific lexical repertoires in each of her languages pretty much from the beginning of word production onwards (in addition to words that exist in both Catalan and Spanish).

> In order to study the specific issues presented by Spanish and Catalan because of their large overlapping lexicons, Águila *et al.* (2005, 2007) developed a special bilingual parent report instrument. It consists of 148 Spanish–Catalan translation equivalents divided into 14 lexical categories. Nearly two-thirds (62%) of the 148 translation equivalents were cognates (see the first section on 'The words that BFLA children hear'). In fact, you could say that between Spanish and Catalan, such cognates are often pretty much language neutral, and certainly can be so in children's immature speech. Non-cognates accounted for the remaining 38%.
>
> Águila and colleagues used their bilingual parental report instrument for monolingual Catalan, monolingual Spanish and BFLA Spanish–Catalan infants and toddlers. All the children overwhelmingly first produced cognates rather than non-cognates (84% in the Águila *et al.* 2005 study). When they got older, the proportion diminished a bit, but was still higher than expected based on the proportion present on the list (76% at age 18–20 months and 73% at age 22–24 months).
>
> In a similar setting involving two very close languages, Galician and Spanish, only a Galician CDI form was used to assess Galician–Spanish bilingual children's lexical knowledge (Pérez Pereira & García Soto, 2003). As Pérez Pereira (2008) explains, it would have been very strange if the parents had been asked to also fill in the Spanish CDI. That is because the Galician CDI has only 12% of words that are not identical or nearly identical to Spanish words.

At the age of two, Roger and María del Mar had close to a third or more language-neutral words in their vocabulary (see Box 6.17). Águila *et al.*'s (2005, 2007) findings show that this high use of a lot of language-neutral words is a general characteristic of other Spanish–Catalan bilingual children, as well as Spanish and Catalan monolingual infants and toddlers.

For very closely related languages like Catalan and Spanish, then, it is not enough to distinguish between words from either Catalan or Spanish, but it is important to take into account cognates or language-neutral words, that is, words that are common to both languages and that have the same form and meaning (see also Box 6.10(adv.) earlier).[13]

Box 6.17	Language-neutral and language-specific words in BFLA word production			
Age 2	% Words in Catalan	% Words in Spanish	% Language neutral words	Total word production
Roger	22.30	45.70	32.00	247
María del Mar	13.50	48.40	38.10	215
Adapted from Vila, 1984: 37				

For lexically quite distinct languages like Dutch and French, there will be rather few language-neutral words, especially for the semantic domains that small children meet with. Children acquiring Dutch and French, then, will be expected to have mostly language-specific words in their production vocabularies. Manuela, who was acquiring Spanish and English, two lexically rather unrelated languages, produced only 13% language neutral words at age 1;10 (Quay, 1995). This contrasts with findings for other BFLA children who were also acquiring Spanish from birth, but in combination with a lexically close language, Catalan (see earlier).

Most of the words that young BFLA children produce, if they are interpretable at all, can be related to specific adult targets. BFLA children's production vocabularies will exist of (a) language-neutral words and (b) words that clearly belong to only one of their two languages.

Language-neutral words are in fact translations of a word in the other language, but you can't tell, because the pronunciation is the same. As suggested before, it will depend on the historic relation between the two languages involved how many language-neutral words a BFLA child needs to use in day-to-day life.

Words that clearly belong to one of the input languages may have a straightforward translation equivalent in the other one. Others will not. For words that children have heard TEs for, they may produce either doublets (that is, both members of the TE; for an explanation, see the section on comprehension earlier). Children may also produce singlets, that is, a single member of a TE (see also earlier). In addition, children may produce words in each language that do not have straightforward translation equivalents in the other language.

I summarize these points in Box 6.18. I discuss the production of translation equivalents in a separate section below.

Box 6.18 BFLA children's word production vocabularies

(1) Language neutral words;
(2) Words that clearly belong to one of the input languages:
   (2a) words with a TE in the other input language:
       – children may produce both these words (doublets);
       – children may also produce just one of these words (singlets).
   (2b) words without a TE in the other input language:
       – children may produce language-specific words.

Lexical gaps and adding new words

One typical aspect of children's word productions is that compared to adults, they know so few. This means there are large gaps in children's early lexical knowledge (Clark, 1995). We as adults continue to have lexical gaps – nobody knows all the words available in a particular language, and we continue to fill these gaps when required.

Of course, because they know so many words already, adults have fewer gaps to fill. When they are very little, children know next to no words and need to overcome this communicative problem. Lexical development is very much driven by filling lexical gaps.

A lexical gap arises when children want to express something but lack the words. For BFLA children this includes lacking the words in the right language.

Children fill lexical gaps by quickly adding more words to their repertoire. In learning new words, children often use what is called 'fast mapping' (Carey, 1978). This means that depending on the circumstances very young children are able to assign some sort of appropriate meaning very quickly to an unfamiliar word. They may require just a single instance of hearing a new word in their input in order to be able to say it in an appropriate context. You see an example of this for BFLA in Box 6.19.

Box 6.19 Learning to fill a lexical gap for the other member of a TE pair

At age 3;4, German–Italian Lukas is talking to an Italian-speaking investigator, Anna. He shows her a picture he's just drawn and says: 'adesso ho fatto una **kreuz**' (now I've made a cross; this is a mixed utterance consisting mostly of Italian, but with a German word at the end).

Anna then asks him in Italian: 'che cos'hai fatto?' (what did you make?). Lukas answers in German: 'kreuz' (cross).

Anna responds in Italian: 'non ho capito che cos'è?' (I didn't get it, what is it?). Lukas answers once more in German: 'kreuz' (cross).

Anna looks at the picture and then says in Italian: 'la croce' (the cross). Lukas repeats with excitement: 'la croce!' (the cross).

Adapted from Cantone, 2007: 104

The example in Box 6.19 shows that the BFLA child in question, Lukas, only knew one of the words making up a TE pair. This is clear from the fact that he does not produce the word in the expected language even after the interlocutor made it repeatedly clear to him that she did not understand him. Given that on the whole children do want to be understood and can easily adjust to their interlocutors' language choice, certainly by age three (see later), Lukas most likely did not know the Italian word for 'cross'. This is a clear example of a lexical gap.

Once he heard the needed word in the 'right' language from the interlocutor, Lukas was happy to repeat it, and had learned to say a new word. Because he already knew the word in the other language, he was able to use the equivalent in the other language immediately.

The example from Lukas here shows that the filling of lexical gaps in BFLA is partly driven by a communicative need to express oneself in one particular language rather than another. In BFLA, children's learning to fill lexical gaps may be much aided by their prior knowledge of one member of a TE pair. That's because it's generally easier to build on something you already know than to start from scratch.

Creating new words

Filling lexical gaps can also happen in other ways. When they are still very young, children may overuse all-purpose forms such as 'that' or 'this'. As they get a bit older, they may also make up novel words such as 'door-feather' – a feather that they just put in a screen door (Clark, 1995). However, these novel words will often appear only a few times, until children have learned the conventional words for what they intended to express (or they just don't talk about door feathers anymore).

Children may make new words on the basis of word formation processes that are common in their input language such as compounding, which makes a new word out of two separate words (as in 'door-feather'). They may also add bound morphemes to stems in ways that are patterned after productive processes in their input, as in 'grow-ly', to refer to a fierce dinosaur or 'superman-ning', to refer to being like Superman or 'story-er' instead of 'story teller' (all examples here from Clark, 1995: 401–403; for examples from Dutch MFLA, see Elbers & van Loon-Vervoorn, 1998). Like MFLA children, BFLA children also use compounding to make up new words (Cruz-Ferreira, 2006: 174–180; Nicoladis, 2002).

Children may occasionally make up new words based on bits of old ones. In BFLA, words may contain syllables or phoneme combinations from two words from a different language. That results in 'bilingual blends'. An example is 'bydersehen', a blend that Leopold's second daughter produced on the basis of English 'bye bye' and the equivalent German 'auf Wiedersehen' (Leopold, 1970: 182).

Such bilingual blends are usually pretty rare though. That is most likely because adults will react incredulously or laugh when children say such words. Some of the words may 'stick', though, as a family joke (or because parents find these blends cute). Monolingual children may produce blends as well. For example, the non-existent word 'mieg' was Dutch-speaking Luuk's attempt at 'mug' (mosquito) or 'vlieg' (fly) – he took the first sound of 'mug' and added the vowel and final consonant of 'vlieg' (Tinbergen, 1919).

Bilingual blends at the word level are different from words from one language that also contain a morpheme from the other (see also Chapter 7).

Changes in word production repertoires

In production, early words come and go. Children do not use all the words they have previously produced every day. They will learn a new word, use it a few times, stop using it for a while and then after some time use it again. The same thing can happen in BFLA children. Hildegard, for instance, used two members of a translation equivalent pair at a given age, later used only one of them, and later yet used only the other member of the TE pair (Leopold, 1970: 176–177). Of course, some words will be used on a pretty much daily basis as well, and will thus show more stability.

Once children are beyond the very earliest stages of word production their word production vocabularies may grow quite fast. It is difficult to fully assess children's lexical repertoires on the basis of transcripts of recorded interactions (see also Chapter 3). These are by necessity too limited – a child might be using all sorts of different words the moment you have stopped your recording, except you didn't 'catch' them on tape. Diary studies can do better in this respect, but they need to be very dense in order to be anywhere near complete. They are quite effective for the very earliest stages of word production (Reznick & Goldfield, 1994).

Again, a very useful instrument for assessing children's lexical production repertoires is the CDI (see Chapter 3 and above). Important to know here is that when scholars discuss the number of words that children produce, they almost exclusively talk about the *different* words that children produce, thus the word types, rather than their amount of talk (word tokens). The section below discusses the rate at which children add new words to their production repertoires.

The rate of lexical development in bilingual production

Overall rates of change

It is well known from studies of monolingual acquisition that children vary considerably in the rate at which they learn to produce new words. Some children develop much more slowly than others. The resulting differences in how many words children are able to say at a particular age can therefore be quite great (more about this in the next section). For instance, based on norming data for the Dutch CDI, girls who are in the normal range of development produce one to five words at age 11 months, and six to 47 words just two months later, at age 13 months (Zink & Lejaegere, 2002).

Some children start off saying several different words from early on and their production vocabularies show a fairly gradual rate of change. Other children may say very few words for several months and then all of a sudden start saying hundreds of new words within two months' time (e.g. De Houwer & Gillis, 1998: 51). This usually happens somewhere in the second half of the first year. Children who show a sudden and dramatic increase in lexical production are said to experience a **vocabulary spurt** (Goldfield & Reznick, 1990).[14] Similar to MFLA, Pearson and Fernández (1994) found evidence of a vocabulary spurt in some English–Spanish BFLA children, but not in others.

Just before he was 21 months old, Japanese–English Jessie had a total production lexicon of just 28 words (Wanner, 1996: 23). About half of these were Japanese. Then, all of a sudden, on one and the same day, the day he became 21 months old, Jessie added 14 words to his production vocabulary. After another month's time, Jessie's total number of words had more than tripled. By the time he was 22 months old he produced 94 different words. There were slightly more words in English.

Vila (1984) also reports a vocabulary spurt for two Catalan–Spanish BFLA children. The spurt took place a little after the children were a year and a half old. Deuchar and Quay's (2000) table 4.1 shows a vocabulary spurt for English–Spanish Manuela, who went from producing 58 words at age 1;5 to more than double that at age 1;7. In contrast, the three Portuguese–Swedish children studied by Cruz-Ferreira (2006) all produced several different words from around their first birthdays and added on words at a fairly steady rate.[15]

The evidence we have so far for BFLA children suggests that like MFLA children, they show a lot of differences between each other in the rates with which their levels of word production change (Holowka *et al.*, 2002; Pearson & Fernández, 1994). On average, girls are a bit faster in their lexical development than boys (see, e.g. Fenson *et al.*, 1994; Zink & Lejaegere, 2002). For BFLA this has been shown as well: the seven English–French BFLA girls in David and Li's (2008) study were well ahead in total word production compared to the six boys. The same was true for the 50 Spanish–English girls in Patterson's (1998) study, compared to the 52 boys.

Do both languages develop at the same rate?

There may also be differences between the rates of change in BFLA children's two languages (Patterson, 1998). For the two Catalan–Spanish BFLA children observed by Vila (1984), there was a vocabulary spurt at the same time for words specific to Spanish and language-neutral words. Vila noted a vocabulary spurt for words specific to Catalan one or two months later. Yip and Matthews (2008) report an early vocabulary spurt for Cantonese but an initially more gradual lexical development in English for Cantonese–English Sophie. In Box 6.20 I contrast the rates of change in early word production for French–English Anna and Olivier (David & Li, 2003).

As you can see from Box 6.20, Anna first used many more English than French words, and English words saw a much steeper increase than French words. Soon after her second birthday, though, French took over. Olivier shows a different pattern, with first equal numbers and rates of learning of English and French words, but after his second birthday, English just 'took off' and left French behind a bit, although there was still growth in French.

Prior to his overall vocabulary spurt, about half of Japanese–English Jessie's words were Japanese (Wanner, 1996). This proportion stayed just about the same in the month after the vocabulary spurt, although now there were slightly more words in English. Jessie's early pattern resembles that of Olivier.

We learn from this that, once again, there is great variability between languages, between children and also between different times of development for the same child.

The potentially quite different developmental rates for each language in BFLA imply that at any given age, the numbers of words produced in one language may differ quite a bit from the number produced in the other (see further in the next section).

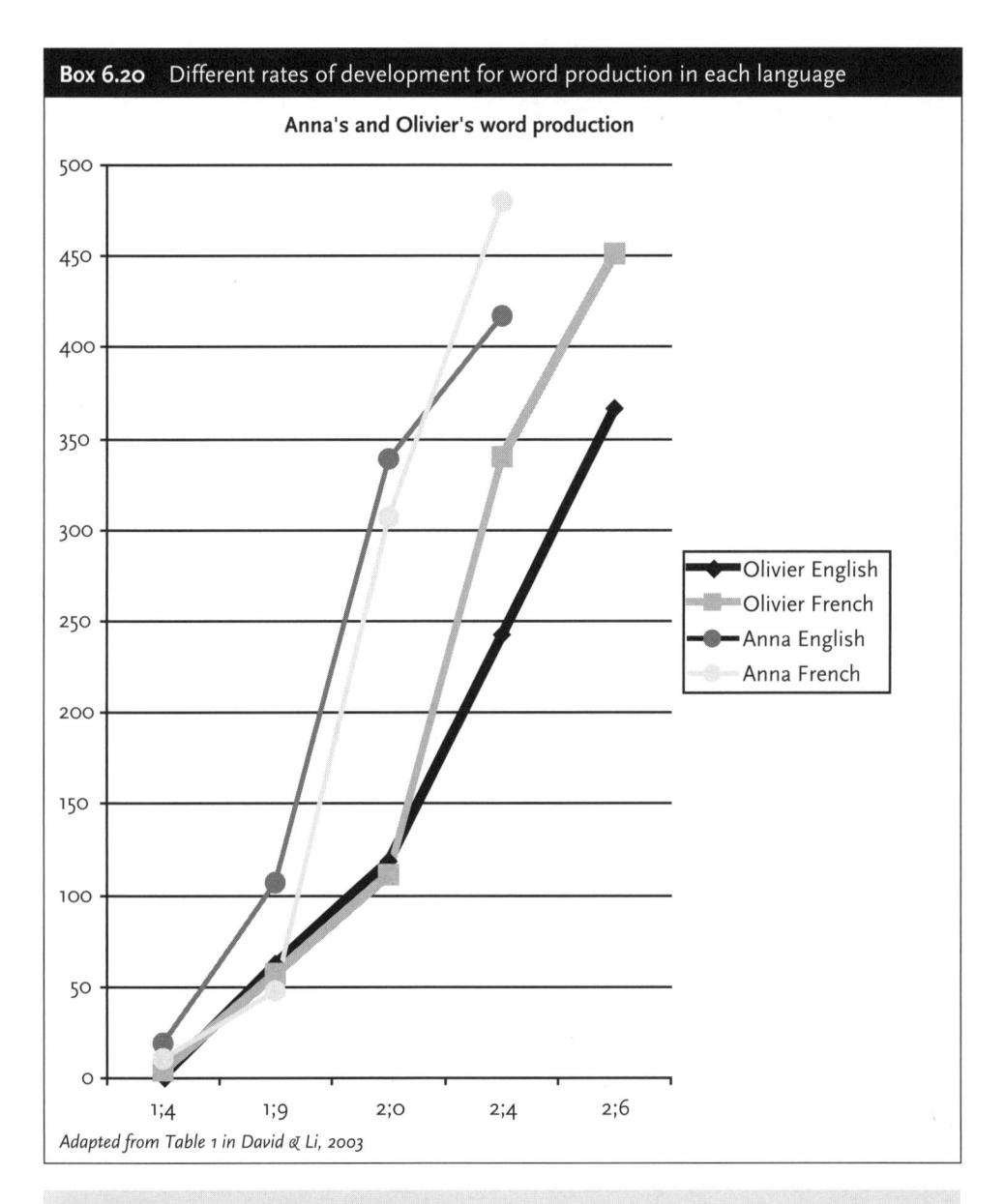

Box 6.20 Different rates of development for word production in each language

Anna's and Olivier's word production

Legend: Olivier English, Olivier French, Anna English, Anna French

Adapted from Table 1 in David & Li, 2003

Stability in word production

As we have seen, children differ a lot from each other in the number of words that they say. At the same time, individual children learn to use more words at different rates. In this highly variable situation, it is amazing to find that children show stability in early word production. This refers to the fact that compared to age-matched peers, children who produce more words at age X also produce more words several months later. In other words, early good talkers (compared to others) are also good talkers later on.

In MFLA children, children's level of word production before the age of 16 months as compared to children of the same age predicts their relative level of word production between age 18 and 24 months (e.g. for English, see Fenson *et al.*, 1994; for Dutch, see Bornstein *et al.*, 2006). We also find this in BFLA. For a group of 31 Dutch–French BFLA children (the same group as mentioned earlier), the levels of word production at 13 months predicted the levels of word production at 20 months (De Houwer *et al.*, 2007). This was true for both languages separately and for total vocabulary. This means that relative to others, young BFLA children who were good talkers in Language A at 13 months were good talkers in Language A at 20 months. The same goes for Language Alpha and total word production (Languages A+Alpha summed).

The findings in the previous subsection of possible differences between the numbers of words a BFLA child produces in each language are not in contradiction with this. This is because when you investigate stability, you do not compare the difference between individual BFLA children's production in each language. Rather, you compare Language A at Time 1 with Language A at Time 2, Language Alpha at Time 1 with Language Alpha at Time 2, and Language A+Alpha at Time 1 with Language A+Alpha at Time 2.

How many words do BFLA children produce?

Knowing many words is important. Knowing a lot of words allows you to be able to talk about a lot of different things. Also, the number of words that children know at an early age is important for their later linguistic and cognitive skills (Marchman & Fernald, 2008).

Large differences between children

The fact that children's rate of growth in lexical production can be so variable from child to child, and the fact that children start to first produce words at such hugely varying ages (relative to the length of time since birth) results in vast differences between the same aged children in the number of different words they produce. For instance, at age 16 months there are MFLA children who produce 154 words, while at the same age there are MFLA children who produce no words at all (Bates *et al.*, 1995: 104).

Such large differences between children also exist for BFLA (see Box 6.21). The most dramatic difference that you see in Box 6.21 is the range for total word production at 20 months, when one child in the group says only 14 words and another one well over a thousand (1,234)!

Patterson (2000, 2002), Marchman *et al.* (2004) and Conboy and Thal (2006) also report large differences within each language and across children for groups of somewhat older English–Spanish bilingual children.[16]

> **Box 6.21** Variation in early word production in BFLA
>
> The number of words produced by a group of 31 BFLA children at age 13 and 20 months (group scores) as measured by the CDI
>
> | Number of words produced | Mean | S.D. | Range |
> | --- | --- | --- | --- |
> | Dutch (13 m) | 10.13 | 13.02 | 0–68 |
> | Dutch (20 m) | 126.65 | 128.35 | 0–642 |
> | French (13 m) | 6.84 | 7.65 | 0–31 |
> | French (20 m) | 144.77 | 156.72 | 4–592 |
> | Total production (13 m) | 16.97 | 17.89 | 0–82 |
> | Total production (20 m) | 271.42 | 265.77 | 14–1234 |
>
> Adapted from De Houwer et al., 2007

Children who say more words in one language also say more words in the other

The fact that BFLA children's word production in both languages may grow at different rates does not mean that there is no relation between them. For the 31 Dutch–French children you have come to know pretty well by now, the number of different words produced in Dutch correlated significantly with the number of words produced in French both at the ages of 13 and 20 months (De Houwer *et al.*, 2007). Conboy and Thal (2006) also report a correlation between young bilingual toddlers' word production in each language.[17] Likewise, for the BFLA girls Maija and Sofia, word production measured in terms of the number of different words in each language showed a strong parallelism between the two languages: increases in word production in one language mirrored increases in the other (Schelletter *et al.*, 2001). If you look at the graphs in Box 6.20 again, you will see a similar picture for Anna and Olivier's word production in French and English.

In the following, when I talk about numbers of words, I am referring to children's production of different words, so, for instance, 'ball' and 'run' (this is also called 'word types'). I'm not referring to how many times they say 'ball' or 'run' (that would be 'word tokens').

The number of words that children say in each language at a given time can be quite different

As young BFLA children learn to say more words in one language, then, they learn to say more words in the other (cf. also Conboy & Thal, 2006). Yet, as mentioned in the previous section, the number of words that individual BFLA children produce at a given age can be quite different for each of their languages (Patterson, 1999, 2000).[18]

For instance, around the age of 1;2, an English–Portuguese boy produced 17 word types in Portuguese but 85 in English (that's 102 in total). This child thus produced five times as many words in English as in Portuguese (Nicoladis, 1998, table 3, observation sessions 6–9).

In contrast, when English–French Anna was at a similar total word production level as this English–Portuguese boy at age 1;7 with a total vocabulary of 101, she produced only twice as many words in one language as in the other (65 in English, 36 in French; David & Li, 2003, table 1). Junker and Stockman (2002[19]), Holowka et al. (2002) and David and Li (2008) also show that at any given age, children may produce quite a different number of word types in each language (see also Box 6.22). Yet different findings are reported for English–German Sofia and English–Latvian Maija. For any one specific age, these two BFLA girls showed no differences between their two languages in the number of word types they produced in each (Schelletter et al., 2001).[20]

Box 6.22 Differences between languages in the proportions of words produced

Nelson, Joseph and Mario are three boys who heard both English and Spanish. When they were 23 months old, the three produced very different proportions of English and Spanish words

Words produced in...	English	Spanish
Nelson	61%	39%
Joseph	81%	19%
Mario	6%	94%

Adapted from Patterson, 1999

Thus, there is a great deal of variation between bilingual toddlers in how many different words they produce in each language at any given time. The number of different words that BFLA children produce at a given age can also differ greatly from child to child. Does this variation mirror what we know for monolingual children? I explore this issue in the next section.

The size of BFLA early production vocabularies compared to MFLA

When BFLA or very young ESLA children are compared to MFLA children as regards the total number of words produced, studies have found no major differences for overall vocabulary (Águila et al., 2005; De Houwer et al., 2006b; Rimel & Eyal, 1996; Pearson et al., 1993), or much *larger* average total vocabulary in bilingual than monolingual toddlers (Águila et al., 2007; Junker & Stockman, 2002; Thordardottir et al., 2006). Four of the studies here concern BFLA (viz., Águila et al., De Houwer et al. and Pearson et al.). Junker and Stockman mention input in two languages from birth or infancy. The study by Rimel and Eyal does not say anything about the bilingual acquisition environments. Thordardottir *et al.*'s bilingual subjects included children whose input in the second language started only at age one (Thordardottir, personal communication).

> I list some basic additional information about these studies in Appendix F.

In spite of different languages, different measures, different age ranges, different data collection procedures, variation between children within each group, varying numbers of subjects and potentially different input settings, none of the studies in the previous paragraph found that bilingual children produce fewer words than monolingual ones.

This shows that contrary to what is often claimed, a bilingual input setting is not a 'danger' for the acquisition process. The fact that three studies found an *advantage for bilinguals* rather than monolinguals is even more convincing proof of this.

The studies here that compared the total number of meanings (or conceptual vocabulary, see Box 6.10(adv.) earlier) that bilingual children expressed with monolingual children's total number of meanings found no differences between the two groups either (De Houwer *et al.*, 2006b; Junker & Stockman, 2002; Rimel & Eyal, 1996; Pearson *et al.*, 1993; Thordardottir *et al.*, 2006[21]). Again, this finding goes against the fairly common idea that bilingual input leads to grave insufficiencies in language learning.

When comparisons were made for one of the bilinguals' languages only, the strictly BFLA studies found no differences with monolinguals (De Houwer *et al.*; Pearson *et al.*). In a study that controlled for the relative amount of input to young bilinguals, Barreña *et al.*, (2008) found no difference between levels of Basque word production in monolingual Basque toddlers and age-matched children with over 60% input in Basque and less than 40% input in Spanish or French. However, comparisons between the monolinguals and bilingual children with less than 60% input in Basque did show the bilinguals to know fewer words in Basque (their other language was not assessed).

Two other studies found that, on average, bilinguals produced fewer words in a single language than monolinguals acquiring that language (Junker & Stockman; Rimel & Eyal; Thordardottir *et al.*). Here, the issue of potentially large differences between the period of time that children had occasion to hear a language spoken to them might be an important intervening factor. It is a foregone conclusion that ESLA children who have had a much shorter experience with a language will know fewer words in that language than MFLA or even BFLA children who have heard that language all their lives.

At the same time, comparing average levels masks the fact that at the individual level, bilingual children may do just as well in one of their languages as monolingual children: seven of the ten bilingual children in the Junker and Stockman study produced as many English words as their monolingual English-speaking peers.

Returning to just the BFLA studies, we can conclude for now that as a group, BFLA children's levels of word production are the same as those of age-matched monolinguals, both in terms of total vocabulary and in terms of vocabulary in a single language. Many more studies are needed, however, to see to what extent this finding is generalizable.

Most of the studies of young BFLA children's lexical knowledge focus on their production of translation equivalents. This is what I turn to next.

Translation equivalents in production

Young bilingual children cannot only understand translation equivalents. They also produce them. The literature appears to show that all BFLA children studied so far produce TEs by the time they are two years old.

The status of translation equivalents in early BFLA production

Young BFLA children have been reported to say words from both their input languages with apparently the same meaning. As discussed previously, children's meanings are often difficult to pinpoint. Are BFLA children really expressing the same thing when they produce words that from a bilingual adult perspective are translation equivalents?

As I discussed before, children may use underextension, that is, they use words with a more restricted meaning than in the adult language. Such underextensions are often difficult to detect in MFLA. In BFLA, you may notice young children's use of underextensions when they happen to use each member of a translation equivalent pair with somewhat different meanings that are clearly underextended in each language. An example is the Dutch–English BFLA child who said 'car' for the family car, but used 'auto' (Dutch car) only to refer to the car that his favorite aunt was driving (example courtesy of Seline Benjamins). Yet the child had definitely heard both the Dutch and English words for 'car' with reference to both the family car and the aunt's car. For another example, see Box 6.23.

> **Box 6.23** An example of the underextension of each member of a TE pair
>
> Spanish–Catalan María del Mar (1;9) is looking at a picture book with her Spanish-speaking (but bilingual) mother. Mother points to a picture of an apple and asks María del Mar what it is. The child answers (in Spanish): 'manzana' (apple).
>
> A little later that same day, at snack time, mother says to María del Mar (in Spanish): 'mira, María del Mar, traigo una manzana' (look, María del Mar, I'm bringing you an apple). But María del Mar says (in Catalan): 'poma' (apple). Her mother repeats what she had said earlier: 'una manzana' (an apple). But the child does not agree, and says: 'no, poma', using the Catalan word again for the 3D apple, whereas before, she had had no problem saying the Spanish word for apple in reference to a picture of an apple.
>
> This example shows an underextended use of the words in each language (and perhaps more; see the Suggestions for study activities).
>
> *Adapted from Vila, 1984: 42*

What we might call a translation equivalent, then, may in fact not have that status for young bilingual children. Some studies have taken this into account. Quay (1995: 378) considered a word to be a translation equivalent only if her English–Spanish BFLA subject Manuela produced a word interchangeably with a word from the other language to refer to the very same object, event or process. Similarly, in her study of a Portuguese–English-learning boy, Nicoladis (1998) took great care to count only those words as translation equivalents that after careful examination appeared to be used with the same meaning.

The fact remains that because young children's early meanings are very fluid, we cannot always really know what a child meant by any specific word. In the remainder of this chapter, I will use the term translation equivalents to refer to words from different languages that could be seen as translations from an adult point of view. This is also the position taken by most scholars who have examined BFLA children's production of TEs.

First occurrence

When do young BFLA children first produce two words that from an adult point of view are 'everyday' translation equivalents? This question appears to have as many different answers as there have been relevant studies. This means there is a great deal of variation between BFLA children.

In their CDI study of 27 English–Spanish BFLA children between the ages of 0;8 and 2;6, Pearson *et al.* (1995) find the earliest production of TEs at the age of ten months (for two children), but many children produced their first TEs somewhat later. English–Spanish Manuela produced one set of doublets at age one, so that two of the three words she produced at that age made up a TE pair (Quay, 1995). The English–Portuguese boy referred to above also produced his earliest TE's from a very early age, that is, shortly after his first birthday (Nicoladis, 1998). In contrast, Porsché (1983: 88–89) reports that German–English Nicolai's production of cross-language synonyms was only slowly developing towards the end of the second year. Similarly, Mandarin–English James did not produce any translation equivalents in the first stages of word production (Qi *et al.*, 2006). Box 6.24 lists a few more examples of BFLA children's earliest documented use of TEs.

Box 6.24 The earliest documented production of TEs in some BFLA children

Age[b]	Child	TE pair [b]	Source
0;9	Karin	Portuguese papa (stress on final syllable) Swedish pappa (stress on first syllable) [c]	Cruz-Ferreira, 2006: 149
1;2	'the child'	Portuguese bola English ball	Nicoladis, 1998
1;4	Louis	German Brot French pain	Ronjat, 1913: 75
1;9	Jessie	Japanese taiyo English sun	Wanner, 1996: 24

[a] Age of first documented production of two members of a TE pair.
[b] Does not list the actual child forms in phonetics, but the adult targets.
[c] It should be noted that Karin not only used different stress patterns, but also different qualities of the vowels, and appropriate lengthening of the middle /p/ in Swedish 'pappa', so through her pronunciation she showed that she was using words from different languages.

This variation between children in when they first produce their first TE isn't surprising, given that they differ so widely in the ages at which they produce their first word, and in the length of time between their first production of a word in Language A and their first production of a word in Language Alpha (see Box 6.16 earlier).

Compared to other BFLA children, German–English Nicolai was quite late in producing his first TEs. Maybe that has something to do with his pretty late start in producing words. At age 19 months, Nicolai produced only six or seven words in total (Porsché 1983: 86). If you compare this level of total word production with the levels for word production at age 20 months in a group of 31 BFLA children (see Box 6.21 earlier), Nicolai is definitely on the slow side here. With his seven words at 19 months, he says only half of the number of words produced by the slowest BFLA child in the Dutch–French BFLA group a month later. In fact, he does not even reach the mean level of total word production that the Dutch–French BFLA group reached six months earlier, at age 13 months.

This raises the question of whether the production of TEs relates to overall word production, that is, whether the first appearance of TEs in children relates to their early lexical production. There have not been any systematic studies of this, but a little reanalysis I did of some published data as set out in Box 6.25(adv.) seems to indicate that there really isn't much of a link between children's overall initial language production and their early use of TEs.

Box 6.25(adv.) Is there a relation between the early production of words and the early production of translation equivalents in BFLA?

Children did not produce any TEs			Children produced at least one TE		
ID	Age	Total production vocabulary	ID	Age	Total production vocabulary
6I	0;8	2	72	1;2	3
6A	0;9	2	Manuela	1;0	3
6D	0;11	2	68	0;10	9
6I	1;3	10	69	1;6	8
V4	1;7	17	6C	1;6	15
			6I	1;3	15
0D	2;6	46	66	1;6	46

All the children here were acquiring Spanish and English from birth; the children with the ID numbers are children studied by Pearson et al., 1995; Manuela is Quay's (1995) and Deuchar and Quay's (2000) subject

The left-hand side of the table here shows all the children in Pearson et al.'s (1995) Table 2 who did not produce any translation equivalents. Then I looked for children in that same Table 2 who had similar or the same levels of total production, but who *did* produce TEs (at least one). Since I found only one child for the smallest total production vocabularies I added the information from Manuela. The table here is divided into four 'bands', one for each different total number of words produced by the children without TEs. As you can see from the right-hand side of the table, it was no problem to find children in each 'band' who did produce TEs.

This little exercise shows that there is little, if any, connection between overall production levels and TE production.

How many TEs do young BFLA children produce and what is their rate of development?

Just as young BFLA children differ widely as far as the time of first TE production is concerned, they differ widely in the number and proportion of translation equivalents that they produce (David & Li, 2008; Pearson *et al.*, 1995). This proportion may also vary within the same child over time (David & Li, 2008; Deuchar & Quay, 2000 table 4.1; Lanvers, 1999). As for MFLA children, the total number of meanings expressed through words also varies considerably from BFLA child to BFLA child (Marchman *et al.*, 2004: 217).

Using a careful and conservative method to trace TE production, Nicoladis (1998) could trace only ten translation equivalents in a six-month period of weekly observations of an English–Portuguese BFLA boy (from age one up). Yet in that same period of time the boy had produced a total of 85 different words. Thus, the 20 word types featuring in the ten translation equivalent pairs accounted for not even a fifth of all the word types produced by this child. Most of his translation equivalent pairs emerged around the age of 1;5, when there was a 'dramatic increase in the number and percentage of TEs' (Nicoladis, 1998: 111).

This pattern of use is to some extent mirrored by Deuchar and Quay's (2000) English–Spanish Manuela. Up until the age of 1;5 Manuela produced 14 TE pairs, but she started to produce a lot more of them at age 1;5. That is also when she started to produce many more words in total.

In a study of an Italian–English-learning boy between the ages of 1;3 and 2, Mcclure (1997) found that translation equivalents were used throughout this period. The proportion of TEs was close to 30% (77 out of a total of 258 word types), which is quite a bit higher than the one found for the Portuguese–English-learning boy studied by Nicoladis.

On the day that Japanese–English Jessie showed evidence of a vocabulary spurt, he also produced his first translation equivalent (Wanner, 1996: 23). In contrast, for the two Catalan–Spanish BFLA children Roger and María del Mar studied by Vila (1984), no relation was seen between an overall increase in vocabulary and the children's first use of translation equivalents. In fact, Roger and María del Mar produced very few TEs compared to their overall word production. When he used a total of 247 words, Roger produced 14 TEs. When she used a total of 616 words, María del Mar produced 65 TEs. You will remember that Roger and María del Mar produced a large proportion of language-neutral words (see Box 6.17 earlier). Perhaps this preempted their need to learn to use a lot of translation equivalents that differ in form across the two languages (but remember that their two languages, Spanish and Catalan, resemble each other a lot on the lexical level).

Finally, just as early words come and go in children's production in the second year of life, some of their translation equivalents may disappear and reappear. Children may produce a TE pair, a bit later only the Language A member of the TE pair, and yet later only the Language Alpha member (Leopold, 1970). In contrast, other children may continue to use both members of a TE pair once they have started to produce them for the first time (Deuchar & Quay, 2000).

Summing up, then, there is a great deal of variation between and within BFLA children in the extent to which they produce TEs. They may produce quite a lot of them, or not so many. Their TEs may make up a large proportion of their overall word production, or not so much.

The kinds of meanings expressed in TEs

Porsché (1983) reports that German–English Nicolai's first translation equivalents only expressed functional, pragmatic meanings such as 'non-existence' (German 'nein', English 'no and 'un-unh', which belongs to both). It is only well after his second birthday that Nicolai started to use translation equivalents that were content words such as {'allein' and 'alone'} and {'Ecke' and 'corner'}.

It seems that Nicolai was a bit of an exception. Most examples of translation equivalents produced by young BFLA children that I have seen in the literature reflect the variety that is present in their other vocabulary, that is, in words they say only in one language. Some examples of such early TEs expressing all kinds of different meanings are listed in Box 6.26.

Box 6.26 Some examples of translation equivalents in the second year of life that show a wide variety of distinct meanings

Italian 'scendere'	and	English 'down'	(Mcclure, 1997)
Italian 'ciao'	and	English 'bye'	(Mcclure, 1997)
Portuguese 'bola'	and	English 'ball'	(Nicoladis, 1998)
Portuguese 'oi'	and	English 'hi'	(Nicoladis, 1998)
Portuguese 'chave'	and	English 'key'	(Nicoladis, 1998)
Spanish 'bajar'	and	English 'down'	(Deuchar & Quay, 2000)
Spanish 'más'	and	English 'more'	(Deuchar & Quay, 2000)
Spanish 'zapato'	and	English 'shoe'	(Deuchar & Quay, 2000)
Spanish 'abuelo'	and	English 'grandpa'	(Deuchar & Quay, 2000)

Young translators?

The use by young BFLA children of the members of a translation equivalent pair on different occasions does not imply that BFLA children are translating in any sense (see also Ronjat, 1913: 76). So when one day a child calls a pipe 'pipe' in French, and the next day 'Pfeife' in German (example taken from Ronjat, 1913: 76), the child is not translating 'pipe' into 'Pfeife' or the other way round. Rather, the child is using each word to express a particular meaning in particular circumstances.

This is not to say that BFLA children cannot on occasion seem to be actually translating (or, more accurately, since we are not talking about writing, interpreting). This occurs when children say two words from different languages for the same thing within one utterance (Box 6.27).

> **Box 6.27** Some examples of translation equivalents used side by side in a single utterance, as if to show translation

Louis	20 m	'oeil Auge' (French and German renditions of 'eye')
Louis	20 m	'Schiff bateau' (German and French renditions of 'boat')
From Ronjat, 1913: 81		
María del Mar	24 m	'pato, ànec' (Spanish and Catalan renditions of 'duck')
From Vila, 1984: 42		

'Real' translating or interpreting is also in evidence when children repeat something they said in Language A to one person in Language Alpha directed at another person, or the same person. It is also evident when children repeat a word in Language Alpha that they just heard in Language A. Some early examples of this are shown in Box 6.28.

> **Box 6.28** Examples of 'real' translations by young BFLA children
>
> 'There is one instance in which Hildegard performed a purely linguistic translation, and it was early, B 1;6. Her mother told her not to do something. When she did not obey, the mother asked "What did Mama tell you?" Hildegard reproduced the injunction, *No, no*. Driving home the point, the mother continued: "Don't you know what 'no, no' means?" Hildegard's answer was: *Nein, nein*.'
>
> *From Leopold, 1970: 179–180*
>
> At age 1;9, Louis said something in German to a German-speaking cook, and then repeated it in French for the benefit of other servants who spoke only French. At age 2;2, the servants use Louis to interpret messages to other servants who speak a different language.
>
> Louis can interpret from German to French and the other way round. He will even interpret between his parents, knowing full well that they both understand each other's language. At age 2;2, Louis interprets quite deliberately: 'Montagne, dass heißt Berg' {'mountain (in French), that's called mountain (in German)}.
>
> *Adapted from Ronjat, 1913: 82, 85*
>
> Christopher lives in El Paso, Texas, in the USA. He has heard Spanish and English from birth. At home, his family speaks both (and understands both!). One day, when Christopher is just over two years old, a wrapped box arrives in the mail. Christopher is at home with his two aunts. They are talking to each other about the box, and one of them says in Spanish: 'es una caja llena de dulces.' (It's a box full of candy.)
>
> Christopher had heard this. He points to the box and says in English: 'cany, cany!' (candy, candy). Christopher has appropriately translated 'dulces' in Spanish into 'candy' in English.
>
> *Adapted from Huerta, 1977*
>
> Anouk is two and a half years old and speaks Dutch and French. Her Dutch-speaking father asks her: 'wat is dit?' (what's this?). Anouk answers in Dutch: 'boot' (boat). Her father then asks her: 'en wat zegt mama hiervoor?' (and what does mummy call this?). Anouk correctly answers in French: 'bateau' (boat).
>
> *Adapted from van der Linden, 2000: 46*

A special status for TEs?

Junker and Stockman (2002) found that all the ten bilingual two-year-olds in their study (not all with bilingual input from birth, though) produced translation equivalents. Indeed, I have seen no examples from BFLA children in the literature who did not produce any TEs by the time they were two. Similarly, there are no reports of BFLA children who do not produce words by age two. Like earliest word production, TE use may start around children's first birthdays. Like earliest word production, some children may show a rapid increase in the number of TEs produced while others do not. Like earliest word production, children vary widely in the number of TEs they produce. So what is so special about TEs?

What's special for TEs is that they allow you to talk about the same things with people who speak different languages. That will become clear from the section on language choice later. But first we look at what might be behind TE production.

What drives the production of TEs, or what hinders it?

Why do children learn to say the two members of one particular TE, but only one member of another TE? Of course, one major reason can be that they have only heard one member of a TE in their input. This means they just haven't had the occasion to learn the other member. For studies of early word knowledge in bilingual children, then, it is important to know what words they heard in what language.

When children do have access to both members of a TE pair, some scholars have argued that it is the phonological shape of members of a TE pair that determines which member a child will try to produce or not.

Similar sounding TEs

It has been suggested that in learning to produce translation equivalents, BFLA children are aided by the fact that some words sound pretty much the same in both input languages (for instance, English 'bed' and German 'Bett'; Schelletter, 2002). Celce-Murcia (1978) has made the opposite claim, stating that her French–English daughter Caroline was 'confused' (p. 49) when the words were similar. Celce-Murcia interpreted Caroline's use of hesitations or saying two TEs one after the other as signs of 'confusion'.

Sometimes it is also claimed that BFLA children try to avoid saying TEs that show a lot of overlap in their adult forms, or it is claimed that children do not really distinguish between such words. However, the evidence does not support this. Cruz-Ferreira's (2006: 64–65; 149) three Portuguese–Swedish BFLA children did not avoid similar sounding TEs at all, but readily incorporated them in their speech (see also Box 5.9 in Chapter 5). They said similar sounding adult words in two languages, such as Portuguese 'salame' and Swedish 'salami' (for 'salami'), but they would say them in such a way that the words in each language sounded as differently as possible.[22] Leopold (1970: 178) also gives examples of Hildegard producing both members of a TE pair that are formally very close in the input languages (Ei-egg; Ball-ball).

TEs that are quite distinct in form

As regards TEs with quite distinct forms in the input, some authors have suggested that young BFLA children avoid saying those members of a TE in the adult language that are supposedly more difficult phonetically (Celce-Murcia, 1978; Yavas, 1995). As Celce-Murcia (1978) noted, MFLA children may appear to show avoidance strategies as well. It is quite difficult to prove that children are actively avoiding saying certain words, though.

While it is possible that some BFLA children do use avoidance strategies, so far the evidence for any general use of such strategies is very thin.

Form similarity as a basis for TE learning?

Claims of an influence of cross-linguistic form similarity (Schelletter's 2002 term) in the early production of TEs rest on an implicit assumption that children somehow have an idea in mind of the meanings and forms of different translation equivalent pairs, then see to what extent the forms differ or not, and based on this comparison make a decision whether or not to say a particular form.

Such an approach seems unlikely. It is more likely that children are interested in saying the words they want to say in order to communicate with the world around them (Bloom, 1993). If they were generally led by phonological avoidance strategies, it is hard to see how children would attempt to produce 'difficult' words at all. They do not appear to avoid those as a general strategy, however. They do try to produce more 'difficult' words, but use phonological simplification processes in their own productions (see Chapter 5). Of course, there may be different strategies that different children use.

Children are unlikely to be swayed by form differences and similarities, however, when they need to learn to *understand* both members of a TE pair. Rather, they need to learn to understand more words as they hear them being used, regardless of the words' phonological shapes (see the section on the comprehension of TEs).

It is more likely that it is children's *communicative need* that drives their production of TEs. If a child wants to talk to monolingual English grandma about things she knows only in Spanish, it will help her to communicate with grandma if she learns to say the equivalent English word. This brings us to the next section.

Translation equivalents and language choice

It will be clear by now that not all of BFLA children's words are TEs. BFLA children will produce both members of a TE pair, one member of a TE pair, words in each language that don't have a direct translation in the other language and language-neutral words.

Language-neutral words, by definition, 'work' in both languages. For all the others, children have to select the words from the 'right' language. In principle, then, they can also make the 'wrong' choice.

As little as they still are, though, BFLA children in the second year of life usually select the words from the 'right' language. That means that, on the whole, BFLA children between the age of one and two can already adjust their language choice to their interlocutor (see also Chapter 4 earlier). They hardly ever speak the 'wrong' language (Cantone, 2007: 126). I show a few examples of this in Box 6.29.

Box 6.29 Appropriate word choice in the second year of life and beyond

Maija

English–Latvian Maija produced 273 utterances in a recording at the age of 1;3 (15 months). Of these 93% were in the 'right' language. That is, they were Latvian in conversation with a Latvian interlocutor, or English in conversation with an English interlocutor. This percentage dropped to 85% (out of 426 utterances) at the age of 1;9 but rose to 96% (out of 647 utterances) by the age of 2;2 (see Tables 3 and 4 in Sinka, 2000).

Mara

English–Latvian Mara produced 414 utterances in a recording at the age of 1;6 (18 months). Of these 86% were in the 'right' language. That is, they were Latvian in conversation with a Latvian interlocutor, or English in conversation with an English interlocutor. This percentage was the same at the age of 2;1 but rose to 99% (out of 656 utterances) by the age of 2;5 (see Tables 1 and 2 in Sinka, 2000).

Lukas

At age 1;8 (20 months) German–Italian Lukas said close to 40 utterances in Italian when he was speaking to an Italian-speaking interlocutor. There were also about ten single word utterances in German. On the same day, Lukas said over 80 utterances in German to a German-speaking interlocutor. None of his utterances in the recording with a German-speaking interlocutor contained any Italian (see Figure 6.2. in Cantone, 2007: 118).

Carlotta

At age 1;10 (22 months) German–Italian Carlotta said close to 80 utterances in Italian when she was speaking to an Italian-speaking interlocutor. There was one utterance that contained some German. On the same day, Carlotta said 80 utterances in German to a German-speaking interlocutor. In addition, she said about five single word utterances in Italian; that's about 6% of all recorded utterances with a German-speaking interlocutor (see Figure 6.1. in Cantone, 2007: 117).

> **Box 6.29** Appropriate word choice in the second year of life and beyond continued
>
> *Aurelio*
> At age 1;11 (23 months) German–Italian Aurelio said close to 40 utterances in Italian when he was speaking to an Italian-speaking interlocutor. There were also about four utterances that contained some German. On the same day, Aurelio addressed just over 30 utterances in German to a German-speaking interlocutor. None of his utterances in the recording with a German-speaking interlocutor contained any Italian (see Figure 6.4. in Cantone, 2007: 121).
>
> *Sofia*
> English–German Sofia said 95% of the 392 word tokens recorded in the four-month period between 1;11 and 2;3 in the 'right' language. That is, they were German in conversation with a German interlocutor, or English in conversation with an English interlocutor. This percentage rose a little in the course of the third year (to 97% between 2;4 and 2;6, and 96% between 2;7 and 2;9) (see Table 1 in Schelletter, 2002).
>
> *Jessie*
> Jessie lives in an extended household where mostly Japanese is spoken, except that he also hears his father speak English to him. Jessie's father is also proficient in Japanese, and addresses his wife and her live-in parents in Japanese. While Jessie's mother is also fluent in English, Jessie has no day-to-day experience of this, since she only speaks Japanese when he is around. Towards the end of the second year, Jessie uses English single- and multi-word utterances to address his father. Jessie hardly ever uses English to address his mother and grandmother. Rather, he speaks to them in Japanese. Jessie also speaks Japanese to his father, though (Wanner, 1999).
>
> *Anouk*
> Anouk lives in the Netherlands and has heard Dutch and French from birth. In recordings made at age two and a half, Anouk produced mostly Dutch words in a Dutch context (89%), and mostly French words in a French context (88%) (see Table 1 in van der Linden, 2000).

BFLA children do differ from each other, though, in the exact ages at which they first show evidence of adjusting their language choice. Children also differ in the extent to which they produce words from the 'wrong' language (in spite of the fact that, on the whole, they do speak the 'right' language) (see also Cantone, 2007: 116).

This brings us back to translation equivalents. One good reason for knowing how to say two labels for the same thing is that this helps you to speak the right language (Quay, 1995; Deuchar & Quay, 2000). Yet it isn't really clear what the precise relation is between the learning of TEs and learning to speak the 'right' language. In some children, the first regular production of TEs goes together with mostly speaking the 'right' language. In others, it does not. I describe a few contrasting examples in Box 6.30.

> You might think that the Japanese–English boy in Box 6.30 first needed some additional words in order to be able to choose the 'right' language. That's possible. But if there is a strong link between children's overall production vocabularies and their ability to adjust their language choice, children with fairly large production vocabularies (and many TEs!) should definitely be adjusting their language choice. The example from the English–Italian boy in Box 6.30 suggests that that doesn't hold either. As of now, it isn't clear

whether appropriate language choice in BFLA children under age two mostly relates to their knowledge of translation equivalents or to the size of children's lexicons. It is possible that there is very little link, and that the early use of words from the 'right' language is primarily linked to the interlocutor's use of monolingual discourse strategies (Lanza, 1997; see also Chapter 4 and Deuchar & Quay, 2006: 104–106). It is also possible that different BFLA children just follow different paths (Cantone, 2007). This awaits investigation, however.

Box 6.30 Appropriate language choice and early TE production

Appropriate language choice appears together with TEs

Up until age 1;9, Japanese–English Jessie produced no TEs. He produced a total of 28 words. There were both English and Japanese words in his vocabulary. Jessie did not address his interlocutors in the 'right' language. Once Jessie started to produce translation equivalents (at 1;9), he also started to mostly address his interlocutor in the 'right' language (Wanner, 1996).

Appropriate language choice appears prior to TEs

Nicoladis (1998) finds that at age 1;6, her Portuguese–English subject had already adjusted somewhat to his interlocutor's language choice before TEs had really set in.

Many TEs but no appropriate language choice

Mcclure (1997) found that her Italian–English subject did not really adjust his language choice to the interlocutor's until age two. Nevertheless, the boy did produce many translation equivalents prior to that age.

Even BFLA children who on the whole pretty much use the 'right' language may produce the 'wrong' member of a TE pair. Ronjat (1913: 7) notes that when his son Louis was 20 months old, he often would insert a German word in his otherwise French utterances when addressing his French-speaking bilingual father (the very first use of German to his father instead of French is the example in Box 6.12 earlier). Ronjat's response to such mixed utterances was to say (in French): 'Oh, you mean X', and then he said the translation equivalent of the German word that Louis had used. Ronjat is here using what Lanza (1997) has termed a monolingual discourse strategy (see Chapter 4). As Louis got a bit older and knew more TEs, he did speak more and more French to his father.

One reason, then, for using the 'wrong' member of a TE pair is that BFLA children do not know the other member of a TE pair (see also, e.g. Nicoladis & Secco, 2000). That means they have a lexical gap for that particular TE pair (see the earlier section on 'Words and meanings in early production'). They know just one member of the pair of doublets. Leaning how to say the label from the other language for the same thing will increase their ability to speak the 'right' language. Strategies such as those used by Ronjat will help in teaching children the words they need.

Not all uses of words in the 'wrong' language can be explained by lexical gaps, though (Cantone, 2007; David & Li, 2003; De Houwer, 1990: 107–113; Deuchar & Quay, 2000). Children may have recently produced both members of a TE pair, and yet they will occasionally select the member from the 'wrong' language. Often, when somewhat older

BFLA children do not say a member of a TE in the right language, they *can* say the other member if you ask them or show them you don't understand (that fits in with their overall capability of repairing their utterances; see Chapter 7). Why they first selected the word from the 'wrong' language isn't certain. Fully proficient bilingual adults may sometimes use a word from the 'wrong' language as well (e.g. La Heij, 2005).

BFLA children who generally use words from the 'right' language do occasionally use words from the 'wrong' language. Often, though, they will tend to do this for only one language. That means they will occasionally say words from Language A when they are addressing someone who speaks Language Alpha, but they do not say words from Language Alpha when they are addressing someone who speaks Language A. For instance, returning to the example from Louis a few paragraphs earlier, Ronjat (1913) notes that his German-speaking wife and the German-speaking nanny did not have to use any 'Oh you mean X' strategies, since Louis hardly ever said any French words when he addressed his mother or the nanny. It so happens that at the time, Louis heard a lot more German than French. That means that he heard many words in German for which he did not hear a French TE. Once again, we see that the input really matters a whole lot.

The fact that from early on, Ronjat was attentive to Louis' production of words from the 'wrong' language and offered him the 'right' word most likely contributed to the fact that Louis soon leaned a lot more TEs and no longer needed to resort to the 'wrong' language. The example from Louis shows that TE word learning opportunities and discourse strategies are closely connected.

In conclusion

BFLA input can speed up the rate of word learning

The learning of new words is intimately bound up with conversation in interaction (Clark, 2007). Children need adult experts to guide them in their word learning, and are able to learn new words quite fast, especially after age two.

There is nothing in the research literature to suggest that these basic facts about word learning are different for BFLA and MFLA children. However, young BFLA children may generally be at an advantage compared to MFLA children in their word learning. Certainly, they learn new words, or 'labels for concepts', at a much faster pace that monolingual children, both in comprehension and production. That is, BFLA children show levels of total comprehension and production vocabularies that it takes MFLA children a lot longer to reach.

This is not surprising, given BFLA children's communicative need to understand people referring to the same thing in two languages. In comparison with MFLA children, BFLA children need to pay extra attention to what speakers intend to say, since the variation in the different words they hear is so much greater than in a bilingual setting, and the variation from speaker to speaker can be so large as to involve a change of language.

The fact that BFLA children can learn to understand words with the same overall ease as MFLA children, and learn to understand more words than MFLA children at the same age (and thus, in the same amount of time) suggests that the learning of words in MFLA children is delayed in comparison to BFLA children – simply because the MFLA children have not had as differentiated a learning opportunity.

Two separate lexical 'systems'?

In the literature on BFLA the question is often asked whether children's word production development in the second year of life shows evidence of children learning one 'global' lexical system or two separate ones.

The discussions in this chapter will have hopefully made you realize that the question of whether BFLA infants and toddlers develop two separate lexical 'systems' from the start is an oversimplified one. Lexical development has many different aspects and is a very gradual and slow process at first. When it 'takes off' (with, for instance, the vocabulary spurt in production), BFLA children may produce many translation equivalents or not so many, many words in one language but not so many in the other or equal numbers of words in each. The variability is enormous.

Then there are the more fundamental issues of whether bilinguals have two separate lexical 'systems' in the first place (see also Kroll & Tokowicz, 2005; La Heij, 2005) and what sort of empirical evidence would be needed to examine whether young BFLA children are building up two separate lexical systems from the beginning onwards. The answers here are not clear.

Remember, though, that BFLA children perceive their two languages as different from infancy (Chapter 5). This may help them to develop processing strategies that keep the words of each of their languages in separate 'mindfiles'.

Regardless of whether or not there are two separate lexical systems developing in the minds of young BFLA children, we do have substantial evidence that they build up comprehension and production lexicons in each of their languages at the same time, that they use similar semantic processes in each and sometimes can even actively translate between them. At the same time, lexical comprehension and/or production in one language are not necessarily at the same level in the other: BFLA children can know more words in Language A than Language Alpha. This balance can change over time, however.

Bilingual lexical development beyond the toddler years

Most of the research on young BFLA children's lexical development is limited to the age of around two and a half. One reason is methodological: the CDI Toddler form goes up to that age.[23] In turn, the reason for that is that two and a half-year-olds know so many words that it becomes very difficult for parents to report on the specific words their children know.

When BFLA children are very young, they learn words in both their languages. That's probably because the things people talk to them about are, on the whole, pretty similar across both languages. This also explains why BFLA children learn so many translation equivalents.

As they start going to school, BFLA children will be hearing many more new words for new things in one language only. That means that their worlds start to be more 'compartmentalized', that is, each language will more and more be heard and used in different circumstances.

I know of no group studies involving just BFLA school-age children's lexical development. My personal experience with BFLA school-age children suggests that both in comprehension and production they will develop one language more for one particular set of domains, and the other one for others. For instance, bilingual children may hear about mathematics only in Language A, but have tennis lessons in Language Alpha. It shouldn't come as much of a surprise, then, that BFLA school-age children may not be able to talk about mathematics in Language Alpha and may not know the specific vocabulary necessary for tennis in Language A.

This is what Oller and colleagues (e.g. Oller, 2005; Oller et al., 2007) have called the 'distributed characteristic' of bilingual word learning. Bilingual children will increasingly have specialized vocabularies in each language.[24] This implies several things: (1) that assessing just one language generally underestimates bilingual children's lexical knowledge and, hence, (2) that comparing bilingual children's lexical knowledge in just a single language to norms made for monolingual children is an unfair comparison. Bilingual children's total lexical knowledge should be taken into account.

Fostering lexical development in two languages

BFLA children who go to school in Language A may soon start to experience a stagnation in their lexical development in Language Alpha, simply because they spend so much time hearing Language A and learning to read in it. In order to aid a continuous increase in BFLA children's lexical knowledge of Language Alpha as well, parents may want to invest time in explaining concepts and vocabulary learnt at school in Language A. They may also teach children to read books in Language Alpha once children are comfortable with reading in Language A. Trips to places where Language Alpha is spoken by children will also help (for examples of how some BFLA families have done all this, see, e.g. Caldas, 2006 and Saunders, 1988).

In general, it is also advisable to try and use a diversified and sophisticated vocabulary with school-age children – of course, as part of conversations on topics that children are interested in (Weizman & Snow, 2001).

This sounds like a lot of work. And, indeed, it is (Okita, 2002). Parents may not have the willingness, energy or the resources to give much attention to their school-aged children's continued development in the non-school language. This might hinder harmonious bilingual development or, depending on one's expectations, it may not (see Chapter 8).

Yet, the important point here is that lexical development can increase quite fast in school-aged children with increased input, and that includes reading. Reading is a wonderful source for vocabulary development (and can be a lot of fun, too!). Reading books is one possibility, but in this day and age children may be more inclined to read on the Internet. Given proper parental guidance, this is a great opportunity for children all over the world.

Also school-age children who are learning a new second language at school will be much aided by teaching programs developed to boost their input and thus their lexical development. Again, increased input can quickly lead to more learning.

As we have seen in this chapter, the role of input frequency is also important at the very earliest stages of BFLA lexical development. For MFLA, the articulatory clarity with which adults speak to infants in the first year of life plays an important role in determining how well infants will perceive speech sounds (Liu *et al.*, 2003). A high degree of input clarity coupled with a high frequency of input may explain much of the interindividual variation we already see in BFLA children's lexicons at the age of 13 months. BFLA children who know a lot of words relative to others at age 13 months keep their advantage at age 20 months. To what extent such an early advantage remains in effect as children get older has not yet been studied for BFLA, but studies from MFLA children suggest it may (Marchman & Fernald, 2008).

There is much more to be learned about lexical development in BFLA. It is clear, though, that words are BFLA children's greatest opportunity. They can learn many of them and there is no limit to how many they can learn (cf. also Oller, 2005). Given sufficient learning opportunities lexical gaps can be quickly filled, in one language or in two. We all continue to be able to do this throughout our lives.

The number and kinds of words that young children know is an important basis on which they can build to do what the adults around them do much of the time when they speak: combine words into sentences. This leads us to the next chapter.

Notes

1. It is possible that each language carries with it different associations for the child. 'Time to go to sleep' might be associated with reading a favorite picture book in bed, while 'Tijd om te gaan slapen!' might be more associated with putting on pyjamas and brushing teeth.

2. However, Vila's study concerned just two children. David and Li (2008) rely on data from 13 children and Pearson *et al.* (1997) on 25.

3. In contrast, the total number of meanings that the 113 BFLA children in this study expressed through words did not relate to different proportions of exposure to each language (Marchman *et al.*, 2004: 217).

4. The studies by Patterson (2002) and Pearson *et al.* (1997) may have included some cases of ESLA as well.

5. Although age of first regular exposure to each language for the bilinguals is not specified, the children had bilingual input from birth (Barbara Pearson, personal communication).

6. However, see Pearson (1998) for an in-depth discussion of the deeper question to what degree it makes sense to compare bilingual and monolingual child populations and, especially, to what extent the results of such comparisons can be used in assessments of purported language delay.

7. The children were all first born and lived with both their biological parents in middle-class homes.

8. In testing with the PPVT, children are asked to point to the one of four pictures that shows the word that the investigator said. There are many different pages with pictures. The PPVT is not a global test of how many words children understand, but rather of how many carefully chosen words from a pre-set list children are able to match to the right picture. Norms have been developed for the PPVT that allow children to be compared to each other.

9. The deeper question, of course, is to what extent we ever really know what someone meant to say. A discussion of this would lead me too far, though.

10. Fifty-five of the 64 toddlers in the Conboy and Thal study were BFLA and the other nine were ESLA, with input in their L2 starting prior to age six months (Barbara Conboy, personal communication).

11. Eight months is the lowest age for which the CDI asks information.

12. In comparison, the Infant forms of the CDI contain more than 400 lexical items and the Toddler forms around 700; precise numbers depend on the specific language adaptation.

13. It may also be necessary to include a fourth category of words that are 'semi-cognates' (Águila *et al.*, 2007).

14. But see Bates *et al.* (1995) for a critical appraisal of the notion of vocabulary spurt or 'burst', as they call it.

15. My interpretation here is not based on quantitative analyses but on the great variety in word use that is evident from the many different examples that Cruz-Ferreira (2006) gives.

16. Most of the children in the Patterson studies were BFLA, but some were ESLA (Janet Patterson, personal communication); the 113 children in the Marchman *et al.* study were mostly exposed to their two languages from birth; see note 10 for the Conboy and Thal study; all the studies here look at children of different ages and combined cover the age range from 17 to 31 months.

17. This correlation was measured for data collapsed across an age range from 19 to 31 months.

18. Most of the children in these studies were BFLA, but some were ESLA (Janet Patterson, personal communication).

19. The ten children in this study did not all hear their two languages from birth, though.

20. It should be noted though, that unlike the other studies, Schelletter *et al.*'s (2001) results are based on transcripts of conversations. This methodological difference could account for the different results.

21. Note that Thordardottir *et al.* compared bilinguals to somewhat older monolinguals in each language and found no differences for one comparison (bilinguals and French monolinguals) but did find differences for another comparison (bilinguals and English monolinguals, where the monolinguals scored better). This strange result hangs together with the fact that the French monolinguals scored lower than the English monolinguals. Small sample sizes may be an explanation.

22. While this is what it looks like from an adult point of view, it is most likely the children's early use of some language-specific phonological devices such as stress patterns that caused the differences, rather than any conscious attempt on their part to push the two languages apart – but this, of course, we shall never find out.

23. For BFLA children's weaker language it may be useful to continue with the CDI beyond the age of 2;6, though.

24. The studies by Oller and colleagues here (see also Oller & Eilers, 2002) involve both ESLA and not so early SLA (there is no mention of BFLA children).

25. This exercise is meant to show you just how far the specialization in lexical knowledge can go. I learned French at school and speak it pretty well, but when I first moved into my house in the French-speaking part of Belgium, I couldn't talk to plumbers or electricians, since I just didn't know the words you need 'around the house'. I still need a dictionary for some words on the French CDI – even though French-learning toddlers may know them.

26. In Chapter 7, word knowledge and use are discussed until p. 157; the rest of the chapter deals with BFLA children's early word combinations and early morphosyntactic development. This is also important, but fits in better with the next chapter in this book.

Summary box

- Bilingual infants have learned to understand quite a few words from both their languages by their first birthdays. Around that time they also start to produce a few words.
- Both MFLA and BFLA children's early word production shows great interindividual variability. In spite of this variability, there are no group differences between MFLA and BFLA in the number of words they know for each language separately. BFLA children's total word knowledge exceeds that of age-matched monolinguals.
- BFLA children use the same sorts of semantic processes as children acquiring just one language.
- BFLA children's lexicons may develop at different rates for each language separately. Such differences may be related to overall differences between the global input frequencies in each language. Yet, children with relatively larger vocabularies in the one language will also have larger vocabularies in the other.

Summary box continued

- BFLA children clearly learn to understand and produce words from each of their two target languages. They also learn to understand and produce words that can be considered as translations of each other. Yet is not clear whether it makes any sense to speak of two developing lexical 'systems'.
- BFLA children say words from the language that they are addressed in. The first appearance of this ability to select the 'right' language varies considerably from child to child, but certainly by age two most BFLA children are able to speak the language that is expected from them.

Suggestions for study activities

1. *Project*: If you speak only one language: are there any topics you can talk about very easily, others that you don't feel so comfortable with, yet others you really cannot discuss? (e.g. types of tools for building a house, different kinds of trees, the ins-and-outs of film directing). Have a conversation about this with other students in your class and compare notes. Why do you think there are these differences between topics in how easily you can discuss them?
2. *Project*: If you speak two languages (also if you don't speak them equally well): are there any topics you can talk about very easily in one language but not the other? Select ten topics that you can talk about in at least one language. Draw up a little table in which you check off for each language which topic you can discuss easily. Have a conversation about this with other students in your class and compare notes. Why do you think there are these differences between topics in how easily you can discuss them in one language versus the other?
3. *Project/WEB*: Obtain a copy of a CDI Infant form in a language you learned at school, but do not speak at home (see http://www.sci.sdsu.edu/cdi/adaptations_ol.htm for information on which languages are available). Depending on which language you need, obtaining a copy may be more, or less difficult.

    3.1 Once you have the two forms, select one of the parts (the same for each language) that contains mostly nouns. Following the procedure in Box 6.9(adv.), determine which items in your selection are cognates, translation equivalents and list specific. Make lists of each of these. What problems did you encounter? How did you solve them? (advanced)

    3.2 Once you have the form, fill it in for yourself. Which words do you understand but have never said? Which words do you understand and have used yourself?[25]

4. If there are several students in your class who know the same set of languages, then activity 3.1 can be done jointly, and can be expanded to cover the entire two CDI Infant forms. For larger groups of students, the CDI Toddler forms can be compared (these contain more items). (advanced)
5. *Project*: Find a family with a child between one and one a half (monolingual or bilingual, it doesn't matter, as long as you understand the language(s) that is spoken). Ask whether you can come and visit for an hour or so at a time when the family is not having dinner and the child is awake and alert. Ask whether you can make a video recording of whatever goes on between the child and other people in the family. Explain that you are studying child language development. Parents may say, 'oh, he's not talking yet'. Then you can say that you're also interested to find out what he can understand. Make your video recording (try to be as unobtrusive as possible and don't talk whileyou're doing it). Analyze all or part of the following (you can do this activity with a friend in

> **Suggestions for study activities continued**
>
> your class): (1) what are the sorts of words the parents and/or older siblings use to talk to the child? (2) which are the words or phrases that the child appeared to understand? (3) if the child was saying words, what were they and what do you think they meant?
>
> 6. *Project*: Do this activity with a friend who can help out with the filming. Find a family with a child who is nearly two years old (monolingual or bilingual, it doesn't matter, as long as you understand the language(s) that is spoken). Ask whether you can come and visit at a time when the family is not having dinner and the child is awake and alert. Ask whether you can make a video recording of you playing for half an hour with the child using the child's own toys, and that you'll bring a friend to do the recording. It's fine if the parents are in the room during the recording. Explain that you are studying child language development.
>
>   Once you get the OK, make your video recording (but give the child a few minutes to get acquainted with you and the filmer first). I suggest you bring an attractive children's book without words that you can use during the session to elicit speech from the child. You can then give this book to the child afterwards as a gift. Analyze all or part of the following (you can do this activity with a friend in your class): (1) which words or phrases did the child appear to understand? (2) could you mostly understand the child (you might have needed some time to 'warm up')? (3) if you could, what were the child's words and what do you think they meant? (4) did you notice any 'strange' uses of words? explain; (5) was the child saying only single words or already seeming to combine words?
>
> 7. Look at the list of Spanish and English equivalent words that Manuela produced between age ten months and 1;10 (Deuchar & Quay, 2000: 59–60); you don't have to know Spanish to do this activity. Try to categorize these words into different 'semantic' domains (e.g. words for people, words for objects, words for places, words for actions/processes, social words). How many are there in every domain? Which domain has the most?
>
> 8. Look at the example in Box 6.23. Re-read the section on the Mutual Exclusivity Bias. Does the example in Box 6.23 bear any connection to this Bias? If so, how? (advanced)
>
> 9. Obtain copies of the articles by Conboy and Thal (2006), Marchman *et al.* (2004) and Patterson (1998). Find the figures these publications give for word production in Spanish and English and/or both languages combined. Note the means, ranges and standard deviations where available. Compare the figures to each other. What can you conclude? Write up a two-page discussion. (advanced)

Recommended reading (advanced)

Chapters 7 and 8 in Cruz-Ferreira (2006) offer excellent summaries of many important theoretical and methodological issues involved in studying early word knowledge, with plenty of examples from three BFLA children.[26] Pages 78–86 in the same source are also relevant. Chapter 8 also leads into BFLA children's early use of word combinations.

Quay (1995) was the first to point out the potential importance of BFLA children's production of translation equivalents for the interpretation of language choice in the second year of life.

Patterson (2004) forcefully and succinctly explains why it is so important to pay attention to methodological issues such as the use of conceptual vocabulary in bilingual–monolingual comparisons. For a discussion of important issues regarding the assessment of lexical knowledge in school-aged bilingual children (not necessarily BFLA), see Oller and Jarmulowicz (2007).

7
Sentences in BFLA

The need for more meanings	253
The grammatical status of early word combinations	254
Different paths in learning to combine words	255
When do BFLA children first start to combine words from scratch?	256
Variation in the ages of first use of word combinations	256
Lexical support for first word combinations	258
Which language are BFLA children's early word combinations in?	258
Lexical development and the transition into sentences	259
The continued role of overall lexicon size	259
Grammatical categories in the lexicon	260
Beyond early word combinations: sentences	263
The overall structure of BFLA children's early sentences	263
Increased utterance length means increased grammatical complexity within each language	265
Sentences and BFLA children's language repertoires and language choice	267
BFLA children's language repertoires	267
Language choice	269
Repairing language choice	270
Unequal skill in Language A and Language Alpha	272
Comparing utterance length across languages	273
Differences in talkativeness in each language	274
Implications of the potentially large differences in skill between a BFLA child's languages	276

The Separate Development Hypothesis: BFLA children's sentences develop separately in each language   277

The Separate Development Hypothesis: methodological issues   280

    The SDH applies only to unilingual utterances   280

    Separate development can only be seen for aspects that differ in the input languages   280

    The SDH is only valid if children show separate development for most of the morphosyntactic features that differ in their input languages   282

    The SDH cannot be investigated on the basis of comparisons with monolingual acquisition   283

What makes separate development possible?   284

Crosslinguistic influence in unilingual utterances   287

BFLA compared to MFLA   288

    General level of morphosyntactic development   288

    Comparisons with monolingual children acquiring the same language   289

BFLA compared to ESLA   290

The structural features of mixed utterances   291

The development of narrative   293

In conclusion   295

Summary box   299

Suggestions for study activities   299

Recommended reading   301

In this chapter I try to explain how BFLA children get from saying single words to producing sentences. Rather than focus just on specifically bilingual aspects, I look at BFLA children's language use more globally.

The need for more meanings

Children's single early words have specific meanings. As I discussed in Chapter 6, these meanings can be quite 'big', as in holophrases, where 'doggie!' doesn't just refer to a dog, but may mean 'I see a dog and I want you to know that' or 'there's an animal on four legs and I want to look at it up close'. The words can also be used with a more specific lexical meaning that is closer to the adult meaning.

If children only say single words and want to express a 'big' meaning they will often not be well understood. Their meanings are too implicit. It helps if they are more explicit and express relations between words. First and foremost, then, combining words helps children to better express what they want to say. Combining words helps them to create more meanings. Saying 'more' by itself doesn't mean much. The question will be: 'more what?'. Saying 'more juice' rather than just 'more' will improve children's chances of getting more juice, rather than, for instance, another piece of toast. It helps us to understand children better when we hear them trying to relate things to each other. The meaning of two words that are put together is bigger than the sum of the meanings of the separate words.

Often it is difficult to interpret the meaning of early word combinations, though. Meanings of early combinations are still very much linked to the context of speech, as was also the case earlier for children's single word productions, and one needs to know that context in order to be able to interpret children's early word combinations. But there is a little bit less need for that context than when children were saying only single words.

The meaning relations between two words that are expressed in children's early word combinations are pretty similar, regardless of which language children are learning (Clark, 2003: 167). For instance, they may express what belongs to whom, or what somebody is doing. They may also describe where something is, or describe some characteristic of a particular entity. Clark notes that children's earliest word combinations are used with fairly similar functions across different languages. Typically, they are used to make requests, ask permission, negate some state of affairs, express disagreement or refusal, or simply comment on some state of affairs.

As shown in Box 7.1, we find similar meaning relations and functions in BFLA children's early word combinations.[1]

> **Box 7.1** Some meanings and functions of early word combinations in BFLA
>
> *Describing what somebody is doing*
>
> | | |
> |---|---|
> | Karin (1;10) | mamã peix (Portuguese) |
> | gloss: | mummy fish |
> | context: | mother is drawing a fish |
>
> *Adapted from Cruz-Ferreira, 2006: 155*
>
> *Expressing what belongs to whom*
>
> | | |
> |---|---|
> | Mikael (1;5) | roupa papá (Portuguese) |
> | gloss: | clothes daddy |
> | context: | sorting out laundry and spotting one of daddy's shirts |
>
> *Adapted from Cruz-Ferreira, 2006: 155*
>
> *Describing some characteristic of a particular entity*
>
> | | |
> |---|---|
> | Mikael (1;10) | cabelo amarelo (Portuguese) |
> | gloss: | hair yellow |
> | context: | discussing hair colors while looking through family photographs; this utterance was said when Mikael pointed to himself |
>
> *Adapted from Cruz-Ferreira, 2006: 157*
>
> *Refusing something*
>
> | | |
> |---|---|
> | Manuela (1;7) | no cama (Spanish) |
> | gloss: | not bed |
> | context: | not wanting to go to bed |
>
> *Adapted from Deuchar & Quay, 2000: 139*
>
> *Requesting something*
>
> | | |
> |---|---|
> | Manuela (1;7) | mummy off (English) |
> | gloss: | mummy off |
> | context: | wanting mother to take mother's coat off |
>
> *Adapted from Deuchar & Quay, 2000: 139*

The grammatical status of early word combinations

When children are combining words into single utterances, they must put them into a particular order. However, whether the order they use in early two or three word combinations has any grammatical role is not clear (Clark, 2003: 171). The other element that plays a role in making sentences, bound morphology (see Chapter 2), is often absent in early word combinations as well. In fact, there is considerable controversy about whether children's early word combinations are attempts at real sentences and whether they can be described in terms of grammatical categories such as 'subject' or 'main verb' (compare, e.g. Lieven *et al.*, 1997 and Vihman, 1999).

In this chapter, I will not consider children's early word combinations as showing any sign of grammatical or morphosyntactic development as yet (see also Meisel, 1994). As I will explain in the section 'Lexical development and the transition into sentences', however, the kinds of words children use in their early two or three word combinations may already reflect certain grammatical preferences that are present in their input languages.

Different paths in learning to combine words

When they first start producing words, children will usually say one word at a time. Many children continue to do this for a long time and will use the 'holophrases' typical of this early stage (see Chapter 6).

Some children do not go through a distinct 'one word stage' but start combining words just a few weeks after they have produced their first word (Clark, 1993: 37). Such very early word combinations may be original creations of the type shown in Box 7.1 earlier. They usually consist of just two words. You can see that those two word combinations differ quite a bit from adult sentences.

Some children may start to combine three words from early on and skip the period often seen in other children where they use a lot of two word combinations. These, also, will be quite different from adult utterances at the beginning. Two or three word combinations usually coexist with the sorts of single word utterances typical of young children.

Besides these 'creative' word combinations, some children may use a fairly large proportion of formula-type phrases in the earliest stages of word production (Lieven *et al.*, 1992). An example that Lieven *et al.* mention is 'there it is' (p. 296). Such phrases sound like perfect little sentences, but it is unlikely that children have created them on the basis of putting separate words together from their limited lexicons in the right order and with correct subject–verb agreement. Rather, such phrases are imitations of adult phrases that are used as 'unanalysed wholes' (Peters, 1983), that is, multi-word chunks that form just a single lexical unit in the child's mind. These multi-word chunks may continue to be used as 'wholes' for quite some time afterwards (Lieven *et al.*, 1992, 1997).

An example of the use of such set phrases or formulas in BFLA is the expression 'un peu chaud' (French for 'a bit hot') that English–French Anna (1;10) used as a single lexical item. She did not use 'peu' or 'chaud' on their own (David & Li, 2003). Leopold (1953: 11) mentions that English–German Hildegard said complete sentences like 'I see you' at age 1;5, but he discounted such 'mechanical', 'stereotype phrases', as he calls them, from his analyses because he thought they had nothing to do with children's learning to produce sentences.

More recent thinking on how children learn to produce sentences is quite different, and sees the frequent use of such formula-like phrases and their later 'unravelling' into smaller units as an important step in early morphosyntactic development. Wray and Namba (2003) show how a Japanese–English BFLA boy's production of sentences in both languages was aided by his reliance on formulaic speech well into the sixth year of life. Qi's (2005) Mandarin–English subject James relied a lot on formulaic speech in English, but not in Mandarin.

When children appear to start combining words 'from scratch', that is, make word combinations that do not sound like adult sentences, these combinations rely on their lexicon. That is, known words that children previously produced separately can now be used in combination with other previously used words. At the same time, children continue to learn many more new words that they can immediately combine with other words (Clark, 1993: 22).

Finally, children's earliest attempts at sentences may be marked by a particular kind of prosody. Pauses and the use of intonation contours signal to adults that maybe children are attempting to say sentences. Because of children's general articulatory immaturity, though, their attempts at using this sentence-like prosody may result in less-than-fluent word articulation, also in BFLA children (Cruz-Ferreira, 2006: 119–123). Many of children's early longer utterances may still be quite unintelligible because of this.

When do BFLA children first start to combine words from scratch?

Variation in the ages of first use of word combinations

MFLA children vary considerably in the ages at which they start to combine words. By the age of 1;8, some may be saying many multi-word sentences, while others will still be limited to single words (Goldfield, 2000). Although there is a lot of variation between children, first word combinations usually start between the ages of 1;3 and 1;8 (Clark, 2003). However, there are MFLA children who still are not combining words by the age of 1;10 (Fenson *et al.*, 1993: 22). Boys are a bit slower in starting to combine words than girls (Fenson *et al.*, 1993: 22): while 87% of the girls in their large study had started putting words together by age 1;10, only 75% of boys had started to produce word combinations at that age.

We find the same range of variation in BFLA (see Box 7.2). Certainly, by the time they are two, most BFLA children are combining words, as are MFLA children (see also Junker & Stockman, 2002; Patterson, 1998). Dutch–French Anouk is very slow in the earliest stages of development, then, since her first word combination appeared only at age 2;3,13 (Hulk & Müller, 2000).

Box 7.2 The earliest production of word combinations in some BFLA children as found in some published sources

Age[a]	Child	Utterance[b]	Language	Gloss	Source
1;3	Karin	é mamã?	Portuguese	is it mummy?	Cruz-Ferreira, 2006: 192
1;4	Louis	thé papa	works both in French and German	tea daddy	Ronjat, 1913: 64
1;4	Mikael	papa (smacking sounds) uva	Portuguese	papa is eating grapes	Cruz-Ferreira, 2006: 126
1;5	Anna	this à boire	mixed	this to drink	David & Li, 2003
1;6	Mikael	mama sko?	Swedish	mommy shoe?	Cruz-Ferreira, 2006: 85
1;7	Hildegard	down bitte	mixed	down please	Leopold, 1970: 181
1;9	Nicolai	die da	German	that one there	Porsché, 1983: 90
1;11	Olivier	cut encore	mixed	cut more	David & Li, 2003

[a] Age of first documented production of a spontaneous two word utterance, i.e. the earliest age found in the relevant source (the actual age could be earlier).
[b] Does not list the actual child forms but the adult targets for the separate words.

Spanish–English Manuela started to say two word utterances at the age of 1;7, about six months after she produced her first word (Deuchar & Quay, 2000). She continued to use two word utterances for about five months (Deuchar, 1992). Dutch–English Susan started to use a lot of two word utterances at the age of 1;3. This was about five months after the first word production (my diary notes). Once she started to produce a lot of two word combinations, she continued to say single word utterances. The words she used in these single word utterances never appeared in her word combinations, though. About a month after she first started to produce two word combinations, Susan started saying three word combinations as well. French–German Louis' first two word combination appeared three months after his first word (so at age 1;3), and he started saying three word combinations at the age of 1;6, just two months after his first two word combination (Ronjat, 1913). English–German Hildegard also started saying three or four word combinations after she had first started to regularly use two word combinations at the age of 1;8 (Leopold, 1953, 1970).

As I explained in Chapter 4, some people think that a 'one person, one language' input setting is beneficial to children's bilingual development. If this were the case, you might expect that children raised in this setting would be quicker to start combining words than children raised in settings where the same person addresses them in two languages. However, this is not the case. There is no group difference in the timing of first word combinations in children raised in circumstances where parents each address them in one language only and those where parents both speak two languages to them (Patterson, 1999; see also Chapter 4).[2]

All in all, there is no evidence to suggest that the second big 'milestone' in language development,[3] viz., the appearance of combinatorial speech, is generally 'delayed' in BFLA children. Instead, we see the same range of variation that has been noted for monolingual acquisition.

Lexical support for first word combinations

How can we explain the variation in the ages at which children start to combine words? You will remember from Chapter 6 that same-aged children differ a lot from each other in the number of words they produce. Scholars have tried to find an explanation for the variation between the ages that children start to regularly produce word combinations by looking at differences between the numbers of words that they produce. Typically, it is only when children are able to say a fair number of words that they start to combine words into utterances that are not clearly formulas (Bloom, 1993; Marchman & Bates, 1994). This means there must first be a 'critical mass' (Marchman & Bates, 1994) of words that children know before they can start to combine them in meaningful ways.

Children with fewer than 50 words in their production vocabulary will rarely produce word combinations that are not clearly formulas. The available data for BFLA support this as well. Patterson (1998: 50) found that in a group of 102 English–Spanish bilingual children between the ages of 1;9 and 2;1, 'most children with [total production] vocabularies of 50 words or more were combining words, most children with vocabularies smaller than 30 words were not combining words, and some children with vocabularies between 30 and 50 words were combining words'.

All ten German–English bilingual two-year-olds (between 2;0 and 2;3) in Junker and Stockman's (2002) study had well over 50 words in their total production vocabularies and 'all parents reported emerging word combinations' (p. 390). English–French Anna produced her first two word utterances (at age 1;5) when she had a total of 51 words (for both languages combined) in her production lexicon (David & Li, 2003). English–French Olivier started saying two word utterances a full half year later (at age 1;11). At that time he had a production repertoire of 76 words in English, and 80 in French – so a total of 156 words, which is three times as many as Anna had when she first started to combine words. Spanish–English Manuela said her first two word utterance when she had a total of 125 words in her production vocabulary (Deuchar & Quay, 2000: 70).

Which language are BFLA children's early word combinations in?

Some BFLA children start to combine words in each of their two languages at around the same time. They may also produce mixed word combinations at that time. For instance, English–Spanish Manuela's earliest two word combinations around age 1;8 consisted of

Spanish, English and mixed utterances (Deuchar & Quay, 2000: 107). English–Spanish Nicolas started to regularly produce two word utterances in both Spanish and English around age 1;9 (Silva-Corvalán & Sánchez-Walker, 2007: 12).

German–French Louis, on the other hand, first produced two word combinations that could be in either language and combinations that were clearly German (Ronjat, 1913). Clearly French word combinations appeared a few months later. Ronjat does not mention early mixed word combinations. Similarly, Dutch–English Susan first produced word combinations that could be in either language and combinations that were clearly Dutch (my diary notes). Only later did she produce word combinations that were clearly English. My notes do not mention early mixed word combinations. Similar to Ronjat's Louis, this doesn't imply there weren't any, but it does suggest they were not common.

Lexical development and the transition into sentences

The continued role of overall lexicon size

We have already seen that the size of BFLA children's production lexicons plays an important role in the timing of their very earliest word combinations. This link continues to be present as children start to use longer and more complex word combinations that are more and more like the sentences that adults use.

Marchman *et al.* (2004) first investigated this link for BFLA in an important CDI study. They looked at the relation between overall vocabulary size (in production) and the complexity of BFLA children's utterances in each language.[4] They found that within each language separately, there was a high degree of correlation between them (see Box 7.3 for an explanation of the measures used to determine utterance complexity). Vocabulary size in Spanish highly correlated with sentence complexity in Spanish, and vocabulary size in English highly correlated with sentence complexity in English. These within-language correlations were much stronger than correlations across languages. For instance, Spanish vocabulary related much more strongly to Spanish sentence complexity than to English sentence complexity.[5]

For a subset of 22 children used in their CDI study, Marchman *et al.* (2004) also had observational data with free speech samples in each language. The findings here confirmed the findings from the CDI study. For each language separately, children's average length of utterance measured in words was highly correlated with the number of different words they produced in that same language. In contrast, correlations between languages were very weak. Thus, we see that for each of BFLA children's languages separately, lexicon size is linked to utterance length.

> **Box 7.3** CDI-based measures of utterance complexity used in recent studies of BFLA
>
> Two recent CDI group studies of young bilingual children have measured the complexity of children's utterances in two ways (these are the studies by Marchman *et al.*, 2004 and Conboy & Thal, 2006).
>
> First there is the **M3Lw measure**. This is the average length in words of the three longest utterances produced by children in each language based on parent report. For instance, if the three longest Spanish utterances that a parent wrote down for her child consisted of 3, 2 and 2 words each, the child's M3Lw for Spanish would be 3+2+2 = 7 divided by 3 = 2.3.
>
> Then there is a second measure, which Marchman *et al.* (2004) call 'grammatical complexity' and Conboy and Thal (2006) call 'Sentence Complexity (SC)'. I will use the latter term in this chapter. The **Sentence Complexity measure** is based on a set of 37 pairs of phrases or sentences listed on the Spanish and English CDIs that children might say. One member of each pair is a structurally reduced form typical of linguistically more immature children, and the other member is a more complete form that linguistically more developed children might use. Examples are, 'more cookie!' vs. 'more cookies!' and 'that my truck' vs. 'that's my truck' (these are taken from the English CDI Toddler form, part E, Fenson *et al.*, 1993). Parents have to indicate which of these forms is more representative of the types of utterances their child is producing at the time.

Grammatical categories in the lexicon

Because of the overall immaturity of children's early words and word combinations, many scholars are reluctant to describe them in terms of adult grammatical categories such as 'subject' or 'object' (see, e.g. Clark, 2003; see also the section earlier on the grammatical status of early word combinations). However, as children's words become more adult-like, it is possible to describe them in terms of their main parts of speech, such as noun, verb and adjective (see Chapter 6 for a discussion of this for children's earliest word productions). The fact that we can do this does not imply, however, that children have any abstract knowledge of these categories. In reading the rest of this subsection, you must keep in mind that the terms 'nouns', 'verbs' and so forth refer to adult grammatical categories we conveniently use to categorize words, nothing else.

Maratsos (1990) has convincingly argued that nouns form a lexical category that is different from all other possible categories, and that children can learn to treat nouns as a separate lexical category because they are used to refer to concrete objects. This is perhaps one reason why in many languages, monolingual children's production lexicons usually contain more nouns than verbs by the age of 1;8 (Bornstein & Cote, 2004). Other lexical categories were also found in Bornstein and Cote's study, but much less strongly so. This was true for most children studied, regardless of their total level of word production.

Yet in some languages, such as Korean, young children have been found to produce as many verbs as nouns (Choi & Gopnik, 1995). Such differences between language-in-acquisition are most likely related to how obvious (or salient) verbs are in the input and how caregivers speak to children in ways that support an early learning of verbs (Choi, 1999; Kim *et al.*, 2000).

This implies that in BFLA, there might, in principle, be differences between a child's two languages in the proportion of nouns and verbs used at a given age.

A transcript-based longitudinal study of Hannah, a Japanese–English BFLA girl, shows that between the ages of 1;11 and 4;0, Hannah produced many more nouns than verbs in both languages (Itani-Adams, 2007). A comparison of the use of nouns and verbs by two other BFLA girls shows this to be the case too (see Box 7.4).

Box 7.4 Nouns and verbs in the speech of two BFLA girls

	Language A[a]		English	
Child, age	Noun types	Main verb types	Noun types	Main verb types
Maija, 1;8	ca. 24	18	ca. 38	11
Maija, 1;11	ca. 35	21	ca. 25	12
Sonja, 2;3	ca. 28	11	ca. 20	9
Sonja, 2;7	ca. 20	13	ca. 18	11

[a] Language A is Latvian for Maija and German for Sonja
Table made on the basis of information available in Sinka et al. (2000) and Schelletter et al. (2001); in these studies, the data for each age are based on occurrences within a 250 word sample for each language drawn from transcriptions of natural interaction; the precise numbers here are based on the numbers in Tables 3a, 3b, 4a and 4b in Sinka et al. (2000); the numbers that are preceded by 'ca.' are read off from the graphs in Figures 4 and 5 in Schelletter et al. (2001), and therefore can only be approximate.

Box 7.4 draws on Sinka et al.'s (2000) and Schelletter et al.'s (2001) longitudinal transcript-based studies of English–Latvian Maija in the second year of life and English–German Sofia in the third year of life. Both children had about equal exposure to their two languages. As shown in Box 7.4, both children produced more noun types than verb types in each of their languages (that is, different nouns and verbs), notwithstanding the fact that the children differed quite a bit from each other in their use of common noun types (Schelletter et al., 2001).

Similarly, in a CDI study of 13 English–French BFLA children growing up in the United Kingdom or France, David and Li (2005) found that in both languages, children produced more nouns than any other category.[6] However, there were also indications that action words and adjectives, which David and Li group into one category that they call predicates, were acquired earlier in English than in French.

The much larger CDI study by Conboy and Thal (2006) also found a preponderance of nouns in both languages.[7] Social terms such as games and names of people were second most common in both Spanish and English, predicates were third (also in both languages) and closed class words such as articles, modal verbs and question words were the least frequent in either language.[8] In both languages separately, the proportions of use of each of these four types of words changed as a function of children's vocabulary size. For instance, closed class items made up 5% of children's production vocabularies in each language when children produced 51 to 100 words per language, but this percentage doubled by the time children produced 301 to 400 words per language.

In spite of these overall similarities between the composition of the lexicon in the 64 bilingual children studied by Conboy and Thal (2006), there were some differences as well. Predicates were acquired earlier in Spanish than in English. Conversely, children produced proportionally more closed class words in English than in Spanish when they had a production vocabulary of between 26 and 50 words in each language. Such differences may reflect differences in the two input languages as regards the proportions of closed class items used in the input.

Conboy and Thal (2006) also looked at developmental changes from age 1;8 to 2;6 over three consecutive time points in a subset of 31 bilingual children, again based on CDI data. It won't surprise you that there was an increase in children's proportional use of predicates and closed class words and in their utterance complexity (see Box 7.3). These changes, however, were not only linked to increasing age.

> First, Conboy and Thal compared changes in children's use of predicates and closed class words in each language. These sorts of words are particularly important for building 'real' sentences in Spanish and English. Conboy and Thal found that changes in one language were **not** correlated with changes in the other language. They also found that total conceptual vocabulary (see Chapter 6) did not predict children's use of predicates or closed class words in either Spanish or English. Rather, it was the total vocabulary size in each language separately that predicted how many predicates or closed class words children would use in that same language.
>
> Second, children who added new words to their production vocabularies faster than other children were also more quickly able to produce longer utterances. They also made faster gains in levels of sentence complexity. This was the case for each language separately (Conboy & Thal, 2006). Thus, the growth curve in children's vocabulary sizes in English highly correlated with their degree of growth in English utterance complexity (for a description of measures used to assess utterance complexity, see Box 7.3 earlier). The same was the case for Spanish. Correlations between languages were mostly not significant.[9]

Conboy and Thal (2006: 727) interpret their findings as supporting the view that BFLA children's early morphosyntactic development proceeds in a language-specific manner, and separately for each language.

Sinka *et al.* (2000) also find evidence that each of the two young BFLA children they studied longitudinally was 'developing the system of main verbs independently for each language' (p. 186). For instance, as you can see from Maija's data in Box 7.4 above, she was using a lot more verb types in Latvian than in English, which shows a faster development of verbs in Latvian than in English. The differences between Sonja's German and English verb types are much less pronounced.

Summing up, all the studies of BFLA that have looked at children's production of nouns vs. verbs have found that nouns are used more often than verbs in both BFLA children's languages. The languages investigated so far have been French, German, Japanese, Latvian and Spanish, each in combination with English. At the same time, BFLA children produce different proportions of specific grammatical categories in each of their languages. This shows an early lexically based orientation towards each language that is grammatically significant at the same time.

> While it remains unclear to what extent early lexical and grammatical knowledge are related to each other (Dixon & Marchman, 2007), many studies have emphasized the lexical basis of early grammatical learning, showing that individual children learn to use particular structures first with just a few different verbs, which form the basis for later more across the board rule application (Gathercole *et al.*, 1999; Lieven, 2008; Lieven *et al.*, 1997; Veneziano, 1999; for a different view, see Vihman, 1999). Deuchar and Vihman (2005) show how item-by-item learning may explain the occurrence of early mixed word combinations in a BFLA (Manuela) and ESLA (Raivo[10]) child.

Beyond early word combinations: sentences

The overall structure of BFLA children's early sentences

When children are using mostly single words and later on two word combinations they do not say a whole lot yet. Typically, transcripts of children in these stages of development contain few child utterances. As children grow older, they will have more to say and generally start to talk more. They will also need to be able to express themselves more explicitly than is possible with two word combinations.

Three or four word combinations offer children this opportunity. Some of these longer utterances may still be quite unlike adult sentences, such as the utterance 'bad wate tutteke' (Dutch utterance that translates as: bath water pacifier), said by Dutch–English Susan at age 1;4 as she held her pacifier under the running tap of the bathtub. Simply putting three nouns one after the other in a seemingly random order as Susan did here doesn't make a sentence, though.

Real sentences combine words from different grammatical categories, such as nouns and verbs. Also, real sentences put these words from different grammatical categories in a particular order that is specific to a particular language (see Chapter 2). In addition, they contain bound morphemes and/or closed class items.

Children's early multi-word utterances usually follow the word order that is most common in their input language (Clark, 2003: 172). This is also the case for BFLA. For instance, when Ronjat's Louis started producing a lot of utterances with more than two words at age 19 months, he said 'mama Apfelbrei essen' (German; literally: mummy applesauce eat; Ronjat, 1913: 65). Ronjat doesn't explain whether it was Louis' mother who was eating applesauce, or whether Louis wanted his mother to give him applesauce to eat, but the order in which Louis put the words was already pretty close to the more common word order in German, where a verb (here: eat) follows an object (here: applesauce) and where a verb often appears at the very end of a sentence. Louis did not say 'essen mama Apfelbrei', for instance, which would be very unGerman.

It is not easy for young children to produce utterances with more than two words. That's understandable if you consider all they have to coordinate: they have to select the words they want to express some particular meaning with, they have to get the phonological form of those words straight, they have to put the words in some order that makes sense and they have to use the proper intonation pattern. Adults are experienced at doing all this and at doing it all more or less at once, but young children have no experience with any of this and need practice before they can become fluent (see also Clark, 2003).

Given all this, it is no wonder that children's early sentences are not always fluent. They may contain short pauses, as further described in Box 7.5.

Box 7.5 Developmental disfluencies in BFLA children's sentences

Developmental disfluencies consist of the use of pauses that appear when children are trying to say longer and more complex sentences than they were using before. Once children have gained more experience with such longer and more complex sentences these disfluencies disappear. You could compare these disfluencies to the 'ehms' and hesitations that often occur in people's oral presentations – these are signs that people are a bit overstretched in their abilities to express themselves.

At age 2;1, German–English Hannah was producing a fair number of three word utterances. Hannah would usually insert a pause somewhere in the utterance (between two words), and she didn't produce more than two words without a pause between them. This state of affairs was apparent up until age 2;6. The longer Hannah's utterances became, the more likely it was that they contained a pause. This was the case for Hannah's German, English and mixed utterances. German–English Laura showed similar characteristics.

(From Gut, 2000a: 146–147 and 150–153)

When children are somewhat older and start to produce a fair number of complex sentences consisting of at least two clauses, they may all of a sudden start to sound so disfluent that they appear to be stammering and stuttering. Monolingual children do this, as do BFLA children. For instance, Gut (2000a: 157) reports that at age 3;10, German–English Adam's speech in both languages suddenly became 'very disfluent and [..] full of restarts, stammering and interruptions'. However, the pauses that Adam inserted were not random. For instance, he did not insert pauses between a determiner and a noun.

Dutch–English Kate also showed quite a few disfluencies in her attempts to say more complex sentences, such as Dutch 'wa – was – wa wat zeggen ze als ze in eem boeke zijn' at age 3;3 (literal gloss: wha – wha's – wha what say they when they in a book are; meaning: what do they say when they're in a book; the conversation is about the sounds that the pigeons from a particular picture book make; De Houwer, 2004). This is quite a complex sentence for a child this age that combines a question with a dependent clause.

Likewise, Dutch–English Susan went through a period of about two months at the age of three and a half when she was trying to express all sorts of complicated ideas and obviously couldn't do it, giving rise to many hesitations and restarts as well (my diary notes).

Children's increased use of sentences often coincides with their phonologies becoming more stable. For BFLA children this has the implication that the earlier problems in identifying the language sources for children's words (Chapter 5) start to steadily decrease.

When children first start to say multi-word utterances, they typically do not yet speak in the 'full', 'complete' forms required by their input language. Their early multi-word utterances often seem to show 'gaps'. For instance, when Louis said 'Ofen heiss brennt' (German; literally: oven hot burns; Ronjat, 1913), you could easily think that this was an attempt at the sentence 'der Ofen ist heiss denn er brennt' (the-oven-is-hot-since-it-burns), with the 'little bits' simply left out. The 'little bits' here are closed class items such as the article 'der' (the), the auxiliary 'ist' (is), the conjunction 'denn' (because/since) and the pronoun 'er' (it). Indeed, many of young children's early sentences sound funny because they lack those closed class items.

When monolingual children are still producing only two word combinations, they are definitely lacking in such closed class items. They are usually lacking in bound morphology as well. This is also the case for BFLA. Both Ronjat (1913) and Leopold (1953, 1970) note that the very first word combinations by Louis and Hildegard lacked bound morphemes. These came in only later, as in Ronjat's Louis' 'mama Deckel drauf gemacht' (German; literally: mummy lid on-there did; Ronjat, 1913: 65), where the past participle form 'gemacht' consists of the discontinuous bound past participle morpheme 'ge-t' and the stem form 'mach' (do).

Just how early children start to use bound morphemes and closed class items depends very much on the language they are trying to speak. This finds illustration in the speech of English–Latvian Maija, who used quite a bit of bound morphology in her early Latvian utterances but none in English (Sinka & Schelletter, 1998). Adult Latvian relies heavily on bound morphology, whereas adult English does not. As we see in the next subsection, another explanation for the increased use of bound morphology and closed class items lies in the length of children's utterances.

Increased utterance length means increased grammatical complexity within each language

Gradually, BFLA children's utterances become more and more complex. They start to use many more bound morphemes and closed class items. You may think that this increase in grammatical complexity is a function of getting older and hence, smarter. That is of course an important factor, but there is more.

When BFLA children first start to produce multi-word utterances they are typically between the ages of one and a half and two and a half. At this time, the grammatical complexity of early child speech depends to a large extent on the length of children's utterances. That is, within each language separately, those BFLA children who compared to others produce longer utterances in one language also produce more complex utterances in that same language (Marchman *et al.*, 2004).[11] In Marchman *et al.*'s study, the length of children's utterances (measured in number of words) in Language A did not relate to the length of their utterances in Language Alpha. Furthermore, children's overall grammatical complexity in Language A appeared to be fairly independent of the degree of complexity in Language Alpha.

Even when just very global measures such as the maximum length of children's utterances and parents' assessments of their children's sentence complexity are used, BFLA children thus show different developmental paths in each language at the earliest stages of grammatical development (Marchman *et al.*, 2004). I pick up this thread again in the section on the Separate Development Hypothesis.

It is clear from examples in the many studies of BFLA children's morphosyntactic development that, just like MFLA children, BFLA children gradually produce longer utterances as they get older. These longer utterances have increasingly more bound morphemes and closed class items that are more and more adult-like. In the fourth year of life BFLA children start to be able to produce utterances that combine two or three clauses. Box 7.6 shows a few examples of Dutch–English Kate's overall morphosyntactic development between ages 2;7 and 3;4 (De Houwer, 2004).

Box 7.6 Increased grammatical complexity in the utterances of a Dutch–English girl

Age 2;7.12
*CHI: ik ben nie moe (Dutch; single clause consisting of 4 words)
words: 3 different closed class items: pronoun 'ik' (I), copula 'ben' (am), negative adverb 'nie(t)' (not); 1 open class item: adjective 'moe' (tired)
gloss: I am not tired

Age 2;10.5
*CHI: I am not going to go to Amsterdam (English; single clause consisting of 8 words)
words: 4 different closed class items: pronoun 'I', copula 'am', negative adverb 'not', particle 'to'; 2 different open class items: 'go' and 'Amsterdam'; 2 morphologically different forms of the same word: 'going' and 'go'

Age 2;11.14
*CHI: mommy I think it's bleeding! (English; a vocative followed by a complex sentence consisting of a main clause and a complement clause)
words: 3 different closed class items: pronouns 'I' and 'it', abbreviated copula 's'; 3 different open class items: 'mommy', 'think', 'bleed'; bound morpheme -ing

Age 3;1.6
*CHI: what comes if we don't brush our teeth? (English; complex sentences with a main clause and a subordinate clause)
words: 5 different closed class items: pronouns 'what', 'we' and 'our'; conjunction 'if' and abbreviated negative adverb 'not'; 4 different open class items: 'come', 'do', 'brush', 'teeth'; bound morpheme -s

Age 3;3.16
*CHI: maaR maaR as ik in 't school ben, dan zing ik (Dutch; complex sentence consisting of a subordinate clause and a main clause)
words: 6 different closed class items: conjunctions 'maar' (but), 'a(l)s' (when) and 'dan' (then), pronoun 'ik' (I), preposition 'in' (in), abbreviated article 't' (the), copula 'ben' (am); 2 open class items: 'school' (school) and 'zing' (sing)
gloss: but but when I in the school am, then sing I

All examples from the Kate corpus in De Houwer, 2004

Note that once children start to produce real sentences they may still be using some two word combinations that sound much more immature. These will soon disappear, though. Single word utterances will continue to occur throughout, but will be quite different from before, in the sense that they will often consist of brief responses to questions such as 'yes' and 'no' or vocatives such as 'mummy?', pretty much like in adult speech.

Once BFLA children start to produce sentences in at least one of their languages they may also produce sentences in the other, or they may produce mixed utterances. The next section takes a closer look at BFLA children's language repertoires and their language choice.

Sentences and BFLA children's language repertoires and language choice

BFLA children's language repertoires

When children are still producing mainly single words, they cannot yet produce mixed utterances unless the words are bilingual blends (see the subsection 'Lexical gaps and adding new words' in Chapter 6). As children start to combine words into one utterance, they may combine words from two languages (see the example from English–Spanish Manuela in the subsection 'Which language are BFLA children's early word combinations in?' earlier). Other children may not produce such clearly mixed utterances.

When BFLA children start to produce sentences, there continues to be this variation between children in whether they produce mixed utterances or not. However, so far I have seen no reports of BFLA children producing more mixed utterances than utterances with words and morphemes from just a single language (i.e. unilingual utterances). Mixed utterances always constitute a minority of BFLA children's total language production at any given age.[12] Their proportion typically ranges from 0 to 30%. Note that I continue to use the term 'utterances' here because not all of children's speech production consists of sentences even when they have started to produce sentences (see the end of the previous section).

BFLA children also differ in the proportions with which they produce unilingual utterances in Language A and Language Alpha. Box 7.7 represents the variation that is seen between BFLA children who are producing sentences in the proportions with which they use mixed utterances and unilingual utterances in Language A and Language Alpha. In Box 7.7, Language Alpha is English for all four children.

As you can see in Box 7.7, some children produce no mixed utterances (Maija) or just very few (Sonja). Other children produce more (Tiffany and Odessa). Some BFLA children produce about equal proportions of unilingual utterances in each of their two languages (Sonja and Maija) (Schelletter et al., 2001). Others say markedly more in Language A than in Language Alpha (Tiffany and Odessa) (Jisa, 1989).

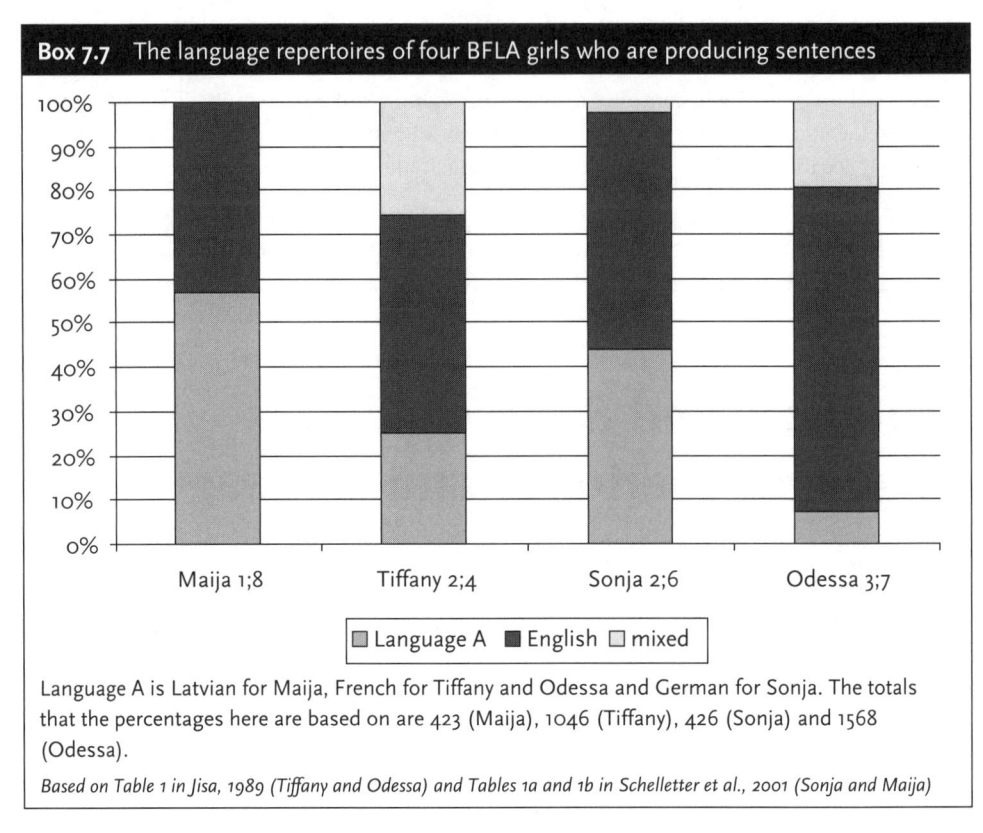

> **Box 7.7** The language repertoires of four BFLA girls who are producing sentences
>
> [Bar chart showing language repertoires: Maija 1;8, Tiffany 2;4, Sonja 2;6, Odessa 3;7, with bars divided into Language A, English, and mixed]
>
> Language A is Latvian for Maija, French for Tiffany and Odessa and German for Sonja. The totals that the percentages here are based on are 423 (Maija), 1046 (Tiffany), 426 (Sonja) and 1568 (Odessa).
>
> *Based on Table 1 in Jisa, 1989 (Tiffany and Odessa) and Tables 1a and 1b in Schelletter et al., 2001 (Sonja and Maija)*

The proportion of mixed utterances in individual children can fluctuate with age. For instance, the percentage of mixed utterances in German–English Hannah's speech between the ages of 2;1 and 2;6 was on average 8%, but peaked at age 2;4 with 16% (Gut, 2000a: 148). Box 7.8 gives a few more examples of fluctuations in the same individual children with regards to their use of mixed utterances.

> **Box 7.8** Fluctuations in the proportion of mixed utterances in individual BFLA children
>
> | Age | Child | Languages | Proportion of mixed utterances | Source |
> |---|---|---|---|---|
> | 1;9 | Eta | Serbocroatian–Hungarian | 5% | Mikes, 1990 |
> | 1;11 | | | 4% | |
> | 1;9 | Vuk | Serbocroatian–Hungarian | 15% | |
> | 1;11 | | | 2% | |
> | 2;9 | Kate | Dutch–English | 3% | De Houwer, 1990 |
> | 3;1 | | | 15% | |
> | 3;3 | | | 6% | |

Similarly to mixed utterances, the proportion with which BFLA children say unilingual utterances in Language A rather than Language Alpha may also fluctuate within the same child.

Finally, as children become better able to articulate they will be using fewer and fewer 'floating utterances' (Chapter 2), that is, utterances whose language orgin is difficult to trace. Similarly, 'indeterminate utterances' (Chapter 2) that could be interpreted as being in Language A just as well as in Language Alpha may still occur, but the chance they do lowers as utterances generally become longer.

Language choice

Just like when they were younger (see Chapter 6), BFLA children who are producing sentences usually choose the 'right' language in the 'right' circumstances. Depending on communicative need and their interlocutor's expectations (see Chapter 3), they will produce utterances in Language A rather than Language Alpha, or the other way round. Another reason may be children's level of proficiency in each language (Jisa, 2000); children may prefer to speak the language they are better able to express themselves in and hence feel most comfortable in.

There are also many factors that may help explain why BFLA children produce mixed utterances (see also Chapter 3). Children's mixed utterances may function as attention-grabbers or for emphasis (Goodz, 1989). Or children may use them because the adults they are talking to also use them and don't mind if children do too (Allen *et al.*, 2002; Huerta-Macías, 1981; Lanza, 1992; Mishina, 1999; Quay, 2008). Lexical gaps are another reason why children may use mixed utterances (see Chapter 6). Alternatively, the virtual lack of mixed utterances in some BFLA children's speech may be a result of the fact that children are socialized into using only unilingual utterances (see Chapter 3).

When children are raised in settings in which the use of a single language is encouraged, their language choice is often appropriate from very early on, and children rarely use mixed utterances or utterances from the 'wrong' language. Other children raised in similar circumstances may need some time to learn to restrict the use of mixed utterances or utterances from the 'wrong' language. For instance, when English–Spanish Manuela was still mainly using two word combinations at ages 1;7 and 1;9, she used a fairly large proportion of mixed utterances or utterances from the 'wrong' language (see Box 7.9). As she got older, and started to use more sentences rather than two word combinations, she used far fewer mixed utterances or utterances from the 'wrong' language (Deuchar & Muntz, 2003).

Generally, if BFLA children use mixed utterances, they mainly use them with bilinguals who they know will understand them. For instance, around age three, Dutch–English Kate used mixed utterances much more often in speaking to her father and myself (who she knew spoke both her languages fluently) than to her mother, who was fluent in English but clearly was just a beginning speaker of Dutch (De Houwer, 1983, 1990; see also Chapter 4).

Box 7.9 Learning to restrict the 'wrong' language

Manuela	Proportion of unilingual utterances in the 'right' language	Proportion of unilingual utterances in the 'wrong' language and mixed utterances	Total number of recorded utterances
1;7	75%	25%	137
1;9	72%	28%	334
1;11	91%	9%	306
2;1	96%	4%	252
2;2	93%	7%	285
2;5	97%	3%	467
2;6	95%	5%	230

Based on information in Table 4 in Deuchar & Muntz, 2003

There has been so much emphasis in the literature on trying to explain young BFLA children's mixed utterances that it is easy to forget that children usually talk in just one language. In the following sections after the next subsection I redress that balance and look at different aspects of children's unilingual utterances beyond the age of two. I come back to mixed utterances and their structural characteristics towards the end of the chapter.

Repairing language choice

When parents are together with their children, they do not always respond to children's prompts for attention. For example, when children do something that is socially inappropriate such as ask a rude question, give an order or whine, parents may ignore them. This is quite a normal way for parents to behave with children who have started to talk (Hart & Risley, 1999: 104–107). When parents wait with their response, children often rephrase what they had first said (this is called *repairing*), and parents finally respond when they hear something they find appropriate. This is part of normal socialization.

Similarly, in a bilingual setting, parents may not immediately respond when children say something. Monolingual children only have the option of rephrasing a sentence they didn't receive any response to using the same language. Bilingual children have the option of using the other language for rephrasing and thus trying to get the response they want (for an example, see Box 7.10). Children who do this are actually correcting, or repairing, their language choice.

The ability of BFLA children to repair their language choice when their interlocutor indicates lack of understanding appears to be subject to considerable individual variation (see Box 7.11). Of course, children who usually use the 'right' language will normally not be asked for a clarification that requires a repair to language choice.

> **Box 7.10** Making yourself understood through rephrasing in the other language
>
> At the age of 4;3, German–Italian Carlotta said to an Italian-speaking adult: 'staubsauger' (German for vacuum cleaner).
>
> The adult didn't understand, and asked in Italian: 'come?' (what?).
>
> In response, Carlotta repeated in Italian: 'un'aspirapolvere!' (a vacuum cleaner; Cantone, 2007: 103).
>
> *We see here an example of a BFLA child using the 'wrong' language and then, after a request for clarification, translating the utterance into the 'right' language.*

> **Box 7.11** Individual variation in repairing language choice
>
> - When Norwegian–English Siri was 2;2, she repaired a mixed utterance ('klappe hand', where Norwegian 'klappe' means 'clap') to fully English 'clap hand' after her English-speaking mother indicated lack of understanding through 'Hm?' (Lanza, 1997: 279).
> - On the other hand, French–English Jennifer at the same age of 2;2 never repaired her 'wrong' language choices (Comeau *et al.*, 1997).
> - At age 3;1, Dutch–English Kate repaired the mixed utterance 'jij white!!' (where 'jij' is the Dutch word for 'you') into the fully Dutch utterance 'jij wit!' after getting a sign of lack of understanding by her Dutch-speaking interlocutor (De Houwer, 1990: 323).
> - In contrast, French–English William at a fairly similar age (3;0) never repaired his 'wrong' language choices (Comeau *et al.*, 1997).

Comeau and colleagues have systematically investigated the use of language choice repairs using an experimental design where an investigator playing with a child indicated lack of comprehension every time the child used the 'wrong' language. Their combined studies (Comeau *et al.*, 1997, 2007; Comeau & Genesee, 2001) cover the use of language choice repairs in about 35 French–English BFLA children between the ages of 1;11 and 5;8. An important overall finding is that bilingual children can reliably repair their language choice starting from about two and a half years of age.

You can see here that there is a link between parental discourse strategies (Chapter 4) and BFLA children's growing ability to interpret adults' lack of understanding as a request to change over to the 'right' language. While children under age two and a half do not generally respond to signs of lack of understanding by switching languages, children beyond that age do start to do this.

Thus, there is hope for parents who previously might have thought they could not change anything with regards to young children's 'wrong' language choice. Parents can start to use the monolingual discourse strategies described in Chapter 4 and with sensitivity, some persistence and luck, they may stand a good chance of being able to create or re-create a need for children to use the 'right' language (see also Lanza, 1997 on repairs and the use of parental discourse strtategies).

Part of the reason that parents may succeed (at least for some time) lies in young children's overall interest in being understood and avoiding communication breakdown. This is why in the course of the third year, children will pay attention to signs of misunderstanding and will act on them. As I noted earlier for Dutch–English Kate, most signs of misunderstanding or lack of understanding by the adult of one of Kate's utterances met with some sort of repair (De Houwer, 1990: 321; see also Jisa, 1991 for an analysis of French–English Odessa's repairs). This mirrors what MFLA children do (Anselmi *et al.*, 1986).

BFLA children's ability to repair language choice when they hear the interacting adult express lack of understanding goes hand in hand with children's growing ability to repair other aspects of their utterances when asked for clarification. For instance, they may add grammatical elements in a repaired utterance that were lacking before, as in three-year-old French–English Odessa's '**she has** little head like that?' which she said after her mother indicated lack of understanding of Odessa's previous utterance: 'has little head like that? little head like that?' (Jisa, 1991: 187).

BFLA children not only repair their utterances in response to signs of misunderstanding or explicit requests to say something again, they also correct themselves upon their own initiative. Starting at age 2;4, German–English Hannah increasingly inserted pauses into her utterances just before self-corrections (Gut, 2000a: 149), as in: 'I'm – I make you much better'. Before age 2;4, 'Hannah never interrupted her speech in order to repair an utterance' (Gut, 2000a: 149). A somewhat later example from German is 'ich hab kein ba – hab kein Barfüße' (age 2;6). German–English Laura's first self-correction was recorded at age 2;5. It was: 'Adam gibt – geht auf den tree' (Adam gives – goes on the tree; Gut, 2000a: 154). Dutch–English Kate also used self-corrections (De Houwer, 1990: 317). Most of these made the utterance better, regardless of whether the utterance was in English or Dutch. In fact, BFLA children's growing ability to repair utterances appears to be independent of a specific language (De Houwer, 1990: 312).

Children's use of repairs is seen as a growing sign of metalinguistic awareness (e.g. Clark, 1978). Correcting other people's speech is another sign of this. For instance, at age 2;7, German–French Louis corrected his mother when he thought she said something wrong (Ronjat, 1913: 85). This would appear to be quite early in comparison with monolingual children.

Unequal skill in Language A and Language Alpha

Some BFLA children seem to speak their two languages at similar levels. Other children clearly do not speak their two languages equally well and thus show 'uneven development' (see Chapter 2). The first two BFLA children who were studied at length represent each of these two typical cases: in the third year of life, Ronjat's Louis produced sentences in both French and German (Ronjat, 1913). In contrast, in the third year of life, Leopold's Hildegard produced sentences in English but only single words in German (Leopold, 1970). For Louis, his two languages seemed to be pretty much on a par. Hildegard had a clearly stronger and weaker language.

Comparing utterance length across languages

In young BFLA children differences between the overall length of their utterances in Language A and Language Alpha may be a clear sign of unequal skill in their two languages. Similar to Leopold's Hildegard, the children Odessa (Jisa, 1995), Andreu (Juan-Garau & Pérez-Vidal, 2000), Jean, Mimi, Anne (Schlyter, 1995), Céline (Müller & Kupisch, 2003), James (Qi, 2005) and Natalie (Stefánik, 1995) at one point produced sentences in only one of their languages but hardly ever combined words in the other.

This brings me to the issue once more of the comparability of the mean length of utterance measure (MLU) across languages (Chapter 3). If children are regularly combining words in one language their MLU in that language will be around 2. If they are not yet regularly combining words in the other language, their MLU in that language will be around 1. Such a difference between languages is quite clear and does not depend much on the specific languages involved. Thus, at the very early stages of language development, that is, before bound morphology has appeared, MLU can globally be compared across languages, especially if it is counted in words.

It becomes much more difficult to compare MLU across languages once bound morphology comes in. What does it mean if an Italian MLU is 3.87 and a German one at the same age only 3.15? Does this mean that German is behind Italian? As I explained in Chapter 3 and elaborate on in Box 7.12(adv.), we cannot really draw any major conclusions on the basis of these kinds of differences. But when children have only an MLU of 2 in one of their languages, and one of 3 or 4 in the other, there is a real difference.

For a study reporting on a BFLA child with fairly low MLUs in each language (and with severe phonological problems), see Müller and Pillunat (2008).

Box 7.12(adv.) More on why caution is needed in using MLU as a basis for comparing different languages in BFLA

Cantone (2007: 100–101) shows two graphs of the MLU progression in Italian and German in the speech of five German–Italian BFLA children between the ages of 1;8 and 5;4 (the data stop earlier for some of the children). In spite of the individual differences between the children, each language shows its own characteristic pattern of growth in MLU.

The overall picture for Italian is one of a steady increase until an MLU of 4.0 is reached (for most of the children, by age three), with a levelling off after that during the fourth year of life. For German, there is much more of a continuing, steady increase (with most children not reaching an MLU of 4.0 until the age of three and a half), and there is much less of a levelling-off pattern. The German MLU continues to rise up to 5.0, but the increase is less obvious than before. The initial rise is not as sharp in German as it is in Italian.

These quite different overall patterns of the MLU progression in each language confirm that one should be careful in making crosslinguistic comparisons based on MLU. A concurrent MLU of 3.50 in Language A and 3.70 in Language Alpha, for instance, may mean something very different depending on which particular languages are involved.

Children may at first show a clear difference of morphosyntactic skill in each of their two languages that later disappears. For instance, Ronjat (1913: 65) writes that in the second half of the second year, his son Louis' German was in advance of French as far as the construction of early multi-word sentences was concerned. After the age of two, Louis' French caught up with his German and both languages were used pretty much at equal levels of overall skill. In other BFLA children, the same language may be their weaker language for a long time, as in Leopold's Hildegard, whose English was far in advance of her German between the ages of one and a half and five (Leopold, 1970). Also, Mandarin–English James was far ahead in Mandarin up until the age of four (Qi, 2005). In yet other children, the language that first was their weaker one may become their stronger one. At age five, in fact, Hildegard's previously weaker language, German, became her stronger one (in the course of a stay in Germany), and Hildegard even seemed to have lost much of her English for a while (Leopold, 1970).

And, of course, there are children who do not have a clearly weaker or stronger language. Instead, they are pretty much at the same overall level of development in both their languages throughout the early childhood years. For instance, by the time English–Spanish Nicolas was 2;9, he was saying sentences in both his languages with, on average, about six words in them (Silva-Corvalán & Sánchez-Walker, 2007: 12).

Even these children may lose one of their languages, at least in production. As I describe a bit more in Chapter 8, this happened to Dutch–English Kate: she lost Dutch. In Chapter 4 I described how Dutch–English Susan lost English. In Susan, though, the loss appeared to be total. BFLA children who lose a language along the way can relearn it later, though (as did Susan). Some people say that they do this relearning faster than children who never knew the lost language before. This did seem to be the case for ten young adults who had been fluent in a later lost (but relearned) language up until age seven (Au *et al.*, 2008). More studies are needed to investigate this further.

Differences in talkativeness in each language

MLU usually increases as children get older but occasionally there can be dips. That may depend on how much children happen to talk at a given time. Indeed, there can be a lot of difference in children's talkativeness from recording to recording. However, some children seem to be pretty talkative all the time, while others are much less so (see also Kupisch, 2008).

For BFLA children there can be consistent differences in how talkative they are in each language. On the other hand, BFLA children may talk quite a bit in both languages.

Sometimes it is said that BFLA children have a weaker language if they talk very little in that language and talk more in the other. Lina (see the top part of Box 7.13) is an example of such a child. She was consistently talkative in Italian but not in Swedish (data from Bernardini, 2003). At the same time, Lina consistently had an MLU of 2 and above in Italian, but of around only 1 in Swedish.

Box 7.13 Talkativeness and mean length of utterance in each language

	Weaker language		Stronger language	
Child, age	MLU	Number of utterances	MLU	Number of utterances
Lina, 2;2,16	1.0	12	2.0	111
Lina, 2;8,21	1.0	22	2.4	251
Lina, 2;10,24	1.3	32	2.7	483
Lina, 3;6	–	1	2.8	282
Lukas, 2;0	1.1	133	1.9	191
Lukas, 2;2	1.1	71	2.3	249
Lukas, 2;5	1.5	111	3.1	288
Lukas, 2;11	1.5	151	3.1	263
Lukas, 3;3,15	2.3	246	4.2	304
Lukas, 3;7,4	2.0	118	4.2	92

Table based on information in Tables 5 and 6 in Bernardini, 2003

Based on MLU measures, Lina's weaker language was Swedish and her stronger language Italian. For Lukas it's the other way round: Swedish was his stronger language and Italian his weaker one. We already met up with Lina and Lukas in Chapter 4 (Box 4.17). The numbers here are based on analyses of transcriptions at each age of twice 30-minute interactions between Lina and either an Italian- or Swedish-speaking investigator, and of 45 minutes of interaction between Lukas and an Italian-speaking investigator and of 20 minutes of interaction between Lukas and a Swedish-speaking investigator (Bernardini, 2003: 56).

However, even if BFLA children talk quite a bit in a particular language, that language may be consistently less well developed than the other one. Lukas (see the middle part of Box 7.13) represents children who are in that situation. The length of Lukas' utterances was consistently much lower in Italian than in Swedish, even up until the middle of his fourth year. We can safely say that Italian was Lukas' weaker language. Yet, Lukas did talk quite a bit in Italian. There was no sign of any reluctance to speak Italian.

When we compare Lukas with Lina we see both a similar and a different picture. Similar, because like Lukas, Lina also showed a consistently much lower MLU in one of her languages compared to the other. She never started to regularly combine words in Swedish. In Lina's case, Swedish was clearly the weaker language, but in addition, Lina also hardly ever spoke any Swedish. Ultimately, she stopped speaking Swedish altogether.

In contrast, Lukas did develop in his weaker language, albeit very slowly. He started to regularly use two word combinations in his weaker language by age 3;3. This is about a year later than in his other language. Another striking difference with Lina is that Lukas did talk quite a bit in his weaker language. On the whole, more than a quarter (27.4%) of the 4,543 utterances that Lukas produced in all the recordings made between age 2;0 and 3;7 were in his weaker language. The proportion for Lina was much lower (10.5% out of 3,248 utterances between ages 1;8 and 3;7) (information based on Tables 5 and 6 in Bernardini, 2003).

Thus, degree of talkativeness in each language is not necessarily a measure that says much about whether children have a stronger or weaker language.

Implications of the potentially large differences in skill between a BFLA child's languages

If we look only at Lina's and Lukas' weaker language we see that at the age of 2;11, Lina's MLU was 1.3 and Lukas' 1.5 (Box 7.11). In general, though, we would expect young children at the end of their third year to be well into the stage where they are producing sentences, which requires an average utterance length of at least 2.5 words. The values of 1.3 and 1.5 are well below this.

Furthermore, Lukas only started to regularly combine words in his weaker language at age 3;3 (Box 7.13), more than a full year after children are expected to have this ability. A monolingual child who only starts to regularly combine words at age 3;3 definitely is in need of professional help, since we would be seeing a severe language delay.

If we were to look only at Lukas' weaker language, he would appear to be in the same situation. But when we look at his stronger language, he is doing just fine, with a 'normal' MLU of 4.2. Language delay as a general outcome of an underlying language problem, then, can be excluded, even though Lukas' weaker language is indeed much delayed in comparison with his stronger one and in comparison with monolingual children.

Lina's development in her stronger language is not as advanced as is Lukas',[13] but with an MLU of 2.8 in Italian at age 3;6 she is well into the sentence production stage, an expected result for that age range. Even though she has stopped speaking her earlier weaker language, her development is within the expected range of normal variation.

If we had available only the information about Lina's and Lukas' weaker language we would have to be worried about them. Their profiles for their weaker language show a language delay in comparison with most monolingually raised children. Fortunately, we can exclude the possibility of a language learning problem in both children because of their good performance in their stronger language.

A first implication of the potentially large differences in skill between a BFLA child's languages, then, is that in order to assess BFLA children's levels of language development you need to take into account *both* their languages. If BFLA children are slow in only one of their languages, but fast or 'normal' in their other one, there is no need for professional help.

However, if both languages are developing slowly and BFLA children are not producing two word combinations in either language by age two, as in Dutch–French Anouk, whose first intelligible word combinations were not produced until the age of 2;3,13 (Hulk & Müller, 2000: 230), it is advisable to at least carefully check whether children's hearing is developing normally and to closely follow up on children's language development (in Anouk's case, even though she had a very slow start, she caught up quickly and at age 3;10 had age-appropriate MLUs of 4.52 in Dutch and 5.53 in French; Hulk & Müller, 2000, tables 3 & 4).

Second, the fact that there can be clear differences between BFLA children's two languages when you look at their overall utterance length implies that the two languages take quite separate routes in development. One language can 'take off', as it were, and not have to worry about what's going on in the other language. I elaborate on this separate morphosyntactic development in the next section.

The Separate Development Hypothesis: BFLA children's sentences develop separately in each language

We have already seen that there are differences in BFLA children's early use of grammatical categories in each of their languages. Also, some BFLA children's morphosyntactic development may be much faster in Language A than in Language Alpha.

These facts are consistent with what I have called the Separate Development Hypothesis (SDH) and what Meisel (2001) has called the Differentiation Hypothesis. The SDH originally stated that children with regular input in two languages from birth who are growing up according to the 'one person, one language' principle develop two distinct morphosyntactic systems. This means that 'the morphosyntactic development of the one language does not have any fundamental effect on the morphosyntactic development of the other' (De Houwer, 1990: 66). Rather, children produce sentences with words from a single language that use the structural possibilities of that same language (see Box 7.14 for a few examples).

Since I proposed the SDH, it has become clear that the condition of the 1P/1L principle can be omitted: BFLA children who have regularly heard or overheard their two languages as spoken by the same person also develop two separate morphosyntactic systems. Furthermore, strictly speaking, the 1P/1L setting most likely is very rare, especially if you include overheard language as being part of children's relevant input (see Chapter 4). Even Kate, the child whose speech patterns first led me to formulate the SDH, did hear the same people speak two languages quite regularly, even though they addressed her in only a single language at the time of my study.

> **Box 7.14** Some examples of unilingual sentences by BFLA children that show morphosyntactic structures belonging to the same language as the words
>
> *CHI: das solln doch hunde gar nicht essen
> age: 2;9,18
> gloss: that should however dogs absolutely not eat (= but dogs aren't supposed to eat that)
>
> *The child here is Italian–German Lukas; example from Kupisch, 2007: 74*
>
> This German unilingual sentence has very German-like word order and topicalization. It contains German bound morphemes and closed class items as well as proper subject–verb agreement. It also appropriately uses a bare noun rather than a noun preceded by an article.
>
> *CHI: you bought this for me
> age: 2;7,11
>
> *The child here is Cantonese–English Timmy; example from Yip & Matthews, 2000: 3*
>
> This English unilingual sentence has English word order and uses the correct irregular past tense form of the verb 'buy'.
>
> *CHI: maintenant faire autre chose
> age: 2;11,27
> gloss: now do other thing
>
> *The child here is French–Dutch Anouck; example from Hulk & Müller, 2000: 237*
>
> This French unilingual utterance has French word order even though it lacks a subject and a finite verb (this is a sign of grammatical immaturity rather than influence from Dutch).
>
> *CHI: no tiene frío
> age: 1;10
> gloss: not has cold (= he's not cold)
>
> *The child here is English–Spanish Nicolas; example from Silva-Corvalán & Sánchez-Walker, 2007: 17*
>
> This Spanish unilingual utterance has Spanish word order. It does not have a subject pronoun. Instead, the subject is expressed in the verb ending -e. Nicolas should have used a different ending (-o, as in 'tengo'), though, since he's referring to himself; his sentence was a reply to his grandmother asking him: '¿tienes frío, Nicolás?' (are you cold, Nicolas?). This error is a language-internal one, though, not one that shows influence from Nico's other language, English (there you would also expect a first person singular marking). Not using a subject pronoun is common in Spanish. Using a subject pronoun here as would be expected in English would not be wrong but quite strange here.

The evidence for the SDH is very robust. BFLA children with regular input in two languages from birth use the word orders and morphosyntactic devices (closed class items, bound morphemes) from Language A in utterances with words from Language A. The same goes for Language Alpha.

> The implication of this is that generally utterances with words from Language A do not follow a word order from Language Alpha that would be wrong in Language A. Neither do BFLA children attempt to 'import' morphosyntactic features from Language Alpha that do not exist in the adult version of Language A. For instance, Dutch–English Kate did not attempt to impose any sort of gender distinction for English nouns even though

she marked gender for Dutch nouns through the use of different articles (it is in fact quite difficult to come up with possible scenarios that would show a mixing of morphosyntactic devices for unilingual utterances, which by definition contain only words and morphemes from a single language). Even studies that focus only on those BFLA children's sentences possibly showing an influence from the other language (e.g. Yip & Matthews, 2007) do not claim that BFLA children generally produce sentences according to a mixture of rules from both languages.

Appendix G lists the bulk of the studies to date that document separate morphosyntactic development in young BFLA children. The studies in Appendix G do not necessarily explicitly address the issue of separate development, and some look only at children's unilingual utterances in one language. However, they all show morphosyntactic developments that are language specific and, as such, relatable to only one of the children's input languages. Most of the studies are case studies that rely on transcriptions of audio or video records of child–adult interactions.

As I have suggested previously (De Houwer, 2005), the SDH is also supported when children seem to push the limits of their two languages further apart than is needed. That is, even when their two input languages are fairly similar with regard to a particular aspect, children may use forms that are quite different in each. I explain this more in Box 7.15.

Box 7.15 Using different forms in each language although the input does not require it

Dutch–English Susan referred to herself using the personal pronoun 'I' in English but didn't use the corresponding pronoun 'ik' in Dutch. Rather, when she spoke Dutch she used her own name (see Box 4.9 in Chapter 4).

As I explained in Chapter 4, the proper use of personal subject pronouns can often only be learned from overhearing third-party conversations. Until Susan had the chance to observe such conversations in Dutch she probably didn't quite know how she should use the subject pronouns in Dutch and hence used a form she knew was unambiguous.

Other BFLA children may take different routes in each language for referring to themselves in spite of frequently overhearing third-party conversations. In Mandarin and in English adult speakers refer to themselves using a subject pronoun. However, Mandarin–English James only resembled one of his input languages when he started referring to himself (Qi et al., 2006). When he spoke English, James used the adult forms 'I', 'mine' and 'my' correctly from the start. In Mandarin, however, James first referred to himself using his own name or nickname (Auchee). This is something that normally you don't do in Mandarin. Only much later did James use the Mandarin first person singular pronoun to refer to himself. But once he started using that pronoun, he continued to refer to himself by his own name. These two forms existed side by side for quite some time. In contrast, in English James never referred to himself by name. Thus, James's development of self-reference took a very different route in both languages.

Another example of BFLA children following a different route in developing their two languages comes from Basque–Spanish Mikel (Almgren & Idiazabal, 2001). Mikel started using imperfective pasts to refer to imaginary events in Spanish nine months before he did this in Basque. Yet imperfective pasts can be used to refer to imaginary events in both Spanish and Basque.

The Separate Development Hypothesis: methodological issues

The SDH applies only to unilingual utterances

If we want to know to what extent BFLA children develop each of their languages in ways that reflect the grammatical properties of each of their input languages it is obvious that only unilingual utterances can serve as a basis for analysis. What we need to figure out is to what extent children's unilingual utterances in Language A and in Language Alpha resemble the regularities from Language A and Language Alpha, respectively. Children's mixed utterances that clearly combine words and/or morphemes from two languages by definition do not match up with just a single language and so cannot be compared to just Language A or just Language Alpha.

It seems counterintuitive to speak of separate development of two languages if a child only produces unilingual utterances in one of them, and mixed utterances. I elaborate on this in Box 7.16.

> **Box 7.16** No unilingual utterances in two languages: no evidence of separate development
>
> O'Neill (1998) claims separate development in Russian–English Alexei based on the child's unilingual utterances in English and mixed Russian–English utterances (you already met up with Alexei in Chapter 4). Alexei did not produce any Russian unilingual utterances (he was growing up in an English-speaking environment and his Russian-speaking mother did not insist on him speaking Russian).
>
> O'Neill looked at the child's use of articles. In English, Alexei used articles appropriately and frequently (including 'zero article'). In front of Russian nouns that appeared in mixed utterances, Alexei never used an article (adult Russian doesn't have articles). O'Neill interprets this as evidence of separate development of the two languages.
>
> For English, it would indeed seem to be the case that there is no influence from Russian: otherwise, we would expect the lack of articles in English, but in fact, Alexei uses them in abundance in front of English nouns in fully English utterances. But for Russian, O'Neill's conclusion is based on mixed utterances. By definition, mixed utterances consist of two languages. They cannot be used in support of the SDH or as evidence against it. Just consider what you would be able to conclude if English articles *had* appeared in front of Russian nouns in otherwise entirely English utterances. Would this have constituted an argument against separate development? My answer is that whatever Alexei did in his mixed utterances cannot say anything about separate development since it is not clear what language Alexei was aiming at in his mixed utterances.

Separate development can only be seen for aspects that differ in the input languages

You can only hope to find evidence for separate development for morphosyntactic aspects that differ across one particular pair of languages (De Houwer, 1990; Meisel, 1989;

Serratrice, 2002). The aspects you are comparing should also be comparable in the two languages, that is, your comparison should make sense. In Box 7.17(adv.) I elaborate on the kinds of comparisons that potentially allow you to investigate the SDH and on those that do not.

> **Box 7.17(adv.)** The SDH can only be addressed on the basis of morphosyntactic aspects that differ across BFLA children's two input languages
>
> *Similar morphosyntactic characteristics: the SDH cannot be addressed*
> Let's take a look at English and Spanish word order in affirmative sentences with an object. In adult English, objects appear usually at the end of sentences, after the verb, as in 'I'm cooking **dinner**' or 'They've been doing **a lot of work**'. Spanish does mostly the same, as in 'Hablan **ingles**' (they speak English) or 'Tenemos **un gato**' (we have a cat).
>
> If you wanted to know whether Spanish–English BFLA children are developing two different morphosyntactic systems, it would not be very informative to look at object placement in children's Spanish and English utterances. If you found that in both languages they were correctly placing the object after the verb, at the end of sentences, you wouldn't know whether they were using a language-specific strategy, since the predicted outcomes would be the same for English and Spanish.
>
> Of course, children could be imposing some difference on the two languages, but I have so far not seen any examples of this except for aspects that are more pragmatic–semantic in nature, such as children's use of their own name for self-reference instead of a subject pronoun (see the end of the previous section).
>
> *Different morphosyntactic characteristics: the SDH can in principle be addressed*
> Let's take another look at English and Spanish, but now for an aspect that clearly differs across the two languages: negative sentences with a lexical verb. In English, you need to use DO-support as in '**I don't speak** Spanish'. This is an 'absolute' rule, meaning you have no choice as an English speaker. In Spanish, there is no DO-support, and negatives are formed by putting 'no' in front of the verb, as in '**No hablo** ingles'. Again, you have no choice as a Spanish speaker.
>
> The formation of negatives with a lexical verb is an excellent topic for investigating whether or not English–Spanish BFLA children develop two separate grammatical systems. You would not expect children to use DO-support in Spanish unilingual utterances, but you would expect them to use it in English unilingual utterances.
>
> If children actually use DO-support in their English sentences, but not in Spanish, you have clear evidence of separate development, and the SDH is confirmed.
>
> The problem is that the results aren't always so clear-cut: young children are immature speakers and need to learn to use particular structures. In getting there, they often use structures that are not adult-like. In this particular case, you might predict that children's early negative sentences in English will not in fact be employing any DO-support. If you find that a Spanish–English BFLA child produces early sentences such as 'no like carrots' the question will be: does this show influence from Spanish, and hence evidence against separate development? It might appear to do so, but then an alternative explanation is that what you are seeing is a development specific to the development of English by young children, whether or not they are acquiring English as their only language, or as one of their two languages (in fact, English monolingual children have been documented to produce early sentences like 'no like carrots', even though DO-support in negative present tense sentences appears quite early in English monolingual children; see Wells, 1985).

> Bilingual First Language Acquisition

> **Box 7.17(adv.)** The SDH can only be addressed on the basis of morphosyntactic aspects that differ across BFLA children's two input languages continued
>
> For cases like these, the SDH cannot be confirmed, nor disconfirmed. Similarly, it would be wrong to conclude that children are operating with a single grammatical system (see also Meisel, 2001: 27).
>
> *Partly overlapping morphosyntactic characteristics: the SDH can probably be addressed*
>
> Finally, many language pairs will overlap somewhat for a particular area of morphosyntax in the structural means they use. For instance, let's have a look at question formation in Spanish and English yes–no questions. Both languages use rising intonation, as in 'You have water?' or its Spanish translation, '¿Tienes agua?', but English in addition uses DO-support, and the more complete, 'full' version of 'You have water?', which is very informal, is '**Do** you have (any) water?'. For English question formation, then, there is what is called 'input ambiguity'. This means there is more than one way of expressing something (in this case, there is more than one way to ask English questions).
>
> Again, the SDH could possibly be addressed in this case, since there is some difference between the languages. The case for the SDH would be fairly clear if in Spanish, Spanish–English BFLA children were to use just rising intonation, without any attempt to translate English 'do' for DO-support, and if at the same time, they were using DO-support (with rising intonation) in their English yes–no questions. The use of rising intonation in Spanish, though, could in princple still be influenced by English, since the English input supports it as well. Indeed, when both input languages share particular properties, it is impossible to say which language is acting as children's model. At any rate, children using just rising intonation in Spanish and DO-support with rising intonation in English are showing patterns in each language that are supported by each of their input languages.
>
> If Spanish–English children were to rely only on rising intonation in their yes–no questions either in Spanish or English, the issue would again not be settled. There might be separate development, or there might not. Again, though, children using just rising intonation in both Spanish and English are showing patterns in each language that are supported by each of their input languages.
>
> Clear evidence against separate development would only exist if in their Spanish, children were attempting to say un-Spanish questions like '¿**Haces** querer chocolate?' (do-you want chocolate), which translate English 'do'. So far, such evidence is lacking, though.

The SDH is only valid if children show separate development for most of the morphosyntactic features that differ in their input languages

For any general statement to hold, there shouldn't be too much evidence against it. For the SDH, this means that separate development should be in evidence for a wide range of morphosyntactic feaures as used by a particular child. The SDH is not confirmed if there is only separate development for just a few morphosyntactic features in one particular child's sentences, but clear and systematic influence in many other sentences at the same time.

Occasional examples of crosslinguistic influence, that is, clear influence from one language on the other, do not detract from the validity of the SDH as long as they do not show any systematicity. With systematicity I mean that they are used in a majority (more than three-quarters) of relevant contexts at a particular age or within a short period of time (say, two weeks). In order to know whether there is any systematicity, then, you need quantitative data that measure the total number of utterances in a corpus and then on the basis of this you can select a subset of relevant sentences. Here we see the methodological need for having transcript-based rather than diary-based studies. Diary-based studies typically cannot 'catch' enough utterances at the stage when children are producing sentences.

So far, there have been relatively few studies that have investigated many different morphosyntactic characteristics of the same BFLA child's sentences. However, there are now detailed findings available on nearly 50 BFLA children (19 girls) who are together acquiring 17 different language combinations (see Appendix G), including typologically very distinct languages such as Inuktitut and English as well as languages that are structurally much more similar, such as French and German. Many different aspects of morphosyntax have been looked at in these studies. You can find these in Appendix H. As such, you could view the totality of these studies as a kind of random sample. It is striking that all these studies support the SDH. If the SDH were not valid, the existence of a varied database such as the one in Appendices G and H would be improbable.

The SDH cannot be investigated on the basis of comparisons with monolingual acquisition

Often, BFLA children's non-adult-like sentences in Language A could be interpreted as showing influence from Language Alpha or could be interpreted as being just a stage in the development of Language A. In those cases it is tempting to look for a possible solution at what monolingual children are doing who are acquiring Language A (De Houwer, 1994: 45), but as Leopold (1970) already noted, this still leaves you with the problem of interpreting what BFLA children are doing (see Box 7.18).

> If monolingual children are at some stage in development saying the same sorts of things in Language A as BFLA children even though they make you think of structural features of Language Alpha, it is clear that for the monolingual children you cannot say they are being influenced by Language Alpha. After all, they have never heard Language Alpha. But for the BFLA children the possibility remains that they *are* being influenced by Language Alpha. So even if BFLA children are saying the same sorts of things as monolingual children, this doesn't mean that the reason for it is the same. Similar forms do not imply similar processing. There are several different ways of getting to the same 'product'.
>
> Also if you *don't* find that monolingual children are making the same sorts of errors as BFLA children in Language A, there is no reason to use evidence from monolingual acquisition to settle an interpretative problem that only arises in BFLA (or other acquisition settings where two languages are involved). Likewise, interpretative problems in monolingual acquisition are not settled by looking at what BFLA children are doing, nor should they.

Although comparisons between MFLA and BFLA are interesting in themselves (see the section 'BFLA compared to MFLA'), they can never settle the issue of whether BFLA children are approaching their two input languages as two separate morphosyntactic systems or not. Monolingual acquisition is not a 'standard' for bilingual acquisition, or the other way round.

> **Box 7.18** The problem of ambiguous forms cannot easily be solved by referring to MFLA
>
> Ronjat (1913: 66) notes that French does not have a fixed word order for the position of adjectives and nouns within the same noun phrase. He notes the frequent error 'des noirs souliers' instead of 'des souliers noirs' as produced by a French monolingual child of his acquaintance. French–German bilingual Louis also made quite a few similar word order errors in French, but almost always used the correct (fixed) word order in German, which places the adjective in front of the noun. Even though bilingual Louis made errors in French that also occur in monolingual acquisition, it remains impossible to say whether Louis was in this particular instance influenced by German or not (on the whole, though, Louis developed his two languages separately as far as morphosyntax went; Ronjat, 1913).
>
> Leopold (1970: 185) reports that when she first started to clearly use verbs, English–German Hildegard did not use infinitive endings on German verbs. She just produced the stem forms, as she did in English. Leopold writes how in monolingual German acquisition many children start off using the infinitive forms, but some do not. He leaves open the possibility that had Hildegard been monolingual, she might have taken the latter route. Leopold explains how it is impossible to say whether Hildegard's early lack of infinitive endings in German was due to an influence from English, since the German input also uses bare stem forms.
>
> Leopold is being appropriately cautious here. Indeed, sometimes it is not possible to say whether you are seeing separate development or not. And just on practical grounds, looking at what monolingual children are doing may not give you much of an answer either, since there is so much variation between them in the early stages of morphosyntactic development. Also, methods used for collecting monolingual data are not necessarily the same as used for the BFLA cases you are comparing them with (Hulk & Müller, 2000). There may be information gaps that make it difficult to interpret the findings from monolingual acquisition.

What makes separate development possible?

So far it isn't clear how it is possible that BFLA children take separate routes for each of their languages in learning to produce sentences. Earlier in this book I emphasized the important role of the input. In Chapter 5 on phonological development I stressed the fact that children are able to distinguish between unilingual utterances in their two input languages from early on. Most likely, that ability depends on children picking up on consistent prosodic differences between unilingual utterances in Language A and Language Alpha.

From early on, then, BFLA children are used to distinguishing between the unilingual utterances that they hear in Language A and Language Alpha. This most likely paves the way for them to be able to just focus on the morphosyntactic regularities of input utterances in Language A or just on those in Language Alpha. Indeed, without close attention to the input in each language separately it is hard to imagine how BFLA children could, in fact, start producing unilingual sentences that show morphosyntactic features of the appropriate language (De Houwer, 1990).

In order to investigate the possible link between the actual input that BFLA children hear in both languages and BFLA children's morphosyntactic development, you of course need to examine the actual input that BFLA children hear. Only a few studies have emerged that have begun to pay attention to the morphosyntactic characteristics of BFLA children's actual language input. I discuss five of these in Box 7.19(adv.).

> **Box 7.19(adv.)** Studies relating BFLA children's morphosyntactic development to the actual input
>
> (1) In **De Houwer (1997)** I investigated the adult use of past and perfect tenses of lexical verbs in the Dutch and English input to Dutch–English Kate between the ages of 2;7 and 3;4. I then compared this input to Kate's use of past and perfect tenses of lexical verbs in Dutch and English, which previously I had determined showed separate development (De Houwer, 1990). That is, even though both Dutch and English use past and perfect tenses of lexical verbs to refer to the past, Kate produced many more perfect tense forms in Dutch than she did in English. In English, she produced simple past forms rather than perfect tense forms. I found that in Dutch, the input contained many more perfect tenses than past tenses, but that in English, it was the other way round. Kate reflected this difference in her own speech.
>
> | | *Dutch* | | *English* | |
> | --- | --- | --- | --- | --- |
> | *Number of occurrences* | Kate | Adult | Kate | Adult |
> | Perfect tense | 43 | 221 | 0 | 15 |
> | Simple past tense | 5 | 32 | 44 | 128 |
>
> *Based on Table 4 in De Houwer, 1997*
>
> (2) **Paradis and Navarro (2003)** analyzed the Spanish parental input to English–Spanish Manuela to see how Manuela's use of subjects in Spanish related to that input. The findings from these analyses were compared to those for two monolingual Spanish-speaking children and their Spanish adult input. Manuela used relatively more overt subjects than the two monolingual children. She also heard many more of these than the two monolingual children, especially from her mother, for whom Spanish was not a first language. Paradis and Navarro (2003) do not go as far as to claim that these input differences actually account for the findings for the children, but suggest that 'the potential impact of the child's input should be considered' (p. 389).
>
> (3) **Rieckborn (2006)** found that in referring to the past through German verb forms, German–French Annika used almost exclusively the perfect tense for lexical verbs but the past tense for modals and the copula. An analysis of adult German spoken to Annika reveals that this was very similar: lexical verbs referring to the past appeared almost exclusively in the perfect tense, while modals and the copula hardly ever did, but instead occurred in the simple past tense. Thus, Annika's frequency of use matched that of the adult's.

Box 7.19(adv.) Studies relating BFLA children's morphosyntactic development to the actual input continued

Three German–French children (Annika, Ivar and Pascal; see also Appendix G) acquired the French 'futur proche' much earlier than the French 'futur simple' and the German future form (Rieckborn 2006). Analyses of adult speech to the children revealed that in the German input there was hardly any use of the future form, whereas in the French input the 'futur proche' was used quite frequently. The 'futur simple' was about as infrequent as the German future form. Rieckborn explains the timing and the frequency of the children's use of the various future tenses as a result of the distribution and frequency of these forms in the adult input.

(4) **Macrory (2007)**, in her study of French–English-speaking Adèle's question formation, analyzed the kinds of questions that Adèle heard from each of her parents. Macrory finds a strong relation between the kinds of questions that Adèle heard from her sole source of input in French, her mother, and the kinds of questions that she produced in French. There was a slightly less direct link between the kinds of questions that Adèle heard from her English-speaking father and Adèle's own English questions, but as Macrory points out, Adèle's input in English was by no means limited to her father. Thus, Adèle had other speakers of English that she could use as models for her own use of English.

The fact remains that there was a strong relation between the kinds of questions Adèle heard from her mother in French and Adèle's own use of questions in French.

(5) **Silva-Corvalán and Montanari (2008)** analyzed the actual input to Spanish–English Nicolas and compared it to Nicolas' language production between the ages of 1;6 and 3. Silva-Corvalán and Montanari looked at the use of the copula BE, progressive BE and passive BE in English, and at the use of the copula SER, the copula ESTAR, ESTAR followed by a past participle form with adjectival function and progressive ESTAR. They found very high correlations between these various uses of English BE and Spanish ESTAR and SER by the adults talking to Nicolas and the child's own use of these forms. This is shown in the following graph, which shows percentages of the total use of BE (296 instances for Nicolas, 117 for the adults) and SER and ESTAR combined (400 instances for Nicolas, 393 for the adults).

Proportion of different uses of BE/SER/ESTAR by a BFLA child and the adults talking to him

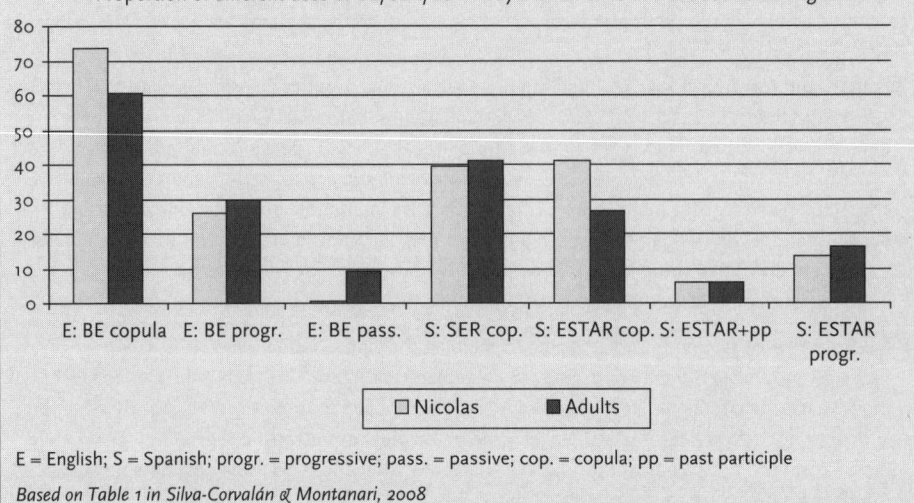

E = English; S = Spanish; progr. = progressive; pass. = passive; cop. = copula; pp = past participle

Based on Table 1 in Silva-Corvalán & Montanari, 2008

The few studies that have looked at the actual input to BFLA children and compared aspects of that input to aspects of children's speech production were all able to find correlations between them.[14] Correlations do not automatically imply causality, but the fact that there are such clear correlations in any study to date that has cared to investigate them suggests that exploring links between BFLA children's actual input and their speech production is a promising avenue for finding explanations of why BFLA children speak the way they do.

Crosslinguistic influence in unilingual utterances

You might think that when BFLA children have a clearly stronger and weaker language, the stronger language may sometimes influence the weaker one. Such occasional crosslinguistic influence from one language on the other in BFLA is certainly possible, but there is no evidence that BFLA children's weaker Language A systematically uses morphosyntactic rules from Language Alpha (for a review of this issue, see Meisel, 2007; see also Müller & Kupisch, 2003 and Bonnesen, to appear).

> **Box 7.20** The importance of the actual input for deciding whether there is crosslinguistic influence
>
> Crosslinguistic influence can only be established for sentences that have not been modelled in the input in either language.
>
> For instance, if a Spanish–English BFLA child were to try using DO-support in Spanish yes–no questions like '¿**Haces** querer chocolate?' (do-you want chocolate; see Box 7.17(adv.) earlier), this would be a clear instance of crosslinguistic influence – except, of course, if the child had actually heard these kinds of questions in Spanish. This is unlikely, since the example with 'hacer' adds an element that is superfluous.
>
> However, BFLA children may indeed hear sentences that sound quite wrong in a particular language. It all depends on who is saying them where.
>
> Many people who speak to BFLA children are L2 learners of a particular language, or speak a variety that does not wholly follow the rules of the standard variety (see Chapter 4). This implies that sometimes children will hear sentences that compared to the standard version of a language are, in fact, sentences with errors. As I explained in Box 4.10 in Chapter 4, in the English that is spoken in Singapore, sentences without an auxiliary such as 'Today I going swimming' are just fine (although the auxiliary BE could be used, too). It shouldn't be surprising, then, if BFLA children acquiring English in Singapore were to use such sentences. Explaining them as a result of children's knowledge of Cantonese would be a possibility, but just as likely a possibility is that English sentences without BE are simply modeled after the kind of English that children are hearing either from adults or from other children.

BFLA children's clearly weaker language does not seem to influence their stronger language. You will remember from earlier that in her third year of life, Leopold's Hildegard had only a limited command of German. Leopold (1970: 187) reports that her English developed rapidly and 'normally', and that it showed no influence from German, her weaker language.

Crosslinguistic influence is in evidence if children's unilingual sentences in Language Alpha use a structure from Language A that does not exist in the version of Language Alpha that children are hearing (see more on this in Box 7.20). Sentences with such crosslinguistic influence are not adult-like.

Clear examples of crosslinguistic influence in young BFLA children are very hard to find. For a total of 4,144 utterances transcribed for Dutch–English Kate, I found perhaps ten utterances that might have shown crosslinguistic influence (De Houwer, 1990). Likewise, Latvian–English Mara and Maija respectively said just two and 13 out of a total of 5,275 and 5,537 unilingual utterances that might be cases of crosslinguistic influence (Sinka, 2000: 171). In fact, then, BFLA children's sentences are usually modeled upon sentences they are hearing around them.

> For advanced readers, Appendix I elaborates on a topic that has been of great interest in the BFLA literature in the last few years and that relates to the issue of crosslinguistic influence. This topic links up with the next section.

BFLA compared to MFLA

General level of morphosyntactic development

'At the early age of two, many children's speech is better developed than Hildegard's was, but many others speak less well' Leopold (1970: 187). This quotation from Leopold captures BFLA children's overall morphosyntactic development in comparison to monolingual children quite nicely. It expresses the fact that there is variation in both MFLA and BFLA, and that a given BFLA child might be developing faster than a given MFLA child, or the other way round.

As I already explained in Chapter 2, there is no evidence that as a group, BFLA children develop morphosyntax faster or slower than MFLA children. However, for BFLA children who have a clearly stronger language this generalization is only accurate for that stronger language.

The general course of morphosyntactic development is similar in BFLA and MFLA. Both MFLA and BFLA children start off their conventionally meaningful language production using single words. They then go on to produce two word combinations, and after producing multi-word sentences for a while they start to use complex sentences as well.

Both young BFLA and MFLA children clearly speak a particular language from a very early age onwards, yet both still differ a lot from how the adults in their environment speak that language. Prior to age six, both BFLA and MFLA children make morphosyntactic errors. Also, they both produce only a portion of the wide range of morphosyntactic devices available to more mature speakers.

There are also quite detailed similarities between MFLA and BFLA children acquiring the same language. These are discussed in the next subsection.

Comparisons with monolingual children acquiring the same language

Whenever scholars have compared the kinds of sentences that age- or MLU-matched BFLA and MFLA children acquiring the same language say, they have found qualitatively similar structures. In some cases, they have found even identical utterances (De Houwer, 1990). It is often impossible to say on the basis of a transcript of unilingual utterances whether the child saying them was raised bilingually or monolingually. Thus, BFLA and MFLA children acquiring the same language produce the same sorts of utterances, with similar types of errors and similar characteristics. Box 7.21(adv.) briefly discusses a few recent studies that have compared BFLA and MFLA acquisition.

Box 7.21(adv.)   Comparisons of BFLA and MFLA children acquiring the same language

(1) Pérez Vidal and Juan Garau (2002) compared Catalan–English Andreu's use of tense and aspect in both languages to findings from monolingual children and found evidence for developmental paths in each language that are similar to monolingual acquisition.

(2) Unsworth (2003) looked at lexical verb forms used without a subject (these are so-called 'root infinitives', although the forms Unsworth looked at included past participle forms as well as stem forms in German, which are not infinitival in form). She found that German–English Annie's lexical verb forms used without a subject in German were similar to those used by monolingual German-speaking children. The ones Annie used in English were similar to those used by monolingual English-speaking children.

(3) Schmitz and Müller (2008) compared the use of French and Italian clitic and strong subject and object pronouns by four BFLA children with that of monolingual children speaking only Italian or French (the BFLA children had German as their Language A and either French and Italian as their Language Alpha). Schmitz and Müller conclude from their comparison that 'the order of appearance of clitic and strong pronouns shows no difference in monolingual and bilingual children' (p. 31).

Languages that have been compared between BFLA and MFLA so far include Basque, Dutch, English, French, German, Inuktitut, Italian and Spanish.

More and more, data from only one of the languages a BFLA child speaks are taken and analyzed by themselves (e.g. Bernardini, 2003; Ezeizabarrena, 2003; Kuchenbrandt, 2005). The implication is that each language forms its own morphosyntactic 'problem space'. In some studies, this has first been established through prior studies regarding the same children's development of morphosyntax (e.g. Ezeizabarrena, 2003); in others, it is simply assumed. It is interesting to note that the only detailed case study of a child with regular input in three languages from birth that I know of also shows considerable similarities between the child's use of English questions and their use in MFLA as well as BFLA (Barnes, 2006).

Occasionally, small differences may emerge between BFLA and MFLA children in the order in which they learn to use particular forms. There are also occasional differences between the proportions with which BFLA and MFLA children use particular structures. It isn't clear what the reasons for such small discrepancies are, given that on the whole, BFLA and MFLA children are so similar in the way they speak a particular language. Again, it might be of interest to investigate the actual input. As shown in Box 7.19 earlier, the fact that English–Spanish Manuela heard her English–Spanish bilingual mother speak Spanish to her in ways that differed somewhat from how monolingual adult users of Spanish speak the language might be a reason that Manuela's Spanish wasn't quite like that of children with Spanish input from only monolingual speakers of Spanish (Paradis & Navarro, 2003).

When Ronjat (1913) wanted to compare his bilingual son's development to monolingual children he complained that he couldn't do this in any real sense simply because there were no sources for monolingual comparisons available. The existence of the CHILDES database (see Chapter 3) which contains data from both monolingual and bilingual children fortunately now makes it possible to compare data from BFLA children to MFLA for many different languages. Yet even when CHILDES transcripts are available for the language you want to look at, it isn't always easy to draw valid comparisons between BFLA and MFLA. One problem is that age cannot be taken as a basis for comparison. That's because there is a great deal of variation between MFLA children in the ages at which they learn to use particular forms, as there is between BFLA children. A better basis for comparison is MLU, which fortunately can be compared for different children speaking the same language as long as the same rules for computing MLU have been used (this is often not the case, though).

BFLA compared to ESLA

Like BFLA children, ESLA children learn to say unilingual sentences in two languages. ESLA children say unilingual utterances in their first language (L1) which sound very much like utterances in that language as said by monolingual children (e.g. Pfaff, 1994; Prévost, 2003; Li & Hua, 2006). L1 may stagnate, though, once children start to be able to speak in the L2 (Li & Hua, 2006). When they are older, ESLA children might also show systematic structural influence in their L1 from their L2 if their L2 is prominently present and they speak it well (Bolonyai, 2007).

In their L2 children may use the same sorts of learning strategies that occur in BFLA (as well as in MFLA). For instance, they may use frequent repetition as a learning strategy (Pallotti, 2002). This may help them in learning to say sentences in their new language. In some children, their early L2 sentences may soon be target-like, and resemble structural features of younger MFLA children acquiring the same language (Rothweiler, 2006). In addition, once children under age six have had one or two years of exposure to their second language, they may use certain aspects of the L2 in much the same way as MFLA or BFLA children. As in MFLA and BFLA, there is a lot of individual variation here, though (Möhring, 2001).

ESLA children who have started to regularly hear a second language in the fourth year of life or somewhat later show a number of different patterns in how they construct sentences compared to children acquiring that language as a first language (either in BFLA or MFLA). Yet those different patterns do not necessarily show any direct influence from the ESLA children's first language (Granfeldt *et al.*, 2007). In a unique comparison between young L2 learners of French and the French of age-matched BFLA children, Meisel (2008) found that the young L2 learners made errors that the BFLA children did not.[15]

There is quite a lot of evidence from different languages-as-L2 that ESLA children also show clear signs of morphosyntactic influence from their first language once they are producing unilingual sentences in their second language that are not formulas (Ervin-Tripp, 1974; Tabors, 1987; Wong Fillmore, 1979; Zdorenko & Paradis, 2007). ESLA children under age six who are in the early stages of producing unilingual sentences in their L2 may use structural elements from their L1 (e.g. Ekmekçi, 1994; Fantini, 1985; Pfaff, 1994). An example is the German unilingual sentence by a Turkish L1 child (Pfaff, 1994: 86): 'alle Kinder is Jocken anziehen' (all-children-is-jogging-suit-on-put; all children are putting on their jogging suits; this sentence contains an attempt at a progressive that does not exist in German but does exist in Turkish). The proportion of these kinds of sentences in relation to the child's overall production in L2 is not known, but they appear to be quite common. We do not normally see these kinds of sentences in BFLA children. What we do find in both BFLA and ESLA children is mixed utterances. These are discussed in the next section.

The structural features of mixed utterances

When they start to combine words, some BFLA children may already produce mixed utterances (e.g. Deuchar & Quay, 2000). Other BFLA children start to produce mixed utterances only once they are able to produce real sentences. Mixed utterances as defined in this book are utterances that contain words or morphemes from two languages (Chapter 2). As discussed earlier in this chapter, mixed utterances always represent a minority of BFLA children's total language repertoire.

It is hard to say anything with certainty about the structural features of children's mixed utterances when children are not yet producing real sentences (but see Deuchar & Vihman, 2005). Once children start producing mixed utterances that are more like adult sentences, though, we can start to see some general characteristics.

A first characteristic is that for the language combinations investigated so far, most of BFLA children's mixed utterances insert a single word from Language A into Language Alpha rather than a bound morpheme (that's for children up until around age four). In a corpus of 801 mixed utterances from 11 BFLA children acquiring five different language pairs I found no examples of children inserting just a bound morpheme of Language A into an utterance that otherwise is entirely in Language Alpha (De Houwer, 1995b). This is not to say that these kinds of mixed utterances cannot occur, but it does suggest that if do, they are an extremely peripheral phenomenon.

The single word from Language A that children insert into Language Alpha most often is a noun (see, e.g. Cantone, 2007: 173; De Houwer, 1990, 1995a; Saunders, 1988; Sinka, 2000; Wanner, 1996).[16] When children combine a determiner from Language A with a noun from Language Alpha, the gender of the determiner and the noun mostly match up (Radford *et al.*, 2007). Mixed utterances with noun insertions, then, are structurally not very different from unilingual utterances. Somewhat older BFLA children (after age four), who are typically able to produce complex sentences in at least one of their languages, mainly insert noun phrases in their mixed utterances, in addition to single nouns (Bentahila & Davies, 1994). Bilingual adults also use more noun insertions than any other category in mixed utterances (see, e.g. Romaine, 1995).

In their mixed utterances that do not contain just a noun from the other language, young bilingual children follow structural constraints that have also been found for adults (Paradis *et al.*, 2000). These constraints apply language-specific structural knowledge (Cantone & Müller, 2005; Paradis *et al.*, 2000).

In fact, the few studies that have compared BFLA children's unilingual and mixed utterances show that there are no clear differences between them in terms of overall length and complexity (e.g. De Houwer, 1990; Sinka, 2000). As such, mixed utterances appear not to have any special status other than that they include words from two languages.

Mixed utterances may contain words that combine a free morpheme from Language A with a bound morpheme from Language Alpha. In these cases, the rest of the utterance will usually be in Language Alpha. An example is 'I'm just **schraub**ing this on', where four-year-old English–German Thomas inserted the German verb stem 'schraub-' (screw) into an otherwise completely English sentence, and where he attached the English -ing morpheme to the German verb stem, just as if that stem was an English verb (Saunders, 1988: 182; see also Box 3.2 in Chapter 3).

Such combinations of a free morpheme from Language A with a bound morpheme from Language Alpha are pretty rare, though. In the corpus of 801 mixed utterances that I compiled on the basis of data from several BFLA children acquiring different languages (De Houwer, 1995b; see above) there were only 28 instances of such combinations (that's only 3.5%).

In summary, the structure of mixed utterances is usually not very different from that of children's unilingual utterances. Young BFLA children's mixed utterances mostly involve the insertion of a noun from Language A into Language Alpha, and that noun is mostly treated as being in Language Alpha.

The development of narrative

Just like MFLA children, BFLA children start to be able to tell short connected stories at around the age of four (Schlyter, 1996). Among others things, telling a good story requires linking sentences one after the other in ways that are engaging and make sense. Languages differ in how they do this. That is, they differ in the structural devices that they use, as well as in the kinds of things they prefer to focus on in stories, and on the degree of 'drama' that is required in their telling, just to name a few possibilities. At the same time, languages are similar in various aspects of storytelling such as making a distinction between old and new information. BFLA children, then, must learn how to tell stories in ways that are sufficiently different in their two languages. They must learn the storytelling styles that are specific to their two languages.

Telling a story is not restricted to telling an imaginary tale or describing a picture book. However, it is these sorts of things that children are used to hearing, and it is these kinds of narrowly defined stories that BFLA children have been asked to tell so researchers could study them. In particular, most of the studies looking at BFLA children's storytelling abilities have relied on a wordless picture book that has been used extensively in studies of children's narrative development (Berman & Slobin, 1994). This is the book *Frog, where are you?* by Mercer Mayer. In Box 7.22 I give an overview of studies of BFLA that have relied on children's telling or retelling (after they heard the story from an adult) of the story depicted in this picture book.

Box 7.22 Studies of BFLA children's story telling that have relied on the picture book *Frog, where are you?*

Child	Age(s)	Language A	Language Alpha	Study
Boy	3;6–5;2	French	German	Schneider, 1999
Kaja	4;6	Norwegian	English	Lanza, 2001
Nicolas	5;2 and 5;7	Spanish	English	Silva-Corvalán, 2003[a]
Alice	6;10	Norwegian	English	Lanza, 2001
Jan	6;11	Spanish	English	Álvarez, 1999, 2003, 2008
12 children	between 6;11 and 8;4	Italian	English	Serratrice, 2007b
Jan	7;11	Spanish	English	Álvarez, 2003, 2008
Nina	8;8	Norwegian	English	Lanza, 2001
Jan	8;11 and 9;11 and 10;11	Spanish	English	Álvarez, 2003, 2008

[a] This study introduces a very useful scoring system that takes into account both narrative and morphosyntactic elements

The studies in Box 7.22 have analyzed different issues, but one issue in all studies has been to what extent BFLA children use narrative devices in language-specific ways. All studies find that children do use different devices in both languages. Still, it is often difficult to determine what sorts of devices are really language specific and what sorts of evidence one would need to show there is a real difference between children's narrations in both languages.

One obvious difference between the languages occurs when children clearly lag behind in one of their languages in terms of their narrative abilities (e.g. Silva-Corvalán, 2003).[17] Another difference occurs when children use specific narrative devices much more frequently in one language than in the other. For instance, the Norwegian–English BFLA children in Lanza's (2001) study used temporal connectors with different frequencies in Norwegian and English. Spanish–English Jan introduced new characters in English mostly by means of grammatical objects, whereas in Spanish new characters were mostly introduced by means of grammatical subjects (Álvarez, 2003). The combined evidence suggests that BLA children learn to use two different rhetorical styles.

BFLA children's stories have also been analyzed in terms of their morphosyntactic characteristics per se. All relevant studies find that children mainly use the structural possibilities of their two input languages. Hence, their two morphosyntactic systems operate separately from each other. For instance, in his German stories the German–French boy studied by Schneider (1999) relied a lot on particle verbs and many different verb types to express various actions, whereas in French he showed much less variation in the number of different lexical verbs but nuanced their meanings using a great variety of adverbs. Serratrice's (2007b) study constitutes the largest database so far of BFLA children's narrations in one particular pair of languages. She concludes on the basis of analyses of many different morphosyntactic structures as well as narrative devices that her 12 Italian–English subjects achieved 'remarkable levels of nativeness in both of their languages' (p. 1083).

Again, the overall separate development in older BFLA children's languages as evidenced by their narrations does not mean there can be no influence from one language on the other. Some clear examples are 'Then it was water down there' and 'Then they got mad on the dog', which show influence from Norwegian on English (Lanza, 2001).

As for younger BFLA children, subtle influence from one language on the other has been claimed on the basis of comparisons with stories from monolingual children in terms of the frequency with which particular narrative devices occur. As before, I maintain that crosslinguistic influence cannot be determined on the basis of just comparisons with MFLA. MFLA is not the norm for BFLA.

At the same time, many parallel developments have been noted between narratives by BFLA and MFLA children concerning the same language. For instance, a study of ten English–French BFLA five-year-olds that was based on the retelling of a story other than the *Frog story* in both languages found that the children did not tell shorter or less lexically varied stories than a group of ten somewhat older (average age: 5;5) English-speaking children or a group of even much older (average age: 6;4) French-speaking children (Nicoladis *et al.*,

2007). The length of Lanza's (2001) three Norwegian–English subjects's stories was also similar to that of monolingual children reported on in the literature. Silva–Corvalán (2003) notes that in spite of her BFLA subject Nicolas having a clearly stronger and weaker language, his level of narrative ability in each falls within the range of monolingual development. Serratrice (2007b: 1083) compared her data for 12 BFLA children to twice 12 MFLA children and finds that: 'With one exception, the linguistic choices made by the bilinguals in [her] sample were significantly similar to the choices made by their monolingual peers in both languages'.

Finally, and not surprisingly, BFLA children also get better at telling a story as they get older. This may manifest itself in an increased length (Lanza, 2001), an increased richness of the stories (Lanza, 2001; Silva-Corvalán, 2003), the increased use of subordinators rather than just sequential markers like 'and then' (Lanza) or the more consistent use of one temporal perspective (Lanza).

In conclusion

Children's early combinatory speech builds on their earlier acquired lexical knowledge. This sounds very obvious, but is much more of a complex issue than it appears. In this chapter I have been able to refer only very fleetingly to theoretical issues concerning the early relation between words and grammatical knowledge. There is a large literature on this (see, for instance, several chapters in Hoff & Shatz, 2007).

Research on BFLA has only just started to pay attention to these larger issues. Whatever evidence there is for BFLA suggests that relations between the lexicon and grammar are language specific from the outset. That is, relations can be observed between the lexicon and grammar within each language separately.

This most likely is the foundation for the basic fact about BFLA children's morphosyntactic development that we see in children's sentences after the age of two, namely that they mainly say sentences that show no structural influence from the other language. This is evidence for the Separate Development Hypothesis: children speak according to the structural rules of each of their languages separately. The effect is that they say sentences that don't make you think of another language much at all.

For BFLA children who speak two languages, there can be a difference in the frequency with which they speak the one rather than the other, and the level of proficiency with which they speak the one rather than the other. But there are also plenty of BFLA children who show no obvious differences between their languages in terms of how often they use them or how well they speak them. The Separate Development Hypothesis obtains even for the former type of BFLA children who speak only one of their languages frequently and well. Their weaker language develops without noticeable systematic influence from their stronger one.

It isn't clear yet why some BFLA children have a clearly stronger and weaker language, but as Qi (2005) and others have suggested (see Chapter 4), differences in the overall frequency with which children hear each of their languages may be an important factor.[18]

In fact, the frequency of various morphosyntactic forms in the input and the different distributions of this input for the two languages, in addition to children's lexical basis in each language, may be fundamental reasons why we see separate development in the first place. Several scholars in BFLA have recently turned their attention to examining the actual input that BFLA children hear. This is a promising research direction that can yield important findings.

The fact that there is separate development does not imply that there cannot be any influence from one language on the other. Indeed, such influence may occur, but so far the evidence for it is slim. Certainly so far there is no evidence of any systematic crosslinguistic influence from Language A on Language Alpha in BFLA children under age four. Even in cases where some scholars predict that crosslinguistic influence (in BFLA) will occur, it in fact does not (Larrañaga, 2008).

As I proposed earlier (De Houwer, 1994), somewhat older BFLA children might start to show some crosslinguistic influence for certain kinds of structures, if only because the more you know, the more you can in fact bring together. In addition, increased metalinguistic awareness may bring about changes in how children speak. There is some experimental evidence that older BFLA children (eight-year-olds) do show some signs of crosslinguistic influence for some aspects of speech (Argyri & Sorace, 2007; Serratrice, 2007a).

However, we know very little of BFLA children's morphosyntactic development beyond age five. Some of the research that has examined BFLA children's stories tells us more about somewhat older BFLA children's morphosyntactic development. The available evidence suggests that separate development continues as children get older. Yet it is still unclear to what extent this finding is generalizable. We know very little about whether school-age BFLA children continue to show separate development or not, and what the circumstances are in which separate development continues or ceases to exist. It is clear, though, that five-year-old children have by no means finished developing as far as morphosyntax is concerned. This means that the issue of separate development into the school years is certainly of interest.

Once children with bilingual input from birth start to produce sentences they may produce three types of utterances: (1) lexically unilingual utterances in Language A; (2) lexically unilingual utterances in Language Alpha; and (3) mixed utterances, which contain lexical items and/or bound morphemes from Languages A and Alpha. BFLA children's choice between these three kinds of utterances is usually appropriate, as it is in ESLA children as well (e.g. Arias & Lakshmanan, 2005).

ESLA children, however, may produce sentences in their L2 that are quite different from those that BFLA children produce, in that they may show clear morphosyntactic influence from the other language they know, their L1. Such clearly structurally influenced sentences 'give away' the fact that children did not hear a particular language from birth.

In contrast, BFLA children's unilingual utterances usually resemble those of more or less age- and MLU-matched monolingual peers speaking that same language. The big difference, of course, is that BFLA children can say unilingual utterances in two languages, whereas MFLA children are limited to just one.

BFLA children's mixed utterances, finally, are not as interesting structurally as you might think. They mainly involve insertions of a single word from the other language. As Cantone (2007) has recently argued, you don't need complicated constraints to explain young BFLA children's mixed utterances. Yet most of their mixed utterances are similar to many adult utterances that combine words from two languages. The very complicated code switching used by some adult bilinguals, however, is not a feature of young BFLA children's speech.

Older BFLA children continue to use the kinds of mixed utterances that young BFLA children use (e.g. Saunders, 1988). An example of a rare mixed utterance by Dutch–English Susan at age ten is 'gaat dat niet melten?' (goes that not melt?; isn't that going to melt?; my notes), where the English verb 'melt' is inserted into an otherwise completely Dutch utterance and has a Dutch infinitive ending attached to it. This kind of mixed utterance is occasionally produced by younger BFLA children as well.

Summing up, young BFLA children's morphosyntactic development shows that in children with regular bilingual input from birth each language has its own separate learning space. The role of the input in this needs more investigation.

Notes

1. The only study I have been able to find that explicitly refers to the kinds of meaning relations present in BFLA children's early word combinations is the one by Itani-Adams (2007). Itani-Adams (2007: 17) notes that between the ages of 1;11 and 2;4, English–Japanese Hannah 'used arguments that express agent, theme/patient and goal/location in both Japanese and English'.

2. However, an individual BFLA child may combine words earlier or later than an individual MFLA child.

3. The first big milestone is the appearance of the first words.

4. The group of 113 children between the ages of 17 and 30 months that Marchman *et al.* studied were mostly children with bilingual input from birth.

5. Another important finding from the Marchman *et al.* study is that the total number of meanings that children expressed across their two languages ('conceptual vocabulary'; see Chapter 6) did not correlate with grammatical complexity once the language-specific scores were controlled for.

6. David and Li (2005) used English and French versions of the toddler form of the CDI and collected data between the ages of 16 and 30 months. They present their findings in function of the total number of words that children produced, irrespective of age.

7. Conboy and Thal (2006) studied 55 BFLA Spanish–English children as part of a group of 64 bilingual children between the ages of 19 and 31 months.

8. Conboy and Thal (2006) subsumed the following under predicates: main verbs (excluding Spanish state verbs), adjectives and several Spanish words listed as quantifiers and adverbs.

9. The one exception was that English vocabulary from 28 to 31 months in the sample of 31 children *did* contribute to children's utterance length in Spanish, over and above Spanish vocabulary at that age (Conboy & Thal, 2006: 727).

10. 'Raivo (was) exposed to Estonian in the home from birth but with regular exposure to English from six months on' (Vihman, 1999: 270).

11. More specifically, in their CDI study of 113 English–Spanish bilingual children (see above), Marchman *et al.* (2004) found that both measures of utterance complexity (ML3w and sentence complexity; see Box 7.3) were highly correlated within each language separately.

12. Mixed utterances were also a minority in a trilingual child's speech (Barnes, 2006).

13. But note that I am here comparing MLU's across different languages (Swedish and Italian), which isn't quite appropriate (see earlier).

14. Many studies of BFLA do refer to children's input, but only in an abstract manner where they describe general structural features of a particular language or variety rather than the actual forms that children hear spoken to them.

15. The errors involved saying non-finite verbs where finite forms were required. Although Meisel (2008) does not discuss the children's knowledge of their L1, German, their ages (three and four) imply that they were using finite forms in German, so there is no reason to suspect L1 influence.

16. Interestingly, for two older children with trilingual input from birth in English, Hebrew and Spanish (aged seven and nine) the most frequently inserted category in mixed utterances was the verb (Stavans & Muchnik, 2008). When the same children were younger, the by far most frequently inserted category was a noun or noun phrase (Hoffmann & Stavans, 2007). Nouns were also the most commonly inserted category in the speech of another child (Robin) with trilingual input from birth (in English, French and Italian) (Hoffmann & Widdicombe, 1999; Robin was studied at the ages of 4;4 and 4;5). These findings are similar to the findings from BFLA for children under age five.

17. Such differences also occur in young ESLA children, whose narratives in the new L2 are predictably incoherent and lack sufficient cohesion because children simply do not as yet have the sufficient structural knowledge necessary for being able to produce good narratives in their L2, even though they are able to do so in their L1 (Montanari, 2005).

18. In the case of Qi's (2005) subject James, he heard his weaker language (English) much less often than his stronger one.

Summary box

- Whether children's early word combinations are 'real' sentences is a controversial issue. But gradually, children do start to say utterances that show morphosyntactic structure and so are real sentences.
- BFLA children who are producing sentences mostly produce unilingual utterances. BFLA children's early unilingual sentences show a language-specific development. This means that they are not influenced by the other language. This confirms the Separate Development Hypothesis.
- Each of BFLA children's languages develops as it does in MFLA children, but there are differences with ESLA.
- BFLA children's morphosyntactic development in Language A may be more advanced than in Language Alpha. BFLA children, then, may have a clearly stronger and weaker language. This does not affect the SDH.
- BFLA children also produce mixed utterances but these are much less common than unilingual utterances. Most mixed utterances have words of Language A in them and in addition a single word from Language Alpha.
- From early on, BFLA children are able to produce unilingual utterances in Language A where Language A is expected. The same goes for Language Alpha. From the middle of the third year onwards, BFLA children are able to repair their language choice when their conversational partner expresses lack of understanding.

Suggestions for study activities

1. Look at the list of early word combinations that Manuela produced between ages 1;6;25 and 1;7,26 (Deuchar & Quay, 2000: 137–141). If you know Spanish, work with all the utterances here that are entirely in Spanish. If you don't know Spanish, work with all the utterances that consist of only English words. Try to categorize these utterances into different groups based on the different kinds of meaning relations they seem to express. Look for the following kinds of relations (the order doesn't matter): actor–action, entity–possessor, entity–quality/state, location–entity. Create new categories if you need to. How many utterances are there in each group? Which group has the most? Do the orders of the words follow any kind of pattern?
2. For those of you who know something about French and Dutch: French–Dutch Anouck produced the following French unilingual sentence at age 2;7,28: 'je cherche petit nounours' (Müller & Hulk, 2001: 13). Does this utterance confirm or disconfirm the SDH? Why (not)? Does the utterance match French? How so?
3. The following activity is easier if you know Dutch, French and English but can be done with knowledge of just English, too.
    Dutch–French Anouk often used the particles 'ook' (Dutch) and 'aussi' (French) (somewhat similar to English 'also, too') in a language-appropriate manner in terms of where she placed them (Hulk, 2003), as did Dutch–English Kate (De Houwer 1990).
    In her Dutch, Anouk occasionally also used Dutch 'ook' at the very end of sentences. This is common in adult French. Adult Dutch occasionally also places 'ook' at the very end of sentences, as in 'wil je deze ook?' (want you this also?), or 'ik wil die ook!' (I want that also!). However, the Dutch utterances in which Anouk put 'ook' at the end aren't the kind of utterances where adult Dutch speakers would also do so. Examples from Anouk are: 'Mara nu op vakantie ook' (Mara now on holiday also; age 2;11)'; 'een heel ver land ook' (a very far country also; 3;7); 'erg veel kleurtjes ook' (very many colors also; 2;10) (Hulk, 2003: 251). The word order of Anouk's utterances here makes you think of French. In adult Dutch these utterances should be: 'Mara nu ook op vakantie', 'ook een heel ver land' and 'ook erg veel kleurtjes'.

> ### Suggestions for study activities continued
>
> Dutch–English Kate also occasionally used Dutch 'ook' at the very end of sentences. This isn't common in adult English. Similar to Anouk, the Dutch utterances in which Kate put 'ook' at the end aren't the kind of utterances where adult Dutch speakers would also do so. Examples from Kate are: 'ik heef kaas en en tofu ook hé!' (I have cheese and and tofu also, huh!; age 3;3) and 'en da's de koe ook' (and that's the cow also; age 2;11). The word order of Kate's utterances here doesn't make you think of English. In adult Dutch these sentences should be: 'ik heb ook kaas en tofu hé!' and 'en da's ook de koe'.
>
> Analyze these examples in terms of input ambiguity. What do the children's unusual usages of 'ook' mean for the SDH? Is there crosslinguistic influence? (advanced)

4. For this activity you just need to know English. German–English Hannah produced the following mixed utterance at age 2;4, '**ich hab ge**made you much better' (I made you much better; Gut, 2000a: 148). The utterance starts with the German first singular pronoun 'ich' (I), then continues with an auxiliary 'hab' (have), and then there is a past participle which consists of the German past participle morpheme (ge-) and an English verb form that could be either a past participle or a simple past verb. The rest of the utterance is in English.
   Is this the kind of mixed utterance you would expect from young BFLA children? Why (not)?

5. *Project*: Try to gain access to a gregarious BFLA child between the ages of three and five who you share one language with. Ask the parents if you can come and play with the child for an hour or so. Bring some interesting age-appropriate toys to the appointment. Make a recording of the interaction as you play with the child (preferably, without any one else in the room). Talk your overlapping language with the child. Also talk to the parents to find out more about the child's input in the language you used with the child.
   Afterwards, do one of the activities (or take more than one) listed below. All except 5.1 involve making a full transcript of the recorded interaction using the CHAT system (see Chapter 3) and including your own utterances.

   5.1. Listen to the recordings a few times. Find a friend who knows the same language. Try to have that friend listen to the recording, too. Talk about how the child sounds. Does the child talk the way you would expect a child their age to sound? Are there any strange or funny things that the child says? Do they just sound 'child-like' or do you think something else is going on?

   5.2. Categorize the child utterances into:
      – unilingual in the language you were using
      – unilingual in the other language the child is acquiring
      – mixed utterances.

      What is the proportion of each? For the mixed utterances and the unilingual utterances in the other language the child is acquiring (if there are any) try to figure out what triggered them. Is it anything you said or did? Was there a change of topic? Someone who called out to the child from another room?

   5.3. Categorize the child's unilingual utterances in the language you used into:
      – single word utterances
      – two word utterances
      – utterances with more than two words but a maximum of one clause
      – utterances combining two or more clauses.

      What was the proportion of each? Determine the average length of utterances in words. How many words did the child's longest utterance contain?

> **Suggestions for study activities continued**
>
> 5.4. Take the child's unilingual utterances in the language you were using that sound non-adult-like to you (if there are any). Try to determine what makes them non-adult-like. Do you think there is any possible sign of influence from the other language? (advanced)
>
> 5.5. Take the child's unilingual utterances in the language you were using that contain a verb (any kind of verb). How were the subjects expressed? What was the word order? Can you see any patterns? Do the patterns fit the language you were using? (advanced)

Recommended reading (advanced)

Deuchar and Muntz (2003) carefully address several theoretical accounts for the explanation of some BFLA children's early use of the 'wrong' language. De Houwer (2005) addresses the Separate Development Hypothesis in more detail and with more background than I have been able to do here. You will find a penetrating discussion of similar issues from a different theoretical perspective in Meisel (2001). Serratrice *et al.* (2004) offer a balanced discussion of the issue of crosslinguistic influence in BFLA. Deuchar and Vihman (2005) offer an original approach for the structural analysis of the earliest mixed utterances.

8 Harmonious bilingual development

The whole child — 305
   Few studies of BFLA connect up different levels of language functioning — 305
   Yet again some methodological points — 306
   The psycholinguistic perspective — 306
BFLA: good or bad? — 307
Comparisons with monolinguals — 308
Harmonious bilingual development or the lack of it — 310
   Not speaking a particular language — 310
   Assessing BFLA children for language learning problems — 312
   Language choice — 312
   Language and identity — 313
   Professional advice to give up one of the languages — 315
   Language and emotion — 316
   Negative attitudes from outside the family — 317
   Uneven development — 317
   Hotchpotch? — 318
   Parental expectations — 320
   Parental input frequency — 321
   Parental work — 322
   Children's expectations — 323

And what happens when BFLA children get older?	324
Needed: an alternative research paradigm	326
In conclusion	327
Summary box	330
Suggestions for study activities	330
Recommended reading	331
Resources for parents and educators	331

The whole child

The detailed descriptions of bilingual children's language development in this book have been discussed in separate chapters for the use of sounds, words and sentences. These aspects, however, are not developing separately. Children are developing different language-related skills at the same time.

Also, the boundaries that we as linguists draw between different aspects of language use are not necessarily the same boundaries that language learning children make as they tackle the task of becoming competent hearers and speakers of their input languages. In addition, the fact that different aspects are discussed within one chapter with the same title does not mean that even within one chapter or one level of language functioning there is a unified whole. Phonological development, for instance, includes learning about intonation contours and smaller units, but the two are not necessarily related, or may even be quite unrelated (Gut, 2000a: 170).

For bilingual language development this implies that the 'big' issue of whether children develop two separate languages from the beginning onwards may have different answers depending on what you are looking at. A child may be using different words orders in the two languages from the beginning of multi-word speech, but may use similar phonological processes in both languages that make it difficult to see whether their segmental phonology is developing in a language-specific manner.

Few studies of BFLA connect up different levels of language functioning

There are few in-depth studies of the acquisition of phonological, lexical and morphosyntactic development in the same BFLA child. Leopold's (1970) monumental four-volume work spanned five years in the life of a single child (and even more). This allowed him to observe a large range of linguistic phenomena. However, even this to date most comprehensive case study of BFLA says very little about morphosyntactic development (but all the more about phonological and lexical development).

Cruz-Ferreira's (2006) book on three children also focuses mostly on phonological and lexical development. Other recent book-length studies of BFLA have focused mainly on one area of linguistic functioning (e.g. Cantone, 2007, on the use of mixed utterances and language choice; Yip & Matthews, 2007, on a selection of morphosyntactic structures in the speech of six English–Cantonese bilingual children).

One reason why studies focus on mainly one particular area of language functioning is that different kinds of linguistic knowledge appear at different ages. For instance, you cannot analyze morphosyntactic development in 12-month-olds except that you can investigate aspects of their ability to detect different sentence patterns. A new exciting line of research in BFLA started up at the International School for Advanced Studies (SISSA) in Trieste, Italy, does just that (Kovács & Mehler, 2008). My comments here lay bare the general limitation of studies of BFLA in that they have tended to focus mainly on what children say rather than also on what they understand. Fortunately, with the relatively new research on BFLA children's language perception (Chapter 5) and word comprehension (Chapter 6), this imbalance is starting to be redressed.

Yet again some methodological points

Ideally, in order to understand the emerging connections between different aspects of BFLA children's language development before age five we would need to have longitudinal data from the same children from birth up to age five. The monumental database that Virginia Yip and Stephen Matthews have compiled and which they have now started to mine for other than morphosyntactic aspects (Yip & Matthews, 2008) is an example of just the kind of rich data set that is needed.

Case studies aren't the only ones that can address the issue of connections between various levels of language functioning in BFLA children. The CDI studies by Marchman *et al.* (2004) and Conboy and Thal (2006) referred to in Chapter 6 are examples of group studies that can address links between lexical and morphosyntactic development. Also, the ongoing study of 31 French–Dutch BFLA children that I have been coordinating with Marc Bornstein, with data collected at the ages of 5, 13, 20 and approximately 48 months, holds promise for the analysis of the data at different levels of language functioning.

The projects mentioned in the previous paragraph are also exemplary of the general new trend in BFLA research to direct more attention to the very early stages of BFLA children's language development, prior to the onset of sentences. The work on early bilingual perception (Chapter 5) is an example of this. These more recent research directions form an important counterweight to the dominance of studies of morphosyntactic development in BFLA that was especially in evidence until the mid-1990s.

Regardless of the area investigated, the last decade has seen a great expansion in the number of languages and language pairs-in-acquisition studied. In addition, the use of experimental designs in BFLA marks a wholly new approach.

Also quite new is the interest in the role of linguistic input, that is, in the structural form of parental utterances as an explanatory factor for the emergence of certain structures as produced by bilingual children (Chapter 7). However, with a few exceptions, this interest has so far not led to many published reports that provide analyses of actual speech to bilingual children.

The psycholinguistic perspective

It is still the case today, as it was when I was preparing the overview chapter on bilingual acquisition that appeared in the mid-1990s (De Houwer, 1995a), that most of the work in bilingual acquisition is done from a psycholinguistic perspective. This means it focuses mainly on the structures that bilingual children produce and on trying to find explanations for why specific structures occur. Sociolinguistic approaches are rare, and even more rare are approaches that combine the two perspectives.

It is of course important to know what kinds of structures bilingual children use, and how they develop on a psycholinguistic level. It is important to know this from a theoretical perspective, so that we gain more scientific insight into processes of human language acquisition. At the beginning of this book I wrote that I wouldn't dwell much on theoretical issues. I want to stress, though, that research on BFLA plays an important role in theory development in psycholinguistics, from early speech perception (e.g. Werker & Byers-Heinlein, 2008) over the early link between the lexicon and grammatical development (e.g. Marchman *et al.*, 2004) to the issue of language-specific vs. language-universal processes in morphosyntactic development (De Houwer, 1990). After all, psycholinguistic theories of child language development should be able to account for all children, not just those with just a single input language.

Knowing what kinds of structures bilingual children use is also important from an applied perspective. There is a great demand from speech therapists and educators for more knowledge about bilingual children's language development. They want to know what kinds of language use they can reasonably expect from bilingual children, so that they know whether a child needs intervention, and what kind.

The field's obvious response to this demand has been to attempt to determine what types of structures are to be expected from bilingual children, and which are not, so that any 'deviations' may be properly assessed as perhaps constituting a language learning problem that needs to be attended to by a language and speech professional. This is obviously an important issue. Language is crucial in human functioning, and the basis for children's active participation in all aspects of life. Problems in language expression need to be addressed. If not, children's overall development will be at risk.

Indeed, it is children's overall development that should really be at the forefront. Children are not only developing different language-related skills. They are simultaneously developing their personalities and their cognitive, emotional and social skills. In this final chapter, I want to put the whole child back in the picture.

BFLA: good or bad?

When parents or teachers find out that I study bilingual children's language development, the first question I usually get is: 'And, what did you find, is it good for children or bad?'. I'm always a bit embarrassed when I get that question, since I really don't have an answer to it. One reason is that I disagree with one of the assumptions of the question, namely that bilingualism is somehow a choice (more about this in a bit). Another reason is that I'm not always sure what people mean by 'good' or 'bad' here. Of course, I do usually answer people's question and try to explain that it isn't my role to judge, but to find out in what circumstances a bilingual upbringing turns out well for all involved, and in what circumstances it might lead to trouble.

And indeed, I think that we as researchers owe it to parents, teachers and children to know more about those circumstances. When a bilingual upbringing turns out well for all involved, there is what I call 'harmonious bilingual development'. When it doesn't, there obviously isn't. While many children growing up in bilingual families fortunately go through a harmonious process of language development, many others do not.

Before I go on to the next section, I want to discuss the frequent assumption that a bilingual upbringing is a choice. It is true, future parents who as a couple know more than one language can very consciously decide whether or not to speak one or two languages to their children. As I described at the beginning of Chapter 4, different decisions are possible in different circumstances.

Yet in many cases, there is no 'free' choice, since choosing against a bilingual upbringing for the children would imply cutting off part of the family from communicating with the new child, and the other way round. Also, even when parents are proficient bilinguals, it may be emotionally hard or even impossible for them to speak to their newborn baby other than in the language they themselves were raised in. In addition, as I discussed in Chapter 4, the language 'constellation' within the couple of parents-to-be is an important factor in determining what the range of 'choices' really is.

Completely monolingual future parents who each speak just one and the same language have no choice as regards the language they will address their offspring in. Their single language is just the default. This is maybe why no one ever asks me whether monolingual acquisition is good. For many bilingual future parents, there isn't necessarily that much of a choice either. The issue of 'good' or 'bad', then, doesn't seem to be very relevant – bilingual acquisition often is also just the default.

The perceived special status of bilingual acquisition as the 'unusual' case for children to develop language skills is at the back of many people's minds, including those of parents in bilingual families. Implicit in many lay people's and scholars' approaches to bilingual acquisition is the idea that bilingual children should resemble monolingual ones. I discuss this further in the next section.

Comparisons with monolinguals

People who have been brought up bilingually often say of themselves that 'of course, I don't speak either of my languages as well as a monolingual', or, 'in school I was behind the monolingual children'. Others feel no such misgivings, and do not compare themselves to monolinguals.[1]

Indeed, I think that one of the basic problematic issues with regard to how bilingually raised people regard themselves and how other people regard *them* lies in the constant comparison between bilingualism and monolingualism. Somehow, people expect bilinguals to be two monolinguals in one – and not just any monolinguals, but monolinguals with highly advanced language skills.

People expect this also from children. They worry that bilingual input burdens children's minds, to the extent that children will have a delayed development, that is, in comparison to monolingual children. Even among some scholars there still is an idea that bilingual input somehow overburdens young children's minds.[2]

This fear must have already existed in Ronjat's time (1913). You will remember that he was the first to publish a study on BFLA. He already found it necessary to state that his bilingual son's development was no different from monolingual children's in terms of the timing of important milestones and in terms of many other aspects of linguistic development. This implies that in Ronjat's time educated people were worried about that.

These ideas about children not being able to handle two languages persist until today. Many parents, schoolteachers and child health professionals believe that bilingual input could be a threat to children's development. As researchers, we can say time and again that comparisons with monolinguals are not necessary to understand the bilingual acquisition process; and that bilingual development should be studied in its own right, without reference to monolinguals. But that doesn't help bilingual families. They invariably meet up with the myth of bilingual input as a threat.

Researchers must address this fear, then, and compare bilinguals to monolinguals to see how they are doing. Also in Chapters 5, 6 and 7 in this book I have drawn comparisons between bilingual and monolingual children in their language development. That's not because in fact BFLA *should* be compared to MFLA or because MFLA should be seen as the standard. That's because it still unfortunately needs to be proved to many people that child bilingualism does not 'hurt' a child or impedes children's language development.[3]

There is no intrinsic reason why bilinguals should be the same as monolinguals, just as there is no reason why monolinguals should be the same as bilinguals. However, the evidence to date, as discussed also in this book, shows that in fact bilingual and monolingual children develop language in extraordinarily *similar* ways. Certainly, you do also find differences between a particular bilingual and monolingual child, but the magnitude of these differences is no greater than the range of variation there is between monolingual children among themselves, or bilingual children among themselves. As I wrote in Chapter 2, young MFLA children of the same age can differ widely in their level of proficiency in just one language, and so can BFLA children.

Sometimes the literature comparing monolingual and bilingual children's language development gives the impression that there is a competition going on: who is doing better – the bilingual children or the monolingual ones? I think this is the wrong question. What we need to focus on is which circumstances lead to harmonious development in all children, regardless of whether they have monolingual or bilingual input.

At the same time, it is true that children growing up bilingually often seem to experience problems in their developmental path that are not experienced by monolingual children. I here make abstraction from the many children, whether with monolingual or bilingual input, who have neurophysiological limits on their functioning. It is obvious that in many cases where children are severely hearing impaired, suffer from neurodegenerative diseases or do not have access to sufficient food and medical care – just to name a few of the difficult circumstances that so many children in this world unfortunately have to deal with – harmonious development is an ideal that seems beyond reach.

For BFLA children, harmonious development may be hindered because of the bilingual setting they find themselves in. One of the reasons why BFLA children do not develop harmoniously is that often parents and teachers, and later children themselves, have an ideal in mind of the bilingual as two highly proficient monolinguals in one who can do everything in both languages. While there are highly proficient bilinguals who function very well in their two languages and can talk about just anything in either of them, for most people this will be an ideal that is impossible to attain. As Wölck (1987/88: 7) explains, one reason is that for most bilinguals, 'there is a contextual separation or preference for one language over the other in a number of [lexical] domains'. Indeed, people tend to experience and learn certain things in just one of their two languages. This is because a single person does not lead two lives.

The next section elaborates on situations where bilingual development may be most vulnerable.

Harmonious bilingual development or the lack of it

Not speaking a particular language

In monolingual families where all family members speak the majority language, it is expected that young children will grow up to soon speak the language they hear around them. Language is not usually an issue, unless a child does not start talking, or continues to speak very unclearly or strangely beyond the earliest stages of language development. When monolingually raised children fail to understand and/or speak that single language, this is seen as an abnormal, even pathological situation that needs urgent attention, and rightly so. Children who fail to communicate through language in a MFLA setting may have a hearing or neurological disorder that needs to be remedied for the sake of their overall development. There are several additional possible reasons for why monolingual children may be experiencing language learning problems.

In order to help monolingual children with communication problems, their families may be involved in a professional treatment schedule (for instance, through playing language games with children), but there will be no mention of stopping to speak to the children or switching to another language. Rather, families will be encouraged to interact and talk *more* with the children. The choice of language used is not a point of concern. Not speaking well or not speaking at all is of course a very difficult situation for both child and family, but rarely will any blame be put on the family or child, and usually no blame will be laid with the fact that the child is in the process of learning a particular language.

For monolingually raised children with language learning problems, language development will not be very harmonious. For almost all other children growing up monolingually, language acquisition usually is one of those things in life that receives fairly little attention and that seems to just develop 'naturally'.

Things are quite different in a setting where children are raised bilingually. In bilingual family settings, harmonious bilingual development for children who have no intrinsic language learning or neurophysiological problems is not a given. Children may not speak both languages to the extent that their environment expects or wants them to, or they may not speak the languages in the situations required of them, or they may simply not speak one of the languages involved.

Even though children may speak two separate languages in the third and fourth year of life, they may stop using one of those languages as they start to attend preschool or school (see Chapter 4). Dutch–English Kate, who was a competent bilingual at age 3;8 (De Houwer, 1990) stopped speaking Dutch very soon after the family moved from Belgium to the United States, even though her father continued to address her in Dutch and she met up with other Dutch (bilingual) speakers as well.[4]

Similar changes have been reported for ESLA. For instance, the girl Michal moved from Israel to the United States when she was two and a half years old. At that point, she was a fluent monolingual speaker of Hebrew. Input in Hebrew continued at home through both parents and two older siblings while English exposure started at nursery school. As Michal learned to speak English, she became less and less able and willing to speak Hebrew. By the time she was four and a half she spoke fluent English but could hardly be said to speak Hebrew any more. Hebrew-like word roots were inserted into English utterances in ways that showed more influence from English than from Hebrew (Kaufman & Aronoff, 1991).

Michal's example is by no means exceptional. Also the case of BFLA children not speaking one of 'their' languages is quite common (Chapter 4). In some cases, it may be no problem that the child speaks only one language. My many conversations with parents of such children, however, suggest otherwise: usually it does become quite a problem for the parents in these bilingual families that their children speak only one language. Often, also, as the children grow up, they are very sorry not to be able to communicate with some members of their extended family, and not being able to function in the country where the language they don't speak is being used.

What's more, not speaking the same language as your parents is not conducive to a good parent–child relationship. For instance, survey results from adolescents from immigrant families in the United States found that 'Adolescents who conversed with their parents in different languages felt more emotionally distant from them and were less likely to engage in discussions with them than were youths who shared the same language with their parents' (Tseng & Fuligni, 2000: 473). Also, speaking Language A but not Language Alpha may lead to a large discrepancy between both languages in comprehension as well. Ultimately, bilingual children may understand very little of one of their languages. This may lead to grave communication problems between parents and children (e.g. Shin, 2005; Wong Fillmore, 1991).

In these cases where children and their families experience frequent negative feelings because in spite of bilingual input, children speak only one language, bilingual development has not been harmonious (see also, Guardado, 2002). Trying to 'turn the tide' is not impossible, but difficult. First of all, this requires motivation on the part of the children that may simply not be there. Second, there most likely needs to be an increased input frequency, with many different and interesting opportunities for learning.

Assessing BFLA children for language learning problems

If BFLA children do not speak any language at all, or speak two languages very haltingly or badly, this is a major cause for concern. The problem in a bilingual setting, however, often is that it isn't always clear whether BFLA children's communicative problems are typical second language learning problems or whether there is a deeper underlying cause that points to a language learning impairment (Abudarham, 1980). Ways to help in the first case are fairly straightforward: increased input, and ample time and opportunity for learning the language or languages that are giving problems. In the second case, speech and language therapists will have to try and find a solution.

As Abudarham wrote nearly three decades ago, a serious obstacle towards determining whether a bilingual child simply needs more opportunities to learn or has impaired language learning abilities is the issue of valid assessment. By and large, unfortunately that situation still remains the same (e.g. Thordardottir *et al.*, 2006). This is one reason why monolingual tools are still being used to assess bilingual children (about the issues involved in assessing young bilingual children's speech, see, e.g. Pearson, 1998). As I indicated in Chapter 7, however, if BFLA children are speaking quite well in Language A, a language learning problem can be ruled out as a possible cause for why Language Alpha is not well developed. Of course, you can only find out if you assess both of BFLA children's languages. This is an absolute must in all cases where language learning problems are suspected in bilingual settings.

Finally, in cases where BFLA children do have overall communication problems, that is, in both their languages, medical personnel often lays the blame with a bilingual family environment. In a monolingual environment, problems with language learning are usually addressed with *more* input (see above). In contrast, many doctors and speech therapists see *less* input in a language as a 'cure' for perceived language learning problems in a bilingual setting. In fact, when doctors and speech therapists find out that children are growing up with two languages, they will often advise to stop talking the minority language at home.[5] They often do this without addressing what later often surfaces as the real underlying problem for the fact that children have problems with both their languages, for instance, deafness (see Chapter 2 and later in this chapter). In such cases there is of course no harmonious bilingual development, although with early proper treatment of the real cause of the communication problems, it could in many cases have had a chance (see also Saunders, 1988).

Language choice

Children raised bilingually who speak two languages may not always select the language that is expected of them in a particular situation. They may do this without being aware of it, or they may do it intentionally. Since language choice is so inextricably bound with identity (see also below), a child who frequently 'mis-selects' will encounter negative reactions, which may result in less than harmonious development.

As I have indicated throughout this book, BFLA children actually choose their languages appropriately in function of what their addressee expects. These expectations are communicated through more monolingual or more bilingual parental discourse strategies (Chapter 4). Children who do not usually choose their language appropriately may be reprimanded for this or otherwise meet with negative reactions. BFLA children are able to switch between utterances in each language without any interruption in the flow of conversation. Children who do not switch easily between languages will have to overcome this hurdle in order to become a proficient bilingual.

Even if bilingual children choose their language appropriately, they may be faced with contradictory expectations. For instance, a child may speak Danish with a parent, and French at school, but may be overheard speaking Danish to their mother at the school gate and be ridiculed for it by the other children. This will cause a dilemma.

Instances of this kind can be just mildly annoying, but when the bilingual child becomes the object of severe bullying on the basis of language choice, bilingual development can no longer be seen as harmonious.

Language and identity

As Letitia Raubichek already noted in 1934, 'the tie which binds together the speakers of a common tongue often serves to isolate one language group from another' (p. 18). This notion of language simultaneously connecting and disconnecting people not only applies to large groups of speakers but also to individual members of bilingual families.

Whether or not parents are very conscious of which language they use when (many parents indeed are not, or not all the time – see Goodz, 1989), their language choices will have an effect on how they are perceived by the other members of the family, including the children, and how they eventually perceive themselves. Patterns of language choice and the resulting use are a vital aspect of one's identity.

In bilingual individuals, these identities may shift over time and may be problematic. There may be struggles between the identity one knows others want and other identities one wishes for oneself. Especially in highly emotionally loaded relationships, such as those of many couples, linguistic choices are not emotionally neutral (Piller, 2002; see also Chapter 4). A monolingual father may resent a bilingual mother speaking a language with the children that he does not understand. This feeling of not being part of the rest of the family may affect the way the father interacts with the children, and the continuous frustration of not being able to be fully involved with the rest of the family may lead to conflict and divorce. This is why in Chapter 4 I emphasized the fact that couples in this situation need to consider very carefully how they will organize themselves as a bilingual family. In the case of a monolingual and a bilingual parent, I suggested that one fairly simple way of preventing exclusionary dynamics from appearing is for the bilingual parent (and later on the children) only to use the language the monolingual parent does not understand in the latter's absence. Of course, this may still create feelings of exclusion, but then not on the basis of not understanding what is being said.

Exclusion from full and free communication through linguistic choices in a bilingual family is a very real problem, then, that can adversely affect family harmony and the well-being of individual family members (see Box 8.1 for a particularly poignant example).

The example in Box 8.1 is one reason that I always advise parents to treat all their children similarly in terms of language choice. The example in Box 8.1 also links up with the language use by siblings in the same family. Unlike in Karniol's (1982) study, children in bilingual families tend to speak similarly: either they all speak the same two languages or they speak just the majority language (De Houwer, 2007).

> **Box 8.1** An example of exclusion through language choice
>
> Karniol (1992)[6] describes the language development of a child who lives In Israel and is raised in Hebrew and English. The child showed repeated problems in communicating after age two. Prior to that age, the child spoke English and Hebrew fluently. After age two, there were long periods of severe stuttering, especially in English. The child eventually stopped speaking English altogether, but continued developing in Hebrew.
>
> Karniol claims that the child was stuttering because he was cognitively overloaded. Apart from the fact that there is generally no ground for positing a cognitive overload for children raised bilingually since in fact so many children do grow up bilingually without stuttering, there is an alternative explanation for Karniol's subject's communication problems that I believe is far more likely.
>
> The child heard English from his parents, who addressed each other in Hebrew. He had an older sister who his parents addressed in Hebrew and English, but who was instructed to speak only English to him. Hungarian relatives who visited spoke English to the child but not to his parents and sister. Thus, the child was the only one in his family to be exclusively addressed in English. All the other family members shared something he was not part of at home: Hebrew.
>
> Karniol provides many quotes of the child requesting that his parents speak Hebrew to him, and of him saying he does not want to speak English. Clearly, the child was not developing language harmoniously. The reason for this, I believe, is an emotional one, viz., the child felt excluded from the rest of the family because he was not spoken to in the same way as the other family members.

Besides language choice possibly acting as an instrument for exclusion (or inclusion), the fact that the use of a particular language is for many people inextricably bound to a person's identity means that language choice can be a powerful symbol in family interaction. Language choice is certainly not a neutral phenomenon.

In a monolingual setting, children have the choice between speaking and not speaking. Silence where parents expect talk is often interpreted as a rejection of the parents or an expression of rebellion.

Similarly, in a bilingual setting, if children speak Language A where parents expect Language Alpha this can be interpreted as a sign of rejection or rebellion on the individual level. To parents, children's language choices may also signal acceptance or rejection of parents' ethnic identities (Schecter & Bailey, 1998).

It also works the other way round. Children may interpret their parents' switch to Language A when they normally address children in Language Alpha as a sign of rejection or even punishment (see Chapter 4 for an example from Dutch–English Susan). Children of all ages may have this reaction, but especially children under age five may be very susceptible to negative emotions and feelings of loss when a parent who used to address the child only in Language A switches completely to Language Alpha.

Professional advice to give up one of the languages

In connection with the point in the previous sentence, it is important to point out that even in families where children are quite happily becoming bilingual, interference from outside the family may cause unnecessary problems, leading to non-harmonious bilingual development. Preschool teachers, medical personnel or speech therapists often advise parents in bilingual families to stop using the minority language at home, even for children who fluently speak two languages (this advice is most likely based on the unwarranted overt belief that early bilingualism is bad for children; see Chapter 4).

Parents often take this advice, since they want to do what is best for their children and believe that teachers, doctors, nurses and language professionals know best. The results of this can be quite negative. Parents may in many cases no longer be able to communicate well with their children (since they may be switching to a language they hardly know), and the children are bewildered and upset that their parent all of a sudden speaks another language to them; this, many young children see as putting an undesirable distance between the parent and themselves that they may find hard to bear.

There is no need to upset children and parents like this. First off, a bilingual input situation is not a danger for children. In fact, bilingual children have been found to perform better in difficult cognitive tasks including those requiring a lot of attention (Barac *et al.*, 2008; Bialystok, 2001, 2007; Martin-Rhee & Bialystok, 2008), understand more words than monolingual children (Chapter 6), have higher degrees of metalinguistic awareness (Cromdal, 1999) and are able to take into account someone else's needs, beliefs and intentions[7] better than monolingual children (Goetz, 2003; Kovács, 2008), just to name a few areas where bilingual children are at an advantage.

Second, the advice to stop talking one language seems to stem from the unfounded idea that speaking a second language takes away from the other one. Indeed, if our minds were boxes the same way our heads are, this might make sense: there is only so much space in a box, and if it's full you have to take something out before you can put something else in there (Box 8.2.).

Fortunately, our minds are not like boxes, and we can learn new things, including new vocabulary and even new languages until we are quite old. Little children, of course, still have a lot of opportunities for learning. And so far, there is no evidence that BFLA children who stop receiving input in their Language A suddenly increase their skill in Language Alpha. In fact, parents who stopped talking Language A to preschool-aged children who were fluent in two languages have told me how their children seemed to miss Language A and were very unhappy when parents who had previously spoken Language A to them no longer did. Furthermore, parents themselves may become quite unhappy when they feel no longer allowed to use the language they have an emotional attachment to with their children. They may feel an emotional distance between themselves and their children if they address them in a language that is an L2 to them, even though they might be quite proficient in it (Pavlenko, 2004; Yamamoto, 2005). Such feelings may affect parents' interaction with their children and do not contribute to children's harmonious bilingual development (see also Wong Fillmore, 2000).

> **Box 8.2** Our mind is not a box!
>
> FULL?
> OUR MIND IS NOT A BOX

I want to stress here that the advice to parents in bilingual families to stop speaking one of the languages to their children can be harmful to children and also is unethical. The fact that parents are never advised to give up speaking the majority language also shows an ideological bias that is not professional. Furthermore, it shows no respect for families' cultural heritage.

Language choice, then, is very much connected with identity and with emotional attachment. To ignore this can be quite detrimental to children's harmonious bilingual development.

Language and emotion

Patterns of language choice may act as expressors of attitudes and emotional stances towards a particular language. If parents always express anger or discontent in Spanish, but discuss neutral topics and fun things in French, it will come as no surprise if their children end up disliking Spanish and not wanting to speak it, since for the children Spanish has become associated with negativity.

Parents should be aware of this, and should avoid expressing negative emotions just in one particular language (this is not a call for expressing more negative emotions! just for making sure there is no specific language link). Also, if arguments between bilingual siblings are usually expressed in one particular language only, negative attitudes may be created towards that language.

If one particular language is usually connected with negative feelings or used to express anger, this will hinder harmonious bilingual development. Thus, language is very much tied up not only with identity but also with emotion (in a monolingual setting this link is not so clear).

Negative attitudes from outside the family

There are many contributing factors within the family that may explain why in the one case children develop bilingualism harmoniously, and in the other not. There are family external factors as well: no bilingual family that lives a community life can avoid influence from that community.

Negative stereotyping of particular languages can be detrimental to children's harmonious bilingual development (for an in-depth discussion, see Saunders, 1988), as can negative ideas about child bilingualism. Educators or pediatricians who advise parents to stop speaking a particular language to their children are expressing negative attitudes to that language and/or to child bilingualism.[8] As I noted earlier and in Chapter 4, such negative attitudes can have a tremendously negative effect on bilingual families. As Saunders (1982b) has already observed, non-antagonistic attitudes towards bilingualism 'make it easier for both parents and children to establish and maintain a minority language in the immediate family' (p. 283).

Uneven development

In editorial comments to her edited volume on second language acquisition, Evelyn Hatch noted 30 years ago: 'Uneven development of the two languages is common in all studies of infant bilingualism. The child develops faster in the language which is used most in his environment' (1978: 38).[9] When this was written, there were not many studies of BFLA. Also, many of those that were available had methodological problems that made it hard to see what was really going on (for a review, see De Houwer, 1990).

The evidence available today shows that Hatch was right in stating that BFLA children often develop faster in one language than the other. The recent literature on BFLA children's language development has fortunately started to pay more attention to children who have a 'weaker' and a 'stronger' language.

Most likely, differences in proficiency between languages are due to a combination of input factors in children's socializing environment. In order to better understand the bilingual acquisition process, these input factors must be known. Unfortunately, that is often not the case. Because of this crucially missing information, it is often difficult to know why BFLA children as discussed in the literature are presenting with a particular language profile.

The little evidence there is, though, shows that, as Hatch suggested, input frequency most likely plays a major role. The discourse strategies as proposed by Lanza (1997) may play an important role as well. In addition, there are several other factors relating to BFLA children's language environments that may help determine the level of skill BFLA children develop in each of their languages, such as changes in the average daily quantity of input in each language and the distribution of the languages among the people interacting with the child (Chapter 4).[10]

When BFLA children are much less proficient in one of their languages than in the other, this may cause problems within the family. You may remember the example from the American father in Bruges (Chapter 4) who quoted Chomsky to me as an explanation for why it was fine for him not to spend much time talking to his daughter, although he was her sole source of input in English. As I also mentioned in Chapter 4, the father was very angry with his three-year-old daughter for not being fluent in English (she was quite proficient in Dutch). He accused the poor child of rejecting him. The bewildered child was very upset. Even when I tried to explain to the father that the child needed more input in English in order to be able to speak better English, he continued to attribute to the child conscious attempts to reject him. For outsiders such a case seems somewhat unbelievable, but for the insiders – the child in question in particular – it is a tragedy.

Even if quite dissimilar levels of language proficiency for the two languages are not seen as a problem within the family, low proficiency in one of the languages may cause problems outside the confines of the nuclear family. It may be the cause of real communicative problems within the extended family, at preschool or elsewhere where children need to socialize. There may just be repeated miscommunication or the child may be ridiculed for not speaking well enough. There is no harmonious bilingual development in these cases.

The variability that we see between BFLA children's two languages is also found in children who are second language learners.[11] 'Profile effects' (Oller *et al.*, 2007) are quite common in both bilingual and second language acquisition, with children perhaps reading better in one language but being better at listening comprehension in another (Gutiérrez-Clellen & Kreiter, 2003). Language proficiency in child bilinguals, then, can best be seen as being a dynamic feature on a continuum of proficiencies in both languages (Valdés & Figueroa, 1994).

Hotchpotch?

Lay people cannot be blamed for thinking that young bilingual children start out talking in some weird garbled kind of way, a hotchpotch, if you like. After all, for a long time this idea was promoted by scholars such as Volterra and Taeschner (1978). Also, there seems to be a general idea that bilingual children produce a great deal of mixed utterances. Many people see these as as signs of a hotchpotch, too.

Three decades with much excellent research later, we know that bilingual children don't make a 'hotchpotch' out of their two separate input languages. Also, they don't use all that many mixed utterances. And even when they do, these utterances with words from two languages mainly show the structural properties of just a single language.

Note that when lay people think that BFLA children speak in some kind of amalgamated manner, they are not talking about the first two years of life, but about the preschool age, when children typically are saying sentences. With regard to BFLA children's sentences, it is safe to say that they are *not* a hotchpotch. Rather, BFLA children say many sentences in each language separately that don't show any evidence of them knowing another language (Chapter 7). This is also why it is possible that we often see that BFLA children's two languages do not develop at the same pace.

Box 8.3   Making trouble where there isn't any

SCHOOL COUNSELING

I'M 5
ICH BIN 5

SHOULD I TEACH HER TO READ GERMAN? SHE'S BRIGHT!

NO NO! SHE NEEDS SPECIAL EDUCATION!

('Ich bin 5' means 'I'm 5')

PS Like some students that I explained this box to in a guest lecture for a course on bilingualism you may not believe it. The instructor, however, noted that just this same thing had happened to her and her daughter. Unfortunately my examples are real.

Hopefully, with this solid evidence, the pervasive myth can be dispelled that young bilingual children are confused and cannot get their languages straight. This myth unfortunately persists in large sections of society all over the industrialized world. Possibly, this myth is also at the basis of many people's belief that bilingual input is harmful to children.

As I have already explained earlier, people with such beliefs, and hence negative attitudes, may make trouble for bilingual-families-to-be and their children. This does not foster harmonious bilingual development. An example of negative attitudes from children's environments getting in the way of harmonious development even when a child is a proficient speaker of two languages is illustrated in Box 8.3.

Parental expectations

Many parents in bilingual families have 'great expectations' for their children and see childhood bilingualism as an investment in their children's economic and cultural future (e.g. Piller, 2002). However, children may not become excellent speakers of two languages as their parents wanted them to be (Piller, 2002: 264). Or children may reject one of the languages at some point. As a result, many parents may experience a sense of failure (Okita, 2002; Piller, 2002).

Given many parents' high expectations, Piller sees this outcome as not surprising. In Chapter 4 I explained that environmental support with positive attitudes and an impact belief on the part of the parents are crucial in fostering bilingual development. Parents with an impact belief rightly believe that how they themselves communicate with their children has an effect on their children's language development. These are the same parents who may actively socialize their children into particular patterns of language choice (see further below). While many scholars doing research on child language acquisition will agree that this impact belief is valid, many parents do not in fact have such an impact belief. Parents that do not have an impact belief may take no specific steps to foster their children's bilingual development and run a great chance of having bilingually raised children who speak only a single language (Chapter 4).

Environmental support of bilingual acquisition and an impact belief are no guarantees, however, that BFLA children become fluent and proficient speakers of two languages. As the results of my large survey show (Chapter 4), in almost two-thirds of the bilingual families where both parents used the majority language at home and only one parent used the minority language, children did not end up speaking two languages, but instead only spoke the majority language. Yet the parents in those families might have used socialization strategies expressing an impact belief, and there might have been positive environmental support. It is likely that in those families a very crucial element was missing, namely sufficient input in the minority language (see the next subsection).

Back to parents' expectations. Some bilingual parents don't mind if their child speaks only one language at the beginning of speech. They are just happy that their infant can talk, and will respond to the child's utterances without focusing on the actual language the child used (Chapter 4). However, as children get a bit older, parents may start to wonder when children will start to use the 'right' language to them. Parents with an impact belief who first were using bilingual discourse strategies by allowing their children to respond in the 'wrong' language may start to use more monolingual discourse strategies in order to 'turn the tide'.

Changing from bilingual to monolingual discourse strategies may not be easy, but as for instance Juan-Garau and Pérez-Vidal (2001) have shown, it is possible (see also Taeschner, 1983). The strategy needed for this is pretending not to understand children's use of the 'wrong' language: 'the role of being a bilingual can be negotiated in ongoing interaction as the mother feigns the role of a monolingual speaker' (Lanza, 1988: 75). Another strategy that might work is asking children expressly to repeat their utterance in the other language. Asking children to do so is in essence no worse than asking them to say 'please' when they want something.

Still, parents should be sensitive to children's reactions, and use such strategies sparingly and carefully, especially if previously, children were used to parents speaking to them in Language Alpha and apparently not minding that children responded in Language A (see also Barron-Hauwaert, 2004: 36–39). Using such strategies may have the desired effect when children are around three years old or so. After the preschool years, it becomes virtually impossible to change children's habit of addressing bilingual parents in the 'other' language. This again has to do with that very important link between language and identity.

Parents should be aware, though, that if they allow their young children's use of Language Alpha in all circumstances, children have no need for speaking Language A, and will become part of that large group of children raised bilingually who understand two languages but speak only one.

In spite of the many possibilities for guiding and supporting bilingual children's language development, the complex and changing nature of a bilingual input setting as well as children's own developing personalities and learning styles make it very difficult to predict just how it will proceed. If parents have realistic expectations and do not expect their children to become two highly proficient monolinguals in one, this will make life easier for them and avoid the disappointments that may stand in the way of harmonious bilingual development.

Parental input frequency

Many parents, whether in monolingual or bilingual families, are not aware of the importance of their role as providers of language input to their children. In a monolingual setting, if the parents do not speak much to the child or speak in ways that are not conducive to language learning, there will most likely be other sources of input that can help the child in learning language. Yet even in a monolingual setting, there is a direct relationship between frequency of input and lexical learning, which is the cornerstone of language development (Chapters 4 and 6).

In a bilingual setting, language input is by definition spread out over two languages. This does not mean that any one bilingual child will receive less input in each of those languages as compared to a monolingual child, given the huge variation that can exist within a monolingual group (Chapter 4). But a bilingual setting is indeed much more fragile than a monolingual one, since the input in one of the languages may be limited to just one parent. That parent then has the burden of providing sufficient input of the right kind to the child in order for the child to be able to learn the language.

My advice to parents in a bilingual situation is that they should talk to their children in two languages as much as possible. For instance, I often see people with young children stand silently in supermarket lines. I understand that sometimes parents need a break from talking, but still, such times are great opportunities to talk to children. In fact, the first thing parents should do when there are concerns about children not developing well in one of their languages is drastically increase the amount of input in that language. Reading books with children is an excellent way of doing this.

So far, there have not been all that many studies of BFLA that have empirically shown the link between input frequency and development, but the fact that this link has been found for monolingual acquisition demonstrates its importance. Future research will have to show precisely what the links are between frequency of input and bilingual acquisition. In the meantime, my advice to talk as much as possible to children cannot harm them and most likely will be of benefit to them.

In her textbook on first language acquisition, Eve Clark (2003) includes a section entitled 'Practice makes Perfect', in which she emphasizes the fact that children need to practice a lot in order to be able to say the sounds and words they need. I would like to extend this notion of 'practice makes perfect' to BFLA children's language use in general. Indeed, talking does not happen 'like that'. It requires a lot of practice, a lot of use. The supermarket line mentioned above and similar situations like car rides offer good opportunities for engaging children in conversation at a time that they are not busy playing, watching television or doing their homework.

Children who are talkative, and so practice their verbal skills a lot, will become better and better speakers. For BFLA children this need to talk a lot is perhaps greater than in a monolingual setting, because here, indeed, children have to divide their time over two languages. However, parents may get very tired from talkative children and just not have the energy for all this extra work. In the next section I further discuss this very real problem of extra work.

Parental work

Some parents are not aware of their very important role as input providers, but may provide sufficient input anyhow. Others may be all too aware of their crucial role. In some cases this may not be a problem, but in others, parents may find the task too daunting and may worry that they cannot succeed.

As Okita (2002) has admirably shown for a group of Japanese mothers residing in the United Kingdom, there may be far too much stress involved and far too much language-related work for isolated bilingual parents to ensure that their children become bilingual.

Indeed, making sure that children in a bilingual family become actively bilingual and speak two languages in acceptable ways may involve a great deal of work. The tips that 'help' publications for bilingual families offer are quite a lot of work to put into effect: for instance, getting videotapes in the two languages, seeking out playgroups where the minority language can be used, standing up to health professionals, family members and teachers who have a negative view of child bilingualism, teaching your child words in Language Alpha for words in Language A you never knew existed, reading books in two languages and so forth and so forth. And what if you don't succeed? As Okita points out, the guilt can be overwhelming, and the sense of failure can cause family breakdown.

Similarly, Lanza (2007: 46) points out that

> 'many parents face problems as they attempt to raise their children bilingually. Many receive unfounded advice and lack the general support from any bilingual community,

and hence abandon any attempts to establish individual bilingualism in the home [..] some of the important social repercussions of this failure include the inability of the child to communicate with grandparents and other family in the [..] homeland'.

Nevertheless, many bilingual parents do manage to raise bilingual children, even without a lot of extra work or feelings of inadequacy. However, they may be aided in this by the many publications that contain practical tips on how to raise bilingual children. At the end of this chapter, I have included a selection of some useful publications that fully take into account the latest research results.

Parents and educators should be warned that not all 'help' publications actually are well informed. For instance, recently I read in a general child development book for parents that they shouldn't worry about mixed utterances too much since, after all, bilingual children stop using mixed utterances by the time they are four. It is not generally true that bilingual children stop using mixed utterances by the time they are four. Thus, this book raises unrealistic expectations. Also, the implication here is that mixed utterances are a bad thing. They are not. While I do not particularly want to encourage the use of mixed utterances, parents should know that in conversations with bilinguals sharing the same two languages, mixed utterances may increase the power of expression. They also can serve as important markers of social identity. They are not signs of mental confusion but entirely normal in bilingual speakers of any age.

Children's expectations

Most young children look up to their parents. In general, parents know everything better and are the 'teachers' of many skills. But in a bilingual situation, children may actually speak a particular language better than their parents. Children don't necessarily like this, and they may have less respect for their parents because of it, or may feel ashamed (see Box 8.4). Again, this points to the important link between language and personal identity.

> **Box 8.4** Children feeling awkward because of their parents' insufficient language proficiency
>
> W. Theodor Elwert, who wrote a wonderful book about his own experiences as a multilingual person, always spoke English with his mother. When Theodor was very young, his family lived in Italy and he learned Italian from a very young age onwards. Later, the family moved to Germany, and Theodor and his sister quickly learned to speak German, too. Theodor's mother spoke German reasonably well, but did make errors.
>
> Theodor writes: 'Diese mangelhafte Beherrschung des Deutschen wirkte störend; nicht nur, daß die Mutter uns in deutscher Sprache fremd vorkam; es war uns auch ausgesprochen peinlich, sie "falsch" sprechen zu hören, sie in einer Situation der Unterlegenheit zu erleben' (Elwert, 1973: 27; my translation: 'This lack of proficiency in German was a problem, not only because Mother seemed like a stranger to us when she spoke German, but above all because it was very painful for us to hear her make errors and thus experience her in a situation where she did not have the upper hand').

Just feeling awkward isn't that much of a problem. Children's negative feelings about their parents' perceived insufficient language proficiency may have more serious consequences at a later stage of development such as adolescence. At this time, children often start to revolt against their parents. Family relations may become very strained when children then start to belittle or ridicule their parents' less than perfect speech (Raubichek, 1934), and in those circumstances it may be very difficult for parents to continue playing their guiding and supporting roles.

At an earlier age, BFLA children may also correct their parents' language use (see Chapter 7 and Box 8.5).

> **Box 8.5** Children correcting their parents' language use
>
> Portuguese–Swedish Karin (2;9) is talking to her mother, who speaks Portuguese to her. They are discussing the past summer vacation in Sweden. Karin's mother says: 'e veio o Carl' (and Carl came, too), but she pronounces the name 'Carl' in a Swedish manner. Karin frowns and sits still for a while. Then she says: 'não é [a], mamã, é [here rounded a:]' (it's not [a], mommy, it's [rounded a:]). Karin thus is correcting a particular sound that her mother 'misused', i.e. used from the 'wrong' language.
>
> *Adapted from Cruz-Ferreira, 2006: 91*
>
> English–German Thomas (3;10) is looking in the boot of the car. He asks his English-speaking mother: 'what's that?'. She replies: 'that's the Ersatzrad' (that's the spare wheel; the mother used a German noun here). Thomas comments very emphatically: 'no, you say spare wheel, not Ersatzrad'. Thomas is here correcting a word that his mother used from the 'wrong' language.
>
> *Adapted from Saunders, 1988: 76*

And what happens when BFLA children get older?

By the time that they are six and ready to go to school, many BFLA children are able to speak two languages fluently. The question is what happens then. Do BFLA school-aged children continue to use their two languages actively if that's what they were doing as a small child? Do they continue to understand them? Do any advantages in dual language proficiency that they might have had before age six stay with them once they are a bit older? Or, alternatively, do any differences that there might have been between the proficiency levels in each language continue to exist?

The dynamic perspective that had been adopted in this book would say that 'it all depends…': it depends on BFLA children's continued exposure to two languages at increasingly more complex levels, on their continued communicative need to speak two languages, on their opportunities for learning to read and write the two languages, on their attitudes towards the two languages, on their motivations to continue being engaged with them. Other factors no doubt are the attitudes that school and peers have towards the two languages involved and towards child bilingualism in general.

We know very little about the later lives of children who grew up with two languages from birth. Some exceptions are the descriptions of later language development in BFLA children in Caldas (2006), Cruz-Ferreira (2006), Leopold (1970) and Saunders (1988). The evidence suggests that the wide variability seen in the early phases of bilingual development continues later on, with some older children continuing to use both their languages with great skill, and others focusing more and more on just one language. Others still might be replacing both their initial languages by a third. Thus, older BFLA children's language use profiles can change dramatically over time.

Anecdotal evidence suggests that some older BFLA children continue to develop two languages easily and without personal problems, whereas others feel that they have had a troubled childhood because of a bilingual upbringing.

Mixed utterances may remain part of some older BFLA children's repertoires but not of others'. Although there are no studies on older BFLA children's proportion of mixed utterances, my contacts with BFLA children and their families and my reading indicate that some children only occasionally use mixed utterances but others more frequently (see also Saunders, 1988).

Is it an advantage for later language learning to have learned two languages at an early age? The jury is still out on that question. We would need systematic large longitudinal group studies of BFLA children with matched groups of MFLA and ESLA children to investigate this. This is the sort of database we would need in order to start to settle the question of the influence of a BFLA input setting on later linguistic functioning. I know of no relevant studies so far.

However, there are fortunately more and more studies of adult bilinguals that take into account their subjects' language learning histories. Studies that then compare adults who heard two languages since birth and others who started learning an L2 a few years after they had been monolingual could tell us more about whether the difference between BFLA and ESLA matters in the long run. There is evidence that adult bilinguals who heard their two languages from birth are, on average, better at discriminating between sounds in each of their languages than adults who learned one language after the other (Sebastián-Gallés & Bosch, 2005; Sundara & Polka, 2008). Granfeldt-Saavedra (2007) showed that bilingual adults who acquired their two languages from birth did better on vocabulary and pronunciation tests than other bilingual adults who learned their second language at a later age.

This suggests that the distinction I make between BFLA and ESLA may be important even for children's later language functioning, even though some BFLA children become good speakers of just one of their languages, and some ESLA children become highly proficient speakers of two. Certainly the possible importance of the distinction between BFLA and ESLA in older individuals is worthy of systematic investigation.

Needed: an alternative research paradigm

On the whole, studies of BFLA have focused on children who have been successful in their bilingual acquisition. Yet it is abundantly clear that there are many children who are not so successful. They may understand two languages, but speak only one, much to their own chagrin or that of their family members, or they may speak two languages in ways that are unsatisfactory to their environment. In addition, frictions may arise in bilingual families that are attributed to the fact of bilingualism. In all these cases, there is no harmonious bilingual development, and children's and families' lives are adversely affected.

There is little systematic research at the moment that can fully address the question what factors lead to harmonious bilingual development. This means that a psycholinguistic approach will have to be combined with a more sociolinguistic one that fully takes into account the macro- and micro-contexts within which children grow up bilingually.

It is only by having a very wide range of information on different aspects of bilingual children's linguistic environments that we will be able to discover what makes the difference between harmonious and unsuccessful bilingual development, and thus, what contributes to bilingual children's well-being. Methodologically, this implies a new focus on the bilingual family as the unit of analysis. So far, it is the bilingual child's language use that has been at the center of research attention.

What we need to find out is which kinds of bilingual family environments, within specific societal settings, give rise to harmonious bilingual development in the children in these families, and which kinds do not. Is there more chance of harmonious bilingual development in multilingual societies that are used to people speaking several languages? Or does the difference with more monolingual societies not matter? With the exception of the studies coming out of Montreal most of the studies reviewed in this book were conducted in basically monolingual societies. Is bilingual development more harmonious in bilingual Montreal than in monolingual Flanders, for instance? So far, we don't know.

Perhaps much depends on the specific languages that are being learned in a particular setting. For instance, when teachers in Flanders heard that my daughter was bilingual, they frowned and were ready to start protesting – but then I said: 'Yes, she learned English from her father', and their reaction changed completely. English was fine! French is probably what they expected, and many people in officially Dutch-speaking Flanders don't like it if people there raise their children in French. On the other hand, I've been consulting for an English–Dutch family in Flanders where the preschool teacher was very much against the fact that the child in that family was learning English. We need research that addresses the potential importance of different societal settings for bilingual development.

Becoming bilingual involves a lot more than the 'dry' learning of two separate linguistic systems. Learning two languages in a bilingual family setting, or, as the case may be, *not* learning two languages in such a setting, involves a family dynamic in which language may take on a much more emotionally loaded meaning than is usually the case in wholly monolingual families where all members share the same linguistic identity. It is also this dynamic as part of the child's bilingual family environment that needs to be given more research attention.

We also need a more in-depth characterization of what constitutes harmonious bilingual development, and we need tools that help us to measure it. In this chapter, I have been fairly vague in characterizing harmonious vs. non-harmonious bilingual development and have not properly defined either. We need to develop a set of criteria to specify whether BFLA children are developing harmoniously or not. Many of these criteria, though, will depend on how children and their families are feeling. It may not always be possible to draw a distinction between harmonious and non-harmonious bilingual development based on externally observable phenomena.

In order to construct a typology of kinds of linguistic environments, we need in-depth case studies of individual families, as well as group studies in which we can focus on a limited number of variables that have so far been identified as possibly playing a role. Obviously, not all aspects of a family's environment will matter: it is important to try and find the most relevant characteristics. Thus, whether the family drinks tea or coffee won't matter, but personality profiles of the parents may be quite relevant, since these will influence communicative styles.

This also implies that we have to compare children to each other and ask why some children seem to develop harmoniously and others not. Group studies using similar methods for collecting data on a fairly large number of children are a must. At the same time, in-depth case studies that pay full attention to various aspects of a child's linguistic environment are a necessary complement to such group studies.

We do need to investigate what determines whether children in bilingual families grow up without experiencing problems directly related to their bilingual environment. It is unlikely that insights from any single discipline will be sufficient for this kind of complex study. Interdisciplinary cooperation is really the only way to go (see also Okita, 2002). Only by having a very wide range of information on different aspects pertaining to a bilingual child's life will we be able to discover what makes the difference between harmonious and unsuccessful bilingual development. We owe it to the many bilingual families in the world to try and solve this issue.

In conclusion

With ever increasing mobility worldwide, there are more and more young couples consisting of partners from different linguistic and cultural backgrounds. The children born of these partnerships often grow up bilingually, meaning that they hear different people speak different languages on a pseudo-daily basis. These children have two first languages, A and Alpha.

In the last two decades, there has been a burgeoning of publications aimed at educating and supporting the parents in these bilingual families (see, e.g. *The Bilingual Family Newsletter* published by Multilingual Matters, and the resources listed at the end of this chapter).

Child bilingualism as fostered in bilingual families has also become an increasingly popular topic in the child language acquisition literature. The result of this research on young bilingual children's language development shows that, on the whole, they try to speak like the people acting as models for their two input languages. This is true for any language and any language combination that BFLA children are hearing around them.

As such, there is no evidence for the pervasive myth that young bilingual children are confused and cannot get their languages straight. This myth unfortunately persists in large portions of society but at least now there is scientific evidence that shows it to be what it is, viz., an unfounded myth.

Throughout this book, I have discussed examples from different languages and different language combinations, as if the particular languages do not matter. Also, the conclusions I have offered after each chapter make abstraction of the particular languages being learned. And, indeed, learning to distinguish between two languages in perception, understanding and producing translation equivalents, using the 'right' language in the right circumstances, producing unilingual utterances that follow the morphosyntactic rules of one particular language only, these are all features that all BFLA children share, irrespective of the particular languages they are acquiring.

Where it has been possible to make comparisons with monolingual acquisition, bilingual children have been found to develop their two languages in ways that are very similar to monolingual children. The important milestones of language development are reached at similar ages in monolingual and bilingual children alike. However, all too often, researchers in bilingual acquisition hold up monolingualism as a standard. Monolingual acquisition, though, is not the norm for bilingual acquisition, nor should it be. Bilingual acquisition can and needs to be studied in its own right. It is encouraging to see that established scholars in monolingual acquisition are emphasizing this as well (e.g. Kuhl *et al.*, 2008).

Whereas it is important to continue documenting the various characteristics of BFLA children's language use, it is of great societal interest to start to map out in which kinds of situations children develop bilingually as a matter of course (harmonious bilingual development), and in which situations early bilingual acquisition becomes a source of concern and problems (non-harmonious bilingual development).

There are no statistics available on the incidence of harmonious vs. non-harmonious bilingual development in young children raised in bilingual families. Yet anecdotal evidence and reports in the literature suggest that non-harmonious bilingual development occurs quite frequently. Non-harmonious bilingual development may cause some or all of the following: insecure emotional attachment between child and parent, extreme feelings of sibling rivalry, difficulties in forming early friendships, disadvantage in educational settings, non-acceptance by family members, feelings of inadequacy, depression, and many more negative sociopsychological events.

Harmonious bilingual development is, of course, no guarantee for these negative effects not to occur (neither is monolingual development!). But in harmonious bilingual development language use and language choice are not problematized, and the child does not feel bad because he or she is in a bilingual situation.

As this book has shown, children can learn to understand and fluently speak two languages at a very early age. BFLA children can distinguish between their two languages in perception from the time they are born. By the time they are ten months old, they understand words in each of their two languages. By the time they are 14 months old, some can already say the right words from the right language to a bilingual adult. By the time they are two years old, some can say sentences in each language that do not show any influence from the other language.

Clearly, then, young children are fully equipped to learn more than one language from early on. Yet there seem to be all sorts of processes that can interfere with a carefree learning of two languages from birth. What these processes consist of is finally starting to be investigated. For now, we can already identify a few factors that we know support the learning of any language: a warm, nurturing environment in which children are free to learn, and plenty of opportunities to hear and use whatever language or languages they are learning.

Notes

1. Personally, I'm in the latter category. I am very grateful I had the chance to learn a second language from early on, and others afterwards. This has widened my world tremendously.
2. For an excellent overview of some of the negative views of bilingualism held by scientists in the first half of the 20th century, see Hakuta (1986).
3. Of course, comparing BFLA to MFLA also gives us greater insight into theoretical issues about how children learn language.
4. Kate started to use Dutch again in her teens, when she got interested in corresponding with a cousin in Belgium who didn't know any English. Kate is now in her twenties and can still speak, understand and read Dutch, but her English is much better. She also speaks excellent Spanish (I know all this because I am still in touch with Kate and her family).
5. There are of course also doctors and speech therapists who are supportive of bilingual families.
6. Note that Karniol does not interpret her diary data the way I do here.
7. This is the kind of social competence that is known in the research literature as Theory of Mind and that is very important in developing social relations.
8. Of course, fortunately there are many educators and pediatricians who do not hold such negative attitudes.

9. I first used the term 'uneven development' myself in 2002 (De Houwer, 2002b), but it is only recently that I discovered it had been used with reference to BFLA in print before. I have not seen earlier references than the one by Hatch.
10. For ESLA, the following input factors and their interaction have been proposed as playing a role in the speed of acquisition of an L2: age of first exposure to the L2, the length of exposure and the intensity of the exposure (Unsworth, 2007).
11. Such variability is also seen in somewhat older and adult bilinguals.

Summary box

- Even though BFLA children are able to develop two separate languages, many people are in doubt of this. This may negatively affect bilingual children and their families.
- Within families, language choice may become a problem and cause families great upset. Research needs to address these issues systematically and investigate in what circumstances children develop without any negative effects from the bilingual input setting.
- Plenty of children experience positive effects from being raised with two languages. Both cognitively and socially, they show advantages in comparison to monolingual children. The very fact, though, that bilingual children can understand two languages and often communicate in both is a great human resource that can open many doors.

Suggestions for study activities

1. (if you didn't do this activity for Chapter 1) *Project:* Ask around in your circle of friends and family about whether they know anyone who was raised with two languages from birth. Try to get in touch with them and have a conversation with them about their early bilingual experience. What languages were involved? Did they learn to understand them? Did they learn to speak them? How do they feel about their early bilingualism?
2. (if you didn't do this activity for Chapter 1 or 2) *Project:* Ask around in your circle of friends and family about whether they know anyone who is raising a child with two languages from birth. Try to get in touch with them and have a conversation with them about their child's overall linguistic development. What languages are involved? Does their child *understand* them both? Does their child *speak* them both? Are they happy about how their child is developing?
3. (if you didn't do this activity for Chapter 4) *Project:* Find people in your environment who because of their profession deal with young children (or, find people who are studying in preparation of such professions). Possibilities are: pediatric nurses, pediatricians, family health practitioners, preschool teachers, childcare workers and the like. Have a conversation with two such individuals built around the following questions: would they advise people to raise their child with two languages? Why (not)? Be courteous with your interviewees even if you disagree with their points of view. Report on your findings in class and discuss the answers you gained in terms of the issues raised in this chapter.
4. (this activity is part of one already listed for Chapter 4) *WEB:* Locate three websites in the language you know best (or, if you cannot find any, in another language you know) that discuss child bilingual development. Browse through those websites and rate them on whether in general you find the information on the website accurate and realistic judging from your understanding of this book. Explain why.

> **Suggestions for study activities continued**
>
> 5. (if you didn't do this activity for Chapter 4) Read four recent issues of the *Bilingual Family Newsletter* or a similar magazine and identify two main concerns that parents have about raising bilingual children

Recommended reading

Wong Fillmore's (1991 or 2000) articles discuss in a very penetrating way what the tragic effects can be of children speaking only one language to their parents. Pearson (2007) addresses several issues relating to bilingual children societal and environmental influences. Pavlenko (2004) discusses emotional aspects of language use in bilingual families. Bialystok (2005) reviews the evidence showing bilingual children's cognitive advantage over monolingual children.

Resources for parents and educators

Ada, A.F. & Baker, C. (2001). *Guía para padres y maestros de niños bilingües*. Clevedon: Multilingual Matters (in Spanish).

Baker, C. (2007). *A parents' & teachers' guide to bilingualism* (3rd revised edition). Clevedon: Multilingual Matters.

Cunningham-Andersson, U. & Andersson, S. (2004). *Growing up with two languages. A practical guide* (2nd edition). London: Routledge.

Harding-Esch, E. & Riley, P. (2008). The bilingual family: A handbook for parents. Cambridge: Cambridge University Press.

Montanari, E. (2002). *Mit zwei Sprachen groß werden: Mehrsprachige Erziehung in Familie, Kindergarten und Schule*. München: Kösel (in German).

Montanari, E., Aarssen, J., Bos, P. & Wagenaar, E. (2004). Hoe kinderen meertalig opgroeien. Amsterdam: PLanPlan (in Dutch).

Pearson, B.Z. (2008). Raising a bilingual child. A step-by-step guide for parents. New York: Living Language.

Appendix A

Subject selection: making sure you are dealing with BFLA

(links up with Chapter 3)

First you need to know which varieties of which two languages are involved (see also the section on 'Language models' in Chapter 4). It is not enough to know the parents' citizenship. Sometimes published reports in the literature just mention that a child's mother was Polish and her father Bulgarian, for instance. The implication seems to be that the child was raised in Bulgarian and Polish from birth. However, Polish and Bulgarian nationals speak many more languages than just Polish and Bulgarian, and not every Polish or Bulgarian national actually speaks Polish or Bulgarian. And even if the child's mother now speaks Polish to her and the child's father Bulgarian, this does not mean that this was the case immediately after the girl was born.

Equally important is to know who has been speaking the two languages when and to whom. You need to know about the children's linguistic environments (including input outside the home) and main patterns of language input to the children (see Chapter 4).

You need to have this information from the time the target children were born until the time you are asking questions about it. You will also need to follow up on this until the end of your study if there is any kind of longitudinal design. After all, as shown in Chapter 4, BFLA children's linguistic environments may undergo quite dramatic changes. It is especially important to know about longer periods of time that children may not have heard one of their languages.

It is crucial for a study on BFLA to know what the input patterns to a particular child were in terms of ages and times of regular exposure to each language. Having this information can help you decide whether or not to include a particular child or family in your study. Also when you want to study things that are more concerned with a bilingual family's life you will need to find out about changes in the family's residence, travel patterns and the like.

If you want to study children in a situation where most people address them in only one language (1P/1L; see Chapter 4) then you have to make sure at the start that, in fact, the family you might want to recruit for your study falls in that category. In case anyone in the child's close environment (one of the parents, or both parents, or other family members or caregivers) regularly speak two languages to the child you would need to find out about that, too. In any case, knowing about children's linguistic backgrounds is crucial for the later interpretation of research results (see Chapter 4). And, of course, if you are setting up a comparative group study in which you want to study the effect of changes in the input over time, you will most definitely need precise information about the BFLA learning context.

There is really only one way of finding out about all the aspects mentioned above, and that is to ask parents or other members of the household you are interested in. The protocol below contains an outline of the aspects of a bilingual child and family's background that you need to know about before you can start to study BFLA. You can use this outline as a guide for talking to parents to obtain the required information. Alternatively, you could develop a written questionnaire. However, it is better to talk to the parents directly (either in person or by telephone). Generally by talking you get a better sense of what's going on, and you can ask clarification questions as needed.

One final remark here: when you talk to parents, be sensitive about their linguistic needs. Do not assume that they will be able to talk to you in the language you choose – ask them about which language they are most comfortable in and be prepared to adjust accordingly. If you use a written questionnaire, be sure to have available different language versions and select the one that parents prefer.

The protocol lists only the kind of information that it is crucial to collect before you start your actual study. You can add to it at will.

Protocol for obtaining information about a BFLA context [a]

1. Family composition

Family member	Date of birth	Country of origin	Gender	Employment status
Parent1				
Parent2				
Target child				n.a.
Sibling 1				
Sibling 2				
Other 1: ___				
Other 2: ___				

Appendices

2. Current patterns of home language use

Family member	Speaks to parent2	Speaks to parent1	Speaks to target child	Speaks to sibling 1/2/3	Speaks to other 1/2
Parent1		n.a.			
Parent2	n.a.				
Target child			to self:		
Sibling 1					
Sibling 2					
Sibling 3					
Other: ___					
Other: ___					

Cells here can of course be filled in with more than one language

Have there been any big changes in home language use since the targets child's birth? If so, please explain.

Can you confirm that the target child has heard two languages from birth regularly?

3. Target child care history in and outside the home

In the home

	From (m,y)	Until (m, y)	Main caregiver(s)	Average number of hours per week	Language(s) spoken to child by caregiver(s)
Period 1					
Period 2					
Period 3					
Period 4					

Start a different period when the child care environment clearly changed
(m, y) = month, year

Outside the home

	From (m,y)	Until (m, y)	Main caregiver(s)	Average number of hours per week	Language(s) spoken to child by caregiver(s)
Period 1					
Period 2					
Period 3					
Period 4					

Start a different period when the child care environment clearly changed
(m, y) = month, year

If the child was taken care of in a group setting, specifiy the number of other children in the group.

4. Target child residence and long-term travel (>1 week) since birth

From (m,y)	Until (m,y)	Residence/Place visited	Language(s)

Please list closest city and country; which language(s) are used there in public life?
(m, y) = month, year

Not counting the first week of life, has the child ever been hospitalized for a period longer than a week? If so, please specify the dates (from – until).

5. Target child health

Has (s)he experienced any health problem that affects hearing, cognitive functioning and/or language use?

6. Family contact information and date that this information was received

Note: try to obtain dates rather than ages throughout. This is much easier for later analysis.

[a] This protocol is a modified version of a background information form that I used when I was collecting Dutch–English data in Belgium in the late 1970s. Answers to many of the questions here for one of the bilingual families I collected data on are reflected on pages 71–74 in the book where I present my study of Kate, a young bilingual girl (De Houwer, 1990).

Appendix B

Behavioral studies of early speech perception in BFLA infants

(links up with Chapter 5)

Average infant ages (in months)	Number	Languages	Focus on the discrimination of....	Main findings: BFLA infants...	Source
4 m	?	Catalan–Spanish	contrast between [o] and [u] (phonemic in Catalan and Spanish)	can discriminate this contrast (as can monolingual infants[a])	Bosch & Sebastián-Gallés, 2005
4 m	?	Catalan–Spanish	contrast between [e] and [u] (phonemic in Catalan and Spanish)	can discriminate this contrast (as can monolingual infants[a])	Bosch & Sebastián-Gallés, 2005
4.2 m	10	Catalan–Spanish	passages of sentences recorded in English contrasted with passages in Catalan or Spanish	responded differently to either of their languages than to English, as did monolingual infants learning either Catalan or Spanish; bilinguals were faster to respond to English (the opposite holds for monolinguals)	Bosch & Sebastián-Gallés, 1997
4.5 m	10	Catalan–Spanish	passages of sentences recorded in Italian contrasted with passages in Catalan or Spanish	responded differently to either of their languages than to Italian, as did monolingual infants learning either Catalan or Spanish; bilinguals were faster to respond to English (the opposite holds for monolinguals)	Bosch & Sebastián-Gallés, 1997

Average infant ages (in months)	Number	Languages	Focus on the discrimination of....	Main findings: BFLA infants...	Source
4.5 m	10	Catalan–Spanish	passages of sentences recorded in Catalan or Spanish	responded similarly to either of their languages (no difference in the speed of response); their response pattern was the same as that by monolingual infants for each language separately	Bosch & Sebastián-Gallés, 1997
4.5 m	28	Catalan–Spanish	passages of sentences recorded in Catalan and Spanish	were able to detect a change from Catalan to Spanish and the other way round (as were matched monolinguals in each language)	Bosch & Sebastián-Gallés, 2001b
4.5 m	12	Catalan–Spanish	contrast between [e] and [ɛ] (phonemic in Catalan but not in Spanish)	were able to discriminate this contrast (as were matched monolinguals in each language)	Bosch & Sebastián-Gallés, 2003
6.3 m	10	Catalan–Spanish	passages of sentences recorded in English contrasted with passages in Catalan or Spanish	responded differently to one of their languages than to English (they were faster to respond to English); this is the opposite of what monolingual infants learning either Catalan or Spanish did; all infants responded the same way to English, but bilingual infants were much slower to respond to passages in one of their familiar languages	Bosch & Sebastián-Gallés, 2001a
6.9 m	16	English–French[b]	contrast between French dental [d] and English alveodental [d]	were able to distinguish between the two 'd's (like monolingual infants learning either French or English)	Sundara et al., 2008

Average infant ages (in months)	Number	Languages	Focus on the discrimination of....	Main findings: BFLA infants...	Source
7.2 m	9	English–French	contrast between [ba] & [pʰa] after hearing [pa] (French-speaking adults hear [pa] as /pa/, and English-speaking adults hear [pa] as /ba/; there are differences in **Voice Onset Time** in both languages)	were able to discriminate a change from [pa] to [ba] but not from [pa] to [pʰa] (like matched monolingual English infants); both groups thus behaved like French-speaking adults	Burns et al., 2007[c]
8 m	24	Catalan–Spanish	contrast between /o/ and /u/, which exists in both Catalan and Spanish	can**not** discriminate this contrast (but 4-month-olds could, see earlier); monolingual infants can, though[a]	Bosch & Sebastián-Gallés, 2005
8 m	?	Catalan–Spanish	contrast between /e/ and /u/, which exists in both Catalan and Spanish	can discriminate this contrast (like 4-month-olds, see earlier), as can monolinguals[a]	Bosch & Sebastián-Gallés, 2005
8.1 m	12	Catalan–Spanish	contrast between /e/ and /ɛ/, which exists in Catalan but not in Spanish	did not discriminate this contrast very well, and did worse than at 4.5 m; matched Catalan monolinguals did discriminate the contrast, but matched Spanish monolinguals did not	Bosch & Sebastián-Gallés, 2003
11 m	18	English–French	contrast between [ba] and [pʰa] after hearing [pa] (see above)	were able to discriminate a change from [pa] to [ba] and from [pa] to [pʰa] (unlike matched monolingual English infants, who only discriminated a change from [pa] to [pʰa])	Burns et al., 2007

Average infant ages (in months)	Number	Languages	Focus on the discrimination of....	Main findings: BFLA infants...	Source
11.4 m	16	English–French	contrast between French dental [d] and English alveodental [d]	were able to distinguish between the two 'd's (like monolingual infants learning English; but not like monolingual infants learning French, who failed to discriminate)	Sundara et al., 2008
12.3 m	12	Catalan–Spanish	contrast between /e/ and /ɛ/, which exists in Catalan but not in Spanish	were able to discriminate this contrast, like Catalan monolinguals at 8 m	Bosch & Sebastián-Gallés, 2003
14.3 m	12	English–French	contrast between [ba] & [pʰa] after hearing [pa] (see above)	were able to discriminate a change from [pa] to [ba] and from [pa] to [pʰa] (unlike matched monolingual infants, who only discriminated a change from [pa] to [pʰa])	Burns et al., 2007

[a] The study does not specify which language these monolinguals were acquiring.
[b] All the English and French bilingually raised infants in this table heard Canadian English and Canadian French; the Spanish in the table refers to Spanish as spoken in Catalunya, Spain.
[c] Preliminary results of this study were earlier published in Burns et al., 2003.

Appendix C

Behavioral studies of early phonetic word learning in BFLA infants

(links up with Chapter 5)

Average infant ages (in months)	Number	Languages	Focus on the contrast between....	Main findings: the BFLA infants...	Source
14.3 m	16	English + 1 of several other languages	novel English nonsense words 'bih' and 'dih'	did not make a difference between 'bih' and 'dih' (like monolingual English infants at 14 m)	Fennell *et al.*, 2007
17 m	16	English–Chinese	novel English nonsense words 'bih' and 'dih'	did not make a difference between 'bih' and 'dih' (**un**like monolingual English infants at 17 m)	Fennell *et al.*, 2007
17 m	14	English–French	novel English nonsense words 'bih' and 'dih'	did not make a difference between 'bih' and 'dih' (**un**like monolingual English infants at 17 m)	Fennell *et al.*, 2007

Average infant ages (in months)	Number	Languages	Focus on the contrast between....	Main findings: the BFLA infants...	Source
17.5 m	16	English + 1 of several other languages	novel English nonsense words 'bih' and 'dih'	did not make a difference between 'bih' and 'dih' (**un**like monolingual English infants at 17 m)	Fennell *et al.*, 2007
17.5 m	16	English–French	nonsense words 'bowce' and 'gowce' pronounced in an English and French manner	had no trouble perceiving these contrasts (but infants monolingual in either English and French did have trouble)	Mattock *et al.*, 2008b
19.7 m	16	English + 1 of several other languages	novel English nonsense words 'bih' and 'dih'	made a difference between 'bih' and 'dih' (like monolingual English infants at 20 m)	Fennell *et al.*, 2007
20 m	12	English–Chinese	novel English nonsense words 'bih' and 'dih'	made a difference between 'bih' and 'dih' (like monolingual English infants at 20 m)	Fennell *et al.*, 2007
20 m	11	English–French	novel English nonsense words 'bih' and 'dih'	made a difference between 'bih' and 'dih' (like monolingual English infants at 20 m)	Fennell *et al.*, 2007

[a] All the English and French bilingually raised infants in this table heard Canadian English and Canadian French.

Appendix D

Studies of the use of speech rhythm in young BFLA children

(links up with Chapter 5)

Studies are ordered according to the ages of the children studied

Child	Age[a]	Languages[b]	Focus	Source
Arsham	0;9–2;0	English–Farsi	word stress and syllable structure	Keshavarz & Ingram, 2002
Irene	1;1–2;4	German–Spanish	syllable codas	Lleó et al., 2003
Robert	1;1–2;4	German–Spanish	syllable codas	Lleó et al., 2003
"	1;6–2;4	German–Spanish	pauses in two word utterances	Lleó & Rakow, 2006
Stefan	1;2–2;3	German–Spanish	syllable codas	Lleó et al., 2003
Nils	1;3–1;9	German–Spanish	syllable codas	Lleó et al., 2003
"	1;6–2;2	German–Spanish	truncation	Lleó, 2002
Simon	1;3–2;4	German–Spanish	syllable codas	Lleó et al., 2003
"	1;6–2;2	German–Spanish	truncation	Lleó, 2002
"	1;6–2;4	German–Spanish	pauses in two word utterances	Lleó & Rakow, 2006
"	no info	German–Spanish	speech rhythm	Lleó et al., 2007

Child	Age[a]	Languages[b]	Focus	Source
"	2;10–3;1	German–Spanish	pitch accent	Lleó et al., 2004
Louis	1;3–2;6	French–German	word stress	Ronjat, 1913: 14–15
Hildegard	1;6–2;0	English–German	syllable structure	Paradis, 1996
Jens	1;6–2;3	German–Spanish	truncation	Lleó, 2002
Jens	1;6–2;4	German–Spanish	pauses in two word utterances	Lleó & Rakow, 2006
"	1;6–2;3	German–Spanish	truncation	Lleó, 2002
"	2;10–3;1	German–Spanish	pitch accent	Lleó et al., 2004
"	no info	German–Spanish	speech rhythm	Lleó et al., 2007
'Mu'	no info	German–Spanish	speech rhythm	Lleó et al., 2007
Tom	1;8–2;6	French–English	word stress	Brulard & Carr, 2003
Andreas	1;9	English–Norwegian	syllable structure	Johnson & Lancaster, 1998
N=17[c]	1;11–2;11	French–English	truncation	Paradis, 1998
'L'	2;0	English–Italian	syllable structure	Ingram, 1981/82
Hannah	2;1–2;6	German–English	pitch; word and sentence stress	Gut, 2000a
"	"	German–English	pauses in multi-word utterances	Gut, 2000a
Laura	2;5–4;3	German–English	pitch; word and sentence stress	Gut, 2000a
"	"	German–English	pauses in multi-word utterances	Gut, 2000a
Adam[d]	3;6–5;5	German–English	pitch; word and sentence stress	Gut, 2000a
"	"	German–English	pauses in multi-word utterances	Gut, 2000a

Child	Age[a]	Languages[b]	Focus	Source
N=10[e]	4;0–5;2	English–Spanish	speech rhythm	Bunta & Ingram, 2007
Leonore	5;0	English–German	rhythmic variability	Whitworth, 2002

[a] Ages were rounded off to the nearest month.
[b] The language used in the greater community is listed first.
[c] Note that this study collapses results from children with bilingual input from birth and from children with input in a second language prior to age six months (p. 24). It is not mentioned where the children grew up, so the order 'French–English' might not in fact be correct.
[d] Adam is Laura's older brother.
[e] One of these children had input to the second language starting at nine months of age.

Appendix E

Studies of the use of speech segments in young BFLA children

(links up with Chapter 5)

Studies are ordered according to the youngest ages of the children studied

Child	Age[a]	Languages[b]	Focus	Source
Louis	0;8–3;0	French–German	vowels and consonants	Ronjat, 1913
Arsham	0;9–2;0	English–Farsi	consonants	Keshavarz & Ingram, 2002
Hildegard	0;9–2;0	English–German	vowels and consonants	Leopold, 1953, 1970
Fernando	1;1–3;9	Spanish–English	vowels and consonants	Schnitzer & Krasinski, 1994
Jens	1;4–3;0	German–Spanish	fricative and stop consonants	Lleó & Rakow, 2005
"	1;10–2;6	German–Spanish	vowels	Kehoe, 2002
Nils	1;7–3;0	German–Spanish	fricative and stop consonants	Lleó & Rakow, 2005
"	1;10–2;6	German–Spanish	vowels	Kehoe, 2002
Zevio[c]	1;6–4;6	Spanish–English	vowels and consonants	Schnitzer & Krasinski, 1996
Simon	1;7–3;0	German–Spanish	fricative and stop consonants	Lleó & Rakow, 2005
"	1;10–2;6	German–Spanish	vowels	Kehoe, 2002

Child	Age[a]	Languages[b]	Focus	Source
Andreas	1;9	English–Norwegian	vowels and consonants	Johnson & Lancaster, 1998
Manuela	1;10	English–Spanish	vowels and consonants	Deuchar & Quay, 2000: 29–34
"L"	2;0	English–Italian	consonants	Ingram, 1981/82
N=11[d]	2;10–3;0	English–Spanish	vowels and consonants	Pearson *et al.*, 1995; Pearson & Navarro, 1996

[a] Ages have been rounded off to the nearest month.
[b] The language used in the greater community is listed first.
[c] Zevio is Fernando's older brother.
[d] One or two of these children might not be cases of BFLA.

Appendix F

Studies comparing lexical development in MFLA and BFLA/ESLA

(links up with Chapter 6)

	Number	Age(s)	Measure	Language(s)
Águila et al., 2005				
Bilinguals	15	12–14 m	own bilingual report instrument	Catalan–Spanish
Monolinguals	13	12–14 m	same	Spanish
Monolinguals	8	12–14 m	same	Catalan
Bilinguals	15	18–20 m	same	Catalan–Spanish
Monolinguals	15	18–20 m	same	Spanish
Monolinguals	15	18–20 m	same	Catalan
Bilinguals	11	22–24 m	same	Catalan–Spanish
Monolinguals	15	22–24 m	same	Spanish
Monolinguals	14	22–24 m	same	Catalan
Águila et al., 2007				
Bilinguals	24	12–15 m	own bilingual report instrument[a]	Catalan–Spanish
Monolinguals	17	12–15 m	same	Spanish
Monolinguals	20	12–15 m	same	Catalan
Bilinguals	44	16–24 m	same	Catalan–Spanish
Monolinguals	21	16–24 m	same	Spanish
Monolinguals	44	16–24 m	same	Catalan

	Number	*Age(s)*	*Measure*	*Language(s)*
De Houwer et al., 2006b[b]				
Bilinguals	31	13 m	Dutch and European French CDI	Dutch–French
Monolinguals	30	13 m	Dutch CDI	Dutch
Junker & Stockman, 2002				
Bilinguals	10	24–27 m	see below[c]	English–German
Monolinguals	10	24–27 m	see below[c]	German
Monolinguals	10	24–27 m	see below[c]	English
Rimel & Eyal, 1996				
Bilinguals	20	18–30 m	English and Hebrew CDI	English–Hebrew
Monolinguals	20	18–30 m	Hebrew CDI	Hebrew
Pearson et al., 1993				
Bilinguals	25	16–27 m	English and Spanish CDI	English–Spanish
Monolinguals	32	16–27 m	English CDI	English
Monolinguals	3	16–27 m	Spanish CDI	Spanish
Thordardottir et al., 2006[d]				
Bilinguals	8	32 m (average)	English and Canadian French CDI	English–French
Monolinguals	10	33 m (average)	English CDI	English
Monolinguals	10	33 m (average)	Canadian French CDI	French

[a] This is an improved version of the one used in Águila *et al.*, 2005.
[b] All the infants in this study were firstborn, middle-class children living with both their biological parents.
[c] This study used a standardized English report instrument, the Language Development Survey (LDS; Rescorla, 1989) for the bilinguals and the English-speaking monolinguals, and a translation of that instrument into German for the bilinguals and the German-speaking monolinguals (translated by the first author).
[d] The bilingual children were not necessarily BFLA but all started hearing a second language by age 1 (Elin Thordardottir, personal communication); ages have been rounded off to the nearest month.

Note 1: For each of the groups and age ranges indicated, there was just one measurement for all the children here except for the Pearson *et al.* study. Pearson *et al.* used repeated measures for some of the same children at different ages.

Note 2: For the De Houwer *et al.* study, up to three people per language filled out a CDI form for both the bilingual and the monolingual group (see the procedure described in Box 3.8 in Chapter 3). For the bilingual group in the Junker and Stockman study, one person filled out the LDS in two languages.

Appendix G

Studies of BFLA supporting the Separate Development Hypothesis

(links up with Chapter 7)

Child	Languages	Age(s)[a]	Study/Studies
Mikel	Basque–Spanish	1;6–3;0	Almgren & Barreña, 2000; Barreña & Almgren, 2000
		1;6–3;6	Barreña, 1997
		1;6–4;0	Barreña, 2001
		1;7–4;0	Almgren & Idiazabal, 2001; Ezeizabarrena & Larrañaga, 1996; Larrañaga, 2008
Peru	Basque–Spanish	1;11–4;0	Barreña, 2001; Larrañaga, 2008
Zevio	Spanish–English	0;11–4;6	Krasinski, 1995
Nicolas	Spanish–English	1;5–2;9	Silva-Corvalán & Sánchez-Walker, 2007
		1;6–3;0	Silva-Corvalán & Montanari, 2008
Manuela	Spanish–English	1;7–3;2	Deuchar, 1992
		1;8–2;3	Deuchar & Quay, 2000: 82–87
		1;11–2;6	Berger-Morales et al., 2005
Simon[b]	Spanish–English	2;4–4;11	Liceras et al., 2008
Leo[b]	Spanish–English	2;4–4;11	Liceras et al., 2008
Ken	Japanese–English	1;11–3;2	Mishina-Mori, 2005
		2;8–3;2	Mishina-Mori, 2002
Hannah	Japanese–English	2;2–2;4	Itani-Adams, 2007

Child	Languages	Age(s)[a]	Study/Studies
Rie	Japanese–English	2;4–2;10	Mishina-Mori, 2002
		2;4–3;3	Mishina-Mori, 2005
Carlo	Italian–English	1;10–3;2	Serratrice, 2001, 2002
Natalie	Slovak–English	1;3–5;7	Stefánik, 1995, 1997
Maija	Latvian–English	1;2–1;11	Sinka & Schelletter, 1998
Andreu	Catalan–English	1;3–4;2	Juan-Garau & Pérez-Vidal, 2000
Kate	Dutch–English	2;7–3;4	De Houwer, 1990, 1997
Sonja	German–English	2;0–2;6	Sinka & Schelletter, 1998
Annie	German–English	2;3–2;10	Unsworth, 2003
Ralph	Mandarin–English	0;10–2;9	Chang-Smith, 2008
James	Mandarin–English	1;0–4;0	Qi et al., 2006
AW (girl)	Inuktitut–English	1;8–2;6	Zwanziger et al., 2005
SR (boy)	Inuktitut–English	2;0–2;10	Zwanziger et al., 2005
SA (girl)	Inuktitut–English	2;5–3;2	Zwanziger et al., 2005
MT (boy)	Inuktitut–English	2;5–3;3	Zwanziger et al., 2005
PN (girl)	Inuktitut–English	2;8–3;5	Zwanziger et al., 2005
AI (boy)	Inuktitut–English	2;11–3;9	Zwanziger et al., 2005
Mathieu	French–English	1;9–2;11	Paradis & Genesee, 1997
Olivier	French–English	1;11–2;10	Paradis & Genesee, 1996
Yann	French–English	1;11–3;0	Paradis & Genesee, 1997
Gene	French–English	1;11–3;1	Paradis & Genesee, 1996
William	French–English	2;2–3;3	Paradis & Genesee, 1996
Adèle	French–English	2;3–3;6	Macrory, 2007
Odessa	French–English	2;7–2;9	Jisa, 1995
Jason	French–English	2;9–3;3	Nicoladis, 1999
Jean	French–Swedish	1;10–3;9	Granfeldt, 2000; Schlyter, 1995
Mimi	French–Swedish	2;0–4;2	Granfeldt, 2000; Schlyter, 1995
Anne	French–Swedish	2;3–4;0	Granfeldt, 2000
		2;3–4;4	Schlyter, 1995

Child	Languages	Age(s)[a]	Study/Studies
Anouk	French–Dutch	2;3–3;4	Hulk & van der Linden, 1996
		2;3–3;10	Hulk & Müller, 2000
		2;5–3;10	Hulk, 2003
Caroline	French–German	1;0–3;6	Meisel, 1985
		1;0–3;1	Meisel, 1990
		1;6–3;0	Müller, 1995
		1;6–5;0	Meisel & Müller, 1992; Müller, 1990a, 1994a, 1994b
		1;10–3;10	Meisel, 1986, 1989
		1;11–2;8	Meisel, 1994
		1;11–4;6	Klinge, 1990
Pierre	French–German	1;0–3;6	Meisel, 1985
		1;0–4;0	Meisel, 1990
		2;6–4;0	Meisel, 1989
		2;7–3;3	Meisel, 1994
		2;7–3;8	Meisel, 1986
		unknown[c]	Bonnesen, 2007, 2008
Christophe	French–German	1;1–3;8	Parodi, 1990
		1;11–3;5	Schlyter, 1990b
		2;3–3;7	Bonnesen, 2007, to appear
		2;3–3;8	Klinge, 1990
Ivar	French–German	1;4–2;9	Meisel, 1990
		1;5–3;0	Müller, 1994a
		1;5–4;3	Meisel & Müller, 1992; Müller, 1990b
		1;5–5;0	Koehn, 1994
		1;5–5;10	Müller, 1994b
		1;6–5	Rieckborn, 2006
		1;10–3;0	Kaiser, 1994
		1;10–3;5	Schlyter, 1990b; Müller, 1993

Child	Languages	Age(s)[a]	Study/Studies
		2;0–2;8	Meisel, 1994
		2;2–3;5	Klinge, 1990
		2;2–2;6	Köppe, 1994a
		2;4–3;5	Müller et al., 1996
Pascal	French–German	1;5–3;6	Möhring & Meisel, 2003
		1;5–4;0	Meisel & Müller, 1992; Müller, 1990b
		1;5–4;7	Müller, 1994b
		1;6–5	Rieckborn, 2006
		1;8–4;10	Stenzel, 1994
		1;9–2;11	Kaiser, 1994
		1;10–2;5	Köppe, 1994a
		1;10–3;5	Müller, 1993
Annika	French–German	2;4–4;7	Stenzel, 1996
		1;9–2;9	Möhring & Meisel, 2003
		2;0–3;11	Stenzel, 1994
		unknown[c]	Bonnesen, 2007, 2008
François	French–German	2;0–4;0	Bonnesen, 2007, to appear
		2;4–3;4	Schlyter, 1990b
Daniel	German–Portuguese	1;7–3;11	Hinzelin, 2003
Luís	German–Portuguese	2;2–3;6	Hinzelin, 2003
Carlotta	German–Italian	1;9–3;2	Hulk & Müller, 2000
Leo	German–Italian	2;0–2;7	Berger-Morales et al., 2005; Salustri & Hyams, 2006

This table is a modified extension of Table 1 in De Houwer 2005 (with kind permission from the editors, J. Kroll and A. de Groot).

[a] Ages are indicated in years;months (months have been rounded up to the next month for children who were at least 20 days into the next month); a dash between ages means 'from age X to age Y'.
[b] Simon and Leo are twin brothers.
[c] Data are presented for the third and fourth year of life.

Appendix H

Main morphosyntactic topics investigated in empirical studies of BFLA supporting the SDH

(links up with Chapter 7)

Topic   **Study/Studies**

Morphology of the nominal constituent
> Almgren & Barreña, 2000; Barreña, 1997; Barreña & Almgren, 2000; Chang-Smith, 2008; De Houwer, 1990; Deuchar & Quay, 2000: 82–87; Ezeizabarrena & Larrañaga, 1996; Koehn, 1994; Meisel, 1986; Müller, 1995; Parodi, 1990; Sinka & Schelletter, 1998; Stefánik, 1995, 1997; Stenzel, 1994, 1996

Word order in compound nouns
> Nicoladis, 1999

Syntactic gender
> De Houwer, 1990; Müller, 1990a, 1994a, 1995; Sinka & Schelletter, 1998; Stefánik, 1995, 1997

Determiners
> Barreña, 1997; De Houwer, 1990; Granfeldt, 2000; Müller, 1994b; Paradis & Genesee, 1997

Pluralization
> Barreña, 1997; De Houwer, 1990; Müller, 1994a; Sinka & Schelletter, 1998

Pronouns/Clitics
> Almgren & Barreña, 2000; Bonnesen, to appear; De Houwer, 1990; Kaiser, 1994; Müller *et al.*, 1996; Serratrice, 2002; Qi *et al.*, 2006; Liceras *et al.*, 2008

Prepositions
> Klinge, 1990

Subject realization
> Bonnesen, to appear; Juan-Garau & Pérez-Vidal, 2000; Hinzelin, 2003; Liceras *et al.*, 2008; Serratrice, 2002; Silva-Corvalán & Sánchez-Walker, 2007; Zwanziger *et al.*, 2005

The use of root infinitives
> Berger-Morales *et al.*, 2005; Hulk & Müller, 2000; Itani-Adams, 2007; Salustri & Hyams, 2006; Unsworth, 2003

The use of finiteness
> Berger-Morales *et al.*, 2005

Imperatives
> Salustri & Hyams, 2006

Congruence/Agreement
> Almgren & Barreña, 2000; De Houwer, 1990; Deuchar, 1992; Meisel, 1989, 1990, 1994; Meisel & Müller, 1992; Müller, 1990b; Paradis & Genesee, 1996; Serratrice, 2002; Sinka & Schelletter, 1998; Liceras *et al.*, 2008

Verb morphology
> Almgren & Barreña, 2000; Almgren & Idiazabal, 2001; Barreña & Almgren, 2000; De Houwer, 1990; Deuchar, 1992; Deuchar & Quay, 2000: 82–87; Ezeizabarrena & Larrañaga, 1996; Jisa, 1995; Itani-Adams, 2007; Meisel, 1996; Meisel & Müller, 1992; Müller, 1990b; Paradis & Genesee, 1997; Serratrice, 2001; Sinka & Schelletter, 1998

Aspect and/or time markings
> Almgren & Barreña, 2000; Almgren & Idiazabal, 2001; De Houwer, 1990, 1997; Jisa, 1995; Krasinski, 1995; Meisel, 1985, 1994; Mishina-Mori, 2002; Rieckborn, 2006; Serratrice, 2001; Schlyter, 1990b, 1995

The use of the copula and/or auxiliaries
> De Houwer, 1990; Silva-Corvalán & Montanari, 2008

Negation
> Bonnesen, to appear; Mishina-Mori, 2002; Paradis & Genesee, 1996, 1997

Question formation
> De Houwer, 1990; Macrory, 2007; Mishina-Mori, 2005

The placement of particles
> De Houwer, 1990; Hulk, 2003

Syntactic word order
> Almgren & Barreña, 2000; Bonnesen, 2007, 2008; De Houwer, 1990; Hulk & van der Linden, 1996; Köppe, 1994a; Larrañaga, 2008; Meisel, 1986, 1989; Meisel & Müller, 1992; Möhring & Meisel, 2003; Müller, 1990b, 1993; Parodi, 1990; Sinka & Schelletter, 1998

Complex sentences
> Barreña, 2001; De Houwer, 1990; Müller, 1993, 1994b

General development
> De Houwer, 1990; Juan-Garau & Pérez-Vidal, 2000

This table is a modified extension of Table 2 in De Houwer, 2005 (with kind permission from the editors, J. Kroll and A. de Groot).

Appendix I

Not using particular kinds of grammatical elements and what this might mean in terms of crosslinguistic influence

(links up with Chapter 7)

The SDH is based on what children actually say: the morphological forms they use, the word orders they produce. There have been a number of studies that focus on what young BFLA children do *not* say. You may think this is very strange. But, indeed, different languages make different choices as to what they express through words and morphemes, and children have to learn to use those choices.

For instance, in Spanish you can just say 'no hablo español' (I don't speak Spanish). The subject is not expressed by a pronoun but by the 'o' in 'hablo'. You also have the option of saying 'yo no hablo español', where you add the subject pronoun 'yo'. Here you're emphasizing it's you rather than someone else who doesn't speak Spanish. It is pragmatic rules – for instance, about whether you are giving new information – and the discourse context that determine whether you have to use a pronoun or not. In contrast, in English, you need subject pronouns pretty much all the time except with imperatives and in questions like 'want some?' in informal speech. In addition to differing in the degree to which languages require overt subjects, languages may also differ with regard to the degree to which they express objects.

Müller and Hulk (2001) have suggested that BFLA children who are acquiring two languages that differ in how obligatory it is to use particular kinds of elements and where that obligation depends on discourse–pragmatic rules may show crosslinguistic influence in the particular domain where the two languages differ (in spite of children generally showing separate development). They have explained the early non-use of object pronouns in French and Italian by three BFLA children acquiring French and Italian as Language A as showing influence from their Language Alpha, German or Dutch. Depending on the context, both German and Dutch allow object omission more than French or Italian (Müller and Hulk do not show data from the children's German or Dutch, though). The reason that Müller and Hulk are arguing for crosslinguistic influence is that the BFLA children use object omissions much more often than MFLA children acquiring just French or Italian. The kinds of sentences in which the bilingual children omit objects, though, are the same as the ones in which monolingual children omit them.

Müller and Hulk's (2001) study has been quite influential. Other studies involving different language pairs have tried to find more evidence for Müller and Hulk's claim that crosslinguistic influence in BFLA occurs when languages show partial overlap for certain areas of grammar and where competing ways of grammatical expression in one of the languages depend on pragmatic factors. Müller and Hulk's claim of crosslinguistic influence crucially depends on comparisons with monolingual children, however.

One of the studies examining Müller and Hulk's proposal is that by Serratrice *et al.* (2004) that compared English–Italian Carlo's use of overt and non-overt subjects and objects with that of Italian and English monolingual children (Italian is like Spanish in its use of subject pronouns; see above). Rather than using more non-adult-like *omissions* than was the case in the Müller and Hulk study, bilingual Carlo used more non-adult-like *overt subjects* in Italian than the Italian monolinguals. Serratrice *et al.* did not find any evidence for strong crosslinguistic influence from Italian on English that would lead to Carlo not using any overt subjects in English. Rather, they stress the point that individual learning styles may exert an influence. They also stress that it is important to investigate the pragmatic discourse contexts for children's use of overt or non-overt subjects and objects, something that Müller and Hulk did not do (see also Schlyter, 2001)[1].

Zwanziger *et al.* (2005) looked at the rate of subject omission in the English and Inuktitut of six BFLA children. Inuktitut is like Italian and Spanish in also having the option of using a subject pronoun or not. However, that option is not possible for first and second persons, only for third persons. Zwanziger *et al.* (2005) found clear differences between the children's English and Inuktitut. When they compared the bilingual children's proportions of non-adult-like subject omissions, there were no differences with monolingual children in either language, although in English, the bilingual children used adult-like subjects sooner than the monolinguals. Zwanziger *et al.* (2005) conclude that they found no evidence of crosslinguistic influence. Their data also show a fair amount of variation between the six bilingual children in the proportions with which they expressed subjects in each language.

Paradis and Navarro (2003) compared the use of Spanish subjects by English–Spanish Manuela to their use by two Spanish monolingual children growing up in Spain. They find differences between Manuela and the monolingual children in the extent to which they used overt subjects in Spanish (Manuela used more). Paradis and Navarro suggest, however, that differences in the adult speech may account for these differences, rather than crosslinguistic influence (although they still leave open the possibility that there is such influence; see Box 7.19 in Chapter 7). Paradis and Navarro (2003: 388) found that in adult speech to the two monolingual Spanish children overt subjects were used in about 40% of the cases, whereas Manuela heard overt subjects in Spanish in about 60% of the relevant cases.

Continuing this much needed focus on the input, Silva-Corvalán and Sánchez-Walker (2007) present empirical data based on adult speech that show actual percentages of the use of overt subjects in different varieties of Spanish. In their study of subject omissions by

Spanish-English Nicolas they explain part of their findings in terms of the frequencies in the Spanish input that Nicolas is likely to have heard (there are no analyses of his actual language input). Silva-Corvalán and Sánchez-Walker find no evidence of any influence of the one language on the other, and demonstrate that Nicolas knows the discourse–pragmatic rules of both Spanish and English from a very early age onwards (from 20 to 22 months of age). Silva-Corvalán and Sánchez-Walker stress that it is each input language that determines the development of language-specific usage.

It is in fact very difficult to explain why children do *not* express something. It is easier to try and explain why they say what they do. Nevertheless, children's non-adult-like omission of sentence elements needs to be explained. The explanation may be developmental (children are just too immature; or children have different learning styles), or it may be based on the input, or indeed, in BFLA children, there may be subtle signs of crosslinguistic influence.

However, the issue of the relation between a BFLA child's developing languages, including crosslinguistic transfer, cannot be decided on the basis of comparisons with monolingual acquisition (Chapter 7). The issue must be settled on the basis of bilingual data. It might be instructive, as Serratrice *et al.* (2005) suggest, to compare many BFLA children to each other who are acquiring different pairs of languages that do or do not differ with regard to how frequently they express overt subjects or objects. Indeed, such comparisons would be able to say how often and in what circumstances crosslinguistic influence occurs. Still, crosslinguistic influence is a phenomenon that operates at the individual level and can strictly speaking only be analyzed on a case-by-case, bilingual child-by-child basis.

Note

1. In order to carry out such an investigation, one needs access to video recordings. Otherwise, it is impossible to accurately assess the context.

Glossary

- *Terms in the explanations that are themselves explained elsewhere in the glossary appear in bold face*
- *As noted in the Preface, the explanations in this Glossary are only meant to facilitate the understanding of this book. Different linguists may lay different emphases.*

1P/1L
A **language presentation** setting following the 'one person, one language' principle, where the important people (mostly the parents) in a child's **linguistic soundscape** each address the child using one language only.

1P/2L
A **language presentation** setting in which the important people (mostly the parents) in a child's **linguistic soundscape** each address the child in two languages.

1P/1L & 1P/2L
A **language presentation** setting in which some important people (including one parent) in a child's **linguistic soundscape** each address the child in two languages and in which other important people (including the other parent) address the child in one language only.

Absolute frequency (of language input)
The number of **utterances** or **words** that children hear in a particular time frame.

Adult-like
Pronounced or said or used the way adults speaking the same language would.

Adverbials
Sentence elements that add more information about what is expressed in the **verb**. They tend to refer to meanings expressing the manner, place or time of the event or action expressed in a **sentence**.

Articulators
Parts of the body used for articulating speech sounds (for instance, lips and tongue).

BFLA
See **Bilingual First Language Acquisition**.

BFLA children
Children who heard two languages spoken to them from birth.

Bilingual couple
Both persons in the couple speak two languages X and Y and use these two languages between them.

Bilingual First Language Acquisition (BFLA)
The development of language in young children who heard two languages spoken to them from birth.

Bilingual/monolingual couple
One person in the couple speaks two languages X and Y but the other person does not understand language X and speaks only language Y; within the couple, only language Y is used.

Bilingual community
A particular kind of personal social network and 'street' environment where many people regularly use two languages either in **comprehension** or **production** and where the use of more than one language is acknowledged and accepted.

Blend
Novel **word** creation constructed on the basis of parts of two separate words (either taken from two different languages, or from the same language).

Bound morphemes
Single **phonemes** or **syllables** (one or more than one) that are attached to **free morphemes** or **word roots** to express all kinds of different grammatical meanings.

Canonical babbling
Infants' **production** of **vowel–consonant** combinations that sound like they could be **words**, but infants produce these without any apparent communicative meaning. Often starts around eight months of age.

CDI
Communicative Development Inventory, a **parental report instrument** used to find out about overall communicative development in very young children with a focus on children's understanding and saying of **words**.

CHILDES
The international archive of standardized **transcripts** of human speech including supporting software and other tools; *see* http://childes.psy.cmu.edu/.

Codas
Syllable final **consonants**.

Coding
Categorizing **data** (for instance, in **transcripts**) according to previously established and clearly specified categories.

Cognates
Words that have the same **phonological** form and basic meaning across two languages in the input; there might be slight differences in meaning between the two words in the adult input, though; such forms I here also call '**language neutral words**'.

Complex sentences
Utterances that consist of more than one **sentence** (or, more accurately, or more than one clause). Complex sentences can be coordinating (combining two clauses on the same level) or subordinating (one clause is dependent on another), or a combination of these. Examples are: 'I am going for a walk but I won't be long' (coordinating); 'I am going for a walk because I need some fresh air' (subordinating); 'I am going for a walk and I'll try to stop by the store if I don't forget' (coordinating and subordinating).

Comprehension
The understanding of **words** and **sentences** in a language.

Consonant harmony
A **phonological** substitution process whereby the **consonants** in a **word** all get the same place and manner of articulation (although they may differ in **voice**). For instance, a child may say 'dit' instead of 'dish', and so make the final consonant of 'dish' more like its first: like [d], [t] is pronounced with

the tongue close to the teeth (closer than the last consonant of 'dish'); like [d], [t] is pronounced with a momentary full closure of the mouth (by contrast, the last consonant of 'dish' is a **fricative**).

Consonants
Speech sounds that are produced with a restriction in the mouth of the air flow from the lungs through the vocal cords. The restriction can be total (as in sounds like [m] where the lips stop the airflow for a moment) or less so, like in **fricatives** (there are various degrees here).

Corpus (plural: corpora)
A collection of **transcripts** that represents one particular research project (for instance, all the transcripts of longitudinal recordings involving one child; or all the transcripts of one-off recordings involving several children).

Cross-sectional design
A study that collects **data** for different children at different ages and then combines these data as if they came from just one child.

Data
Information gathered for a scientific study.

Deletion
Here used most often to describe children's omission of a **phoneme** where there should have been one.

Determiners
A type of **word** that accompanies a **noun** and that can express whether the noun is definite or indefinite, plural or singular, male or female, the topic of the sentence or the object, close or distant, already mentioned previously or new, and many other meanings.

Devoicing (of consonants)
A **phonological** process whereby a voiced **consonant** is pronounced in a **voiceless** manner.

Dilingual conversations
Conversations in which one partner consistently speaks a different language than the other one. For this to be possible, both partners must understand the other one's language.

Diphthongs
Speech sounds that involve a movement of the mouth that seems to go (or glide) from one **vowel** to another.

Discourse strategies
Meaning in this book: conversational habits that encourage or discourage the use of a particular language.

Doublet
You know a doublet if you know both members of a pair of **words** making up a **translation equivalent**, such as English 'word' and Spanish 'palabra'.

Early Second Language Acquisition (ESLA)
The situation where children first hear and learn one language (**Language 1**) from birth but where there is a change in children's language environments such that they start to hear and learn a second language after the first (**Language 2**).

Empirical research
Scientific research for which **data** have been systematically collected that can be used as evidence for a particular phenomenon.

ESLA
See **Early Second Language Acquisition**.

Experimental setting/study
In the context of child language research this refers to a situation or study in which you observe children carrying out a particular linguistic or communicative task or structured activity that was specifically designed to elicit the kind of behavior you want to study.

Floating utterances
Child utterances that seem to bear little or no relation to a child's **input** language(s).

Free morphemes
Words with referential meaning that can be used on their own (see Box 2.6 for more explanation).

Fricatives
Consonantal **speech segments** pronounced with a partial closure of the mouth, so the air can still escape with a sort of hissing sound. Examples of English fricatives are /f/ and /z/.

Grammatical words
For any particular language, there may be a limited set of **free morphemes** that have primarily grammatical meanings and that are combined with words in sentences that have more referential meanings. Examples are the German article 'ein', the Spanish preposition 'en', the French personal pronoun 'moi', the Dutch relative pronoun 'dat' and the English conjunction 'if'.

Holophrases
Early child **utterances** consisting of single **words** that appear to have much bigger meanings than the words by themselves have in adult usage.

Iambic stress
Final stress on words with more than one syllable (e.g. French 'papier' – paper) (the opposite of **trochaic stress**).

Impact belief
The belief that how and how frequently a child is talked to has an effect on children's language development.

Indeterminate utterances
Utterances spoken by a bilingual person that could belong to either of two languages. An example is 'ja!'. This could be Dutch or German.

Infant-directed speech (IDS)
The particular way of speaking many people use to address young children.

Input
The speech that children hear.

Interaction
A communicative setting in which people relate to each other face to face through verbal or non-verbal means.

Interlocutor
A participant in an **interaction**.

Glossary

Intersubjective learning
Learning through and in communication with others.

Intonation
See **prosody** below.

IPA
International Phonetic Alphabet: the set of symbols developed by the International Phonetic Association to represent human speech sounds.

Joint attention
The situation where two participants in an **interaction** are focused on the same topic, entity or activity.

Language A
One of a **BFLA** child's two first input languages.

Language Alpha
One of a **BFLA** child's two first input languages.

Language 1
A child's first or only input language (in **MFLA** and **ESLA**).

Language 2
A child's second input language (in **ESLA**).

Language choice
The choice between languages that a bilingual person necessarily has to make when speaking and that results in the use of one particular kind of **utterance** rather than another (for instance, speaking French rather than Japanese, in the case of a person who can speak both French and Japanese).

Language models
The language varieties and the speech characteristics that children hear.

Language neutral words
Words in the speech of a bilingual person that could belong to either of two specific languages.

Language orientation
A psychological orientation that sets up expectations regarding **language choice** in a particular linguistic enviroment.

Language presentation
Refers to who speaks which language(s) to a child and how many: one or two.

Lexical comprehension
The understanding of **words**.

Lexical verb
A **verb** with a lexical, referential meaning such as 'run', 'put', 'sleep'; this excludes auxiliary verbs such as 'be' or 'have'. Also excluded are modal verbs such as 'need' (although often it is difficult to draw a clear distinction between modal and lexical verbs) and copular verbs such as 'be'. Note that English 'be' can be a lexical ('To be, or not to be...' – W. Shakespeare), copular (e.g. in: 'I'm ill') or auxiliary (e.g. in: 'I'm going home') verb.

Lexicon
The totality of **word** knowledge that a person has.

Linguistic soundscape
Meaning in this book: the totality of the various uses of spoken language that individuals encounter. This includes language use by people in one's social network, media and overheard speech by people who are not part of one's social network.

Longitudinal design
A study that aims to collect **data** about the same **subjects** at different times.

Maturation
The process of physical, neurological and cognitive development that unfolds as babies grow older.

MFLA
See **Monolingual First Language Acquisition**.

Mean Length of Utterance (MLU)
The average length of the **utterances** that a person says during a particular time frame. Length can be measured in **morphemes** or **words**.

Methodological issues
Issues relating to the various aspects of an empirical (**data**-based) scientific study such as **subject** selection, data collection methods, coding of the material, analysis and reporting.

Mixed utterances
Utterances with **words** or **morphemes** from two languages.

Modeling
Part of **socialization**; process whereby someone is taught something indirectly by observing a particular behavior.

Monolingual First Language Acquisition (MFLA)
The situation where children learn to understand and speak just one language, since they are hearing only one language (**Language 1**) from birth.

Morphemes
Grammatically or referentially meaningful parts of **words** (an entire word may consist of just one morpheme).

Morphology
The study of how **words** are constructed; the construction of words.

Morphosyntactic development
The development in young children of the ability to construct **words** and **sentences**.

(Morpho)syntax
(the study of) how **sentences** are put together.

Mutism
A socially problematic condition where people who clearly understand language and who have reached an age at which they would be expected to speak do not actually speak.

Mutual Exclusivity Bias
A lexical learning strategy which leads children to assume that every class of objects can only have one name.

Glossary

Native contrasts
Different speech sounds that are distinct **phonemes** in a particular language (also called phonemic contrasts).

Naturalistic study
In the context of child language research this is a study of a child's communicative behavior as it would most likely occur if your purpose wasn't to study it.

Non-native contrasts
Different speech sounds that are not distinct **phonemes** in a particular language.

Noun
A type of **word** that typically refers to classes of perceivable entities (and to a multitude of other things such as abstract ideas). Examples from English are 'miracle', 'beauty', 'table', 'girl'.

Object
Sentence element that is closely connected to the **verb** of a **sentence** and usually expresses what or who is affected by that which is said in the verb. There are many sentences without objects.

Observational study
In the context of child language research this is a study in which you record children's communicative behavior. You can do this simply by taking notes, or by using audio and video recordings.

Oral variety
The particular regionally and/or socially determined spoken form of a particular language.

Overextension
The use of **words** in a way that includes much more than the common meaning, as in 'ball' to refer to any round object.

Parental rating instruments
Methodological tools that use evaluations or ratings by adults such as parents in order to assess children's language knowledge (an example is the **CDI**; see Chapters 3 and 6).

Particles
These **sentence elements** are often difficult to distinguish from **adverbials** but in general add important nuances of meaning to a situation expressed in the rest of the **sentence**.

Phonemes
Single speech sounds that can make for changes of meaning in a particular language. Phonemes are usually put between slashes, as for English /n/, for instance.

Phonetic transcriptions
Transcriptions of human speech that record the sounds produced. The level of detail can be quite high (narrow, more phonetic transcription) or less so (broad phonetic transcription). Phonetic transcriptions may be limited to **segments** (i.e. speech sounds or phones), or may also include suprasegmental information (e.g. the overall sound melody or intonation pattern of a word, or stress patterns) – see more on this in Chapter 5.

Phonological contrasts
Contrasts between **phonemes** (see also **native contrasts**).

Phonological development
The learning of the sound system of a language.

Phonological processes
Processes that from an adult point of view are used by children in attempting to produce speech segments and that involve mainly the **deletion** of particular **phonemes** or their substitution (compared to the adult form).

Phonotactics
The specific characteristics of a language that determine the structure of **syllables**, **consonant** clusters and **vowel** sequences. Phonotactics thus refers to the rules for the combination of **phonemes**. For instance, a sequence of /d/ and /n/ at the beginning of a word is not allowed in English, but is fine in Russian.

Pitch
The acoustic frequency of (speech) sounds.

Pitch contours
Variations in the frequency of speech sounds that are articulated in one breath.

Positive attitude
An internal, psychological orientation towards a particular object, phenomenon or person that is favorable and that guides behavior towards that object, phenomenon or person.

Pragmatic meaning
A meaning that mainly has to do with communicative effect and function (rather than naming or reference as such).

Pragmatics
Usually defined as the study of how language expresses communicative functions at the **utterance** or discourse level.

Pragmatic words
Words that do not really refer to a particular entity or process but that are used with an **interaction**al meaning, such as 'up!' or 'out!'. Pragmatic words are meant to trigger an action on the part of the interlocutor.

Production
Saying (producing) sounds, **words** or **sentences** that have meaning in a particular language.

Production vocabulary
The (number of) **words** that an individual is able to say.

Proficient speaker
A person who understands a language in most day-to-day circumstances and who speaks it well enough to be able to express most of what (s)he wants to say.

Pronouns
A type of **word** that can be used in a **sentence** instead of a **noun**.

Prosody
Used in this book to refer to the overall 'melody' of an **utterance** or combination of **syllables**.

Recruiting subjects
The process of selecting **subjects** for a study and getting them to agree to be part of the study.

Reduplicated babbling
Infants' repeated **production** of the same **vowel–consonant** combinations in one breath. Typical of the end of the first year of life.

Glossary

Reduplication
A **phonological process** whereby one **syllable** of an adult target **word** is repeated, as in 'toto' for 'chaussure' (shoe), where the first syllable, 'chau-' is repeated – here also with a substitution of the first **consonant** (example from Brulard & Carr, 2003: 188).

Referential
Intended to mainly just name something.

Relative frequency (of language input)
The proportion with which a particular language is addressed to a child (compared to another language or compared to **mixed utterances**).

SDH
See **Separate Development Hypothesis**.

Segments
See **speech segments**.

Semantic
That which has to do with meaning.

Sentence
It is impossible to formulate a definition of 'sentence' that all or even most linguists will agree on. I will use the term 'sentence' in this book to refer to **utterances** containing at least a **verb**-like element. For sake of simplicity, I here equate the notion sentence with that of 'clause'.

Sentence elements
The building blocks of **sentences** above the **word** level (e.g. the **object**, **adverbials**).

Separate Development Hypothesis (SDH)
Children regularly exposed to two separate languages from birth develop two distinct **morphosyntactic** systems.

Singlet
You know a singlet if you know just one member of a pair of **translation equivalents**, so only English 'word', for instance, rather than also French 'mot'.

Socialization
The process whereby people learn the cultural behaviors expected from them in the environments they live in.

Social words
Words that are used with an **interaction**al meaning, such as 'bye bye' and 'thank you' (there is some overlap with **pragmatic words**).

Speaking rate
Number of **words** or **utterances** spoken by a particular person within a particular time unit.

Speech segments
Consonants and **vowels**.

Stability (in early word production)
This refers to the fact that children who relative to others produce more **words** at age X also produce more words relative to others several months later. In other words, early good talkers (compared to others) are also good talkers later on.

Stop consonant
A **consonant** produced in such a way that the air flow from the lungs is momentarily stopped in the oral cavity. This is the case, for instance, for [b], [t] or [k].

Subject (grammatical term)
Again, a term that is impossible to correctly define. Usually it refers to a **sentence element** that in many languages expresses the topic that is being talked about. Not all **sentences** have subjects.

Subjects
Participants in a scientific study; the people that scientists study.

Substitution
In particular for **phonological** development: the use of a related **phoneme** instead of the one you would expect to hear from an adult. There are different kinds of substitutions (e.g. **consonant harmony**). An example of a substitution is saying 'fis' instead of 'fish'.

Syllables
Combinations of **consonants** and **vowels**.

Target child(ren)
The child(ren) that a study is about.

Target-like form
A form that sounds like one that the adults **interacting** with a child might use.

Transcript (or transcription)
A written record of previously audio or video recorded language use

Translation equivalent
A **word** that in the lives of young children adequately translates a word in the other language that children are hearing or speaking.

Trilingual acquisition
The learning of three languages in early childhood.

Trochaic stress
Initial stress on **words** with more than one **syllable** (e.g. English 'paper') (the opposite of **iambic stress**).

Truncation
As used here, the omission of **syllables** in a word compared to the adult target form, as in 'nana' for 'banana'.

Underextension
The use of **words** in a way that is much more restricted than the regular meaning, for example, when a child says 'bus' only for the bus she takes with her mother to go shopping, but not for other buses.

Uneven development
That is, between a **BFLA child**'s two languages: lack of parallel development, so the languages are used with different levels of proficiency.

Unilingual utterances
Utterances with **words** from one language only (both mono- and bilingual speakers can produce unilingual utterances).

Glossary

Upper Bound (UB)
The number of **morphemes** in the longest utterance in a **transcript**.

Utterances
Speech sounds usually produced in one breath as part of a conversation or monologue, however short. Utterances can be **sentences** but they need not be (for instance, babbling 'baba' or saying 'Yes' constitute utterances but not sentences; saying 'I'll do it' is an utterance that is also a sentence).

Verb
This is again a term that is very difficult to define correctly. It often refers to a **sentence element** that expresses an action or state. It is a central part of **sentences**. The term 'verb' also refers to what class of **word** a word is.

Verbal interaction
Communication between two people that involves the use of language.

Vocabulary spurt
A sudden increase in early **word** knowledge (either in **comprehension** or in **production**).

Vocalization
A sound made by human **articulators** that is not physiologically determined. Burping, for instance, does not normally count as a vocalization. Although in principle verbal **utterances** are vocalizations, the term vocalization usually implies an absence of recognizable speech.

Voice (in phonology)
Characteristic of speech sounds in terms of the degree of vibration of the vocal cords.

Voiceless sound
A sound produced without vibration of the vocal cords.

Voice onset time (VOT)
The time period between the release of air just after the **production** of a **stop consonant** and the moment that the vocal cords start to vibrate (or the other way round).

Vowels
Speech sounds that are produced without restricting the air flow coming from the vocal cords and that do not involve a clear movement of the oral cavity (as is the case for **diphthongs**).

Word
It is impossible to really define what a word is. In this book I loosely define it as a part of language structure that typically you would find as a lemma in a dictionary (since all the languages I am referring to have a written form, the question of what would happen for unwritten languages does not arise).

Word roots
Words that have a dictionary meaning but that cannot be used by themselves (see Box 2.6 for more explanation).

Bibliography

Abudarham, S. (1980). The role of the speech therapist in the assessment of language-learning potential and proficiency of children with dual language (DL) systems or backgrounds. *Journal of Multilingual and Multicultural Development*, 1, 187–206.

Ada, A.F. & Baker, C. (2001). *Guía para padres y maestros de niños bilingües*. Clevedon: Multilingual Matters.

Águila, E., Ramon, M., Pons, F. & Bosch, L. (2005). Efecto de la exposición bilingüe sobre el desarrollo léxico inicial. In A. Mayor Cinca, B. Zubiauz de Pedro & E. Díez-Villoria (eds), *Estudios sobre la adquisición del lenguaje* (pp. 676–692). Salamanca: Universidad de Salamanca.

Águila, E., Ramon-Casas, M., Pons, F. & Bosch, L. (2007). La medida del léxico productivo inicial: aplicación de un cuestionario para la población bilingüe. In E. Diez-Itra (ed.), *Estudios de desarrollo del lenguaje y educación* (pp. 163–172). Oviedo, Spain: ICE Monografiasde Aula Abierta, 32.

Akhtar, N. (2005). The robustness of learning through overhearing. *Developmental Science, 8 (2)*, 199–209.

Allen, S. (2007). The future of Inuktitut in the face of majority languages: Bilingualism or language shift? *Applied Psycholinguistics, 28*, 515–536.

Allen, S., Genesee, F., Fish, S. & Crago, M. (2002). Patterns of code mixing in English–Inuktitut bilinguals. In M. Andronis, C. Ball, H. Elston & S. Neuvel (eds), *Proceedings of the 37th Annual Meeting of the Chicago Linguistic Society* (Vol. 2, pp. 171–188). Chicago, IL: Chicago Linguistic Society.

Almgren, M. & Barreña, A. (2000). Bilingual acquisition and separation of linguistic codes: Ergativity in Basque versus accusativity in Spanish. In K. Nelson, A. Aksu-Koç & C. Johnson (eds) *Children's language* (Volume 11). Mahwah, NJ: Lawrence Erlbaum Associates.

Almgren, M. & Idiazabal, I. (2001). Past tense verb forms, discourse context and input features in bilingual and monolingual acquisition of Basque and Spanish. In J. Cenoz & F. Genesee (eds), *Trends in bilingual acquisition* (pp. 107–130). Amsterdam/Philadelphia: John Benjamins.

Álvarez, E. (1999). The role of language dominance in two narratives of a 7-year-old Spanish/English bilingual. *AILE (Acquisition et Interaction en Langue Etrangère), 1*, 83–95.

Álvarez, E. (2003). Character introduction in two languages: Its development in the stories of a Spanish–English bilingual child age 6;11–10;11. *Bilingualism: Language and Cognition, 6(3)*, 227–243.

Álvarez, E. (2008). The simultaneous development of narratives in English and Spanish. In Ca. Pérez-Vidal, M. Juan-Garau & A. Bel (eds), *A portrait of the young in the new multilingual Spain. Issues in the acquisition of two or more languages in multilingual environments* (pp. 159–182). Clevedon: Multilingual Matters.

Anderson, R.T. (2001). Lexical morphology and verb use in child first language loss: A preliminary case study investigation. *International Journal of Bilingualism, 5(4)*, 377–401.

Anselmi, D., Tomasello, T. & Acunzo, M. (1986). Young children's responses to neutral and specific contingent queries. *Journal of Child Language, 13*, 135–144.

Argyri, E. & Sorace, A. (2007). Crosslinguistic influence and language dominance in older bilingual children. *Bilingualism: Language and Cognition, 10*, 79–99.

Arias, R. & Lakshmanan, U. (2005). Code switching in a Spanish–English bilingual child: A communication resource. In J. Cohen, K.T. McAlister, K. Rolstad & J. MacSwan (eds), *ISB4: Proceedings of the 4th International Symposium on Bilingualism* (pp. 94–109). Somerville, MA: Cascadilla Press.

Au, T., Oh, J., Knightly, L., Jun, S. & Romo, L. (2008). Salvaging a childhood language. *Journal of Memory and Language, 58,* 998–1011.

Baetens Beardsmore, H. (1982). *Bilingualism. Basic principles.* Clevedon: Tieto Ltd (which later became Multilingual Matters).

Baker, A. (2006). Taalontwikkelingsstoornissen ten gevolge van visusproblemen [Developmental language disorders in children with sight problems]. In H.M. Peters (ed.), *Handboek Stem-, spraak- en taalpathologie [Handbook Voice, speech and language pathology]* (pp. 1–16). Houten: Bohn Stafleu en van Loghum.

Baker, A. & van den Bogaerde, B. (2008). Codemixing in sign and words in input to and output from children. In C. Plaza Pust & E. Morales Lopez (eds), Sign bilingualism: Language development, interaction and maintenance in language contact situations (pp. 1–28). Amsterdam/Philadephia: John Benjamins.

Baker, C. (2007). *A parents' & teachers' guide to bilingualism* (3rd revised edition). Clevedon: Multilingual Matters.

Ball, M.J., Müller, N. & Munro, S. (2001). The acquisition of the rhotic consonants by Welsh–English bilingual children. *International Journal of Bilingualism, 5(1),* 71–86.

Barac, R., Bialystok, E., Blaye, A., & Poulin-Dubois, D. (2008). Word learning and executive functioning in young monolingual and bilingual children. Poster presented at IASCL 2008, The XI Congress of the International Association for the Study of Child Language, Edinburgh, United Kingdom, July 28–August 1.

Barlow, J. (2002). Error patterns and transfer in Spanish–English bilingual phonological development. In B. Skarabela, S. Fish & A.H. Do (eds), *Proceedings of the 26th Boston University Conference on Language Development* (pp. 60–71). Somerville, MA: Cascadilla Press.

Barnes, J.D. (2006). *Early trilingualism. A focus on questions.* Clevedon: Multilingual Matters.

Barreña, A. (1997). Desarrollo diferenciado de sistemas gramaticales en un niño vasco-español bilingüe. In A. Pérez-Leroux & W. Glass (eds), *Contemporary perspectives on the acquisition of Spanish. Volume 1: Developing grammars* (pp. 55–74). Somerville, MA: Cascadilla Press.

Barreña, A. (2001). Grammar differentiation in early bilingual acquisition: Subordination structures in Spanish and Basque. In M. Almgren, A. Barreña, M.J. Ezeizabarrena, I. Idiazabal & B. MacWhinney (eds), *Research on Child Language Acquisition. Proceedings of the 8th Conference of the International Association for the Study of Child Language* (pp. 78–94). Somerville, MA: Cascadilla Press.

Barreña, A. & Almgren, M. (2000). Marcas de sujetos y objetos en euskara y español y separación de códigos lingüísticos. *Infancia y Aprendizaje, 91,* 31–54.

Barreña, A., Ezeizabarrena, Mª.J. & García, I. (2008). Influence of the linguistic environment on the development of the lexicon and grammar of Basque bilingual children. In C. Pérez-Vidal, M. Juan-Garau & A. Bel (eds), *A portrait of the young in the new multilingual Spain. Issues in the acquisition of two or more languages in multilingual environments* (pp. 86–110). Clevedon: Multilingual Matters.

Barrett, M. (1995). Early lexical development. In P. Fletcher & B. MacWhinney (eds), *The handbook of child language* (pp. 362–392). Oxford: Blackwell.

Barron-Hauwaert, S. (2004). *Language strategies for bilingual families.* Clevedon: Multilingual Matters.

Barton, M. & Tomasello, M. (1994). The rest of the family: the role of fathers and siblings in early language development. In C. Gallaway & B. Richards (eds), *Input and interaction in language acquisition* (pp. 109–134). Cambridge: Cambridge University Press.

Bates, E. (1993). Comprehension and production in early language development: Comments on Savage-Rumbaugh et al. *Monographs of the Society for Research in Child Development Serial No. 233, 58,* 222–242.

Bates, E., Dale, P. & Thal, D. (1995). Individual differences and their implications for theories of language development. In P. Fletcher & B. MacWhinney (eds), *Handbook of child language* (pp. 96–151). London: Blackwell.

Bayley, R., Schecter, S.R. & Torres-Ayala, B. (1996). Strategies for bilingual maintenance: Case studies of Mexican-origin families in Texas. *Linguistics and Education, 8,* 389–408.

Behrens, H. & Gut, U. (2005). The relationship between syntactic and prosodic organisation in early multiword speech. *Journal of Child Language, 32,* 1–34.

Bentahila, A. & Davies, E. (1994). Two languages, three varieties: A look at some bilingual children's code-switching. In G. Extra & L. Verhoeven (eds), *The cross-linguistic study of bilingual development* (pp. 113–128). Amsterdam: North-Holland.

Berger-Morales, J., Salustri, M. & Gilkerson, J. (2005). Root infinitives in the spontaneous speech of two bilingual children: Evidence for separate grammatical systems. In J. Cohen, K.T. McAlister, K. Rolstad & J. MacSwan (eds), *ISB4: Proceedings of the 4th International Symposium on Bilingualism* (pp. 296–305). Somerville, MA: Cascadilla Press.

Berman, R. (1979). The re-emergence of a bilingual: a case study of a Hebrew–English speaking child. *Working Papers on Bilingualism, 19,* 157–180.

Berman, R. (ed.) (2004). *Language development across childhood and adolescence.* Amsterdam/Philadephia: John Benjamins.

Berman, R. & Slobin, D.I. (1994). *Relating events in narrative: A crosslinguistic. developmental study.* Hillsdale, NJ: Lawrence Erlbaum Associates.

Bernardini, P. (2003). Child and adult acquisition of word order in the Italian DP. In N. Müller (ed.), *(In)vulnerable domains in multilingualism* (pp. 41–81). Amsterdam/Philadelphia: John Benjamins.

Bialystok, E. (2001). *Bilingualism in development: Language, literacy, and cognition.* Cambridge: Cambridge University Press.

Bialystok, E. (2005). Consequences of bilingualism for cognitive development. In J. Kroll & A. de Groot (eds), *The handbook of bilingualism* (pp. 417–432). Oxford: Oxford University Press.

Bialystok, E. (2007). Cognitive effects of bilingualism: How linguistic experience leads to cognitive change. *International Journal of Bilingual Education and Bilingualism, 10,* 210–223.

Bloom, L. (1993). *The transition from infancy to language: Acquiring the power of expression.* Cambridge: Cambridge University Press.

Bolonyai, A. (2007). (In)vulnerable agreement in incomplete bilingual L1 learners. *International Journal of Bilingualism, 11(1),* 3–23.

Bonnesen, M. (2007). V2 ou V3? La position du verbe fléchi en français chez des enfants bilingues français-allemand. *Aile: Acquisition et Interaction en Langue Etrangère, 25,* 103–127.

Bonnesen, M. (2008). On the "vulnerability" of the left periphery in French/German balanced bilingual language acquisition. In P. Guijarro-Fuentes, M.P. Larrañaga & J. Clibbens (eds), *First language acquisition of morphology and syntax. Perspectives across languages and learners* (pp. 161–182). Amsterdam/Philadelphia: John Benjamins.

Bonnesen, M. (to appear). The status of the "weaker" language in unbalanced French/German bilingual language acquisition. *Bilingualism: Language and Cognition.*

Bornstein, M.H. (2002). Parenting infants. In M.H. Bornstein (ed.), *Handbook of parenting Vol. 1 Children and parenting* (2nd edition) (pp. 3–43). Mahwah, NJ: Lawrence Erlbaum Associates.

Bornstein, M.H. & Lamb, M.E. (2008). *Development in infancy: An introduction* (5th edition). Mahwah, NJ: Lawrence Erlbaum Associates.

Bornstein, M.H. & Cote, L. R. with Maital, S., Painter, K., Park, S.-Y., Pascual, L., Pêcheux, M.-G., Ruel, J., Venuti, P. & Vyt, A. (2004). Cross-linguistic analysis of vocabulary in young children: Spanish, Dutch, French, Hebrew, Italian, Korean, and American English. *Child Development, 75,* 1115–1139.

Bornstein, M.H., De Houwer, A., Park, Y., Suwalsky, J.T. & Haynes, O.M. (in preparation). Belgium: Monolingual versus bilingual rearing from infancy. In M.H. Bornstein (ed.), Infancy, parenting, culture: Argentina, Belgium, Israel, Italy, The United States. SRCD Monograph.

Bornstein, M.H., Haynes, O.M. & Painter, K.M. (1998). Sources of child vocabulary competence: A multivariate model. *Journal of Child Language, 25,* 367–393.

Bornstein, M.H., Haynes, O.M., O'Reilly, A.W. & Painter, K.M. (1996). Solitary and collaborative pretense play in early childhood: Sources of individual variation in the development of representational competence. *Child Development, 67,* 2910–2929.

Bornstein, M.H., Putnick, D.L. & De Houwer, A. (2006). Child vocabulary across the second year: Stability and continuity for reporter comparisons and a cumulative score. *First Language, 26,* 299–316.

Bosch, L. & Sebastián-Gallés, N. (1997). Native-language recognition abilities in 4-month-old infants from monolingual and bilingual environments. *Cognition, 65,* 33–69.

Bosch, L. & Sebastián-Gallés, N. (2001a). Early language differentiation in bilingual infants. In J. Cenoz & F. Genesee (eds), *Trends in bilingual acquisition* (pp. 71–93). Amsterdam/Philadelphia: John Benjamins.

Bosch, L. & Sebastián-Gallés, N. (2001b). Evidence of early language discrimination abilities in infants from bilingual environments. *Infancy, 2,* 29–49.

Bosch, L. & Sebastián-Gallés, N. (2003). Simultaneous bilingualism and the perception of a language-specific vowel contrast in the first year of life. *Language and Speech, 46,* 217–243.

Bosch, L. & Sebastián-Gallés, N. (2005). Developmental changes in the discrimination of vowel contrasts in bilingual infants. In J. Cohen, K.T. McAlister, K. Rolstad & J. MacSwan (eds), *ISB4:*

Proceedings of the 4th International Symposium on Bilingualism (pp. 354–363). Somerville, MA: Cascadilla Press.

Bowerman, M. (1985). What shapes children's grammar? In D. Slobin (ed.), *The crosslinguistic study of language acquisition* (pp. 1257–1320). Hillsdale, NJ: Lawrence Erlbaum Associates.

Braunwald, S. & Brislin, R. (1979). The diary method updated. In E. Ochs & B. Schieffelin (eds), *Developmental pragmatics* (pp. 21–42). New York: Academic Press.

Breznitz, Z. & Sherman, T. (1987). Speech patterning of natural discourse of well and depressed mothers and their young children. *Child Development, 58(2),* 395–400.

Bridges, K. (2008). Home language use and family structure as influences on bilingual development: The role of siblings. Poster presented at IASCL 2008, The XI Congress of the International Association for the Study of Child Language, Edinburgh, United Kingdom, July 28–August 1.

Brohy, C. (1992). *Das Sprachverhalten zweisprachiger Paare und Familien in Freiburg/Fribourg (Schweiz).* Germanistica Friburgensia, 14. Freiburg, Schweiz: Universitätsverslag Freiburg.

Brown, R. (1973). *A first language. The early stages.* Cambridge: Harvard University Press.

Brulard, I. & Carr, P. (2003). French–English bilingual acquisition of phonology: One production system or two? *International Journal of Bilingualism, 7(2),* 177–202.

Bunta, F. & Ingram, D. (2007). The acquisition of speech rhythm by bilingual Spanish- and English-speaking 4- and 5-year-old children. *Journal of Speech, Language, and Hearing Research, 50,* 999–1014.

Burns, T., Werker, J.T. & McVie, K. (2003). Development of phonetic categories in infants raised in bilingual and monolingual environments. In B. Beachley, A. Brown & F. Conlin (eds), *BUCLD 27: Proceedings of the 27th annual Boston University Conference on Language Development* (pp. 120–128). Boston, MA: Cascadilla Press.

Burns, T., Yoshida, K., Hill, K. & Werker, J.T. (2007). The development of phonetic representation in bilingual and monolingual infants. *Applied Psycholinguistics, 28,* 455–474.

Byers-Heinlein, K., Werker, J.T. & Burns, T. (2008). Language preference and discrimination in newborns with prenatal bilingual exposure. Poster presented at the XVIth International Conference on Infant Studies, Vancouver, March 27–29.

Caldas, S. (2006). *Raising bilingual–biliterate children in monolingual cultures.* Clevedon: Multilingual Matters.

Caldas, S.J. & Caron-Caldas, S. (2000). The influence of family, school and community on bilingual preference: Results from a Louisiana/Québec case study. *Applied Psycholinguistics, 21,* 365–381.

Cantone, K.F. (2007). *Code-switching in bilingual children.* Dordrecht: Springer.

Cantone, K.F. & Müller, N. (2005). Codeswitching at the interface of language-specific lexicons and the computational system. *International Journal of Bilingualism, 9(2),* 205–225.

Carey, S. (1978). The child as word learner. In M. Halle, J. Bresnan & G.A. Miller (eds), *Linguistic theory and psychological reality* (pp. 264–293). Cambridge, MA: MIT Press.

Caselli, M.C., Casadio, P. & Bates, E. (1999). A comparison of the transition from first words to grammar in English and Italian. *Journal of Child Language, 26,* 69–111.

Celce-Murcia, M. (1978). Phonological factors in vocabulary acquisition: A case study of a two-year-old, English–French bilingual. In E. Hatch (ed.), *Second language acquisition. A book of readings* (pp. 39–53). Rowley, MA: Newbury House.

Chang-Smith, M. (2008). 2L1 Acquisition of the determiner phrase by a simultaneous Mandarin–English bilingual. Poster presented at IASCL 2008, The XI Congress of the International Association for the Study of Child Language, Edinburgh, United Kingdom, July 28–August 1.

Chapman, R. (2000). Children's language learning: An interactionist perspective. *Journal of Child Psychology and Psychiatry, 41(1),* 33–54.

Choi, S. (1999). Early development of verb structures and caregiver input in Korean: Two case studies. *International Journal of Bilingualism, 3(2–3),* 241–265.

Choi, S. & Gopnik, A. (1995). Early acquisition of verbs in Korean: A cross-linguistic study. *Journal of Child Language, 22,* 497–529.

Chomsky, N. (1980). *Rules and representations.* Oxford: Basil Blackwell.

Clark, E.V. (1978). Awareness of language: Some evidence from what children say and do. In A. Sinclair, R. Jarvella & W. Levelt (eds), *The child's conception of language* (pp. 17–43). Berlin: Springer-Verlag.

Clark, E.V. (1987). The principle of contrast: A constraint on language acquisition. In B. MacWhinney (ed.), *Mechanisms of language acquisition* (pp. 1–33). Hillsdale, NJ: Lawrence Erlbaum Associates.

Clark, E.V. (1993). *The lexicon in acquisition.* Cambridge: Cambridge University Press.

Clark, E.V. (1995). Later lexical development and word formation. In: P. Fletcher & B. MacWhinney (eds), *The handbook of child language* (pp. 393–412). Oxford: Blackwell.

Clark, E.V. (2003). *First language acquisition.* Cambridge: Cambridge University Press.

Clark, E.V. (2006). Color, reference, and expertise in language acquisition. *Journal of Experimental Child Psychology, 94,* 339–343.

Clark, E.V. (2007). Young children's uptake of new words in conversation. *Language in Society, 36,* 157–182.

Clark, E.V. & Hecht, B.F. (1983). Comprehension, production, and language acquisition. *Annual Review of Psychology, 34,* 325–349.

Clark, J. & Yallop, C. (1995). *An introduction to phonetics and phonology* (2nd edition). London: Blackwell.

Clyne, M. (1987). "Don't you get bored speaking only English?" Expressions of metalinguistic awareness in a bilingual child. In R. Steele & T. Threadgold (eds), *Language topics. Essays in honour of Michael Halliday* (pp. 85–103). Amsterdam/Philadelphia: John Benjamins.

Collins, A.W., Maccoby, E.E., Steinberg, L., Hetherington, M.E. & Bornstein, M.H. (2000). Contemporary research on parenting: The case for nature and nurture. *American Psychologist, 55(2),* 218–232.

Comeau, L. & Genesee, F. (2001). Bilingual children's repair strategies during dyadic communication. In J. Cenoz & F. Genesee (eds), *Trends in bilingual acquisition* (pp. 231–256). Amsterdam/Philadelphia: John Benjamins.

Comeau, L., Genesee, F. & Lapaquette, L. (2003). The Modeling Hypothesis and child bilingual codemixing. *International Journal of Bilingualism, 7(2),* 113–126.

Comeau, L., Genesee, F. & Mendelson, M. (2007). Bilingual children's repairs of breakdowns in communication. *Journal of Child Language, 34,* 159–174.

Comeau, L., Genesee, F., Nicoladis, E. & Vrakas, G. (1997). Can young bilingual children identify their language choice as a cause of breakdown in communication? In E. Hughes, M. Hughes & A. Greenhill (eds), *Proceedings of the 21th annual Boston University Conference on Language Development* (pp. 79–90). Somerville, MA: Cascadilla Press.

Conboy, B.T. & Mills, D.L. (2006). Two languages, one developing brain: Event-related potentials to words in bilingual toddlers. *Developmental Science, 9,* F1–F12.

Conboy, B.T. & Thal, D. (2006). Ties between the lexicon and grammar: Cross-sectional and longitudinal studies of bilingual toddlers. *Child Development, 77,* 712–735.

Conboy, B., Rivera-Gaxiola, M., Klarman, L., Aksoylu, E. & Kuhl, P.K. (2005). Associations between native and nonnative speech sound discrimination and language development at the end of the first year. In A. Brugos, M.R. Clark-Cotton & S. Ha (eds), *Supplement to the Proceedings of the 29th Boston University Conference on Language Development* (available online only, at http://www.bu.edu/linguistics/APPLIED/BUCLD/supp29.html).

Conboy, B.T., Rivera-Gaxiola, M., Silva-Pereyra, J. & Kuhl, P.K. (2008). Event-related potential studies of early language processing at the phoneme, word, and sentence levels. In A.D. Friederici & T. Guillaume (eds), *Early language development. Bridging brain and behaviour* (pp. 23–64). Amsterdam/Philadelphia: John Benjamins.

Cortés, S., Lleó, C. & Benet, A. (2008). The acquisition of Catalan vowel contrasts by bilingual children in two districts of Barcelona. Poster presented at IASCL 2008, The XI Congress of the International Association for the Study of Child Language, Edinburgh, United Kingdom, July 28–August 1.

Cromdal, J. (1999). Childhood bilingualism and metalinguistic skills: Analysis and control in young Swedish–English bilinguals. *Applied Psycholinguistics, 20,* 1–20.

Cruz-Ferreira, M. (2006). *Three is a crowd? Acquiring Portuguese in a trilingual environment.* Clevedon: Multilingual Matters.

Crystal, D. (1974). Review of Roger Brown's 'A first language'. *Journal of Child Language, 1,* 289–334.

Cunningham-Andersson, U. & Andersson, S. (2004). *Growing up with two languages. A practical guide* (2nd edition). London: Routledge.

David, A. & Li, W. (2003). To what extent is code-switching dependent on a bilingual child's lexical development? *Sociolinguistica, 18,* 1–12.

David, A. & Li, W. (2005). The composition of the bilingual lexicon. In J. Cohen, K.T. McAlister, K. Rolstad & J. MacSwan (eds), *ISB4: Proceedings of the 4th International Symposium on Bilingualism* (pp. 594–607). Somerville, MA: Cascadilla Press.

David, A. & Li, W. (2008). Individual differences in the lexical development of French–English bilingual children. *International Journal of Bilingualism and Bilingual Education, 11,* 1–21.

Davidson, D., Jergovic, D., Imami, Z. & Theodos, V. (1997). Monolingual and bilingual children's use of the mutual exclusivity constraint. *Journal of Child Language, 24,* 3–24.

de Boysson-Bardies, B. & Vihman, M.M. (1991). Adaptation to language: Evidence from babbling and first words in four languages. *Language, 67,* 297–319.

de Boysson-Bardies, B., Sagart, L. & Durand, C. (1984). Discernible differences in the babbling of infants according to target language. *Journal of Child Language, 11,* 1–15.

De Houwer, A. (1983). Some aspects of the simultaneous acquisition of Dutch and English by a three-year-old child. *Nottingham Linguistic Circular, 12,* 106–129.

De Houwer, A. (1990). *The acquisition of two languages from birth: A case study.* Cambridge: Cambridge University Press.

De Houwer, A. (1994). The Separate Development Hypothesis: method and implications. In G. Extra & L. Verhoeven (eds), *The cross-linguistic study of bilingual development* (pp. 39–50). Amsterdam: North-Holland.

De Houwer, A. (1995a). Bilingual language acquisition. In P. Fletcher & B. MacWhinney (eds), *Handbook of child language* (pp. 219–250). London: Blackwell.

De Houwer, A. (1995b). Alternance codique intra-phrastique chez des jeunes enfants bilingues. *AILE (Acquisition et Interaction en Langue Etrangère), 6,* 39–64.

De Houwer, A. (1997). The role of input in the acquisition of past verb forms in English and Dutch: evidence from a bilingual child. In E. Clark (ed.), *Proceedings of the 28th Stanford Child Language Research Forum* (pp. 153–162). Stanford, CA: CSLI.

De Houwer, A. (1998). By way of introduction: Methods in studies of bilingual first language acquisition. *International Journal of Bilingualism, 2(3),* 249–263.

De Houwer, A. (1999). Environmental factors in early bilingual development: the role of parental beliefs and attitudes. In G. Extra & L. Verhoeven (eds), *Bilingualism and migration* (pp. 75–95). Berlin: Mouton de Gruyter.

De Houwer, A. (2000). Children's linguistic environments: a first impression. In M. Beers, B. van den Bogaerde, G. Bol, J. de Jong & C. Rooijmans (eds), *From sound to sentence: Studies on first language acquisition* (pp. 57–68). Groningen: Centre for Language and Cognition.

De Houwer, A. (2002a). Comparing monolingual and bilingual acquisition. *Alkalmazott Nyelvtudomány [Hungarian Journal of Applied Linguistics], II,* 5–19.

De Houwer, A. (2002b). Uneven development in bilingual acquisition. Keynote lecture, Joint meeting of the IASCL and the SRCLD, Madison, WI, USA, July 16–21.

De Houwer, A. (2003). Home languages spoken in officially monolingual Flanders: A survey. *Plurilingua, 24,* 71–87.

De Houwer, A. (2004). *A. DeHouwer Corpus.* Pittsburgh, PA: Talkbank (can be downloaded from http://childes.psy.cmu.edu).

De Houwer, A. (2005). Early bilingual acquisition: focus on morphosyntax and the Separate Development Hypothesis. In J. Kroll & A. de Groot (eds), *The handbook of bilingualism* (pp. 30–48). Oxford: Oxford University Press.

De Houwer, A. (2006). Bilingual development in the early years. In K. Brown (ed.), *Encyclopedia of Languages and Linguistics* (2nd edition) (pp. 781–787). Amsterdam: Elsevier.

De Houwer, A. (2007). Parental language input patterns and children's bilingual use. *Applied Psycholinguistics, 28(3),* 411–424.

De Houwer, A. & Gillis, S. (1985). Language and communication during the second year of life. *Journal of Pragmatics, 9,* 683–704.

De Houwer, A. & Gillis, S. (1998). Dutch child language: an overview. In S. Gillis & A. De Houwer (eds), *The acquisition of Dutch* (pp. 1–100). Amsterdam/Philadelphia: John Benjamins.

De Houwer, A., Bornstein, M.H. & De Coster, S. (2006a). Early understanding of two words for the same thing: A CDI study of lexical comprehension in infant bilinguals. *International Journal of Bilingualism, 10(3),* 331–347.

De Houwer, A., Bornstein, M.H. & Leach, D.B. (2005). Assessing early communicative ability: a cross-reporter cumulative score for the MacArthur CDI. *Journal of Child Language, 32,* 735–758.

De Houwer, A., Bornstein, M.H. & Putnick, D.L. (2006b). Bilingual infants know more words: A monolingual–bilingual comparison of lexical development at 13 months using the CDI. Poster presented at the Language Acquisition and Bilingualism Conference, Toronto, Canada, May 4–7.

De Houwer, A., Bornstein, M.H. & Putnick, D.L. (2007). The relation between lexical comprehension and production: evidence from bilingual infants and toddlers. Poster presented at the Biennal Meeting of the Society for Research on Child Development, Boston, MA, USA, March 29–April 1.

Deprez, C. (1995). *Les enfants bilingues: Langues et familles.* Paris: Didier.

Deuchar, M. (1992). Can government and binding theory account for language acquisition? In C.M. Vide (ed.), *Lenguajes Naturales y Lenguajes Formales VIII* (pp. 273–279). Barcelona: University of Barcelona.

Deuchar, M. & Clark, A. (1996). Early bilingual acquisition of the voicing contrast in English and Spanish. *Journal of Phonetics, 24,* 351–365.

Deuchar, M. & Muntz, R. (2003). Factors accounting for code-mixing in an early developing bilingual. In N. Müller (ed.), *(In)vulnerable domains in multilingualism* (pp. 161–190), Amsterdam/Philadelphia: John Benjamins.

Deuchar, M. & Quay, S. (1999). Language choice in the earliest utterances: A case study with methodological implications. *Journal of Child Language, 26,* 461–475.

Deuchar, M. & Quay, S. (2000). *Bilingual acquisition: Theoretical implications of a case study.* Oxford: Oxford University Press.

Deuchar, M. & Vihman, M.M. (2005). A radical approach to early mixed utterances. *International Journal of Bilingualism, 9(2),* 137–157.

Diesendruck, G. (2007). Mechanisms of word learning. In E. Hoff & M. Shatz (eds), *Blackwell handbook of language development* (pp. 257–276). Oxford: Blackwell.

Dixon, J.A. & Marchman, V.A. (2007). Grammar and the lexicon: Developmental ordering in language acquisition. *Child Development, 78(1),* 190–212.

Dore, J., Franklin, M.B., Miller, R.T. & Ramer, A.L.H. (1976). Transitional phenomena in early language acquisition. *Journal of Child Language, 3,* 13–28.

Dunn, L.M. & Dunn, M.L. (1981). *Peabody Picture Vocabulary Test – Revised Manual.* Circle Pines, MN: American Guidance Service.

Dunn, L.M., Thériault-Whalen, C.M., & Dunn, M.L. (1993). *Echelle de vocabulaire en images Peabody.* Toronto: Psycan.

Ekmekçi, Ö. (1994). Bilingual development of English preschool children in Turkey. In G. Extra & L. Verhoeven (eds), *The cross-linguistic study of bilingualism* (pp. 99–112). Amsterdam: North-Holland.

Elbers, L. & Josi, T. (1985). Play pen monologues: the interplay of words and babbles in the first words period. *Journal of Child Language, 12*, 551–565.

Elbers, L. & van Loon-Vervoorn, A. (1998). Acquiring the lexicon. Evidence from Dutch research. In S. Gillis & A. De Houwer (eds), *The acquisition of Dutch* (pp. 301–377). Amsterdam/Philadelphia: John Benjamins.

Elwert, T.W. (1973). *Das zweisprachige Individuum und andere Aufsätze zur romanischen und allgemeinen Sprachwissenschaft*. Wiesbaden: Franz Steiner Verlag.

Ervin-Tripp, S. (1974). Is second language learning like the first? *TESOL Quarterly*, 111–127.

Ervin-Tripp, S. & Reyes, I. (2005). Child codeswitching and adult content contrasts. *International Journal of Bilingualism, 9(1)*, 85–102.

Evans, M. (1987). Linguistic accommodation in a bilingual family: one perspective on the language acquisition of a bilingual child being raised in a monolingual community. *Journal of Multilingual and Multicultural Development, 8*, 231–235.

Extra, G., Aarts, R., van der Avoird, T., Broeder, P. & Yağmur, K. (2002). *De andere talen van Nederland. Thuis en op school [The other languages of the Netherlands. At home and at school]*. Bussum: Uitgeverij Coutinho.

Ezeiabarrena, M. (2003). Null subjects and optional infinitives in Basqué. In N. Müller (ed.). *(In) vulnerable domains in multilingualism* (pp. 83–106). Amsterdam/Philadelphia: John Benjamins.

Ezeizabarrena, M. & Larrañaga, M. (1996). Ergativity in Basque: a problem for language acquisition? *Linguistics, 34*, 955–991.

Fantini, A. (1985). *Language acquisition of a bilingual child: a sociolinguistic perspective (to age ten)*. Clevedon: Multilingual Matters.

Fennell, C.T., Byers-Heinlein, K. & Werker, J.F. (2007). Using speech sounds to guide word learning: The case of bilingual infants. *Child Development, 78(5)*, 1510–1525.

Fenson, L., Dale, P., Reznick, S., Bates, E., Thal, D. & Pethick, S. (1994). Variability in early communicative development. *Monographs of the Society for Research in Child Development, 59*, (5, Serial No. 242).

Fenson, L., Dale, P., Reznick, S., Thal, D., Bates, E., Hartung, J., Pethick, S. & Reilly, J. (1993). *MacArthur Communicative Development Inventories: User's guide and technical manual*. San Diego, CA: Singular Publishing Group, Inc.

Fenson, L., Marchman, V.A., Thal, D., Dale, P., Reznick, S. & Bates, E. (2006). *MacArthur-Bates Communicative Development Inventories (CDIs)* (2nd edition). Baltimore, MD: Brookes Publishing.

Fernald, A. (2006). When infants hear two languages: Interpreting research on early speech perception by bilingual children. In P. McCardle & E. Hoff (eds), *Childhood bilingualism. Research on infancy through school age* (pp. 19–29). Clevedon: Multilingual Matters.

Finnegan, R. (2005). *Communicating. The multiple modes of human interconnection*. London: Routledge.

Floor, P. & Akhtar, N. (2006). Can 18-month-old infants learn words by listening in on conversations? *Infancy, 9*, 327–339.

Fortescue, M. (1984). Learning to speak Greenlandic: a case study of a two-year-old's morphology in a polysynthetic language. *First Language, 5(14)*, 101–112.

Fox, A. (2000). *Prosodic features and prosodic structure: The phonology of suprasegmentals*. Oxford: Oxford University Press.

Frank, I. & Poulin-Dubois, D. (2002). Young monolingual and bilingual children's responses to violation of the Mutual Exclusivity Principle. *International Journal of Bilingualism, 6(2)*, 125–146.

Friederici, A.D. & Thierry, G. (eds) (2008). Early language development. *Bridging brain and behaviour*. Amsterdam/Philadelphia: John Benjamins.

Gallaway, C. & Richards, B. (eds) (1994). *Input and interaction in language acquisition*. Cambridge: Cambridge University Press.

García, E. & Carrasco, R., 1981. An analysis of bilingual mother–child discourse. In R. Durán, (ed.), *Latino language and communicative behavior* (pp. 251–269). Norwood, NJ: Ablex Publishers.

Gathercole, V. (1986). The acquisition of the present perfect: explaining differences in the speech of Scottish and American children. *Journal of Child Language, 13*, 537–560.

Gathercole, V.M. & Hoff, E. (2007). Input and the acquisition of language: three questions. In E. Hoff & M. Shatz (eds), *Blackwell handbook of language development* (pp. 107–127). Oxford: Blackwell.

Gathercole, V.C., Sebastián, E. & Soto, P. (1999). The early acquisition of Spanish verbal morphology: Across-the-board or piecemeal knowledge? *International Journal of Bilingualism, 3*, 133–182.

Genesee, F. (1989). Early bilingual development: one language or two? *Journal of Child Language, 16*, 161–179.

Genesee, F. (2005). The capacity of the language faculty: Contributions from studies of simultaneous bilingual acquisition. In J. Cohen, K.T. McAlister, K. Rolstad & J. MacSwan (eds), *ISB4: Proceedings of the 4th International Symposium on Bilingualism* (pp. 890–901). Somerville, MA: Cascadilla Press.

Genesee, F., Boivin, I. & Nicoladis, E. (1996). Talking with strangers: A study of bilingual children's communicative competence. *Applied Psycholinguistics, 17*, 427–442.

Genesee, F., Nicoladis, E. & Paradis, J. (1995). Language differentiation in early bilingual development. *Journal of Child Language, 22*, 611–631.

Gerhardt, K. & Abrams, R. (2000). Fetal exposures to sound and vibroacoustic stimulation. *Journal of Perinatology, 20*, S20–S29.

Gillis, S. (1984). *De verwerving van talige referentie [The acquisition of verbal reference]*. Unpublished PhD dissertation. Antwerp, Belgium: University of Antwerp.

Gindis, B. (1999). Language-related issues for international adoptees and adoptive families. In T. Tepper, L. Hannon & D. Sandstrom (eds), *International adoption: challenges and opportunities* (pp. 98–108). Meadow Lands, PA: PNPIC.

Goetz, P. (2003). The effects of bilingualism on theory of mind development. *Bilingualism: Language and Cognition, 6*, 1–15.

Goldfield, B. (2000). Nouns before verbs in comprehension vs. production: The view from pragmatics. *Journal of Child Language, 27*, 501–520.

Goldfield, B. & Reznick, J.S. (1990). Early lexical acquisition: rate, content, and the vocabulary spurt. *Journal of Child Language, 17*, 171–183.

González-Bueno, M. (2005). Articulatory difficulties in the acquisiton of Spanish /r/ in a bilingual context. In J. Cohen, K.T. McAlister, K. Rolstad & J. MacSwan (eds), *ISB4: Proceedings of the 4th International Symposium on Bilingualism* (pp. 914–934). Somerville, MA: Cascadilla Press.

Goodz, N. (1989). Parental language mixing in bilingual families. *Infant Mental Health Journal, 10*, 25–44.

Goodz, N. (1994). Interactions between parents and children in bilingual families. In F. Genesee (ed.), *Educating second language children* (pp. 61–81). Cambridge: Cambridge University Press.

Gorter, D. (ed.) (2006). *Linguistic landscape. A new approach to multilingualism.* Clevedon: Multilingual Matters.

Grabe, E., Post, B. & Watson, I. (1999). The acquisition of rhythmic patterns in English and French. In *Proceedings of the 14th International Congress of Phonetic Sciences* (pp. 1201–1204). Berkeley, CA: University of California.

Granfeldt, J. (2000). The acquisition of the determiner phrase in bilingual and second language French. *Bilingualism: Language and Cognition, 3(3)*, 263–280.

Granfeldt, J., Schlyter, S. & Kihlstedt, M. (2007). French as cL2, 2L1 and L1 in pre-school children. In J. Granfeldt (ed.), *Studies in Romance bilingual acquisition – Age of onset and development of French and Spanish* (pp. 7–42). Lund, Sweden: Lunds Universitets Språk- och Litteraturcentrum.

Granfeldt-Saavedra, P. (2007). Adquisición de vocabulario y pronunciación en L1 y L2. Estudio comparativo de los factores edad e input en el castellano de suecos bilingües. In J. Granfeldt (ed.), *Studies in Romance bilingual acquisition – Age of onset and development of French and Spanish* (pp. 43–89). Lund, Sweden: Lunds Universitets Språk- och Litteraturcentrum.

Grenon, I., Benner, A. & Esling, J.H. (2007). Language-specific phonetic production patterns in the first year of life. In J. Trouvain & W.J. Barry (eds), *Proceedings of the 16th International Congress of Phonetic Sciences* (pp. 1250–1253). Saarbrücken, Germany.

Grosjean, F. (1989). Neurolinguists, beware! The bilingual is not two monolinguals in one person. *Brain and Language, 36*, 3–15.

Grosjean, F. (2001). The bilingual's language modes. In J.L. Nicol (ed.), *One mind, two languages: Bilingual language processing* (pp. 1–22). Malden, MA: Blackwell Publishers.

Grosjean, F. (2008). *Studying bilinguals.* Oxford: Oxford Unversity Press.

Guardadao, M. (2002). Loss and maintenance of first language skills: Case studies of Hispanic families in Vancouver. *Canadian Modern Language Review, 58(3)*, 341–363.

Gupta, A.F. (1994). *The step-tongue. Children's English in Singapore.* Clevedon: Multilingual Matters.

Gut, U. (2000a). *Bilingual acquisition of intonation: A study of children speaking German and English.* Tübingen: Max Niemeyer Verlag.

Gut, U. (2000b). Cross-linguistic structures in the acquisition of intonational phonology by German–English bilingual children. In S. Döpke (ed.), *Cross-linguistic structures in simultaneous bilingualism* (pp. 201–225). Amsterdam/Philadelphia: John Benjamins.

Gutiérrez-Clellen, V.F. & Kreiter, J. (2003). Understanding child bilingual acquisition using parent and teacher reports. *Applied Psycholinguistics, 24*, 267–288.

Hakuta, K. (1986). *Mirror of language. The debate on bilingualism.* New York: Basic Books.

Harrison, G., Bellin, W. & Piette, B. (1981). *Bilingual mothers in Wales and the language of their children.* Cardiff: University of Wales Press.

Hart, B. & Risley, T. (1995). *Meaningful differences in the everyday experiences of young American children.* Baltimore, MD: Paul Brookes.

Hart, B. & Risley, T. (1999). *The social world of children learning to talk.* Baltimore, MD: Paul Brookes.

Hart, B. & Risley, T. (2003). The early catastrophe. *American Educator, Spring 2003,* 4–9. (available online at: http://www.aft.org/pubs-report/american-educator/spring2003/catastrophe.html).

Hatch, E. (ed.) (1978). *Second language acquisition. A book of readings.* Rowley, MA: Newbury House.

Hazen, N. & Black, B. (1989). Preschool peer communication skills: the role of social status and interaction context. *Child Development, 60,* 867–876.

Heath, S.B. (1989). The learner as cultural member. In M. Rice & R. Schiefelbusch (eds), *The teachability of language* (pp. 333–350). Baltimore, MD: Paul H. Brookes.

Herman, S. (1961). Explorations in the social psychology of language choice. *Human Relations, 14,* 149–164.

Hinzelin, M.O. (2003). The acquisition of subjects in bilingual children. Pronoun use in Portuguese–German children. In N. Müller (ed.), *(In)vulnerable domains in multilingualism* (pp. 107–137). Amsterdam/Philadelphia: John Benjamins.

Hoff, E. (2003). The specificity of environmental influence: socioeconomic status affects early vocabulary development via maternal speech. *Child Development, 74(5),* 1368–1378.

Hoff, E. & Shatz, M. (eds) (2007). *Blackwell handbook of language development.* Oxford: Blackwell.

Hoff-Ginsberg, E. (1991). Mother–child conversation in different social classes and communicative settings. *Child Development, 62(4),* 782–796.

Hoffmann, C. & Stavans, A. (2007). The evolution of trilingual codeswitching from infancy to school age: The shaping of trilingual codeswitching from infancy to school age: The shaping of trilingual competence through dynamic language dominance. *International Journal of Bilingualism, 11,* 55–72.

Hoffmann, C. & Widdicombe, S. (1999). Code-switching and language dominance in the trilingual child. *AILE (Acquisition et Interaction en Langue Etrangère), 1,* 51–81.

Holmberg, M.C. (1980). The development of social interchange patterns from 12 to 42 months. *Child Development, 51(2),* 448–456.

Holowka, S., Brosseau-Lapré, F. & Petitto, L.A. (2002). Semantic and conceptual knowledge underlying bilingual babies' first signs and words. *Language Learning, 52,* 205–262.

Hua, Z. & Dodd, B. (eds) (2006). *Phonological development and disorders in children. A multilingual perspective.* Clevedon: Multilingual Matters.

Huerta, A. (1977). The acquisition of bilingualism: A code-switching approach. *Sociolinguistic Working Paper Number 39.* Austin, Texas.

Huerta-Macías, A. (1981). Codeswitching: all in the family. In R. Durán (ed.), *Latino language and communicative behavior* (pp. 153–168). Norwood, NJ: Ablex Publishers.

Hulk, A. (2003). Merging scope-particles. Word order variation and the acquisition of *aussi* and *ook* in a bilingual context. In C. Dimroth & M. Starren (eds), *Information structure and the dynamics of language acquisition* (pp. 211–234). Amsterdam/Philadelphia: John Benjamins.

Hulk, A. & Müller, N. (2000). Bilingual first language acquisition at the interface between syntax and pragmatics. *Bilingualism: Language and Cognition, 3(3)*, 227–244.

Hulk, A. & van der Linden, E. (1996). Language mixing in a French–Dutch bilingual child. *Toegepaste Taalwetenschap in Artikelen, 2*, 89–101.

Ingram, D. (1981/82). The emerging phonological system of an Italian–English bilingual child. *Journal of Italian Linguistics, 2*, 95–113.

Ingram, D. (1989). *First language acquisition. Method, description, and explanation.* Cambridge: Cambridge University Press.

Itani-Adams, Y. (2007). Lexical and grammatical development in Japanese–English bilingual first language acquisition. In F. Mansouri (ed.), *Second language acquisition research: Theory-construction and testing* (pp. 173–198). Newcastle: Cambridge Scholars Press.

Jisa, H. (1989). The process of language replacement. In *Actes du symposium AILA/CILA: Minorisation linguistique et interaction* (pp. 125–134). Commission Interuniversitaire Suisse de Linguistique Appliquée.

Jisa, H. (1991). Les réformulations d'un bilingue dans sa langue non dominante: observation de la zone proximale de développement. In C. Russier, H. Stoffel & D. Véronique (eds), *Interactions en langue étrangère* (pp. 179–191). Aix-en-Provence: Publications de l'Université de Provence.

Jisa, H. (1995). L'utilisation du morphème be en anglais langue faible. *AILE (Acquisition et Interaction en Langue Etrangère), 6*, 101–127.

Jisa, H. (2000). Language mixing in the weak language: Evidence from two children. *Journal of Pragmatics, 32*, 1363–1386.

Johnson, C. & Lancaster, P. (1998). The development of more than one phonology: A case study of a Norwegian–English bilingual child. *International Journal of Bilingualism, 2(3)*, 265–300.

Johnson, C.E. & Wilson, I.L. (2002). Phonetic evidence for early language differentiation: Research issues and some preliminary data. *International Journal of Bilingualism, 6(3)*, 271–289.

Juan-Garau, M. & Pérez-Vidal, C. (2000). Subject realization in the syntactic development of a bilingual child. *Bilingualism: Language and Cognition, 3*, 173–191.

Juan-Garau, M. & Pérez-Vidal, C. (2001). Mixing and pragmatic parental strategies in early bilingual acquisition. *Journal of Child Language, 28*, 59–86.

Junker, D. & Stockman, I. (2002). Expressive vocabulary of German–English bilingual toddlers. *American Journal of Speech–Language Pathology, 11*, 381–394.

Kaiser, G. (1994). More about INFL-ection and agreement: the acquisition of clitic pronouns in French. In J. Meisel (ed.), *Bilingual first language acquisition. French and German grammatical development* (pp. 131–160). Amsterdam/Philadelphia: John Benjamins.

Karniol, R. (1992). Stuttering out of bilingualism. *First Language, 12*, 255–283.

Kasuya, H. (1998). Determinants of language choice in bilingual children: The role of input. *International Journal of Bilingualism, 2*, 327–346.

Kaufman, D. & Aronoff, M. (1991). Morphological disintegration and reconstruction in first language attrition. In H. Seliger & R. Vago (eds), *First language attrition* (pp. 175–188). Cambridge: Cambridge University Press.

Kehoe, M. (2002). Developing vowel systems as a window to bilingual phonology. *International Journal of Bilingualism, 6(3),* 315–334.

Kehoe, M., Lleó, C. & Rakow, M. (2004). Voice onset time in bilingual German–Spanish children. *Bilingualism: Language and Cognition, 7,* 71–88.

Kent, R.D. (1976). Anatomical and neuromuscular maturation of the speech mechanism: Evidence from acoustic studies. *Journal of Speech and Hearing Research, 19,* 421–447.

Kern, S. (2007). Lexicon development in French-speaking infants. *First Language, 27,* 227–250.

Keshavarz, M.H. & Ingram, D. (2002). The early phonological development of a Farsi–English bilingual child. *International Journal of Bilingualism, 6(3),* 335–353.

Khattab, G. (2002). /l/ production in English–Arabic bilingual speakers. *International Journal of Bilingualism, 6(3),* 335–353.

Khattab, G. (2006). Phonological acquisition by Arabic–English bilingual children. In Z. Hua & B. Dodd (eds), *Phonological development and disorders in children. A multilingual perspective* (pp. 383–412). Clevedon: Multilingual Matters.

Kielhöfer, B. & Jonekeit, S. (1983). *Zweisprachige Kindererziehung.* Tübingen: Stauffenberg Verlag.

Kim, M., McGregor, K.K. & Thompson, C.K. (2000). Early lexical development in English- and Korean-speaking children: language-general and language-specific patterns. *Journal of Child Language, 27,* 225–254.

King, K. & Fogle, L. (2006a). Bilingual parenting as good parenting: Parents' perspectives on family language policy for additive bilingualism. *International Journal of Bilingual Education and Bilingualism, 9(6),* 695–712.

King, K. & Fogle, L. (2006b). Raising bilingual children: Common parental concerns and current research. *CALdigest,* April 2006. Washington, D.C.: Center for Applied Linguistics.

Kitamura, C. & Burnham, D. (2003). Pitch and communicative intent in mother's speech: adjustments for age and sex in the first year. *Infancy, 4(1),* 85–110.

Klammler, A. (2006). Erwerb und Beschaffenheit des deutsch–italienisch bilingualen Lexikons in der holophrastischen Phase. Eine quantitative und qualitative Analyse. Unpublished MA thesis, Graz, Austria, Karl-Franzens-Universität.

Klinge, S. (1990). Prepositions in bilingual language acquisition. In J. Meisel (ed.), *Two first languages. Early grammatical development in bilingual children* (pp. 123–156). Dordrecht: Foris Publications.

Koehn, C. (1994). The acquisition of gender and number morphology within NP. In J. Meisel (ed.), *Bilingual first language acquisition. French and German grammatical development* (pp. 29–51). Amsterdam/Philadelphia: John Benjamins.

Köppe, R. (1994a). NP-movement and subject raising. In J. Meisel (ed.), *Bilingual first language acquisition. French and German grammatical development* (pp. 209–234). Amsterdam/Philadelphia: John Benjamins.

Köppe, R. (1994b). The DUFDE project. In J. Meisel (ed.), *Bilingual first language acquisition. French and German grammatical development* (pp. 15–27). Amsterdam/Philadelphia: John Benjamins.

Köppe, R. (1996). Language differentiation in bilingual children: the development of grammatical and pragmatic competence. *Linguistics, 34,* 927–954.

Kovács, Á.M. (2008). Early bilingualism enhances mechanisms of false-belief reasoning. *Developmental Science* (online: DOI: 10:1111/j.1467-7687.2008.00742.x).

Kovács, Á.M. & Mehler, J. (2008). Simultaneous learning of two linguistic rules in monolingual and bilingual infants: Evidence from eye tracking. Poster presented at the XVIth International Conference on Infant Studies, Vancouver, March 27–29, 2008.

Krasinski, E. (1995). The development of past marking in a bilingual child and the punctual–nonpunctual distinction. *First Language, 15,* 277–300.

Kroll, J. & de Groot, A. (eds) (2005). *Handbook of bilingualism.* Oxford: Oxford University Press.

Kroll, J.F. & Tokowicz, N. (2005). Models of bilingual representation and processing: looking back and to the future. In J. Kroll & A. de Groot (eds), *The handbook of bilingualism* (pp. 531–554). Oxford: Oxford University Press.

Krueger, C., Holditch-Davis, D., Quint, S. & DeCasper, A. (2004). Recurring auditory experience in the 28- to 34-week-old fetus. *Infant Behavior and Development, 27(4),* 537–543.

Kuchenbrandt, I. (2005). Gender acquisition in bilingual Spanish. In J. Cohen, K.T. McAlister, K. Rolstead & J. MacSwan (eds). *ISB4: Proceedings of the 4th International Symposium on Bilingualism* (pp. 1252–1263). Somerville, MA: Cascadilla Press.

Kuhl, P.K. (2007). Is speech learning 'gated' by the social brain? *Developmental Science, 10(1),* 110–120.

Kuhl, P.K. & Meltzoff, A.N. (1996). Infant vocalizations in response to speech: Vocal imitation and developmental change. *Journal of the Acoustical Society of America, 100,* 2425–2438.

Kuhl, P.K., Conboy, B.T., Coffey-Corina, S., Padden, D., Rivera-Gaxiola, M. & Nelson, T. (2008). Phonetic learning as a pathway to language: new data and native language magnet theory expanded (NLM-e). *Philosophical Transactions of the Royal Society of London B, 363,* 979–1000.

Kuhl, P.K., Stevens, E., Hayashi, A., Deguchi, T., Kiritani, S. & Iverson, P. (2006). Infants show a facilitation effect for native language phonetic perception between 6 and 12 months. *Developmental Science, 9(2),* F13–F21.

Kuhl, P.K., Tsao, F.M. & Liu, H.M. (2003). Foreign-language experience in infancy: Effects of short-term exposure and social interaction on phonetic learning. *Proceedings of the National Academy of Sciences, 100,* 9096–9101.

Kuhl, P.K., Williams, K.A., Lacerda, F., Stevens, K.N. & Lindblom, B. (1992). Linguistic experience alters phonetic perception in infants by 6 months of age. *Science, 255,* 606–608.

Kulick, D. (1992). *Language shift and cultural reproduction. Socialization, self, and syncretism in a Papua New Guinean village.* Cambridge: Cambridge University Press.

Kupisch, T. (2003). The DP, a vulnerable domain? Evidence from the acquisition of French. In N. Müller (ed.), *(In)vulnerable domains in multilingualism* (pp. 1–39). Amsterdam/Philadelphia: John Benjamins.

Kupisch, T. (2006). The emergence of article forms and functions in a German–Italian bilingual child. In C. Lleó (ed.), *Interfaces in multilingualism: Acquisition, representation and processing* (pp. 45–109). Amsterdam/Philadelphia: John Benjamins.

Kupisch, T. (2007). Determiners in bilingual German–Italian children: What they tell us about the relation between language influence and language dominance. *Bilingualism: Language and Cognition, 10(1)*, 57–78.

Kupisch, T. (2008). Dominance, mixing and cross-linguistic influence: On their relation in bilingual development. A French/German case study. In P. Guijarro-Fuentes, M.P. Larrañaga & J. Clibbens (eds), *First language acquisition of morphology and syntax. Perspectives across languages and learners* (pp. 209–234). Amsterdam/Philadelphia: John Benjamins.

Kuppens, A. & De Houwer, A. (2006). De relatie tussen mediagebruik en Engelse taalvaardigheid [The relation between media usage and English proficiency]. Internal report. Antwerp, Belgium: University of Antwerp.

Kwan-Terry, A. (1992). Code-switching and code-mixing: the case of a child learning English and Chinese simultaneously. *Journal of Multilingual and Multicultural Development, 13*, 243–259.

La Heij, W. (2005). Selection processes in monolingual and bilingual lexical access. In J. Kroll & A. de Groot (eds), *The handbook of bilingualism* (pp. 289–307). Oxford: Oxford University Press.

Lanvers, U. (1999). Lexical growth patterns in a bilingual infant: the occurrence and significance of equivalents in the bilingual lexicon. *International Journal of Bilingual Education and Bilingualism, 2*, 30–52.

Lanvers, U. (2001). Language alternation in infant bilinguals: A developmental approach to codeswitching. *International Journal of Bilingualism, 5(4)*, 437–464.

Lanza, E. (1988). Language strategies in the home: linguistic input and infant bilingualism. In A. Holmen, E. Hansen, J. Gimbel & J.N. Jørgensen (eds), *Bilingualism and the individual* (pp. 69–84). Clevedon: Multilingual Matters.

Lanza, E. (1992). Can bilingual two-year-olds code-switch? *Journal of Child Language, 19*, 633–658.

Lanza, E. (1997). *Language mixing in infant bilingualism. A sociolinguistic perspective.* Oxford: Clarendon Press (See also the 2004 second, paperback edition with a new afterword published by Oxford University Press).

Lanza, E. (1998). Raising children bilingually in Norway. *International Journal of the Sociology of Language, 133*, 73–88.

Lanza, E. (2001). Temporality and language contact in narratives by children acquiring Norwegian and English simultaneously. In L. Verhoeven & S. Strömqvist (eds), *Narrative development in a multilingual context* (pp. 15–50). Amsterdam/Philadelphia: John Benjamins.

Lanza, E. (2007). Multilingualism and the family. In P. Auer & W. Li (eds), *Handbook of multilingualism and multilingual communication* (pp. 45–68). Berlin/New York: Mouton de Gruyter.

Larrañaga, M.P. (2008). The subjects of unaccusative verbs in bilingual Basque/Spanish children. In P. Guijarro-Fuentes, M.P. Larrañaga & J. Clibbens (eds), *First language acquisition of morphology and syntax. Perspectives across languages and learners* (pp. 183–207). Amsterdam/Philadelphia: John Benjamins.

Leopold, W. (1953). Patterning in children's language learning. *Language Learning, 5*, 1–14.

Leopold, W. (1970). *Speech development of a bilingual child. A linguist's record.* New York: AMS Press (original work published 1939–1949).

Leopold, W. (1978). A child's learning of two languages. In E. Hatch (ed.), *Second language acquisition. A book of readings* (pp. 24–32). Rowley, MA: Newbury House (article first published elsewhere in 1954).

Li, W. (1994). *Three generations, two languages, one family. Language choice and language shift in a Chinese community in Britain.* Clevedon: Multilingual Matters.

Li, W. & Hua, Z. (2006). The development of code-switching in early second language acquisition. *BISAL, 1,* 68–81.

Li, W. & Moyer, M. (eds) (2008). *The Blackwell guide to research methods in bilingualism and multilingualism.* London: Blackwell.

Liceras, J.M., Fernández Fuertes, R. & Pérez-Tattam, R. (2008). Null and overt subjects in the developing grammars (L1 English/L1 Spanish) of two bilingual twins. In C. Pérez-Vidal, M. Juan-Garau & A. Bel (eds), *A portrait of the young in the new multilingual Spain* (pp. 111–134), Clevedon: Multilingual Matters.

Lieven, E. (1994). Crosslinguistic and crosscultural aspects of language addressed to children. In C. Gallaway & B. Richards (eds), *Input and interaction in language acquisition* (pp. 56–73). Cambridge: Cambridge University Press.

Lieven, E. (2008). Learning the English auxiliary: A usage-based approach. In H. Behrens (ed.), *Corpora in language acquisition research. History, methods, perspectives* (pp. 61–98). Amsterdam/Philadelphia: John Benjamins.

Lieven, E., Behrens, H., Speares, J. & Tomasello, M. (2003). Early syntactic creativity: A usage-based approach. *Journal of Child Language, 30,* 333–370.

Lieven, E., Pine, J. & Baldwin, G. (1997). Lexically-based learning and early grammatical development. *Journal of Child Language, 24,* 187–219.

Lieven, E., Pine, J. & Barnes, H. (1992). Individual differences in early vocabulary development: redefining the referential-expressive distinction. *Journal of Child Language, 19,* 287–310.

Liu, H.M., Kuhl, P.K. & Tsao, F.M. (2003). An association between mothers' speech clarity and infants' speech discrimination skills. *Developmental Science, 6(3),* F1–F10.

Lleó, C. (1990). Homonymy and reduplication: on the extended availability of two strategies in phonological acquisition. *Journal of Child Language, 17,* 267–278.

Lleó, C. (2002). The role of markedness in the acquisition of complex prosodic structures by German–Spanish bilinguals. *International Journal of Bilingualism, 6(3),* 291–313.

Lleó, C., Kuchenbrandt, I., Kehoe, M. & Trujillo, C. (2003). Syllable final consonants in Spanish and German monolingual and bilingual acquisition. In N. Müller (ed.), *(In)vulnerable domains in multilingualism* (pp. 191–220). Amsterdam/Philadelphia: John Benjamins.

Lleó, C. & Rakow, M. (2005). Markedness effects in the acquisition of voiced stop spirantization by Spanish–German bilinguals. In J. Cohen, K.T. McAlister, K. Rolstad & J. McSwan (eds). *ISB4: Proceedings of the 4th International Symposium on Bilingualism* (pp. 1353–1371). Somerville, MA: Cascadilla Press.

Lleó, C. & Rakow, M. (2006). The prosody of early two-word utterances by German and Spanish monolingual and bilingual children. In C. Lleó (ed.), *Interfaces in multilingualism* (pp. 1–26). Amsterdam/Philadelphia: John Benjamins.

Lleó, C., Rakow, M. & Kehoe, M.M. (2004). Acquisition of language-specific pitch accent by Spanish and German monolingual and bilingual children. In T. Face (ed.), *Laboratory approaches to Spanish phonology* (pp. 3–27). Berlin/New York: Mouton.

Lleó, C., Rakow, M., & Kehoe Winkler, M. (2007). Acquiring rhythmically different languages in a bilingual context. In J. Trouvain & W.J. Barry (eds), *Proceedings of the 16th International Congress of Phonetic Sciences* (pp. 1545–1548). Saarbrücken, Germany.

Macrory, G. (2007). Constructing language: Evidence from a French–English bilingual child. *Early Child Development and Care, 177(6),* 781–792.

MacWhinney, B. (2000). *The CHILDES Project: Tools for analyzing talk* (3rd edition). Mahwah, NJ: Lawrence Erlbaum Associates.

MacWhinney, B. & Snow, C. (1985). The child language data exchange system. *Journal of Child Language, 12,* 271–295.

Maneva, B. & Genesee, F. (2002). Bilingual babbling: evidence for language differentiation in dual language acquisition. In B. Skarabela, S. Fish & A. Do (eds) *BUCLD26: The Proceedings of the 26th Boston University Conference on Language Development* (pp. 383–392). Somerville, MA: Cascadilla Press.

Männel, C. (2008). The method of event-related potentials in the study of cognitive processes: A tutorial. In A. Friederici & T. Guillaume (eds), *Early language development. Bridging brain and behaviour* (pp. 1–22). Amsterdam/Philadelphia: John Benjamins.

Maratsos, M. (1990). Are actions to verbs as objects are to nouns? On the differential semantic bases of form, class, category. *Linguistics, 28,* 1351–1379.

Marchman, V.A. & Bates, E. (1994). Continuity in lexical and morphological development: a test of the critical mass hypothesis. *Journal of Child Language, 21,* 339–366.

Marchman, V.A. & Fernald, A. (2008). Speed of word recognition and vocabulary knowledge in infancy predict cognitive and language outcomes in later childhood. *Developmental Science, 11(3),* F9–16.

Marchman, V.A. & Martínez-Sussmann, C. (2002). Concurrent validity of caregiver/parent report measures of language for children who are learning both English and Spanish. *Journal of Speech, Language & Hearing Research, 45(5),* 983–998.

Marchman, V.A., Martínez-Sussmann, C. & Dale, P.S. (2004). The language-specific nature of grammatical development: evidence from bilingual language learners. *Developmental Science, 7(2),* 212–224.

Markman, E.M. (1989). *Categorization and naming in children: Problems of induction.* Cambridge, MA: MIT Press.

Markman, E.M. & Wachtel, G.F. (1988). Children's use of mutual exclusivity to constrain the meanings of words. *Cognitive Psychology, 20,* 121–157.

Martin-Rhee, M. & Bialystok, E. (2008). The development of two types of inhibitory control in monolingual and bilingual children. *Bilingualism: Language and Cognition, 11,* 81–93.

Masataka, N. (2003). *The onset of language.* Cambridge: Cambridge University Press.

Mattock, K., Molnar, M., Polka, L. & Burnham, D. (2008a). The developmental course of lexical tone perception in the first year of life. *Cognition, 106(3)*, 1367–1381.

Mattock, K., Polka, L., Rvachew, S. & Krehm, M. (2008b). Phonetic variability affects word learning in 17m old monolinguals and bilinguals. Poster presented at IASCL 2008, The XI Congress of the International Association for the Study of Child Language, Edinburgh, United Kingdom, July 28–August 1.

Mcclure, K. (1997). Evidence against mutual exclusivity. *Proceedings of the 1997 GALA conference on Language Acquisition: Knowledge Representation and Processing*, Edinburgh, pp. 102–108.

McLaughlin, B. (1984). *Second-language acquisition in childhood: Volume 1. Preschool children* (2nd edition). Hillsdale, NJ: Lawrence Erlbaum Associates.

Mehler, J. & Christophe, A. (1994). Language in the infant's mind. *Philosophical Transactions of the Royal Society of London B, 346*, 13–20.

Mehler, J., Dupoux, E., Nazzi, T. & Dehaene-Lambertz, G. (1996). Coping with linguistic diversity: The infant's viewpoint. In J. Morgan & K. Demuth (eds), *Signal to syntax. Bootstrapping from speech to grammar in early acquisition* (pp. 101–116). Mahwah, NJ: Lawrence Erlbaum Associates.

Meisel, J. (1985). Les phases initiales du développement de notions temporelles, aspectuelles et de modes d'action. Etude basée sur le langage d'enfants bilingues français-allemand. *Lingua, 66*, 321–374.

Meisel, J. (1986). Word order and case marking in early child language. Evidence from simultaneous acquisition of two first languages: French and German. *Linguistics, 24*, 123–183.

Meisel, J. (1989). Early differentiation of languages in bilingual children. In K. Hyltenstam & L. Obler (eds), *Bilingualism across the lifespan. Aspects of acquisition, maturity and loss* (pp. 13–40). Cambridge: Cambridge University Press.

Meisel, J. (1990). INFL-ection: Subjects and subject-verb agreement. In J. Meisel (ed.), *Two first languages. Early grammatical development in bilingual children* (pp. 237–298). Dordrecht: Foris Publications.

Meisel, J. (1994). Getting FAT: finiteness, agreement and tense in early grammars. In J. Meisel (ed.), *Bilingual first language acquisition. French and German grammatical development* (pp. 89–130). Amsterdam/Philadelphia: John Benjamins.

Meisel, J. (2001). The simultaneous acquisition of two first languages. Early differentiation and subsequent development of grammars. In J. Cenoz & F. Genesee (eds), *Trends in bilingual acquisition* (pp. 11–41). Amsterdam/Philadelphia: John Benjamins.

Meisel, J. (2007). The weaker language in early child bilingualism: Acquiring a first language as a second language? *Applied Pycholinguistics, 28*, 495–514.

Meisel, J.M. (2008). Child second language acquisition or successive first language acquisition? In B. Haznedar & E. Gavruseva (eds), *Current trends in child second language acquisition: A generative perspective* (pp. 55–80), Amsterdam/Philadelphia: John Benjamins.

Meisel, J. & Müller, N. (1992). Finiteness and verb placement in early child grammars. Evidence from simultaneous acquisition of two first languages: French and German. In J. Meisel (ed.), *The acquisition of verb placement. Functional categories and V2 phenomena in language acquisition* (pp. 109–138). Dordrecht: Kluwer.

Meltzoff, A.N. & Moore, M.K. (1977). Imitation of facial and manual gestures by human neonates. *Science, 198,* 75–78.

Métraux, R. (1965). A study of bilingualism among children of U.S.–French parents. *The French Review, 38(5),* 650–665.

Mikes, M. (1990). Some issues of lexical development in early bi- and trilinguals. In G. Conti-Ramsden & C. Snow (eds). *Children's language. Volume 7* (pp. 103–120). Hillsdale, NJ: Lawrence Erlbaum Associates.

Mishina, S. (1999). The role of parental input and discourse strategies in the early language mixing of a bilingual child. *Multilingua, 18,* 1–30.

Mishina-Mori, S. (2002). Language differentiation of the two languages in early bilingual development: A case study of Japanese/English bilingual children. *International Review of Applied Linguistics, 40(3),* 211–233.

Mishina-Mori, S. (2005). Autonomous and interdependent development of two language systems in Japanese/English simultaneous bilinguals: evidence from question formation. *First Language, 25(3),* 291–315.

Miyawaki, K., Strange, W., Verbrugge, R., Liberman, A., Jenkins, J.J. & Fujimura, O. (1975). An effect of linguistic experience: The discrimination of [r] and [l] by native speakers of Japanese and English. *Perception & Psychophysics, 18,* 331–340.

Möhring, A. (2001). The acquisition of French by German pre-school children. An empirical investigation of gender assignment and gender agreement. *EUROSLA Yearbook 1* (pp. 171–193). Amsterdam/Philadelphia: John Benjamins.

Möhring, A. & Meisel, J. (2003). The verb-object parameter in simultaneous and successive acquisition of bilingualism. In N. Müller (ed.), *(In)vulnerable domains in multilingualism* (pp. 296–334). Amsterdam/Philadelphia: John Benjamins.

Montanari, E. (2002). *Mit zwei Sprachen groß werden: Mehrsprachige Erziehung in Familie, Kindergarten und Schule.* München: Kösel.

Montanari, S. (2005). "Sol! 'GANDA, cute!": A longitudinal study of language choice in a developing trilingual child. In J. Cohen, K.T. McAlister, K. Rolstad & J. MacSwan (eds), *ISB4: Proceedings of the 4th International Symposium on Bilingualism* (pp. 1662–1678). Somerville, MA: Cascadilla Press.

Moon, C. & Fifer, W. (2000). Evidence of transnatal auditory learning. *Journal of Perinatology, 20,* S36–S43.

Morgan, G. & Woll, B. (eds) (2002). *Directions in sign language acquisition.* Amsterdam/Philadelphia: John Benjamins.

Müller, N. (1990a). Developing two gender assignment systems simultaneously. In J. Meisel (ed.), *Two first languages. Early grammatical development in bilingual children* (pp. 193–236), Dordrecht: Foris Publications.

Müller, N. (1990b). Erwerb der Wortstellung im Französischen und Deutschen. Zur Distribution von Finitheitsmerkmalen in der Grammatik bilingualer Kinder. In M. Rothweiler (ed.), *Spracherwerb und Grammatik. Linguistische Untersuchungen zum Erwerb von Syntax und Morphologie* (pp. 127–151). Opladen: Westdeutscher Verlag.

Müller, N. (1993). *Komplexe Sätze. Der Erwerb von COMP und von Wortstellungsmustern bei bilingualen Kindern (Französisch/Deutsch)*. Tübingen: Gunter Narr Verlag.

Müller, N. (1994a). Gender and number agreement within DP. In J. Meisel (ed.), *Bilingual first language acquisition. French and German grammatical development* (pp. 53–88). Amsterdam/Philadelphia: John Benjamins.

Müller, N. (1994b). Parameters cannot be reset: evidence from the development of COMP. In J. Meisel (ed.), *Bilingual first language acquisition. French and German grammatical development* (pp. 235–270). Amsterdam/Philadelphia: John Benjamins.

Müller, N. (1995). L'acquisition du genre et du nombre chez des enfants bilingues (français–allemand). *AILE (Acquisition et Interaction en Langue Etrangère), 6*, 65–99.

Müller, N. & Hulk, A. (2001). "Comment expliquez-vous?" Null objects in adults and children. *Bilingualism: Language and Cognition, 4(1)*, 49–63.

Müller, N. & Kupisch, T. (2003). Zum simultanen Erwerb des Deutschen und des Französischen bei (un)ausgeglichen bilingualen Kindern. *Vox Romanica, 62*, 145–169.

Müller, N. & Pillunat, A. (2008). Balanced bilingual children with two weak languages. A French/German case study. In P. Guijarro-Fuentes, M.P. Larrañaga & J. Clibbens (eds), *First language acquisition of morphology and syntax. Perspectives across languages and learners* (pp. 269–294). Amsterdam/Philadelphia: John Benjamins.

Müller, N., Crysmann, B. & G. Kaiser (1996). Interactions between the acquisition of French object drop and the development of the C-system. *Language Acquisition, 5(1)*, 35–63.

Myers-Scotton, C. (2006). *Multiple voices. An introduction to bilingualism*. Oxford: Blackwell.

Naigles, L.G. & Gelman, S.A. (1995). Overextensions in comprehension and production revisited: Preferential-looking in a study of dog, cat, and cow. *Journal of Child Language, 22*, 19–46.

Navarro, A.M., Pearson, B.Z., Cobo-Lewis, A. & Oller, K.D. (1998). Identifying the language spoken by 26-month-old monolingual- and bilingual-learning babies in a no-context situation. In A. Greenhill, M. Hughes, H. Littlefield & H. Walsh (eds). *Proceedings of the 22nd Annual Boston University Conference on Language Development Vol. 2* (pp. 557–568). Somerville, MA: Cascadilla Press.

Navarro, A.M., Pearson, B.Z., Cobo-Lewis, A. & Oller, K.D. (2005). Differentiation, carry-over and the distributed characteristic in bilinguals: differentiation in early phonological adaptation? In J. Cohen, K.T. McAlister, K. Rolstad & J. MacSwan (eds), *ISB4: Proceedings of the 4th International Symposium on Bilingualism* (pp. 1690–1702). Somerville, MA: Cascadilla Press.

Nazzi, T., Bertoncini, J. & Mehler, J. (1998). Language discrimination by newborns: Toward an understanding of the role of rhythm. *Journal of Experimental Psychology: Human Perception and Performance, 24*, 756–766.

Neiss, L., De Houwer, A. & Bornstein, M.H. (2008). Uneven development in Bilingual First Language Acquisition: Evidence from 4-year-olds. Conference on Bilingual Acquisition in Early Childhood, Hong Kong, December 11–12.

Newman, R., Bernstein Ratner, N., Jusczyk, A.M., Jusczyk, P.W. & Dow, K.A. (2006). Infants' early ability to segment the conversational speech signal predicts later language development: A retrospective analysis. *Developmental Psychology, 42(4)*, 643–655.

Nicoladis, E. (1998). First clues to the existence of two input languages: Pragmatic and lexical differentiation in a bilingual child. *Bilingualism: Language and Cognition, 1*, 105–116.

Nicoladis, E. (1999). "Where is my brush-teeth?" Acquisition of compound nouns in a French–English bilingual child. *Bilingualism: Language and Cognition, 2*, 245–256.

Nicoladis, E. (2002). What's the difference between 'toilet paper' and 'paper toilet'? French–English bilingual children's crosslinguistic transfer in compound nouns. *Journal of Child Language, 29*, 843–863.

Nicoladis, E. & Grabois, H. (2002). Learning English and losing Chinese: A case study of a child adopted from China. *International Journal of Bilingualism, 6(4)*, 441–454.

Nicoladis, E. & Secco, G. (2000). The role of a child's productive vocabulary in the language choice of a bilingual family. *First Language, 20*, 3–28.

Nicoladis, E., Palmer, A. & Marentette, P. (2007). The role of type and token frequency in using past tense morphemes correctly. *Developmental Science, 10(2)*, 237–254.

Okita, T. (2002). *Invisible work. Bilingualism, language choice and childrearing in intermarried families.* Amsterdam/Philadelphia: John Benjamins.

Oller, D.K. (1980). The emergence of the sounds of speech in infancy. In G. Yeni-Komshian, J. Kavanagh & C. Ferguson (eds), *Child Phonology: Vol. 1. Production* (pp. 93–112). New York: Academic Press.

Oller, D.K. (2000). *The emergence of the speech capacity.* Mahwah, NJ: Lawrence Erlbaum Associates.

Oller, D.K. (2005). The distributed characteristic in bilingual learning. In J. Cohen, K.T. McAlister, K. Rolstad & J. MacSwan (eds), *ISB4: Proceedings of the 4th International Symposium on Bilingualism* (pp. 1744–1749). Somerville, MA: Cascadilla Press.

Oller, D.K. & Eilers, R.E. (eds) (2002). *Language and literacy in bilingual children.* Clevedon: Multilingual Matters.

Oller, D.K. & Jarmulowicz, L. (2007). Language and literacy in bilingual children in the early school years. In E. Hoff & M. Shatz (eds), *Blackwell handbook of language development* (pp. 368–386). Oxford: Blackwell.

Oller, D.K., Eilers, R.E., Urbano, R. & Cobo-Lewis, A.B. (1997). Development of precursors to speech in infants exposed to two languages. *Journal of Child Language, 24*, 407–425.

Oller, D.K., Pearson, B.Z. & Cobo-Lewis, A.B. (2007). Profile effects in early bilingual language and literacy. *Applied Psycholinguistics, 28*, 191–230.

O'Neill, M. (1998). Support for the independent development hypothesis: Evidence from a case study of a bilingual Russian- and English-speaking child. In A. Greenhill, M. Hughes, H. Littlefield & H. Walsh (eds). *Proceedings of the 22nd Annual Boston University Conference on Language Development Vol. 2* (pp. 586–597). Somerville, MA: Cascadilla Press.

Oshima-Takane, Y., Takane, Y. & Shultz, T.R. (1999). The learning of first and second person pronouns in English: network models and analysis. *Journal of Child Language, 26(3)*, 545–575.

Ota, M. (2003). *The development of prosodic structure in early words.* Amsterdam/Philadelphia: John Benjamins.

Pallotti, G. (2002). Borrowing words: appropriations in child second language discourse. In J. Leather & J. van Dam (eds), *The ecology of language acquisition* (pp. 183–202). Amsterdam: Kluwer.

Pancsofar, N. & Vernon-Feagans, L. (2006). Mother and father language input to young children: Contributions to later language development. *Journal of Applied Developmental Psychology, 27,* 571–587.

Papoušek, M. (2007). Communication in early infancy: An arena of intersubjective learning. *Infant Behavior and Development, 30,* 258–266.

Papoušek, M. & Papoušek, H. (1989). Forms and functions of vocal matching in interactions between mothers and their precanonical infants. *First Language, 9,* 137–158.

Paradis, J. (1996). Phonological differentiation in a bilingual child: Hildegaard revisited. In A. Stringfellow, D. Cahana-Amitay, E. Hughes & A. Zukowski (eds), *BUCLD 20: Proceedings of the 20th annual Boston University Conference on Language Development* (pp. 528–539). Boston, MA: Cascadilla Press.

Paradis, J. (1998). Do bilingual two year olds have separate phonological systems? *International Journal of Bilingualism, 5(1),* 19–38.

Paradis, J. (2001). Are object omission in Romance object clitic omissions? *Bilingualism: Language and Cognition, 4(1),* 36–37.

Paradis, J. (2007). Early bilingual and multilingual acquisition. In P. Auer & W. Li (eds), *Handbook of multilingualism and multilingual communication* (pp. 15–44). Berlin/New York: Mouton de Gruyter.

Paradis, J. & Genesee, F. (1996). Syntactic acquisition in bilingual children: autonomous or interdependent? *Studies in Second Language Acquisition, 18,* 1–25.

Paradis, J. & Genesee, F. (1997). On continuity and the emergence of functional categories in bilingual first-language acquisition. *Language Acquisition, 6(2),* 91–124.

Paradis, J. & Navarro, S. (2003). Subject realization and crosslinguistic interference in the bilingual acquisition of Spanish and English: what is the role of the input? *Journal of Child Language, 30,* 371–393.

Paradis, J. & Nicoladis, E. (2007). The influence of dominance and sociolinguistic context on bilingual preschoolers' language choice. *International Journal of Bilingual Education and Bilingualism, 10,* 277–297.

Paradis, J., Nicoladis, E. & Genesee, F. (2000). Early emergence of structural constraints on code-mixing: evidence from French–English bilingual children. *Bilingualism: Language and Cognition, 3(3),* 245–261.

Parodi, T. (1990). The acquisition of word order regularities and case morphology. In J. Meisel (ed.), *Two first languages. Early grammatical development in bilingual children* (pp. 157–192). Dordrecht: Foris Publications.

Patterson, J. (1998). Expressive vocabulary development and word combinations of Spanish–English bilingual toddlers. *American Journal of Speech–Language Pathology, 7,* 46–56.

Patterson, J.L. (1999). What bilingual toddlers hear and say: Language input and word combinations. *Communication Disorders Quarterly, 21(1),* 32–38.

Patterson, J.L. (2000). Observed and reported expressive vocabulary and word combinations in bilingual toddlers. *Journal of Speech, Language and Hearing Research, 43,* 121–128.

Patterson, J.L. (2002). Relationships of expressive vocabulary to frequency of reading and television experience among bilingual toddlers. *Applied Psycholinguistics, 23(4)*, 493–508.

Patterson, J.L. (2004). Comparing bilingual and monolingual toddlers' expressive vocabulary size: Revisiting Rescorla and Achenbach (2002). *Journal of Speech, Language and Hearing Research, 47*, 1213–1215.

Patterson, J.L. & Pearson, B.Z. (2004). Bilingual lexical development: influences, contexts and processes. In B.A. Goldstein (ed.), *Bilingual language development and disorders in Spanish-English speakers* (pp. 77–104). Baltimore, MD: Paul H. Brooks Publishing.

Pavlenko, A. (2004). "Stop doing that, ia komu skazala!": Emotions and language choice in bilingual families. *Journal of Multilingual and Multicultural Development, 25*, 179–203.

Pearson, B.Z. (1998). Assessing lexical development in bilingual babies and toddlers. *International Journal of Bilingualism, 2(3)*, 347–372.

Pearson, B.Z. (2007). Social factors in childhood bilingualism in the United States. *Applied Psycholinguistics, 28*, 399–410.

Pearson, B.Z. (2008). *Raising a bilingual child. A step-by-step guide for parents.* New York: Living Language.

Pearson, B.Z. & Fernández, S. (1994). Patterns of interaction in the lexical development in two languages of bilingual infants. *Language Learning, 44*, 617–653.

Pearson, B.Z. & Navarro, A.M. (1996). Do early simultaneous bilinguals have a "foreign accent" in one or both of their languages? In A. Aksu-Koç, E. Erguvanli-Taylan, A. Sumru Özsoy & A. Küntay (eds), *Perspectives on language acquisition: Selected papers from the VIIth International Congress for the Study of Child Language* (pp. 156–168). Istanbul: Bogaziçi University.

Pearson, B.Z., Fernández, S., Lewedeg, V. & Oller, D.K. (1997). The relation of input factors to lexical learning by bilingual infants. *Applied Psycholinguistics, 18*, 41–58.

Pearson, B.Z., Fernández, S. & Oller, D.K. (1993). Lexical development in bilingual infants and toddlers: comparison to monolingual norms. *Language Learning, 43*, 93–120.

Pearson, B.Z., Fernández, S. & Oller, D.K. (1995). Cross-language synonyms in the lexicons of bilingual infants: one language or two? *Journal of Child Language, 22*, 345–368.

Pearson, B.Z., Navarro, A. & Gathercole, V.M. (1995). Assessment of phonetic differentiation in bilingual learning infants. In D. MacLaughlin & S. McEwen (eds). *Proceedings of the 19th Annual Boston University Conference on Language Development* (pp. 427–438). Somerville, MA: Cascadilla Press.

Pérez Pereira, M. (2008). Early Galician/Spanish bilingualism: Contrasts with monolingualism. In C. Pérez-Vidal, M. Juan-Garau & A. Bel (eds), *A portrait of the young in the new multilingual Spain. Issues in the acquisition of two or more languages in multilingual environments* (pp. 39–62). Clevedon: Multilingual Matters.

Pérez Pereira, M., & García Soto, X.R. (2003). El diagnóstico del desarrollo comunicativo en la primera infancia: Adaptación de las escalas MacArthur al gallego. *Psicothema, 15(3)*, 352–361.

Pérez-Vidal, C. & Juan-Garau, M. (2002). A contrastive study of tense and aspect in the Catalan–English oral production of a young bilingual. *Atlantis, 24(2)*, 169–182.

Peters, A. (1983). *The units of language acquisition.* Cambridge: Cambridge University Press.

Pfaff, C. (1994). Early bilingual development of Turkish children in Berlin. In G. Extra & L. Verhoeven (eds), *The cross-linguistic study of bilingualism* (pp. 75–97). Amsterdam: North-Holland.

Piller, I. (2002). *Bilingual couples' talk: The discursive construction of hybridity*. Amsterdam/Philadelphia: John Benjamins.

Porsché, D. (1983). *Die Zweisprachigkeit während des primären Spracherwerbs*. Tübingen: Gunter Narr Verlag.

Poulin-Dubois, D. & Goodz, N. (2001). Language differentiation in bilingual infants: Evidence from babbling. In J. Cenoz & F. Genesee (eds), *Trends in bilingual acquisition* (pp. 95–106). Amsterdam/Philadelphia: John Benjamins.

Prévost, P. (2003). Truncation and missing inflection in initial child L2 German. *Studies in Second Language Acquisition, 25*, 65–97.

Putnick, D.L., Suwalsky, J.T. & Bornstein, M.H. (2007). Firstborn and secondborn infants and their mothers: differential behaviors. Poster presented at the 2007 Biennial Meeting of the Society for Research in Child Development, Boston, MA, March 29–April 1.

Pye, C. (1992). Language loss among the Chilcotin. *International Journal of the Sociology of Language, 93*, 75–86.

Qi, R. (2005). From nominal to pronominal person reference in the early language of a Mandarin–English bilingual child. In J. Cohen, K.T. McAlister, K. Rolstad & J. MacSwan (eds), *ISB4: Proceedings of the 4th International Symposium on Bilingualism* (pp. 1893–1909). Somerville, MA: Cascadilla Press.

Qi, R., di Biase, B. & Campbell, S. (2006). The transition from nominal to pronominal person reference in the early language of a Mandarin–English bilingual child. *International Journal of Bilingualism, 10(3)*, 301–329.

Quay, S. (1995). The bilingual lexicon: implications for studies of language choice. *Journal of Child Language, 22*, 369–387.

Quay, S. (1998). One parent, two languages? In A. Aksu-Koç, E. Erguvanli-Taylan, A. Sumru Özsoy & A. Küntay (eds), *Perspectives on language acquisition: Selected papers from the VIIth International Congress for the Study of Child Language* (pp. 140–155). Istanbul: Bogaziçi University.

Quay, S. (2008). Dinner conversations with a trilingual two-year-old: Language socialization in a multilingual context. *First Language, 28*, 5–33.

Radford, A., Kupisch, T., Köppe, R. & Azzaro, G. (2007). Concord, convergence and accommodation in bilingual children. *Bilingualism: Language and Cognition, 10*, 239–256.

Ramon-Casas, M., Swingley, D., Sebastián-Gallés, N. & Bosch, L. (under review). Vowel categorization during word recognition in bilingual toddlers.

Raubichek, L. (1934). Psychology of multilingualism. *The Volta Review, 36*, 17–20.

Rescorla, L. (1989). The Language Development Survey: A screening tool for delayed language in toddlers. *Journal of Speech and Hearing Disorders, 54*, 587–599.

Rescorla, L. & Okuda, S. (1987). Modular patterns in second language acquisition. *Applied Psycholinguistics, 8*, 281–308.

Reznick, J.S. & Goldfield, B.A. (1992). Rapid change in lexical development in comprehension and production. *Developmental Psychology, 28(3)*, 406–13.

Reznick, J.S. & Goldfield, B.A. (1994). Diary vs. representative checklist assessment of productive vocabulary. *Journal of Child Language, 21*, 465–472.

Rice, M. (1993). "Don't talk to him; He's weird": A social consequences account of language and social interactions. In A. Kaiser & D. Gray (eds), *Enhancing children's communication: Research foundations for intervention* (pp. 139–158). Baltimore, MD: Brookes.

Rieckborn, S. (2006). The development of forms and functions in the acquisition of tense and aspect in German–French bilingual children. In C. Lleó (ed.), *Interfaces in multilingualism* (pp. 61–89). Amsterdam/Philadelphia: John Benjamins.

Rimel, A. & Eyal, S. (1996). Comparison of data on the lexical knowledge of bilingual vs. monolingual toddlers collected by their parents, using the MacArthur Communicative Development Inventory (CDI). *Speech and Hearing Disorders, 19*, 212–219.

Romaine, S. (1995). *Bilingualism* (2nd edition). Oxford: Blackwell.

Ronjat, J. (1913). *Le développement du langage observé chez un enfant bilingue*. Paris: Champion.

Rothweiler, M. (2006). The acquisition of V2 and subordinate clauses in early successive acquisition of German. In C. Lleó (ed.), *Interfaces in multilingualism* (pp. 91–113). Amsterdam/Philadelphia: John Benjamins

Rowe, M.L., Coker, D. & Pan, B.A. (2004). A comparison of fathers' and mothers' talk to toddlers in low-income families. *Social Development, 13(2)*, 278–291.

Rubin, K.H., Hemphill, S.A., Chen, X., Hastings, P., Sanson, A., Lo Coco, A., Zappulla, C., Chung, O.B., Park, S.Y., Doh, H.C., Chen, H., Sun, L., Yoon, C.H. & Cui, L. (2006). A cross-cultural study of behavioral inhibition in toddlers: East-West-North-South. *International Journal of Behavioural Development, 30*, 219–226.

Salustri, M. & Hyams, N. (2006). Looking for the universal core of the RI stage. In V. Torrens & L. Escobar (eds), *The acquisition of syntax in Romance languages* (pp. 159–182). Amsterdam/Philadelphia: John Benjamins.

Saunders, G. (1982a). *Bilingual children: guidance for the family*. Clevedon: Multilingual Matters.

Saunders, G. (1982b). Infant bilingualism: a look at some doubts and objections. *Journal of Multilingual and Multicultural Development, 3*, 277–292.

Saunders, G. (1988). *Bilingual children: from birth to teens*. Clevedon: Multilingual Matters.

Saville-Troike, M. (1987). Dilingual discourse: the negotiation of meaning without a common code. *Linguistics, 25*, 81–106.

Schaerlaekens, A., Huygelier, N. & Dondeyne, A. (1988). Language adjustments in international adoptions: an exploratory study. *Journal of Multicultural and Multilingual Development, 9*, 247–266.

Schecter, S.R. & Bayley, R. (1997). Language socialization practices and cultural identity: case studies of Mexican-descent families in California and Texas. *TESOL Quarterly, 31(3)*, 513–541.

Schecter, S.R. & Bayley, R. (1998). Concurrence and complementarity: Mexican-background parents' decisions about language and schooling. *Journal for a Just Caring Education, 4(1)*, 47–64.

Schelletter, C. (2002). The effect of form similarity on bilingual children's lexical development. *Bilingualism: Language and Cognition, 5,* 93–107.

Schelletter, C., Sinka, I. & Garman, M. (2001). Early nouns in bilingual acquisition: a test of the separate development hypothesis. In M. Georgiafentis, P. Kerswill & S. Varlokosta (eds), *Working papers in linguistics 5* (pp. 301–317). Reading: University of Reading.

Schlyter, S. (1990a). Introducing the DUFDE project. In J. Meisel (ed.), *Two first languages. Early grammatical development in bilingual children* (pp. 73–86). Dordrecht: Foris Publications.

Schlyter, S. (1990b). The acquisition of tense and aspect. In J. Meisel (ed.), *Two first languages. Early grammatical development in bilingual children* (pp. 87–122). Dordrecht: Foris Publications.

Schlyter, S. (1994). Early morphology in Swedish as the weaker language in French–Swedish bilingual children. *Scandinavian Working Papers on Bilingualism, 9,* 67–86.

Schlyter, S. (1995). Formes verbales du passé dans des interactions en langue forte et en langue faible. *AILE (Acquisition et Interaction en Langue Etrangère), 6,* 129–152.

Schlyter, S. (1996). Bilingual children's stories: French passé composé/imparfait and their correspondences in Swedish. *Linguistics, 34,* 1059–1085.

Schlyter, S. (2001). Pragmatic rules, C-domain, and language dominance. *Bilingualism: Language and Cognition, 4(1),* 40–42.

Schlyter, S. & Granfeldt, J. (2008). Is child L2 French like 2L1 or like adult L2? Presentation at IASCL 2008, The XI Congress of the International Association for the Study of Child Language, Edinburgh, United Kingdom, July 28–August 1.

Schmitz, K. & Müller, N. (2008). Strong and clitic pronouns in monolingual and bilingual acquisition of French and Italian. *Bilingualism: Language and Cognition, 11,* 19–41.

Schneider, R. (1999). L'expression des procès dans les récits d'un enfant bilingue. *AILE (Acquisition et Interaction en Langue Etrangère), 1,* 63–82.

Schnitzer, M. & Krasinski, E. (1994). The development of segmental phonological production in a bilingual child. *Journal of Child Language, 21,* 585–622.

Schnitzer, M. & Krasinski, E. (1996). The development of segmental phonological production in a bilingual child: a contrasting second case. *Journal of Child Language, 23,* 547–571.

Sebastián-Gallés, N. (2006). Native-language sensitivities: evolution in the first year of life. *Trends in Cognitive Sciences, 10(6),* 239–241.

Sebastián-Gallés, N., & Bosch, L. (2005). Phonology and bilingualism. In J. Kroll & A. de Groot (eds), *The handbook of bilingualism* (pp. 68–87). Oxford: Oxford University Press.

Serratrice, L. (2001). The emergence of verbal morphology and the lead-lag pattern issue in bilingual acquisition. In J. Cenoz & F. Genesee (eds), *Trends in bilingual acquisition* (pp. 43–70). Amsterdam/Philadelphia: John Benjamins.

Serratrice, L. (2002). Overt subjects in English: evidence for the marking of person in an English–Italian bilingual child. *Journal of Child Language, 29(2),* 1–29.

Serratrice, L. (2005). Language mixing and learning strategy. *International Journal of Bilingualism, 9(2),* 159–177.

Serratrice, L. (2007a). Cross-linguistic influence in the interpretation of anaphoric and cataphoric pronouns in English–Italian bilingual children. *Bilingualism: Language and Cognition, 10,* 225–238.

Serratrice, L. (2007b). Referential cohesion in the narratives of bilingual English–Italian children and monolingual peers. *Journal of Pragmatics, 39,* 1058–1087.

Serratrice, L., Sorace, A. & Paoli, S. (2004). Transfer at the syntax–pragmatics interface: subjects and objects in Italian–English bilingual and monolingual acquisition. *Bilingualism: Language and Cognition, 7,* 1–23.

Shin, S. (2005). *Developing in two languages. Korean children in America.* Clevedon: Multilingual Matters.

Silva-Corvalán, C. (2003). Linguistic consequences of reduced input in bilingual first language acquisition. In S. Montrul & F. Ordóñez (eds), *Linguistic theory and language development in Hispanic languages* (pp. 375–397). Somerville, MA: Cascadilla Press.

Silva-Corvalán, C. & Montanari, S. (2008). The acquisition of *ser, estar* (and *be*) by a Spanish–English bilingual child: the early stages. *Bilingualism: Language and Cognition* 11, 341–360.

Silva-Corvalán, C. & Sánchez-Walker, N. (2007). Subjects in early dual language developmnt. A case study of a Spanish–English bilingual child. In K. Potowski & R. Cameron (eds), *Spanish in contact. Policy, social and linguistic inquiries* (pp. 3–22). Amsterdam/Philadelphia: John Benjamins.

Sinka, I. (2000). The search for cross-linguistic influences in the language of young Latvian–English bilinguals. In S. Döpke (ed.), *Cross-linguistic structures in simultaneous bilingualism* (pp. 149–174). Amsterdam/Philadelphia: John Benjamins.

Sinka, I. & Schelletter, C. (1998). Morphosyntactic development in bilingual children. *International Journal of Bilingualism, 2(3),* 301–326.

Sinka, I., Garman, M. & Schelletter, C. (2000). Early verbs in bilingual acquisition: a lexical profiling approach. In R. Ingham & P. Kerswill (eds), *Working papers in linguistics 4* (pp. 175–187). Reading: University of Reading.

Slobin, D. (1973). Cognitive prerequisites for the development of grammar. In C. Ferguson & D. Slobin (eds). *Studies of child language development* (pp. 175–208). New York: Holt Rinehoert and Winston.

Slobin, D. (ed.) (1985). *The crosslinguistic study of language acquisition.* Hillsdale, NJ: Lawrence Erlbaum Associates.

Snow, C. (1977). The development of conversations between mothers and babies. *Journal of Child Language, 4,* 1–22.

Snow, C. & Ferguson, C. (eds) (1977). *Talking to children. Language input and acquisition.* Cambridge: Cambridge University Press.

Snow, D. & Balog, H. (2002). Do children produce the melody before the words? A review of developmental intonation research. *Lingua, 112,* 1025–1058.

Spence, M.J. & Moore, D.S. (2003). Categorization of infant-directed speech: Development from 4 to 6 months. *Developmental Psychobiology, 42,* 97–109.

Stavans, A. & Muchnik, M. (2008). Language production in trilingual children: Insights on code switching and code mixing. *Sociolinguistic Studies, 1,* 483–511.

Stefánik, J. (1995). Grammatical category of gender in Slovak–English and English–Slovak bilinguals. *Journal of East European Studies, 4,* 155–164.

Stefánik, J. (1997). A study of English–Slovak bilingualism in a child. *Journal*, 30, 721–734.

Stenzel, A. (1994). Case assignment and functional categories in bilingual children. In J. Meisel (ed.), *Bilingual first language acquisition. French and German grammatical development* (pp. 161–208). Amsterdam/Philadelphia: John Benjamins.

Stenzel, A. (1996). Development of prepositional case in a bilingual child. *Linguistics*, 34, 1029–1058.

Stern, C. & Stern, W. (1965). *Die Kindersprache*. Darmstadt: Wissenschaftliche Buchgesellschaft (first published in 1907).

Stoel-Gammon, C. & Vogel Sosa, A. (2007). Phonological development. In E. Hoff & M. Shatz (eds), *Blackwell handbook of language development* (pp. 238–256). Oxford: Blackwell.

Sundara, M. & Polka, L. (2008). Discrimination of coronal stops by bilingual adults: The timing and nature of language interaction. *Cognition*, 106(1), 234–258.

Sundara, M., Polka, L. & Genesee, F. (2006). Language-experience facilitates discrimination of /d-ð/ in monolingual and bilingual acquisition of English. *Cognition*, 100, 369–388.

Sundara, M., Polka, L. & Molnar, M. (2008). Development of coronal stop perception: Bilingual infants keep pace with their monolingual peers. *Cognition*, 108, 232–242.

Swain, M. (1972). Bilingualism as a first language. Unpublished PhD dissertation, University of California.

Swain, M. (1976). Bilingual first-language acquisition. In W. von Raffler-Engel & Y. Lebrun (eds), *Baby talk and infant speech* (pp. 277–280). Amsterdam: Swets & Zeitlinger.

Swingley, D. & Aslin, R. (2002). Lexical neighborhoods and the wordform representations of 14-month-olds. *Psychological Science*, 13, 480–484.

Tabors, P. (1987). *The development of communicative competence by second language learners in a nursery school classroom: An ethnolinguistic study*. Unpublished doctoral dissertation. Boston: Harvard University.

Taeschner, T. (1983). *The sun is feminine: A study on language acquisition in bilingual children*. Berlin: Springer Verlag.

Tare, M. & Gelman, S. (2008). Pragmatic language use during bilingual parent–child conversations. Poster presented at IASCL 2008, The XI Congress of the International Association for the Study of Child Language, Edinburgh, United Kingdom, July 28–August 1.

Test, J. (2001). Bilingual acquisition in the first year: could gestures provide prelinguistic support for language differentiation? A case study. In M. Almgren, A. Barreña, M.J. Ezeizabarrena, I. Idiazabal & B. MacWhinney (eds), *Research on child language acquisition: Proceedings of the Eighth Conference of the International Association for the Study of Child Language* (pp. 160–173). Somerville, MA: Cascadilla Press.

Thierry, G. & Vihman, M.M. (2008). The onset of word form recognition: A behavioural and neurophysiological study. In A. Friederici & G. Thierry (eds), *Early language development. Bridging brain and behaviour* (pp. 115–136). Amsterdam/Philadelphia: John Benjamins.

Thordardottir, E., Rothenberg, A., Rivard, M.-E. & Naves, R. (2006). Bilingual assessment: Can overall proficiency be estimated from separate measurement of two languages? *Journal of Multilingual Communication Disorders*, 4(1), 1–21.

Tinbergen, D. (1919). Kinderpraat. *De Nieuwe Taalgids, 13*, 1–16/65–86.

Tomasello, M. (1992). The social bases of language acquisition. *Social Development, 1(1)*, 67–87.

Tomasello, M. & Mervis, C. (1994). The instrument is great, but measuring comprehension is still a problem. *Monographs of the Society for Research in Child Development, 59(5)*, 174–179.

Tsao, F.M., Liu, H.M. & Kuhl, P.K. (2004). Speech perception in infancy predicts language development in the second year of life: A longitudinal study. *Child Development, 75*, 1067–1084.

Tseng, V. & Fuligni, A.J. (2000). Parent–Adolescent Language Use and Relationships among Immigrant Families with East Asian, Filipino, and Latin American Backgrounds. *Journal of Marriage and the Family, 62(2)*, 465–476.

Turian, D. & Altenberg, E.P. (1991). Compensatory strategies of child first language attrition. In H.W. Seliger & R.M. Vago (eds), *First language attrition* (pp. 207–226). Cambridge: Cambridge University Press.

Umbel, V., Pearson, B., Fernández, M. & Oller, D.K. (1992). Measuring bilingual children's receptive vocabularies. *Child Development, 63*, 1012–1020.

Unsworth, S. (2003). Testing Hulk & Müller (2000) on crosslinguistic influence: root infinitives in a bilingual German/English child. *Bilingualism: Language and Cognition, 6(2)*, 143–158.

Unsworth, S. (2007). Age and input in early child bilingualism: The acquisition of grammatical gender in Dutch. In A. Belikova, L. Meroni & M. Umeda (eds), *Galana 2: Proceedings of the Conference on Generative Approaches to Language Acquisition North America 2* (pp. 448–458). Somerville, MA: Cascadilla Proceedings Project.

Valdés, G. & Figueroa, R.A. (1994). *Bilingualism and testing: A special case of bias*. Norwood, NJ: Ablex.

van den Bogaerde, B. & Baker, A. (2002). Are young deaf children bilingual? In G. Morgan & B. Woll (eds), *Directions in sign language acquisition* (pp. 183–206). Amsterdam/Philadelphia: John Benjamins.

van der Linden, E. (2000). Non-selective access and activation in child bilingualism. The lexicon. In S. Döpke (ed.), *Cross-linguistic structures in simultaneous bilingualism* (pp. 37–56). Amsterdam/Philadelphia: John Benjamins.

van der Stelt, J. (1993). *Finally a word. A sensori-motor approach of the mother–infant system in its development towards speech*. Amsterdam: IFOTT.

van de Weijer, J. (1997). Language input to a prelingual infant. In A. Sorace, C. Heycock & R. Shillcock (eds). *Proceedings of the GALA '97 Conference on Language Acquisition* (pp. 290–293). Edinburgh, UK: University of Edinburgh.

van de Weijer, J. (2000). Language input and word discovery. In M. Beers, B. van den Bogaerde, G. Bol, J. de Jong & C. Rooijmans (eds), *From sound to sentence: Studies on first language acquisition* (pp. 155–162). Groningen: Centre for Language and Cognition.

van de Weijer, J. (2002). How much does an infant hear in a day? In J. Costa & M. João Freitas (eds), *Proceedings of the GALA2001 Conference on Language Acquisition* (pp. 279–282). Lisboa: Associação Portuguesa de Linguistíca.

Varro, G. (1998). Does bilingualism survive the second generation? Three generations of French–American families in France. *International Journal of the Sociology of Language, 133*, 105–128.

Veneziano, E. (1999). Early lexical, morphological and syntactic development in French: Some complex relations. *International Journal of Bilingualism, 3*, 183–217.

Vihman, M.M. (1999). The transition to grammar in a bilingual child: Positional patterns, model learning, and relational words. *International Journal of Bilingualism, 3(2–3)*, 267–301.

Vihman, M.M. (2002). Getting started without a system: From phonetics to phonology in bilingual development. *International Journal of Bilingualism, 6(3)*, 239–254.

Vihman, M.M. & Nakai, S. (2003). Experimental evidence for an effect of vocal experience on infant speech perception. In M.J. Solé, D. Recasens & J. Romero (eds), *Proceedings of the 15th International Congress of Phonetic Sciences* (pp. 1017–1020). Barcelona: Universitat Autònoma de Barcelona.

Vihman, M.M., Lum, J.A.G., Thierry, G., Nakai, S. & Keren-Portnoy, T. (2006). The onset of word form recognition in one language and in two. In P. McCardle & E. Hoff (eds), *Childhood bilingualism. Research on infancy through school age* (pp. 30–44). Clevedon: Multilingual Matters.

Vihman, M.M., Macken, M.A., Miller, R., Simmons, H. & Miller, J. (1985). From babbling to speech: A re-assessment of the continuity issue. *Language, 61(2)*, 397–445.

Vihman, M.M., Nakai, S. & DePaolis, R.A. (2006). Getting the rhythm right: A cross-linguistic study of segmental duration in babbling and first words. In L. Goldstein, D. Whalen & C. Best (eds), *Laboratory phonology 8* (pp. 341–366). New York/Berlin: Mouton de Gruyter.

Vihman, M.M., Thierry, G., Lum, J., Keren-Portnoy, T. & Martin, P. (2007). Onset of word form recognition in English, Welsh, and English–Welsh bilingual infants. *Applied Psycholinguistics, 28*, 475–493.

Vila, I. (1984). Yo siempre hablo catalan y castellano: datos de una investigacion en curso sobre la adquisicion del lenguaje en niños bilingües familiares. In M. Siguan (ed.), *Adquisición precoz de una segunda lengua* (pp. 31–51). Barcelona: Publicacions i edicions de la Universitat de Barcelona.

Volterra, V. & Taeschner, T. (1978). The acquisition and development of language by bilingual children. *Journal of Child Language, 5*, 311–326.

von Raffler-Engel, W. (1965). Del bilinguismo infantile. *Archivio Glottologico Italiano, 50*, 175–180.

Vygotsky, L.S. (1975). *Thought and language.* Cambridge: MIT Press.

Wanner, P.J. (1996). A study of the initial codeswitching stage in the linguistic development of an English–Japanese bilingual child. *Japan Journal of Multilingualism and Multiculturalism, 2*, 20–40.

Wanner, P.J. (1997). A longitudinal linguistic study of language differentiation in a Japanese and English bilingual child from 1;0–1;9. *Memoirs of the Faculty of Engineering and Design Kyoto Institute of Technology, 45*, 25–37.

Wanner, P.J. (1999). A secondary stage in the linguistic development of a bilingual child. *Memoirs of the Faculty of Engineering and Design Kyoto Institute of Technology, 47*, 41–68.

Weikum, W.M, Vouloumanos, A., Navarra, J., Soto-Faraco, S., Sebastián-Gallés, N. & Werker, J.F. (2007). Visual language discrimination in infancy. *Science, 316(5828)*, 1159.

Weizman, Z.O. & Snow, C.E. (2001). Lexical input as related to children's vocabulary acquisition: Effects of sophisticated exposure and support for meaning. *Developmental Psychology, 37(2)*, 265–279.

Wells, G. (1985). *Language development in the pre-school years.* Cambridge: Cambridge University Press.

Werker, J.F. & Byers-Heinlein, K. (2008). Bilingualism in infancy: first steps in perception and comprehension of language. *Trends in Cognitive Sciences, 12(4)*, 144–151.

Werker, J.F. & Yeung, H.H. (2005). Infant speech perception bootstraps word learning. *Trends in Cognitive Sciences, 9(11)*, 519–527.

Werker, J.F., Fennell, C.T., Corcoran, K. & Stager, C.L. (2002). Infants' ability to learn phonetically similar words: Effects of age and vocabulary size. *Infancy, 3*, 1–30.

Whitworth, N. (2002). Speech rhythm production in three German–English bilingual families. *Leeds Working Papers in Linguistics and Phonetics, 9*, 175–205.

Wölck, W. (1987/1988). Types of natural bilingual behavior: A review and revision. *The Bilingual Review/La Revista bilingüe, 14*, 3–16.

Wong Fillmore, L. (1979). Individual differences in second language acquisition. In C. Fillmore, D. Kempler & W. Wang (eds), *Individual differences in language ability and language behavior* (pp. 203–228). New York: Academic Press.

Wong Fillmore, L. (1991). When learning a second language means losing the first. *Early Childhood Research Quarterly, 6*, 232–346.

Wong Fillmore, L. (2000). Loss of family languages: Should educators be concerned? *Theory into Practice, 39(4)*, 203–210.

Wray, A. & Namba, K. (2003). Use of formulaic language by a Japanese–English bilingual child: a practical approach to data analysis. *Japan Journal of Multilingualism and Multiculturalism, 9(1)*, 24–51.

Yamamoto, M. (2001). *Language use in interlingual families: A Japanese–English sociolinguistic study*. Clevedon: Multilingual Matters.

Yamamoto, M. (2005). What makes who choose what language to whom?: Language use in Japanese–Filipino interlingual families in Japan. *International Journal of Bilingual Education and Bilingualism, 8(6)*, 588–606.

Yavas, M. (1995). Phonological selectivity in the first fifty words of a bilingual child. *Language and Speech, 38(2)*, 189–202.

Yip, V. & Matthews, S. (2000). Syntactic transfer in a Cantonese–English bilingual child. *Bilingualism: Language and Cognition, 3(3)*, 193–208.

Yip, V. & Matthews, S. (2005). Dual input and learnability: Null objects in Cantonese–English bilingual children. In J. Cohen, K.T. McAlister, K. Rolstad & J. MacSwan (eds), *ISB4: Proceedings of the 4th International Symposium on Bilingualism* (pp. 2421–2431). Somerville, MA: Cascadilla Press.

Yip, V. & Matthews, S. (2007). *The bilingual child. Early development and language contact*. Cambridge: Cambridge University Press.

Yip, V. & Matthews, S. (2008). Lexical development in Cantonese–English bilingual children. Poster presented at IASCL 2008, The XI Congress of the International Association for the Study of Child Language, Edinburgh, United Kingdom, July 28–August 1.

Yow, W.G. & Markman, E. (2007). Monolingual and bilingual children's use of mutual exclusivity assumption and pragmatic cues in word learning. Poster presented at the Biennal Meeting of the Society for Research on Child Development, Boston, MA, March 29–April 1.

Yow, W.Q. & Markman, E. (2008). Understanding speaker's communicative intent – bilingual children's heightened social awareness of referential gestures. Poster presented at the XVIth International Conference on Infant Studies, Vancouver, March 27–29.

Zdorenko, T. & Paradis, J. (2007). The role of the first language in child second language acquisition of articles. In A. Belikova, L Meroni & M. Umeda (eds), *Galana 2: Proceedings of the Conference on Generative Approaches to Language Acquisition North America 2* (pp. 483–490). Somerville, MA: Cascadilla Proceedings Project.

Zentella, A.C. (1997). *Growing up bilingual. Puerto Rican children in New York.* Oxford: Blackwell.

Zink, I. & Lejaegere, M. (2002). *N-CDIs: Lijsten voor communicatieve ontwikkeling. Aanpassing en hernormering van de MacArthur CDIs van Fenson et al.* Leuven: Acco.

Zlatić, L., MacNeilage, P.F., Matyear, C.L. & Davis, B.L. (1997). Babbling of twins in a bilingual environment. *Applied Psycholinguistics, 18,* 453–469.

Zukow-Goldring, P. (2002). Sibling caregiving. In M.H. Bornstein (Ed.), *Handbook of parenting Vol. 3 Status and social conditions of parenting* (2nd edition) (pp. 253–286). Mahwah, NJ: Lawrence Erlbaum Associates.

Zukow-Goldring, P. & Arbib, M.A. (2007). Affordances, effectivities, and assisted imitation: Caregivers and the directing of attention. *Neurocomputing, 17,* 2181–2193.

Zwanziger, E., Allen, S. & Genesee, F. (2005). Crosslinguistic influence in bilingual acquisition: subject omission in learners of Inuktitut and English. *Journal of Child Language, 32,* 893–909.

Child index

Adam, 181, 186, 264, 272, 344, 345
Adèle, 286, 351
Alexei, 138, 280
Andreu, 70, 139, 140, 273, 289, 351
Anna, 221, 224–225, 227–228, 255, 257–258
Anne, 159, 273, 351
Annie, 289, 351
Annika, 285–286, 353
Anouk, 137, 235, 239, 256, 277, 299–300, 352
Arsham, 173, 175, 343, 346
Aurelio, 239

Carlo, 3, 35, 44, 80, 351, 357
Carlotta, 238, 271, 353
Céline, 47, 50, 130, 273
Christopher, 235

Daniel, 36, 353

Ed, 216, 218
Eta, 268

Hannah, 181, 186, 261, 264, 268, 272, 297, 300, 344, 350
Hildegard, 11, 60, 81, 130–131, 168, 170, 178–179, 182, 196, 198–199, 201, 210, 212, 214, 217, 222, 235, 237, 255, 257, 265, 272–274, 284, 288, 344, 346

Ivar, 286, 352

James, 80, 214, 231, 256, 273–274, 279, 298, 351
Jane, 216, 218
Jean, 273, 351
Jennifer, 271
Jessica, 69, 143
Jessie, 197, 223–224, 231, 233, 239–240
Joanna, 111
Joseph, 144, 228
Julia, 133, 135

Karin, 69, 171, 198–199, 218, 231, 254, 257, 324
Kate, 62, 69, 116, 118, 145, 264, 266, 268–269, 271–272, 274, 277–278, 285, 288, 299–300, 311, 329, 336, 351
Ken, 42, 138–139, 350

Laura, 130, 160, 167, 181–182, 264, 272, 344–345
Leila, 69, 143
Lina, 36, 115, 274–276
Lisa, 63
Louis, 10, 130, 166, 168, 171, 173, 177–178, 181, 184, 196, 212, 231, 235, 240–241, 257, 259, 263–265, 272, 274, 284, 344, 346

Maija, 227–228, 238, 261–262, 265, 267–268, 288, 351
Manuela, 58, 68–69, 110–111, 145, 184, 189, 202, 210–211, 220, 224, 231–233, 248, 254, 257–258, 263, 267, 269–270, 285, 290, 299, 347, 350, 357
Mara, 238, 288, 299
María del Mar, 200, 218–220, 230, 233, 235
Marta, 136, 144
Mikael, 69, 129, 168, 198–199, 202, 213, 216, 218, 254, 257
Mikel, 80, 279, 350
Mimi, 273, 351
Monika, 133, 135

Natalie, 273, 351
Nicolai, 32, 43, 211–212, 215, 231–232, 234, 257
Nicolas, 136, 259, 274, 278, 286, 293, 295, 350, 358

Odessa, 130, 267–268, 272, 273, 351
Olivier, 67–70, 224–225, 227, 257–258, 351

Pascal, 286, 353

Rie, 42, 351
Roger, 37, 218–220, 233, 376
Rosita, 133–135

Shelli, 128, 210
Siri, 42, 81, 271
Sofia, 69, 198, 227–228, 239, 261
Sophie, 42, 70, 218, 224
Susan, 103, 117, 130, 140, 170, 181, 183, 214, 217, 257, 259, 263–264, 274, 279, 297, 315

Thomas, 63, 130, 292, 324
Tiffany, 268

Timmy, 36, 42, 70, 278
Tom, 173, 181–183, 344

Vuk, 268

William, 271, 351

Language index

Arabic, 34, 94, 180, 384

Basque, 64, 80, 89, 229, 279, 289, 350, 370–371, 379, 386

Cantonese, 36, 42–43, 70, 80, 105, 224, 278, 287, 305, 402
Chinese, 28, 97, 105, 110, 341–342, 386–387, 392
Danish, 67, 69, 91–92, 313

Dutch, 2, 8–9, 13, 24–25, 28–31, 34, 43, 45, 49, 59, 62, 69, 74–75, 84, 93, 103, 107, 116–119, 121–123, 126, 130, 137, 140, 145, 154, 170, 178–179, 181, 183, 187, 193–194, 201, 203–205, 208, 210–211, 213–218, 220, 222–223, 226–227, 230, 232, 235, 239, 256–257, 259, 263–264, 266, 268–269, 271–272, 274, 277–279, 285, 288–289, 297, 299–300, 306, 311, 315, 318, 326, 329, 331, 336, 349, 351–352, 356, 362, 373, 377–379, 383, 400

English, 2, 3, 8, 11–13, 25–28, 30–36, 41–44, 49–50, 56, 58, 60, 62–63, 65–70, 72–73, 79–80, 87, 89, 93–95, 100, 103, 105–106, 108–111, 116–119, 123–125, 128–131, 133–134, 136, 138–140, 143–145, 147, 149, 153, 155–157, 159–161, 163, 165–171, 173–175, 178–189, 193–197, 199, 201–202, 205–218, 220, 222–240, 246, 248, 254–269, 271–272, 274, 278–290, 292–295, 297, 298–300, 305, 311, 314–315, 318, 323–324, 326, 329, 336–347, 349–351, 356–358, 361–363, 365–368, 370–379, 381, 383–384, 386–388, 390, 392–395, 397–403

Farsi, 173, 175, 343, 346, 384
French, 7, 8, 10, 12–13, 15, 25, 28–30, 34, 41, 43, 45, 47, 50, 59, 62, 67, 69–70, 74–75, 78, 80, 93–95, 100, 103, 130, 137, 143–144, 156, 159, 163, 165–166, 168–169, 173, 177–179, 181–184, 187–188, 193–196, 201, 203–204, 208–209, 211–212, 214, 216–218, 220, 224–229, 231–232, 234–236, 239–241, 246, 255–259, 261–262, 268, 271–272, 274, 277–278, 283–286, 289, 291, 293–294, 297–299, 306, 313, 316, 326, 338–342, 344–346, 349, 351–353, 356–357, 362–363, 367, 373–376, 381, 383–386, 388–393, 396–397, 399–401

Galician, 208, 219, 394
German, 7, 10–13, 15, 32, 34, 36, 43–44, 46–47, 60, 63, 65, 68–69, 78, 80, 84, 95, 103, 106–107, 111, 121–123, 126, 130–131, 134–136, 142, 144, 154, 159, 166–168, 170, 172, 173–178, 181–182, 184, 186, 193–196, 198–199, 201–202, 210, 212, 214–215, 221–222, 228, 231–232, 234–236, 238–241, 255, 257–259, 261–265, 268, 271–274, 278, 283–286, 288–289, 291–294, 298, 300, 323–324, 331, 343–346, 349, 351–353, 356, 362, 373, 381–391, 395–396, 399–400, 402
Greek, 100

Hebrew, 34, 128, 145, 210, 298, 311, 314, 349, 372–373
Hokkien, 105
Hungarian, 66, 195, 268, 314, 377

Inuktitut, 33, 66, 124–125, 283, 289, 351, 357, 370, 403
Irish, 100
Italian, 3, 11, 33, 35–36, 43–44, 46, 63, 68–69, 80, 87, 100, 115, 131, 134–136, 142, 144, 160, 194, 198, 221, 233–234, 238–240, 271, 273–276, 278, 289, 293–294, 298, 323, 337, 344, 347, 351, 353, 356–357, 372–374, 383, 386, 397–398

Japanese, 8, 25, 27, 34, 42, 67, 69, 100, 108, 110, 129, 138–139, 179, 184–185, 197, 213, 223– 224, 231, 233, 239–240, 256, 261–262, 297, 322, 350–351, 363, 383, 390, 401–402

Korean, 100, 260, 373, 375, 384, 398

Latvian, 228, 238, 261–262, 265, 268, 288, 351, 398

Malay, 105
Mandarin, 28, 80, 110, 194, 214, 231, 256, 274, 279, 351, 375, 395

Norwegian, 13, 42, 130, 271, 293–295, 344, 347, 383, 386

Portuguese, 23, 31, 36, 69, 129, 164, 166–168, 171, 190, 199, 202, 208, 210, 213, 216, 218, 224, 228, 231, 233, 234, 236, 240, 254, 257, 324, 353, 376, 382

Serbocroatian, 195, 268
Slovak, 351, 398–399
Spanish, 13, 26, 33–34, 56, 58, 64, 66, 68–70, 73, 80, 89, 100, 109–110, 124–125, 133–136, 138, 145, 149, 160–161, 165, 168, 172, 175, 180–182, 184–185, 189, 197, 200, 202, 206–208, 211, 214, 218–220, 223–224, 226, 228–235, 237, 248, 254, 257–262, 267, 269, 274, 278–279, 281–282, 285–287, 289–290, 293–294, 297–299, 316, 329, 331, 337–340, 343–350, 356–358, 361–362, 370–371, 373–374, 378, 380–381, 384–388, 393–394, 398
Swahili, 34
Swedish, 23, 36, 69, 94–95, 115, 129, 164, 166–168, 171, 190, 199, 202, 210, 213, 216, 218, 224, 231, 236–237, 257, 274–275, 298, 324, 351, 376, 397

Tagalog, 157, 160
Taiap, 92, 101–102
Thai, 155–156
Tok Pisin, 101–102

Vietnamese, 91–92

Welsh, 165, 187, 371, 401

Xhosa, 24

Subject index

1P/1L, *see* language presentation
1P/1L & 1P/2L, *see* language presentation
1P/2L, *see* language presentation

adult-like, 23, 30-31, 43, 174, 176, 181-83, 199, 260, 266, 281, 283, 288, 301, 357-59
attitude, 88-92, 96, 101, 131, 134, 148-49, 316, 324, 377
– negative attitude, 89-92, 317, 319, 329
– positive attitude, 86-94, 96, 148, 320, 366

babbling, 29, 30, 37, 81, 151, 167-71, 176, 186-88, 360, 366, 369, 376-77, 388, 395, 401, 403
– canonical babbling, 168-69, 360
– reduplicated babbling, 168, 170, 366
bilingual community, 76, 105, 111, 322, 360
bilingual couple, 7-8, 86, 89, 359, 395
bilingual/monolingual couple, 88, 359
blend, 42-43, 62, 222, 267, 360
bound morpheme, *see* morphology

CDI, 51, 53, 55, 59, 71-76, 79, 200-204, 206-208, 211, 214, 217-19, 223, 227, 231, 242, 245-47, 259, 260-62, 297-98, 306, 349, 360, 365, 378-79, 396, 403
CHILDES, 36, 51, 53, 61, 63, 66-71, 79-81, 149, 188, 290, 360, 377, 388
codas, *see* speech sounds
coding, 53, 60, 61, 62, 63, 64, 67, 68, 71, 79, 360, 364
cognates, 165, 194, 203, 219, 220, 245, 247, 360
complex sentence, *see* sentence
comprehension, 2, 4-6, 11, 37, 39, 48, 51, 72, 75, 126, 190-91, 193-94, 196, 198-206, 208-12, 217, 220, 237, 241-43, 271, 306, 311, 318, 360, 363, 369, 372, 375, 378, 380, 391, 396, 400, 402
consonant, *see* speech sounds
consonant harmony, *see* speech sounds
corpus / corpora, 36, 41, 44, 51, 60, 61, 66-71, 80, 149, 188, 266, 283, 292, 361, 377, 387
crosslinguistic influence, 282, 287-88, 294, 296, 300-301, 356-58, 370, 392-93, 400, 403
cross-sectional design, 58, 361, 376

deletion, *see* speech sounds
determiner, *see* parts of speech
devoicing, *see* speech sounds
doublet, 203-204, 211, 220, 231, 240, 361

Early Second Language Acquisition / ESLA, *see* second language

falling intonation, *see* intonation
floating utterance, *see* utterance
free morpheme, *see* morphology
frequency
– absolute frequency, 97, 124, 127, 359
– input frequency, *see* input
– relative frequency, 124-27, 367
fricative, *see* speech sounds

grammatical word, 34-37, 362

holophrase, 31-32, 215, 253, 255, 362

iambic stress, *see* speech sounds
impact belief, 92, 95-96, 102, 134, 148, 320, 362
indeterminate utterance, *see* utterance
input, 4, 6, 15, 27-28, 39, 49, 57-59, 76-79, 83-84, 86, 92-97, 101-102, 104, 106-108, 110, 113-14, 116, 119-29, 131-32, 138, 144, 146-49, 151, 156, 159, 169, 174-75, 179, 183, 185, 187, 190-92, 195-97, 199, 202, 208, 210, 213, 221-22, 228-29, 236-37, 241, 243-46, 252, 257, 260, 262, 277, 279, 282, 284-87, 290, 296-98, 300, 303, 306, 311-12, 315, 317-18, 320-22, 325, 330, 333-34, 345, 357, 358-60, 362, 367, 370-71, 375, 381, 383, 386, 390, 393-94, 398, 400-402
– bilingual input, 38-39, 57, 77-79, 87, 89-91, 96, 105-106, 120, 126, 154, 163, 206, 229, 236, 244, 296-97, 308-309, 311, 315, 319, 321, 330, 345
– input frequency, 40, 97, 99, 113, 119, 125-27, 148, 244, 264, 317, 321-22
– input language, 27, 30, 35, 44-45, 51, 58, 107, 138, 146, 153-54, 158, 160, 162, 165, 169, 170, 172, 175, 183, 185, 187, 194-95, 208, 220, 222, 230,

409

237, 255, 262-63, 265, 279, 280-82, 284, 294, 305, 307, 318, 328, 358, 362-63, 392
– input pattern, 10, 78, 110-13, 129, 148, 333, 377
– language model, 76, 97, 104, 174, 333, 363
– monolingual input, 6, 91, 120, 186
– regular input, 4-5, 98, 126, 190, 199, 208, 277-78
interaction, 4, 15, 17, 19-23, 28, 41, 46, 50-51, 55, 71, 88-89, 97, 99, 114, 120-21, 126, 135, 143, 145-46, 173, 176-78, 188, 241, 261, 275, 300, 314, 316, 320, 330, 362-63, 369, 371-72, 377, 380-82, 385, 387, 391, 394, 399
intersubjective learning / intersubjectivity, 19, 51, 363, 393
intonation, 23, 27-28, 136, 147, 151, 153-57, 166-68, 171, 176, 186, 188, 215, 256, 264, 305, 363, 365, 381, 398
– falling intonation, 154-56, 158, 215
– rising intonation, 153, 155, 158, 215, 282
IPA, 24, 81, 363

joint attention, 21-22, 363

language choice, 7, 13, 46-47, 63-64, 71, 81, 97, 110, 114, 116, 119, 132-35, 138, 141-45, 149, 188, 221, 236, 238-40, 248, 267, 269-72, 299, 305, 312-14, 316, 320, 329-30, 363, 376, 378, 382-83, 387, 390, 392-95
language model, *see* input
language neutral word, 203, 220, 360, 363
language orientation, 60, 116-19, 138, 140, 363
language presentation, 84-85, 97, 99, 107-14, 131-32, 359, 363
– 1P/1L, 107-13, 120, 128, 131-32, 138, 164, 277, 333, 359
– 1P/1L & 1P/2L, 110-13, 359
– 1P/2L, 108-13, 120, 132, 359
lexical development, 12-13, 75, 79, 124, 186, 192, 206, 223-24, 242-44, 305, 348, 372, 375-76, 378, 384, 390, 394, 396-97, 402
lexicon, 4, 72, 76, 197, 223, 251, 256, 258-60, 262, 295, 363, 307, 371, 375-76, 378-79, 384, 386, 395, 400
linguistic soundscape, 83-84, 97, 99-101, 104, 106-107, 111, 113, 116, 127-28, 130, 132-33, 146, 148-49, 359, 364

maturation, 20, 23, 28, 50, 364, 384
'mixed sort of language', 12, 58, 60

mixed utterance, *see* utterance
monolingual (first language) acquisition / MFLA, 4-7, 11, 29, 38, 40-41, 45, 48-50, 56-58, 60-62, 64-66, 104, 114, 127, 154, 157, 159-60, 162, 170, 172, 174, 176, 178-79, 182, 185, 195, 198-99, 205-206, 208, 210, 214, 217, 219, 222-24, 226, 228-30, 233, 237, 241-42, 244, 246, 256, 266, 272, 283-84, 288-91, 293-97, 299, 309-10, 322, 325, 328-29, 348, 357, 363-64, 370, 398
morphology, 33, 35, 58, 65, 254, 265, 273, 354-55, 364, 370, 373, 380, 384, 386, 391, 393, 397
– bound morpheme, 33-37, 41, 65, 215, 222, 263, 265-66, 278, 292, 296, 360
– free morpheme, 33-34, 36, 41, 43, 292, 360, 362
morphosyntax / morphosyntactic development, 13, 33-36, 48, 71-72, 178, 246, 255-56, 262, 266, 274, 277-91, 294-99, 305, 306-307, 328, 354, 364, 367, 373, 377, 398
multi-word utterances, 30, 44, 239, 255-56, 263, 265, 274, 288, 305, 344, 372
mutism, 44, 364
Mutual Exclusivity (Bias), 191, 205-206, 248, 364, 376, 380, 388-89, 402

narrative, 293-95, 298, 370, 372, 386, 398
native contrast, *see* phonological contrast
non-native contrast, *see* phonological contrast
noun, *see* parts of speech

object, *see* sentence element
observational study / observational data, 55, 59, 73, 79, 80, 125, 147, 162, 259, 365

parental rating instrument, 5, 365
parental report, 147, 217, 219, 360
particle, *see* parts of speech
parts of speech, 215, 260
– determiner, 35, 264, 292, 361, 375, 381, 386
– noun, 34, 36, 41, 110, 131, 194, 198, 215-16, 247, 260-64, 278-80, 284, 292, 298, 324, 354, 361, 365-66, 380, 388, 392, 397
– particle, 34, 36, 42, 266, 294, 299, 355, 365, 383
– verb, 32-36, 47, 62-63, 194, 215-16, 254-55, 260-63, 278, 281, 284-85, 292, 294, 297-98, 300-301, 359, 363, 365, 367, 369-70, 375, 377, 380, 386, 388-90, 398

phoneme, 24-27, 30, 33, 154-55, 157-58, 160, 162, 175-77, 179, 181, 183, 187, 189, 222, 360, 361, 365-66, 368, 376
phonological contrast, 28, 365
– native contrast, 25-26, 28, 365
– non-native contrast, 25, 26, 365
phonology / phonological development, 26, 48, 167, 171, 176-79, 186-87, 190, 284, 305, 365, 368-69, 371, 374-75, 380-84, 388, 392, 397, 399, 401
phonological process, *see* speech sounds
phonotactics, 154, 157-58, 366
pitch, 23, 30, 107, 153-57, 167, 173, 186, 344, 366, 384, 388
– pitch contour, 23, 156, 366
pragmatic(s), 31, 72, 103, 109, 127, 153, 170, 205, 214, 234, 281, 356, 357-58, 366-67, 374, 378, 380, 383, 385, 392, 397-99, 402
production vocabulary, 32, 223, 258, 262, 366 *see also* word production
pronoun, 34-36, 102-103, 215, 265-66, 278-79, 281, 289, 300, 354, 356-57, 362, 366, 382-83, 392, 397, 416
prosody, 23, 154, 158, 160, 166-67, 256, 363, 366, 388

reduplication, 167-68, 170, 176, 182, 366-67, 387
referential, 31, 33, 170, 216, 362-64, 367, 387, 398, 403
rising intonation, *see* intonation
root, 33-35, 36, 81, 289, 311, 354, 360, 369, 372, 400

second language, 4-6, 45, 59, 65, 77, 88, 95, 106, 208, 229, 244, 291, 312, 315, 317-18, 325, 329, 345, 349, 375, 381-83, 387, 389, 393, 395, 399, 402-403
– Early Second Language Acquisition / ESLA, 4-7, 29, 45, 48, 77, 79, 129, 147, 180, 185, 208, 228-29, 244-46, 263, 290-91, 296, 298-99, 311, 325, 330, 348, 361-63, 387
– second language learner/learning, 70, 106, 147, 174, 318, 379, 399
semantic, 31, 72, 214-16, 220, 242, 246, 248, 281, 367, 382, 388
sentence, 5-6, 14, 27, 30-37, 39, 43, 50, 62, 72-73, 95, 104, 117, 146,155, 158, 160-61, 163, 167, 171, 176, 186, 188, 198, 215-16, 244, 253-54, 256, 259, 260, 262-70, 272-74, 276-79, 281-85, 287-93, 295-96, 299-300, 305, 306, 319, 329, 337-38, 344, 357-62, 364-69, 376-77, 400
– complex sentence, 36, 37, 66, 264, 266, 288, 292, 355, 360
sentence element, 33-36, 358-59, 365, 367-69
– object, 33-34, 263, 281, 289, 294, 356-58, 361, 365, 367, 390-91, 393, 398, 402
– subject, 33-36, 105, 254, 260, 278-79, 281, 285, 289, 294, 301, 354, 356-57, 368, 379, 382, 383-84, 386-87, 389, 393, 397-98, 403
separate development hypothesis / SDH, 12, 35, 48, 58, 104-105, 261-62, 265-66, 277, 279-82, 284-85, 294, 295-99, 301, 305, 311, 318-19, 326, 330, 350-56, 367, 372, 377, 397
sibling, 19, 70, 99, 101, 126-28, 147, 164, 169, 174, 248, 311, 314, 316, 328, 334-35, 372, 374, 403
singlet, 204, 220, 367
social words, 214, 248, 367
socialization, 7, 19, 20, 24, 28, 50, 88, 97, 99, 119, 133, 142, 149, 270, 320, 364, 367, 385, 395-96
speaking rate, 119-21, 123, 367
speech sounds
– codas, 172, 343, 360
– consonant, 23, 24, 157-58, 165, 167-69, 171-72, 177, 181-82, 184, 187, 222, 346-47, 360, 361-62, 366-68, 371, 387
– consonant harmony, 182, 360
– deletion, 30, 171-72, 180-81, 361, 366
– fricative, 175-76, 180-83, 346, 361-62
– iambic (stress), 173, 362, 368
– phonological process, 177, 180-83, 189, 361, 366-67
– speech segment, 175-77, 179, 181, 187, 346, 362, 367
– stop consonant, 175, 180-81, 184, 368-69
– substitution, 30, 180-83, 360, 366-68
– syllable, 23, 33, 37, 155, 166, 168-75, 177, 180, 187-88, 231, 343-44, 360, 362, 366-68, 387
– trochaic (stress), 173, 362, 368
– truncation, 172, 343-44, 368, 395
– voiced (voicing), 25, 181-85, 187, 361, 378, 387
– voiceless (devoicing), 25, 30, 181-82, 184, 187, 361
– vowel, 23-26, 166-71, 175, 177, 181, 186, 217, 222, 231, 346-47, 360-61, 366-69, 373, 376, 384, 395
speech segment, *see* speech sounds
stability, 183, 222, 225-26, 367, 373
stop consonant, *see* speech sounds

story telling (as part of narrative development), 37, 40, 50, 293-94 (*see also* narrative)
subject, *see* sentence element
subject (as participant of study), 44, 55-56, 59, 78-81, 118, 161, 168, 179, 187, 210, 229, 231-32, 240, 256, 294-95, 298, 314, 325, 333, 364, 366, 368
substitution, *see* speech sounds
syllable, *see* speech sounds

transcription, 36, 60-62, 67-68, 71, 79, 81, 178, 184, 261, 275, 279, 365, 368
translation equivalent / TE, 137, 191-95, 197, 198, 202-205, 207, 211-12, 219-22, 230-42, 247, 248, 328, 361, 367-68
trochaic, *see* speech sounds
truncation, *see* speech sounds
two word utterance, 44, 137, 257-59, 300, 388

underextension, 31, 199, 216, 230, 368
uneven development, 47-48, 272, 317, 330, 368
unilingual utterance, *see* utterance
utterance
– floating utterance, 42-43, 362

– indeterminate utterance, 41-44, 62, 64, 68, 121-22, 178, 269, 362
– mixed utterance, 41-47, 51, 62-64, 68-69, 79, 84, 105-106, 108-10, 113, 125-27, 133-36, 138-39, 142, 144, 146-49, 178, 198, 202, 221, 240, 252, 257-59, 263-64, 267-71, 280, 291-92, 296-301, 305, 318, 323, 325, 364, 367, 378
– unilingual utterance, 41-46, 51, 62-66, 79, 106, 109, 122, 125-27, 133, 138, 143, 146, 267, 269-70, 278-81, 284, 288-90, 292, 296, 299, 300-301, 328, 368

verb, *see* parts of speech
vocabulary spurt, 223-24, 233, 242, 245, 369, 380
vocalization, 22, 43, 51, 167-68, 188, 213, 369, 385
voiced (voicing), *see* speech sounds
voiceless, *see* speech sounds
vowel, *see* speech sounds

word production, 72-73, 191-92, 199, 200, 209-11, 213-15, 217-29, 231, 232, 233-34, 236, 242, 246, 248, 253, 255, 257, 260, 367, *see also* production vocabulary